The Jacob Engelbrecht Marriage Ledger

of

Frederick County, Maryland

1820 - 1890

Including fathers, non-Frederick County marriages, black couples, 2nd and 3rd marriages, non-traditional family name spellings, military units in which the groom is currently enlisted, New York Society headliners, royalty, politicians and other information to help the Frederick County researcher.

Compiled by:
Trudie Davis Long and Edith Olivia Eader

Technical Assistance by:
Ronald William Long

Paw Prints, Inc.
PO Box 52
Monrovia, MD 21770-0052

This book was published by and may be purchased from:

Paw Prints, Inc.
PO Box 52
Monrovia, MD 21770-0052

Library of Congress
Catalog Card Number 94-67326

ISBN 0-9642239-0-2

Copyright 1994 by Paw Prints, Inc.

Printed in the United States of America

Table of Contents

Acknowledgment i

Foreword ii

Introduction and Notes about Using this Book 1

Marriage Ledger 3

Addendums to Marriage Ledger 144
    1) Loose sheet on family of Mrs. Christianna **HUMMELL**
    2) List of Births on last page of ledger (page 236)
    3) List of Deaths on last page of ledger (page 236)

Index of Names 145

Index of Places 264

Foreword

The following marriages were abstracted from the Engelbrecht Diaries and compared with the recorded marriages at the Frederick County Court House, Frederick, Maryland. When available, additional information was inserted. This compilation was a result from many long, tedious, caring and exhausting hours, which were necessary to make this project become a reality. When this publication was in the making, there was at least one thought in mind; that was: making accessible more valuable records for research. Upon the use of these entries, the work and research of historians, genealogists, family historians, and many others, will be made a lot easier.

                                        Margaret E Myers
                                        28 April 1994

Acknowledgment

We wish to acknowledge the assistance of Angie Brosius, Librarian, and Bill Willmann, Executive Director, of the Historical Society of Frederick County, Maryland, for permission to publish the Marriage and Death Ledgers which are part of the society's Engelbrecht Diary collection.

Thanks to Ron Long for his technical expertise in producing the finished product.

We wish to thank Bob Fout for suggesting the project, and Velma Defibaugh for showing Bob the information in the first place.

Our thanks to Helen Six for suggestions, proofing and support, and to Margaret E Myers for her encouragement, the use of her published works and for 'volunteering' to write a foreword.

The compilers appreciate the assistance of the staff of the Frederick County Courthouse, and the title searchers who answered questions, for their helpfulness and courtesy.

Thanks to Edie's brother, Allan Johnson, who answered her late night programming questions.

Thanks to all our family members and friends who had to put up with time taken away from other family events with the excuse that this is `important and valuable'.

Trudie Davis Long
Edith Olivia Eader

Introduction

Jacob Engelbrecht was a tailor in Frederick, Maryland, where he lived until his death in 1878. A one time mayor of the city, he was very interested in the happenings around him and wrote down his observations in a series of loose papers and short note books that became known as the Engelbrecht Diaries. When his original manuscripts became wet after a flood in 1868, he went through them and started individual ledgers for deaths, marriages, and property, abstracting his previously written diary.

We are publishing both the marriage and death ledgers; adding place and name indexes. The original marriage ledger is 176 pages, and the original death ledger is 304 pages.

Both ledgers are headed by Mr Engelbrecht as:
"Alphabetical list of marriages {or deaths} commencing about 1820, by Jacob Engelbrecht, Frederick City, Maryland, copied from my Diaries which were very much defaced by the freshet in Carroll's Creek July 24 1868. The water was on the first floor of my house about six feet."

Mr Engelbrecht's marriage ledger is compiled as it was written by him, and, after his death, by his son, until the son's death, and after that, by one or more of his grandchildren until 1891.

Notes about Using this Book

Each marriage is given a number. The numbers in the index refer to that record, or an addendum number, and not to any page number. Some marriage records have as many as 3 related individuals whose names appear in the index. The marriage record is listed in the order: groom's last name (with the one exception of Victoria, Queen of England), first name, possibly a note, bride's last name, first name, usually a note, and the date. The date listed by Mr Engelbrecht is the date of marriage and has no relation to the license dates recorded at the courthouse. The compiler has found, in verifying marriage partners, there are time spans up to and greater than 3 months between the time of application for the license and the date of marriage. Licenses marriage dates could include the same time span or not ever be returned to the courthouse by the minister. The surnames of the contracting parties appear in ***bold italics***.

The compilers have attempted a verbatim listing of Mr Engelbrecht's ledgers. That being the case, there are times when words that don't appear to have a relationship to the 2 marriage partners are included in the entry. Where possible we have interpreted these additional words as either places or surnames. It is more likely that places will be listed as surnames than vice versa.

Unless noted otherwise, each female partner to the marriage is listed in the ledger as Miss.

The only other word dropped in any of the records is the word "*to*" between the groom and bride's names.

After 1878, the quality of the handwriting becomes very poor, and there are blotches and missing letters. We have endeavored to correctly interpret the handwriting.

Other secondary references have been used to verify these marriage records when the names appear ambiguous. They are each given a key reference symbol. (#) Names in Stone by Jacob Mehrling Holdcraft, (*) Marriages of Frederick County by Margaret E Myers, and (@) for the license books at the Frederick Court House. Notes by the compiler are listed with {parentheses}.

There are 3 addendums to the marriage ledger. One addendum is a loose sheet of paper on the HUMMELL family. The other 2 addendums are a list of births and a separate list of deaths of Mr Engelbrecht's extended family members. There are no surnames for the births listed, but, according to Margaret E Myers, these births are all for members of the Ramsburg family, and they are included in the index with the surname Ramsburg. Items from the addendum are listed in the index by the addendum number, not the page number.

The inside front and back covers of the original ledger books have numerous recipes and newspaper clippings which are not included in this book.

Mr Engelbrecht would insert sheets of paper into the marriage ledger without numbering them, or use other sheets from the end of the ledger. In cases where there is no numbering of the ledger, the first page after a number is that number with the letter "a". Between 66 and 68 there are pages 66a, 66b, 66c, 66d, and then 68.

In addition to inserting pages in the ledger, Mr Engelbrecht would omit pages. The missing page numbers in the marriage ledger are: 5, 19, 29, 37, 47, 55, 67, 71, 81, 89, 101, 107-109, 115, 124, 151-153, and 155.

Trudie Davis-Long
July 1994

1 ADAMS, Valentine, 1st wife, THOMAS, Sevilla, of Mich'l, January 8 1822, 1
2 ARMOUR, James U, 3d wife, SAUNDERS, Catherine, of John, Nov 14 1823, 1
3 ALBAUGH, William H, SNYDER, Susanna (Mrs), HICKSON, Septr 9 1824, 1
4 ALBACH, John W, PETERS, Elizabeth, Augt 20 1825, 1
5 ALBERT, John L, STICKEL, A Mary Ann, Octr 20 1825, 1
6 ALLISON, John, DADISMAN, Sophia, March 27 1826, 1
7 ARMSTRONG, Wm (Rev), JOHNSON, Eliza, March 28 1826, 1
8 ALBACH, Valentine A, BRUNNER, Rebecca, Augt 6 1826, 1
9 AUBERT, Jacob, GROVE, Hannah, April 26 1827, 1
10 ARMOUR, James U, 4th wife, FLEMING, Charlotte, 20 Septr 1830, 1
11 ABBOTT, John, DORFF, Juliann, of Geo, June 17 1832, 1
12 ARNOLD, James Madison, PHEBUS, Elizabeth, July 16 1833, 1
13 ALLEN, Mervin (Rev), SIMMONS, Balinda E, of Col John, Decr 31 1833, 1
14 ANGELBERGER, Joseph, MARTZ, Elizabeth, Feby 18 1836, 1
15 ATTIG, Philip, KESSLER, Maria, May 5 1836, 1
16 AUL, Jacob, WAGNER, Margaret, Decr 26 1839, 1
17 ALLEN, Isaac Hollingsworth, TITLOW, Evelina, of Geo, Jan 16 1840, 1
18 NO SURNAME GIVEN, Albert, Duke of Saxe Coburg, GUELPH, Victoria, Queen of Eng, Feby 10 1840, 1
19 ANDERSON, J W, HECKENTHORN, Sophia, Dec 24 1840, 1
20 ARMOUR, James E U, NOBLE, Sarah E, of Va, May 16 1841, 1
21 ALBACH, Allen, KELLER, Adeline, Nov 20 1841, 1
22 ALBACH, Grafton, of Solomon, HARRIS, My Elizabeth, May 31 1842, Balto, 1
23 ANDERSON, No first name given, GETZENDANNER, Rebecca, Octr 1842, Cumberland, 1
24 ANSPACH, Fred'k R, 1st wife, REINHART, Lilly, January 25 1844, Va, 1
25 ANDERSON, Wm S, DELAUTER, Ann S, Feby 6 1845, 1
26 ARTZ, Christian Burr, THOMAS, Margaret C, of Michael, June 23 1845, 1
27 ALLAND, Frederick, SCHAEFFER, Mary Ann, of Peter, April 9 1846, 1
28 APP, Conrad, ALLAND, Mrs, March 27 1846, 1
29 ANGELBERGER, David S, STONER, Lydia Ann, May 31 1846, 1
30 ALLEMAN, Munroe J (Rev), SCHELLMAN, Catherine E, of Wm, Octr 13 1846, 1
31 ALLEND, Henry, LENTZ, Ann, Septr 25 1847, 1
32 ANDERSON, Wm Pickney, MORGAN, Sophia Rollington, of Tho's W, Nov 21 1848, 1
33 ANGELBERGER, Jacob M, RENNER, Rebecca, Feby 24 1848, 1
34 ANDERS, Aaron, STONER, Mary Ann, March 15 1849, 1
35 AGASSIZ, Louis (Prof), CAREY, Elizabeth C, April 1850, Mass, 2
36 ALBAUGH, Maurice, CRUM, Frances Matilda, Octr 23 1850, KESSLER, 2
37 ADAMS, Valentine, 2d wife, REICH, Sarah, June 4 1851, 2
38 ANGEL, Wm H, EVERHART, Serauda E C, Septr 21 1851, 2
39 ALLISON, Richard T, TANEY, Maria Key, of Roger B, Feby 9 1852, 2
40 ALBAUGH, Jeremiah W, CRUMBAUGH, Harriet E, May 6 1852, Glade, 2
41 ALTMAN, John Michael, 2d wife, STEINBRECHER, Elizabeth, June 11 1852, 2
42 ALBAUGH, Abraham A, SUMMERS, Mary A, of Jacob, June 17 1852, 2
43 ADAMS, Washington, JOHNSON, Ellen Cuyler, of Col Tho's, Decr 8 1852, 2
44 ALBERT, Augustus, HATCH, Madaline C, of Wm S, May 26 1853, Balto, 2
45 ADAM, Henry, 2d wife, RAAC, Sophia, June 14 1853, 2
46 ATTIG, John, ADAMS, Martha Jane, June 28 1853, 2

47 ANDERS, Wm, *DOMER*, Susan Elizabeth, Septr 1 1853, 2
48 ADAMS, Ab'm Tho's, of Valentine, *KEMP*, Sarah A, of David, Decr 14 1853, 2
49 ANGELBERGER, Geo D, *WACHTER*, Elizabeth, Octr 30 1854, 2
50 ANDERS, Upton, 1st wife, *KREIS*, Lydia A S, Decr 7 1854, 2
51 ALBAUGH, Joshua, of Val A, *HAUGH*, Susannah, March 20 1855, 2
52 ANDERSON, Geo W (Rev), *WINTER*, Anna M, Septr 25 1855, 2
53 ABRECHT, Luther N, *SHIPLEY*, Eliza A, Nov 15 1855, 2
54 ANDREWS, Solomon (Jun'r Dr), *BUNKLEY*, Josephine M, "Nun", Jany 9 1856, 2
55 ACHEY, Charles F, *SCHULTZ*, Amelia S, of H'y, Feby 5 1856, 2
56 ANDERS, Thomas, *WAGNER*, Amelia J, March 4 1856, 2
57 ANDERS, George J, *HILTON*, Lucretia, March 18 1856, Montgomery, 2
58 AUBERT, Albert H, *BRUNNER*, Henrietta, of Jacob, Decr 2 1856, 2
59 ANGELBERGER, Luther Henry, *STALEY*, Juliann Cath, April 12 1857, 2
60 ABEL, Jacob, *SCHMIDT*, Elizabeth, April 19 1857, 2
61 ALBAUGH, Christian T, 1st wife, *ABBOTT*, Elenora V, May 20 1857, DORFF, 2
62 ASCHEMEIER, William, *LAMPE*, Louisa, Augt 18 1857, 2
63 ANDERS, Caleb A, *HALLER*, Alice Virginia, of Ch W, Septr 22 1857, 2
64 ANGELBERGER, John P, *STALEY*, Mary S, Septr 24 1857, 2
65 ALEXANDER, G W, *YOUNG*, Henrietta C, of John of P, Nov 9 1857, 2
66 ANDERSON, Tho's W, *TURNER*, Jennie R, of Tho's, June 1 1858, 2
67 ABBOTT, Francis P (Dr), of Maine, *FAY*, Caroline C, of Thodore S, June 14 1858, "SCHWIETZ", 2
68 ANDERS, Upton, 2d wife, *BARNHART*, Sarah Jane (Mrs), Nov 2 1858, Balto, 2
69 ALBAUGH, Henry Clay, of Val A, *HULL*, Sarah J, Dec 21 1858, Balto, 2
70 ADDISON, John D, *HENDRY*, Martha C, of Cha's, January 12 1859, 2
71 ALTMAN, Jacob G, *HALLER*, Julia Virginia, March 16 1859, 2
72 ARTHUR, S A McNair, *PICKING*, Annie E, of Tho's, March 24 1859, 2
73 ASHBAUGH, Wm H, *DYER*, Martha J, April 5 1859, 2
74 ALBAUGH, Daniel I, of Absolom, *LINK*, Mary F, April 20 1859, Balto, 2
75 ANDERS, Joshua, *REIDENAUER*, Catherine (Mrs), April 3 1859, 2
76 ANDERS, John M, *ANDERS*, Margaret, May 1859, Woodsboro, 2
77 ARMSTRONG, Archibald, *VANFOSSEN*, Mary A, of Levi, June 9 1859, "Artesian", 3
78 ANDERSON, Archer, *MASON*, Mary Ann, of John Y MASON, Augt 9 1859, Paris, 3
79 APPLER, Arthur M, *ETCHISON*, Helen M, of Tho's H, Septr 14 1859, 3
80 ANGELL, David, *SHUCK*, Mary E, January 3 1860, 3
81 ANSPACH, Fred'k R (Rev), 2d wife, *GALE*, Susan M (Mrs), April 10 1860, Balto, 3
82 ANDERS, James W, *REED,*, Lethe Ann, May 24 1860, 3
83 ALBACH, Andrew H, *CLEM*, Miranda Priscilla, Nov 22 1860, 3
84 ADELSBERGER, Daniel G, *BUSBY*, Marg't M J, January 29 1861, 3
85 ANDERS, Wm H, *LEAKINS*, Senia E, February 4 1861, 3
86 ADAM, Andrew J, *JOHNSON*, Jane E, of Col Tho's, May 23 1861, 3
87 ASHERMAN, Tilghman, *WETNIGHT*, Elizabeth, Augt 15 1861, 3
88 ARMOUR, Charles Lee, *NO BRIDES NAME GIVEN*, Miss, Septr 5 1861, 3
89 AHALT, Joshua, *MACHT*, Sarah E, Nov 7 1861, 3
90 ALBAUGH, Charles E, *LITTLE*, Isabella, Nov 15 1861, 3
91 ABBOTT, George A, *BURUCKER*, Clementine, Feby 4 1862, 3
92 AHALT, Carlton P, *WILLARD*, Manzilla M, Jany 30 1862, 3

93 AAB, John, BOBST, Rowanna, Feby 27 1862, 3
94 ARAGO, Cha's Gabriel, MONTHOLON, Albine Ann Yolande, March 11 1862, N York, 3
95 AHALT, Matthias S, SHEFFER, Martha Jane, of Dan'l, Decr 4 1862, 3
96 ALBAUGH, Edward, of Lewis A, UNKEFER, Lucy R, UNGEFEHR, Dec4 23 1862, Liberty, 3
97 ASHERMAN, David, RAMSBURG, Amanda L, March 4 1863, 3
98 NO SURNAME GIVEN, Albert Edward, Prince of Wales, NO BRIDES NAME GIVEN, Alexandra, Princess/of Denmark, March 10 1863, 3
99 ARTZ, Edwin, Hospital Steward USA, DIXON, Hellen, March 19 1863, 3
100 ARNOLD, James M, SINN, Martha, of Jacob, Septr 23 1863, 3
101 ALBAUGH, Wm H, his 2d wife, HOLLIDAY, Susan (Mrs), her 3rd husband, Octr 8 1863, 3
102 ALBAUGH, Daniel (Elder), PETERHOFF, Catherine, Octr 13 1863, 3
103 ANDERSON, Oliver P, YOUNG, Laura V, Nov 10 1863, DERTZBAUGH, 3
104 ANDERSON, Wm R, KOHLENBERG, Harriet A, of Adam, April 12 1864, 3
105 ANDERS, Cha's A, HOLBRUNNER, Maria L, May 12 1864, 3
106 ABSHESKY, Theodore F, CONRAD, Fannie M, Augt 11 1864, Connecticut, 3
107 ATHERTON, Benjamin, BENDER, Elizabeth J, of John, July 10 1864, Va, 3
108 ANGEVINE, Wm H, HEMMELL, Rosie, of Jacob, Octr 5 1864, 3
109 ASCHBACH, Aquilla, SUMAN, Ellen, May 6 1865, 3
110 ANDERS, Wm H, CREAGER, Clarissa E, Octr 18 1865, Glade, 3
111 ALTMAN, John M, 2d wife, WILES, Ann M, Feby 26 1866, 3
112 ATLEE, Abe J, CROMWELL, Netta, April 16 1867, 3
113 AMBROSE, Henry W, TINTERMAN, Mary Ellen, July 23 1867, 3
114 ATKINSON, J Edward (Dr), KEMP, Virginia R, Octr 17 1867, 3
115 AHL, Romma, MCCAFFERTY, Mary Ellen, of John, Octr 14 1867, Balto, 3
116 ASHBAUGH, Sam'l D, DUVALL, Julia A, of Wm T, April 23 1868, 3
117 ANDERSON, Julius H, THOMAS, Alice, of C Keefer THOMAS, July 23 1868, 3
118 ALBAUGH, Geo F, WECKLER, Vickie R, of Fred'k, Octr 27 1868, Boonsboro, 3
119 ABBOTT, John H, HANSHEW, Julia M, of Henry, Octr 29 1868, 4
120 ALBAUGH, Christian T, 2d wife, SHANK, Carrie V, of Ezra, Octr 13 1868, 4
121 ANNAN, Robert L (Dr), MOTTER, A C, Feby 11 1869, Emmittsburg, 4
122 AMES, Hon, of Miss, BUTLER, Blanche, of B F, July 21 1870, 4
123 ADAMS, John Q, of Washington City, BRUNNER, Susan, of Lewis, Septr 6 1870, 4
124 ANGELBERGER, Philip S, STONE, Sarah T, Feby 1 1871, 4
125 ADAM, Henry, of Andreas, FISCHBACH, Margaret, Septr 15 1872, 3
126 ALAND, Carlton E, CRUMBAUGH, Flora C, Octr 14 1873, 4
127 NO SURNAME GIVEN, Ernst Alfred, Prince of England, NO BRIDES NAME GIVEN, Alexandrovna, of Russia, Jany 23 1874, St Petersburg, 4
128 ASHENHUST, John J, STEINER, Alice Ida, of Rev Jesse, March 18 1874, Ohio, 4
129 ALTPETER, George, THIEMEYER, Emilie, Jan 19 1875, Balto, 4
130 ATWATER, Dorrence, US Consul, NO BRIDES NAME GIVEN, Princess Mastia, Tahiti society, Octr 27 1875, 4
131 ALBAUGH, Edward S, of Solo, GEHRNETT, Barb Ann (Mrs), Decr 26 1875, 4
132 ADAM, William, of Andreas, BRENNER, Mary J, Decr 21 1876, 4
133 ALDRIDGE, Singleton A, SCHULTZ, Emma, Nov 14 1877, 4
134 ATTICK, Albert S, HAUGH, Clemmie A, Jan 1 1878, 4
135 ANDERS, Charles C, FRAZIER, Lillie R, of David, Jan 22 1878, 4
136 ALBAUGH, James S, FOGLE, Flora E, February 8 1888, 4

137 ANNAN, Andrew A, WHITE, Luella, February 15 1888, 4
138 ANDERSON, Jesse, EVERHART, Cornelia, April 30 1889, 4
139 ANDERSON, Edward, POOLE, Ella, October 1 1889, 4
140 ALSTON, David M, SWAN, Nellie P, November 27 1889, 4
141 BRIGHTLY, Marcy, FOUT, Sophia, of Jacob, March 29 1821, 6
142 BRUTCHEY, Jacob, HARTZ, Catherine, April 23 1821, "FRANTZ", 6
143 BRENGLE, Wm, of Jacob, GROVE, Margaret, May 8 1821, 6
144 BENDER, John, KEHLER, Elizabeth, of Henry, June 1 1821, 6
145 BARRICK, Samuel, RICE, Miss, of James/(*Sophia), Augt 27 1821, 6
146 BALTZELL, John (Dr), RIDGELY, Ruth, Decr 24 1821, in Balto, 6
147 BAGER, Samuel B, SMITH, Elizabeth, March 14 1822, 6
148 BIGGS, William, 2d wife, HATTON, Nancy, Octr 14 1822, 6
149 BOWLUS, David, BECKENBACH, Sophia, January 5 1823, 6
150 BERRY, John, GETZENDANNER, Mary, of Col Jacob, April 8 1823, 6
151 BRENNER, Wm, 1st wife, ENGLAND, Sarah, Octr 11 1823, 6
152 BACHMAN, George, KNAUFF, Elizabeth, April 15 1824, 6
153 BALTZELL, John, (Hatter), MILLER, Charlotte, of Dr J Sam'l, Octr 12 1824, 6
154 BAER, John, ROWE, Catherine, Nov 14 1824, 6
155 BAETZHOTZ, John, ERNSTBERGER, Catherine, Nov 25 1824, 6
156 BRISH, Henry C, CAREY, Eleanor, Decr 7 1824, 6
157 BURKITT, Newton, CREAGER, Rebecca, of Dr Lewis, Jany 8 1825, 6
158 BRISH, John M, HOUCK, Eliza, of John, Feby 3 1825, 6
159 BENTZ, John, GETZENDANNER, Rebecca, April 19 1825, 6
160 BAKER, Ezra, SOUDER, Miss, (*Mary), May 3 1824, Glade, 6
161 BROWN, D Anderton, PAYNE, Sarah C D, May 1825, N Carolina, 6
162 BRIEN, Robert Coleman, TIERNAN, Ann Elizah, of Luke, Nov 8 1825, Balto, 6
163 BAER, Ezra, of John, KNOTT, Rosella, May 11th 1826, 6
164 BELL, John, (Negro), PRESTON, Susan (Mrs), (Negress), June 11 1826, 6
165 BINGHAM, Daniel H, BACON, Ann, Augt 20 1826, 6
166 BRUBACHER, John, FREY, Mary P, (not listed as Miss), February 8 1827, 6
167 BURKHART, Charles H, NEIGHBORS, Elizabeth R, May 3d 1827, 6
168 BROOKE, John Thompson (Rev), HUNTER, Rebecca, May 8 1827, Va, 6
169 BRIEN, John McPerson, MERIDETH, Rebecca, March 25 1828, Balto, 6
170 BIRNIE, Clotworthy (Jun'r), WORTHINGTON, Harriott A, of Wm, June 24 1828, 6
171 BRENGLE, Lawrence J, of Capt John/1st wife, SHRIVER, Cath C, of And'w/(not listed as Miss), Decr 2 1828, 6
172 BLESSING, Abraham (Jun'r), ENT, Mary, of Capt Geo W, Feby 3 1829, 6
173 BISER, Tilghman (Dr), LAMAR, Miss, (*Mary Ann), Feby 3 1829, 6
174 BROWN, Wm S, TROUT, Charlotte, June 2 1829, 6
175 BRENNER, William, 2d wife, ENGLAND, Catherine, Decr 5 1829, 6
176 BRUNNER, John, of J/2d wife, DOLL, Sophia, of Jos, March 23 1830, 6
177 BANTZ, Nimrod, HARDING, Mary, July 27 1830, 6
178 BAYER, Thomas, KELLER, Sophia, July 29 1830, 6
179 BRASHEAR, Thomas, ROHR, Louisa, of Jacob, Septr 12 1830, 6
180 BOWLUS, George, his 2d wife, BENSON, Ann, Nov 23 1830, 6
181 BOTELER, Henry, LEVY, Ann R C, of David, Feby 22 1831, 6
182 BUCKEY, Washington, HERD, Catharine, March 3 1831, 6

183 *BRENGLE*, Cha's, of Christ'n, *BAER*, Sarah A (Mrs), February 5 1832, 7
184 *BEALL*, Geo W, of Elisha, *COCKEY*, Caroline C, Feby 9 1832, 6
185 *BRUNNER*, Jonathan, of Elias/1st wife, *MIDDELKAUFF*, Sarah, May 10 1832, 6
186 *BRENGLE*, Alfred F, of Jacob, *BRENGLE*, Louisa, of Nich, May 17 1832, cousins, 7
187 *BLAIR*, John, *HALLEY*, Mary A, Augt 21 1832, 7
188 *BRIEN*, John McPherson, 2d wife, *BARON*, Isabella, Octr 23 1832, 7
189 *BLACKSTONE*, Benjamin C, *HART*, Catherine (Mrs), "HERRING", March 3 1833, 7
190 *BRUNNER*, Lewis, *RAMSBURG*, Ann Rebecca, March 21 1833, 7
191 *BREEDY*, George, *BUTLER*, Ann E, of Ormond F, May 28 1833, 7
192 *BUCKEY*, Jacob, *TITLOW*, Juliann, June 16 1833, 7
193 *BARKER*, Samuel, *MCLANAHAN*, Martha A, Augt 29 1833, 7
194 *BRIEN*, Wm C, *HUGHES*, Catharine, Octr 10 1833, 7
195 *BRUNNER*, Jonathan, 2d wife, *MIDDELKAUFF*, Mary, Octr 20 1833, 7
196 *BENTZ*, Daniel, *SCHOLL*, Mary Elizabeth, of Christ'n, Nov 21 1833, 7
197 *BEST*, John F, *CRAMER*, Catharine, Nov 21 1833, 7
198 *BLACKBURN*, Richard S, *THOMAS*, Sarah A E, Nov 13 1833, 7
199 *BRENGLE*, Daniel, of Capt'n John, *THOMAS*, Caroline, of Wm, Decr 3 1833, 7
200 *BOSTON*, Jacob, 2d wife, *ENGLES*, Cristianna, of Silas, Decr 16 1833, 7
201 *BEAHEY*, John, *KELLY*, Margaret A, Feby 4 1834, in Balto, 7
202 *BEALL*, James B, *WILCOXON*, Louisa, of Wm, April 14 1834, 7
203 *BANTZ*, Gideon (Junior), *HARTMAN*, Juliann, April 23 1834, York, 7
204 *BRENGLE*, Lewis A, of Peter, *CARLTON*, Ann Rebecca, of Tho's, May 22 1834, 7
205 *BENTZ*, Ezra, of Geo, *ASHBURY*, Prudence, May 23 1834, Georgetown, 7
206 *BUTLER*, Pierce, *KEMBLE*, Fanny, June 7 1834, Phila, 7
207 *BRUMETT*, Michael, *ROLLINGTON*, Eleanor (Mrs), July 6 1834, 7
208 *BOWLUS*, Samuel, *GAVER*, Mahala, March 17 1835, 7
209 *BRENGLE*, Lawrence J, Capt John/2d wife, *SHRIVER*, Eliza, of And'w, May 12 1835, 7
210 *BAKER*, John, *COE*, Catherine (Mrs), "BERNHART", Septr 7 1835, SOWER, 7
211 *BOLLEBACHER*, Peter, *RENN*, Amelia, Septr 27 1835, 7
212 *BOSSLER*, David (Rev), *EMMITT*, Emily, Octr 29 1835, 7
213 *BRENGLE*, Christian (Sen'r), 2d wife, *SCHABACKER*, Barbara, Feby 2d 1836, 7
214 *BUCKEY*, Daniel, of Geo/2d wife, *HITE*, Caroline M, July 26 1836, 7
215 *BRENGLE*, Francis, of Peter, *DOWNEY*, Maria, of Wm, Augt 2 1836, 7
216 *BEVAN*, Joseph, 1st wife, *FISCHER*, Sarah, of Adam, Nov 14 1836, 7
217 *BAST*, Elias, *LAMBERT*, Mary, April 13 1837, 7
218 *BEATTY*, Afrebee Philip, *TRAPNELL*, Sarah, April 254 1837, 7
219 *BRENGEL*, Daniel (Sen'r), 2 wife, *KULLMAN*, Caroline (Mrs), March 13 1838, 7
220 *BLOCHER*, John, *DURBIN*, Elizabeth, of Wm, April 2 1838, Cuml'd, 7
221 *BENNETT*, Tilghman B, *SHIPLEY*, Catharne, Augt 14 1838, 7
222 *BAYER*, Henry, *HILTON*, Rosanna, Octr 23 1838, 7
223 *BENTLINGER*, Frederick, *SPONSELLER*, Amanda A, of Adam, Octr 25 1838, 7
224 *BOONE*, Tho's J, *BOOGHER*, Elizabeth A, Nov 6 1838, 7
225 *BUCKEY*, Michael, 2 wife, *ADAMS*, Mary (Mrs), Decr 1838, Georgetown, 8
226 *BASCOM*, Henry B (Rev DD), *VAN ANTWERP*, Eliza, March 5 1838, 8
227 *BEALL*, Enoch, *KNAUFF*, Maria, March 14 1839, "CANOUGH", 8
228 *BALCH*, Lewis P W (Rev), 1st wife, *JAY*, Anna, of Wm, April 10 1839, N York, 8
229 *BRANE*, Henry, *LAUMAN*, Margaret, (not listed as Miss), May 12 1839, 8

230 *BEARD*, Solomon, *EULER*, Margaret, April 24 1839, Woodsboro, 8
231 *BAKER*, Henry, *DUVALL*, Rebecca, May 30 1839, 8
232 *BRANE*, George, *HOFFMAN*, Sarah, June 5 1839, 8
233 *BERGER*, Philip, of Henry, *NULL*, Mary Jane, June 13 1839, Tiffin, Ohio, 8
234 *BAST*, Israel, *BURTON*, Mary Parks, July 28 1839, 8
235 *BURNES*, Cha's W, *MASON*, Mary, late of England, July 20 1839, 8
236 *BRENT*, R W H (Rev), *MILLER*, Catharine E, of Geo W, Augt 27 1839, 8
237 *BROWN*, E Lincoln (Dr), *FUNDENBURG*, Ann Maria, Octr 31 1839, 8
238 *BARRICK*, John W, *DEVILBISS*, Cath Sophia, of Geo, Octr 29 1839, 8
239 *BARRICK*, Ezra E, *CRAMER*, Harriet, Nov 19 1839, 8
240 *BOTHEIMER*, Ferdinand, *NEUBRANDT*, Christianna, Feby 27 1840, 8
241 *BRUNNER*, Isaac, *SCHULTZ*, Ann Sophia, of Geo, March 26 1840, 8
242 *BODISCE*, Alexander de, His Excellency, *WILLIAMS*, Harriett, April 9 1840, 8
243 *BINNIX*, Tho's H, *MOXLEY*, Margaret C, April 23 1840, 8
244 *BRENGLE*, Geo L, *NEILL*, Susan, of John W, May 7 1840, 8
245 *BAKER*, Wm Harrison (Dr), *FOX*, Margaret, July 31 1840, 8
246 *BAST*, Isaac, *FRAZIER*, Margaret, of Jeremiah, Augt 27 1840, 8
247 *BISER*, John G, *JARBOE*, Eleanor Ann, Nov 1 1840, 8
248 *BUCHHEIMER*, Conrad, *BRENGEL*, Elizabeth, Nov 3 1840, 8
249 *BENNETT*, Lewis H, *SUMAN*, Mary A M, of Isaac, Nov 5 1840, 8
250 *BANTZ*, William S, his 1st wife, *WARFIELD*, Caroline, January 5 1841, 8
251 *BUDDINTON*, Wm Ives (Rev), *GUNTON*, Elizabeth Livingston, Jany 5 1841, Washington, 8
252 *BELL*, Thomas, *MCDADE*, Mary, March 25 1841, 8
253 *BOSTEAN*, Solomon, *FOGLE*, Margaret, March 25 1841, 8
254 *BEALL*, Wm T, *SPONSELLER*, Mary R, of Jacob, April 8 1841, 8
255 *BRUNNER*, Henry, *SCHULTZ*, Margaret J, of Geo, May 19 1841, 8
256 *BOWMAN*, Tho's (Rev), *HARTMAN*, Matilda, July 1 1841, York, Pa, 8
257 *BLUME*, Michael, *BADEN*, Eliza Ann, July 29 1841, 8
258 *BLUMENAUER*, George, *SENTZELL*, Catharine, Augt 12 1841, 8
259 *BAKER*, Edward, *SCHULTZ*, Maria Louisa, of Geo, Septr 16 1841, 8
260 *BECK*, Edward, *OURAND*, Ann L (Mrs), "WALKER", Octr 31 1841, 8
261 *BURKHART*, Wm F, *LECHLEITER*, Agnes, Octr 28 1841, 8
262 *BALL*, Owen D, *BOYD*, Elizabeth, of David, Nov 18 1841, 8
263 *BIGGS*, James M, son of old Billy, *BROWN*, Mary L, Decr 12 1841, Balto, 8
264 *BRANDT*, Henry, *NAZERENUS*, Elizabeth, Feby 24 1842, 8
265 *BURUCKER*, John Simon, *LANGE*, Sophia (Mrs), (ROELKE), March 27 1842, 8
266 *BOLUND*, Daniel, *SIMPSON*, Sophia, of John, April 8 1842, Geotown, 8
267 *BAUERLEIN*, John Geo, *SAHM*, Mary, April 12th 1842, 9
268 *BAILEY*, Otho, *MOBBERLY*, Louisa, April 19 1842, 9
269 *BLUMENAUER*, Nicholas, *MEYER*, Fredericca, (not listed as Miss), April 19 1842, 9
270 *BAKER*, Wm B, *MANTZ*, Elizabeth, of Cyrus, May 31 1842, 9
271 *BOYD*, Andrew, *MANTZ*, Caroline, of Cyrus, Septr 1 1842, 9
272 *BEATTY*, Elie, Cashier Hagerstown Bank/2d wife, *YARNELL*, Mary D, Septr 8 1842, 9
273 *BROWN*, John R, *WEBB*, Mercy Elgar, of Jos B, Nov 10 1842, 9
274 *BANTZ*, Theodore S, *HARTMAN*, Cecelia, March 7 1842, York, Pa, 9
275 *BRENGEL*, J Nicholas, 1st wife, *SCHWALM*, Catharine, April 7 1843, 9
276 *BAUGHER*, Daniel B, *SHAFFER*, Susanna, widow of Jacob, April 6 1843, 9

277 BREIDTHAUPT, Frederick, *SAUMAN*, Wilhelmina, April 17 1843, 9
278 BROWER, Isaac (Maj), *CLEMSON*, Juliett, May 23 1843, 9
279 BERGER, Philip, *ROTH*, Mary, Septr 21 1843, 9
280 BIRELY, John Wm, *CRAMER*, Mary R, of Philip H, Octr 29 1843, 9
281 BUTLER, Richard F, *CLEVELAND*, Deborah A, Octr 15 1843, 9
282 BAYLEY, George W, *DILL*, Ellen Virginia, of Ezra, Nov 1 1843, 9
283 BARGEE, Miles, *LINTHICUM*, Ellen M, Feby 1 1844, 9
284 BUCKEY, Jacob M, *BUCKEY*, Harriott C, of Dan'l, May 9 1844, 9
285 BACHMAN, John W, *JAMISON*, Mary Jane, May 27 1844, 9
286 BOYLE, James, *WALLING*, Adelia H, of James, July 10 1844, 9
287 BOOTH, Nathaniel, *LIPSCOMB*, Mary Ellen, Octr 24 1844, 9
288 BLUMENAUER, Michael, *OESTERLE*, Mary Ann, Nov 21 1844, 9
289 BAUMAN, George, *GEITZ*, Miss, of Charles/(*Marg't), Decr 26 1844, 9
290 BECHTEL, J, (*John), *GETZENDANNER*, Mary A, May 20 1845, 9
291 BAER, George, *DUNLOP*, Mary Ann, May 18 1845, 9
292 BARTIS, Frederick Trenck, *FOX*, Maria, June 5 1845, 9
293 BECKLIE, Gabriel, *HALLER*, Elizab, of Henry, Augt 24 1845, 9
294 BRISCOE, Andrew Jackson, *SNELL*, Mary E, Augt 24 1845, 9
295 BRETTELL, J Cha's (Rev), *CROMWELL*, Elizabeth R, Octr 9 1845, 9
296 BUTLER, Ormond F (Junior), *HURDLE*, Malinda, Decr 11 1845, 9
297 BOTELER, Henry, *PHILPOT*, Violetta, Jany 8 1846, Merryland Tract, 9
298 BARRICK, Geo P, *DERR*, Catharine E, Jany 8 1846, Glade, 9
299 BAER, Cha's J (Dr), *SPRINGER*, Margaret, of Balto, Jany 27 1846, 9
300 BARTGIS, Geo Washington Lafayette, *ORTNER*, Elizabeth, of John, Feby 22 1846, 9
301 BOONE, Edward, *KEEFER*, Catharine, Feby 25 1846, 9
302 BUCKEY, George Wm, *RHODERICK*, Elizabeth, March 10 1846, 9
303 BARTGIS, John M, *BURGESS*, Mary Catharine, March 1 1846, Balto, 9
304 BRANDENBURG, John N, *SMITH*, Mary B, March 26 1846, 9
305 BRUNNER, John H, *BENTZ*, Mary Elizabeth (Mrs), widow of Dan'l, March 31 1846, 9
306 BIXLER, Wm Tell, *BALTZELL*, Clara L, of Tho's, March 31 1846, 9
307 BELL, Tho's, 2d wife, *REED*, Caroline, (PITTS), May 7 1846, 9
308 BALDERSON, John, his 3d wife, *LEE*, Margaret (Mrs), May 10 1846, 9
309 BRUNNER, Jonathan, 3d wife, *MICHAEL*, Mary E A, June 2d 1846, 10
310 BLUMENAUER, Michael, of George, *SCHRODER*, Johanna D, July 30 1846, "RETTGERING", 10
311 BIRELY, Valentine, 2d wife, *SEEVERS*, Eveline H, Augt 25 1846, 10
312 BARTHMANN, Valentine, *HAYS*, Marietta, Octr 25 1846, 10
313 BECKENBAUGH, Wm W, *STEWART*, Margaret Ann, Nov 12 1846, 10
314 BOONE, H Jerningham (Dr), *EICHELBERGER*, Mary Jane, Feby 2 1847, 10
315 BENTZ, Horatio Wm, *FAUBEL*, Catharine A, of Jacob, Feby 16 1847, 10
316 BOYD, John J, *SIFFORD*, Adelaide Frances, of John, March 10 1847, 10
317 BRECKINRIDGE, Robert J (Rev), 2d wife, *SHELBY*, Virginia (Mrs), April 1 1847, Kentucky, 10
318 BARRICK, John W, *HORNER*, Elizabeth, May 20 1847, 10
319 BROWN, Wm S, *IJAMS*, Josham M, of Plummer, May 20 1847, 10
320 BOLINGER, Werner, *EICHELBERGER*, Catherine, July 5 1847, 10
321 BENTZ, Jacob M, of Wm, *METZGER*, Ann M, Augt 17 1847, 10
322 BEALL, John H, *LEASE*, Matilda, Octr 14 1847, Linganore, 10

323 **BRIEN**, Luke Tierman, of Rob't C, *WILSON*, Mary V, Nov 2 1847, Balto, 10
324 **BAUGHER**, Oscar, of Isaac, *HILLEARY*, Elizabeth M, Decr 14 1847, 10
325 **BERGER**, Francis A, *BENDER*, Mary Catharine, of John (not listed as Miss), Decr 23 1847, 10
326 **BOBST**, William, *LEASE*, Sarah E, of Geo, April 19 1848, 10
327 **BLUMENAUER**, George, *ALBERT*, Margaret, May 4 1848, 10
328 **BECK**, John, *PFAUB*, Catharine, May 10 1848, 10
329 **BRENGLE**, Wm H, *BRISH*, Mary, of David, July 27 1848, of Christian Jun'r, 10
330 **BANTZ**, Edward (Dr), *COBLENTZ*, Malinda A, Septr 13 1848, Dayton, Ohio, 10
331 **BAKER**, Francis M (Rev), *TYLER*, Lucy F, of Dr Wm, Octr 3d 1848, 10
332 **BROWN**, Zachariah, *HYATT*, Lucy M, of Asa, Nov 23 1848, 10
333 **BLISS**, Wm W S (Col), *TAYLOR*, Betty, of Gen'l Zachary, Nov 23 1848, 10
334 **BLAKE**, William, 1st wife, *HERGESHEIMER*, Catherine, of Dan'l, Decr 6 1848, 10
335 **BENNETT**, Joseph S, *GROVE*, Lydia Ann, of Reuben, Decr 26 1848, 10
336 **BAKER**, Camillus S, *GAITHER*, Annie E, of Stuart, Jany 2 1849, 10
337 **BYERLY**, Jacob, 2d wife, *HAUER*, Catharine E, of Dan'l, Jun'r, Jany 23 1849, 10
338 **BARTGIS**, Hiram, *CARLIN*, Matilda E, of James, February 27 1849, 10
339 **BECK**, Osborn, *GILDZ*, Rebecca, April 10 1849, 10
340 **BURTON**, John C, *MCCLEERY*, Ellen, of Wm, June 30 1849, Brookville, Ind, 10
341 **BENDER**, John H, *LEASE*, Barbara Ann, of Geo, July 22 1849, 10
342 **BRUTCHEY**, Henry, *WOODS*, Eleanora, Octr 4 1849, 10
343 **BRENGLE**, Jacob, of Wm, *BUCHER*, Sarah Elizabeth, Octr 10 1849, 10
344 **BELT**, T Hanson, *BOONE*, Clara, of Benedict, Octr 23 1849, 10
345 **BECK**, John J, *FINCH*, Ann Catharine, of John, Octr 31 1849, 10
346 **BELMONT**, August, *PERRY*, Miss, of Com Mathew C, 7 Nov 1849, ROTHSCHILD agent NY/SCHONBURG, 10
347 **BUCKEY**, Geo Jacob, *BOBST*, Sarah A, Feby 10 1850, 10
348 **BENTZ**, Lawrence, *LAMBRECHT*, Ann Sophia, of Mich'l, March 19 1850, 10
349 **BALCH**, Lewis P W (Rev), his 2d wife, *WIGGIN*, Emily, (of London), April 25 1850, 10
350 **BRUNNER**, Lewis A (Rev), *SHEARMAN*, Jane E, Octr 1 1850, Delaware, Ohio, 10
351 **BARTGIS**, James, (Mayor), *SHAWEN*, Mary E, Octr 30 1850, 11
352 **BISHOP**, Edwin, *DIDIER*, Josephine, Nov 6 1850, Balto, 11
353 **BUHRMAN**, Alfred (Rev), *SCHULTZ*, Elizabeth Ann, Jany 16 1851, 11
354 **BEIDEL**, Christopher, *SCHWIN*, Elizabeth, Jany 20 1851, 11
355 **BLUMENAUER**, Henry, *ABB*, Margaret, January 28 1851, 11
356 **BROWN**, Nelson, "SANDERSON'S", *MARTIN*, Sophia, June 5 1851, Colored Friends, 11
357 **BROBST**, John Frederick (Rev), *KOLB*, Ann R, of Raemer, Nov 26 1851, 11
358 **BRUTCHEY**, Jacob (Sen'r), his 2d wife, *TURNER*, Ann Barbara (Mrs), Jany 6 1852, 11
359 **BUCKEY**, Richard Root, *WOLFE*, Susan Elizabeth, of John, Jany 6 1852, 11
360 **BECHT**, Wm H, *WEINBRENNER*, Harriott, Feby 24 1852, 11
361 **BALTZELL**, James M, *STAUFFER*, Mary A, March 25 1852, 11
362 **BOLLER**, Henry A, *HAHN*, Matilda, March 25 1852, 11
363 **BOYD**, Charles (Doctr), of David, *REEDER*, Charlotte M, April 8 1852, Cincin, O, 11
364 **BROWN**, William, *WOLFE*, Mary Margaret, of Adam (not listed as Miss), June 29 1852, 11
365 **BUDDY**, Philip, *STEIN*, Sophia H, Septr 1 1852, Globe Inn, 11
366 **BRAWNER**, Joseph, *YERK*, Catharine (Mrs), (LAMBRECHT), Augt 29 1852, Emmittsburg, 11
367 **BENTZ**, Henry, of Wm, *DEGRANGE*, Catharine M, of John, Septr 9 1852, 11
368 **BUZZARD**, David, *HEIM*, Susan C, Septr 9 1852, 11

369 *BANTZ*, A Sydney, *PORTER*, Isabella S, Septr 22 1852, 11
370 *BECHTEL*, Samuel, *WICKES*, Mary P, of Rev Wm, Oct 1852, Carlisle, Pa, 11
371 *BURKHART*, Ezra G W, *WARD*, Elizabeth M, Octr 14 1852, 11
372 *BROWN*, Benjamin F, *REICH*, Dorcus H, of Philip, Nov 2 1852, 11
373 *BALCH*, Thomas, *SWIFT*, Emily, Octr 5 1852, Phila, 11
374 *BARTGIS*, Dewitt Clinton, *LAMBERT*, Mary, of John, Nov 30 1852, 11
375 *BARTHOLOW*, John, 2d wife, *MCLAUGHLIN*, Sarah (Mrs), Decr 2 1852, 11
376 *BRUNNER*, Edward Jacob, *COX*, Caroline, Decr 23 1852, Delaware, O, 11
377 *BENDER*, Edward, of John, *CAREY*, Annie M, of John, Decr 26 1852, 11
378 *BOGUE*, John J, *DONNALLY*, Elizabeth R, of Patrick, Jany 20 1853, 11
379 *BONAPARTE*, Louis Napoleon 3d, *de MONTIJO*, Eugenia, of Spain, Jany 29 1853, 11
380 *BROWN*, Wm A, *PEARCE*, Emily B, February 17 1853, Balt, 11
381 *BRUNNER*, Valentine Stickel, *PYFER*, Margaret M, of Ph, March 8 1853, 11
382 *BENDER*, Jacob, of John, *SMALL*, Charlotte, March 14 1853, 11
383 *BUTLER*, Ormon Fischer, *BRENGLE*, Barbara (Mrs), March 24 1853, "SCHABACKER", 11
384 *BATSON*, John B, *PIMM*, Mary, May 5 1853, 11
385 *BRENGLE*, Sam'l Tho's, *FULL*, Madera, May 5 1853, 11
386 *BANTZ*, Wm S, 2d wife, *BRUNNER*, Caroline, of John of J, June 1st 1853, 11
387 *BAKER*, Ephraim, *WEINBRENNER*, Julia, June 2 1853, 11
388 *BORGER*, William, *FISCHER*, Mary, May 15 1853, 11
389 *BECKER*, George, *MAY*, Magdalena, July 3 1853, 11
390 *BOBST*, Joshua D, *FLEMING*, Julia A E, of Jos P, Augt 10 1853, 11
391 *BURRIER*, Wm H, *DRAPER*, Margaret, Septr 11 1853, 11
392 *BAER*, Henry, *CARNES*, Sarah Ann, (KERN), Decr 25 1853, 11
393 *BARRICK*, Joseph, *DIXON*, Caroline, of Haines, Feby 23 1854, 12
394 *BEIDEL*, Andrew, *BEALL*, Mary E, March 6 1854, 12
395 *BURALL*, William, *REAM*, Elizabeth Ann, March 28 1854, 12
396 *BUCHHEIMER*, George, *GLEIS*, Mary M, Septr 5 1854, 12
397 *BRUTSCHY*, Basil, *MCDEVITT*, Elizabeth, Septr 10 1854, 12
398 *BENDER*, John, 2d wife, *CARLIN*, Eliza A, Septr 19 1854, 12
399 *BLESSING*, Parker George, *YONSON*, Wilhelmina, Septr 19 1854, 12
400 *BALLINGER*, Herrman, his 2d wife, *EICHELBERGER*, Mary, Octr 22 1854, 12
401 *BARTGIS*, Martin L, *EBNECHT*, Ann Rebecca, of John, Nov 5 1854, 12
402 *BENNETT*, Robert, *GUIE*, Margaret, July 30 1854, Kaighns Point, NJ, 12
403 *BEST*, Henry L, *LAMBRECHT*, Mary Jane, of Jacob, Jany 18 1855, Glade, 12
404 *BALTZELL*, Wm H (Dr), *NELSON*, Josephine V, of Madison, Feby 14 1855, 12
405 *BENNETT*, David T, *JAMES*, Charity A, of Washington, May 8 1855, 12
406 *BRUGONIER*, Wm W, *HULL*, Lydia A, May 3 1855, Glade, 12
407 *BOND*, John R, *MORGAN*, Virginia D, of Thomas W, June 26 1855, 12
408 *BOWERS*, Daniel, 2d wife, *WILLIAR*, Margaret Ann (Mrs), Augt 26 1855, 12
409 *BAUMGARTNER*, Henry, *SCHABACKER*, Caroline, of Jacob, Decr 1855, 12
410 *BISHOP*, Mark, *BECK*, Agnes, of Adam, Decr 25 1855, Woodsborough, 12
411 *BASFORD*, J Henry, *TROUT*, Julian, January 17 1856, 12
412 *BLESSING*, Francis T, *KERTZENDORFFER*, Henrietta, of Jos, Jany 29 1856, 12
413 *BARTHOLOW*, J Presley, his 2d wife, *PHILIPS*, Isabella, Feby 14 1856, 12
414 *BOWERS*, Wm D, *ROUTZAHN*, Charlotte E, of Joseph, March 20 1856, 12
415 *BAUGHER*, John F, of Isaac, *WINCHESTER*, Evaline Kirkham, of Hiram, March 26 1856, 12

416 BUSEY, Ezra F (Rev), *CORNER*, S Jane, of James, April 17 1856, Balto, 12
417 BURALL, Oliver, *NICHOLS*, Ann, May 1 1856, 12
418 BUCKEY, Geo P, *SCHRINER*, Elizabeth R, of Carroll Co, May 29 1856, 12
419 BLACKSTONE, Benjamin H, *WARTHEN*, Josephine A, June 25 1856, 12
420 BROADRUF, Cornelius A, 1st wife, *CREAGER*, Eliza A, July 25 1856, 12
421 BURCK, Wm, of Philip, *REEL*, Miss, of Otho/(*Ann C), Augt 18 1856, 12
422 BEDDINGER, John A, *ANDERS*, Susan, Septr 5 1856, 12
423 BAYER, Jacob M, of Tho's, *GUYTON*, Mary, Septr 17 1856, 12
424 BOWERS, Allen T, *HOY*, Clementine V, Septr 25 1856, 12
425 BERTERMAN, John, *LAMPE*, Henrietta, Octr 13 1856, 12
426 BALTZELL, Hezekiah, *HETTERLY*, Elizabeth C, Octr 30 1856, 12
427 BIBBY, James Monroe, *HEISKELL*, Elizabeth K, Octr 30 1856, NEEDWOOD, 12
428 BUCK, John M, 2d wife, *COE*, Emma, Nov 12 1856, Balto, 12
429 BLANK, John H, *HARGETT*, Harriott V, Nov 18 1856, 12
430 BUCKEY, Charles, of Mich'l, *SHOEMAKER*, Elizabeth, of Geo, Nov 20 1856, Georgetown, 12
431 BAKER, Ezra, 2d wife/of Ohio, *GRIMM*, Ann Sophia, Decr 2 1856, 12
432 BREWER, Jacob Newton, "BRUA", *BREWER*, Eliza Jane, January 13 1857, 12
433 BAKER, Joseph G, *DEVILBISS*, Hannah, January 29 1857, 12
434 BAILE, David C, *NAILL*, Mary Elizabeth, of David W, Feby 26 1857, 12
435 BELL, H, *SMALL*, Lizzie A, of Capt Wm, April 8 1857, Balto, 13
436 BRANDENBURG, Joel, *HEWITT*, Melissa, April 23 1857, 13
437 BENTZ, George W, of Wm, *BELL*, Sarah Catharine, May 6 1857, 13
438 BOYD, Asbury McKendree, of David, *BAKER*, Julia E, of Jacob, May 12 1857, Winchester, Va, 13
439 BONINE, Tho's W, *HALLER*, Maria L, of Philip, May 12 1857, Balto, 13
440 BURCK, John, *STUBBINS*, Eliza, July 17 1857, KLEIN, 13
441 BOWERS, Alfred B, *SMITH*, Henrietta E, Octr 8 1857, 13
442 BOTELER, Jefferson O, *KEEFER*, Alice V, of J Henry, Octr 28 1857, 13
443 BRADY, George C, *HILL*, Margretta E, Nov 18 1857, 13
444 BOWERS, John, *MILLER*, Sarah A E, January 12 1858, 13
445 BENTZ, Daniel, of Wm, *YOUNG*, Frances H, Feby 18 1858, 13
446 BRUTSCHY, Joseph, *MINNICH*, Ann C, April 6 1858, 13
447 BAUMAN, Frederick, *HARTBAUER*, Charlotte, of Wm, April 11 1858, 13
448 BERGER, John W, *SEEMAN*, Elizabeth, of Christian, May 2 1858, 13
449 BOWERS, Wm W (Rev), *COSSMAN*, Louisa M A, June 1 1858, Lunenburg, N Scotia, 13
450 BECK, Nicholas, *GRUNDEL*, Eve Mary, Septr 23 1858, 13
451 BEARD, John W, *COLE*, Mary Emily, Octr 13 1858, 13
452 BOND, Isaac, (Civil Engineer), *ORR*, Caroline E, of Rev A V B ORR, Nov 4 1858, 13
453 BARRICK, Josiah, *MCCORMACK*, Jane Rebecca, Nov 18 1858, 13
454 BROOKS, Cha's S, *CUMMING*, Mora B, of Aug's J, Nov 28 1858, York, 13
455 BOGGERT, Harvey, *FOGEL*, Rebecca, Decr 25 1858, Woodsboro, 13
456 BUTLER, Samuel J, *RODENEISZER*, Catharine, Decr 28 1858, 13
457 BAYER, Francis, *SCHMIDT*, Elizabeth, of Jacob, Jany 11 1859, 13
458 BOTTLEMAY, Vernon, *STEWART*, Margaret, Jany 12 1859, 13
459 BURGHEIM, Philip Fahnenberg de, Baron, *STROTHER*, Miss, of J F S, Jany 5 1859, at Brussels, 13
460 BARRICK, Christian, *SMITH*, Nancy, March 6 1959, Glade, 13

461 BRENGLE, John W, CROMWELL, Ann Rebecca, March 3 1859, 13
462 BRANDENBURG, James A, WAHRENFELSZ, Mary A R, March 22 1859, Middletown valley, 13
463 BOYER, Oliver, RICE, Martha M, April 5 1859, Harmony Grove, 13
464 BLUMENAUER, Henry, SMITH, Anna M, April 21 1859, Cumberland, Md, 13
465 BRECKINRIDGE, Wm C P, CLAY, Miss, of Tho's Hart CLAY, April 1859, Kentucky, 13
466 BROWN, Wm H, CARMACK, Mary E, May 1 1859, Graceham, 13
467 BUCKIGNANI, Antonio, age 19, EATON, Mary L (Mrs), (TIMBERLAKE)/age 65/her 3d husband, June 7th 1859, Washington, 13
468 BURTON, James H, 3rd wife, MAUZY, Eugenia H, {his 1st wife is her sister/complr}, June 7 1859, Harpersferry, 13
469 BRUST, Conrad, SANDMEYER, Louisa, July 19 1859, 13
470 BELL, Emanuel, BASFORD, Elizabeth, Septr 15 1859, 13
471 BURALL, Oliver, GRAY, Ann E, Octr 17 1859, N Market, 13
472 BISER, Daniel G, SHAFER, Albenia E, Octr 11 1859, 13
473 BALL, William, TRAIL, Theresa Ann, Nov 11 1859, 13
474 BIRELY, George Krebs, SCHLEY, Ann E, of Edward, Decr 13 1859, 13
475 BARRICK, Theodore, BALTZELL, Juliann, Nov 17 1859, 13
476 BROWN, Geo H, (of Wm S), GINN, Mary, Decr 14 1859, Balto, 13
477 BITTEL, Tho's F, WATERS, Mary Elizabeth, Decr 22 1859, Middletownvalley, 14
478 BOWERS, Wm H, MCMULLIN, Rose Ann, Decr 27 1859, Berlin, 14
479 BUTTS, Joseph, ASHERMAN, Mary M, Jany 12 1860, 14
480 BUSING, Wm F, HOBBS, Amelia, Feby 21 1860, 14
481 BRUNNER, Wm L, MILLER, Juliann H, Feby 23 1860, 14
482 BUSEY, Wm G, DUNLOP, Lizzie, (of Col Henry), Feby 1 1860, 14
483 BOYD, Wilson Rowan, ROCHE, Lizzie H, March 6 1860, Balto, 14
484 BARRICK, Wm T, BECK, Harriett E, March 4 1860, Woodsboro, 14
485 BAKER, R B, WAYS, Harriet A, March 28 1860, Balto, 14
486 BEALL, Evan F, DUNAWIN, Phebe A, of Tho's, April 5 1860, 14
487 BAUGHER, John David, SCHENKEL, Sarah L, April 10 1860, 14
488 BALTZELL, Wesley, DARNALL, Rachel, of Rob't, April 24 1860, 14
489 BARCLAY, R G (Dr), US Consul at Beyroot{Beirut comp}, HAMPTON, Louisa, March 1860, 14
490 BOULIGNY, J E (Hon), PARKER, Miss, May 1 1860, Washington/N Orleans, 14
491 BECHTOLL, Harvey, HARBAUGH, Harriott Josephine, April 24 1860, 14
492 BROWN, John Wilson, BAER, Elizabeth Schellman, of Dr Mich'l, Septr 6 1860, Balto, 14
493 BARBER, Cha's, RIDDELMOSER, Ann, Septr 4 1860, 14
494 BREWER, John H C, CUMMING, Fannie, of Aug's J, Augt 30 1860, 14
495 BRUTSCHY, John H, TURNER, Margaret A, Septr 25 1860, 14
496 BLANEY, Cha's E, LOANE, Martha F, Octr 1 1860, Balto, 14
497 BECKENBAUGH, George W, KLEIN, Mollie A, of Andrew, Octr 23 1860, 14
498 BROCKE, Theodore, WERNER, Annie, (not listed as Miss), Octr 25 1860, 14
499 BACHMAN, Henry C (Rev), of Nazereth, Pa, GERNAND, Sarah E, of Jacob, Octr 28 1860, 14
500 BRUGONIER, Alfred, MCGEE, Elizabeth, Nov 8 1860, 14
501 BAKER, Camillus W, BAUGHER, Ann E, of Isaac, Nov 22 1860, 14
502 BROWNING, Basil D, DIXON, Mary Jane, Nov 27 1860, 14
503 BRISH, Wm H, (of John H), WACHTER, Margaret S, of Dan'l, January 29 1861, 14

504 *BEST*, George W, *CRAMER*, Catharine B, March 5 1861, Glade, 14
505 *BLUMENAUER*, Michael (Sen'r), *KETTLER*, Catherine (Mrs), "BINGER" "LANGE", March 26 1861, 14
506 *BAUER*, John G, *FISCHER*, Catharine B, March 11 1861, 14
507 *BLUNT*, Wm W, *DORSEY*, Lizzie M, of Harry W, March 28 1861, 14
508 *BRENGLE*, Lewis A (Junior), *RAMSBURG*, Ellen R, of Wm H, April 30 1861, 14
509 *BRADY*, David F S, *KERN*, Bettie, of James, May 23 1861, 14
510 *BROWN*, John, *KNIPPLE*, Mary A, May 19 1861, Carroll Co, Md, 14
511 *BOYER*, Jesse J, *PAINE*, Mary E, May 31 1861, 14
512 *BAKER*, Harrison, *MEALEY*, Jemima, July 9 1861, 14
513 *BISER*, David, *CRONE*, Charlotte A V, Augt 6 1861, Middletownvalley, 14
514 *BAER*, Henry, *CROMWELL*, Susan, June 6 1861, 14
515 *BAKER*, John P, *MATHEWS*, Mary Rebecca (Mrs), BIRELY RICE MATTHEWS, Septr 15 1861, {BAKER her 3d husband compilr}, 14
516 *BOWERS*, Reuben G, *HEFFNER*, Mary L, Septr 26 1861, 14
517 *BRADENBERG*, Matthias, *BLESSING*, Loretto A, Octr 1 1861, 14
518 *BUCKEY*, Edward E, *OGBORN*, Fannie, of John W, Octr 29 1861, 14
519 *BANTZ*, Peter Sowers, 1st wife, *MURPHY*, Sarah A P, Octr 30 1861, St Louis, 15
520 *BAST*, Israel, his 2d wife, *OTT*, Mary Jane, January 15 1862, 15
521 *BRENGLE*, Nicholas, 2d wife, *ROSS*, Christianna (Mrs), Jany 23 1862, 15
522 *BITTLE*, Wm Metzger, *RAUZAHN*, Catharine, Jany 30 1862, 15
523 *BROWN*, Martin L, 1st wife, *BUHRMAN*, Mary E, Jany 12 1862, 15
524 *BAKER*, Nathan L, *EILER*, Juliann, Jany 6 1862, 15
525 *BECROFT*, John L, *HENNINGTON*, Frances, March 11 1862, 15
526 *BRUST*, Caspar (Jun'r), *HABERCORN*, Sarah, March 31 1862, 15
527 *BUHRMAN*, Ephraim H, *HALE*, Ann Virginia, April 10 1862, 15
528 *BRUNNER*, Charles A, (of Lewis), *GANNON*, Catharine C, May 15 1862, 15
529 *BEST*, Wm H, *HALLER*, Elizabeth C, of Mich'l H, Augt 28 1862, 15
530 *BISER*, John W, *REEDER*, Jane E, Octr 20 1862, 15
531 *BROADRUP*, Cornelius A, 2d wife, *CANNON*, Anna S, Nov 13 1862, 15
532 *BRIDGES*, Wm James, *JONES*, Susan H G, of Aubury, Decr 11 1862, "Boyd", 15
533 *BOHN*, Daniel, *LEAKINS*, Mary E, March 12 1863, 15
534 *BAUMGERTNER*, John, *SINN*, Franny E, of Dan'l, March 31 1863, 15
535 *BAKER*, Nathan, *ADAMS*, Elizabeth, April 7 1863, Woodsboro, 15
536 *BIGGS*, Elisha H, 1st wife, *CROWN*, Elizabeth V, April 15 1863, "Manor", 15
537 *BOWLUS*, Josiah, *KOOGLE*, Emiline, April 1863, Middletownvalley, 15
538 *BEATTY*, Wm H, *NUSZ*, Anna Mary, of Wm, April 30 1863, 15
539 *BRADSHAW*, Wm H, *HAUER*, Annie M, of John, April 25 1863, 15
540 *BOARDWELL*, Daniel B, *LOVELY*, Amantha E, EBRECHT, Septr 13 1863, 15
541 *BENNETT*, John H, (of Lewis H), *CROUSE*, Nannie H, Septr 10 1863, 15
542 *BILLY*, John C, "96 Pa Regt", *STONER*, Anna Mary, Nov 5 1863, 15
543 *BOPST*, John H, *MISS*, Laura, Nov 3 1863, 15
544 *BUTLER*, Kennedy H (Lieut), 2nd wife, *RISER*, Sarah E W, of Geo H, Nov 12 1863, 15
545 *BRENGLE*, Jacob, of Christian, *TAYLOR*, Margaret, Decr 1 1863, 15
546 *BECKENBAUGH*, George (Sen'r), 2d wife, *CRAFT*, Sophia, Feby 3 1864, Balto, 15
547 *BURRIER*, Cha's D, *HOKE*, Catharine, of Sam'l "HOCH", March 1 1864, 15
548 *BASFORD*, Jacob, *RENN*, Harriett, March 3 1864, 15

549 BUHRMAN, Jacob, MANTZ, Elizabeth (Mrs), widow of Edward, Feby 18 1864, 15
550 BLESSING, Wm H, THOMAS, Mary A, March 23 1864, 15
551 BROADRUP, George E, HELDEBRAND, Ann M, March 31 1864, 15
552 BEST, Nathaniel L, (US Army), HARRIS, Josephine, April 5 1864, 15
553 BEST, John T, DORSEY, Joanna M, April 7 1864, 15
554 BASFORD, George, RENN, Lauretto, April 13 1864, 15
555 BEATTY, Joseph E (Dr), TRAPNELL, Emily, of Jos (Jun'r), May 2d 1864, "cousins", 15
556 BETSON, Samuel P, MEASELL, Amanda, April 4 1864, 15
557 BARRICK, Presley Jones, LEASE, Margart E, Sept 10 1864, 15
558 BANTZ, Peter Sowers, 2d wife, REESE, Mattie T, of Rev D E, Nov 3 1864, 15
559 BEACH, Philip S, NUSZ, Eleanora V, of Wm, Nov 29 1864, 15
560 BUHRMAN, David H, HARBAUGH, Susan, Decr 1 1864, 15
561 BOWEN, James E, JAMES, Mary M, of Washington, Decr 28 1864, 16
562 BANDELL, Geo W, SMITH, Lucretia, of David F, Feby 15 1865, 16
563 BALL, Cha's N, 2d wife, KOONTZ, Margaret C (Mrs), (widow of Henry of John), Feby 2 1865, 16
564 BROOKER, Joseph H, KRAUTH, Louisa A, March 20 1865, 16
565 BECKER, John, (US Army), WHITEFORD, Anna M V, April 2 1865, 16
566 BAER, George W, RAUZAHN, Catharine, of Adam, April 13 1865, 16
567 BRENGLE, James S, (of Law J), GAW, U Annie, April 27 1865, Phila, 16
568 BECK, James M, BOTELER, Alice V (Mrs), widow of Jefferson O, April 9 1865, 16
569 BUCK, Jerome B, LEILICH, Maria L, of Jacob, April 13 1865, 16
570 BAST, John H, TITLOW, Maggie E, July 18 1865, 16
571 BONN, Frederick (Rev), GUMMEL, Louisa, July 26 1865, Balto, 16
572 BLESSING, George W, WEAGLEY, Valetta S T, Val ADAM's daughter, Augt 3 1865, 16
573 BROWN, Martin L, 2d wife, CREEGER, Henrietta S, Septr 17 1865, Hauvers, 16
574 BURTON, James Henry, REYNALDS, Mary Ellen, Septr 18 1865, 16
575 BURRIER, Simon E, POOLE, Emma J, of John (Butcher), Septr 21 1865, 16
576 BENTZ, Lewis, ENGEL, Lydia A, Septr 21 1865, 16
577 BILLINGSLEA, James L (Dr), COVER, Lizzie, Sept 27 1865, 16
578 BAER, John R, SCHWAERIN, Maggie, Octr 12 1865, 16
579 BUXTON, Brook (Jun'r), BAKER, Emma J (Mrs), Decr 7 1865, BUXTON, 16
580 BETTS, Samuel C, NELSON, Emma F, of Madison, April 4 1866, 16
581 BALTZELL, Robert C, FORNEY, Susan S, April 16 1866, 16
582 BROADBENT, Wm (Jun'r, Dr), MCCRON, Jennie, of Rev Jon, Septr 4 1866, Balto, 16
583 BISER, Wm Henry, SHOOK, Clementine M, Octr 9 1866, 16
584 BLESSING, S V, SIMMONS, Emma, of John A, Octr 31 1866, 16
585 BAER, James J, (of Dr Mich'l S), FESSLER, Susan, of Henry B, Nov 23 1866, 16
586 BEEBE, Charles, DAVIS, Laura V, of Tyler, Feby 21 1867, 16
587 BROADRUP, Cornelius A, his 3d wife, MCPHERSON, Alphemia J, Feby 26 1867, 16
588 BUCKEY, Geo Wm, 2d wife, COLLINS, Lydia A (Mrs), March 5 1867, 16
589 BISER, James P, DIXON, Sophia E, of Wm H, April 9 1867, 16
590 BANTZ, Eugene H, of Gideon, FRANCE, Louisa M, June 4 1867, Balto, 16
591 BOPST, Milton B, CONLEY, Rose A, of Harrison, July 22 1867, 16
592 BUTLER, John Geo (Rev DD), 2d wife, BAKER, Lizzie A (Mrs), Octr 16 1867, "BAUGHER", 16
593 BAKER, A H, MILLER, Sallie A J, of Jacob T C, Nov 28 1867, 16

The Joseph Engelbrecht Marriage Ledger of Frederick Co., MD 1820-1890 *Marriage List*

594 BAUMGERTNER, Charles, **KING**, Henrietta, (KONIG) of Henry, Jany 6 1868, 16
595 BURRIER, John W, **BRUTSCHY**, Mary C, Feby 18 1868, 16
596 BRENDEL, Cha's H, **WALTERS**, Isabella, March 24 1868, 16
597 BURUCKER, J Louis, **GRUMBEIN**, Alice M, March 29 1868, 16
598 BARNEY, Jerome A, **WHITNEY**, Maria, March 21 1868, California, 16
599 BOWIE, Washington, **SCHLEY**, Nettie, of Geo, June 23 1868, Hagerstown, 16
600 BROWN, Henry, **HEIM**, Euphrosina (Mrs), widow of Lewis A, Septr 17 1868, 16
601 BECHENBAUGH, John M (Dr), of Geo, **DOUGLASS**, Annie, of Rev Rob't, Nov 24 1868, 16
602 BARNES, Samuel T, of Tho's, **KEHLER**, Ella V, of Frederick (#), Nov 25 1868, 16
603 BOYD, A McKendree, of David/2 wife, **ROY**, Mary Mason, of Wm H, Jany 7 1869, Mathews Co, Va, 17
604 BLAND, I H, of Gloucester Co, Va, **BURTON**, Columbia T, of R Henry BURTON, Jany 7 1869, 17
605 BREADY, C Edward, **LAMAR**, Annie M, Jany 14 1869, 17
606 BARNES, John R, of Balto, **BARTGIS**, Maggie E, of Geo W L, Jany 21 1869, 17
607 BEAN, Samuel, of Nebraska, **MANTZ**, Mary E, of Cha's, Feby 4 1869, 17
608 BABEL, J Christian, **ASHBAUGH**, Mary J, of John, Feby 2 1869, 17
609 BECKLEY, Constantine F, of Gabriel, **KOONTZ**, Cornelia E, of Edward, Feby 15 1869, 17
610 BRENGLE, George M, **ECKSTEIN**, Lizzie, of Ch'n, April 29 1869, 17
611 BRUNNER, John H, of John H, **DOWNING**, Maggie W, May 5 1869, 17
612 BROSIUS, John W, **TEHAN**, Anna, of John, May 11 1869, 17
613 BROWN, No first name given, **MCCLEERY**, Lizzie Hanna "KNIGHT", Nov 5 1868, ommitted before, 17
614 BYERLY, J Davis, of Jacob, **MARKELL**, Mary, of Geo, Octr 27 1869, 17
615 BIRCH, Joseph H, **CONNER**, Mollie E, of James, Nov 1 1869, "Zeph HARRISON", 17
616 BELL, Herbert, **NEAL**, Sophia F, of Sam'l, Nov 23 1869, col'd friends, 17
617 BELT, T H (Jun'r), **TYLER**, Maria, of Dr Wm Bradley, Decr 8 1869, 17
618 BENNER, Francis, of Va, **DILL**, Emma J, of John F, Decr 16 1869, 17
619 BABCOCK, Hiram, **GETZENDANNER**, Margaret (Mrs), "SENTZELL", Octr 7 1867, Coridon, Ia, 17
620 BUSHEY, Jacob M, 2d wife, **BROMWELL**, Gussie, of Balto, Jany 18 1870, 17
621 BANTZ, Harry H, of Wm T, **BARNETT**, Annie E, Jany 25 1870, Balto, 17
622 BANNISTER, R Harry, of Ohio, **BUSHEY**, Frances V, of J M, Feby 10 1870, 17
623 BROADBENT, G S (Rev), **CREAGER**, Carrie E, of Eph'm, Feby 23 1870, 17
624 BAST, Samuel L, of Isaac, **CUTSAIL**, Ann J, March 24 1870, 17
625 BROWNING, Elias, **HOWARD**, Sarah Ann (Mrs), Augt 15 1870, 17
626 BUCKEY, Francis T, **GROVE**, Louisa, Septr 5 1870, 17
627 BUL, Ole, the Fidler, **THORPE**, Sarah, of Madison, Wisc, Septr 6 1870, 17
628 BRUNNER, Edward Livingston, of Lewis, **HERSCHMAN**, Anna M, Octr 27 1870, 17
629 BANTZ, Theodore Marion, of Gideon, **EADER**, Annie E, of Wm, Feby 21 1871, 17
630 BRENDEL, Franklin A, of H'y G, **ZIEGLER**, Alice S, of Henry L, Mar 7 1871, 17
631 BUSHEY, T Frank, of Jacob, **WILE**, Annie C, of Dan'l, March 28 1871, 17
632 BONAPART, Jerome Napoleon (Col), **EDGAR**, Caro'e Leroy (Mrs), Septr 7 1871, 17
633 BRENGLE, Edward A, **LEACHEY**, Annie E, Jan 2 1872, 17
634 BAUFELTER, George, **FRALEY**, Jennetta, of H'y, Jan 5 1872, 17
635 BARTON, John, **DUVALL**, Annie D, Jan 18 1872, 17
636 BURRIER, Lewis H, **BEARD**, Sarah V, March 26 1872, 17

637 BROWN, Daniel, RIDGELY, Ellen, May 7 1872, F F Seminary, 17
638 BABEL, George Andrew, KOLB, Marceline, of J Mich'l, May 22 1872, 17
639 BAKER, James T, MANN, M Virginia, of Stephen S, Septr 3 1872, 17
640 BIRELY, Philip Henry Clay, of J Wm, BAILE, M Ellen, of Jesse, Octr 1 1872, 17
641 BANTZ, Wm S, his 3rd wife, LEITER, Elizabeth (Mrs), Octr 31 1872, 17
642 BRUNNER, Franklin, of Lewis/1st wife, STOTTELMEYER, Susan M, Decr 8 1872, 17
643 BROOKS, David W, RICE, Harriett A, of Geo, Feb 13 1873, 17
644 BENTLINGER, Adam T, MURPHY, Sarah A, Feb 20 1873, 17
645 BOWLUS, Edw (Dr), of David, CLAGETT, Mollie, of Tho's, April 22 1873, 18
646 BIRELY, Wm C, of J Wm, SINN, Laura V, of Edw, Octr 21 1873, 18
647 BURRIER, Calvin S, CRUMBAUGH, Flora C, of F B, Octr 14 1873, 18
648 BLACK, Geo W Z (Col), PIGMAN, Mary Briscoe, of Hanson, Octr 30 1873, 18
649 BIGGS, Elisha H, 2d wife, NUSZ, Clara, of Hiram M, Decr 17 1873, 18
650 BANTZ, Clarence, BLACKISTON, Jennie, of W Va, Nov 26 1873, 18
651 BELKNAP, Wm W (Hon), Sec of War/2d wife, BOWERS, H A (Mrs), Decr 12 1873, 18
652 BUHRMAN, Harvey (Dr), FOX, Sophia, of Geo H, Decr 26 1873, 18
653 BRUST, Henry, of Caspar, STULL, Ann Florence, March 1 1874, 18
654 BOUIC, Rufus A, of Rockville, SELLMANN, Maggie V (Mrs), March 19 1874, "HOLLOW", 18
655 BEAMER, Nelson, CLARK, Carrie (Mrs), "PALMER", March 11 1874, of Wm T PALMER, 18
656 BRUST, George, of Caspar, BIELFELD, Salome, Augt 2 1874, 18
657 BECKER, Louis P, of Henry, PHEBUS, Mary E, of Ja's H, Augt 4 1874, 18
658 BARNUM, Phineas Taylor, 2d wife/aged 67, FISH, Nancy, aged 26, Septr 15 1874, 18
659 BAER, William H, THOMPSON, Mary J, Septr 1 1874, 18
660 BAKER, Edward, of Fred'k/2d wife, HAYS, Harriet A, Septr 14 1874, 18
661 BENDER, Francis T, COLLIER, Sarah, May 28 1874, Va, 18
662 BARNES, John, COVELL, Lydia (Mrs), Nov 2 1874, Bartonsville, 18
663 BRUST, Charles, of Caspar, STULL, Annie S, Nov 3 1874, 18
664 BOYD, David, of David, PARSONS, Mamie D, Decr 15 1874, Balto, 18
665 BARRICK, John C, WACHTER, Florence E, Jan 19 1875, Glade, 18
666 BRUBAKER, John Wm, 2d wife, HOOVER, Julia C, "PUTTS", May 11 1875, 18
667 BUTLER, Charles E, of Cha's J, CONNOR, Ida M, June 17 1875, 18
668 BRENGLE, Wm H (Jun'r), SCHMIDT, Annie G, of Jacob, July 8 1875, 18
669 BONAPART, Cha's Joseph, DAY, Ellen Channing, Septr 1 1875, 18
670 BUHRMAN, Cha's A, of Upton, RAYMER, Cordelia F, Aug 26 1875, 18
671 BARTHOLOW, Wm H, FOX, Ida V, of Ernst A C, Octr 17 1875, 18
672 BOYER, Samuel L, 2d wife, ROELKEY, Anne, Nov 11 1875, of Wm, 18
673 BARRICK, Cha's J, EICHELBERGER, Emma J, Jan 11 1876, 18
674 BUCKEY, Basil V, HERGESHEIMER, Emma, of Ja's, March 1 1876, 18
675 BACHARACH, N E, LAUPHEIMER, Belle, March 9 1876, Balt, 18
676 BURCK, Joseph, BRENNER, Applonia, Decr 28 1875, 18
677 BIGGS, James, BUCKEY, Mary L, of Jacob, July 4 1876, 18
678 BURGER, Henry C, BARNES, Alice, of Tho's, Septr 12 1876, 18
679 BURCK, Francis Tho's (Dr), CRAMER, Mary E, Nov 29 1876, 18
680 BLUMENAUER, John N, MILLER, Susan, Decr 28 1876, 18
681 BUCKEY, Geo J, ROSS, Maria A, March 15 1877, 18
682 BENNETT, Lewis T, of Lewis H, SILENCE, Emma A, May 28 1877, 18
683 BEATTY, Alex'r P, ROUZER, Sallie J, Aug 9 1877, 18

The Joseph Engelbrecht Marriage Ledger of Frederick Co., MD 1820-1890 *Marriage List*

684 BROWN, Daniel E, *KING*, Mary A, of Balto, Aug 23 1877, 18
685 BAKER, Joseph D, *CUMMINGHAM*, Emma N, Nov 13 1877, 18a
686 BAKER, John, his 3d wife, *DAVIS*, Annie, Nov 25 1877, 18a
687 BRENGLE, Cha's B, *HALLER*, S Loretto, of Mich'l H, Decr 20 1877, 18a
688 BLUMENAUER, Geo W, *BAUFELTER*, Sallie R, Jan 17 1878, 18a
689 BAYER, Lewis, *FRITZ*, Laura V, March 6th 1878, 18a
690 BARTHOLOW, Marshall A, *STONER*, Alice A, Mar 27 1878, 18a
691 BURCK, Philip H, *KREH*, Lizzie, June 18th 1879, 18a
692 BURRAS, Daniel E, *FAUBLE*, Barbara, (not listed as Miss), Feb 4th 1880, 18a
693 BAUGHER, Charles H, *DALL*, Meloria, (not listed as Miss), June 17th 1880, 18a
694 BAYLY, F W, *HALLER*, Mary M, of M H (not listed as Miss), June 28th 1880, 18a
695 BUTTLER, Geo C, of Georgetown, DC, *DELASHMUT*, Margaret M, of Basel (not listed as Miss), Apr 20 '81, 18a
696 BAUGHMAN, L Victor (Col), of the "Citizen", *ABELL*, Helen M, of A S/(not listed as Miss), Sep 27th 1881, 18a
697 BAKER, Benjamin E, of Washington, *JOHNSON*, Mary A, of Wm F/(not listed as Miss), Octber 5th 1881, 18a
698 BURALL, George W, *STIMMEL*, Joanna, Nov 6th 1881, 18a
699 BARTGIS, Mathias E, (of Doc)/1st wife, *CRAMER*, Ida V, of E Joh, Feb 15th 1882, 18a
700 BUTLER, Frank G, (of Va), *THOMAS*, Jennie, (of Col C KEEFER), Feb 20th 1882, BRUMSPING match, 18a
701 BOPST, John, *DERTZABAUGH*, Georgetta, March 8th 1882, 18a
702 BURK, Lewis A, *KOONTZ*, A Lilly, April 5th 1882, 18a
703 BRAGONIER, Charles H, *FULLER*, Adelia, Sept 17 1882, 18a
704 BOULDIN, William J (Jr), *RITCHIE*, Bettie M, of John, Oct 19th 1882, 18a
705 BAKER, Henry W, *HILLEARY*, Emma W, of Wm, April 12th 1883, 18a
706 BARTGIS, James W, *JONES*, Emma F, (not listed as Miss), June 20th 1883, 18a
707 BAYER, John H F, *SCHELL*, Bettie, Septembr 27th 1883, 18a
708 BENTZ, Geo Wm Wallace, *LOWE*, Sarah Jane Amelia, May 29 1884, 18a
709 BELT, Alfred M (Dr), *TRAIL*, Ariana T, of Col C E, Septr 21 1884, 18a
710 BARTGIS, John A, *GROVE*, R Bella, March 3 1885, 18a
711 BROWN, S Elmer, *WILCOXON*, Clara M, March 11 1885, 18a
712 BISHOP, Joseph, (POOLE)/(@), *ELLIS*, Mollie V, April 30 1885, 18a
713 BERGAN, Joshua, (@), *WINCHESTER*, Alice N (Mrs), (INGMAN), May 7 1885, 18a
714 BOBST, William M, *BRUNNER*, Annie M, (@), May 13 1885, 18a
715 BEDHEIMER, George, *MISS*, Tillie O, May 14 1885, 18a
716 BURGER, Charles E, (@), *BENNETT*, Nettie J, November 25 1885, 18a
717 BOUST, Lewis C, *RIEHL*, Princella, of John, December 10 1885, 18a
718 BROWN, R M G (Lieut), *DAVIS*, Katie B, January 6 1886, (BANTZ), 18a
719 BERGEN, Louis, *GREENBAUM*, Rachel, March 10 1886, 18a
720 BEAR, Cha's J (Dr), 2d wife, *SCHLY*, Rosa, (@), March 24 1886, 18a
721 BULER, Henry S, (@ BEELER), *MANTZ*, Minnie, March 31 1886, 18a
722 BRADY, Charles G, (@ BLANDY), *PURNELL*, Elizabeth H, of Wm H, Aug 17 1886, 18a
723 BIRELY, Charles S, *GITTINGER*, Margaret J, November 30 1886, 18b
724 BARBER, Llyod H, *SMITH*, Hattie E, January 27 1887, of Liberty, 18b
725 BUCKEY, Jacob E, *BARGEE*, Caroline C, June 5 1887, in Baltimore, 18b
726 BOWES, Harry W, of Wm D, *FOX*, Ann J, of Cha's B, July 18 1877, 18b

727 BLUMENAUER, Nicholas J, *ELY*, Maggie, of Isaac, August 16 1887, 18b
728 BEACHT, Joseph F, *JAMISON*, Lucinda B, September 13 1887, 18b
729 BROSIUS, John W, 2d wife, *COCKEY*, Nannie, September 15 1887, 18b
730 BUTLER, Edward M, (@ BOETLER), *SIX*, Mamie K, of John, October 16 1887, 18b
731 BLUMENAUER, John, *KLINE*, Julia A, of H Tho's, December 11 1887, 18b
732 BITTLE, Elmer, *BUHRMAN*, Mollie, of Upton, January 25 1888, 18b
733 BAKER, Cha's J, *MOTTER*, Mabel, January 26 1888, 18b
734 BURUCKER, Oscar M, *LANGLEY*, Grace, January 31 1888, 18b
735 BUSSARD, Daniel R, *ROBERTS*, Sallie, February 21 1888, 18b
736 BAUMGARDNER, Geo T, of Jno, *VANFOSSEN*, Hattie L, of Geo, February 29 1888, 18b
737 BENNETT, Frank, of Daniel, *UHER*, Nelsie, April 17 1888, 18b
738 BLACKSTONE, Wm C, of B H, *CRAMER*, Katie J, April 22 1888, 18b
739 BEST, Cha's E T, *KNAUFF*, F Gertrude, of C E, May 16 1888, (@), 18b
740 BURGESS, John E F, *HAMMOND*, Nettie L, of Grafton, May 30 1888, (@), 18b
741 BISER, Clarence S, *WHISTNER*, Mollie V, (@ Mary WINDSOR), Oct 25 1888, 18b
742 BLUMENAUR, Daniel, *MOTT*, Emma, (@), Nov 15 1888, 18b
743 BAUMAN, George W, *HOOPER*, Ettie, (@ Marietta), Nov 21 1888, 18b
744 BRADLEY, Wm H, *RITLER*, Eartheldia, of J Alf/(@ Erthida), Nov 21 1888, 18b
745 BROWN, James, *GETZENDANNER*, Nettie, Dec 6 1888, 18b
746 BRUST, O Nicholas, (@ John Nicholas), *TREAGO*, Mary, February 9 1889, 18b
747 BLAUDEN, James H, (@ BLADEN), *GILSON*, Ella B, (@ Ella Bruce), Febraury 21 1889, 18b
748 BYRNS, S L, (@ Samuel L), *LEWIS*, Imogene, (@ Emogine), April 24 1889, 18b
749 BEALE, Wm T, *KOLB*, Mary Alice, May 14 1889, 18b
750 BRACE, Wm D, *SCHULTZ*, Sophia K, June 11 1889, 18b
751 BARTHELOW, Wm D, *BA??ER*, Julia C, (surname illegible), Jun 19 1889, 18b
752 BURCK, Cha's W, *MCHENRY*, Mollie, June 30 1889, 18b
753 BOPST, Byron, (@ Bine), *BRUTCHEY*, Mary E, August 11 1889, 18b
754 BENTZ, Daniel, *SHIPLEY*, Mary E, August 13 1889, 18b
755 BALL, John, *CHISWELL*, Virginia, Sept 21 1889, 18b
756 BURALL, Cameron, *FOX*, Corona, (@ Sophronia), November 13 1889, 18b
757 BLACK, Cha's G, *SLICK*, Laura, November 26 1889, 18c
758 BISER, G S, (@ Thaddeus M), *THOMAS*, Jennie I, (@ Jennie Irene), December 31 1889, 18c
759 BATSON, Daniel, *FIELD*, Maggie, March 3 1890, 18c
760 BIRELY, Wm F, *MITCHEL*, Ella M, (@ HARWETEL), March 25 1890, 18c
761 BANTZ, Daniel Z, of Wm, *LINN*, Maud E, May 2 1890, 18c
762 BARRICK, George D, *CUTSHALL*, Katie M, May 29 1890, 18c
763 BAKER, Joseph D, 2d wife, *MARKELL*, Mary M, June 12 1890, 18c
764 BELT, J Lawrence, *STAHLE*, Katie A, (DOLL), June 12 1890, 18c
765 BOYER, Tho's S, *RODRICK*, Ella E, (@ RODERICK), August 6 1890, 18c
766 BRUST, Cha's C, *EBAUGH*, Emma, December 24 1890, 18c
767 BROWNING, Richard M, *TOMLINSON*, Catharine B, Dec 24 1890, 18c
768 CROSS, Lewis (Junior), *JONES*, Charlotte, Augt 2 1821, 20
769 CUSHMAN, Philip, *SMITH*, Elizabeth, Augt 14 1821, 20
770 CURFMAN, William, *STRAEFFER*, Miss, (* Margaret), June 16 1822, 20
771 CARLIN, James, *WHITTINGTON*, Miss, of John/(* Mary), Augt 4 1822, 20
772 CAMPBELL, Randolph, *BUTTERWORTH*, Marian, Nov 14 1822, 20
773 CONRADT, Christian G, *HUGHES*, Emily, Decr 23 1823, Hagerstown, 20

774 CROMWELL, Richard, 2d wife, *BOONE*, Caroline, of Alexius, Jany 13 1824, 20
775 CHANEY, Elias, *EASTBURN*, Sarah, of Robinson, Feby 26 1824, 20
776 CAREY, Cyrus, *ARBUCKLE*, Mary, July 22 1824, Va, 20
777 CLARK, Samuel (Rev), *REYNALDS*, Elizabeth, Decr 9 1824, 20
778 CRONISE, Samuel, of John, *MYERS*, Mary, of Rudolph, March 3 1825, 20
779 CROMWELL, John, his 3d wife, *SINN*, Margaret, of Henry, May 17 1825, 20
780 CHARLTON, John W, *KEMP*, Susan, May 31 1825, 20
781 CLINGAN, Winchester, *KOLB*, Sophia, of Mich'l, July 10 1825, 20
782 CUNNINGHAM, Daniel T, *KELLY*, Miss, Nov 22 1825, 20
783 CLINGHAN, Wm (Rev), 2d or 3d wife, *GUYTON*, Sarah (Mrs), Nov 20 1825, 20
784 COLEMAN, George, *RICE*, Louisa, of Geo, March 28 1826, 20
785 CAMPBELL, Edward, *JOHNSON*, Ann J, TANKAFIELD, Decr 12 1826, 20
786 CARMACK, Jacob, *WINNULL*, Ann, Feby 18 1827, 20
787 CROUGH, Michael, *CONNOR*, Rosanna, of Tho's, July 26 1827, 20
788 COLEMAN, Chester, *GRAHAM*, Eliza, of Augustus, April 10 1828, 20
789 CARLIN, Wm, of Tho's, *LEASE*, Sarah, of Geo, June 22 1828, 20
790 CAMPBELL, Abner, *HELFENSTEIN*, Catharine, of Rev Jonathan, Octr 21 1828, 20
791 CROCKEN, James J, *BARTGIS*, Eliza, Nov 18 1828, 20
792 COLE, George A, *HILTON*, Ann F, of Clement, Nov 22 1829, 20
793 COOK, John, *MANTZ*, Christianna E, of Isaac, Decr 24 1829, 20
794 CARLIN, Tho's (Junior), *WILLIS*, Sarah Ann, of Wm, July 18 1830, 20
795 CRUM, Isaac, *KESSLER*, Catharine, of David, Septr 12 1830, 20
796 CRIST, Joseph, *KEYSER*, Elizabeth, Decr 30 1830, 20
797 CARLIN, Henry, of Tho's, *KEHLER*, Sarah, of Henry, Jany 30 1831, 20
798 CRUM, William, of Isaac, *PHILLIPS*, Ann, April 26 1831, 20
799 COBURN, James R, *MORGAN*, Mary Ann, Mrs Geo Webster's sister, June 23 1831, 20
800 CAHOON, Joel B, *VAN ALLEN*, Margaret (Mrs), July 14 1831, 20
801 CHARLESWORTH, Solomon, *MCVICKER*, Mary, Septr 25 1832, 20
802 CRUM, John, of Isaac, *GETZ*, Mary A, Feby 26 1833, 20
803 CARNES, William, (KERN), *TROGLER*, Ann (Mrs), Feby 19 1833, MAHONEY, 20
804 CARMACK, Ephraim, *KUHN*, Mary M, of Henry, March 4 1833, 20
805 CROPSEY, Frances J, *STOUFFER*, Miranda E, May 20 1833, 20
806 CROMWELL, George W, 1st wife, *STORM*, Mary A E, of Peter, July 25 1833, 20
807 CARLIN, James, 2d wife, *HEMSWORTH*, Eliza A, Nov 17 1833, 20
808 CURRANS, Elijah, *REINDOLLAR*, Amelia J, April 10 1834, 20
809 CASTLE, James (Jun'r), *HOFFMAN*, Mary A, Septr 25 1834, 20
810 CLUNETT, Victor, *SUMMERS*, Miss, Jany 27 1835, Balto/Jane, 21
811 COCKEY, Sebastian G, *SPRIGG*, Elizabeth, June 2 1835, 21
812 CRONISE, Isaac, of John/1st wife, *WHITE*, Elizabeth, of John, June 11 1835, 21
813 CAMBRELING, Churchill C (Hon), *GLOVER*, Phebe, Nov 17 1835, New York, 21
814 COLEGATE, George, *POOL*, Elizabeth, Feby 24 1836, 21
815 CARMACK, Christian S, *SPRINGER*, Mary, of Wm, May 5 1836, 21
816 CLARY, Upton, *WEAVER*, Theodosia, May 17 1836, 21
817 CONVERSE, Freeman, *MILLER*, Emily, Augt 17 1836, Leesburg, Va, 21
818 CONNOR, Henry, of Tho's, *MCGLENNEN*, Margaret, Octr 11 1836, 21
819 CRAMER, Jacob, *DEVILBISS*, Lucretia A, of David, Octr 18 1836, 21
820 CUNNINGHAM, Benj'n Amos, 2d wife, *CANDLER*, Eveline, Decr 6 1836, 21

821 *CULLER*, Daniel, of Henry, *HARGETT*, Ann M, April 13 1837, 21
822 *CONLEY*, Harrison, 1st wife, *SCHELL*, Rosanna Elizabeth, of Ezra, Feby 15 1838, 21
823 *CARLIN*, David, of Tho's, *KENEGE*, Mary, of David, March 22 1838, 21
824 *CONOWAY*, Solomon Freeborn, *DIXON*, Ann Reb, of Haines, May 29 1838, 21
825 *CRUM*, Stephen Basford, *KLEIN*, Harriott, of Caspar, May 29 1838, 21
826 *COOK*, Alexander A, *MANTZ*, Mary, of Isaac, Augt 9 1838, Hagerstown, 21
827 *CROMWELL*, Tho's T, of Philemon, *STAUFFER*, Catharine, of Jos, Nov 8 1838, 21
828 *CANDLER*, Daniel H, *BAER*, Ann E, of Mich'l, Decr 4 1838, 21
829 *CARMACK*, Hanson, *CLAYBAUGH*, Harriott, March 13 1839, Taneytown, 21
830 *CONRAD*, John, of Jos, *TITLOW*, Margaret, March 21 1839, 21
831 *CANTWELL*, James, *JOHNSON*, Sophia, of Baker, Feby 19 1839, Florida, 21
832 *CLOSE*, Elijah, *BIGGS*, Susan, of Frederick, May 1 1839, 21
833 *CROSS*, Robert, *TIGHDY*, Harriett, May 2 1839, Balto, 21
834 *CONRAD*, Wm, of Jos, *STEINER*, Margaret, of Ezra, July 14 1839, "FOGLER", 21
835 *COPPERSMITH*, Lewis F, *BAUGHER*, Louisa, of Isaac, Nov 4 1839, 21
836 *CLEM*, Peter C, *BRUNNER*, Rhoda, Nov 4 1839, 21
837 *CLINGMAN*, Enoch G, *LYON*, Sarah, of Dr Isaac, Nov 15 1839, Cincin, O, 21
838 *CRUTCHLEY*, Elias, 2d wife, *BEALL*, Lucinda, January 30 1840, 21
839 *COLLIFLOWER*, Wm F (Rev), *FISCHER*, Ann E, Feby 12 1840, 21
840 *CLEM*, A, (* George A), *DEVILBISS*, Eliza, April 9 1840, Glade, 21
841 *CARLTON*, William, *NEILL*, Mary P, of John W, June 25 1840, 21
842 *CUSTUS*, Wm H, *MARTIN*, Rosanna, Septr 8 1840, 21
843 *CURFMAN*, Wm, 2d wife, *YANDLEY*, Ann, Octr 6 1840, 21
844 *CLEMSON*, Harrison T, *BENNETT*, Ann Elizabeth, Octr 15 1840, 21
845 *COLEGATE*, Edward, *STITCHER*, Catharine (Mrs), Octr 28 1840, 21
846 *CLEMENT*, Wm H, *STEINER*, Elizabeth, of Capt'n Henry, Decr 31 1840, Sandusky, O, 21
847 *CASTLE*, George T, *HARGETT*, Catharine B, of John, March 11 1841, 21
848 *CURTIS*, John, *HAMILTON*, Isabella, March 23 1841, Liberty, 21
849 *COLE*, Wm G, *RICE*, Juliann, of Geo (Sen'r), May 25 1841, 21
850 *CRIST*, Jacob, *MELDRUM*, Elizabeth A, June 3 1841, 21
851 *CULLER*, Peter, *BECHTEL*, Miss, (* Hannah), Nov 18 1841, 21
852 *CARPENTER*, John M, *IJAMS*, Rebecca, of Plummer, Nov 25 1841, 22
853 *CONNER*, James A O, *MOORE*, Margaret H, of George, Nov 10 1840, 22
854 *COOK*, John, 2d wife, *RUE*, Ellen, Decr 14 1841, Hagerstown, 22
855 *CONNOR*, James, *HARRISON*, Lydia Ann, of Zephaniah, Jany 2 1842, 22
856 *COLE*, Lewis M, *RUTHERFORD*, Caroline, of Benj'n, May 24 1842, 22
857 *COLLINS*, Elisha, *ROBINSON*, Martha Ann, of Rev Henry, Augt 17 1842, 22
858 *CRONISE*, Joseph, of John, *BRUNNER*, Rebecca, Nov 24 1842, 22
859 *COOMES*, Joseph W, *MORGAN*, Sarah J, of Tho's W, Decr 6 1842, 22
860 *CRONISE*, Isaac, of John/2d wife, *BARRICK*, Juliann, of Fred'k, May 16 1843, 22
861 *COLLINS*, Wm O, *WEVER*, Catharine Willis, of Caspar W, Nov 8 1843, WEVERTON, 22
862 *CARTY*, Joseph W L, 1st wife, *HARDT*, Margaret C, April 3 1844, 22
863 *CARLIN*, Joseph, of Tho's, *GETZENDANNER*, Sarah L, of Adam, July 21 1844, 22
864 *CLARKSON*, Freeman (Rev), *BALCH*, Catharine, of L P W (Sen'r), July 30 1844, Leetown, Va, 22
865 *CULLER*, Philip, of Henry, *DIXON*, Ann R, Septr 24 1844, 22
866 *CULLER*, Henry (Jun'r), *WARFIELD*, Eliza Ann, Feby 10 1845, 22

867 CHAMBERS, William, HART, Ann Margaret, of John, May 6 1845, 22
868 CASTLE, Abraham H, KEEFER, Adelia Margaret, of Jacob, May 15 1845, 22
869 CRAMER, George, REYNALDS, Catharine A, of Sam'l, June 10 1845, 22
870 CAMPBELL, John B H, RICHARDSON, Ann U, of Davis, June 17 1845, 22
871 CLEM, Philip H, MCCORMICK, Catharine Ann, Feby 24 1846, 22
872 CRONISE, J Stoll (Dr), of Jacob, FLEMMING, Marianna, April 28 1846, 22
873 CLAY, Adam H, BEDFORD, Mary E, May 4 1846, 22
874 CROW, John, KOONTZ, Elleanor Matilda, of John, May 14 1846, 22
875 COLE, Charles, MOORE, Ann R, of George, May 20 1846, 22
876 COLVOCORESSES, Geo M, (US Navy), HALSEY, Eliza F, May 17 1846, 22
877 CLEAVLAND, Sylvester, LOKEY, Virginia R, May 27 1846, 22
878 CRONISE, B Franklin, LEASE, Elizabeth, of Wm, July 23 1846, 22
879 CRAMPTON, John W, HOSKINSON, Mary P, Septr 22 1846, 22
880 CONRADT, Theophilus M, SHERWOOD, Emma B, April 20 1847, Balto, 22
881 CHISWELL, Geo W, GRIFFITH, Leah, April 27 1847, 22
882 CRAVER, Simon P, STULL, Susanna R, May 6 1847, 22
883 CORBIN, Samuel M, STOWELL, Mary A, May 20 1847, 22
884 CRAMER, Jeremiah H, STIMMEL, Elizabeth C, Feby 15 1848, 22
885 COOPER, David, ADAMS, Ellenora M, of Valentine, May 30 1848, 22
886 CLABAUGH, Norman B, FOUT, Margaret E, of Peter S, May 30 1848, 22
887 CRAMER, John David, 1st wife, KEMP, Mary Ann, of Peter, June 13 1848, 22
888 CUNNINGHAM, Philip, VANFOSSEN, Susan, of Levi, Feby 19 1849, 22
889 CRAMER, Jacob, LAMBRECHT, Susan T E, January 1 1850, 22
890 CHAMBERS, James, 2d wife, FETTE', Johanna, May 16 1850, Boonsboro, 22
891 CAIN, John, SHRYOCK, Louisa E, May 30 1850, 22
892 CISSELL, Richard S T, BERNARD, Mary, of Rob't, Decr 26 1850, Geo Town, 22
893 CRUM, Geo W (Dr), REMSBERG, Susan S, Feby 18 1851, 22
894 CROMWELL, Joseph W, WISONG, Margaret S, of Isaac, March 20 1851, 23
895 CHANEY, Richard G (Rev), KOONTZ, Sallie E, of Godfrey, April 10 1851, 23
896 CARLISLE, David, GAVER, Elizabeth, April 15 1851, 23
897 CUTTER, Wm J (Rev), missionary to Gontoon, EMERICK, Margaret, June 1 1851, 23
898 CRONISE, Simon, of Sam'l/1st wife, REIN, Matilda A, Octr 14 1851, 23
899 COLE, David, of Geo A, STRAILMAN, Sarah A, of Geo, May 4 1852, 23
900 CREAGER, Esau D, STAUFFER, Ellen Amanda, of John, May 11 1852, 23
901 CONNOR, Geo J, of Tho's, NO BRIDES NAME GIVEN, Miss, July 1852, Carlisle, Pa/ DADISMAN, 23
902 CRAMER, William, HULL, Sarah Ann, Augt 10 1852, Glade, 23
903 CULLER, John J, RAUZAHN, Sarah, of Philip, Septr 23 1852, 23
904 CLEM, John, CLEM, Harriett, Octr 13 1852, at David SCHLEY's, 23
905 COVER, Cyrus, LIDAY, Henrietta, Nov 9 1852, 23
906 CAUGHY, No first name given, TORMEY, Mary Jane, of Patrick, Nov 1852, Balto, 23
907 CLARKE, James Charles, SCHAEFFER, Susanna, of Peter, Decr 23 1852, 23
908 CRITTENDEN, John J, 2d wife, ASHLEY, Elizabeth (Mrs), Feby 27 1853, Kentucky, 23
909 CASSADY, Francis Stansbury (Rev), KREBS, Mary Ann, March 14 1853, 23
910 CRAMER, Ethan Allen, STEINER, Susan R, of Henry, March 23 1853, 23
911 CRUMBAUGH, Simon Calvin, 1st wife, KUSHWA, Kate, of John D, April 12 1853, Mercersburg, Pa, 23

912 COOK, Luther M E, of John, STEPHENS, Mary, of Sam'l, April 19 1853, Liberty, 23
913 CHILCOTE, Thomas M, CRIST, Margret E, of Joseph, May 12 1853, 23
914 CLARY, Frederick S, RUNKELS, Theodocia A, Augt 24 1853, 23
915 CAPEL, Joseph, GUIE, Rebecca, Nov 1853, Kaighns' point, NJ, 23
916 CRUMBAUGH, Geo F B, KEMP, Margaret, Nov 15 1853, Walkersville, 23
917 CROMWELL, Wm H H, FRAZIER, Ann Elizabeth, Feby 22 1854, 23
918 CONDON, Joseph, BRASHEAR, Caroline R, March 9 1854, 23
919 CREIGHTON, Johnston Blakely (Lieut), (USN), STRINGHAM, Edwinna, Augt 1854, 23
920 CLEM, George, BAKER, Catharine, Octr 5 1854, 23
921 CROUSE, George V, LORENTZ, Malinda A, of Jacob, Octr 30 1854, 23
922 CARTER, Henry, NICODEMUS, Margaret E, Nov 23 1854, 23
923 CRAMER, Ezra Lewis, KEMP, Henrietta, of David, Decr 12 1854, 23
924 CLAGGETT, Tho's John, HILLEARY, Ann Perry, Jany 9 1855, 23
925 CUTSAIL, Wm H, NUSZ, Ann R, of Cyrus, May 3d 1855, 23
926 CROMWELL, George W, 2d wife, KNAUFF, Mary A E, of Jacob, Septr 25 1855, 23
927 COOPER, David (Hon), 2d wife, FORWARD, Annie E, Octr 3 1855, Minnisota, 23
928 CRAMER, Columbus A, 1st wife, DAYHOFF, Elizabeth, Octr 30 1855, 23
929 CONRAD, Henry, of Jos, WIEST, Susan, Nov 22 1855, 23
930 CULLER, C C (Rev), DATESMAN, Ann Maria, Nov 27 1855, Milton, Pa, 23
931 CLAY, William, STEEL, Sarah, Nov 27 1855, 23
932 CLINE, Caspar, (KLEIN)/2d wife/sisters, EVANS, Corilla, Feby 5 1856, 23
933 CUTSAIL, Wm H, HULL, Henrietta, of Julius, Feby 21 1856, 23
934 COATES, Isaac, LYONS, Mary, June 12 1856, 23
935 CRUMBAUGH, Simon C (Rev), 2d wife, WOLFE, Ellen, June 18 1856, Chambersburg, Pa, 23
936 CREAGER, Simon, VANSANT, Ellen, Septr 7 1856, 24
937 CUNNINGHAM, John R H, DAVIS, Mattie C, of James L, Septr 9 1856, 24
938 CRUM, William E, GROVE, Susan, of Reuben, Nov 6 1856, 24
939 COOKSON, John C, HOWARD, Emily, of Edward, Decr 10 1856, 24
940 CASTLE, Rezin Josephus, MESSER, Ann Rebecca, Decr 25 1856, 24
941 CONLEY, Harrison, his 2d wife, FRIEND, Rachel Ann, Feby 19 1857, 24
942 COVER, John M, SAYLER, Margret E, of Rev D V, April 9 1857, 24
943 COPELAND, James W, MYERS, Rebecca E, May 5 1857, 24
944 CROWN, S Curtis, BREADY, Elizabeth A, of Geo, March 14 1857, "BRIE", 24
945 CAREY, John T H, SHAW, Mary Elizabeth, June 9 1857, 24
946 CECILL, Samuel T, KEEFER, Margaret, Octr 29 1857, 24
947 CRONISE, Jonathan K, of Sam'l, REIN, Emily C, Octr 27 1857, 24
948 COOK, Benjamin F, STOCKMAN, Sarah Ann E, Nov 19 1857, 24
949 CLINGAN, Thomas, of Pa, CLINGAN, Hester E, of Winchester (#), Decr 22 1857, 24
950 CLARKE, Rolurt B, GAITHER, S Jane, of Stuart, Jany 12 1858, 24
951 CARLIN, Frank B, of James, SHEPPERD, Cecelia, of Abijah, Feby 22 1858, 24
952 CRIMMINS, John, (* CREMINS), SULLIVAN, Miss, (*Mary), April 19 1858, 24
953 CRIST, Grafton B, MICHAEL, Emily J, April 13 1848, 25
954 CARMACK, Sam'l Philip, MULLAN, Sally A, May 18 1858, 24
955 CULLER, David, SLIFER, Margaret Ann, June 10 1858, 24
956 CONDON, Richard W, REESE, Anna M, June 29 1858, Sam's Creek, 24
957 CREAGER, Mannassah, HARDING, Ellen, (en), Octr 17 1858, 24
958 CONN, John T, CROMWELL, Ellen B, of John, Nov 1 1858, Henderson, Ky/SINN, 24

959	CONTEE, Richard, BOWLING, Anna, Nov 23 1858, Prince Geo Co, Md, 24
960	CONRAD, John D, of Va, FOUT, Olivia, of Lewis, Nov 25 1858, 24
961	CISSELL, Wm Martin, HEWETT, Mary Jane, Decr 14 1858, 24
962	CRAMER, Cha's C, OBGORN, Laura J, of John W, Jany 25 1859, 24
963	CRONISE, Geo W, of Fred'k, SHEETS, Anna Mary, Feby 22 1859, 24
964	CASTLE, James W, EICHLER, Mary Ann Elizabeth (Mrs), April 21 1859, 24
965	CURTIS, George C, CASSIN, Sophia A, of Com Stephen, May 5 1859, 24
966	CROUSE, John L (Dr), SEFTON, Mary M, June 8 1859, 24
967	COST, Henry, his 2d wife, SHIPLEY, Mary A S, Septr 29 1959, 24
968	CASSIN, John, of Com Stephen, SCHLEY, Alice, 3rd daughter of Col Edward, Octr 25 1859, 24
969	CARLIN, George T, GRIMES, Ann A W, Nov 24 1859, Georgetown, DCa, 24
970	CLAPHAM, Josiah Henry, GRUBB, Lydia Ellen, Decr 11 1859, Loudon Co, 24
971	CLARY, Nathaniel H, BARTHOLOW, Mary A, Decr 20 1859, 24
972	CULLER, J Harman, KEAFAUVER, Lucinda C, of Jacob, March 1st 1860, 24
973	CRAVER, Grafton H, CLEM, Sarah Ann E, Feby 15 1860, Graceham, 24
974	CAREY, George G, POE, Josephine C, of Neilson, April 10 1860, Balto, 24
975	CLINE, George W, DORSEY, Harriet Ann, of Claggett W, April 5 1860, 24
976	CROOK, Geo Wash Musgrave, LEWIS, Hannah M, of Jacob, May 15 1860, 24
977	COOK, Joseph D, ROELKE, Medora S, of Christian, July 4 1860, 24
978	CRONISE, Simon, of Sam'l/2d wife, OGLE, Eveline, of James, Augt 28 1860, 25
979	CROMWELL, Wm Eldridge, CRAWFORD, Ann Elizabeth, Augt 28 1860, 25
980	CLEM, George H, EATON, Elizabeth A J, Septr 20 1860, 25
981	CRONE, John E, (KROHN), WELKER, Harriett, Octr 4 1860, Midd valley, 25
982	CRAMER, Columbus A, 2d wife, LINK, Catharine, Nov 13 1860, 25
983	CLAPP, C Clinton, KEENAN, Annie Amelia Gibson, of James, Nov 22 1860, Winchester, Va, 25
984	CRUM, John, CRAMER, Mary Ann, (not listed as Miss), Decr 13 1860, Jefferson, 25
985	COBLENTZ, Edward T, MAIN, Catharine E, Nov 16 1860, 25
986	CRAMER, John David, 2d wife, SCHOLL, Annabel, of Elias, Jany 15 1861, 25
987	CRAMER, Albert J, STOTTELMEYER, Rebecca, Jany 1 1861, 25
988	CREAGER, Simon, FROSCHAUER, Ann M, Feby 14 1861, Glade, 25
989	CRAMER, George W, of Ph, GALLION, Molly E, of John P, Feby 21 1861, 25
990	COOPER, John, (brother of Gen'l James)/2d wife, TRIMPER, Maria E, Feby 20 1861, Michigan, 25
991	CARSANOVIA, J N, HARDING, Eleanora, of John L, Feby 8 1861, 25
992	CLINGAN, Lewis S, GOMBER, Minerva E, of Ezra, March 26 1861, 25
993	CASTLE, Tho's F, SMITH, Georgianna, of Andrew, March 20 1861, Fairview, 25
994	CESNOLA, Cavaliere Luigi Palma di, REID, Mary Isabella, of Capt Sam'l, June 11 1861, 25
995	CUNNINGHAM, Wm Armstrong, DAVIS, Molly, of Ja's L, July 31 1861, 25
996	CRUM, Simon, HOLBRUNNER, Margaret, Octr 24 1861, 25
997	CRUM, Isaac B, of Wm, DOYLE, Margaret, of Lawrence, Nov 12 1861, 25
998	CRUM, Lewis, HILDEBRIDEL, Sarah, Nov 28 1861, 25
999	COLLIS, Cha's H T, Capt'n, LEVI, Miss, of Phila, Decr 10 1861, Zouaves de Afrique, 25
1000	CORRISON, Geo Wm, HEIM, Mary Mansilla, Jany 28 1862, 25
1001	CHAMBERS, Tho's J, FOGEL, Emeline, Jany 16 1862, 25
1002	COBB, Edward L, of N York, ETCHISON, Annie M, of Tho's, Augt 7 1862, 25

1003 *CAMPBELL*, Mortimer S, *WINGATE*, Matilda, Augt 1862, 25
1004 *CUMMING*, Wm A, (of Aug's J), *VIERS*, Kate, of Sam'l C, Octr 28 1862, 25
1005 *CLINE*, George Tho's, *LAWRENCE*, Frances, Octr 19 1862, Illinois "of Caspar", 25
1006 *CLARK*, John F, *BAER*, Fannie, of John (ROWE), Decr 16 1862, 25
1007 *CARTY*, Joseph W L, 2d wife, *LUGENBEEL*, Mary Margaret, of Moses, Decr 31 1862, 25
1008 *CRAW*, Edwin A, (14th Regt Conn. Vol), *HECKATHORN*, Susan E, of Ch'n, Jany 6 1863, 25
1009 *COBURN*, Jacob D, of Kentucky, *CARLIN*, Ceclia, of Tho's, March 12 1863, 25
1010 *CRAVER*, George W, *PALMER*, Elmira, (Adamsville), June 4 1863, 25
1011 *CROUCH*, James O, *WISNER*, Caroline, June 8 1863, 25
1012 *CISSELL*, Jonas, *STEWART*, Annie F, Septr 29 1863, 25
1013 *COLLIFLOWER*, Henry, *THOMAS*, Elizabeth (Mrs), Octr 27 1863, Jefferson, 25
1014 *CLARK*, Joseph P, *PALMER*, Carrie, of Wm T, Nov 24 1863, 25
1015 *COLBY*, Wm J, US Army, *BRUTSCHY*, Mary C, Decr 6 1863, 25
1016 *CRAIG*, Geo W, *LOCKNER*, Annie E, of Geo, Decr 26 1863, 25
1017 *CASTLE*, George T (Capt'n), *ENGELBRECHT*, Agnes, of Geo, March 10 1864, 25
1018 *CRUM*, Caspar, *WIRTZ*, Anna M, March 10 1864, 25
1019 *CROUSE*, William A, *BRUST*, Margaret, of Caspar, March 22 1864, 25
1020 *COOPER*, Adderly, of Bermuda, *LOWELL*, Rose, of Wm LOWELL, June 11 1864, 26
1021 *CAREY*, James (Jun'r), *SPECHT*, Mary C, Augt 18 1864, 26
1022 *CHINIGUY*, Charles (Rev), Rom Cath Priest, *ALLARD*, Euphremia, April 26 1864, Illinois, Kankaku, 26
1023 *CRONISE*, Gideon, of Sam'l, *HOLLAND*, Miss, (* Sally), Octr 18 1864, 26
1024 *CREAGER*, John Wesley, *AUBERT*, Louisa, of Jacob, March 2d 1865, 26
1025 *CHARLTON*, John W (Jun'r Rev), *FARROW*, Mollie C, March 6 1865, Snowhill, 26
1026 *CRAMER*, Jacob W, *RAMSBURG*, Cordelia A, March 20 1865, Glade, 26
1027 *COLBATH*, Martin P, *ARNOLD*, Annie E, of Ja's Madison, April 18 1865, 26
1028 *CARROLL*, D H (Rev), *BOYD*, Mary E, of Andrew, July 6 1865, 26
1029 *COLLINS*, Cha's E, (of Rochester, Ny), *SMITH*, Susan R, of David F, July 12 1865, 26
1030 *CARPENTER*, Mark C, *STALEY*, Rowanna R, Septr 13 1865, 26
1031 *CREAGER*, Andrew J, *GEESEY*, Susan R, Septr 26 1865, 26
1032 *CRUM*, Issac L, *HAHN*, Sophia L, Nov 28 1865, 26
1033 *CRAMER*, John P, *EYLER*, Emeline, Decr 21 1865, 26
1034 *CASTLE*, Thomas M, *TRACY*, Molly E, of Balto, Decr 28 1865, 26
1035 *COMFORT*, H C (Rev), 3d wife, *COLLIFLOWER*, Willie A, of Rev Wm F, Jany 30 1866, 26
1036 *CARTER*, Grafton, *TROXELL*, Emma H, of Joshua, Octr 25 1866, 26
1037 *CHAPLINE*, J Thomas, *SCHLEY*, Laura, of Col Edward, January 31 1867, 26
1038 *CECILL*, George M, *ROLKE*, Sarah J, of Wm, April 8 1867, 26
1039 *CRAMER*, Jeremiah C, *CLOSE*, Virginia C, May 14 1867, 26
1040 *CRONISE*, J Calvin, of Jos, *BAKER*, Maggie E, of Aaron, Oct 1 1867, 26
1041 *CARTY*, Cha's P, of Jos W L, *KENEASTER*, Lucy C, of Indianapolis, Octr 29 1867, 26
1042 *CARTY*, Clarance C, of Jos W L/1 wife, *FOX*, Johanna, of Adolphus, Octr 30 1867, 26
1043 *CARTER*, Walter S, *JONES*, Mary A B, of Aubury, Decr 18 1867, 26
1044 *COOK*, Frank W (Dr), *LANDIS*, Emma, of Jesse, Decr 18 1867, 26
1045 *CUNNINGHAM*, Wm F, *SIM*, Bobbie, Jany 9 1868, Liberty, 26
1046 *COBLENTZ*, Stephen B, *POTTERFIELD*, Nettie, Jany 30 1868, 26
1047 *CRONISE*, Wm H V, *PLUME*, Kate C, California, April 2 1868, 26

The Joseph Engelbrecht Marriage Ledger of Frederick Co., MD 1820-1890 *Marriage List*

1048 *CRUM*, Hanson, *BARRICK*, Matilda S, May 5 1868, 26
1049 *COLFAX*, Schuyler, Vice Prest US, *WADE*, Ella M, Nov 18 1868, Ashtobula Co, O, 26
1050 *COLE*, Charles Edwin, of Cha's, *NICHOLS*, Mary Catharine, of Edward, Nov 26 1868, 26
1051 *CONRAD*, Wm J, *MEASELL*, Mary Jane, both of Rocky Spring, Decr 10 1868, 26
1052 *COLBERT*, Wm B, of Louisiana, *WILSON*, Mary E, "SHRIVER"/of Cha's, Jany 20 1869, 26
1053 *CREAGER*, F A W (Lieut), *RENFRO*, Kate, Feby 28 1869, Huntsville, TX, 26
1054 *CROUSE*, Wm F, *NEIDHARDT*, Mary E, of Wm, April 13 1869, 26
1055 *CHISWELL*, John N (Capt'n), *WHITE*, Virginia, Augt 17 1869, 26
1056 *CLINE*, Nicholas O, of Caspar, *KERN*, Annie A (Mrs), "MICHAEL", Nov 23 1869, 26
1057 *CUBITZ*, George, *HANDSCHUH*, Kate, Decr 9 1969, Bethel church, 26
1058 *COBLENTZ*, John C, *SMITH*, Lucinda E M, of Ezra, Decr 13 1869, Middletownvalley, 26
1059 *CARSON*, Alonzo, of Ambrose/(#), *HARRISON*, Georgetta, of Josiah, Decr 26 1869, 26
1060 *CARNS*, Wm H, *PACELEY*, Emily H, of Wm, April 5 1870, 26
1061 *CRUM*, Geo M, *MICHAEL*, Virginia E, April 13 1870, 26
1062 *CROMWELL*, Tho's T, of Philemon/2d wife, *LUGENBEEL*, Jamima A (Mrs), Octr 11 1870, Tiffin, Ohio, 27
1063 *COURTNAY*, James F, *GUERAND*, Leonide M, Feby 2 1871, Balto, 27
1064 *COOMBS*, Wm H O, *HUDSON*, Fannie L, of John A, March 21 1871, 27
1065 *CHAPMAN*, John Lee, of Balt, *THOMPSON*, Alice, July 11 1871, 27
1066 *CONDON*, Frank C, *WILLSON*, Ellie, of John J, July 17 1871, 27
1067 *CONRADI*, F A (Rev), *ABELE*, F W, July 18 1871, Lockport, NY, 27
1068 *COLE*, Wm H, of Wm G, *BRADBURN*, Kate E, in Washington City, July 25 1871, 27
1069 *CORNING*, Albion J, *WOODSIDE*, M Sheppie, of John T, Nov 22 1871, Balto, 27
1070 *CARROLL*, R G Harper, *LEE*, Mary D, of Tho's S, June 1872, 27
1071 *CANN*, Geo W, of Rev Tho's M, *DERBY*, Ella V, July 25 1872, Gardner, Mass, 27
1072 *COCHREN*, Lewis R, *WAITE*, Louisa H (Mrs), of Balto, Nov 26 1872, 27
1073 *CRAMER*, Geo W, *FOX*, Mollie E, of Jacob, Decr 26 1872, 27
1074 *CRUM*, Lewis, *TAYLOR*, Mollie E, of Beallsville, July 3 1873, 27
1075 *CRAMPTON*, Henry G, *CULLER*, Cordelia S, of Peter, Nov 4 1873, 27
1076 *COOKSEY*, Wm T, *FOUT*, Lillie F, of David, Decr 17 1873, 27
1077 *CONRAD*, James P, *BROWN*, Margaret E, Jan 1 1874, 27
1078 *COLE*, Lamartine, of Cha's, *JENKINS*, Ida, Septr 10 1874, Balto, 27
1079 *CULLER*, Henry (Col), 2d wife, *SOWERS*, H L (Mrs), of Va, Octr 6 1874, 27
1080 *CREAGER*, Noble H, of Ephraim, *PITCHER*, Molly N, Octr 31 1874, Balt, 27
1081 *CROMWELL*, Cha's C, of Geo W, *ADAMS*, Phebe H, Nov 26 1874, Illinois, 27
1082 *CLABAUGH*, Usher, *WILLSON*, Mary E, of John J, June 1 1875, 27
1083 *CURFMAN*, Wm H, *KELLER*, Laura V, Nov 30 1875, 27
1084 *CROFT*, S F, *MANN*, Allie, of Stephen S, Feb 2 1876, "SOWERS", 27
1085 *CHRISTIANCY*, J P (Hon), age 64, *LUGENBEEL*, Lillie, age 19, Feb 8 1876, 27
1086 *CRUM*, John, *KREH*, Ann M M (Mrs), widow of John of Theo, Aug 31 1876, 27
1087 *CASTLE*, Abraham P, *DEGRANGE*, Jane R C, March 8 1877, 27
1088 *CARROLL*, John Lee (Gov), 2d wife, *THOMPSON*, Carter, May 14 1877, 27
1089 *CAHEN*, Felix, *RAFF*, Isabelle, Octr 14 1877, Balto, 27
1090 *CRAWFORD*, Tho's L, *HOOD*, Sallie E, Octr 30 1877, 27
1091 *CUSHWA*, Geo W, *BANTZ*, Mollie, March 12th 1878, 27
1092 *CRISE*, Geo H, *SMITH*, Clara C, Dec 2d 1878, 27
1093 *CARLIN*, John T, *HIMMELL*, Francis B, July 31st 1879, 27

1094 *CURTIS*, J B Gregg, *RITTER*, Catharine, Sept 18th 1879, 27
1095 *CRAMER*, Geo L, *WORMAN*, Mary O, (not listed as Miss), Feb 4th 1880, 27
1096 *CROMWELL*, J Charles, *HARDT*, Maggie C, of John/(not listed as Miss), April 21st 1880, 27
1097 *CRAMER*, John A, *STONER*, Hannah E, (not listed as Miss), Dec 23d 1880, 27
1098 *CHEW*, Jos H, *LIDIE*, Clara, (not listed as Miss), April 21st 1881, 27
1099 *CHESTER*, Wm G, *LOGAN*, Mora, of James/(not listed as Miss), May 24th 1881, 27
1100 *CRAMER*, David K, *MERCER*, Fannie, (not listed as Miss), June 1st 1881, 27
1101 *CRAMER*, Ezra L, *CRAMER*, Ada M, Sep 17th 1881, 27
1102 *CASHOUR*, Charles W F, (@), *FLEMING*, Katie H, January 26th 1882, 27
1103 *CASTLE*, Charles A, *PHILLIPS*, Annie M, February 1st 1882, 27
1104 *CHEW*, Thomas, *HOOPER*, Ida L, Septembr 11th 1882, 28
1105 *COUSINS*, Lewis W, *ROSS*, Florence E, of Peter, September 20 1882, 28
1106 *CORNING*, Jasper, *COCKEY*, Bella S, of S G COCKEY, October 25th 1882, 28
1107 *CUTSAIL*, Clayton E, of J J, *KINNEY*, Emma, (@ KINNA), October 31st 1882, 28
1108 *CAMPBELL*, Robert H, (@), *CASTLE*, Jennie, of Daniel, Oct 23d 1883, 28
1109 *CRIST*, William, *MYERS*, Lucy, of Cha's, January 7 1884, 28
1110 *CARTER*, Cha's C, *ADAMS*, Anne E, June 19 1884, 28
1111 *CARTY*, Alton B, *COBLENTZ*, Mollie C, November 6 1884, 28
1112 *CUTSAIL*, Charles, *MOBERLY*, Katie, of Lewis, February 26 1885, 28
1113 *CURRAN*, Robert N, *PATTEN*, Hattie E, May 6 1885, 28
1114 *CLABAUGH*, G M Dall, *SWAIN*, Mollie L (Mrs), May 28 1885, (MOBERLY), 28
1115 *CARTY*, Clarence C, 2d wife, *KEEFER*, Nannie C, November 4 1885, 28
1116 *COOKERLY*, George W, *DELASHMUTH*, Lizzie V, January 13 1886, 28
1117 *CONKLIN*, Wm J, of Boston, *CARTY*, Dassie E, of Jos W L/(@ Daisie), April 26 1887, 28
1118 *CLURER*, Charles W, *WENSING*, Maggie E, June 17 1887, in Balto/(SAHM), 28
1119 *CONNER*, Hebert, *NICHODEMUS*, Addie, November 16t 1887, 28
1120 *CULLER*, John J S, (@), *HARWOOD*, Emma, December 20 1887, 28
1121 *CRUM*, Charles J, *KING*, Katie L, of Henry, January 17 1888, 28
1122 *CHILTON*, Wm F, (@), *CUNNINGHAM*, Celia, of B Amos, January 19 1888, 28
1123 *CLABAUGH*, Geo M, *BIRELY*, Ettie R, (@ BYERLY), January 24 1888, 28
1124 *CHISWELL*, Joseph N, *STOUFFER*, Fannie, (@ SNOUFFER), February 23 1888, 28
1125 *COOK*, Wm F Nelson, *MOSSBURG*, Campsy Dell, March 1 1888, 28
1126 *COBLENTZ*, Geo G, *RUNKLES*, Clara E, March 21 1888, 28
1127 *CRAMER*, Edward A, of Ephraim, *KOOGLE*, Annie, (@ Jennie), July 26 1888, 28
1128 *CHILDS*, Geo F, *EARY*, Theresa, Sept 27 1888, 28
1129 *CHEW*, A Richard, *CROCETCHER*, Jane, Dec 19 1888, 28
1130 *COZENS*, Wm J (Maj), *CLINE*, Maggie C, (@ Margaret), February 5 1889, (of Nicholas), 28
1131 *CRAMER*, Wm C, (@ Willie), *ALBAUGH*, Susie, February 6 1889, 28
1132 *CUTSAIL*, J Milton, (@ Joseph M), *KNODE*, Alice V, February 14 1889, 28
1133 *CROUSE*, Wm A, *MILLER*, Annie, of Milton, March 12 1889, 28
1134 *CUTSHALL*, Wm B, *LOUGH*, Myrtie E, (@ Myrtle), March 21 1889, 28
1135 *CLAGGETT*, Horace W, *WHITE*, Mary E, September 4 1889, 28
1136 *CRAMPTON*, Garrott, (@ J D Garrott), *CLAGGETT*, Sophie E, November 18 1889, 28
1137 *CRAMER*, Harry B, *SNOUFFER*, Bessie M, November 27 1889, 28
1138 *CAREY*, James, *HOLMS*, Emma, December 24 1889, 28
1139 *CHAMBERLAIN*, Benjamin W, *LEWIS*, Katie, of Cha's J, January 25 1890, 28

1140 *CLABAUGH*, Charles B, *BEAR*, Emma L, (@ BAER), April 6 1890, 28
1141 *CRAMER*, Henry E, of E_than, *BRUCHEY*, Sallie A, April 7 1890, 28
1142 *CULLER*, Charles K, *CLERAMER*, Minnie, April 9 1890, 28
1143 *CAMPBELL*, Cha's A, *FORD*, Lulie B, Octr 21 1890, 28
1144 *CARTY*, Joseph W L, *DIXON*, Minnie, of Frank, Nov 5 1890, 28
1145 *CLARK*, Asa, *GRAHE*, Sophia, Nov 25 1890, 28
1146 *CRAWFORD*, Cha's T, *YINGLING*, Laura Belle, Dec 30 1890, 28
1147 *CULLER*, Jacob A, (@ Andrew Jacob), *KELLER*, Grace, (@ Alice Grace), Dec 24 1890, 28
1148 *DEGRANGE*, John, *ARCHBALD*, Elizabeth (Mrs), Nov 30 1820, 30
1149 *DAVIS*, Richard W (Dr), of Ignatius, *BRASHEAR*, Sarah, of Dr Belt/(#), May 8 1821, 30
1150 *DEVITT*, David B, 1st wife, *MANTZ*, Ann, of Isaac, Octr 23 1821, 30
1151 *DOYLE*, Lawrence, *GORDON*, Sarah, Jany 27 1822, 30
1152 *DOLL*, Thomas, *KOLB*, Caroline, (ADLUM), May 12 1822, 30
1153 *DOLL*, Ezra, *ZIELER*, Harriott, of Geo, Octr 14 1823, 30
1154 *DOLL*, David, *KOLB*, Catharine, April 18 1824, 30
1155 *DOUB*, Joshua, *BRUBACHER*, Ann, Septr 16 1824, 30
1156 *DINDEMAN*, Conrad, *HUGHES*, Catharine, Nov 1824, 30
1157 *DOFLER*, Jonathan, *MCKINLEY*, Ann Maria, Feby 3 1825, 30
1158 *DOYLE*, George, *WHITTINGTON*, Margaret, of John, June 7 1825, 30
1159 *DIETRICH*, Henry, *CRONISE*, Eliza, of Jacob, Octr 9 1825, 30
1160 *DU VAL*, Singleton, *CLAGGETT*, Ellen Moale, Octr 18 1825, Balto, 30
1161 *DUNGAN*, Levi, *ELY*, Martha (Mrs), her 2d husband/of Dan'l, March 19 1826, 30
1162 *DRILL*, Andrew, 2d wife, *MORRISON*, Jane, May 11 1826, 30
1163 *DORSEY*, Robert E (Dr), *DUVALL*, Sarah Ann, of Dr Grafton, July 20 1826, 30
1164 *DOWDLE*, Old Wm, *ATKINS*, Polly, Septr 5 1826, 30
1165 *DONNE*, John Augustus, *THOMSON*, Grace, of Andrew, Septr 19 1826, 30
1166 *DAVIS*, Levi, 1st wife, *SHRIVER*, Rebecca, of Isaac, Nov 28 1826, 30
1167 *DERR*, Jacob, 2d wife, *STALEY*, Catharine (Mrs), June 4 1827, 30
1168 *DUCKETT*, Thomas, 1st wife, *GOLDSBOROUGH*, Catharine E W, of Wm, Nov 13 1827, 30
1169 *DEGRANGE*, Peter (Jun'r), *EBBERTS*, Louisa C, of Michael, May 28 1829, 30
1170 *DADISMAN*, Jacob, *STORM*, Lydia Ann, of Peter, June 28 1829, 30
1171 *DEVITT*, David B, 2d wife, *FOUT*, Elizabeth, of Peter, Jany 19 1830, 30
1172 *DERR*, John (Jun'r), *LUGENBEEL*, Elizabeth, April 8 1830, 30
1173 *DAVIDSON*, Samuel P, of Rev Patrick, *RAITT*, Lydia, May 27 1830, Emmittsburg, 30
1174 *DOFLER*, George (Jun'r), *HERBACH*, Mary An, Augt 5 1830, 30
1175 *DODGE*, Daniel (Rev), 2d wife, *MANKIN*, Latitia, Feby 1831, 30
1176 *DAY*, Enoch G, *ENGLAND*, Juliann, May 9 1831, 30
1177 *DAWSON*, Philip, 1st wife, *PEBUS*, Ann, of Jacobus, Nov 6 1831, 30
1178 *DURBIN*, James, *STONER*, Ann E, Nov 29 1831, 30
1179 *DAVIS*, James L, of Ignatius, *HAMNER*, Elizabeth G, Jany 10 1833, 30
1180 *DIXON*, William, *STALLINGS*, Rebecca, of Benj'n, March 25 1834, 30
1181 *DIETRICH*, Christian, *TREFZER*, Ann M, June 19 1834, 30
1182 *DERR*, Daniel, *DERTZBAUGH*, Catharine, of Geo, Septr 21 1834, 30
1183 *DAVIS*, James, *SMITH*, Sophia, of Henry, Septr 28 1834, at Washington City, 30
1184 *DADISMAN*, Ezra, of Jacob, *KELLY*, Catharine, of Va, Decr 22 1834, 30
1185 *DUVALL*, Wm T, of Marsh Mareen, *HAWMAN*, Rebecca, March 31 1835, 30
1186 *DIXON*, Joshua, *GETZENDANNER*, Sophia, of Col Jacob, June 18 1835, 30

1187 DIETRICH, Philip, his second wife, MILLER, Maria M (Mrs), her 3d husband, Septr 8 1835, 30
1188 DEAN, William, BARRICK, Catharine, January 26 1836, 30
1189 DILL, Leonard Augustus, CANNON, Ann Levina, April 17 1836, 30
1190 DAVIS, Tho's I, of Ignatius, WINN, Isabella, Nov 14 1837, 31
1191 DUVALL, John, of Marsh Maureen/1st wife, NOAKES, Christianna, of Rich'd, March 4 1838, 31
1192 DOUGLASS, William, HOUX, Sophia, of Geo Jacob, Decr 23 1838, Washington City, 31
1193 DAVIS, Levi, 2d wife and sisters, SHRIVER, Juliann, of Isaac, March 14 1839, 31
1194 DAVIS, Zachariah H, CLARY, Cordelia Ann, May 2 1839, 31
1195 DORSEY, Augustus P, THOMAS, Martha C, of Va, Octr 22 1839, 31
1196 DAWSON, Philip, his 2d wife, THOMPSON, Mary, Nov 28 1839, 31
1197 DUKE, Green H, OGLE, Elizabeth, of Ja's (Sen'r), March 5 1840, 31
1198 DERR, John, of Lewistown, HALLER, Catharine, of Peter, March 26 1840, 31
1199 DUTROW, Robert H, FELTY, Rachel C, June 2 1840, 31
1200 DUTROW, Randolph, SHRINER, Julia C, Septr 10 1840, 31
1201 DUCKETT, Thomas, 2d wife, CLARKE, Catharine (Mrs), (Miss BOWIE), Nov 12 1840, 31
1202 DOWNS, John T, BURKE, Lucinda, of Wm B, Feby 10 1841, Balto, 31
1203 DILL, Tho's P, of Ezra, ETSCHBERGER, Berthia C, Jany 24 1841, Balto, 31
1204 DUDDERER, Joseph H, CROMWELL, Mary A, March 30 1841, 31
1205 DILL, Wm H, of Ezra, DECKER, Deborah, July 22 1841, Balto, 31
1206 DEPFER, Frederick, LAUERMAN, Charlotte, Augt 30 1841, 31
1207 DUTROW, Philip H, DEVILBISS, Elizabeth Jane, of David, Octr 28 1841, 31
1208 DUVAL, M (Maj'r), (* Malachi), KEITH, Christianna, of James KIETH, Octr 20 1841, 31
1209 DONELSON, Andrew J (Maj), RANDOLPH, Elizabeth A, Nov 10 1841, Tennessee, 31
1210 DOLL, Daniel, of Jacob, PETERS, Mary C, of Cha's, Nov 25 1841, 31
1211 DILL, John F, of Joshua, CLAY, Sarah A, Feby 17 1842, 31
1212 DILL, John Tho's, of Ezra, BAILEY, Sarah, June 23 1842, Balto, 31
1213 DUVALL, Henry, of Dr Grafton, CLAGGETT, Sarah, Nov 29 1842, 31
1214 DOFLER, Jacob, of Geo, MURRAY, Ruth, March 14 1843, 31
1215 DERR, George Washington, SHAW, Ellen E, May 2 1843, Boonsboro, 31
1216 DILL, Edward W, of Ezra, SHIPLEY, Milcah Ann, June 29 1843, Balto, 31
1217 DAVIS, John J, of Ignatius, NELSON, Rosa L, of John, Augt 26 1843, Balto, 31
1218 DORSEY, Harry W, WATERS, Miss, April 9 1844, 31
1219 DERTZBAUGH, John W, METZGER, Catharine E, of Jac, May 30 1844, 31
1220 DUVALL, James L H, KEMP, Rebecca S, Nov 9 1844, 31
1221 DERR, Abraham, MARTIN, Mary Ann, March 25 1845, 31
1222 DUVALL, John, of Marsh Mareen/2d wife, SCHUBEL, Mary, April 26 1846, 31
1223 DAVIS, Geo L L, of Ignatius, CHAMBERS, Laura, of Ezekiel F, Augt 4 1846, 31
1224 DILL, Charles L, of Ezra, BLACK, Mary J, Octr 21 1846, Balto, 31
1225 DERR, Wm H, HEDGES, Julia Ann R, of Enos, Jany 28 1847, 31
1226 DOWNEY, William, WRIGHT, Margaret Jane, of Jesse, Feby 11 1847, 31
1227 DILL, Lewis H, HOUCK, Ellen, of John, March 25 1847, 31
1228 DILLER, Jacob, HOLTZMAN, Eliza A, March 31 1847, 31
1229 DORFFLER, Christian, 2d wife, MAYER, Johanna, April 21 1847, 31
1230 DOUGLASS, John T, MCPHERSON, Cornelia, of Edw B, May 8 1847, Missouri, 31
1231 DEETER, Alexander R, LINTON, Ann Mary, of Benj'n, Augt 12 1847, 31

1232 DELAPLANE, Theodore, WILCOXON, Ann (Mrs), widow of Jesse, Septr 16 1847, 32
1233 DOWNEY, John, JOHNSON, Elizabeth D, of Dr T W, Septr 21 1847, 32
1234 DILL, George T, of Joshua, SCHAFFER, Mary, of Noah A, Septr 23 1847, 32
1235 DAIGEN, Owen, MCKINNEY, Juliann, May 7 1848, NORRIS's Owen & OTT's Julia, 32
1236 DERTZBACH, George Wm, DUVALL, Ellen Jane, of Tho's, May 25 1848, 32
1237 DUVALL, Alex'r Tho's Hawkins, 1st wife, WILLIAMS, Sarah J, July 6 1848, Louisiana, 32
1238 DUVALL, John W, of Tho's, DERTZBAUGH, Christianna, of Geo, March 22 1849, 32
1239 DELASHMUTT, Basil J, SIMPSON, Juliet L, April 26 1849, 32
1240 DEAN, Robert, MONTGOMERY, Emily O, May 31 1849, 32
1241 DOLL, Wm D, OTT, Ann Sophia, of Peter, Octr 18 1849, 32
1242 DIXON, Haines, his 3d wife, HAINES, Dorothy (Mrs), March 14 1850, 32
1243 DEVILBISS, Isaiah, WILES, Mary Ann, April 4 1850, 32
1244 DELAPLANE, Joshua, FOUT, Charlotte, June 11 1850, 32
1245 DIXON, John W, KOHLENBERG, Leonora, June 16 1850, 32
1246 DOUB, Wm H, of Joshua, STALEY, Marietta C, of Cornelius, Decr 3 1850, 32
1247 DELASHMUTT, Basil, EAGLE, E Frances, of Wm, May 26 1851, 32
1248 DELASHMUTT, Andrew J, REICH, Phebe, of Philip, May 28 1851, 32
1249 DOMER, David, DOMER, Maria (Mrs), Augt 7 1851, Woodsboro, 32
1250 DOUB, Valentine Wm Otterbein, SNOOK, Elizabeth A, Septr 16 1851, 32
1251 DUVALL, Benjamin W, EICHELBERGER, Ann M, Jany 6 1852, 32
1252 DOUGHERTY, John S, BYRNE, Mary, of Michael, Jany 8 1852, 32
1253 DENNIS, George R, 1st wife, MCPHERSON, Alice, of Col John, Jany 20 1852, 32
1254 DUNLAP, Worthington, BALEY, Susan, March 21 1852, 32
1255 DOLL, John L, CARLIN, Agnes, of James, April 6 1852, 32
1256 DOLL, Geo Jos, of Ezra, WISONG, Ann E B, of Isaac, April 22 1852, 32
1257 DEVILBISS, Cha's W, WOOD, Nancy, Octr 19 1852, 32
1258 DECK, Joseph, 2d wife, GRACE, Mary, of Harpersferry, Octr 28 1852, 32
1259 DEAN, Wm E, WATERS, Mary Ann, Jany 6 1853, 32
1260 DAVIS, Henry G, BANTZ, Catharine A S, of Gideon, Feby 22 1853, 32
1261 DIXON, Wm H, PERKINS, Mary Jane, July 12 1853, 32
1262 DOUD, Francis A, STURGEON, Margaret, of John, July 31 1853, Balto, 32
1263 DEVITT, David M, PYFER, Elizabeth, of Henry, Nov 1853, in Ohio, 32
1264 DORSEY, Roderick W, BRASHEAR, Bettie, of Col Tho's, Nov 22 1853, 32
1265 DARBY, Darius, MANTZ, Catharine, of Gideon, Feby 22 1854, 32
1266 DUVALL, Wm W, MOLESWORTH, Rachel, May 1854, 32
1267 DUVALL, Alex'r Tho's Hawkins, 2d wife, JOHNSON, Rebecca H, Octr 10 1854, 32
1268 DEVILBISS, Solomon D, CRONISE, Susan H, of Sam'l, Nov 2 1854, 32
1269 DAWSON, Wm C (Hon), He US Senator of Georgia, WILLIAMS, E M (Mrs), Nov 27 1854, 32
1270 DUNGAN, William H, LUGENBEEL, Maria S, of Moses, Feby 14 1855, 32
1271 DEETER, Jacob (Jun'r), EBRECHT, Georgianna, of John, Septr 25 1855, 32
1272 DEGRANGE, George W, of John, WOLFF, Ella S, Octr 4th 1855, Martinsburg, Va, 32
1273 DIXON, B F, (* Benjamin), GREENWALD, Mary C, of Ch'n, Nov 6 1855, 32
1274 DIETRICH, J H, MILLER, Louisa, of Geo, Octr 24 1855, "Hack", 33
1275 DARCUS, William, FLOOK, Sarah A (Mrs), Jany 3d 1856, Woodsboro, 33
1276 DELAPLANE, William, FOX, Ann Elizabeth, of Baltzer, March 4 1856, 33
1277 DEVILBISS, George W, SNYDER, Ann M, March 13 1856, 33

1278 DUGAN, Wm H, *TURNER*, Amelia F, May 22 1856, 33
1279 DAUGHADAY, Joseph, *CHARD*, Henrietta, May 13 1856, Balto, 33
1280 DAVIS, Isaac Y, *KEELIKOLAUI*, H E L, Honolulu, Hawaii, July 3 1856, 33
1281 DEVILBISS, Joseph, *KOLB*, Ann E, Augt 31 1856, 33
1282 DELASHMUTT, Arthur, 2d wife, *DUVALL*, Ruth, of Tho's, Octr 9 1856, 33
1283 DAVIS, S Hamner (Rev), of Ja's L, *CARUTHERS*, Elizabeth W, Octr 28 1856, East VA, 33
1284 DOUGLAS, Stephen Arnold (Hon), 2d wife, *CUTTS*, Ada, Nov 20 1856, 33
1285 DAVIS, Henry Winter (Hon), *MORRIS*, Nancy H, of John B, Jany 27 1857, 33
1286 DEVILBISS, John Hanson, *WACHTER*, Jane R, March 24 1857, 33
1287 DUKEHART, John P, *BANTZ*, Julia Ada, of Gideon, April 28 1857, 33
1288 DYER, Edward, *DUNGAN*, Jane, Octr 1856, omitted before this place, 33
1289 DEVILBISS, George W, *BAILE*, Kitty Ann, Augt 27 1857, 33
1290 DYER, John W, *KAUFFMAN*, Mary E, of Henry, Octr 6 1857, 33
1291 DRILL, Henry C, *KEEFER*, Harriet Virginia, Octr 22 1857, 33
1292 DURGEN, Stephen, *JACLARD*, Clara (Mrs), Nov 29 1857, New York, 33
1293 DORSEY, Nicholas J (Dr), *TALBOTT*, Mattie, Jany 24 1858, Indianapolis, 33
1294 DAVIS, Wm M, *WINDSOR*, Antonie M, Jany 12 1858, 33
1295 DIEHL, Albrecht, 3d wife, *WESTPHALE*, Augustina, Feby 21 1858, 33
1296 DOUB, Ezra (Capt'n), 2d wife, *HOGG*, Lizzie Robinson, of Sam'l R, Feby 25 1858, 33
1297 DANDRIDGE, Philip P, *BLISS*, Betty "TAYLOR" (Mrs), daughter of Gen'l Zack TAYLOR, Feby 11 1858, 33
1298 DIETRICK, Lewis F, *UMSTEAD*, Catharine, of Rev J H UMSTEAD, March 30 1858, 33
1299 DUBOSE, D M, *TOOMBS*, Sallie, of Robert, April 11 1858, Georgia, 33
1300 DE CANNAY, The Marquis, *RIDGEWAY*, Emily, of John/Phila, April 8 1858, Paris, 33
1301 DAY, Daniel, *HAMMOND*, Louisa (Mrs), June 24 1858, Balto, 33
1302 DOLL, Geo W, *LIDAY*, Julia A, May 1858, 33
1303 DUVALL, Grafton, *DUTROW*, Columbia F, of Sam'l, Septr 16 1858, 33
1304 DORSEY, Nimrod, *KLEIN*, Sarah, Nov 17 1858, Unionville, 33
1305 DUTROW, Cromwell, *RAUZAHN*, Loretto, of Jos, Jany 6 1859, 33
1306 DAYHOFF, Joshua T, *LEILICH*, Annie, of Jacob, Feby 3 1859, 33
1307 DORFFLER, Louis, of Ch'n, *MUNZENBERG*, Dora, Decr 31 1858, Milwaukie, Wisc, 33
1308 DORSEY, James, *DIXON*, Elizabeth, of Wm, March 8 1959, 33
1309 DAVIS, William, *KANTNER*, Henrietta F, of Geo, March 10 1859, Reading, Pa, 33
1310 DELASHMUTT, E Van (Dr), *SIFFORD*, Cleantha E, of John, May 25 1859, 33
1311 DIXON, Thomas, *MEASELL*, Margaret S, June 16 1859, Glade, 33
1312 DERR, John P, of John, *WARNER*, Annie C N, of Mich'l, Octr 5 1859, Balto, 33
1313 DORSEY, Harry W (Jun'r Dr), *WATERS*, Annie Pottinger, of Dr Wm, Octr 13 1859, 33
1314 DUDERAR, Dennis, *COLLEBERRY*, Annie R, Octr 13 1859, 33
1315 DIMMICH, Joseph E, *KELLY*, Mary A, Octr 31 1859, Washington City, 33
1316 DUVALL, Benjamin F, *BOYER*, Sydney Jane, Nov 16 1859, 34
1317 DEVILBISS, Ezra M, *RHOADS*, Susan, of Dan'l, Nov 17 1859, 34
1318 DONNEBERGER, Geo, *WRIGHT*, Lydia F, Decr 13 1859, 34
1319 DEMUTH, Josiah, *FRIEZE*, Mary A, Decr 20 1859, 34
1320 DEGRANGE, David J, of John, *RENN*, Ruth A C, of John H, Decr 21 1859, 34
1321 DEVILBISS, Abner C, *SWEADNER*, Lydia, of Dan'l, Jany 3 1860, 34
1322 DERR, John, his 3d wife, *WACHTER*, Elizabeth B (Mrs), (REESE), Jany 3 1860, Middletown, 34

1323 DOLL, Lewis H, OGLE, Annie F, of James (HOUCK), Jany 10 1860, 34
1324 DULANY, James H (Rev), STIER, Mary P, of Hamilton, May 10 1860, N Market, 34
1325 DUVALL, Wm Luther, HILTON, Mary S, of Henry K, May 1 1860, 34
1326 DORSEY, W L, (* Wm L), WORTHINGTON, A D, of Upton, July 7 1860, Urbanna, 34
1327 DIXON, Cha's T, of Wm, MONTGOMERY, Joanna, of Col John, Augt 14 1860, 34
1328 DOUB, Josiah, BEAKLEY, Susan A, Decr 20 1860, 34
1329 DEGRANGE, Wm M, BAUGHER, Sevilla, Feby 5 1861, 34
1330 DORSEY, Joseph J, WHEELER, Mary A (Mrs), widow of Joseph A, April 7 1861, Balto, 34
1331 DUVALL, Wm T, 2d wife/(N Market), BYERS, Ann R, June 1861, 34
1332 DIEFENTHAL, Cha's A, HALLER, Alice Z, of Ezra, Septr 12 1861, Balto, 34
1333 DELAUTER, John H, RENNER, Rebecca, Octr 17 1861, Middletownvalley, 34
1334 DRONEBERGER, John Tho's, BURRIER, Susan, of Eli, Nov 4 1861, 34
1335 DOUB, Lewis P, HARP, Mary A, Decr 3 1861, 34
1336 DEAN, Wm Houston R, 1st wife, GALLION, Ann Louisa, of John P, March 4 1862, 34
1337 DEAN, Henry A, MCDERMOTT, Rosa M (Mrs), Jany 8 1862, St Louis/Porter/Rollington, 34
1338 DIXON, John, MICHAEL, Sarah J, Augt 28 1862, 34
1339 DAYHOFF, John J, HOTZ, Ann Elizabeth, of Martin, Nov 3 1862, 34
1340 DARKUS, David F, CRAMER, Martha, April 7 1863, Woodsboro, 34
1341 DAMON, Cha's L, MARTELL, Mary, of Jacob, July 19 1863, 34
1342 DEAN, Sam'l M, (of US Army), DOFLER, Ruth "MURRAY" (Mrs), Nov 12 1863, widow of Jacob, 34
1343 DAIGER, No first name given, MCDERMOTT, Katie, of John, January 1864, Balto, 34
1344 DADISMAN, Jacob, of Ezra, MCCAFFERTY, Susannah, April 26 1864, Balto, 34
1345 DOLL, Leander Z, LYETH, Anna, of John McF, May 10 1864, 34
1346 DENNIS, Geo R, Col, 2d wife/sisters, MCPHERSON, Fannie, of Col John, June 9 1864, 34
1347 DAVISON, Morris, HILTON, Alice, of H'y K, Septr 23 1864, 34
1348 DEAN, Wm Houston R, 2d wife, STEIN, Elizabeth C, of Louis, Nov 5 1864, 34
1349 DEAN, Geo Albert, GORTON, Emma V, Decr 1864, Balto, 34
1350 DRYSDALE, Lieut, (* James M), NELSON, Molly, of Wm B, Feby 15 1865, 34
1351 DERR, George C, of Dan'l, VANFOSSEN, Frances F, of Eli, Feby 28 1865, 34
1352 DONOLDSON, Donald, JONES, Virginia, March 12 1865, 34
1353 DOUGLASS, Robert, RUSSELL, Ann E, April 9 1865, 34
1354 DEGRANGE, David J, (of John)/2d wife, HOFFMAN, Josephine V, April 25 1865, 34
1355 DERR, Geo F, MCCORMICK, Harriett A, Augt 8 1865, 34
1356 DAVIS, Robert E, of Pittsburgh, STONER, Martha A E, Septr 7 1865, 34
1357 DUST, Lewis, (US Army), HERRMANN, Lena, Octr 1 1865, 34
1358 DIXON, Benjamin S, THOMAS, E Amanda, of Peter Deceased, Octr 17 1865, 35
1359 DRYDEN, J Merideth, COLE, Fannie R, of Lewis M, Octr 10 1865, Balto, 35
1360 DIETRICH, Edington, REIGHLEY, Elise, of Rev Cha's, Nov 2 1865, N York, 35
1361 DEMUTH, Geo A, WILLIAR, Sarah A, Decr 21 1865, 35
1362 DEGRANGE, Henry Clay, of Peter, BENNETT, Mary M, of Tilghman, Decr 21 1865, N Market, 35
1363 DUTROW, Jacob W, ENGLISH, Ruth Ann, of Jonathan W, Jany 18 1866, Wolfsville, 35
1364 DUNOTT, Thomas J (Dr), ZACHARIAS, Lizzie, of Rev Dan'l, May 22 1866, 35
1365 DIXON, Charles F, WILCOXON, Laura J, of John, July 26 1866, 35
1366 DUKEHART, John M, MANTZ, Rebecca, of Henry, Augt 29 1866, Balto, 35
1367 DERR, Luther C, FRALEY, Victoria, (FROLICH) of Henry, Septr 6 1866, 35

1368 DAVIS, William C, *DUDLEY*, Ruth A, Augt 27 1866, 35
1369 DEAN, James H, *PICKING*, Rebecca T, of Tho's, Octr 16 1866, in Balto, 35
1370 DELASHMUTT, Wm G, *REICH*, Virginia S, of Philip, Nov 6 1866, 35
1371 DUDDERAR, David W, *PEARRE*, Maggie A, Octr 14 1866, 35
1372 DUTROW, Samuel, 2d wife, *COST*, Mary A S (Mrs), (widow of Henry), April 17 1867, 35
1373 DOLL, Samuel V, *MCLANE*, Mary Lucretia, of Wm W, May 14 1867, 35
1374 DOLL, Melville E, *DANNER*, Hannah M, Septr 19 1867, Gettysburg, Pa, 35
1375 DORSEY, Wm H B, *EBERT*, Fannie V, of Valerius, Nov 20 1867, 35
1376 DERR, Charles E, *FRALEY*, Alice R, (FROLICH), July 15 1868, 35
1377 DUVALL, James E, of Tho's, *YOUNG*, Maggie A, of Wm/"DERTZBAUGH", Decr 10 1868, 35
1378 DORSEY, Richard H, *HAMMOND*, Mary M, of Dr Richard T, Septr 1 1869, 35
1379 DERR, William R, of John, *GITTINGER*, Frances B, of Wm, Nov 9 1869, 35
1380 DIETRICH, J Stoll, of Henry, *MARKELL*, Hallie, of Geo/3d daughter, Nov 16 1869, 35
1381 DERN, George M, *ROUTZAHN*, Amanda E, Decr 20 1869, Glade, 35
1382 DIEHL, Nelson, of Adam, *GETZENDANNER*, Laura V, of Edw T, Feby 1 1870, 35
1383 DELASHMUTT, Elias L, 2d wife, *HURLEY*, Lucinda Jane, Octr 27 1870, 35
1384 DORSEY, Ignatius W, *HOBBS*, Laura, Jan 17 1871, 35
1385 DEAN, George W, of John, *GONSO*, Laura, of Wm H, Jan 26 1871, 35
1386 DEGRANGE, Wm F, of John, *WILES*, Ellen A C, of Tho's, Jan 19 1871, 35
1387 DEVILBISS, James E (Dr), *BOWERSOX*, Mattie, March 30 1871, 35
1388 DEGRANGE, D W F, of John, *WILLIAMSON*, E V, Octr 17 1871, W Va, 35
1389 DIEHL, Nathan, *KEEN*, Laura Virginia, of Balto, Feby 24 1872, 35
1390 DERR, Millard Taylor, of Dan'l, *SMITH*, Mary E, Nov 5 1872, 35
1391 DINTERMAN, Jacob E, *TITLOW*, Susan E, March 11 1873, 35
1392 DIEHL, Albert (Jun'r), *NOLTE'*, Christianna, April 29 1873, 35
1393 DEAVER, G Clinton (Prof), *HOPKINS*, Harriet O, Decr 24 1873, 35
1394 DUTROW, Joseph S, *FOUT*, Sue A, of Geo H, Jan 27 1874, 35
1395 DIX, Morgan (Rev DD & LLD), *SOUTTER*, Emily Wolsey, June 3 1874, N York, 35
1396 DANDRIDGE, Edmund P, *PITTS*, Elizabeth, of Ch's H, Decr 10 1874, 35
1397 DUVALL, J Ijams, of Tho's, *IJAMS*, Mary V, of J P, Decr 23 1874, 35
1398 DARBY, Zachary Taylor, *CANDLER*, Augusta B, Jan 27 1875, 35
1399 DEAN, John A, *MAINHART*, Mary A, April 29 1875, 35
1400 DERTZBAUGH, Henry, *BENNETT*, Emma J, of Lewis H, July 8 1875, 36
1401 DUTROW, Richard J, *COOPER*, E Minnie, of David, Nov 1875, "ADAMS", 36
1402 DERR, Eugene L, of John, *GROVERMAN*, Fannie, March 20 1876, 36
1403 DOWNEY, Jesse Wright, *HAMMOND*, Miss, of Denton, Apl 25 1876, 36
1404 DUTROW, Randolph, 2d wife, *BAKER*, Mary A (Mrs), "FOUT", April 17 1876, 36
1405 DEAN, Henry C, *HAGAN*, Maggie E, of Igntius, Sept 12 1876, Balto, 36
1406 DAVIS, Sam'l R, *EBERT*, Rebecca M, of Benj, Jan 18 1877, 36
1407 DEGRANGE, Garnett S, *MCQUILKEN*, Sallie M, March 1 1877, 36
1408 DENNIS, Louis E, *FOX*, Emma Francisco, of Adolph, April 26 1877, 36
1409 DOLL, J Edward, of John L, *KEEFER*, M Ella, of John, June 28 1877, 36
1410 DELASHMUTT, Philip R, *BISCH*, Marie, of Col Victor, Aug 27 1877, 36
1411 DILL, Joshua J, of Lewis M, *BARTGIS*, Nellie J, of Ja's, Octr 2 1877, 36
1412 DELASHMUTT, E T H, *THOMAS*, E Alvida, Nov 14 1877, 36
1413 DUVALL, Wilbur H, 1st wife, *FRAZIER*, Ida, (not listed as Miss), February 7th 1878, 36

The Joseph Engelbrecht Marriage Ledger of Frederick Co., MD 1820-1890 *Marriage List*

1414 DIXON, Thomas H, *FRALEY*, Eutoka G, March 14th 1878, 36
1415 DEPKIN, J Harry, *CRISE*, Mollie O, Jan 7th 1879, 36
1416 DERR, Hiram, *MCLAINE*, Florence M, April 17th 1879, 36
1417 DOLL, Clifford H, *WISNER*, Clemma E, Sept 18th 1879, 36
1418 DADE, Maruice, *CHISWELL*, Rachie, (of Joseph)/(not listed as Miss), Jan 7th 1880, 36
1419 DENEGRE, Wm P (@), of NY, *MILLER*, Mamie, of Wm/(not listed as Miss), Feb 4th 1880, 36
1420 DELASHMUT, Elias E, *RAMSBURG*, Susie, of Wm H/(not listed as Miss), June 23d 1880, 36
1421 DEGRANGE, Cha's A, *BROWN*, Florence G, (not listed as Miss), Aug 28th 1880, 36
1422 DUVALL, Wm H E, of Luther, *SHOOK*, Belle E, (not listed as Miss), Nov 12th 1880, 36
1423 DUSCHE, George J, of Pennsylvania, *LEASE*, Emma C, (not listed as Miss), March 15 1881, 36
1424 DUDREAR, Richard R, *GROFF*, Fannie, of Joseph, January 25t 1882, 36
1425 DE GARMADNDIER, Carlos, of NY, *BAUGHMAN*, Corrinne F, of John W, June 21 1882, 36
1426 DIFFINDAL, Charles L, *THOMAS*, Hattie, September 4 1882, 36
1427 DYER, Harry W, *LAYMAN*, Susan H M, September 6th 1882, 36
1428 DYER, John H, *FUNK*, Minnie L, March 27th 1883, 36
1429 DILL, Lewis H, *REPP*, Maggie E, January 24 1884, 36
1430 DUTROW, R Claude, *BECK*, Ida E, February 20th 1884, 36
1431 DELAPLAINE, Wm T, of Theo, *BIRELY*, Fannie, of Geo K, March 2 1884, 36
1432 DIXON, Richard P, *PERRY*, Minnie N, of James P(#), April 10 1884, 36
1433 DUFFINDORFER, Wm E, (@ DIEFFENDERFER), *BARTGIS*, Anna R, Oct 12 1884, 36
1434 DANNER, Robert T, (@), *SUMAN*, Alice O, of Isaac, March 25 1885, 36
1435 DOUBB, Charles V, *BLAIR*, Edmonia, July 9 1885, 36
1436 DAVIDISON, Bradly H, *MOATH*, Miss, November 23 1886, HILTON, 36
1437 DEVILBISS, Lee/Levi (@ #), *SHIPLEY*, Mollie, February 2 1887, 36
1438 DORCUS, Edward T, *ZIMMERMAN*, Alice, (@ Susan A), March 17 1887, 36
1439 DUNGAN, Wm L W, *KEYSER*, Annie, June 22 1887, in Kansas, 36
1440 DIETER, Wm H, (@ DETER), *FRALEY*, Cora H, of August, June 29 1887, 36
1441 DELASHMUTT, John A, *SIMMONS*, Fannie S, October 11 1887, 36
1442 DANNER, Cha's H, *WILLS*, Katie, December 16 1887, 36
1443 DIETRICK, Lewis F, of Balto, *DOMY*, Lilly, January 25 1888, 36a
1444 DUVALL, Wilber H, 2 wife, *RENNER*, Lola E (Mrs), 2 husband, March 8 1888, 36a
1445 DETRICK, Peter, *SHAFER*, Mary C, March 11 1888, 36a
1446 DAVIS, John K, *MOXLEY*, Nora, (#), April 12 1888, 36a
1447 DIFFENDAL, T Bernard, *HOBBS*, Mollie, April 16 1888, 36a
1448 DAYHOFF, F M, *EGLESTOWN*, Lucy, July 10 1888, 36a
1449 DAVIS, Wm, *HUGHES*, Renie, Sept 12 1888, DUVALL, 36a
1450 DIEHL, T S (Dr), *CONN*, Ella T, October 3 1888, 36a
1451 DURMIN, Edward F, *MCPRICE*, Mary M, Jan 8 1889, 36a
1452 DE VIERS, B F, (@ Benjamin DE VRIES), *DEVILBISS*, Ada, January 23 1889, (Liberty, 36a
1453 DYER, Marion, *BOYER*, Emma V, February 27 1889, 36a
1454 DOLL, Cha's J, *CRAMER*, Mamie L, (@ Mary L), March 27 1889, 36a
1455 DAHLGREN, John Vinton, *DRIXELL*, Elizabeth, June 29 1889, 36a
1456 DANNER, Wm H, *STEINER*, Mary, Sept 8 1889, 36a
1457 DE YOE, Luther (Rev), *MCKNIGHT*, Jennie, November 19 1889, 36a

1458 *DOTY*, E W, *ETCHISON*, Lenora, April 22 1890, 36a
1459 *DRILL*, Ollie B, *JANNEY*, Annie V, May 3 1890, 36a
1460 *DANIELS*, M E, *WALTER*, Birdie E, of John, July 11 1890, 36a
1461 *DOLL*, Charles D, of John, *STULL*, Florence J, July 16 1890, 36a
1462 *DYER*, Walter R, *KUHN*, Mollie M, of M, Septr 16 1890, 36a
1463 *DELASHMUTT*, Lynn, *MOFFAT*, Gracie, Nov 5 1890, 36a
1464 *DIXON*, Wm T, *SEACHRIST*, Salome E, of Rev C W, Dec 24 1890, (@ SECHRIST), 36a
1465 *ELVINS*, William R, *BOGEN*, Caroline, of Dr J Nich Andrew BOGAN, Octr 15 1820, 38
1466 *FISCHER*, William (Dr), *GUNTON*, Harriott, Feby 22 1821, 38
1467 *EVITT*, Woodward, 2d wife, *TICE*, Mary (Mrs), (BECKWITH), June 29 1821, 38
1468 *EVITT*, Joseph, of Woodward, *NICHOLS*, Margaret, April 7 1822, 38
1469 *FEW*, William, *RITCHIE*, Susan, of Wm (Co Clerk), April 9 1822, 38
1470 *FOUT*, Baltzer, 2d wife, *KEPHART*, Charlotte, of Geo, Augt 6 1822, 38
1471 *EADER*, Wm, of Ab'm/1st wife, *BUCHER*, Jemima, Nov 24 1822, 38
1472 *ELIOTT*, Robert (Rev DD), 2d wife, *LAMOTT*, Elizabeth, Nov 19 1822, 38
1473 *EADER*, Darias, of Ab'm, *PHILLIPS*, Miranda, Jany 12 1823, 38
1474 *EBERT*, Emanuel, *WOODS*, Mrs, (* Ann Maria), January 1823, 38
1475 *FRAZIER*, Fielder, *DRURY*, Rosanna, April 24 1823, 38
1476 *EADER*, Lewis B, of David, *BRENGLE*, Catharine, of Nicholas, May 6 1824, 38
1477 *FOGLER*, Henry (Jun'r), 1st wife, *FITZGERALD*, Maria, July 25 1824, 38
1478 *EBERT*, John, 3d wife, *KRUG*, Elizabeth, of Rev John Andrew, Jany 13 1825, 38
1479 *ELLIOTT*, Tho's, of Balto, *DANNER*, Charlotte, of York, PA, March 1825, 38
1480 *FINGER*, John Adam, 2d wife, *MARCKLEY*, Barbara (Mrs), April 24 1825, 38
1481 *ENGELBRECHT*, Jacob, of Mich'l, *RAMSBURG*, Eliza, of John, May 29 1825, 38
1482 *EMLEY*, David M, *KLEIN*, Rebecca, of Stephen, Septr 29 1825, 38
1483 *ENGLEBRIGHT*, John, of Mich'l, *LEASE*, Catharine, of Geo, Nov 14 1825, 38
1484 *FITZPATRICK*, Daniel, *KANTNER*, Sarah, Decr 31 1825, 38
1485 *EADER*, George, of Ab'm, *DERR*, Catharine, of Jacob, Feby 5 1826, 38
1486 *EICHELBERGER*, Martin, *ZIMMERMAN*, Maria C, April 13 1826, 38
1487 *ELLSWORTH*, Frederick, teacher in Acadamy, *BEDINGER*, Susan Peyton, of Va, May 11 1826, 38
1488 *ELY*, Ezra, *ROWE*, Ann Eliza, of Michael (Sen'r), Jany 23 1827, 38
1489 *FOUT*, Lewis, 1st wife/of Daniel, *RAUZAHN*, Lydia Ann, Feby 15 1827, 38
1490 *FLEMING*, Joseph P, *HOUCK*, Charlotte, of John, March 27 1827, 38
1491 *EADER*, George, of John, *DRAPER*, Minerva, May 3 1827, 38
1492 *FOUT*, Peter S, *THOMAS*, Susan, of Henry, May 3 1827, 38
1493 *FREY*, Joseph, *NUSZ*, Harriott, Septr 27 1827, 38
1494 *EAGLE*, William, 2d wife, *FOUT*, Margaret, of Wm (not listed as Miss), Decr 30 1827, 38
1495 *FEW*, Howell, *CLARK*, Eliza A L, Decr 27 1827, in Balto, 38
1496 *EATON*, John H (Hon), 2d wife, *TIMBERLAKE*, Margaret L (Mrs), Jany 1829, 38
1497 *FOUT*, Lewis, of Daniel/2d wife, *SCHOLL*, Elizabeth, of John, Feby 5 1829, 38
1498 *EADER*, Edward, of John, *HALLER*, Mary, of Peter, Nov 5 1829, 38
1499 *EATY*, Henry B, *CROMWELL*, Lucy Ann, Nov 3 1829, 38
1500 *EBERT*, Benjamin, of John, *BIRELY*, Caroline, of Wm, Decr 24 1829, 38
1501 *EADER*, George, of John/2d wife, *HOPWOOD*, Mary, of Joshua, Decr 24 1829, 38
1502 *EICHELBERGER*, Lewis (Rev), *MILLER*, Mary Ann, Feby 4 1830, Winchester, Va, 38
1503 *FIRESTONE*, Joshua, *STULL*, Christianna, April 8 1830, 38

The Joseph Engelbrecht Marriage Ledger of Frederick Co., MD 1820-1890 *Marriage List*

1504 FOUT, Lewis, of Daniel/3d wife, *LATE*, Mary A, of Jacob, Augt 31 1830, 38
1505 ENGELBRECHT, William, *WINTER*, Susan, of Benj'n, Octr 3 1830, 38
1506 FOUT, Otho, of Dan'l, *CRUM*, Catharine, of Isaac, Octr 12 1830, 38
1507 EBERT, Augustus F, *BANTZ*, Elizabeth Maria, Octr 19 1830, 39
1508 FLOWERS, Michael, *ARNOLD*, Catharine (Mrs), Jany 27 1831, 39
1509 EBRECHT, John (Jonathan), *WILLS*, Rebecca, of Mich'l, July 10 1831, 38
1510 FROSCHAUER, Adam, 2d wife, *FAUBEL*, Lydia A, Augt 16 1831, 39
1511 FINNEY, James, 2d wife, *BAER*, Charlotte (Mrs), widow of Michael (KEEFER), Jany 15 1832, 39
1512 FAUBEL, David, 1st wife, *DEGRANGE*, Margaret, of Peter, May 1 1832, 39
1513 ENGELBRECHT, George, *BRENGLE*, Ann Maria, of Capt'n John, May 7 1833, 39
1514 FERTICH, John, *ROTHAUER*, Catharine, July 20 1833, 39
1515 FLEMING, Tho's A (Dr), *NUSZ*, Catharine, of Frederick, Octr 22 1833, 39
1516 FLEMING, John, *KESSLER*, Ann Catharine, of Jacob, March 30 1834, Tiffin, Ohio, 39
1517 FERREE, Daniel, *DIXON*, Eliza, of Haines, April 10 1834, 39
1518 FAUBEL, David, 2d wife, *KLEINERT*, Susan, of Frederick, July 31 1834, 39
1519 FESSLER, Henry Baer, *WOOLTZ*, Ann Eliza, of Geo, Septr 2 1834, 39
1520 FRENSCHBACH, Frederick, *BOLASKY*, Susan (Mrs), Septr 18 1834, 39
1521 FOUT, John H, of Wm, *STONER*, Susan, of John, Jany 15 1835, 39
1522 FISCHER, George Jacob, *JOHNSTON*, Isabella, (not listed as Miss), Feby 10 1835, 39
1523 EADER, William, 2d wife, *STALLINGS*, Ann E, of Benj'n, May 31 1835, 39
1524 FRALEY, Henry, (FROLICH), *FAGAN*, Elizabeth, of Geo, June 11 1835, 39
1525 FOX, Charles J, *GETZENDANNER*, Catharine E, of Adam, March 20 1836, 39
1526 FILLER, Eli, *DAYHOFF*, Maria, May 1 1836, 39
1527 ENT, Otho George, *LAMBRECHT*, Lydia, of Mich'l, March 21 1837, 39
1528 FEIT, Jacob, 2d wife, *HENRY*, Barbara, (HEINRICH), April 3 1837, 39
1529 EAGLE, William, his 3d wife, *COOLEY*, Ruth Ann, June 1 1837, 39
1530 FLOWERS, Benjamin C (Rev), *JONES*, Mary Ann, of Rev Josha, Feby 8 1838, 39
1531 FEETE, Harrison, of Henry, *MILLER*, Elizabeth A, (not listed as Miss), March 22 1838, Middletown, 39
1532 FOUT, George, *PICKINS*, Margaret, April 5 1838, 39
1533 ENGELBRECHT, Michael, *MCMULLIN*, Rebecca R, Augt 28 1838, 39
1534 FROSCHAUER, Geo W, *BAER*, Juliann, Jany 29 1839, 39
1535 EATON, Henry, *BURCH*, Sarah A, Jany 29 1839, 39
1536 FAUBEL, Joseph D, of Jacob, *REYNOLDS*, Margaret, Feby 14 1839, 39
1537 FOUT, Greenberry, of Baltzer, *POST*, Eliza (Mrs), (GROVE), Feby 26 1839, 39
1538 EICHELBERGER, Lewis (Rev), 2d wife, *HAY*, Penelope Lynn, March 14 1839, 39
1539 FOUT, Grafton, of Baltzer, *GROVE*, Lauretto, of Jacob, May 16 1839, 39
1540 FRAAS, George, *BERNHARDT*, Margaretta, May 20 1839, 39
1541 EADER, Edward, of John/2d wife, *HALLER*, Mary (Mrs), widow of John (BROWN), Octr 29 1839, 39
1542 EICHENBROD, Daniel, *HARP*, Elizabeth, Octr 8 1839, 39
1543 FISHER, Joseph R, *CARLLEY*, Mary H, Decr 17 1839, Montgy Co, 39
1544 FITZGERALD, Aaron (Capt), *MILLER*, Frances Ann (Mrs), Decr 18 1839, 39
1545 FISH, Preserved, 2d wife, *SHEPHERD*, Mary (Mrs), April 24 1840, N York, 39
1546 FRAZIER, Wm, of Jeremiah, *HALLER*, Margaret, of Henry, April 30 1840, 39
1547 FOGLER, Henry, his 2d wife, *DUNGAN*, Martha (Mrs), her 3rd husband, June 30 1840, 39

1548 FIRESTONE, Henry M, of Jacob, MAHONEY, Mary Ann, of Martin, Augt 21 1840, 39
1549 EBERT, John M, RAMSBURG, Catharine, of John, Decr 24 1840, 40
1550 EBBERTS, Joseph Matthias, FOUT, Catharine, of Peter, Jany 28 1841, 40
1551 EASTERDAY, Daniel, (OSTERDAG), SCHINDLER, Susanna, March 16 1841, 40
1552 ELLIS, William, 1st wife, BEARD, Mary Ann, June 24 1841, 40
1553 FUSS, Jeremiah, WEBB, Naomi Lacy, of Jos B, July 29 1841, 40
1554 FAUBEL, Solomon, CLAPSADDLE, Miss, (* Catharine E), Octr 21 1841, 40
1555 ELLIS, Daniel, 2d wife, GANTZAN, Mary (Mrs), Octr 24 1841, 40
1556 FAGAN, George (Jun'r), WALLING, Elizabeth, of David, Octr 26 1841, 40
1557 FINCH, Wm, of John, STARR, Eliza Ann, Octr 17 1841, 40
1558 EBERT, Valerius, of John, BACHMAN, Charlotte, Octr 25 1842, 40
1559 FIEGE, Philip, of Fred'k, HOOVER, Lucy, Nov 1 1842, Cumberland, 40
1560 FORD, Robert, BALTZELL, Ellen, of Dr John, Decr 13 1842, 40
1561 ELLIS, Crosby W, GRAFF, Mary C, of Geo, July 3 1843, 40
1562 FEAGA, George (Sen'r), (FIEGE)/2d wife, STALEY, Ann E (Mrs), Octr 5 1843, 40
1563 EICHELBERGER, Grayson, BAUGHER, Amanda, of Isaac, May 21 1844, 40
1564 ELLIOTT, James, HOUSTON, Sarah A, of James F, Octr 29 1844, 40
1565 ELKINS, Joseph D, TITLOW, Eleanor, of John, Nov 24 1844, 40
1566 EBRECHT, William, EICHELBERGER, Sarah Jane, Decr 11 1844, 40
1567 FORD, No first name given, (*John B), RICKERD, Catharine, of Henry J/(*RICKETTS), Jany 9 1845, 40
1568 FOX, William A, ADKINS, Mary, Augt 7 1845, 40
1569 FIRESTONE, Frederick, WHITTER, Rebecca, of Tho's, Augt 12 1845, 40
1570 ELLIS, Joseph, TITLOW, Henrietta, of John, Augt 14 1845, 40
1571 FAUBEL, John Jacob, of Jacob, LEAKIN, Julia E, Octr 2d 1845, 40
1572 FLEMING, Wm Randolph, HAUER, Matilda, of Dan'l, Junr, Nov 26 1845, 40
1573 EBBERTS, Wm, of Joseph, CRAMER, Margret, Feby 14 1846, 40
1574 FRIDAY, Henry (Jun'r), DELASHMUTT, Catharine Ann, Octr 22 1846, 40
1575 ENGLISH, James J, of Richard, HERGESHEIMER, Jane Rebecca, of Jos (not listed as Miss), March 4 1847, 40
1576 EYSTER, D A S, (*David), BLESSING, Penelope A M, of Ab'm, April 13 1847, "ENT", 40
1577 FISHER, Lewis, 1st wife, ROSZMAN, Barbara, of Jacob, April 14 1847, 40
1578 ENT, Charles W, of Capt Geo W, EADER, Isabella Ann, of Tho's, April 29 1847, 40
1579 EBERT, Wm, of John, DYE, Elizabeth, Georgetown, DC, May 19 1847, 40
1580 EVANS, M Topham, KEMP, Lavinia Ellen, of Henry, Nov 9 1847, Allegany, 40
1581 FEIGHLER, Joseph, SMELTZER, Sarah Catharine, of Henry R, Feby 9 1848, 40
1582 EADER, Cha's W, of Wm, DADISMAN, Almira E, of Jacob, Septr 8 1848, 40
1583 EADER, Mannassah, of John, LEASE, Mary, Septr 21 1848, Linganore, 40
1584 FRAZIER, Luther, MERMAN, Salina M, Nov 2 1848, 40
1585 ESWORTHY, James, WINDBIGLER, Mary, Decr 5 1848, 40
1586 ENGELBRECHT, John Adam, 2d wife, DANNER, Mary Ann, Decr 14 1848, 40
1587 FAGAN, Thomas, 1st wife, CRIST, Josephine, of Jacob, Feby 13 1849, 40
1588 FLEET, John A, MAYNARD, Lea Ellen, May 7 1849, 40
1589 ELY, David W, of Wm, FINCH, Julia, of John, Jany 7 1850, 40
1590 FOUT, David J, of Baltzer, WINDSOR, Mary Jane, Jany 17 1850, 40
1591 ENGELBRECHT, John Conrad, of John, BALL, Caroline E, Feby 20 1850, 41
1592 FOUT, Michael W, of Wm, MARLOW, Ann R, of Hanson, Nov 22 1844, 41

1593 ESTERLY, Frederick, (OSTERLE), *ROSS*, Maria, (ROSZ), March 10 1850, 41
1594 FRAZIER, David, of Jeremiah, *MARKEY*, Matilda E, of Fred'k, April 10 1850, 41
1595 FEIT, J Jacob, his 3d wife, *FRAAS*, Mrs, April 14 1850, 41
1596 EBERT, Adam S, of Geo Adam, *BURGEE*, Harriott, April 1850, Balto, 41
1597 FRIDAY, Henry, *PRESTON*, Ann E, June 8 1850, 41
1598 ESTERLY, Geo, 1st wife, *BORCHER*, Miss Elizabeth, {Miss given name? compiler}, Octr 27 1850, (*BOYER), 41
1599 FORD, John T, of Jeff Co, Va, *CROMWELL*, Henrietta G, of John, Nov 14 1850, Henderson, Ky, 41
1600 EDMONSTON, Richard A, *CARLIN*, Margaret P, of Wm, Jany 23 1851, LEASE, 41
1601 EDWARDS, Samuel, *EBERT*, Charlotte, of Adam, Feby 4 1851, 41
1602 FULTON, Joseph, *TITLOW*, Caroline, March 24 1851, 41
1603 ELY, Isaac H, *SAHM*, Mary Catharine, June 10 1851, 41
1604 FOUKE, Isaac, *MILLER*, Margaret, Harpersferry, Augt 7 1851, 41
1605 EAGLE, William H, *DUDERRAR*, Charlotte E, Augt 7 1851, 41
1606 EICHELBERGER, J Dix, *CLOUD*, Maria H, of Jesse, Nov 27 1851, 41
1607 EADER, David Nicholas, of L B, *DUFFIE*, Margaret, Decr 4 1851, 41
1608 EVES, Peter, *HELDEBRAND*, Amanda Melvina, of John, Decr 23 1851, 41
1609 FLEMING, Joseph P, his 2d, *BAUGHER*, Susanna (Mrs), her 3d, March 28 1852, 41
1610 EADER, Jonathan, of Lewis B, *BIRDWELL*, Catharine P, Washington City, May 4 1852, 41
1611 EBERT, John, of Benj'n, *SCHREINER*, Mary E, of John, June 17 1852, 41
1612 FLING, Thomas, *CRAMER*, Mary M, Septr 16 1852, 41
1613 FIROR, Ephraim, (FURUHR), *BEGGETT*, Elizabeth, Washington City, Septr 14 1852, 41
1614 EGE, Andrew Gailbraith, *CRAIGHEAD*, Matilda H, Decr 8 1852, Pa, 41
1615 FOUT, George Henry, of Peter S, *SHOOK*, Luretia, May 25 1853, 41
1616 EINSTEIN, Samuel, 2d wife/widower 2 mon 2 days, *STEINBERG*, Miss, June 7 1853, 41
1617 FISHER, Wm H, of Barney, *WRIGHT*, Anna M, Balto, May 31 1853, 41
1618 FETTERLING, Geo R, *BRUBAKER*, Isabella, of John, Octr 14 1853, 41
1619 EISENHAUER, Balthaser, *HOLTZINGER*, Teresa, Nov 27 1853, 41
1620 ECKMAN, John W, *ARTHUR*, Catharine E, Decr 20 1853, 41
1621 FLEMING, Robert C, *EAGLE*, Sally E, of Wm, Feby 21 1854, 41
1622 FLEMING, John C, of Jos P, *SHAFER*, Harriott E, of Jacob, Feby 28 1854, 41
1623 ENGLE, John R, *STONE*, Elizabeth, March 30 1854, Liberty, 41
1624 FRENCH, Ford Jones, *HAUER*, Charlotte C, of Rev Dan'l J, May 4 1854, 41
1625 FISHER, Hugh, 2nd wife, *MILLER*, Maria Ellen, (QUYNN), July 18 1854, 41
1626 FRAZIER, Sylvester A, *CRISSAMER*, Anna, Nov 25 1854, 41
1627 FLEMING, J Alfred, of Jos P, *GLAZE*, Mary Ann, March 21 1855, 41
1628 ENGELBRECHT, George, of John Adam, *DERR*, Elizabeth C, of Dan'l, June 12 1855, 41
1629 FRAZIER, Jeremiah H, *FRAZIER*, Ann Mary, of Gettysburg, Pa, Octr 24 1854, 41
1630 ENGELBRECHT, Philipp Melancthon, *STORM*, Salina Virginia, Octr 17 1855, 41
1631 EBRECHT, Luther N, *SHIPLEY*, Eliza A, Nov 15 1855, 41
1632 FEASTER, Benjamin, *STEIN*, Susan R, Nov 29 1855, 41
1633 EICHHOLTZ, Jesse, *HAHN*, Malinda Ann, (Graceham), March 20 1856, 42
1634 FINNEY, Ch'n Keefer, *GREENTREE*, Eliza W, of Ezra, March 14 1856, 42
1635 FORREST, Summerfield, *CURRANS*, Emma C, of Elijah, May 1856, 42
1636 EAGLE, George W, *BOYER*, Sarah, Sugarloaf Mountain, Augt 5 1856, 42
1637 FISHER, John, (Cashier, Westminster Bank), *MOTHLAND*, Annie E, Nov 13 1856, 42

1638 FOX, Cha's H O, GEISINGER, Sarah Catharine, of Sam'l L, Nov 19 1856, 42
1639 EBEL, Jacob, SCHMIDT, Elizabeth, April 19 1857, 42
1640 FREY, George, MCDADE, Isabella, of Sam'l/Balto, May 17 1857, 42
1641 FLEMING, Charles F, of Dr Tho's A, ELLIS, Susan R, of Dan'l, June 18 1857, 42
1642 EADER, Cha's E, of Lewis B, LAMBRECHT, Ann C, of John, July 17 1857, 42
1643 FALK, John M, AUBEL, Catharine, Augt 30 1857, 42
1644 FIGGINS, James, ORR, Letitia A, of Dr A V B Orr, Nov 5 1857, 42
1645 FAVORITE, Wm L, EICHHOLTZ, Lydia, Glade, Nov 3 1857, 42
1646 FISHER, Lewis, of Barney/2d wife, CRUM, Ann Maria, of Isaac, Jany 12 1858, 42
1647 FILLMORE, Millard (Hon), 2d wife, MCINTOSH, Caroline C, Feby 10 1858, Albarry, NY, 42
1648 FREDERICK, Wm Nicholas Charles, of Prussia, "GULPH", Victoria Adelaide M L, Jany 25 1858, 42
1649 EVANS, F James, BAYER, Annie, of our town/"BOLEY", Jany 16 1858, at York, Pa, 42
1650 ELY, William J, SEABROOK, Martha C, April 7 1858, Creagerstown, 42
1651 FAY, Theodore S, 2d wife, LEUTWEIN, Anna, (not listed as Miss), June 15 1858, Berne "Schweitz", 42
1652 FINNY, Clark, GREENTREE, Isabella, of Ezra, Augt 12 1858, 42
1653 ESTERLY, George (Jun'r), (OSTERLE)/2d wife, ANGELBERGER, Rebecca, of Geo, Augt 24 1858, 42
1654 FULMER, John Lewis, HEIM, Sarah Rebecca, Nov 11 1858, 42
1655 EISENHART, J Schmucker, SMITH, Ellie C, Williamsburg, Pa, Decr 14 1858, 42
1656 FOREMAN, Cha's V, SEFTON, Margaret F, Decr 21 1858, 42
1657 FISHER, William, WEYL, Elleanor, of Rev Cha's G/Balto, Jany 6 1859, 42
1658 EADER, Lewis A, 2d wife, STIPES, Catharine (Mrs), 2d husband, Jany 4 1859, 42
1659 EUSTIS, George (Hon), of N Orleans, CORCORAN, Louisa M, of W W, April 5 1859, 42
1660 EVERHART, O T, KISTER, Sally, April 26 1859, Pa, 42
1661 EADER, Augustus L, of Tho's, MANN, Annie M, of Stephen S, May 11 1859, 42
1662 EICHEL, H L, MANNSTADT, Mary R, Balto, June 12 1859, 42
1663 FOOTE, Henry S, Ex-Gov, SMILEY, Rachel D (Mrs), June 14 1859, Nashville, Tenn, 42
1664 FINE, John, aged 96 years, HARLEY, Elizabeth, aged 37, Augt 12 1859, Davie Co, NC, 42
1665 ECKERD, Titus, SWORMSTEDT, Eliza Catharine, Octr 24 1859, 42
1666 FOX, Joseph C, BUHRMAN, Seraphine, Octr 27 1859, 42
1667 ELLIOTT, Curtis E, WHEELER, Margaret (Mrs), widow of John F R, Nov 15 1859, Balto, 42
1668 FOWLER, Oliver Perry, TURNER, Mary, Nov 24 1859, 42
1669 FRAZIER, Wm H, FIDE, Susan, Nov 13 1859, 42
1670 FOWLER, Samuel L, LARKIN, Olevia M C, of Rev Jacob, Octr 25 1859, 42
1671 ESWORTHY, Joseph W, HICKMAN, Mary E (Mrs), Rockville, Md, Decr 22 1859, 42
1672 EISENBRANDT, Henry W R, WILD, Jeannette C, Balto, Feby 2 1860, 42
1673 EROIN, Wm T, widower, HARBAUGH, Henrietta C (Mrs), "BURKITT"/widow, March 8 1860, 42
1674 FOX, James H, WRIGHT, Mary E, Mount Pleasant, March 22 1860, 42
1675 EICHNER, John, FISCHER, Elizabeth, April 18 1860, 43
1676 FIROR, Calvin L, ROUZER, Josephine, May 1 1860, 43
1677 FLORENCE, No first name given, NATHAN, Miss, of Benj NATHAN, May 22 1860, Phila & NY, 43
1678 ENGEL, Ezra, STULL, Rowanna, June 3 1860, 43
1679 EYLER, Joseph H, WILHIDE, Mary M, June 3 1860, 43
1680 FRIEND, Edward H, ALBERT, Charlotte E, of John L, June 21 1860, Wmsport, 43

1681 *ELKINS*, Henry M (Dr), *CRUMBAUGH*, Margret A, of Gideon, Augt 1 1860, Illinois & Iowa, 43

1682 *EICHELBERGER*, Samuel, *FOGEL*, Margaret R, Augt 11 1860, 43

1683 *FOUT*, Greenbury G, *JARBOE*, Fannie, Septr 20 1860, 43

1684 *FLOOK*, Jonas E, *SLIFER*, Mary C, of Peter/ "SCHLEIFER", Octr 25 1860, 43

1685 *ELGEN*, John, *GOSSNELL*, Ann Firoda, Nov 13 1860, 43

1686 *FOGEL*, Michael, *GARNER*, Caroline, Octr 16 1860, 43

1687 *EADER*, W H, of Lewis B, *KELLY*, Eliza, Memphis, Tenn, Decr 6 1860, Memphis, Tenn, 43

1688 *FOWLER*, David Q, widower, *SMITH*, Laura V (Mrs), widow, Jany 23 1861, HALLEY-GOMBER, 43

1689 *EULER*, Andrew Jackson, *ALBAUGH*, Sarah Susan, Feby 7 1861, 43

1690 *FRALEY*, John F, (FROLICH), *WOODWARD*, Catharine, of Alex'r, March 28 1861, 43

1691 *ELLIOTT*, Grafton W, *BECK*, Cath Ann (Mrs), widow of John J, April 14 1861, "FINCH", 43

1692 *FITCH*, Mortimer C, *BARRICK*, Susan M, April 17 1861, 43

1693 *ESTERLY*, Philip, *DADISMAN*, Sarah, of Ezra, April 25 1861, 43

1694 *FROSCHAUER*, John M, of Adam, *LEASE*, Ann Cath (Mrs), widow of Wm LEASE, Jun'r, June 2d 1861, 43

1695 *FAGAN*, Thomas, 2d wife, *RENN*, Miss, (* Catharine E), July 1861, 43

1696 *FISHER*, Warner, (Barney)/2d wife, *MARSH*, Mary A, of Joel, July 14 1861, 43

1697 *EASTER*, Hamilton, of Balto/2d wife, *HAVILAND*, Anna, of James C, July 23 1861, Brooklyn, NY, 43

1698 *EVANS*, Tho's B (Dr), *MYERS*, Maggie J, of John, Octr 16 1861, 43

1699 *EVANS*, French S (Rev), *MCJILTON*, Margaret C G, Octr 22 1861, Balto, 43

1700 *FRALEY*, Mahlon Augustus, (FROLICH), *YOUNG*, Adaline A, of Henry, Decr 2 1861, 43

1701 *EILER*, Jeremiah, *BETZEN*, Margaret C, Decr 17 1861, 43

1702 *FAVORITE*, Henry, *RENNER*, Elizabeth, Decr 18 1861, 43

1703 *FEITZ*, Geo V, *WARFIELD*, Fanny A, Jany 1 1862, 43

1704 *EICHELBERGER*, Martin J, *FAVOURTIE*, C, Jany 15 1862, 43

1705 *FROSCHAUER*, Geo C, *HAINES*, Hannah A, Feby 20 1862, 43

1706 *FLEMING*, John E, of Dr Tho's A/1st wife, *KELLER*, Ann Amelia, March 19 1862, 43

1707 *FOSSETT*, Francis C, *KEPHART*, Caroline, of Peter, July 17 1862, 43

1708 *FIRESTONE*, Martin Luther, of Joshua, *GALLE*, Catharine V, Augt 14 1862, 43

1709 *ESTERLY*, William, (OSTERLE), *NUNNEMACHER*, Mary, of Hagerstown, Octr 10 1862, 43

1710 *FIEGE*, Charles E, *NICKEL*, Martha S, of Jacob, Nov 18 1862, 43

1711 *EAGLE*, William, *TRAMMEL*, Ann E, March 10 1863, 43

1712 *EBUR*, E M (Lieut), (*Edwin), *FLEMING*, Alice E, of Dr Tho's A, Augt 20 1863, 43

1713 *EAGLE*, Lycurges, *WILLIAMS*, Sarah, of Montgomery Co, Septr 2 1863, 43

1714 *ENRIGHT*, P J, (*Patrick), *RYAN*, Mary A, of Dr John, August 13 1863, 43

1715 *FAGAN*, Charles, *FLEMING*, Fannie, of Dr Tho's A, Septr 24 1863, 43

1716 *FOX*, Orlando B, *BROOKS*, Mora B (Mrs), CUMINGS, Nov 18 1868, Washington, 43

1717 *FULTON*, Lee Calvin L, *SIFFORD*, Georgia, of John, Decr 23 1863, 43

1718 *FEASTER*, John H, *CULLER*, Joanna Virginia, of Peter, Decr 17 1863, 44

1719 *EICHELBERGER*, Singleton, *MARTELL*, Kate, of Jacob, Jany 3 1864, 44

1720 *FOX*, Ernst A C, 2d wife, *BABEL*, Margaret Caroline, of Christian, Feby 2d 1864, 44

1721 *ENGLAND*, John W, *HENDRY*, Mary E, of Cha's, Jany 26 1864, 44

1722 *ENGLAND*, James W, *ENGLAND*, Harriet L, March 1 1864, 44

1723 *FORD*, Wm Henry, *BELT*, Loretto, April 5 1864, 44

1724 FOUTZ, Geo W, (of US Army), SCHMIDT, Mary, of Jacob, June 16 1864, 44
1725 FALLON, John F, SCHILL, Mary E, of Geo, Septr 14 1864, 44
1726 FISHER, Lewis, of Barney/his 3d wife, HAMMACK, Emma L (Mrs), Decr 11 1864, Balto, 44
1727 ENGELBRECHT, Luther M, of Wm, RAUZAHN, Betty, of Adam, Jany 5 1865, 44
1728 EASTERDAY, Martin VanBuren, PALMER, Susan Ellen, March 9 1865, 44
1729 FISHER, Parks, SCHLEY, Antoinette, of John T, June 8 1865, Balto, 44
1730 FREY, Henry, of Ohio, EXNER, Mary (Mrs), widow of J Sebastian, April 5 1866, 44
1731 FOLLAND, John, DIMMICH, Clementine, of Mich'l, May 24 1866, 44
1732 EVERHART, Geo F, HAVER, Mary E, of Rev Danl J, June 5 1866, Pa, 44
1733 FLEMMING, W Norman, WEBSTER, Julia, of Jos, June 7 1866, Balto, 44
1734 EISENHAUER, John, WEHNER, Margaret, Octr 9 1866, 44
1735 EARDMAN, Frederick F, STUBBINS, Frances, Decr 26 1866, 44
1736 FROST, Eli, (of Wyondotte, Ohio), KOONTZ, Annie R, of Geo, Decr 31 1866, 44
1737 FIELDS, James, MAYBERRY, Laura E V, of Justiman, Jany 1 1867, Balto, 44
1738 FOUT, Geo Wm, (VOGHT)/of Henry, ADAM, Catharine C, of Wm, Jany 22 1867, 44
1739 EBERT, Valerius (Jun'r), YARBOROUGH, Hattie L, of N Carolina, Feby 5 1867, 44
1740 EYLER, Ephraim, WALTZ, Sarah C, June 25 1867, 44
1741 ELY, James, of Ezra, BRIGHTWELL, Martha, of Liberty, July 4 1867, 44
1742 FOX, Cha's B, of Adolphus, STORM, Clara, of P L Storm, Octr 2 1867, 44
1743 FULTON, C Henry, RAUZAHN, Harriott A (Mrs), (WEINBRENNER), Decr 10 1867, 44
1744 FOX, Henry C, POOLE, Sarah E, Mount Pleasant, Decr 17 1867, 44
1745 FISHER, Charles, RHODERICK, Elizabeth, "Both Mutes", Decr 19 1867, 44
1746 FLOOK, Jonas, SCHUMACHER, Ann, (SCHENER), Feby 19 1868, 44
1747 ELLIS, John D, CONRAD, Caroline W, June 4 1868, 44
1748 FOUT, Charles B, of Peter S, TABLER, Ida Kate, of Wm B, Nov 25 1868, 44
1749 FISHER, Wm H, DIXON, Mary E A, Decr 13 1868, 44
1750 FARROW, Wm H, of Washington City, CLINGAN, Annie E, of John F, Decr 15 1868, 44
1751 EASTERDAY, Geo E, HORINE, Sarah S, of Tobias, Jany 1869, 44
1752 FINLAYSON, L A, of Phila, HOUSTON, Mary A Trail (Mrs), widow of Sam T, Jany 23 1869, 44
1753 FOX, Singleton E, BRENGLE, M Lizzie, of Ezra M, Feby 11 1869, 44
1754 FLEMING, Robert, of Dr Tho's A/1st wife, YOUNG, Bettie, of Tilghman H, Feby 11 1869, 44
1755 FLOYD, J Walker, of South Carolina, PETTIT, Hattie F, Septr 30 1869, 44
1756 FOX, Thomas E, BENTLINGER, Catharine R, of Fred'k, Octr 18 1869, 44
1757 FOUT, Bradley T, of Peter S, DYER, Mary E (Mrs), "KAUFFMAN", Octr 28 1869, 44
1758 FLEISCHMAN, John H, of Carl, BECKER, Christiana, of Lewis, Nov 25 1869, 44
1759 FAUBEL, John, 2d wife, METZGER, Mattie, of Wm, May 10 1870, 45
1760 EADER, Peter Mantz, of Lewis B, BRUCHEY, Sidney A, May 26 1870, 45
1761 FOX, Ernst Augs, of Ernst A C, MARKEN, Hellen, of Josiah R, Septr 15 1870, 45
1762 EBBERTS, Geo Fred'k Erdman, of Wm, FISCHER, Anna M, Octr 11 1870, 45
1763 EVERS, Wm (Rev), of U Brethren, BUHRMAN, Florence, of Upton, Decr 27 1870, 45
1764 EBERT, Augustus H, of Benj'n, BAUMGARTNER, Elizabeth, Jan 19 1871, 45
1765 EASTERDAY, Joseph, "OSTERTAG"/2d wife, MAHONY, Mary J (Mrs), March 16 1871, 45
1766 EISENHAUER, Joseph F, WATERS, Lizzie, April 27 1871, 45
1767 EICHELBERGER, Wm H, BAER, Rachel Ann, Septr 10 1871, 45
1768 FRISBY, Edgar, EBERT, Laura V, of Wm, Augt 6 1872, DCa, 45

1769 FOUT, Lewis, LOWER, Sarah E, Octr 17 18872, 45
1770 ESTERLY, John P, of Geo ("OSTERLE"), PHOEBUS, Clara V, of John, Feb 23 1873, 45
1771 FEETE, Daniel (Rev), 2d wife, BRANT, Elizabeth (Mrs), March 20 1873, Norristown, Pa, 45
1772 EBRECHT, George F, of Jonathan, ESTERLY, Bettie E, July 17 1873, 45
1773 FLEMING, Richard, ACKERMAN, Lizzie, Septr 11 1873, 45
1774 EBERT, John Wm, of John M, STALEY, Emma E, of John A, Oct 19 1873, 45
1775 FOUT, Lewis F, CONRAD, Ettie, Octr 7 1873, in Balto, 45
1776 EMMART, Joseph, LYETH, Ida, of J McF, Nov 13 1873, Balto, 45
1777 FOUT, Otho F, LEWIS, S Candace, Decr 16 1873, Kemptown, 45
1778 FRIDAY, John M (Rev), WHIP, Ella S, Nov 26 1873, Jefferson, 45
1779 ESKSTEIN, Wm F, of Ch'n, HEISKELL, Mary E, Augt 25 1874, 45
1780 FITCH, Tho's W, U S Engineer, SHERMAN, Maria E, of Gen'l W J, Octr 1 1874, 45
1781 GARVER, Wm H, STEELE, Ann V, Octr 15 1874, 45
1782 GRANT, Fred'k D (Col), of U S, HONORE, Ida M, Octr 20 1874, 45
1783 FROMKE, Henry W, BABEL, Maggie E, Nov 19 1874, 45
1784 ECKSTEIN, Christian H, FEINAUR, Mary K, Mrs written above Miss, June 3 1875, 45
1785 EMERY, John H, TREGO, J, of John T, June 8 1875, NORRIS, 45
1786 ELKINS, Stephen B (Hon), DAVIS, Hallie, of Hon Henry G, April 14 1875, BANTZ, 45
1787 EBRECHT, James, DELAUTER, Sarah, July 27 1875, 45
1788 ELDRIDGE, Olen Emory (Rev), YOE, Mollie E, Octr 7 1875, Calvert, 45
1789 FEETE, Wm C, of Henry, FEESTER, Kate A, Nov 30 1875, Middlen, 45
1790 FOUT, Cyrus A, of P S, RAMSBURG, Mattie M, Decr 15 1875, 45
1791 FORD, A W (Dr), MILLER, Eveline M, of Wm S, June 27 1876, 45
1792 EBERT, Charles S, of Vals, BUSSARD, Lucinda, July 27 1876, 45
1793 FRANKLIN, Benjamin (Dr), of Carroll Co, SHUEY, Aggie, Sep 27 1876, 45
1794 EBERT, Edward C, of John of B, GANSAU, Fannie S, Decr 14 1876, 45
1795 ELDRIDGE, Wm C, of Clarke, SENTZELL, Bettie, Feb 15 1877, 45
1796 FEARHAKE, Adolphus (Jun'r), ELIOTT, Agnes, of Ja's, June 6 1877, 45
1797 FOX, Lewis M, of E A C, BAUMGARDNER, Ida A M, Sep 16 1877, 45
1798 FLEMING, Robert, of Dr Tho's A/2d wife, LILLY, Mattie, Sep 18 1877, 45
1799 FISHER, George J, MUSSETTER, Maggie R, Nov 27 1877, 45
1800 FLEMING, John E, 2d wife, KEHLER, Sallie H, July 3rd 1879, 45
1801 ETCHISON, Marshal C L, MULLINIX, Sybelle M, Oct 7th 1879, 45
1802 EVANS, Richard K, BROWN, Fannie V, Nov 20th 1879, 46
1803 EBBERTS, Thomas H O, of Wm, THOMAS, Emma K, April 6th 1880, 46
1804 EADER, Charles M, of August, MANTZ, Ida, (not listed as Miss), April 7th 1880, 46
1805 EADER, Edward J M, HEARD, Fannie M, (not listed as Miss), May 26th 1880, 46
1806 EADER, Charles E, of Cha's, QUINN, Mary M, of John/(not listed as Miss), Aug 12th 1880, 46
1807 FILBY, Samuel L, BARIER, Saddie E, (not listed as Miss), Oct 13th 1881, 46
1808 EMRY, Wm H, of York, Pa, KEEFER, Katie, of Hiram, June 22d 1881, 46
1809 FLEIGHNER, Charles, of Conn, LOWENSTEIN, Clara M, July 20th 1881, Jews, 46
1810 FAGAN, Allen C, of Thomas, ESTERLY, Clara, (not listed as Miss), October 7th 1881, 46
1811 FOX, John F A, DATZBAUGH, Fannie S, (@ DETZBAUGH), November 15th 1881, 46
1812 FISHER, Moses, ROELKEY, Mary E, February 21 1882, 46
1813 FORMAN, O T/S, CLINGAN, Amanda S H, Oct 24t 1882, 46
1814 FOX, George F V, HERGESHEIMER, Florence R, Nov 21st 1882, 46

The Joseph Engelbrecht Marriage Ledger of Frederick Co., MD 1820-1890 *Marriage List*

1815 EBERT, William H, of John, ZIMMERMAN, Fannie V, Dec 28 1882, 46
1816 FEIGLEY, Daniel F, KOONTZ, Adele, of Ed, Feb 13 1883, 46
1817 FAUST, Wm A J, BRENGLE, Fannie M, of Sam, April 18th 1883, 46
1818 FRAZIER, Ernst D, of David, DUVALL, Annette P, April 16th 1883, 46
1819 EICHELBERGER, Francis M, COUTCHLEY, Lillie M, May 10th 1883, 46
1820 FOUT, Marshal, WOLF, Florence J, of Geo, March 12 1884, 46
1821 EADER, Thomas S, EBERT, Katie R, of John, April 23 1884, 46
1822 ENSHAW, Georg, (@ EARNSHAW), MERCER, Rebecca H, (@ MERCIER), June 12 1884, (REICH), 46
1823 FREED, J D (Rev), HOOPWOOD, Emma J, of Ja's, Sept 2 1884, 46
1824 FIRESTONE, Oscar F, STEINER, Fannie E, 1884, 46
1825 ESTERLY, George, TITLOW, Hester, of Cha's, January 7 1885, 46
1826 ENGLAR, Samuel L, NELSON, Sallie S, May 15 1885, (Adams, 46
1827 FREY, Robert, HALLER, Florence, October 1, 1885, 46
1828 FEAGA, Elmer B, STALEY, Orthena B, (@ Orsena), December 3 1885, 46
1829 ELKINS, Edward J, HARTMAN, Annie O H, February 17 1886, 46
1830 FREEZE, Wm O, NELSON, Fannie C, March 18 1886, U B Church, 46
1831 FOUT, George H, 2d wife, ESWORTHY, Harriet, December 19 1886, 46
1832 EISSLER, Daniel G, BATSON, Ella C, (@ Ellen R), January 6 1887, Glove maker, 46
1833 FIROUR, B U, CHANY, Geneva, April 7 1887, (ECKSTEIN), 46
1834 FOUT, Clayton O, HOFFMAN, Mary, May 12 1887, 46
1835 FISHER, Cha's, DERR, Mary Irene, of Luther, October 25 1887, 46
1836 ENGELBRECHT, George, YOUNG, Susie, November 23 1887, 46
1837 ENGLISH, George N, RAMSBURG, Fannie, March 1 1888, 46
1838 FLEMING, Wm, BAKER, Lucretia, June 18 1888, 46
1839 EMMRUN, Joseph -- (Dr), GREENTREE, Nettie H, of Howard, June 20 1888, 46
1840 ENGELBRECHT, John, of Geo, DEBRING, Gertrude, (@ Ida Gertrude), Oct 11 1888, 46
1841 ETCHISON, Henry N, 3d wife, SMITH, Hester E (Mrs), January 30 1889, 46
1842 FISCHER, Frederick, B____ING, Mary C, {surname blurred and overwritten}, February 20 1889, 46
1843 FAUBLE, John, THOMPSON, Mary W, February 26 1889, 46
1844 FUNK, Wm H, MAY, Lullu E, May 17 1889, 46
1845 FRALEY, Lewis, BURCK, Christiana V, August 4 1889, 46
1846 ENGELBRECHT, Lewis W, STOUFFER, Helen J, Oct 1 1889, 46a
1847 ETCHISON, Frank B, GRIFFITH, Florence C, Oct 15 1889, 46a
1848 EYLER, Tho's W, ESTERLY, Mollie, October 30 1889, 46a
1849 FORD, Cha's W, ANDERSON, Minnie J, November 26 1889, 46a
1850 ECKER, Albert W, DOUGHERTY, Jennie I, November 28 1889, 46a
1851 EYLER, Ephraim, 2d wife, WILES, Mattie W, February 20 1890, 46a
1852 ENGELBRECHT, A Lincoln, AKERS, Nettie V, (@ Jinette V), March 20 1890, ACRES written above AKERS, 46a
1853 FORNEY, Samuel J, RHOADES, Ada E, (@ RHODES), March 27 1890, 46a
1854 EICHELBERGER, Abraham J, GETTINGER, Minnie, of Ed, July 30 1890, 46a
1855 ELLIOTT, James H, COMPHER, Candace V, Dec 31st 1890, 46a
1856 GAITHER, Stuart, SCHELL, of Cha's, Jany 6 1821, 48
1857 GETZENDANNER, Jonathan, of John, DERR, Elizabeth, of John, April 12 1821, 48
1858 GARDNER, Geo, of Henry, GETZENDANNER, Hannah, May 21 1822, 48

1859 GETZENDANNER, Solomon, of Ch'n, *SPALDING*, Susan, June 30 1822, 48
1860 GRAHAME, Tho's J, of Maj John, *JOHNSON*, Caroline, of old Col Baker, Septr 10 1822, 48
1861 GETZENDANNER, Henry, *KEMP*, Catharine, of Fred'k, April 8 1823, 48
1862 GETZENDANNER, Mich'l Jefferson, *BEARD*, Sarah, Augt 7 1823, 48
1863 GETZENDANNER, Daniel, of John, *DERR*, Mary, of John, Decr 21 1823, 48
1864 GEWEYER, George, of Leonard, *HECKMAN*, Sophia, Decr 21 1823, 48
1865 GETZENDANNER, Geo, of Ch'n, *SALMON*, Elizabeth, April 1 1824, 48
1866 GETZENDANNER, Charles, of Ch'n, *GENTZEN*, Susan, (GENSLY), April 10 1825, 48
1867 GETZENDANNER, Henry (Jun'r), *LOWRY*, Miss, March 1825, 48
1868 GLENN, Lewis W, *DUER*, Mary Ann, May 5 1825, Phila, 48
1869 GUYTON, Albert Gallatin, of Ab'm, *GORDON*, Elizabeth, of Wm, June 7 1825, 48
1870 GIBBONS, John, of Jacob, *STILLY*, Lydia (Mrs), widow of John, July 21 1825, 48
1871 GEETIG, John, 1st wife, *KENEGE*, Elizabeth, of Joseph, Nov 17 1825, 48
1872 GARDNER, Frederick, *GROSS*, Catharine, Septr 17 1826, 48
1873 GALLAGHER, Tho's, *HERD*, Elizabeth, Rev Dan'l J HAUER's 1st wedding, Septr 28 1826, 48
1874 GOLDSBOROUGH, Edward Y (Dr), *SCHLEY*, Margaret, of John, Nov 21 1826, 48
1875 GITTINGER, George, 1st wife, *SCHOLL*, Charlotte, of Ch'n, Feby 8 1827, 48
1876 GATRELL, James L, *NICHOLS*, Mary A, Feby 1827, 48
1877 GREEN, Tho's W (Rev), *BURGESS*, Sarah D, Feby 25 1827, 48
1878 GANTT, Edward Anderson, *ANDERSON*, Kitty Ann, Octr 2 1827, 48
1879 GRAHAME, James, *JOHNSON*, Margaret R, Jany 15 1828, 48
1880 GROVE, Leonard S, *FOUT*, Rebecca, of Baltzer, Jany 29 1829, 48
1881 GRIFFITH, Wm T, *MATLOCK*, Elizabeth, March 31 1829, Washington City, 48
1882 GAMBRILL, Cha's A, 1st wife, *SCHRIVER*, Ann M, of Ab'm, April 14 1829, 48
1883 GEBHART, John (Sen'r), 3d wife, *RITTER*, Catharine (Mrs), July 23 1829, 48
1884 GILBERT, David, *KOONTZ*, Margaret, Jany 17 1830, 48
1885 GOLDBOROUGH, Leander W (Dr), *DUNCAN*, Sarah, April 1830, 48
1886 GREENWALD, Christian, 2d wife, *MATTERN*, Catharine, Nov 28 1830, 48
1887 GERE, John A (Rev), (Methodist), *NEAL*, Sarah, Feby 22 1831, Balto, 48
1888 GETZENDANNER, Alexander, of Col Jacob/2d wife, *HILL*, Maria, Feby 24 1831, 48
1889 GETZENDANNER, Josiah, *HULL*, Harriott, Octr 4 1831, 48
1890 GREUZARD, Louis, *LAMBRECHT*, Catharine, of Geo, Jany 30 1832, 48
1891 GARDNER, Jacob, (RIEHL), *KING*, Catharine, April 29 1832, 48
1892 GOMBER, Ezra M, *FISCHER*, Margaret, of Adam, July 5 1832, 48
1893 GETZENDANNER, Abraham, of John, *BUCKEY*, Mary E, of Peter, May 7 1833, 48
1894 GORSUCH, A P, (* Abraham), *ARNOLD*, Sophia, (FLOWERS), July 21 1833, 48
1895 GOODMANSON, Peter, 1st wife, *EBBERTS*, Wilhelmina, of Mich'l, Nov 28 1833, 48
1896 GIST, Newton H, *BACON*, Amelia A, Jany 9 1834, Balto, 48
1897 GETZENDANNER, Cha's, of Ch'n/2d wife, *JONES*, Ann M, March 9 1834, 48
1898 GONTER, John, *NUSZ*, Catharine, of Henry, Augt 21 1834, 49
1899 GREENWALD, Emanuel (Rev), *WILLIAMS*, Livinia, Decr 17 1834, Ohio, 49
1900 GREENHOLTZ, Jacob, *MULHORN*, Barbara (Mrs), "FROSCHAUR", May 31 1835, 49
1901 GILBERT, Daniel, of Gettysburg, *RICE*, Amy, Septr 24 1835, 49
1902 GAMBRILL, Cha's A, 2d wife, *EICHELBERGER*, Nancy, of Col Geo M, Jany 26 1836, 49
1903 GRIM, Edward O, of Balto, *O'NEILL*, Amanda A, May 16 1836, 49
1904 GRINDER, Jacob, *HAY*, Ann, June 2 1836, Glade, 49

1905 GOSZ, Lorentz, LEILICH, Anna Magdelena, Septr 30 1836, 49
1906 GARDNER, Oliver P, of York, Pa, BUCKEY, Elizabeth M, of Mich'l, Nov 21 1838, {prefaced "this is right"}, 49
1907 GOLDSBOROUGH, Cha's W (Dr), POE, Amelia, Nov 24 1836, 49
1908 GRIFFITH, Lebbeus, WOOD, Sarah Ann, March 12 1839, 49
1909 GILBERT, John W, HOOD, Rachel, March 28 1839, 49
1910 GAINES, Edmund P (Gen'l), 2d wife, CLARK, Mary C W, N Orleans, April 17 1839, 49
1911 GRIMES, Gassaway S (Dr), DORSEY, Susan H, Carroll Co, June 27 1839, Carroll Co, 49
1912 GROSHON, Abraham E, EICHELBERGER, Ann Maria, July 11 1839, 49
1913 GITTINGER, J William, BRENGLE, Ann R, of Peter, Augt 7 1839, 49
1914 GIBBS, George W, BUZZARD, Lydia, Octr 17 1839, 49
1915 GOODMASON, Peter, 2d wife, HALLAR, Mary, of Joseph, March 27 1840, 49
1916 GROVER, George M, CRABSTER, Elmira J, April 19 1840, 49
1917 GETZENDANNER, Christian, NICHOLS, Mary, of Peter, May 5 1840, 49
1918 GRIFFITH, Emanuel R, HOOPER, Mary (Mrs), widow of Ab'm (OTT), Septr 3 1840, 49
1919 GRIMES, Albert, EDMONSON, Ellen, Septr 3 1840, 49
1920 GORSUCH, Robert, ANGELL, Sophronia, Nov 23 or 16 1840, 49
1921 GRIER, Robert (Rev), ANNAN, Jane, July 26 1841, Emmittsburg, 49
1922 GARRETSON, Nimrod, BENTZ, Harriott, of Geo, Octr 15 1841, 49
1923 GILBERT, Solomon, SLIFER, Sarah, of Wm, Nov 18 1841, 49
1924 GUNN, Walter (Rev), PULTZ, Lorenia, Augt 30 1843, Luth Mission, 49
1925 GRIM, Tho's C, CRAMER, Catharine, Nov 14 1844, 49
1926 GETZENDANNER, John D, of Jonathan, PATTINGALL, Charlotte E, of Sam'l, April 10 1845, 49
1927 GRAHE, Theodore, STARRE, Louisa, March 19 1846, 49
1928 GEWEYER, William, of Geo, WARTHEN, Balinda, April 23 1846, 49
1929 GRAEF, Gustav, ERDMAN, Barbara, June 1 1846, 49
1930 GWYNN, Robert, HOUSTON, Lizzie, of James F, Septr 22 1846, 49
1931 GEESEY, John T, STULL, Amelia M, Octr 1 1846, 49
1932 GIBSON, J Gregg (Dr), WATERS, Susan, of Dr Wm, May 18 1847, 49
1933 GEPHART, Simon Cronise, of John, BEALL, Eliza, Augt 29 1847, Cumberland, 49
1934 GANZAN, George, GILDZ, Mary Ann C, Septr 9 1847, 49
1935 GAULT, Adam, EBBERTS, Catharine E, of Jos, Septr 30 1847, 49
1936 GALLE', Henry, MARTZ, Catharine S, Octr 28 1847, 49
1937 GEPHART, John (Jun'r), of Balto, STARR, Ann L, Decr 23 1847, 49
1938 GILPIN, Charles, ARMOUR, Julia A, of Ja's U, March 1 1848, 49
1939 GETZENDANNER, Edward T, of Dan'l, SHAFER, Catharine E, of Jacob, Augt 15 1848, 49
1940 GETZENDANNER, Christian, of Cha's, SENTZELL, Margaret, Nov 12 1848, 50
1941 GREEN, John T, 1st wife, LECHLEITER, Harriet T, Jany 2 1849, 50
1942 GAITHER, Lott, COYLE, Margaret, Jany 29 1849, 50
1943 GRIMES, Frances M, SCHEIDEL, Adaline M, (KEEFER), April 25 1849, 50
1944 GEPHART, Solomon A, RICE, Louisa Virginia, of Geo, Octr 30 1849, 50
1945 GITTINGER, Zachariah James, MANTZ, Mary, of Gideon, Nov 29 1849, 50
1946 GRUND, Michael, STAUCH, Catharina, Augt 11 1850, 50
1947 GITTINGER, J Howard, of John, JARBOE, Harriett E, Nov 10 1850, 50
1948 GOLDSCHMIDT, Otto, LIND, Jenny, Feby 5 1852, in Boston, 50
1949 GOUVERNEUR, Samuel L, 2d wife, LEE, Mary Digges, of Wm LEE, Nov 1851, 50

1950 *GLISAN*, Samuel, *HARDING*, Margaret Ann, Feby 24 1852, 50
1951 *GROVE*, Mannassah, *JARBOE*, Martha, March 22 1852, 50
1952 *GETZENDANNER*, Jacob A J, *RAMSBURG*, Amanda Ellen, May 11 1852, 50
1953 *GITTINGER*, George, 2d wife, *YOUNG*, Catharine, Septr 14 1852, 50
1954 *GOSNER*, John, *VANFOSSEN*, Mary E, Decr 7 1852, 50
1955 *GROSSNICKEL*, Peter, *BITTEL*, Elizabeth, M Valley, Decr 23 1852, 50
1956 *GASEY*, Theodore, *WICKHAM*, Martha J, Nov 11 1852, 50
1957 *GANNON*, James M, *BROWN*, Mary C, Decr 13 1853, 50
1958 *GAUGH*, Daniel, *CRONISE*, Lydia A, of Fred'k, Decr 7 1853, 50
1959 *GLESSNER*, Geo W, of Wm, *WEINBRENNER*, Mary Ellen, Decr 19 1853, 50
1960 *GETZENDANNER*, Jacob R, of Jonathan, *FLEMING*, Anna V H, of Jos P, March 14 18854, 50
1961 *GIVINS*, Charles, *WATERS*, Mary Jane, April 20 1854, 50
1962 *GLONINGER*, Frederick, *WISSEL*, Veronica, Balto, May 9 1854, 50
1963 *GREENTREE*, Howard, of Ezra, *GETTINGER*, Harriott R, of John, May 17 1854, 50
1964 *GILBERT*, George, *BROOKS*, Elizab, (sister of David W), Octr 19 1854, 50
1965 *GUIRY*, Wm G, *WALKER*, Mary, Nov 2d 1854, 50
1966 *GETZENDANNER*, Daniel (Jun'r), *WEINBRENNER*, Margaret E, of Ch'n, Decr 12 1854, 50
1967 *GERNAND*, Joseph, *CROUSE*, Harriott S, Jany 25 1855, 50
1968 *GROVE*, David, of Reuben, *BOBST*, Henrietta, May 23 1855, 50
1969 *GLESSNER*, Wm T, of Capt'n Wm, *DADISMAN*, Mary Jane, of Ezra, Septr 19 1855, 50
1970 *GIBSON*, Alexander E (Rev), *MARKEY*, Mary Ellen, of David J, Jany 17 1856, 50
1971 *GEYER*, John Wesley (Dr), of Sam'l, *STERETT*, Ellie R (Mrs), (DRINKHOUSE), June 12 1856, 50
1972 *GELTZ*, John E, *KEYSER*, Ann E, Decr 24 1856, 50
1973 *GROVER*, Leonard B, *SINN*, Laura, of Wm, July 22 1857, Balto, 50
1974 *GRAHAME*, Tho's J (Dr), 1st wife, *BEALL*, Harriott M, Nov 12 1857, Allegany Co, 50
1975 *GIGUS*, Henry, *THOMAS*, Amanda A, Nov 12 1857, 50
1976 *GAITHER*, George, *POOLE*, Kate, Decr 16 1857, 50
1977 *GREEN*, George W, *WELLER*, Catharine E, Nov 19 1857, 50
1978 *GEISELMAN*, Michael, *HANES*, Emeline H, Steubenville, Ohio, Decr 3 1857, 50
1979 *GEAR*, Josiah, of Ohio, *THOMAS*, Martha, of Henry, Feby 9 1858, 50
1980 *GRAY*, Peter, *BRENDEL*, Ann Amelia, of Henry G, April 20 1858, 50
1981 *GLAZE*, Joseph, *CRAMER*, Margaret, of Amos, May 11 1858, 50
1982 *GARNER*, Daniel (Rev), *MILLER*, Emma Virg'a, Bedford, Pa, May 1858, 51
1983 *GENNETZ*, John, *BOYER*, Margaret, Catoctin Furnace, June 4 1858, 51
1984 *GELWICKS*, Cha's A (Rev), *WILSON*, Mary Isabel, Ohio, June 24 1858, 51
1985 *GRIER*, Robert S (Rev), 2d wife, *STEWART*, Margaret (Mrs), Emmittsburg, July 20 1858, 51
1986 *GEARY*, John W (Hon), 2d wife, *HENDERSON*, Mary (Mrs), Nov 2 1858, 51
1987 *GOBRICHER*, Sussman (Rev), *MENDEL*, Regina, First Jew wedding here, Octr 24 1858, 51
1988 *GRABILL*, J M, (Rev), (Luthern), *PRATHER*, Ann, Wash'g Co, Nov 2 1858, 51
1989 *GETZMACHER*, Wm Tho's J, *SLIFER*, Lydia A, Boonsboro, Nov 20 1858, 51
1990 *GORE*, Jonathan, *BLUEJACKET*, Sallie, of Cha's/Kansas, Nov 10 1858, 51
1991 *GILBERT*, John A, *MCGUIGEN*, Sarah J, Graceham, Decr 30 1858, 51
1992 *GRIMES*, Levi F, *WELKER*, Julian, March 10 1859, 51
1993 *GORMLEY*, Thomas, (Tin-Smith)/2d wife, *HARGROVE*, Maggie R, Balto, July 18 1859, 51
1994 *GOLDENBERG*, Henry, *NORDHAUS*, Eva, (VON NECHEIM), Septr 11 1859, 51

1995 GETZENDANNER, Tho's E, of Jonathan/1st wife, WILCOXON, Anna M, of John, Octr 4 1859, 51
1996 GANZAN, Henry, KOLB, Charlotte A, Nov 20 1859, 51
1997 GIESEY, S H (Rev), 2d wife, SPEAR, Sarah Lydia, of Otis, Nov 29 1859, Balto, 51
1998 GALLOWAY, Nelson, GARTER, Clementine V, Decr 23 1859, 51
1999 GITTINGER, Edward Allen, ACKERMAN, Serena Elizabeth, Jany 19 1860, 51
2000 GRAY, John F, CLAGGETT, Laura E, Jany 31 1860, 51
2001 GETZ, Charles B, STEIGERWALD, Rose, (of Meyer), Feby 20 1860, Balto, 51
2002 GEISBERT, Christian, HEFFNER, Catharine A, March 8 1860, Glade, 51
2003 GEISINGER, John J, of Sam'l L, WALTER, Carrie, (of State of NY), June 24 1860, 51
2004 GAMBRILL, James H, STALEY, Antoinette, of Cornelius, July 26 1860, 51
2005 GETZENDANNER, John J, of Col Jacob, KELLER, Kate A, of Theophilus, Septr 25 1860, 51
2006 GREEN, Wm E, WELLER, Amanda C, Nov 29 1860, 51
2007 GROVE, Daniel R, HUFFER, Julia, of Jos L, March 12 1861, Middletown, 51
2008 GUE, William H, GOLDEN, Margaret J, June 8 1861, N Market, 51
2009 GROVE, Elias, of Reuben, KUHNE, Rebecca, (KING), Septr 22 1861, 51
2010 GOLDSBOROUGH, Cha's E, KEMP, Emily B D, Octr 1 1861, Balto, 51
2011 GARLETZSKI, Louis, TYSSOWSKI, Pelagia, Octr 15 1861, Washington City, 51
2012 GROVE, Hiram J, STRAEFFER, Annie M, of John, Decr 12 1861, 51
2013 GOLDENBERG, Daniel, 2d wife, SCHILDESHEIM, Amelia, Decr 8 1861, Balto, 51
2014 GLAZE, Zachariah, ENOLE, Annie R, Jany 7 1862, 51
2015 GALLIAN, John P, 2d wife, ERVIN, Hariett (Mrs), Feby 13 1862, 51
2016 GROFF, Eli G, his 3d wife, LINDSAY, Sarah A (Mrs), her 2d husband/(LUGENBEEL), April 8 1862, 51
2017 GROVE, Jeremiah C, of Jacob, WHITTER, Fanny, of Tho's, Augt 13th 1862, 51
2018 GAYBRECHT, Wm, (GEBRECHT), WENRICK, Rebecca, Octr 14 1862, Manor, 51
2019 GREEN, John T, 2d wife, WEDDELL, Henrietta, Nov 2 1862, 51
2020 GAMBRILL, Horace D, SCHLEY, Ellie E, of Edward, Nov 25 1862, 51
2021 GROVE, Reuben E, MUSSER, Catharine E, Decr 24 1862, 51
2022 GEISENHAINER, Augustus T (Rev), SCHMUCKER, Elleanora S, of S S, Feby 10 1863, 51
2023 GIBSON, Horatio Gates, USA, ATKINSON, Harriott L, March 16 1863, St Louis, 51
2024 GREEN, Hanson T C, CRIST, Annie O, of Joseph, Septr 10 1863, 52
2025 GOLDSBOROUGH, John (Dr), STRIDER, Nannie, of Ja's W, Decr 8 1863, 52
2026 GARROTT, W M, BOTELER, M W, Nov 19 1863, 52
2027 GETZENDANNER, Solomon J, YATES, Georgetta M F, Decr 8 1863, 52
2028 GITTINGER, Lewis C, of Geo, MYERS, Evelina Virginia, of John, Decr 10 1863, 52
2029 GETZENDANNER, Geo W, PROTZMAN, Kate B, March 3 1864, Dayton, Ohio, 52
2030 GOODFELLOW, Charles, HAGER, Lena, April 10 1864, 52
2031 GREENWOOD, Geo E, NEIHOFF, Annie L E, of Christian, July 5 1864, 52
2032 GARDNER, James F, CRUM, Jennie, of Wm, Nov 10 1864, 52
2033 GRIFFING, George H, MYERS, Cleopatra, of Tho's J, Decr 13 1864, 52
2034 GROSSNICKEL, Emanuel, BIECHLEY, Mary, of Conrad, Jany 3 1865, 52
2035 GOLDSBOROUGH, Cha's W (Jun'r Dr), LEE, Henrietta Edmonia, of Va, Nov 7 1865, 62
2036 GALLION, Geo F, of John P, BUSHEY, Ann M, of Jacob M(not listed as Miss), Jany 3 1866, 52
2037 GRAHAME, Tho's J (Dr), of James/ 2d wife, DUKE, Annie M E, of Green H, Feby 1 1866, 52

2038 GIBBONS, David, HARRISON, Sarah Ann (Mrs), March 22 1866, 52
2039 GEDULTIG, Cha's H, WAHRENFELSZ, Sarah A, March 29 1866, 52
2040 GLEIS, George Leonard, 2d wife, CRAWFORD, Malinda (Mrs), June 12 1866, 52
2041 GRACY, John, (Teacher), HAMMOND, Carrie B, Decr 13 1866, 52
2042 GIBSON, Joshua Gregg (Dr), 2d wife, GROVE, Alice B, of Jacob, March 14 1867, 52
2043 GRUMBEIN, Calvin J, of Dan'l, BURUCKER, Mary E, of John S, April 2 1867, 52
2044 GETZENDANNER, John W, (of John D)/1st wife, FOUT, Isadore V, of Grafton, Septr 19 1867, 52
2045 GROSHON, George M, of Geo S/1st wife, KEEFER, Jennie C, of Mich'l, Octr 8 1867, 52
2046 GITTINGER, Tho's C, of Wm, ALBAUGH, Laura V, of Ephraim, Nov 12 1867, 52
2047 GETZENDANNER, M Eugene, of Dan'l, SMITH, Clara V, of Geo, Decr 12 1867, 52
2048 GERLACH, Henry, YINGER, Annie E, of Nicholas, Jany 29 1868, 52
2049 GATCHELL, Hugh McElderry, TYLER, Mary A, of Dr Sam'l, Jany 30 1868, 52
2050 GONDER, Thomas E, HARDING, Alice R, of Norman B, Feby 4 1868, 52
2051 GOMBER, John, of Eza M, HARRISON, Mary E, of Josiah, Feby 6 1868, 52
2052 GROVE, William P, FOUT, Julia M, of Peter S, May 5 1868, 52
2053 GEYER, W F, CUSTARD, Annie Virginia, of Adam, Octr 1 1868, 52
2054 GEISELMAN, Wm H, STITELY, Laura V, Gr dau of Rev J's PFOUTZ, Jany 7 1869, 52
2055 GALBRAITH, Sam'l H, COLLIFLOWER, Laura C, of Rev Wm F, Jany 28 1869, 52
2056 GILBERT, Wm H, ALBAUGH, Annie A, of Val A, Feby 11 1869, 52
2057 GIST, G N, DYER, Sallie C, May 12 1869, 52
2058 GROVE, Emanuel M, WARNER, Hanna M, June 22 1869, 52
2059 GREER, J Allen, POPE, Jennie E, of John H, Nov 10 1869, Balto, 52
2060 GETZENDANNER, Christian, of Christian/2d wife, BOSLEY, Emma, of Balto, Decr 22 1869, 52
2061 GUNDLOCK, August, COCHRAN, Mary, June 7 1870, 52
2062 GRIMES, Napoleon B, WALKER, Mary F, (not listed as Miss), June 15 1870, 52
2063 GARROTT, Joseph B, LOUTHAN, Henrianna, of Va, June 6 1871, 52
2064 GANNON, Wm E, 1st wife, HOOPER, Emma V, of Tho's, Septr 12 1871, 52
2065 GETZENDANNER, Tho's E, of Jonathan/2d wife, CARLIN, Mary E, of Joseph, Feby 4 1872, 52
2066 GROVE, Greenberry F, of Leon'd S, MAHONEY, Margaret, May 21 1872, 53
2067 GEIGER, John W, BRUNNER, Mary L, of Rev Lewis A, Septr 26 1872, Wyandot, Ohio, 53
2068 GETZENDANNER, Edward T, of Daniel/2d wife, YOUNG, Verlinda C, Octr 29 1872, 53
2069 GETZENDANNER, Samuel P, of John D, ZIMMERMAN, Annie M, of Sam'l, Nov 21 1872, 53
2070 GROSHON, George M, of Geo S/2d wife, FILBY, Mary, Nov 18 1872, 53
2071 GITTINGER, John E, of Geo, DEAN, Annie M C, Feb 27 1873, 53
2072 GETZENDANNER, F Marion, YOUNG, Sarah E, March 18 1873, 53
2073 GOODSELL, Wm Henry, NUSZ, Julia Ann, May 29 1873, Fairview, 53
2074 GLADHILL, John T (Rev), WHITE, Mannie M, June 5 1873, 53
2075 GRAHE, John H C, of Julius, SHIVERS, Fannie M, Augt 20 1873, 53
2076 GETZENDANNER, John W (Dr), GETZENDANNER, Martha V, Octr 7 1873, 53
2077 GROVE, Leonard S, YASTE, Cornelia F, Octr 30 1873, Jefferson, 53
2078 GEISINGER, John W, FOX, Maria J, Nov 4 1873, 53
2079 GILBERT, F Marshal, HAMMOND, Emma, of Dr T, Jan 13 1874, 53
2080 GUNDLOCK, Conrad, 2d wife, SCHADE', Wilhelmina (Mrs), March 1 1874, 53

2081 GROSS, Wm H, HARTSOCK, Annie, April 5 1874, 53
2082 GOLDSBOROUGH, Edw Y, AULD, Amy Y, of Ohio, June 10 1874, 53
2083 GARVER, Wm H, STEELE, Ann V, Octr 15 1874, 53
2084 GRANT, Fred'k D (Col), of Ulysses S, HONORE, Ida M, Octr 20 1874, 53
2085 GERDEMANN, J W (Rev), R C Priest, WITTRICK, Margret, Nov 14 1874, 53
2086 GILBERT, James, KOLB, Alice Virginia, of Wm, Nov 17 1874, 53
2087 GILBERT, James L, KAUFFMAN, Emma J, of Wm, Decr 23 1874, Balto, 53
2088 GERLACH, Jacob, BURCK, Anna Mary, Octr 21 1875, 53
2089 GERHART, E V (DD), COBB, Lucie D, Decr 29 1875, 53
2090 GRAHE, Fred'k H, of Julius, FISHER, Ida L, Feb 3 1876, 53
2091 GEISINGER, Tho's E, MORGAN, Sarah, Septr 5 1876, 53
2092 GILBERT, George A, of David/2d wife, HOCKENSMITH, Jennie, April 3 1877, 53
2093 GORMLEY, Matthew, 2d wife, DURNEY, Mary T, (not listed as Miss), Aug 6 1877, 53
2094 GILBERT, H Clay, MCLAIN, Adelade, of Wm, Sep 27 1877, 53
2095 GENZENBACH, Cha's H, SUMAN, Terasa A R, of Rev J J, Nov 8 1877, 53
2096 GANNON, Wm E, 2d wife, BUCKLES, Alice A, Nov 8 1877, 53
2097 GOSNELL, L Ward, DIXON, Ida N, Decr 25 1877, 53
2098 GROVE, Geo W, RIGGS, Jemima B, Jan 30 1878, Ijamsville, 53
2099 GRUMBINE, John A, PAYNE, Ida G, Nov 5th 1878, 53
2100 GLADHILL, J Levi, BEALL, Amelia A, Feb 26th 1880, 53
2101 GARROTT, Edward, HILLEARY, Bertha, of Wm H, Sept 26th 1882, (@ HILLEARY, Laura Clagett), 53
2102 GERSER, George M, MEALEY, Cora A, Nov 30th 1882, 53
2103 GRIFFIN, William H, THOMAS, Jane E, March 9th 1883, 53
2104 GILBERT, Charles M, GLASNER, Annie R, (not listed as Miss), May 24th 1883, 53
2105 GOSSNEL, Stewart F, (@ GOSNELL), HAUGH, Laura C V, July 19th 1883, 53
2106 GITTINGER, Geo M, of Z Ja's, SIMMONS, Emily A, (@ Emlia), June 26 1884, 53
2107 GRUMBINE, Issac M, FOX, Eliza A, Oct 1 1884, 53
2108 GROH, Joseph A, STULL, Nettie V, March 15 1885, 53
2109 GRAHE, Julius A, RICKERDS, Ellen F, (@ Ella F RICKARDS), June 17 1885, 54
2110 GREBRICKKER, Meyer, (@ GOEBRICKER), HOLT, Sophia, January 12 1886, 54
2111 GITTINGER, Myrile, SIMMONS, Susie F, March 16 1886, 54
2112 GREAGER, George, (@ Gottleb YAEGER), MUNDTS, Mary, 2d husband/(@ MUNZ), April 11 1887, HAUSER, 54
2113 GROFF, David, of Middletown, SHAFER, Katie, (@Sarah C), May 10 1887, 54
2114 GROVE, Edward P, SHRIVER, Sallie E, May 31 1887, in York, Pa, 54
2115 GRAYSIN, Lafayette, SINN, Mary K, June 1 1887, 54
2116 GITTINGER, Henry M, SIMMONS, Ludie, November 17 1887, 54
2117 GARDNER, John A P, RAMSBURG, Mollie E, December 21 887, 54
2118 GEISBERT, Wm H, MERCER, Irene, January 9 1888, 54
2119 GROVE, John R, DELASHMUTT, Virginia R, of Andrew J, January 18 1888, 54
2120 GREEN, John Henry Francis, KELLER, Jennie C V, February 15 1888, 54
2121 GARROTT, Willard N, RICE, Ella J, February 21 1888, 54
2122 GROSS, John, KEPLINGER, Annie, April 12 1888, 54
2123 GULL, Ignatius, SCULLY, Brida, April 30 1888, (MCNUNALEY), 54
2124 GRUMBINE, Grayson?, {in obituary-David George d 1949}, ADLESBERGER, George A E, {listed as Georgianna in obituary}, June 9 1888, illegible {HOLDCRAFT file}, 54

2125 **GILDEA**, John H, **YEAKLE**, Mary Adelia, June 24 1888, [BENNETT, 54
2126 **GREEN**, Wm, **DERTZBAUGH**, Katie, August 13 1888, 54
2127 **GEISBERT**, Stephen, (@ Samuel C), **FRAZIER**, Nannie, of D'd, September 4 1888, 54
2128 **GEISINGER**, George D, **GETZENDANNER**, Katie, of Sol, Oct 10 1888, 54
2129 **GILBERT**, Geo A (Jr), **VANFOSSEN**, Annie, of Arnold, October 16 1888, 54
2130 **GEORGE**, Stewart, **BAKER**, Katie, (SHEPHERD), November 6 1888, 54
2131 **GRUMBINE**, Wm, **BECK**, Emma, Nov 28 1888, 54
2132 **GLABSTER**, Martin, **ABBOTT**, Nettie, of George A, Dec 4 1888, 54
2133 **GITTINGER**, Samuel J, **BRUNNER**, Mattie S, March 27 1889, 54
2134 **GILBERT**, Wm L, **EAVES**, Katie, (@ EVES), April 3 1889, 54
2135 **GRAHAM**, Arthur S, **BEATTY**, Nettie, (@ BETTY), August 1 1889, 54
2136 **GRIFFITH**, John J, **ABELL**, Margart, Oct 17 1889, 54
2137 **GRIFFITH**, Clarence, **ETCHISON**, Grace, December 24 1889, 54
2138 **GROFF**, Cha's L R, **DOUB**, Effie R, December 27 1889, 54
2139 **GARROTT**, Lee, **MOORE**, Marie, March 4 1890, 54
2140 **GOLDSMITH**, Myer B, **FELDHEIMER**, Theresa, April 23 1890, [GOLDENBERG, 54
2141 **GAMEZ**, Harold H, **HAMILTON**, Clara, of Wm T, June 18 1890, 54
2142 **GALLAGHER**, Harry P (Dr), **BRODERICK**, Gertrude E, Oct 29 1890, 54
2143 **GISE**, Daniel W, **SINN**, Edith M, of Edward, Nov 26 1890, 54
2144 **GARNAND**, Geo R, **ROWE**, Mary L, (not listed as Miss), Dec 30 1890, 54
2145 **HOPKINS**, Evans, **PATTERSON**, Nancy, Feby 1 1821, 56
2146 **HALLER**, John Alexander, of Christopher, **KAUFFMAN**, Mary, of Henry, April 15 1821, 56
2147 **HEDGES**, Eneas, of Andrew, **SCHOLL**, Catharine, of Ch'n, April 15 1821, 56
2148 **HEYSER**, William, of Chambersburg, **BENTZ**, Elizabeth, of Geo, June 26 1821, 56
2149 **HUMRICHOUSE**, Charles, **LEVY**, Maria C, of David, Septr 4 1821, 56
2150 **HARDT**, John, **ENGELBRECHT**, Catharine, May 9 1822, 56
2151 **HUGHES**, Daniel (Maj), **POTTS**, Elizabeth, of Richard (Sen'r), Septr 3 1822, 56
2152 **HANSHEW**, John, **REMSBERG**, Mary, Nov 26 1822, 56
2153 **HALLER**, Geo W, of Peter, **MUNNICH**, Jemima, March 1823, 56
2154 **HALLER**, Jacob B, **BASCH**, Elizabeth, April 10 1823, 56
2155 **HALLAR**, Philip, (ROCK), **HOWARD**, Dorcus, May 13 1823, 56
2156 **HALLER**, John, of Peter, **BROWN**, Mary, of "Henry BRAUN", Feb 12 1824, 56
2157 **HOUCK**, John (Sen'r), 2d wife, **MCCANN**, Eleanor (Mrs), (BURGESS), May 1824, 56
2158 **HERRING**, Henry, **HOUCK**, Caroline, of Geo, Jany 3 1825, 56
2159 **HANSHEW**, Henry, **STOVER**, Catharine, of John, March 3 1825, 56
2160 **HOWARD**, John S, **MICHAEL**, Catharine, March 24 1825, 56
2161 **HATCH**, William S, **SPURRIER**, Mary (Mrs), widow of Horace, July 21 1825, 56
2162 **HINKEL**, Moses M (Rev), **FLEMING**, Amelia, of Arthur, Augt 16 1825, 56
2163 **HEIM**, Elias, **SHAFER**, Margaret, Septr 1 1825, 56
2164 **HAMMOND**, Grafton, **WILLSON**, Mary E A R, of Tho's P, Octr 11 1825, 56
2165 **HART**, John, **HERRING**, Catharine, Nov 27 1825, 56
2166 **HOWARD**, Tho's, of Charles, **CRUM**, Nancy, Mrs, widow of Isaac, Jany 19 1826, 56
2167 **HOWARD**, Edward, of Cha's, **BUCKEY**, Ann, of Peter, March 9 1826, 56
2168 **HOUCK**, Ezra, of Geo, **BENTZ**, Catharine, of Jacob, March 21 1826, 56
2169 **HARDT**, George, of Peter/1st wife, **BUSER**, Elizabeth, March 30 1826, N Market, 56
2170 **HERGESHEIMER**, Daniel, **ENGLAND**, Caroline, April 9 1826, 56
2171 **HALEY**, William, **FITZPATRICK**, Biddy, Augt 3 1826, 56

2172 HOFFMAN, Wm Christian, of John/1st wife, REICH, Hannah, of John, May 8 1827, 56
2173 HARDY, Benjamin, ROWE, Miss, of Jacob/(*Marg't), June 12 1827, 56
2174 HOSKINS, George, GEBHARDT, Mary Ann, of Geo, Augt 2 1827, 56
2175 HERGESHEIMER, Samuel, 1st wife, ORDNER, Catharine, of Peter, Decr 13 1827, 56
2176 HARRIS, Edward, OYSTER, Joyce, Jany 13 1828, Colored Friends, 56
2177 HADERMAN, Carl Julien, NORMAN, Mary Matilda, June 3 1828, 56
2178 HOFFMAN, Ezra, of Jacob, SMITH, Mary, of Joseph, Augt 10 1828, 56
2179 HAUER, Daniel Jacob (Rev), WARNER, Henrietta, Septr 2 1828, 56
2180 HERGESHEIMER, Peter, WISSINGER, Sophia, of Geo, Octr 9 1828, 56
2181 HOWE, No first name given, (Teacher), WOOLTZ, Lydia, of Geo, July 7 1829, Prin Geo Co, 56
2182 HOUSTON, Samuel, of John, MERRILL, Miss, April 1929, 56
2183 HAWMAN, Philip Jefferson, THOMAS, Margaret, of Gabriel(not listed as Miss), Augt 30 1829, 56
2184 HOFFMAN, John Nicholas (Rev), REESE, Ann, Septr 1829, Balto, 56
2185 HALLER, Joseph, of Peter, DUNN, Miss, Septr 27 1829, Wheeling, Va, 56
2186 HUGHES, Ross, NUSZ, Mary, of Henry, Decr 1 1829, 56
2187 HOPWOOD, Wm, BUSER, Ann, Decr 24 1829, near N Market, 57
2188 HARTZ, Joseph, of Franz, ALEXANDER, Matilda, April 20 1830, 56
2189 HOWARD, Thomas, of Cha's/2d wife, FLEMING, Eleanor, of Jos, May 11 1830, 57
2190 HOFF, Peter, 2d wife, KANDEL, Elizabeth, of Jacob, June 15 1830, 57
2191 HARGETT, John H, of Peter, SHAFER, Henrietta, Augt 9 1830, 57
2192 HALLER, Daniel, of Peter, GELWICKS, Ann Maria, of Geo C, Octr 21 1830, 57
2193 HART, Jacob, of Adam, HERRING, Mary, of Adam, Decr 2 1830, Midd.town, 57
2194 HAMNER, James G (Rev), MCELDERRY, Jane, Decr 9 1830, 57
2195 HALLAR, Philip, 2d wife, WITHY, Louisa (Mrs), widow of Calvin WITHY, Decr 26 1830, 57
2196 HALL, John, FLEMING, Sarah, Feby 25 1831, 57
2197 HAGER, Christian, GEISINGER, Barbara (Mrs), April 28 1831, 57
2198 HOWARD, John C, PHILLIPS, Minerva, of Noah, June 19 1831, 57
2199 HOYT, Henry, Dr, Canal Dover, Ohio, CRABB, Margaret (Mrs), daughter of Wm BAER, June 14 1831, 57
2200 HEMMEL, John D, 1st wife, LEASE, Cath (Mrs), widow of Nicholas, Nov 8 1831, daughter of Geo ZIELER, 57
2201 HOWARD, James, of Balto, ROSS, Cath M, of Wm (JOHNSON), Jany 19 1832, 57
2202 HALLAR, Elisha, BETES, Miss, March 14 1832, New York City, 57
2203 HALLER, Ezra, of Peter, BUCKEY, Elizabeth, of Geo, April 5 1832, 57
2204 HARRISON, Wm G, of Balto, ROSS, Ann E, of Wm (JOHNSON), May 15 1832, 57
2205 HALLER, Michael H, of Tobias, BIRELY, Charlotte C, of Wm, Septr 27 1832, 57
2206 HOBBS, Rezin, GALEZIO, Margaret, of Cha's, Jany 3 1833, 57
2207 HALLER, Samuel, of Peter, LEAH, Charlotte, of Jacob, June 11 1833, 57
2208 HEIM, William D, BENTZ, Louisa, of Jacob, Octr 13 1833, 57
2209 HOUX, David F, of Jacob, KLAUBER, Susan, Decr 1833, DCa, 57
2210 HOBLITZELL, William, of Cumberland, GEPHART, Henrietta, of John, Decr 25 1833, 57
2211 HOFFMAN, Jacob, of Jacob, LIFE, Sarah, Decr 14 1833, 57
2212 HAGAN, John, of Peter, SIFFORD, Maria, of Christ'n, March 20 1834, 57
2213 HARPER, Richard, KELLER, Sophia, of Jacob, April 29 1834, 57
2214 HOPWOOD, James, of Joshua, WALKER, Mary, of John, May 1 1834, 57

2215 HOFFMEIER, John W (Rev), ZIMMERMAN, Lilly Ann, Septr 2 1834, 57
2216 HEINER, Elias (Rev), WOLFE, Mary E, Octr 1 1834, York, Pa, 57
2217 HASSELBACH, George, of John, HARDING, Sarah Ann, Decr 18 1834, 57
2218 HARBAUGH, Morgan, RAUZAHN, Caroline, March 12 1835, 57
2219 HOOPER, Abraham, of John, OTT, Mary, of Peter, July 16 1835, 57
2220 HARN, Levi O, Hagerstown, DUVALL, Zerua Ann, Octr 25 1835, 57
2221 HEDGES, John, WITMER, Mary, Decr 17 1835, 57
2222 HAMILTON, Woodward Evitt, ELY, Catharine, of Wm, Feby 17 1836, 57
2223 HINKEL, Nathaniel H, HURST, Mary Ann, March 14 1836, 57
2224 HUNT, Asbury Hemphill, 1st wife, MCLANAHAN, Zeruah M, April 5 1836, 57
2225 HUGHES, No first name given, (*Edward), ORDNER, Sophia (Mrs), widow of John (SHOPE), Augt 11 1836, 57
2226 HOUCK, Henry, of John, BRENGLE, Mary C, of Peter, Jany 19 1837, 57
2227 HARGETT, Samuel, of John, WATERS, Ellen (Mrs), April 6 1837, 57
2228 HARGETT, Peter, 2d wife, MATTHEWS, Elizabeth, May 18 1837, 57
2229 HARGETT, David, DUTROW, Rebecca, June 6 1837, 58
2230 HEMBRY, John, HOOPER, Juliann, of John, Feby 22 1838, 58
2231 HALLER, Tobias W, of Henry, SUMAN, Juliann C, of Isaac, May 10 1838, 58
2232 HARDING, Norman B, of John L, OGLE, Ann Maria, of James, Sen'r, May 31 1838, 58
2233 HARDT, George, of Peter/2d wife, BALEY, Eliza, Octr 4 1838, 58
2234 HOFFMAN, Wm C, 2d wife, FETTE', Dorothea, of Melle', Septr 30 1838, 58
2235 HALLAR, Cha's W, of Joshua, PRESTON, Sarah B, of Cha's, Octr 31 1838, 58
2236 HAMILTON, Benjamin, DEAN, Margaret Ann, Decr 26 1838, 58
2237 HOGG, William, (brother of Sam'l B), HALL, Mary Ann, Jany 5 1839, Cecil Co, Md, 58
2238 HILTON, Henry Konig, KNAUFF, Margaret, of Jacob, Feby 21 1839, 58
2239 HAUER, John, of Adam, SPIELMAN, Elizabeth, April 9 1839, 58
2240 HILTON, William H, of Clement, LEISHER, Susan, Augt 27 1839, Balto, 58
2241 HOFF, John F (Rev), (of Lancaster, Pa), ROSS, Julianna J, of Wm, Octr 29 1839, 58
2242 HECKENTHORN, Christian, WHEELER, Mary (Mrs), widow of Bennet, Nov 19 1839, 58
2243 HEMSTON, Christian, DADE, Mary A, (HAMPFSTEIN), Decr 19 1839, 58
2244 HORTON, James, HANE, Catharine, of David, Jany 21 1840, 58
2245 HAMILTON, John, of John/1st wife, LEASE, Mary, of Harry, Feby 27 1840, Linganore, 58
2246 HUDSON, John A, MARMAN, Juliann E, March 16 1840, 58
2247 HALLER, David H, of Peter, ROELKE, Eliza, of John, March 31 1840, 58
2248 HARD, Edward D, HILTON, Margaret Ann, March 31 1840, 58
2249 HARTBAUER, William, SAHM, Louisa, of John Peter, May 31 1840, 58
2250 HOUCK, Henry T, (son of Dr Jacob), WILLIAMS, Eleanor M, June 9 1840, Balto, 58
2251 HOFFMAN, Francis, CRUM, Ann Rebecca, June 11 1840, (Jefferson), 58
2252 HALLER, Thomas, of Tobias/1st wife, SHEARER, Lydia Ann, of Lewis, Septr 10 1840, 58
2253 HARGETT, John William, of John, THOMAS, Mary Ellen, of Levin, Septr 15 1840, 58
2254 HULL, Tideman (Dr), DERR, Eliza, of John W, Nov 3 1840, 58
2255 HARDING, James Marshall, of John L, HALL, Sarah, Mrs, (FLEMING), Decr 1 1840, 58
2256 HOUCK, Geo John, of Jacob, JANSEN, Elizabeth, of Erasmus, Decr 29 1840, 58
2257 HAGAN, Stephen, of Peter, WEISZ, Elizabeth, of Middletown, Jany 21 1841, 58
2258 HODDINOTT, Charles, KOONTZ, Henrietta C, of John, Jany 7 1841, 58
2259 HITESHEW, Philip, (HEITSCHUH), RETTGERING, Matilda, of Melle'/(not listed as Miss), March 2d 1841, 58

2260 **HEINER**, John (Dr), **GRABILL**, Charlotte, March 2 1841, 58
2261 **HOUCK**, Jacob, (Country), **POPE**, Catharine (Mrs), widow of Wm, April 25 1841, 58
2262 **HEIDECKER**, Henry, **HUGO**, Wilhelmina (Mrs), (RETTGERING of Melle'), June 8 1841, 58
2263 **HAMMOND**, Charles S, of Cha's, **GILLISS**, Marianne A B, June 8 1841, 58
2264 **HOOD**, Benjamin, **WADSWORTH**, Amelia, Octr 14 1841, 58
2265 **HAMTRAMCK**, John F, of Va/2d wife, **SELBY**, Sarah Elmor, Octr 24 1841, 58
2266 **HEDGES**, Baily, **MEIKSELL**, Eliza, of Jacob, Sen'r, Octr 19 1841, 58
2267 **HUNT**, Samuel, of Job, **BEALL**, Martha M, of Wm M, Jany 11 1842, 58
2268 **HAMMOND**, Richard F (Dr), of Walter C, **CRAMER**, Agnes, of Ezra, Feby 3 1842, 58
2269 **HERGESHEIMER**, James, **HENDERSON**, Maria Cath, of Rob't, Feby 10 1842, 58
2270 **HOUCK**, John (Junior), **EARLY**, Margaret, of John, May 3 1842, 58
2271 **HERGESHEIMER**, Samuel, 2d wife, **MATTEWS**, Elizabeth, March 31 1842, 59
2272 **HINKS**, Samuel, of Balto, **NIXDORFF**, Susan, of Henry, Octr 18 1842, 59
2273 **HALLER**, Nicholas T, **DOLL**, Mary R, of Tho's, Jany 3 1843, 59
2274 **HALLER**, William, of Geo W, **MILLER**, Mary, of John W, March 5 1843, 59
2275 **HOFFMAN**, Ezra, of Jacob, **LIFE**, Miss, May 1843, 59
2276 **HAUER**, Nicholas D, of Dan'l, Junr, **MEYERS**, Ann Kate, of Balto, June 6 1843, 59
2277 **HARRIS**, Henry R, **BARRICK**, Clarissa, July 27 1843, 59
2278 **HEGESHEIMER**, David J, of Joseph, **THOMAS**, Sarah Ellis, of Jacob R, Augt 31 1843, 59
2279 **HOUCK**, Edward, **ROBERTS**, Rachel, Nov 21 1843, 59
2280 **HOLTZMAN**, Bernard H, **HOFFMAN**, Malinda, of Geo, Decr 26 1843, 59
2281 **HOGG**, Samuel R, 2d wife, **TICE**, Barbara (Mrs), widow of Hen Nich, Jany 25 1844, daughter of J KUNKEL, 59
2282 **HAMNER**, Tho's L (Rev), **WILSON**, Harriott H, Jany 25 1844, Leesburg, Va, 59
2283 **HEINTZ**, Adam, **HERTZ**, Elizabeth, Feby 21 1844, 59
2284 **HEIM**, Jacob B, of Andrew, **SMITH**, Ann C, of John D, April 11 1844, GOMBER, 59
2285 **HEFFNER**, Wm W, **FIEGE**, Catharine M, May 1 1844, 59
2286 **HARRISON**, Joshia, of Zeph, **LUDWIG**, Ann Rebecca, May 9 1844, 59
2287 **HOUX**, Matthias, of Geo Jacob, **SHEDD**, Miss, July 1844, Washington, 59
2288 **HEUSER**, Christian, **KERSCHNER**, Elizabeth, Decr 4 1844, 59
2289 **HAMMOND**, Wm P, **UNKEFER**, Harriet L, of Abdiel, Decr 19 1844, "UNGEFEHR", 59
2290 **HURLEY**, George E, **LOKEY**, Catharine, March 27 1845, 59
2291 **HAY**, Charles A (Rev), **BARNITZ**, Sarah R, May 5 1845, York, Pa, 59
2292 **HAMMOND**, Denton, 2d wife, **HAMMOND**, Elizabeth R, Nov 11 1845, 59
2293 **HOUCK**, Daniel J, **AUBERT**, Ann Rebecca, of Jacob, Feby 3 1846, 59
2294 **HARSHBERGER**, Henry S, **WILLIARD**, Sarah Ann, Feby 16 1846, 59
2295 **HELFENSTEIN**, Albert G, of Rev Jonathan, **FRAIM**, Ann M, Feby 17 1846, Lancaster, 59
2296 **HAMMOND**, Dawson V, 1st wife, **HODGEKISS**, Lydia, Feby 25 1846, 59
2297 **HANSHEW**, Henry E, of John/1st wife, **KELLER**, Caroline M, of Jacob, March 24 1846, 59
2298 **HOOD**, James M, **BOGGS**, Sarah Ann, April 7 1846, in Phila, 59
2299 **HUMRICHOUSE**, Cha's W, **HAWKEN**, Mary, May 6 1846, Hagerstown, 59
2300 **HOOPER**, Tho's, of John, **STOWELL**, Lydia Ann, May 10 1846, 59
2301 **HAYS**, No first name given, **PEARRE**, Mary Tabitha, of Wm, May 14 1846, "SPRINGER", 59
2302 **HANE**, Jacob D, of Daniel, **SCHAEFFER**, Anna Mary, of Rev D F, May 19 1846, 59
2303 **HART**, Elias, **TRISLER**, Margaret, of Geo, May 26 1846, 59
2304 **HOUSE**, Martin W E, **KERTZENDORFFER**, Rebecca E, of Jos, May 28 1846, 59

2305 HALLER, Jacob, of Jacob/2d wife, MICHAEL, Ann M (Mrs), "ZIELER", July 2 1846, 59
2306 HERRING, Daniel, THOMAS, Miss, Augt 6 1846, Middletown, 59
2307 HUNT, Asbury Hemphill, 2d wife/HOUCK, HERRING, Ann Sophia, Octr 8 1846, 59
2308 HOUSE, Wm W, BARRETT, Ellen, Octr 13 1846, 59
2309 HALLER, Thomas, 2d wife, FESSLER, Caroline R, of John, Octr 28 1846, 59
2310 HARKEY, James M (Rev), KELLER, Ann Elizabeth, of Jacob, Nov 5 1846, 59
2311 HARRISON, Wm Henry (Rev), of Zeph, WINWOOD, Sarah A, Nov 24 1846, Springfield, O, 59
2312 HEIM, Tho's A, of Andrew, SMITH, Mary Jane, Decr 10 1846, Cincinati, Ohio, 59
2313 HARBAUGH, Geo S, BURKITT, Henrietta C, of Newton, May 6 1847, 60
2314 HAMMOND, Denton, FOX, Rebecca (Mrs), May 14 1847, 60
2315 HAGAN, Henry, of Peter, LEMMON, Miss, June 12 1847, Shepherdstown, Va, 60
2316 HERRING, John H A, ARMPRISLER, Louisa, Augt 3 1847, 60
2317 HALLEBAUGH, Joel V, HERGESHEIMER, Ann Rebecca, of Sam'l, Nov 23 1847, 60
2318 HOUCK, Henry G, STONE, Susannah, Decr 23 1847, 60
2319 HOLMES, John L, ECKES, Harriett E, Jany 11 1848, 60
2320 HEMSTONE, Armstead T, LUCKETT, Harriott B, of Lloyd, Jany 20 1848, 60
2321 HARTSOCK, Noah, ENBELBRECHT, Margaret (Mrs), March 20 1848, 60
2322 HARKEY, Sydney L (Rev), JENKINS, Mary Jane, May 16 1848, 60
2323 HEALD, William, 2d wife, ALLEN, Balinda E (Mrs), "SIMMONS", May 13 1848, Balto, 60
2324 HAGER, John, CARMACK, Ann Sophia, of Sam'l, July 27 1848, 60
2325 HUGHES, Wm H, GETZENDANNER, Ann Rebecca, of Jonathan, Augt 20 1848, 60
2326 HARDT, John Conrad, MCCULLEY, Sarah Jane, of John J, Nov 16 1848, 60
2327 HOUSE, Eli C P, PIERPOINT, Sarah A, Nov 16 1848, 60
2328 HAMMOND, Upton J, BOON, Martha R, Nov 23 1848, 60
2329 HILLEARY, Thomas, WHEELER, Sarah Odel, Nov 28 1848, 60
2330 HOWARD, William, FAGAN, Mary Jane, of Geo, Decr 12 1848, 60
2331 HOLBRUNNER, Tho's M, SMITH, Elizabeth, of John of Midd, Decr 18 1848, 60
2332 HEDGES, Daniel A, of Enos, DEVILBISS, Catharine M, of David, Jany 1849, 60
2333 HILDEBRAND, Wm H, STALEY, Mary Ann R, March 8 1849, 60
2334 HEMMELL, John D, 2d wife, WAITE, Elizabeth B (Mrs), Nov 29 1849, Balto, 60
2335 HOBBS, Jackson, LEWIS, Emily, Nov 22 1849, 60
2336 HEMBRY, Issacher, 1st wife, FLEMING, Elizabeth, Decr 25 1849, Va, 60
2337 HEWELL, James L, BENNETT, Lydia A M, of David, Feby 21 1850, 60
2338 HARGER, M, VAN HORN, Anna E, "SCHMALTZ", March 5 1850, 60
2339 HALLEY, Leonard, CASTLE, Elizabeth, May 16 1850, 60
2340 HOLMES, M Scott, KRAGER, Olevia, "Dan'l CASSEL", May 22 1850, Balto, 60
2341 HOOPER, William, of John, NEWPORT, Mary Jane, of Adam, Octr 1 1850, 60
2342 HENRY, T Walton, COLEMAN, M Ann, Augt 13 1850, Balto, 60
2343 HARRIS, Wm C, HARTMAN, Frances O, Nov 7 1850, York, Pa, 60
2344 HEFFNER, Samuel P, CRUTCHLEY, Lucinda (Mrs), widow of Elias, Decr 12 1850, 60
2345 HAGER, Martin, ALBAUGH, Miss, of Solomon/(*Adeline A), April 24 1851, 60
2346 HEARD, J Wilson, SCHLEIGH, Mary C, April 24 1851, 60
2347 HALLER, Jacob Junior, KANTNER, Sarah, of Geo, April 27 1851, 60
2348 HUNT, Jesse Johns, of Job, ROSZEL, Mary C, of S Calvert ROSZEL, June 17 1851, Balto, 60
2349 HARGETT, David, RENN, Lydia Ann C, June 22 1851, 60

2350 HUNT, Robert J (Dr), WARD, Sallie, late Mrs LAWRENCE, Octr 1 1851, Louisville, KY, 60
2351 HOLTZ, Benedict M, STALEY, Phebe Ann, Nov 12 1851, 60
2352 HAMMOND, Dawson V, 2d wife, HAMMOND, Anna M, Jany 12 1852, 60
2353 HOLLIDAY, Daniel, RUTHERFORD, Fannie M, of Benj'n, Feby 5 1852, Balto, 60
2354 HAGAN, Ignatius, MCMAHON, Mary, "LOWELL", Feby 24 1852, 60
2355 HARDT, George, 3d wife, HISSEY, Mary Ann, April 22 1852, Rockville, 60
2356 HARGETT, John, HOPWOOD, Matilda J, April 29 1852, 61
2357 HOLTZ, John Oliver, CRONISE, Louisa J, of Sam'l, May 18 1852, 61
2358 HILLEARY, Edward J, KIEFFER, Mary A, of Geo, May 19 1852, "STOFFEL", 61
2359 HEAGY, G W (Dr), CLABAUGH, Mary E, of N, May 27 1852, 61
2360 HALLER, William, of Jacob, NO BRIDES NAME GIVEN, July 1852, Carlisle, Pa, 61
2361 HUDSON, Herschel, WEIRMAN, Sarah D, July 28 1852, Pa, 61
2362 HAUGH, Solomon, COLEGATE, Catharine V, Septr 14 1852, 61
2363 HEIM, James, HOLTER, Elizabeth, Octr 26 1852, 61
2364 HINES, James C, MCDADE, Margaret, of Sam'l, Nov 14 1852, 61
2365 HOLLINGSWORTH, J T, O'NEAL, Susan A, of Hon G, Decr 7 1852, 61
2366 HAINES, Granville S, SHEPHERD, Susan, Decr 30 1852, 61
2367 HEIM, Edward P, STREAM, Mary A V, Jany 13 1853, 61
2368 HOFFMAN, Jacob, of Jacob/ 2d wife, NO BRIDES NAME GIVEN, Miss, Feby 1853, 61
2369 HAUGH, Wm H, LEATHER, Henrietta L, of John, April 26 1853, 61
2370 HARBAUGH, Levi C, MILLER, Minerva A, April 21 1853, Creagerstown, 61
2371 HARDEN, William (Rev), SLICER, Lizzie S, of Rev Henry, June 7 1853, Geotown, 61
2372 HARDING, Basil, (HARDINGER), LOWE, Margaret E, June 7 1853, 61
2373 HORNUNG, George, BURKHART, Elizabeth, Augt 9 1853, 61
2374 HOUCK, Peter, STULL, Levina, Septr 4th 1853, 61
2375 HEFFNER, John H, CLEM, Barbara, Septr 15 1853, 61
2376 HAUER, Geo N, of Henry, POOLE, Lucretia, of Wm, Octr 6 1853, 61
2377 HUNT, David Boyd, GORRELL, Molly A H, Octr 25 1853, 61
2378 HERBERT, John, RAUPP, Dorothea, Nov 14 1853, 61
2379 HARMAN, George, STOTTELMEYER, S Ann, Decr 22 1853, 61
2380 HAGAN, Michael P, WILES, Mary P, Jany 11 1854, 61
2381 HILL, Christopher, 1st wife, BRISH, Harriott A R, of John M, Feby 9 1854, 61
2382 HEIT, Jacob, BELL, Caroline (Mrs), (Caroline PITTS), March 3 1854, 61
2383 HOLBRUNNER, John H, HESSEN, Matilda E, March 15 1854, 61
2384 HULL, Joel, STONER, Sarah A (Mrs), (BALTZELL), Apl 13 1854, Tiffin, Ohio, 61
2385 HUGHES, James, WIEST, Mary C, of Jacob, July 11 1854, Balto, 61
2386 HERRINGTON, Geo, PHEBUS, Margaret (Mrs), "GROVE"/widow of Geo, 1854, "Grove", 61
2387 HIPSLEY, Levi F (Dr), TODD, Lucy E, of Benj'n, Octr 10 1854, 61
2388 HUXFORD, David C, STALLINGS, Mary Ann, Nov 28 1854, 61
2389 HOOPER, John, (Jacky), HAMILTON, Catharine (Mrs), widow of Woodward, Decr 31 1854, 61
2390 HARDING, John L, KEMP, Henrietta, of Col Lewis, Feby 7 1855, 61
2391 HINKS, Cha's D, SAUERWEIN, Amelia C, March 6 1855, Balto, 61
2392 HARLEY, G W Truman, TICE, Annie E, (H'y Nichs), April 18 1855, 61
2393 HUBBARD, Alexander J, BROWN, Mary E, of Wm S, June 13 1855, 61
2394 HARPER, Robert G, SHIPMAN, Harriott A, June 28 1855, Gettysburg, 61
2395 HERWIG, August, 2d wife, WERNER, Catherine, July 1855, 61

2396 HARRISON, Edward, of Zeph, GELWICKS, Virginia F, of Geo C, Augt 21 1855, 61
2397 HAMMOND, Augustus (Rev), HAMMOND, Mary Virginia, Octr 2 1855, N Market, 61
2398 HALL, Robert C, CUNNINGHAM, Mary R, of B Amos, Octr 2 1855, 62
2399 HART, Jacob A, of Jacob, HALLER, Eleanora L, of Daniel, Octr 17 1855, 62
2400 HARTT, Frederick P, BLUEMENAUER, Catharine, Octr 21 1855, 62
2401 HARKNESS, John C, LARE, Maria (Mrs), (widow of Henry C LOCHR), Nov 1 1855, "O'NEAL", 62
2402 HORINE, Ezra S, HOUSE, Eliza Ann, Octr 29 1855, 62
2403 HAHN, William, HALLER, Catharine, of Jacob (S & F), Nov 13 1855, 62
2404 HALLER, David E, of Mich'l H, FULTZ, Mary Cath, Decr 27 1855, Balto, 62
2405 HOFFMAN, Jacob, of Ezra, BENNETT, Hannah, of Tilghman, Jany 20 1856, 62
2406 HEISTERMANN, Adolph, BUCHHEIMER, Mary (Mrs), April 6 1856, 62
2407 HEAGY, Jacob, CRONISE, Rebecca, of Frederick, April 17 1856, 62
2408 HAFER, Samuel, GROVE, Catharine, of Reuben, May 6 1856, 62
2409 HARRISON, Nimrod F, GUYTON, Harriott J, of Albert G, May 20 1856, 62
2410 HOOD, George, WOLFE, Sarah, June 12 1856, near Monrovia, 62
2411 HOFFMAN, Daniel, CRAWFORD, Margaret, June 19 1856, 62
2412 HOOVER, Christian, MICHAEL, Cassandra, (not listed as Miss), Augt 19 1856, 62
2413 HELFENSTEIN, Cha's J, TARGEE, Helena, Augt 17 1856, St Louis, Mo, 62
2414 HENDRICKSON, Ephraim, ANDERSON, Cecelia R, Septr 23 1856, 62
2415 HEFFNER, Lewis C, BRUNNER, Frances E, Nov 6 1856, 62
2416 HIGH, Joseph A, MARTIN, Mary A M, of Wm C, Nov 18 1856, Balto, 62
2417 HALLER, Abner Davis, of Phil, WILLSON, Mary A, Nov 27 1856, Balto, 62
2418 HOFFMAN, Jos Cromwell, NUSSBAUM, Henrietta, of Jacob, Decr 11 1856, 62
2419 HEMBRY, Isaacher, 2d wife, HOOPER, Mary, of John, Sen'r, March 2 1857, 62
2420 HOLTZ, Albert B, 1st wife, CROMWELL, Mary E, March 19 1857, 62
2421 HARRISON, Orra, MICHAEL, Sarah C, April 15 1857, (Manor), 62
2422 HELDEBRAND, Lewis H, WINDBIGLER, Amanda L, June 11 1857, 62
2423 HILL, Christopher, 2d wife, EARNSHAW, Olive R, June 30 1857, Martinsburg, Va, 62
2424 HOWARD, Charles E, of Edward, GROVE, Joan, of Jacob, Augt 5 1857, 62
2425 HARDEN, Wm (Rev), 2d wife, MOODY, Mary Winbourne, Augt 1857, Balto, 62
2426 HOSKINSON, Hilleary, HOSKINSON, Elizabeth, Augt 27 1857, 62
2427 HANSON, Geo A, BARRAUD, Courtney C, Sept 23 1857, at Norfolk, Va, 62
2428 HOOPER, Wm H, BRENGLE, Mary Susan, of Ch'n, Sept 30 1857, 62
2429 HERONIMUS, R S Dean, DARBY, Martha A P, of Walter C, Nov 15 1857, 62
2430 HORINE, John F, SMITH, Emma, Nov 23 1857, (Boonsborough), 62
2431 HORSEY, Outerbridge, CARROLL, Anna, of Phila, Nov 24 1857, 62
2432 HERRING, Lloyd H, 2d wife, SMELTZER, Elizabeth, of Henry R, Decr 16 1857, 62
2433 HARBAUGH, John S, HUGHES, Nancy J, Decr 25 1857, Emmittsburg, 62
2434 HOUSTON, Samuel T, of Ja's F, CHARLES, Mary Ann Traill, of Phila, Decr 31 1857, 62
2435 HORNER, Eli, AGNEW, Sophia, "SCHWERTZELL", Decr 31 1857, Emmittsburg, 62
2436 HERGESHEIMER, Geo P, KARNS, M Jane, Jany 5 1858, 62
2437 HELFFENSTEIN, Cyrus G, TRAIL, Ann E, of Edw/(he of Rev Jona), Feby 16 1858, 62
2438 HENDRY, Charles Junior, ENGLAND, Henrietta, March 30 1858, 62
2439 HAUPT, Jacob N D, GLESSNER, Amanda M, of Rev Geo M, April 15 1858, 62
2440 HARGETT, John B, 2d wife, CUBITZ, A Elizabeth, April 15 1858, 63
2441 HOWARD, George W (Prof), (EINSTEIN), MORGAN, Eleanor W, of Tho's W, June 16 1858,

63

2442 HORINE, Adam F, SMELTZER, Deborah F, of Daniel, Augt 18 1858, 63
2443 HARDING, Lewis R, LEATHER, Ann R, of Major John, Augt 26 1858, 63
2444 HEDGES, Lycurgus E, of Enos, BAKER, Amanda S, Octr 5 1858, 63
2445 HOUCK, Charles, of John, STOCKETT, Mary A, Octr 7 1858, Balto, 63
2446 HARRISON, Joseph, BITZENBERGER, Ann Elzab, Octr 12 1858, 63
2447 HARN, Wesley J, MANAHAN, Eurith, Octr 14 1858, 63
2448 HEIM, David C, SMITH, Mary A, Octr 21 1858, 63
2449 HERGESHEIMER, Jacob, of Peter/1st wife, SUMAN, Rachel, of John, Decr 16 1858, 63
2450 HARBAUGH, James P, WEBSTER, Eliza V, Decr 23 1858, (Harbach valley), 63
2451 HANSHEW, Fritchie, of Henry, CUSTARD, Martha A S, of Adam, Jany 19 1859, 63
2452 HIMES, William H, of Ohio, WHITTER, Ella J, of Tho's, Jany 20 1859, 63
2453 HEINLEIN, Frederick, DUNKHORST, Dorus, of H'y, April 5 1859, 63
2454 HAMMOND, Wm Edgar, ETCHISON, Sarah Roberta, of Perry G, March 31 1859, 63
2455 HAMMOND, Grafton, TRAYER, Martha Frances, May 17 1859, 63
2456 HAYS, John B, BOOGER, Susan, ("BUCHER"), July 7 1859, Cumberland, 63
2457 HAMILTON, Wm T (Hon), Hagerstown, JENNESS, Clara, Septr 8 1859, Porthmouth, NH, 63
2458 HOUPT, George W, WAHRENFELSZ, Caroline, Octr 27 1859, 63
2459 HOOPER, James, of John, DAVIS, Mary E, Nov 30 1859, 63
2460 HAINES, Thomas J, CLAY, Cinderella, of Zebulon, Jany 5 1860, 63
2461 HERRING, Geo Edward, SULLIVAN, Agnes, of Dr Dan'l, Feby 16 1860, 63
2462 HAUGH, John W, of Wm, MICHAEL, Mary Ann, March 28 1860, 63
2463 HAMMOND, Oliver B, SIMMONS, Serena, of Maj James, April 27 1860, 63
2464 HAGAN, Wm E, of John, PUTTS, Lizzie C, Augt 15 1860, 63
2465 HOPWOOD, Mahlon Augustus, of Ja's, MILLER, Annie S, of Fred'k D, Septr 15 1860, 63
2466 HOUPT, Josiah, WARRENFELSZ, Amanda, Octr 4 1860, Middletownvalley, 63
2467 HENKE', William D, WILHIDE, Ann Marie, Octr 11 1860, 63
2468 HEIM, Lewis Augustus, FOSTEN, Euphrosina, (GRUSSER), Decr 16 1860, 63
2469 HORWETEL, Lewis, SCHLIMMER, Hannah, Decr 24 1860, Pipe Creek, 63
2470 HESSER, George Jacob, NEROMAN, E Susan, Decr 30 1860, 63
2471 HELDEBRAND, Lewis M, STALEY, Laura V, Jany 1 1861, 63
2472 HEIGERD, Henry (Rev), KILPATRICK, Susan C, Jany 6 1861, Muhlenberg, Africa, 63
2473 HOVES, William, LIGHTNER, Ann M, Jany 31 1861, 63
2474 HAUSER, Dennis D, YOUNG, Mary E, Feby 5 1861, 63
2475 HOBBS, Samuel A, WEDDELL, Candace A, Feby 12 1861, 63
2476 HOUSEHOLDER, Wm H, KEHLER, Mary, of Jacob, Feby 17 1861, 63
2477 HARKER, Joseph, CARLIN, Anne R, of David, Feby 20 1861, 63
2478 HAGER, Lewis, BURCK, Mary F, April 17 1861, 63
2479 HERSCHBERGER, Aaron B, AHALT, Amanda C, of Sam'l, June 18 1861, 63
2480 HARP, Daniel V, SCHEFFER, Lugenia F, Octr 22 1861, 63
2481 HARRIS, Edward, MILLER, Matilda, Nov 7 1861, 63
2482 HAMILTON, John, 2d wife, KIRBY, Elizabeth, of Wm, Nov 21 1861, 64
2483 HOBBS, Charles S, of Rezin, HITESHEW, Sophia E, of Philip, Nov 26 1861, 64
2484 HALLER, Tho's Grason, KOSTER, Martha E, of Henry, Decr 11 1861, 64
2485 HINEA, Jacob H, GAUGH, Eve, Decr 3 1861, 64
2486 HULL, G W, BAKER, Sarah Jane, Nov 26 1861, 64
2487 HOBBS, Albert, UPPERMAN, Margaret (Mrs), (METZGER), Decr 30 1861, 64

The Joseph Engelbrecht Marriage Ledger of Frederick Co., MD 1820-1890 *Marriage List*

2488 HERSCHMAN, David W, OGLE, Annie S, of John, April 24 1862, Glade, 64
2489 HAUSER, Frank T, MUSSETER, Sarah A, April 30 1862, 64
2490 HOUCK, John W, of David, PHEBUS, Ann E, of Geo, May 15 1862, 64
2491 HERNDON, Jackson L, BLUMENAUER, Caroline, Octr 28 1862, 64
2492 HEDGES, Henry S, CRAMER, Maggie E, Nov 4 1862, 64
2493 HARRIS, George W, WILES, Arabella, Nov 18 1862, Glade, 64
2494 HEDGES, Lewis A, RAMSBURG, Mary E, Jany 8 1863, 64
2495 HEETER, John, CONRAD, Margaret, of John, Jany 19 1863, 64
2496 HAMILTON, John W, (of Woodward), YINGER, Mary M, of Nicholas, Feby 5 1863, (not listed as Miss), 64
2497 HUTH, Firdenand W, SCHROEDER, Albertine, (J F ZELLER), Feby 10 1863, 64
2498 HAGAN, John C, of John, BRINING, Kate M, Feby 17 1863, 64
2499 HAINES, Nicholas, (107 Regt Pa Vol), KAUFFMAN, Ann Cath, of Henry, March 18 1863, 64
2500 HARBAUGH, Simon W, SMITH, Lizzie, March 24 1863, 64
2501 HEINTZ, Jacob Junior, EAVES, Mary Jane, April 30 1863, 64
2502 HARRISON, Wm, of Dr Wm, POOLE, Annie E, May 30 1863, Fairview, 64
2503 HARTMAN, Simon, 2d wife both sisters, WERTHEIMER, Sophia, June 14 1863, 64
2504 HARDMAN, Elmore, CONRAD, A Cordelia, July 16 1863, 64
2505 HOUCK, Isaac J, MARTZ, Caroline C, July 30 1863, 64
2506 HEISE, Henry L D, LUGENBEEL, Ann Rebecca, Septr 15 1863, 64
2507 HALLOWAY, A C (Rev), VANDERSLOOT, Salome F, Octr 16 1863, 64
2508 HOFFMAN, John, of Wm C, CROMWELL, Margaret Ellen, Octr 22 1863, 64
2509 HARRIS, John, (of Wisconsin), MILLER, Mary, Nov 5 1863, 64
2510 HEFFNER, John J, RICE, Drucilla, of Perry G, Decr 24 1863, 64
2511 HAMMITT, Thomas P, OGLE, M Tillie, of Joachim, Jany 5 1864, 64
2512 HERRING, Edward L, BRANDENBURG, Lydia, April 12 1864, 64
2513 HARGETT, John E, ZIMMERMAN, Ellen Lucretia, of Sam'l, May 12 1864, 64
2514 HEATH, Grove, CRUM, Alice C, of Wm, Decr 7 1864, 64
2515 HOFFMAN, Henry, SCHMIDTHEIM, Fredericka, of Balto (not listed as Miss), Decr 15 1864, 64
2516 HOLBRUNNER, John M, SAYLER, Catharine E, Decr 25 1864, Glade, 64
2517 HOWARD, John T, (FINCH), HERRMANN, Maggie, of Mich'l, Jany 12 1865, 64
2518 HODDINOTT, Charles, 2d wife, HOOPER, Mary S (Mrs), of Emmittsburg, Jany 19 1865, 64
2519 HEISER, Levi F, STULL, Emma Jane S E, March 23 1865, 64
2520 HALLER, Henry W, of Mich'l H, DARNELL, Lizzie, April 5 1865, 64
2521 HEINTZ, Adam, FORREST, Elizabeth, April 8 1865, 64
2522 HARGETT, Curtis F, of John H, WASKEY, Sallie J, May 3 1865, 64
2523 HARRIS, Chancey (Capt), of NJ, BAKER, Clementine A, of Edw, May 22 1865, 64
2524 HARGETT, David Z, BLESSING, Elizabeth E, June 19 1865, 65
2525 HOLT, Alexander Stephens, of NY, THOMPSON, Susan E, June 20 1865, 65
2526 HERGESHEIMER, Jacob, of Peter/2d wife, GREEN, Sallie E, of Benedict, July 18 1865, 65
2527 HOLDCRAFT, Patrick J, DUTROW, Catharine A, July 16 1865, Glade, 65
2528 HITESHEW, Philip L (Capt'n), WILCOXON, Fannie A, of John, Augt 10 1865, 65
2529 HARRISON, James W, GIBBONS, Susan, Septr 5 1865, Fairview, 65
2530 HOOKER, Joseph (Maj Gen'l), USA, GROSBACH, Olivia, Octr 3 1865, Cincin, O, 65
2531 HELDEBRAND, Joseph D, ZWANZIGER, Annie, (TWENTY), Octr 12 1865, 65

2532 *HUNTRESS*, Hiram, of Wisconsin, *WILLIAMSON*, Manzella, of Warren R, Octr 19 1865, 65
2533 *HEFFNER*, Lewis C, 2d wife, *ANGELBERGER*, Mary S, Nov 9 1865, 65
2534 *HALL*, B Franklin, *SCHUTENHELM*, Syney Ann, Decr 28 1865, 65
2535 *HALLER*, Isaac H, of Tobias W, *BAER*, Mary E, Jany 18 1866, 65
2536 *HARGETT*, Geo B, *FORTNEY*, Lucretia R, Feby 20 1866, 65
2537 *HOFFMAN*, George, of Ezra, *TROUT*, Harriett C E, March 16 1866, 65
2538 *HARRIS*, Geo W, *STALEY*, Mary E, April 1 1866, 65
2539 *HAGAN*, Francis T, *EAKLE*, Susan A, March 25 1866, 65
2540 *HOWARD*, Wm H, of Edward, *CULLER*, Ella R, of Dan'l L, May 15 1866, 65
2541 *HORNER*, O A (Maj'r), *GRIER*, Maggie A, of Rev Rob't S, June 28 1866, 65
2542 *HARRISON*, P Leonard (Rev), of Zeph, *BANTZ*, Fannie M, of Va, Augt 28 1866, 65
2543 *HOUCK*, David E, of David, *BELL*, Laura V, (Caro PITTS), Augt 23 1866, 65
2544 *HARKEY*, Simeon W (Rev DD), 2d wife, *LISCHER*, Louisa R (Mrs), (SCHERER), Augt 28 1866, 65
2545 *HOUCK*, Ezra, of Ezra, *WORMAN*, Margaret R, of And'w D, Octr 2 1866, 65
2546 *HOFFMAN*, Wm Fette', of Wm C, *BROWN*, Helena, of Norfolk, Va, Octr 16 1866, 65
2547 *HAGAN*, Peter A, of John, *HARRISON*, Mary E, Octr 30 1866, Balto, 65
2548 *HOUCK*, Henry J, of Henry/1st wife, *STONE*, Eugenia M, of Wm H, Decr 11 1866, 65
2549 *HOPWOOD*, Charles L, *COPELAND*, Lottie R, March 5 1867, 65
2550 *HILDEBRAND*, Frederick, *KREBS*, Delia, March 7 1867, 65
2551 *HARGETT*, Luther F, *FULMER*, Mary Catharine, March 26 1867, 65
2552 *HOFFMAN*, Wm Christian, 3d wife, *DERING*, Sarach C, April 4 1867, 65
2553 *HARBACH*, Charles M, Ohio, *HOFFORD*, Harriet, (HOUX), Septr 15 1867, 65
2554 *HOLMES*, Charles E H, *STEINER*, Valietta, of David C (WIEST), Nov 4 1867, 65
2555 *HERRMANN*, Michael, 2d wife, *POWERS*, Elizabeth (Mrs), (GRELE'), Decr 8 1867, 65
2556 *HARRISON*, Geo W, *MOBERLY*, Rowanna V, Jany 1 1868, (Midd val), 65
2557 *HOPWOOD*, James W, of Ja's, *BALTZLEY*, Christana, Jany 28 1868, 65
2558 *HOUCK*, George, of Ezra, *DUTROW*, E Frank, of Randolph, Feby 18 1868, 65
2559 *HARRY*, Wm H H, *HARGETT*, Mary C, of Sam'l, March 5 1868, 65
2560 *HARPER*, James Emory, *PRINCE*, Catharine Amelia, of Tho's C, March 31 1868, 65
2561 *HEIM*, Wm H, *WINER*, Annie V (Mrs), (Warner KAUFFMAN), Octr 20 1868, Balto, 65
2562 *HUNTER*, Henry Lee, of S Carolina, *PETTIT*, Lizzie M, Octr 29 1868, "BEALL", 65
2563 *HORINE*, Peter M, *GAVER*, Emma Susan, Nov 24 1868, Jefferson, 65
2564 *HOOD*, James T, of Arrow Rock, Missouri, *GEISINGER*, Annie A, of Sam'l L, Decr 8 1868, 65
2565 *HILDEBRAND*, Geo H, *CREAGER*, Martha S, Decr 10 1868, Rocky Spring, 65
2566 *HARTSOCK*, S M (Rev), *LEWIS*, Mary E, of Jacob, Jany 10 1869, 66
2567 *HOUCK*, Jacob R, *HOUCK*, Mary J, Feby 2 1869, 66
2568 *HAHRMAN*, Wm H, *HALLER*, Mary E, of Jacob L, Feby 9 1869, 66
2569 *HOWARD*, Cha's T, of Tho's, *COVER*, Mary L, of John, Feby 10 1869, 66
2570 *HARKEY*, James S, of Rev S W, *YOUNT*, Addie N, May 4 1869, 66
2571 *HERGESHEIMER*, Cha's A, of Sam'l, *BETTS*, Ida, July 27 1869, Rulo, Nebraska, 66
2572 *HOOVER*, John, *PETERS*, Urith A (Mrs), "DAYHOFF", June 21 1869, Boonsboro, 66
2573 *HOPKINS*, Howard H (Dr), *DOWNEY*, Maggie M, of Wm, Septr 1 1869, 66
2574 *HOUCK*, James, of Ezra, *CRAMER*, Alice, Octr 14 1869, 66
2575 *HOGG*, John Kunkel, of Sam'l R, *MEYER*, Lizzie W, of Geo, Nov 11 1869, 66
2576 *HILDEBRAND*, Samuel T, *SHAFER*, Matilda, Decr 7 1869, 66

2577 HARE, John J, of Balto, FROMKE, Matilda D, of August, Decr 16 1869, 66
2578 HAUGH, Addison G, GROSSNICKEL, Penelope A, of D'l, March 3 1870, 66
2579 HEPBURN, John Marshall, LIDAY, Charlotte (Mrs), "HARDT" "ALLEN" of Geo H, June 14 1870, 66
2580 HARDING, Lewis D, BARRICK, Ella A, Septr 1 1870, 66
2581 HOOPER, Oscar, of Wm, SCHROYER, Mary, Octr 27 1870, 66
2582 HEIM, Charles G, of Jacob B, NICODEMUS, Bessie, Nov 23 1870, Balto, 66
2583 HAYDEN, James E, ZIELER, Anna L, of John D, Nov 24 1870, 66
2584 HOOPER, Wm H, of Ab'm/2d wife, SMITH, Frances R, of Christ'n, Feby 21 1871, 66
2585 HALLER, Daniel G, of Dan'l, CORNELL, Georgie A, Feby 22 1871, Iowa, 66
2586 HOYT, Wm Sprague, CHASE, Nettie, of Judge S P CHASE, March 23 1871, 66
2587 HAINES, Francis R, of Carroll Co, SMITH, Mary Virginia, of John, April 11 1871, 66
2588 HOPWOOD, Francis Tho's, of James, REMSBURG, Kate A C, April 20 1871, 66
2589 HALLER, Charles E, of Jacob, ECKSTEIN, Annie M, of Chr'n, April 26 1871, 66
2590 HOLMES, Sam'l A, NEVINS, Mollie, June 1 1871, Jerseyville, Illinois, 66
2591 HOPKINS, James H, of Pittsburgh, SCHISSLER, Anna Margret, of Hiram, Octr 19 1871, 66
2592 HOUFF, Charles J, "A Bohemian", ROTHENHOEFFER, Catherine, Nov 21 1871, 66
2593 HANSHEW, Daniel Stover, of H'y, BENNETT, Eleanora, Decr 20 1871, 66
2594 HARTMAN, Valentine, HAMILTON, Annie E, of John, April 4 1872, 66
2595 HAYDON, John A, of S Carolina, MCSHERRY, Alice M, of Ja's, May 30 1872, 66
2596 HYACINTHE, Pere (Rev), MERRIMAN, Emilie J (Mrs), Augt 27 1872, in London, 66
2597 HANSHEW, Henry E, 2d wife, MARRIOTT, Lizzie, "Mary Lizzie", Septr 24 1872, 66
2598 HOKE, David, of Sam'l "HOCH", SHAFER, Hallie, of Hanson, Octr 15 1872, 66
2599 HILL, George S, WISONG, Mary D, of Geo R, Decr 18 1872, 66
2600 HANE, Frank T, BAKER, Susan C, of Woodsboro, Feb 26 1872, 66
2601 HAMILTON, Randolph, HARTMAN, Annie M, April 8 1873, 66
2602 HARSHMAN, Israel, HOOPER, Mary Cath, of Cha's, March 27 1873, 66
2603 HILL, Cornelius H, 1st wife, EICHELBERGER, Frances M, of Grayson, June 19 1873, 66
2604 HOOD, James M, 2d wife, SCHOLL, Margaret E, of Dan'l, Octr 21 1873, 66
2605 HAHN, J W, MORGART, Mattie, Octr 23 1873, 66
2606 HULL, H Clay, BARRICK, Lavinia E, of Rand J, Octr 30 1873, 66
2607 HART, Caspar J, of Jacob, EMERY, Olive P, Decr 18 1873, Cedar Rapids, Iow, 66
2608 HORINE, Carlton R, CULLER, America E, March 24 1874, 66a
2609 HAMILTON, Geo W, KELLER, Margaret, April 7 1874, 66a
2610 HILDT, Geo C, son of Rev Geo, THOMAS, Katie, of Lewis M, Apl 14 1874, 66a
2611 HIMES, John A (Prof), HAY, Mary Jane, of Rev Ch A, June 30 1874, 66a
2612 HECK, H Ridgely, of John, HILTON, Lovetto C, of H'y K, Sep 16 1874, 66a
2613 HEIM, Wm G, BAY, Fannie, Nov 10 1874, Balto, 66a
2614 HOOPER, John H, of Tho's, WATERS, Alice V, Nov 26 1874, 66a
2615 HARGETT, Francis A, GOSNELL, Kate C, Decr 24 1874, Balt, 66a
2616 HAHN, Henry A, ZIMMERMAN, Anna M, of Wm H, Jan 13 1875, 66a
2617 HARDING, Marshall F, of James M, SMITH, Clara C, Feb 7 1875, 66a
2618 HADDAWAY, S W (Rev), THOMPSON, Mollie, Feb 24 1875, 66a
2619 HARRISON, Wm H, 2d wife, HOWARD, Caroline M, May 27 1875, 66a
2620 HOKE, George, of Sam'l "HOCH", BROSS, Barbara C A, June 22 1875, 66a
2621 HEFRON, Nathaniel, aged 17, LLOYD, Maggie, aged 16, July 5 1875, 66a
2622 HEYSER, Lewis F, MAIN, Nettie, July 8 1875, 66a

2623 HOTTEL, F B, MANTZ, Emma, of Cha's, Nov 17 1875, 66a
2624 HARRINGTON, Adolphus H, BAER, Kate, Decr 23 1875, 66a
2625 HEIM, Daniel L, WASKEY, Catharine, Decr 16 1875, 66a
2626 HOFFMAN, Wm O, HARDING, Ardene, of O P, Jan 5 1876, 66a
2627 HOOPER, Wm H, of Ab'm/3d wife, ZIMMERMAN, Susan E (Mrs), Feb 1 1876, 66a
2628 HALLER, John P (Rev), of David H, WINE, Laura V, Mar 1 1876, NJ, 66a
2629 HUBBARD, Alexander J, 2/d wife, CARSON, Lyle, May 25 1876, Balt, 66a
2630 HAMILTON, James D, of Venango Co, Pa, JAMES, Julia A C, July 25 1876, 66a
2631 HARGETT, Schaeffer T, of Sam'l, RIZER, Maggie, of Geo H, Sep 26 1876, 66a
2632 HARDY, Hamilton S, THOMPSON, Eleanora V, Octr 2 1876, 66a
2633 HARGETT, Simeon W, GRIFFIN, Mahala C, Octr 1876, 66a
2634 HUGHES, Eugene, ORDEMAN, Emma C, of Capt H D, Nov 21 1876, 66a
2635 HAY, Edwin B, BROWN, Florence, of B F, Decr 21 1876, 66a
2636 HALLER, James S, of Dan'l, RAMKEY, Sophia, Decr 21 1876, Cal'a, 66a
2637 HALLER, Silas L, KOHLENBERG, Emma R, Decr 27 1876, 66a
2638 HARGETT, Luther F, RENN, Emma Frorence, March 29 1877, 66a
2639 HOWARD, James W, MORNINGSTAR, Annie, April 26 1877, 66a
2640 HARGETT, Douglas G, of Sam, WHIP, Emma M, of Geo T, May 22 1877, 66a
2641 HARGETT, Charles E, WILLARD, Cordelia, Octr 9 1877, 66a
2642 HOLMES, Wm F, HULSEMANN, Elizab M, of B H, Decr 26 1877, 66a
2643 HOLBRUNNER, Charles W, CORRICK, Annie S, Jan 3 1878, 66a
2644 HOUCK, D Edward, KEMP, Jennie, of Dan'l S, Jan 23 1878, 66a
2645 HALLER, Nicholas, (of Tobias), MCCLELLAND, Leora, March 6th 1878, 66a
2646 HABERKERN, John L, SHEFFLER, Emeline, March 5th 1878, 66a
2647 HALLER, Wm T, ECKSTEIN, Louisea E, March 25th 1878, 66a
2648 HARDT, Wm Mc, KELLER, Mary Ida, Oct 9 1878, 66a
2649 HOTZ, Charles E, HEFNER, Fannie, Dec 24 1878, both this place, 66a
2650 HILL, C H, 2/d wife, MCGILL, S K, Augt 7th 1879, 66b
2651 HAUER, J Fisher, 1st wife, ROWE, Clara M, Aug 21st 1879, 66b
2652 HALLER, Oscar L, WOODWARD, Cora V, Sept 25 1879, 66b
2653 HORN, Lewis, STRAFFER, Olivia, Sept 23d 1879, 66b
2654 HAHN, Lewis E, OTT, Ada D, Nov 5th 1879, 66b
2655 HEFFNER, John P, 2d wife, RISE, Sarah A (Mrs), Nov 18th 1879, 66b
2656 HERSHBERGER, Tilghman T, THOMAS, Belvae, of John B/(not listed as Miss), April 29th 1880, 66b
2657 HILL, Noah, KING, Jane, of Henry (not listed as Miss), May 13th 1880, 66b
2658 HAGAN, Cha's M C, of Michael, RENNER, Elizabeth, (not listed as Miss), Dec 30th 1880, 66b
2659 HEARD, Wm K, OVERTON, Ella M, (not listed as Miss), April 23rd 1881, 66b
2660 HILTNER, Wm, SIX, Adelia, (@ Adalaine), September 9th 1881, 66b
2661 HALLER, Frank B, of Nich, ECKLES, Grace M, of Chamb'g, Nov 16 1881, 66b
2662 HALLER, Joseph C, of Tobias, VANFOSSEN, Clara V, January 4th 1882, 66b
2663 HALLER, Thomas H, BOWERS, Cora E, of J'm, January 4 1882, 66b
2664 HEFFNER, William A, (@HAFFNER), GERLACK, Annie M (Mrs), April 4th 1882, 66b
2665 HENDRICKSON, John D, HUNT, Louisa Alice, May 2d 1882, 66b
2666 HOUCK, Charles E, BUESING, Etta C, of Wm H, Oct 25th 1882, 66b
2667 HAUER, J Fisher, 2d wife, FRAZIER, Jennie R, of Luther/(@ Virginia R), Nov 7th 1882, 66b

2668 HEMP, Clayton R, NOTNAGLE, Louisa, of Joh J, Dec 20t 1882, 66b
2669 HOOD, Marion E, CRAWFORD, Emma F, March 20 1883, 66b
2670 HAGAN, Eugene M, of John, GRUMBINE, Rosa C, April 18t 1883, 66b
2671 HANN, R F, WOODWARD, Ida E M, of Alex, July 5 1883, 66b
2672 HAUER, Fritchie H, of George, CLABAUGH, Susie E, Dec 19th 1883, 66b
2673 HARDING, John B (Rev), 2 wife, TRAIL, Annie M, of Col C E, Jan 3 1884, 66b
2674 HALLER, David E, of Michael/2 wife, WEBSTER, Rosa A, December 26 1883, 66b
2675 HAHN, Wm H, HOBBS, Mary A, April 9t 1884, 66b
2676 HAFER, Cha's M, (@ Charles N HAHN), SAWYER, Ida A, May 1 1884, 66b
2677 HAFER, Cha's H D, STALEY, Naomi M, June 17 1884, 66b
2678 HOFFMAN, Joseph K, KREH, Mary C, (@ Mollie), June 26 1884, 66b
2679 HOWARD, James M, YASTE, Jane, August 12 1884, 66b
2680 HAYDEN, William, MICKEY, Katie M, Sept 6 1884, 66b
2681 HAUER, Geo Wm, KEMP, A Bella, Sept 11th 1884, 66b
2682 HARRISON, Luther F, MOBERLY, Mary M, of Cha's, April 28 1885, 66b
2683 HALL, Ralph G, KOLB, Sophie M A, January 26 1886, 66b
2684 HAGAN, Norman B H, HOCKENHEIMER, Sadie A, January 27 1886, 66b
2685 HOUCK, Edwin S, HAMMITT, Julia B, (# Susan B), July 21 1886, 66b
2686 HOFF, John J, (@ HOUFF), TOBBINS, Katie E, September 14 1886, 66b
2687 HOWE, Wm E, DIXON, Lilly C, September 24 1886, 66b
2688 HULL, Wm H, BURUCKER, Ida, of John S, October 12 1886, 66b
2689 HERSHBERGER, John, (@ HERSPERGER), HOOPER, Mary K, January 6 1887, 66b
2690 HALLER, Grant L, of Nicholas, SCHRECK, Mary L, January 19th 1887, 66b
2691 HUNEBERG, W B, BULFIELD, Lydia H, of Rev H, March 17 1887, 66b
2692 HEIMS, Maurice H, HOOPER, Laura E, April 10 1887, 66b
2693 HAGAN, Henry J D, BEST, Lydia E, April 27 1887, 66b
2694 HEFNER, Philip, (@ HEEFNER), MOBERLY, Mary O, (May A), May 6 1887, 66c
2695 HAMIL, Henry P (Rev), JONES, Sallie, July 27 1887, 66c
2696 HEFNER, Eugene, of Julius/(@HAFNER), JACOBS, Rosa, September 4 1887, 66c
2697 HULL, C Elmer, HAINES, Annie, November 27 1887, 66c
2698 HILTON, Wm H, KIMMELL, Emma M, January 3 1888, 66c
2699 HARTSOCK, Wm, VANHORN, Annie, January 31 1888, 66c
2700 HEDGES, Samuel H, DULL, Annie M, of H'y, February 29 1888, 66c
2701 HUNTON, Tho's, of Salvation Army, SHIPLEY, Maggie, April 2 1888, 66c
2702 HARGETT, Edward S, WERKIN, Catherine E, April 3 1888, 66c
2703 HARTSOCK, Cha's T, STIMMELL, Mary L, April 11 1888, 66c
2704 HARRIS, Martin E, BELL, Laura, (@ Laura Bell MAIN), May 19 1888, 66c
2705 HENNEY, Edward, (@HERRING), STAUB, Cora L, May 19 1888, 66c
2706 HALLER, Arthur N, LEASE, Maggie V, (@ Margaret), May 19 1888, 66c
2707 HEWES, Cha's K, BRANDENBURG, Mary E, May 23 1888, 66c
2708 HOOD, Wm E, SHIPLEY, Hattie, May 23 1888, 66c
2709 HAUSER, Paul, 2d wife, MAHONEY, Effie A, Sept 11 1888, 66c
2710 HOUSE, George C, RAMSBURG, Lillie M, October 30 1888, 66c
2711 HOUCK, Thomas, (@ Thomas Theodore), SHOEMAKER, Mary S E, Nov 28 1888, 66c
2712 HOLDCRAFT, John, MEHRLING, Ella, of Casper, Nov 29 1888, 66c
2713 HOES, Russell R, GOUVENIR, Rose Di C, Dec 5 1888, 66c
2714 HOOVER, Allen D, FISHER, Grace J, (@Clara Ida), February 13 1889, 66c

2715 HILDEBRAND, Frank T, BENNETT, Anne M, of John, February 15 1889, 66c
2716 HAUER, Cha's N, FILBY, C Lizzie, March 23 1889, 66c
2717 HARTSOCK, Clarence L, MATHIAS, Etta, June 5 1889, 66c
2718 HOOPER, Elmer, (@Almo), ALBAUGH, Blanche, June 5 1889, 66c
2719 HYATT, George W, WHALEN, Lonie C, Septr 3 1889, 66c
2720 HARDING, Bruce, (@Norman Bruce), SMITH, Ann L, Septr 5 1889, 66c
2721 HAMMOND, John D, SIMPSON, Julia A, October 15 1889, 66c
2722 HOKE, George B, GITTINGER, Ella C, (@GITTINGS), November 25 1889, 66c
2723 HEDGE, Christian E, (@Clinton E), SHAW, Estella, December 25 1889, 66c
2724 HIGHTMAN, Frank, STEIN, Amie, December 26 1889, 66c
2725 HELFENSTEIN, Ernest (Rev), NELSON, Grace F, April 8 1890, 66c
2726 HOUGHTON, Cha's S, CASTLE, Birdie B, April 15 1890, 66c
2727 HORINE, Martin L, HIGHTMAN, Mary E, June 26 1890, 66c
2728 HILDEBRAND, Cha's R, WHITMORE, Mermelta, August 28 1890, 66c
2729 HOATS, Morris, NELSON, Nora J, Nov 12 1890, 66c
2730 HUFFER, Cha's S, HIGHTMAN, Jennie, of Jos, Dec 23 1890, 66d
2731 HARP, M D, ADAMS, Ada C, of R J, Dec 24 1890, 66d
2732 HARSHMAN, W W (Prof), ROWE, May, Dec 30 1890, 66d
2733 HAFFNER, Elmer, SULCER, Florence, (not listed as Miss), Dec 31st 1890, 66d
2734 JOHNS, John (Rev), 1st wife, JOHNSON, Julianna, of Col Baker, Nov 21 1820, 68
2735 JORDAN, Lewis, GENZEN, Elizabeth, (GENSLEY)/(not listed as Miss), March 20 1821, 68
2736 JARBOE, Alexander H, GROVER, Theresa, Jany 8 1822, 68
2737 JOHNSON, Worthington, of Col Baker, POTTS, Mary, of Rich'd, May 14 1822, 68
2738 JOHNSON, Cha's D W, MCKONKEY, Eliza, May 23 1822, Harford Co, 68
2739 JOHNSON, Wm, of Col Baker, DORSEY, Maria, Septr 17 1822, 68
2740 JAMISON, Henry M, BARRETTE, Exile, Jany 6 1824, 68
2741 JONES, John, MARSHALL, Hannah, April 25 1824, 68
2742 JACKSON, David, ROBERTSON, Mary (Mrs), (David MANTZ), April 7 1825, 68
2743 JOHNSON, Thomas (Major), COST, Catharine, of Elias, May 9 1826, NY, 68
2744 JOHNSON, John, ENGLISH, Isabella, of Rich'd, July 20 1824, 68
2745 JEFFERSON, Hamilton, KOONTZ, Ann Sophia, of Henry, Decr 7 1826, 68
2746 JAMISON, Joseph, COOMBS, Martha Ann, July 26 1827, 68
2747 JONES, Henry, 1st wife, HAMMOND, Catharine, Decr 6 1827, (Colored friends), 68
2748 JOHNSON, Wm S, of Kentucky, MILLER, Rebecca, of Dr J Sam'l, July 29 1828, 68
2749 JOHNSON, Cha's W (Dr), of Col Baker, TYLER, Eleanor M, Octr 21 1828, 68
2750 JENKINS, Wm (Rev), EULISS, Mary, March 1829, Duck River, Tenn, 68
2751 JARBOE, John, HAYS, Elizabeth (Mrs), June 18 1829, 68
2752 JOHNSON, Tho's W (Dr), 2d wife, DALRYMPLE, Eleanora (Mrs), Decr 1830, 68
2753 JAMES, Washington, HALLER, Catharine, of Jacob, Augt 7 1831, 68
2754 JACKSON, Andrew (Junior), YORKE, Sarah, Nov 24 1831, 68
2755 JACOBS, George W, of Philip, HAMILTON, Ann, (EVITT), April 19 1835, 68
2756 INISHWILLER, H, (* Henry ERNSPWILLER), ZIMMERMAN, Ann E, of John, Octr 27 1835, Emmittsburg, 68
2757 JONES, Morris J, HACK, Mary Ann, May 2 1837, Balto, 68
2758 JAMISON, Henry M, 2d wife, HOLMES, Mary A, Augt 22 1837, 68
2759 JOHNS, John (Rev DD), 2d wife, SCHAAFF, Margaret Jane, of Dr, July 17 1838, 68
2760 JONES, Aubury, 2d wife, BOYD, Mary, of David, Jany 3 1839, 68

2761 INGMAN, Ambrose, BUCKEY, Catharine Louisa, of John, June 25 1839, 68
2762 JOHNSON, Geo H, FUNDENBURG, Juliann, Octr 31 1839, 68
2763 JONES, Henry, 2d wife, TOOGOOD, Mary, Augt 27 1840, (Colored friends), 68
2764 INGMAN, Mahlon, NOLAND, Mary, (TURNER), Septr 24 1840, 68
2765 JARBOE, Henry J, FLOOK, Eveline E, of Jacob, Nov 12 1840, 68
2766 JONES, Thomas, SPIELMAN, Sarah E, April 4 1841, 68
2767 JOHNSON, Wm Francis, WELSH, Elizabeth, May 17 1842, 68
2768 JOHNSON, Worthington R, of Worth, GRAHAME, Ann R, of Tho's J, June 18 1844, 68
2769 JOHNSON, Cha's W, (of Erasmus JANSEN), NEWPORT, Sarah M, of Adam, Nov 18 1844, 68
2770 JOHNSTON, Robert, MARKELL, Mary, of John, Nov 28 1844, 68
2771 JONES, Joshua (Dr), JONES, Ann (Mrs), Augt 26 1845, 68
2772 JOHNSON, Baker A, HUGHES, Victoria A, Oct 12 1846, 68
2773 JACOBS, Michael J, CELAPHANE, Matilda, of Joshua, Nov 25 1846, 68
2774 JONES, Joseph Chas, of Rev Jos H, SHIPMAN, Elizab Jane, "FISCHER", July 29 1847, 68
2775 JUDY, Francis L, GANZAU, Margaret, "GONSO", June 26 1848, 68
2776 JUDY, Wm A, WHITTER, Ann E, of Tho's, Octr 10 1848, 69
2777 JOHNSON, James T (Dr), MOBBERLY, Anna, of Dr Eldred W, Septr 21 1848, 69
2778 JONES, Jos H Claggett, of Rev Jos H, SMITH, Sallie, Decr 24 1848, King and Queen Co, Va, 69
2779 JOHNSON, Rich'd Potts (Dr), of Worth, TAYLOR, Betty Leigh, of Griffin, April 17 1850, 69
2780 IJAMS, Richard, MUSSEETER, Eliza A, Decr 12 1850, 69
2781 JONES, William H, WARFIELD, Annie M, of Suratt D, Feby 11 1851, 69
2782 JOHNSON, Bradley Tyler, of Dr Cha's W, SAUNDERS, Jeannie C, of Romulus/NC, June 25 1851, 69
2783 JOHNSON, Ross, of Worth, HAMMOND, Maria L, Augt 12 1851, 69
2784 JOHNSON, Zachariah, KEPHART, Susan R, of Peter, Augt 15 1851, 69
2785 JOHNSON, David, CROMWELL, Ellen, of Philemon, June 10 1852, 69
2786 JAMISON, Sylvester Baker, BENTZ, Elizabeth, of John, Feby 1 1853, 69
2787 JARBOE, John S W, KEEFER, Ellen S, of Jacob, Nov 16 1853, 69
2788 JONES, John R, ANDERSON, Lavinia, of Aden, May 15 1853, 69
2789 JONES, William H, MOORE, Rachel L, of Geo, May 25 1853, 69
2790 JONES, William T, WATERS, Achsah D, June 29th 1853, 69
2791 JOHNSTON, Leonidas, BRENGLE, Rachel E, of Nicholas, Nov 1 1853, 69
2792 JACOBS, Benjamin L, of Corbin, HOUCK, Catharine S, of Ezra, Decr 14 1853, 69
2793 JENKINS, Geo W, MANNSTAEDT, Catharine T, of Cha's, April 18 1854, Balt, 69
2794 JUNKER, John, BLUMENAUER, Cath (Mrs), widow of Henry, June 4 1854, 69
2795 JOHNSON, Wm T, HOWARD, Hulda M, Nov 1 1854, 69
2796 JENKINS, Martin Luther, of Rev Wm, FERRELL, Martha Ann, Decr 7 1854, "Tennessee", 69
2797 JOHNSON, Samuel, REIFSCHNEIDER, Sarah Jane, Mar 1 1855, "Carroll Co", 69
2798 JOY, George R, HOFFMAN, Ellen E, April 10 1855, "Jefferson", 69
2799 JOHNSON, George (Dr), of Worth'g, CRAWFORD, Emily, April 19 1855, Phila, 69
2800 JONES, J R, (Landon Academy)/(* John R), BRASHEAR, S L, (*S Louisa), May 22 1855, 69
2801 JONES, Philip R, MANTZ, Anna C (Mrs), widow of Milton/"MARKEY", Septr 11 1855, Balto, 69
2802 JONES, Cha's Joseph, of Rev Jos H/2d wife, CLARK, Elizab Jane, Sept 30 1855, Calloway Co, MO, 69

2803 JOHNSON, Thomas R, *BRASHEAR*, Mary C, of Tho's C, Octr 4 1855, 69
2804 JOHNSON, DeWitt Clinton, of Dr Tho's W, *DALL*, Lydia A, of John R, Septr 16 1856, 69
2805 JACLARD, Augustus P, 1st wife, *GIBSON*, Caroline G, NY, Feby 22 1857, 69
2806 JOHNS, John (Rev DD), 3d wife, *SOUTHGATE*, Angeuna E (Mrs), Va, July 14 1857, 69
2807 JOY, Hezekiah, *COOKE*, Mary Ann E, Nov 26 1857, "Jefferson", 69
2808 JOHNSON, John S, *RICE*, Alverta, of Levin, Jany 18 1858, "Harmony", 69
2809 JONES, David T, 2d wife, *REICH*, Mary C, of Philip, March 4 1858, 69
2810 IJAMS, Jacob W, *HOWARD*, Annie M, of Ohio, Decr 23 1858, Balto, 69
2811 JACKLARD, Augustus P, 2d wife, *LEE*, Harriett S, NY, March 6 1859, 69
2812 JOHNSON, Geo H, 2d wife, *WEIRMAN*, Hannah Rose (Mrs), May 12 1859, Mechanickstown, 69
2813 IDE, E Louis (Prof), (* Ernst Henry Cha's), *WOODWARD*, Sally A E, of Baldwin, Septr 7 1859, 69
2814 IDE, Ernst Henry Chas, *MAIN*, Charlotte Cath, Septr 7 1859, 69
2815 JACOBS, Adam L, *LEASE*, Jemima, Decr 27 1859, 69
2816 JOHNSON, John D (Dr), of Va, *MANTZ*, Isabella, of Cha's, Nov 21 1860, 69
2817 ILER, Andrew Jackson, *ALBAUGH*, Sarah Susan, Feby 7 1861, 69
2818 JENKS, W R C, *SCHLEY*, Susan S, of David, April 2 1861, in Indianna, 70
2819 JAMES, Joshua H, *BAKER*, Mary S, April 15 1861, 70
2820 JONES, Benjamin, of Balto, *CRUM*, Susan E, of Isaac/"LEVY", Jany 20 1862, 70
2821 JENKINS, Thomas, *FITZSIMMONS*, Sophia, Feby 25 1862, 70
2822 JONES, Wm H, *MILLER*, Virginia A R, of Jacob T C, Nov 2 1862, 70
2823 JOY, Geo R, 2d wife, *HARGETT*, Ann Eliza, Decr 18 1862, 70
2824 JACOBS, Philip A, *WINDBIGLER*, Laura J, Jany 1 1863, 70
2825 IRVIN, Washington B, *FINK*, Lizzie, March 19 1863, Middletown, 70
2826 JAMES, Wm H, of Washington, *ALBAUGH*, Emma Jane, of Solomon, Septr 24 1863, 70
2827 JAMES, Emmanuel C, *STRAUSBERGER*, Ada J, Decr 28 1863, 70
2828 JOHNSTON, Gershom D, *MCCAHAN*, Mary C, of George, June 29 1864, Balto, 70
2829 JOHNSON, Tho's Roger, *DAVIS*, Miss, of James L/(*Elizabeth), Septr 7 1864, 70
2830 JONES, Allen A, *MCLEAN*, Mary F B, of Cha's, March 8 1865, 70
2831 JONES, A Sherridan (Prof), of Ohio, *ROSZ*, Mary Barbara, "ROSS", Octr 12 1865, 70
2832 JOHNSTON, Henry E, *LANE*, Harriett, Presit BUCHANAN Niece, Jany 11 1866, 70
2833 JONES, Edward, of Liberty/2d wife, *ZOLLICHOFFER*, Carrie S, of Rev D'l, May 9 1866, 70
2834 JONES, Harvey E, of Aubury, *CAMPBELL*, Jennie, in Winchester, Va, Decr 20 1866, 70
2835 JOHNS, Arthur Shaaff, of Rev John, *POTTS*, Eleanor, of Geo M, Octr 15 1867, 70
2836 JENKINS, Edward Austin, *LOWE*, Adelaide Victoire, "Enoch LOUIS", Octr 16 1867, 70
2837 JONES, Maurice, *HOKE*, Rebecca, of Sam'l "HOCH", Feby 11 1868, 70
2838 JOHNSON, Otis, *READ*, L E C, April 16 1868, in Cumberland, 70
2839 JOHNSON, Tho's W, of Worthington R, *EYLER*, Laura, Nov 9 1868, Woodsboro, 70
2840 JOHNSON, Eugene A, son of Cha's W "JANSEN", *SCHEFFLER*, Margaret C, Jany 20 1869, 70
2841 JOHNSON, John, *GREEN*, Mary C, May 31 1869, 70
2842 JONES, Alexander, *WILLIAMS*, Susan, Feby 3 1870, 70
2843 JOURDAN, Charles H (Prof), *DIELMAN*, Addie J, of Prof Henry, July 6 1871, Mt St Mary, 70
2844 JONES, Spencer Cone, of Rev Jos H, *BREWER*, Ellen, Decr 21 1871, 70
2845 JONES, George Francis, of Balto, *KESSLER*, Ida V, of Lloyd A, Jan 30 1872, 70

2846 *JONES*, Wm H, *BIGGS*, Elizabeth M, April 14 1874, 70
2847 *JONES*, Joseph, of NJ, *RITTER*, Rose, of J Alfred, Jan 5 1875, 70
2848 *JEFFERY*, E T, *CLARKE*, Jennie O, of Ja's C, April 21 1877, Chicago, 70
2849 *JONES*, Seth C, *COLE*, Clara V, Septr 18th 1879, 70
2850 *JAMISON*, J Vincent, *SIMMONS*, Mollie, (not listed as Miss), Feb 5th 1880, 70
2851 *JOHNSTON*, Louis, *HAMMOND*, Clara, (not listed as Miss), April 10th 1880, in Baltimore, 70
2852 *JONES*, Cha's A (Rev), "BOYD", *SMITH*, Sallie C, (not listed as Miss), Oct 4th 1881, 70
2853 *JOHNSON*, William C, of Geo, *GOUVENEUR*, Ruth M, of Sam, Dec 6th 1882, 70
2854 *JOHNSON*, J Graham, of Worthington, *SANDERSON*, Elinnor, April 17th 1883, 70
2855 *JOHNSON*, Richard P, *SCHUFF*, Emma F, (@SHUFF), April 28 1885, 70
2856 *JAMISON*, Joseph L, *BALTZELL*, Rosa, of Wm, March 4 1886, 70
2857 *JAMES*, Edward, *STALEY*, Jennie E, October 19 1886, 70
2858 *JOHNSON*, Dall, *WORTHINGTON*, Eleanor, April 26 1888, 70
2859 *JOHNSON*, Geo P, of Dr Geo, *MANSELL*, Jeabel H, Oct 17 1888, 70
2860 *JAMES*, Harry, *FRALEY*, Ella, (@Ellen), June 6 1889, 70a
2861 *JOHNSON*, Wood P, *SMITH*, Jennie, (@Fanny Virginia), April 16 1890, 70a
2862 *KOONTZ*, John, of Henry, *NORRIS*, Margaret, Octr 5 1820, 72
2863 *KEMP*, Daniel, of Henry/1st wife, *KEMP*, Harriott, of Ch'n, Jany 31 1822, 72
2864 *KEMP*, Jonathan, of Rev Peter, *SOUDER*, Miss, (*Susanna), April 1822, 72
2865 *KRAMER*, Daniel, *SCHOLL*, Maria, (of John), April 9 1822, 72
2866 *KNOX*, Samuel (Rev), 2d wife, *MCCLEERY*, Zeraiah, of H'y, April 18 1822, 72
2867 *KELLER*, Rudolph, of Jacob, *HOOPER*, Elizabeth, May 19 1822, 72
2868 *KLEISZ*, Solomon, *GRIM*, Sarah, Septr 12 1822, 72
2869 *KIMMEL*, Anthony, *JAMES*, Sydney Ann, of Dan'l, Octr 17 1822, 72
2870 *KOONTZ*, Edward, of Henry, *LILLY*, Rebecca, March 2 1823, 72
2871 *KLEIN*, Henry, of Stephen, *HARLAN*, Sarah, May 11 1823, 72
2872 *KNAUFF*, Jacob, 2d wife, *PHILLIPS*, Deborah, Septr 4 1823, 72
2873 *KOCH*, Philip, *SCHONHOLTZ*, Mary, of Fred'k, Augt 8 1824, 72
2874 *KEMP*, Peter, of Rev Peter/1st wife, *MYERS*, Elizabeth, of Rudolph, Mar 3 1825, 72
2875 *KOONTZ*, Godfrey, 1st wife, *YEAKLE*, Mary, April 10 1825, 72
2876 *KEMP*, George, *DUNN*, Barbara, July 13 1825, 72
2877 *KUHN*, Henry (Dr), *BALTZELL*, Catharine, Nov 17 1825, 72
2878 *KOONTZ*, George, *PARKS*, Margaret M, April 31 1826, 72
2879 *KNODE*, No first name given, (*John), *CRONISE*, Susan, of Henry, Feby 4 1827, 72
2880 *KEEFER*, Hiram, *HALLER*, Catharine, of Joshua, May 27 1827, 72
2881 *KEMP*, David, *LEAKIN*, Ruth, May 20 1828, 72
2882 *KENT*, Joseph (Gov), *CONTEE*, Alice Lee, July 8 1828, 72
2883 *KEMP*, Henry Junior, *TRAIL*, Amanda, Nov 4 1828, 72
2884 *KAUFFMAN*, John, *POOL*, Susan, of Walter, Jan 22 1829, 72
2885 *KOLB*, Wilson W (Dr), *HARMAN*, Margaret, of Jacob, Feby 24 1829, 72
2886 *KURTZ*, Benjamin (Rev), 2d wife, *BAKER*, Catharine, Feby 8 1830, Va, 72
2887 *KEMP*, Daniel M, *STAUFFER*, Susan M, of Jos, March 23 1830, 72
2888 *KIEFFER*, Peter, (Christian), *MILLER*, Charlotte, of John/"Hatter", May 6 1830, 72
2889 *KEHLER*, Henry Junior, *BRENGLE*, Eliza (Mrs), widow of Jacob of Ch'n, July 13 1830, 72
2890 *KEEFER*, Jacob, "Fifer", *BIGGS*, Rebecca, of Wm, July 25 1830, 72
2891 *KELLER*, Adam, *BECKENBACH*, Maria, Augt 1 1830, Middletown, 72

2892 KIEFFER, Adam, MICHAEL, Othelia, "Deutschlandt", Octr 10 1830, 72
2893 KOLB, Daniel, of Mich'l, BRENGEL, Caroline, of Jacob, Decr 24 1830, 72
2894 KETRO, George, GETZENDANNER, Catherine (Mrs), April 12 1831, 72
2895 KEMP, Daniel, of Henry/2d wife, FAHRENSTOCK, Matilda, July 19 1831, 72
2896 KREBS, Geo W, of Geo, WARNER, Maria, Septr 27 1831, Balto, 72
2897 KESSLER, Henry, 1st wife, BOSWELL, Priscilla, Feby 7 1832, 72
2898 KELLER, Michael, 4th wife, CREAGER, Margaret (Mrs), "SALMON", May 20 1832, Middletown, 72
2899 KAUFFMAN, John Henry, of Conrad, JOHNSON, Elizabeth, Septr 11 1832, Balto, 72
2900 KOSTER, Henry, ROELKE, Christianna, of John, June 16 1833, 72
2901 KNIGHT, John, BEALL, Frances, of Wm M, July 16 1833, 72
2902 KIEFFER, Nicholas, (STOFFEL), FROSCHAUER, Sophia, of Adam, Nov 16 1833, 72
2903 KLESSNER, Wm, (Cabinet maker), ENGEL, Rebecca (Mrs), Decr 26 1833, 72
2904 (KENEGE, David, DOFLER, Rebecca, of Geo, Octr 13 1818), 73
2905 (KANTNER, George, MCNAMAR, Elizabeth, Octr 25 1818), 73
2906 KIEFFER, John Henry, TITLOW, Elizabeth, of John, July 27 1834, 73
2907 KIEFFER, Jacob, (STOFFEL), STEIN, Elizabeth, "Germany", Octr 7 1834, 73
2908 KLEIN, Stephen, of Stephen, POOLE, Mary Ann, of Wm, Octr 28 1834, 73
2909 KOLB, Frederick, of Mich'l, PARKS, Susan, March 24 1835, 73
2910 KELLER, Theophilus, DOLL, Barbara, of Ja's, March 30 1835, 73
2911 KIEFFER, Michael, (STOFFEL), FAUL, Maria, (STEIN), May 31 1835, 73
2912 KNODE, Cornelius, CLAGGETT, Mary, "Washington Co", July 16 1835, 73
2913 KELLER, Jonathan, SPRINGER, Jane L, of Wm, Octr 22 1835, 73
2914 KEMP, Wm M (Dr), 1st wife, JOHNSON, Susan W, of Dr Tho's W, Jany 12 1836, 73
2915 KAUFFMAN, Henry (Jun'r), DOLL, Charlotte, of Jacob, March 31 1836, 73
2916 KELLY, James, DOFLER, Christianna, of Geo, April 12 1836, 73
2917 KOLB, Michael Grosch, of Mich'l, BELL, Ann, Balto, April 7 1836, 73
2918 KOLB, John Michael, of Wm, HANE, Christianna C, of John, June 16 1836, 73
2919 KERSCHNER, Jonathan, MCCAHAN, Catharine, Nov 17 1836, 73
2920 KELLER, Ezra (Rev), (Springfield, Ohio), RAUZAHN, Miss, (*Caroline), April 25 1837, 73
2921 KEPLER, Henry S (Rev), HANSON, Sarah R, June 23 1837, 73
2922 KNODLE, John, 2d wife, MOIECSELL, Violetta B, of Jacob Sen'r, July 13 1837, Washington Co, 73
2923 KIEFFER, Frederick, of Sam'l, HEMBRY, Elizabeth, of Matthew, Septr 7 1837, 73
2924 KURTZ, Benjamin (Rev), 3d wife, CALHOUN, Mary, Octr 25 1837, 73
2925 KEMP, Peter, of Rev Peter/2d wife, DUTROW, Eliza, Feby 13 1838, 73
2926 KOLB, William, of Wm, FOUT, Catharine (Mrs), widow of Otho, March 29 1838, 73
2927 KEALHOFER, George, HAHNENKAMPF, Mary Elizabeth, Hagerstown, May 1838, 73
2928 KEHLER, Frederick, (KELLY) of Henry, ELKINS, Margaret, of Wm, Decr 31 1838, 73
2929 KEAFAUVER, Jacob, COBLENTZ, Leonora, Jany 31 1839, Middletown, 73
2930 KEYSER, Jacob, ZIMMERMAN, Catharine, of Ch'n, March 14 1839, 73
2931 KOHLHAAS, Frederick, MARTIN, Jane, June 18 1839, 73
2932 KENNEDY, John W, MCPHERSON, Mary E, of Dr Wm S, Septr 19 1839, 73
2933 KING, Rufus, MOBBERLY, Amanda Elizab, Octr 28 1839, 73
2934 KEEFER, Michael, of Ch'n, WARFIELD, Catharine A, Octr 29 1839, 73
2935 KAUFFMAN, Warner, of Henry, LITTLE, Harriett Ann, of Jacob, Nov 10 1839, 73
2936 KILLIAN, Philip, HOOPER, Miss, of John/(*Ann Eliza), Decr 24 1839, 73

2937 KIRBY, Charles A, Balto, *NILES*, Ann Sophia, of Wm Ogden, June 18 1840, 73
2938 KEMP, John, *LAKINS*, Martha A M, June 4 1840, 73
2939 KLEIN, Peter, *STRAEFFER*, Henrietta, Septr 17 1840, 73
2940 KELLER, Cha's F, 1st wife, *EADER*, Susan, of Thomas, Septr 30 1840, 73
2941 KREIDLER, James H, *ENGLES*, Catharine, Decr 3 1840, 73
2942 KROHN, Conrad, (*Conrad CRONE), *KARN*, Miss, (*Eliza Ann), Decr 17 1840, Burkitsville, 73
2943 KLEIN, Daniel, of Stephen, *MILLER*, Ann, Feby 23 1841, 73
2944 KELLER, Jacob, of Adam, *EADER*, Jane, of Wm, March 14 1841, 73
2945 KRUMBEIN, Daniel M, *SHAFER*, Mary Ann, of Jacob, June 10 1841, 73
2946 KETROW, Henry, *MAYHEW*, Keziah, May 20 1841, 74
2947 KIDWELL, Henry, *FISH*, Henrietta, June 15 1841, Manor, 74
2948 KONIG, Conrad, (KING), *HERRINGTON*, Elizabeth, Augt 22 1841, 74
2949 KOHLENBERG, Adam, *THOMAS*, Eveline M, Nov 25 1841, Manor, 74
2950 KETLER, George, *BINGER*, Catherine (overwritten), "LANGE", May 17 1842, 74
2951 KLOTZ, James, *SPROUT*, Isabella, from Va, July 31 1842, 74
2952 KUNKEL, John Baker, *PORTER*, Deborah B, Phila, Decr 1 1842, 74
2953 KOONTZ, Godfrey, 2d wife, *EADER*, Ann Maria (Mrs), "HARMAN", May 28 1843, 74
2954 KRAUTH, Charles Porterfield (Rev), *REYNOLDS*, Susan, Nov 12 1844, Balto, 74
2955 KING, Henry, "KONIG", *BURG*, Caroline, of Philip, Nov 7 1844, 74
2956 KIEFFER, Dennis P, of Peter, *DORFF*, Sophia, of Geo, Decr 19 1844, 74
2957 KRAUTH, Frederick K, *SHERWOOD*, Mary J, NY, March 10 1845, 74
2958 KESSELRING, George, *BECKENBACH*, Mary A, May 20 1845, 74
2959 KEYSER, Benjamin, *ZIEGLER*, Frederika, March 24 1846, 74
2960 KRANTZ, John D, *HAGAN*, Mary A, May 12 1846, 74
2961 KREH, John, *KUHNE*, Christianna, "KING", Septr 8 1846, 74
2962 KEMP, William, *STOCKMAN*, Susan, Octr 15 1846, 74
2963 KELLER, Charles J, of Frederick of Conrad, *MORGAN*, Mary C, May 4 1847, Indianna, 74
2964 KOLB, Frederick, of Michael/2d wife, *STUB*, Lydia Ann (Mrs), Decr 31 1846, 74
2965 KILLITTZ, Herrman, *HENDERSON*, Deborah, of Rob't, Septr 16 1847, 74
2966 KELLER, Benjamin H, of Jacob, *BUFFINGTON*, Kate A, Decr 26 1847, 74
2967 KUNKEL, Jacob M, *MCELFRESH*, Anna Mary, of John H, Jany 3 1848, fortune $80,000, 74
2968 KEMP, Wm H C, *KRAMER*, Ann Rebecca, Feby 8 1848, 74
2969 KEMP, Wm M (Dr), 2d wife, *AMELUNG*, Emma, April 11 1848, 74
2970 KELLER, Frederick H, of Jacob, *SMALL*, Mary, of Wm "SHOE", April 10 1848, 74
2971 KOONTZ, Henry, of John/1st wife, *MELCHING*, Margaret, Septr 7 1848, 74
2972 KEEFER, Theodore P, *SAUNDERS*, Eliza, of Walter, Septr 12 1848, 74
2973 KELLER, John H, *KOONTZ*, Minerva, of Geo, Sepr 9 1848, 74
2974 KANN, Jacob, 1st wife, *PEISER*, Ernestine, "Jews", Octr 17 1848, 74
2975 KANTNER, John J, of J, *DOLL*, Susanna E, of David, Nov 9 1848, 74
2976 KUHL, John, *HOEFER*, Sarah, Nov 23 1848, 74
2977 KELLER, Cha's F, of Jacob/2d wife, *HUNT*, Caroline, of Rev Wm, April 26 1849, 74
2978 KERR, John Bosman (Hon), *STEVENS*, Lucy Hamilton, Octr 21 1849, 74
2979 KNAUFF, William, of Jacob, *KINGHORN*, Mary E, Balto, Decr 31 1849, 74
2980 KESSLER, Lloyd A, *HOWARD*, Mary Elizabeth, of Edward, May 7 1850, 74
2981 KEPHART, Geo R, of Peter, *WOODWARD*, Maria, of Jon, Augt 27 1850, 74

2982 KENNY, Moses S, CROMWELL, Margaret (Mrs), "SINN", Decr 11 1850, Kentucky, 74
2983 KREMER, Michael, KRAPT, Dorathea, Feby 23 1851, 74
2984 KINLEY, William, GREENTREE, Mary Elizabeth, March 25 1851, 74
2985 KLAY, William, KIEFFER, Caroline, of Geo, March 25 1851, "STOFFEL", 74
2986 KROH, Henry Ferdinand Theodore, FOX, Christine Wilhelmina, Septr 8 1851, Balto, 74
2987 KANN, Jacob (Sen'r), COHEN, Arnoldine (Mrs), Balto/"Jews", Nov 12 1851, 74
2988 KEMP, Joshua V, CRAMER, Susan D, of Jacob, July 4 1852, 74
2989 KERN, Emeleugene Davoust, HOESTER, Jeanneta Ludovike Christina, Sept 8 1852, 75
2990 KEYS, Charles, MOULDEN, Mary Ann, of Rev Dennis, Octr 12 1852, 75
2991 KELLER, Daniel, MILLER, Jane, Middletownvalley, Decr 2 1852, 75
2992 KNAUFF, Charles E, BROGUMIER, Anna Mary, of Jacob, March 29 1853, 75
2993 KRANTZ, Wm H, BEAVERS, Julia A, Loudon Co, Va, April 7 1853, 75
2994 KOPP, Wolfgang, BAUMANN, Anna B, May 16 1853, 75
2995 KENNEDY, John C, HAMMOND, M A B (Mrs), "GILLISS", May 17 1853, 75
2996 KOLB, Frederick, Woodsboro, FLAREY, Elizabeth (Mrs), June 10 1853, 75
2997 KONIG, John, (KING)/of Lewis, CISSELL, Mary E, July 21 1853, 75
2998 KAUFFMAN, John, of Conrad, DUTROW, Catharine, Octr 30 1853, 75
2999 KOONTZ, Geo S, of Geo, GASTON, Jane, Balto, Octr 18 1853, 75
3000 KOONTZ, Cha's F, CALLAHAN, Rose, Balto, Feby 19 1854, 75
3001 KEMP, Daniel M, 2d wife, BOON, Ann, March 7 1854, 75
3002 KREH, Lewis, FALK, Eva M, June 5 1854, 75
3003 KEEFER, John, of Sam'l, REAGAN, Jane A, June 15 1854, 75
3004 KUNKEL, Philip H, of John, PYFER, Ann C, of Philip, Septr 14 1854, 75
3005 KOSZTA, Martin, MCFALL, Lucinda M (Mrs), Chicago/"Austrian", Decr 12 1854, 75
3006 KRAGLER, Siegmund, MUHL, Sophia, Decr 26 1854, 75
3007 KOLB, Jacob M, of Dan'l, WILSON, Emma (Mrs), "HUGHES", Feby 6 1855, Ohio, 75
3008 KINNA, William, MOTTER, M A Virginia, of John S, March 13 1855, 75
3009 KLEIN, Peter, MIESELL, Catherine Malinda, March 29 1855, 75
3010 KOREL, John, SCHARMANN, Elizabeth, Octr 28 1855, 75
3011 KEMP, Wm H, of Peter, BRENGLE, Henrietta E, of Alfred F, Decr 4 1855, 75
3012 KIEFFER, Hiram M, of Hiram, HALLER, Margaret A C, of Daniel, Decr 31 1855, 75
3013 KEMP, Stephen, of Frederick, KNAUFF, Ann, of Jacob, March 11 1856, 75
3014 KENNEDY, George T, LEONARD, Mary R, May 1856, 75
3015 KOONTZ, Henry, of John/2d wife, WAGNER, Margaret C, May 25 1856, 75
3016 KLINK, John D, GRIMES, Millie, Johnsville, June 5 1856, 75
3017 KAMAHAMAHA 4th, No first name given, King of Hawaii, ROOKE, Emma, "Honolulu", June 19 1856, 75
3018 KEMP, Cha's Wesley, of Peter, RHODES, Columbia A, of John, June 19 1856, 75
3019 KEISER, Samuel, RAILING, Catharine, June 19 1856, 75
3020 KNILL, William, STEIN, Charlotte, of John, Augt 11 1856, Hamburg, 75
3021 KEEFER, Wm E, of Hiram, LEWIS, Susan C, of Wm D, Augt 19 1856, 75
3022 KONIG, Cha's F R, (KING)/of Lewis, MIX, Louisa E, Septr 25 1856, 75
3023 KEMP, Cha's L, of Col Lewis, BRENGLE, Elizabeth C, of Lawrence J, Nov 26 1856, 75
3024 KLEIN, Joseph T, of Jonathan, KIEHNE, Caroline A, "KING", April 9 1857, 75
3025 KOCHLER, Wm, MILLER, Maria, June 4 1857, 75
3026 KELLER, Dewitt Clinton, of Fred'k, CARPENTER, Marcie, Indian, Decr 10 1857, 75
3027 KEEFER, Lewis H, of John Henry, CARLIN, Alverta, of James, Jany 27 1858, 75

3028 *KUHN*, Cyrus C, *GLOVER*, Cora E, Council Bluffs, Iowa, March 14 1858, 75

3029 *KENNEDY*, Joseph, of Ohio, *CLAGETT*, Kate A C, of Dr Grafton A, May 27 1858, near town, 75

3030 *KOLB*, David H, of Dr Wilson W, *SALTER*, Mary E, of Wm E, Augt 5 1858, 75

3031 *KEMP*, Lewis G, of Col Lewis/2d wife, *MILLER*, Sarah M, of Geo/"DIETRICK", Septr 14 1858, 76

3032 *KNODLE*, Josiah, Editor of the Odd Fellow/2d wife, *WELTY*, Marcella, Boonsboro, Septr 14 1858, 76

3033 *KOOGLE*, George, *KAILOR*, Mary Jane, of David, Septr 12 1858, 76

3034 *KIEFFER*, Charles H, of Hiram, *BENTZ*, Anna M, of Dan'l, Octr 19 1858, 76

3035 *KOPP*, William (Rev), *STRICKLER*, Susan, Somerset, Pa, Nov 2 1858, 76

3036 *KOST*, J K (Rev), *ALLEN*, Sallie J, Nov 2 1858, Ohio, 76

3037 *KIEHNE*, Frederick C, ("KING"), *HART*, Alice F, of Jacob, Nov 17 1858, Iowa, 76

3038 *KROHL*, Julius H, *LUCHER*, Sophia, of Francis, Nov 25 1858, Geo.town, DCa, 76

3039 *KAUFFMAN*, Joseph, *WILLIARD*, Margaret Ann, Harbachs valley, Decr 21 1858, 76

3040 *KULLING*, John (Rev), *FISCHER*, Julia, of Stuttgart, Jany 6 1859, in Phila, 76

3041 *KAY*, J W, *MCDULL*, Jennette, Feby 16 1859, 76

3042 *KING*, Jesse W, *FULMER*, Ann R, April 7 1859, 76

3043 *KOONTZ*, Henry, of Edward, *FORD*, Eveline R, April 25 1859, 76

3044 *KRAMER*, John Adam, *SCHOLL*, Serena S, of Henry of John, May 15 1859, 76

3045 *KINNA*, Thomas, *BECKENBACH*, Rebecca, Midd valley, June 12 1859, 76

3046 *KELLER*, Adam, 2d wife, *DUVALL*, A, Middletown, June 16 1859, 76

3047 *KAHENDAH*, No first name given, alias James BUCHANAN, *JEFF*, Ann Liberia, Colored, Liberia, March 17 1859, 76

3048 *KEAFAUVER*, Horatio, *GLESSNER*, Mary C, of Rev Geo W, Octr 27 1859, 76

3049 *KOOGLE*, John, *MARKER*, Rebecca, Octr 27 1859, 76

3050 *KIMMEL*, Anthony Zaarr, *MORGAN*, Mary, of Tho's W, Jany 24 1860, 76

3051 *KEECH*, Henry H (Dr), *PIGMAN*, Hattie B, Cumberland, Jany 25 1860, 76

3052 *KUHN*, Leander H, *PENNELL*, Virginia A, March 6 1860, 76

3053 *KIDD*, John C, *HOWARD*, Ann M, April 5 1860, 76

3054 *KLEIN*, Geo W, *DORSEY*, Harriet Ann, (of Clagett W DORSEY), April 5 1860, 76

3055 *KONIG*, Christian, "KING"/of Lewis, *FROSS*, Mary M, May 13 1860, 76

3056 *KEAFAUVER*, Daniel Carlton, *DUDDERER*, Molly Jane, of John, May 17 1860, 76

3057 *KLEIN*, Wm E, *ENGELBRECHT*, Mary Ann, of Mich'l, June 7 1860, 76

3058 *KAILOR*, David (Capt'n), 2d wife, *KINNA*, Mary (Mrs), Septr 26 1860, 76

3059 *KUHN*, Wm E, *FRALEY*, Lizzie, (FROLICH), Jany 3 1861, 76

3060 *KEYSER*, Philip, of Jacob, *BUCKEY*, Elizabeth, of Washington, Jany 3 1861, 76

3061 *KAUFFMAN*, Jacob H, of Henry, *SCHELL*, Mary M, of Cha's D, Feby 23 1861, 76

3062 *KENNEDY*, Daniel F, *MCLAUGHLIN*, Mary, Septr 15 1861, 76

3063 *KEATINGE*, John M, *WINTER*, Temple Ann, of Tho's, Nov 14 1861, 76

3064 *KEEFER*, Geo W, of Peter, *HEMBRY*, Mary Elizabeth, of John, Nov 20 1861, 76

3065 *KELTY*, Wm H R, *CRAMER*, Catharine S, of Philip, Decr 3 1861, 76

3066 *KELLER*, Charles E, *DEAN*, Margaret, Decr 3 1861, 76

3067 *KOEHLER*, Herrmann C, *MANN*, Josephine, of Stephen S, Feby 25 1862, 76

3068 *KESSLER*, Wm H H, *SHIPLEY*, Susan J, of Tho's, Feby 18 1862, 76

3069 *KANN*, Jacob, 2d wife, *LEWYT*, Caroline, of S H, May 18 1862, Balto/Jews, 76

3070 *KONIGSBACKER*, Solomon, *SEIFFENSIDER*, Miss, Jews, June 2d 1862, 76

3071 KOLB, William H, MARNIE, Sarah J, Augt 7 1862, 76
3072 KELLER, John J, STOCKMAN, Barbara A, Augt 28 1862, 76
3073 KELLER, Andrew M, COOK, Henrietta R, Jefferson, Octr 2 1862, 77
3074 KLEIN, Edward D, GIBBONS, Annie E, Fairview, Octr 7 1862, 77
3075 KLAARMUNN, John, SCHAAR, Rosina, Nov 10 1862, 77
3076 KNODE, Sam'l C, LANE, M Kate, Boonsboro, Decr 11 1862, 77
3077 KEMP, John Milton, HARPER, Emma, Knoxville, Jany 27 1863, 77
3078 KITTO, John T, NEAL, Eliza (Mrs), (Ezra STONER's daughter), March 24 1863, 77
3079 KAILOR, James H, WHITMORE, Mary E, Middletown, April 5 1863, 77
3080 KOLB, Nimrod Owing, of John Mich'l, LOWELL, Miss, of Wm/(*Ellen Maria), May 28 1863, 77
3081 KABLE, John J, of Va, DUDERER, Ellie V, May 28 1863, 77
3082 KELLY, John, OATES, Catharine, of John, June 23 1863, 77
3083 KIEHNE, Augustus, (KING), HECKMAN, A Sophia, Octr 15 1863, 77
3084 KNIGHT, Abel, HOUCK, Elizabeth, of George John, Nov 3 1863, 77
3085 KAUFFMAN, Martin L, MERCER, Sarah A E, Nov 4 1863, 77
3086 KEAFAUVER, Geo H, KELLER, Mary R, of Joel/Middlet, Nov 5 1863, 77
3087 KOHLENBERG, Geo Ragan, of Adam, ANDERSON, Johanna, Decr 8 1863, 77
3088 KEYSER, Cha's David, WILES, Sarah A Missouri, Jany 3 1864, 77
3089 KRAPP, Jabez, aged 83, WILLIAMS, Thankful, aged 81 (not listed as Miss), April 26 1864, Vermont, 77
3090 KEEDY, Walter H, USA, LAMBERT, Hallie A, of Fred'k, June 26 1864, 77
3091 KETZILBERGER, Geo L, DEVILBISS, Mary Catharine, Septr 1 1864, 77
3092 KOCH, Jacob, UPPERMAN, Mary E, Septr 29 1864, 77
3093 KIRKLEY, Joseph W, CRUM, Louisa M, of Isaac/"KESSLER", Octr 16 1864, 77
3094 KARH, Josephus, HORINE, Mary M, of Tobias, Decr 8 1864, 77
3095 KOONTZ, John J, HUGO, Dorothea, (RETTGERING), Jany 25 1865, 77
3096 KELLER, Joel, BECKWITH, Elizabeth, Middletown, May 18 1865, 77
3097 KEYSER, John C, HAHN, Sarah A, July 6 1865, 77
3098 KLEIN, Ephraim H, MOHLER, Margaret, of Ohio, Augt 3 1865, 77
3099 KALKLOSCHER, Zachary Taylor, KALKLOSCHER, Sarah E V, of Va, Augt 7 1865, 77
3100 KNIGHTON, Francis, MABURRY, Fannie L, of Justin, Augt 9 1865, Balto, 77
3101 KEEFER, Edward P, of Hiram, FISHER, Lucinda J, Septr 5 1865, 77
3102 KOOGLE, Geo Washington, MILLER, Clarissa E, Septr 7 1865, 77
3103 KOOGLE, Cha's W, MAIN, Amanda C, Decr 21 1865, 77
3104 KOLB, Wm Augustus, of Wm/1st wife, JONES, Maggie S, of Balto, May 26 1866, 77
3105 KILLINGSORTH, J C, of our City, PRICE, Nannie, of Harford Co, Decr 6 1866, 77
3106 KOLB, Lewis A, SCHIETENHELM, Maggie, Decr 13 1866, 77
3107 KEY, Joseph H, BALTZELL, Fannie, of Dr John, Decr 1866, at Rochester, Ny, 77
3108 KLEIN, John H, BROWN, Mary M E, March 27 1867, 77
3109 KONIGSBACKER, Samson, LOWENSTEIN, Jennie, (Jews), May 6 1867, 77
3110 KEMP, Calvin F, KINTZ, Sarah J, Augt 6 1867, 77
3111 KEMP, Abraham, aged 81/2d wife, MAIN, Rowanna R, 45, Octr 15 1867, 77
3112 KONIG, Henry, (KING)/2d wife, FLEISCHMAN, Elizabeth (Mrs), Feby 8 1868, 77
3113 KLEIN, H Thomas, of Stephen, HEMBRY, Arrabella, of John, Feby 27 1868, 77
3114 KAUFFMAN, Wesley H, ODEN, Mariann, March 18 1868, 77
3115 KREH, John, of Theodore, HESCH, Ann M M, (of Germany), Septr 17 1868, 78

3116 KRANTZ, Wm H, BOYER, Alice E, Nov 17 1868, 78
3117 KOLB, Wm Augustus, of Wm/2d wife & sisters, JONES, Mary A, of Balto, Jany 2 1869, 78
3118 KIEHNE, Lewis F, "KING", SCHOLL, M Jane, of Dennis, Feby 18 1869, 78
3119 KUSSMAUL, John, YOUNG, Carrie V, March 30 1869, 78
3120 KETLER, George F, of Geo, SEIBERT, Anna, of Geo, April 25 1869, 78
3121 KOHLENBERG, George T, of Adam, BECK, Laura V, May 19 1869, 78
3122 KNIGHT, Samuel, POOLE, Laura T, Augt 5 1869, 78
3123 KEMP, David Columbus, of David, WALCUTT, Serena S A, Nov 10 1869, Ohio, 78
3124 KIEFFER, J Spangler (Rev), CLARK, Mary M, of Harrisburg, Pa, Nov 11 1869, 78
3125 KLEIN, Nicholas O, of Caspar, KERN, Annie A (Mrs), "MICHAEL", Nov 23 1869, 78
3126 KNAUFF, Howard A, of Jacob, DIXON, Alice L, Nov 24 1869, 78
3127 KEMP, John Quincy Adams, GROVE, Annie J, of Leon'd S, Feby 1 1870, 78
3128 KEHLER, Frederick W, of Fred'k, SUMAN, Adelia, March 10 1870, 78
3129 KOLB, Valentine Brunner, of Fred'k, BENNETT, C M, March 30 1870, 78
3130 KIMBALL, Julius H, of Iowa/3d wife, MAULSBY, Emily V, of Wm P, July 19 1870, 78
3131 KIRKPATRICK, John C (Dr), CRONISE, Ella, of Joseph, Nov 22 1870, 78
3132 KARN, Lewis H, ENNIS, Mary C, Burkittsville, Nov 22 1870, 78
3133 KAUFFMAN, Edward S, MILES, Mary E, of Chambersburg, Pa, Octr 31 1870, 78
3134 KEEFER, Michael C, of Mich'l, HINKS, Mary V, of Cha's D, March 9 1871, 78
3135 KUNKEL, John J, of Jacob M, MACGILL, Mary E, of Rob't H, July 6 1871, 78
3136 KEYSER, Louis, of KEYSER & SHULL, MCGURN, Alice, July 17 1871, Kansas, 78
3137 KIRACOFE, J W (Rev), "KIRCHHOFF", BUXTON, Susan B, Augt 1871, 78
3138 KOONTZ, Edward, of Edward, ECKSTEIN, Mary C, of Christian, Oct 10 1872, 78
3139 KEMP, Wm H H, KEINS, Laura V, Feb 18 1873, Glade, 78
3140 KUNKEL, John, of J Baker, CAUSTIN, Miss, April 29 1873, Phila, 78
3141 KEMP, Wm L E, LAMBERT, Malinda A C, Octr 29 1873, 78
3142 KILLIAN, John Edward, DEBRING, Lucy M (Mrs), Jan 8 1874, 78
3143 KOLB, David, of Wm, SAYWER, Carrie V, Octr 28 1874, 78
3144 KINTZ, Wm F, KAUFFMAN, Ida A, Decr 24 1874, 78
3145 KIRK, Philip Howard, LITTLE, Nannie E, of John L, Decr 24 1874, 78
3146 KLIPP, Paul, CORNELL, Mary, Sept 12 1875, 78
3147 KLIPP, John, HART, Susan V, Octr 14 1875, 78
3148 KURTZ, Wm Newton, of T Newton, WILLIAMS, Louisa, Octr 14 1875, Balto, 78
3149 KILGOUR, John A (Rev), of J Mortimer, BEAUFORT, Fannie, Nov 1875, 78
3150 KNOTT, Columbus, CAMPBELL, Lizzie, of Abner, May 11 1876, 78
3151 KINTZ, David C, WHIP, Ida E, May 1876, 78
3152 KARN, Ezra L, MACKLEY, Mary A, Augt 1 1876, 78
3153 KELLY, John, MULLEN, Teresa, Nov 21 1876, "TAMMANY", 78
3154 KOONTZ, Samuel C, KARN, Nettie L, of Ezra L, March 29 1877, 78
3155 KEMP, J Wm, of W H Clay KEMP, HALLER, Lucie V, of Tho's, May 9 1877, 78
3156 KAUFFMAN, Clifford T, FOREMAN, Mary W, July 8 1877, 78
3157 KENNEDY, Thomas F, BURCK, Amelia P, (not listed as Miss), Feby 5th 1878, 79
3158 KETTLEWELL, Glover, HALLER, Lottie, Octr 15th 1878, 79
3159 KREH, Theodore F, STULL, Ida M, Augt 12th 1879, 79
3160 KNIGHT, Ealt, KERETZER, Cora, Septr 21th 1879, 79
3161 KINTZ, Cha's F, KEMP, A M, Sept 18th 1879, 79
3162 KILLIAN, James, STEWART, Mary, (not listed as Miss), March 1st 1880, 79

3163 KILLIAM, Wm H, BUCKEY, Laura V, of G Jacob/(not listed as Miss), Mar 25th 1880, 79
3164 KEY, William T, of St Marys, BALTZELL, Josephine, of Dr Wm H/(not listed as Miss), Nov 16th 1880, 79
3165 KUDRY, Clayton O, (@KEEDY), RITTER, Irene, of T Alfred/(not listed as Miss), Nov 24th 1880, 79
3166 KOOGLE, Carleton E, WILES, Mary, (not listed as Miss), Dec 30th 1880, 79
3167 KOONTZ, W A, HAMMOND, Hattie, of Burgess/(not listed as Miss), April 20th 1881, 79
3168 KENNEDY, John, POOLE, Lillie, (not listed as Miss), October 2d 1881, 79
3169 KOLB, Alfred B, SMITH, Alice R, November 7th 1881, 79
3170 KING, Wm, CASTLE, Annie, February 1st 1882, 79
3171 KRANTZ, Frederick, 2 wife, MEALEY, Laura V, February 22 1882, 79
3172 KREH, Charles F, SCHULTZ, Hetta, (@Henrietta), April 12th 1882, of Theodore, 79
3173 KLINE, Charles T, of Wm, YOUNG, Mary K, of David, Nov 22 1882, 79
3174 KNOCK, James H, HOLMES, Alice E, January 4 1883, 79
3175 KOONTZ, Edward, 2d wife, BUTTS, Isabella E, Dec 13th 1882, 79
3176 KOESTER, Lewis, FAUBLE, Alice, April 1st 1883, 79
3177 KEMP, L Brengle, RICHARDSON, Helen, Nov 27th 1883, 79
3178 KLINE, H Lewis, ENGELBRECHT, Florence K, of Geo, Dec 11th 1883, 79
3179 KELLER, Charles E, WEAGLEY, Vallie S, (@WAGLEY), February 6th 1884, 79
3180 KINDLEY, G Wesley, MILLER, Julia B, April 10th 1884, (GREENTREE), 79
3181 KOOGLE, Clinton M, GRUMBINE, Ida M, Oct 22 1884, 79
3182 KELLER, Edward L, MICHAEL, Hattie L, November 24 1884, 79
3183 KREH, John E, of John, BATERY, Annie, November 25 1884, 79
3184 KINTZ, Jacob, ELKINS, Missouri M, March 25 1885, 79
3185 KELLER, Willard C, GAMBRILL, Nettie, September 23 1886, 79
3186 KLOTZ, Robert, TAYLER, Maggie F, October 19 1886, Lewistown, 79
3187 KELLER, Wm H, SINN, Emma, of Ed, October 19 1886, 79
3188 KENDARD, Francis C, KIGNEY, Magy M, May 26 1887, MANTZ, 79
3189 KEEFER, Charles E, WELTY, Lucy J, of Hiram, September 1 1887, 79
3190 KEIFER, John H/(@KEEFER), of George, GROVE, Susan L, October 26 1887, 79
3191 KAUFMAN, Geo L, of John/(@KAUFFMAN), HOUCK, Fannie M, January 18 1888, 79
3192 KEMP, D L, WEANT, Sallie E, January 26 1888, 79
3193 KLING, Tho's E, MONTGOMERY, Fannie R, March 1 1888, 79
3194 KEMP, D Clinton, BRUNNER, Frances E, March 27 1888, 79
3195 KEFFER, Harry W, of Lewis H, BLENDEN, Louisea, April 26 1888, 79
3196 KOONTZ, Robert L, (@KOONS), BIRELY, Lizzie, June 13 1888, 79
3197 KEMP, Wm, WALKER, Nettie, June 13 1888, 79
3198 KEEFER, L Elmer, (@ Lewis Elmer), MANTZ, Quincey, June 27 1888, 79
3199 KEMP, C Edward, (@Charles E), NIXDORFF, Annie M, of Sam, Oct 16 1888, 80
3200 KEOHLER, Reginald, PALL, Sophie, Nov 14 1888, 80
3201 KIDD, Wm, CISIL, Ada, Dec 6 1888, 80
3202 KNOTT, John O (Rev), SINN, Rosie M, of Ed, April 2 1889, 80
3203 KLINE, John F, BIZER, Martha V, May 11 1889, 80
3204 KINTZ, Lewis, BICKHARD, Susie M, Oct 8 1889, 80
3205 KREH, Cha's, LERCH, Lizzie, (@Mary M), November 28 1889, 80
3206 KEISER, Charles, RIDENOUR, Verna, January 1 1890, 80
3207 KREIG, Jesse, (@KRIEG), PADGETT, Ruth A, February 26 1890, 80

The Joseph Engelbrecht Marriage Ledger of Frederick Co., MD 1820-1890 *Marriage List*

3208 **KING**, J Bell, **DUVALL**, Ruth, March 18 1890, 80
3209 **KEMP**, C Thomas, **SCHULTZ**, Mary M, of Theo, March 18 1890, 80
3210 **KNOCK**, Cha's F, **HILDEBRAND**, Annie E, June 11 1890, 80
3211 **KESSLER**, Thomas, **WHALEN**, Lizzie, (@Elizabeth), Sept 16 1890, 80
3212 **KREH**, Frank L A, **BARRETT**, E (Mrs), Oct 3 1890, 80
3213 **KUSSMAUL**, P Frank, **HEDGES**, Julia A, Sept 30 1890, 80
3214 **KANODE**, Jacob, **GRAZER**, Ella M, "Fair Bride"/(@GRASER), Oct 16 1890, 80
3215 **KUSSMAUL**, Lewis F, **BAUMGARDNER**, Carrie V, of Cha's, Nov 18 1890, 80
3216 **KREH**, Henry, of Lewis, **CHALMERS**, Sadie, Dec 31 1890, 80
3217 **LEWIS**, Charles (Capt), of Va, **HOFFMAN**, Ann Mary, of John, March 15 1821, "MULHEIM", 82
3218 **LLOYD**, Wm Ambrose, 2d wife, **SWAINE**, Elizabeth (Mrs), Reading, Pa, Feby 26 1822, 82
3219 **LEE**, George, **HEMMEL**, Margaret, of Jacob, Feby 11 1823, 82
3220 **LINTON**, Henry, **KAUFFMAN**, Louisa, of Henry, March 4 1823, 82
3221 **LEASE**, George (Junior), **GROVE**, Amelia, of Jacob, March 30 1823, 82
3222 **LEHMAN**, Jacob, **FROSCHAUER**, Sevilla, May 8 1823, 82
3223 **LEASE**, George, of Carlisle, Pa, **STEINER**, Mary Ann, of Jacob, May 20 1823, 82
3224 **LEASE**, William, of Geo, **KEEFER**, Rebecca, Decr 1823, 82
3225 **LAMBRECHT**, Henry, **DEVILBISS**, Catharine, "Glade", Feby 19 1824, 82
3226 **LITTLEJOHN**, John, of Geo, **WIEST**, Margaret, of John, Augt 1 1824, 82
3227 **LAMBRECHT**, Jacob, **ROWE**, Catharine, of Jacob, June 22 1824, 82
3228 **LINTON**, Henry, **PATTINGALL**, Ann, May 5 1825, 82
3229 **LITTLE**, William, **STENGER**, Wilhelmina, of Cha's, Augt 28 1825, 82
3230 **LOWE**, George, **ROSE**, Rebecca, Feby 28 1826, 82
3231 **LAMBRECHT**, John, **BIGGS**, Catharine, of Wm, Jany 25 1827, 82
3232 **LEASE**, Otho, **VANFOSSEN**, Edith, Feby 8 1827, 82
3233 **LAMBERT**, John, **SCHIEWEL**, Harriott, Jany 20 1828, 82
3234 **LUELIER**, Francis, **SIMPSON**, Helen Maria, June 3 1828, 82
3235 **LARE**, William, of Geo "LOEHR", **HULL**, Louisa, Nov 20 1828, 82
3236 **LUCKETT**, Nelson (Col), **MCGILL**, Ellen, Feby 3d 1829, 82
3237 **LEVY**, John Leonard, 2d wife, **SAUNDERS**, Sarah, of John, March 14 1830, 82
3238 **LINDSAY**, Samuel J, **ROHR**, Eleanor A, of David, April 29 1830, 82
3239 **LUGENBEEL**, Basil, **SMITH**, Sevilla, Jany 10 1832, 82
3240 **LEE**, John, of Gov Thos S, **CARROLL**, Harriott, Phila, June 5 1832, 82
3241 **LEITER**, Lawson, of Henry, **BOWLUS**, Catharine, Augt 2 1832, 82
3242 **LAMBRECHT**, Jacob, **DAYHOFF**, Nancy G, Jany 24 1833, 82
3243 **LAMBERT**, Frederick, **LAMBRECHT**, Cath E, of Mich'l, Jany 27 1833, 82
3244 **LEOPOLD**, Geo A (Rev), **ARMOUR**, Jane M, of Ja's U, Feby 21 1833, 82
3245 **LARE**, Edward, of Geo "LOEHR"/1st wife, **KELLER**, Rebecca, (of Henry T KELLER), Nov 7 1833, 82
3246 **LEILICH**, Jacob, **BLUMENAUER**, Catharine, of Geo, April 20th 1834, 82
3247 **LEASE**, Henry, (Linganore), **EADER**, Elizabeth (Mrs), July 21 1834, 82
3248 **LAMBRECHT**, Frederick, of Geo, **MILLER**, Ann Maria, Decr 21 1834, 82
3249 **LEMMEIER**, Fred'k G, **BELL**, Catharine, March 23 1835, 82
3250 **LANGE**, Constantin, **ROELKE**, Sophia, of John, Decr 8 1835, 82
3251 **LEWIS**, Wm D, **RIGDEN**, Columbia E, March 3 1836, 82
3252 **LARE**, Henry C, (LOHR), **O'NEAL**, Maria, of Hon G, Decr 7 1837, 82

3253 LIPPS, John, *RITSCHY*, Catharine, of Adam, Jany 25 1838, 82
3254 LEFEVER, John Beforegod, *HOLLODAY*, Margaret, Emmittsburg, April 6 1839, 82
3255 LYNCH, Thomas, *JOY*, Mary Ann, June 9 1839, 82
3256 LOWE, John M, "LOH", *MERMAN*, Sarah, Mrs, June 23 1839, 82
3257 LAMAR, Richard J, 1st wife, *WELSH*, Malinda, Augt 4 1839, 82
3258 LAMBERT, Joseph, *HEIM*, Mary Ann, Septr 24 1839, 82
3259 LLOYD, William, *NICHOLS*, Ann, Jany 23 1840, 83
3260 LAMAR, Benoni S, *THOMAS*, Mary C, March 10 1840, 83
3261 LONGWELL, John K, *MCKALEB*, Sarah H, Taneytown, May 7 1840, 83
3262 LEE, Tho's Lim, *O'DONNEL*, Josephine, of Balto, May 7 1840, 83
3263 LYNCH, Eugene H, *LEE*, Ellen, of Wm, July 7 1840, 83
3264 LEOPOLD, Matthias, *FINK*, Mary, Nov 26 1840, Middletown, 83
3265 LOVELY, Emanuel, *CONNOR*, Mary Ann Margt, of Tho's/(DADISMAN), Jany 10 1841, 83
3266 LEITER, Solomon, *LONG*, Elizabeth, Middletown, July 29 1841, 83
3267 LORENTZ, George, *HERBERT*, Sarah C, Octr 3 1841, 83
3268 LAMBRECHT, Philip D, *MCCARTNEY*, Jane, Octr 28 1841, 83
3269 LUCKETT, Mountjoy Bailey, *NELSON*, Nelly, of Gen'l Roger, Decr 2 1841, 83
3270 LORENTZ, Wm, *MINNICH*, Catharine Ann S, Middletown, March 24 1842, 83
3271 LEITER, Henry Junior, *GETZENDANNER*, Cath E, of Jonathan, Octr 27 1842, 83
3272 LEWIS, Sam'l, *LOWE*, Mrs, widow of John of Jacob/(*Eliza), Jany 17 1843, 83
3273 LAKIN, John H, *MYERS*, Ann Rebecca, of Israel, Feby 14 1843, 83
3274 LAMBRECHT, Perry, of Geo, *BOWERS*, Margaret, of Dan'l, May 14 1843, 83
3275 LEWIS, Samuel B, 2d wife, *WALLING*, Maria, of John, Augt 31 1843, 83
3276 LUGENBEEL, Pickney (Lieut), USA, *WILLIAMS*, Henreitta E, Detroit, Septr 5 1843, 83
3277 LEVERING, Righter, *ANDERSON*, Eugenia H (Mrs), (Fred'k KELLER of C), Mar 28 1844, 83
3278 LITTLE, Daniel, *BUTCHER*, Margaret, April 2 1844, 83
3279 LORENTZ, Henry, *ROBINSON*, Catharine, of Rev Henry, May 14 1844, 83
3280 LOWE, Enoch Louis, of Bradley, *POLK*, Esther W, of James, May 29 1844, 83
3281 LANSDALE, John, *WOODWARD*, Emma Malinda, Decr 19 1844, 83
3282 LAMAR, Richard J, 2d wife, *KEMP*, Caroline A, of David, Jany 2 1845, 83
3283 LEILICH, Michael, *EIDEMILLER*, Mary Ann, Jany 23 1845, 83
3284 LEASE, Geo Henry, of Nicholas, *HALLER*, Catharine A, of Henry, April 8 1845, 83
3285 LALEY, Wm H, 1st wife, *HERGESHEIMER*, Louisa, of Jos, April 10 1845, 83
3286 LITTLEJOHN, Francis Geisinger, *HUDDLESTONE*, Sarah Jane, May 8 1845, 83
3287 LECHLEITER, John H, *CREAGER*, Sophia, Augt 19 1845, 83
3288 LEITER, John, of Henry, *KESSLER*, Rebecca, (Jefferson), March 31 1846, 83
3289 LEASE, Ezra, of Nicholas, *FETTE'*, Eliza M, of Melle', April 14 1846, 83
3290 LANDERKIN, Tho's C, 1st wife, *TRAGO*, Catharine R, of Wm, May 20 1847, 83
3291 LEWIS, John, *WALTER*, Christianna (Mrs), widow of Jacob, May 23 1847, 83
3292 LAWYER, Henry, *WILLS*, Henrietta, Decr 30 1847, "Bobby on the Gray", 83
3293 LEASE, Geo W, of Geo, *BOBST*, Mahala Ann, April 6 1848, 83
3294 LATE, George W, *CREAGER*, Mary A, April 5 1849, 83
3295 LOATS, John, *SIFFORD*, Caroline E, of John, May 2 1850, 83
3296 LIDAY, Joseph, *BITZENBERGER*, Juliann, Octr 27 1850, 83
3297 LAURENT, Frederick C, *DEMME'*, Marianna S, of Rev C K/Phila, Nov 5 1850, 83
3298 LOGUE, Isaac, *NO BRIDES NAME GIVEN*, Miranda, Colored Friends, April 17 1851, 83
3299 LAMBRECHT, Philip, of John, *KUHN*, Matilda, July 10 1851, 83

3300 LADSON, Wm Henry, BRIEN, Isabel Ann, of John MCBRIEN, Septr 18 1851, 83
3301 LEASE, Upton, NUSSBAUM, Margaret C, Decr 4 1851, 84
3302 LAMBRECHT, David, of John, HEFFNER, Susan, Jany 4 1852, 84
3303 LEATHER, James, of John, WINDSOR, Drusilla, of Zadock, May 27 1852, 84
3304 LUGENBEEL, John H, HARN, Elizabeth C, June 24 1852, 84
3305 LEATHERMAN, Josiah, SCHILDKNECHT, Sarah Ann, Decr 23 1852, 84
3306 LYNCH, Wm B, of Wm/1st wife, CHAMBLIN, Laura R, Leesburg, Va, March 29 1853, 84
3307 LOVEJOY, Perry B, MOUNT, Eliza Ellen, July 17 1853, 84
3308 LIPSCOMB, George B, FOUT, Barbara Ann, of Otho, Augt 31 1853, 84
3309 LAMBERT, John George, of John, GROVE, Mary Ann R, of Jacob, Decr 22 1853, 84
3310 LIGON, Tho's Watkins (Gov), (Gov of Md), DORSEY, Mary T, Jany 31 1854, 84
3311 LATE, George, SHAFER, Rebecca C, of Peter, Feby 28 1854, 84
3312 LINDSEY, R Robinson, KIEFFER, Lizzie G C, Decr 7 1854, 84
3313 LITTLE, John L, KEPHART, M Ellen, of Peter, April 19 1855, 84
3314 LANGLEY, John W (Rev), MONTGOMERY, Jennette R, of Col John, July 13 1855, 84
3315 LARE, Wm L, of Wm "LOHR"/1st wife, BARNES, Rachel, Decr 4 1855, 84
3316 LAMBERT, Daniel T, of John, SHOOK, Jane E, Jany 2 1856, 84
3317 LITTLE, Benjamin Rush (Dr), SCHLEY, Anna M, of David, April 23 1856, 84
3318 LOYNS, James W, CURFMAN, Sarah, of Wm, May 11 1856, 84
3319 LAMBRECHT, John W, of John, HARRIS, Ann Virginia, Augt 5 1856, 84
3320 LOGAN, James, BAER, Caroline, of John/(ROWE), Septr 1 1856, 84
3321 LAMBERT, David Michael, of Fred'k, RUTTER, Loretta V, Octr 30 1856, 84
3322 LYNCH, John A, BECKENBAUGH, Isabella C, of Geo, Nov 17 1856, 84
3323 LOCHNER, Wm M, of Geo, NEWPORT, Louisa C, of Adam, Feby 24 1857, 84
3324 LINTON, Samuel, BRUTSCHE, Barbara Ann (Mrs), "HUGHES", May 12 1857, 84
3325 LARE, David W, of Edw "LOHR", LOCKWOOD, Ellisence, Balto, May 6 1858, 84
3326 LEASE, Cha's E, of Geo, BUTLER, Mary Elizabeth, of Harman, May 13 1858, 84
3327 LAMBRECHT, James W, of John, COLYER, Nancy, (surname overwritten), June 10 1858, 84
3328 LENHART, Henry W, STALEY, Julia Ann, June 17 1858, 84
3329 LOVELL, Wm S, Lieut, QUITMAN, Antonia, of Gen'l John A, June 29 1858, 84
3330 LINK, Lewis, SHEETS, Christianna, Mount Pleasant, Augt 24 1858, 84
3331 LEFEVRE, Jacob A (Rev), SAUERWEIN, Kate L, of Geo/Balto, Octr 19 1858, 84
3332 LONG, Charles H, TONEY, Ann R, Jany 2 1859, 84
3333 LARE, George H, of Edw LOHR, INGALLS, Mary J, Balto, Jany 20 1859, 84
3334 LOVELL, Joseph, of NY, QUITMAN, Louisa T, of Gen'l John A/Natches, Jany 18 1859, 84
3335 LEASE, Andrew Jackson, BRANDENBURG, Charlotte, April 12 1859, 84
3336 LUGENBEEL, Tho's E S, POOLE, Ann M, April 20 1859, 84
3337 LEATHER, Luther J, LENHART, Mary A R, May 26 1859, 84
3338 LAKIN, William H, KEMP, Ellen C, Jefferson, Octr 13 1859, 84
3339 LAMBRECHT, Joseph, LECHLEITER, Mary A, Sheph town, Va, Nov 24 1859, 84
3340 LIGHTNER, Jonathan Coleman, BROWN, Mary Elizabeth, Jany 11 1860, 84
3341 LOHMEYER, H H, MOLICH, Eliza, Balto, Feby 14 1860, 84
3342 LEASE, Tho's U, SNYDER, Olevia J, March 20 1860, 84
3343 LOVELEY, John Emanuel, EBRECHT, Amanthe E, of John, Mar 28 1860, 85
3344 LUGENBEEL, Henry G, SINN, Mary A E, of Jacob, May 31 1860, 85
3345 LAMBERT, Charles, of Fred'k, REEVES, Miss, Shepherdstown, Va, June 5 1860, 85

3346 *LALEY*, William H, 2d wife, *WIEST*, Laura V, of Conrad, Jany 9 1861, 85
3347 *LOCHNER*, Nicholas, of Geo, *BAUMGERTNER*, Barbara A, of Tho's, Jany 13 1861, 85
3348 *LARE*, Wm L, of Wm "LOHR"/2d wife, *HOLBRUNNER*, Lydia A, Jany 15 1861, 85
3349 *LIGHTNER*, Presley T, *BARRICK*, Mary J, Feby 12 1861, Glade, 85
3350 *LAMPE*, Julius Junior, *KONIG*, Mary, of Louis "KING", April 24 1861, 85
3351 *LANCASTER*, John Henry, *SHANK*, Margaret A, (PETT) of Ezra, May 31 1861, 85
3352 *LOWELL*, James P, of Wm, *PRICE*, Mary Cath, Westminster, June 11 1861, 85
3353 *LECHLEITER*, Alexander A, *HERR*, Rebecca, at Gettysburg, Pa, Augt 6 1861, 85
3354 *LEATHER*, David, *RIEHL*, Jane, of Otho, Augt 13 1861, 85
3355 *LEASE*, David H, of Wm, *NICHOLS*, Mary Jane, of Wm, Augt 23 1861, 85
3356 *LIDAY*, Henry, 2d wife, *ALLEN*, Charlotte (Mrs), daughter of Geo HARDT, Nov 1861, 85
3357 *LATROBE*, Ferdinand C, *SWANN*, Louisa, of Tho's/Balto, Decr 26 1861, 85
3358 *LINDSEY*, Benjamin F, *NORRIS*, H Annie, of Sam'l, Jany 1 1862, 85
3359 *LEWIS*, Jacob, 2d wife, *WINGER*, Elizabeth, April 3 1862, 85
3360 *LIGGET*, Charles A, *DALE*, M Frances, Parksville, Missouri, April 23 1862, 85
3361 *LEWIS*, William H, *EADER*, Eliza C, of Lewis B, May 1 1862, 85
3362 *LEASE*, Robert, *SCHIETENHELM*, Mary, May 8 1862, 85
3363 *LATRILLE*, Robert Horatio, (of St Louis), *PHEBUS*, Laura Permelia, May 12 1862, 85
3364 *LAYMAN*, Geo H, *SHAW*, Sarah C, May 10 1862, 85
3365 *LEISTER*, Albert, *LENHART*, Juliann L, June 10 1862, 85
3366 *NO SURNAME GIVEN*, Louis, Prince of Hesse, *NO BRIDES NAME GIVEN*, Alice Maude Mary,, Princess 2d daughter of Victoria, July 1 1862, 85
3367 *LOUD*, Granville, *WEYL*, Amanda, of Rev C G/Balto, Augt 19 1862, 85
3368 *LEASE*, Josiah, *KETROW*, Sarah E, Jany 8 1863, 85
3369 *LEASE*, Wm H, *MCALLISTER*, Ann A, of Carroll Co, March 26 1863, 85
3370 *LAVENTUNE*, Samuel, *KEEFER*, Amanda C, of Peter H, May 30 1863, 85
3371 *LINK*, Daniel (Lieut), *WACHTER*, Sophia E, of David F, Augt 12 1863, 85
3372 *LEASE*, Oliver D, *ZIMMERMAN*, Minerva, Septr 21 1863, 85
3373 *LAMPE*, J Henry, *ROSZ*, Elizabeth M, Octr 29 1863, 85
3374 *LONG*, Josephus, *HOLBRUNNER*, Sarah E, May 4 1864, 85
3375 *LAMAR*, Baker J, of Rich'd J, *KEMP*, E Cornelia, of Peter, June 28 1864, 85
3376 *LARE*, Edward, "LOHR"/2d wife, *HENRY*, Cornelia, Balto, Augt 11 1864, 85
3377 *LINDSEY*, George, (of Maine), *DAVIS*, Laura J, Decr 28 1864, 85
3378 *LAMBRECHT*, John W, of John/2d wife, *ADAM*, Annie R, of Andreas, Feby 12 1865, 85
3379 *LEWIS*, John S, of Jacob, *HENDERSON*, Maggie J, of Andrew, May 24 1865, 85
3380 *LEONARD*, Tho's, of Balto, *EBRECHT*, Cornelia, of John, July 17 1865, 85
3381 *LYNCH*, Wm B, of Wm/2d wife, *WILDMAN*, Jane D, Leesburg, Va, Nov 22 1865, 85
3382 *LANDERS*, Wm H, *GROVE*, Christie S, Decr 21 1865, 85
3383 *LEWIS*, George T, *WOODWARD*, Mary Jane, of Alex'r, Feby 1 1866, 85
3384 *LEWIS*, Charles J, *KOOGLE*, Hallie A, of Adam, Feby 8 1866, 85
3385 *LYNN*, A Luther, *DORSEY*, Mary Elleanor, of Rev Edwin/Balto, Octr 18 1866, 86
3386 *LARE*, Lewis G, of Edw "LOHR", *FOSTER*, Rachel, Balto, Nov 15 1866, 86
3387 *LAMAR*, Wm K, of Rich'd J, *CROMWELL*, Annie B, "SINN", July 25 1867, 86
3388 *LEGROFT*, George, *HAUER*, Jane C, of John, Nov 21 1867, 86
3389 *LEITER*, Samuel L H, *COBLENTZ*, Mary Ellen, Jany 2d 1868, 86
3390 *LUTZ*, Charles, *BOBST*, Alice M, Feby 5 1868, 86
3391 *LIPPS*, John C, *MILLER*, Elleanora, Boonsboro, April 23 1868, 86

3392 LESTER, Joseph R, of Balto, MARKEY, Lucy E, of David Jacob, May 5 1868, 86
3393 LINCOLN, Robert T, of Ab'm, HARLAN, Mary, of Hon James, Septr 24 1868, 86
3394 LEWIS, Francis J, TROXELL, Columbia H, of Joshua, Decr 10 1868, 86
3395 LEASE, A Calvin, DYER, Elizabeth Ellen, Feby 3 1869, 86
3396 LAMAR, Robert G, of Rich'd J, SINN, Kate, of Edw, Augt 25 1869, 86
3397 LYETH, John T, of John Mc, FOUT, Mary C, of Geo, Nov 9 1869, 86
3398 LAMAR, Baker J, JOHNSON, Emma, Urbana, Nov 23 1869, 86
3399 LEILICH, Michael, 2d wife, NEUBRANDT, Anna Mary, of John, Jany 20 1870, 86
3400 LEASE, Amos, HOUCK, Mary, of John, Feby 22 1870, 86
3401 LOEWENSTEIN, David, STERN, Clara, of Aaron, May 1 1870, 86
3402 LEASE, Franklin M, NICHOLS, Clara V, May 19 1870, 86
3403 LIPPS, Thomas, of John, POFFENBERGER, Martha, Decr 8 1870, 86
3404 LEVY, Cha's V S, STROBEL, Mary Grace, of Rev Wm D, Jan 5 1871, 86
3405 LIGGET, John J (Dr), HARRIS, Amanda, of Henry R, Feby 21 1871, 86
3406 LAMPE, Christian L C, BABEL, Mary E, of Ch'n, April 26 1871, 86
3407 LEGGE, J Frank, 1st wife, BANTZ, Theodora, of Wm S, June 13 1871, 86
3408 LOHMANN, Edward, NOLLTE', Fredericka, Augt 31 1871, 86
3409 LUCKETT, Wm F (Dr), SELSAM, Emma, Septr 12 1871, 86
3410 LEITER, Ezra K, STULL, Hester Ann Louisa, valley, Nov 16 1871, 86
3411 LEILICH, Francis T, of Michael, EBBERTS, Mary E, of Jos M, Decr 28 1871, 86
3412 LAWRENCE, Richard H, of Otho, NELSON, Rose E, of Madison, Nov 30 1872, 86
3413 LAMAR, Richard D, BORDER, Sallie, W Va, Nov 12 1873, 86
3414 LORENTZ, Charles H, of Henry, MYERS, Clara H, of Cha's E, Nov 13 1873, 86
3415 LEITER, Daniel J, VANANDA, Mollie A, Nov 9 1873, 86
3416 LOWENSTEIN, Isaac, STRAUSS, Carrie, of Mich'l, Jan 4 1874, 86
3417 LEATHERMAN, Marshall (Dr), RAMSBURG, Florence, Feb 3 1874, Glade, 86
3418 LAMBERT, Tho's F, of Fred'k, ZIMMERMAN, Kate E, May 7 1874, 86
3419 LUTZ, John, of Mich'l/2d wife, MEYER, Maria Elizab, of Justus, Sep 21 1874, 86
3420 LONG, P Allison (Rev), HESS, L Araminta, Nov 19 1874, 86
3421 LAKE, Orange E (Rev), ZIMMERMAN, Lillie H M, Jan 18 1876, 86
3422 LAMBRIGHT, Philip H, 2d wife, TOPPER, Clara V, May 4 1876, 86
3423 LORENTZ, Edwin C, of Henry, TAYLOR, Irene, of Ohio, June 24 1876, 86
3424 LIEDEMAN, John L, PROBST, Carrie L, of Rev J F, Septr 7 1876, So Cara, 86
3425 LIPPS, Lewis, of John, MILLER, Clara, May 31 1877, 86
3426 LIGHTNER, Wesley J, HOUCK, Susanna, Oct 30 1877, 86
3427 LITTLE, Harry, EBBERTS, Annie M (Mrs), Nov 22 1877, 87
3428 LANDAUER, Abraham, BLUMENBERG, Katie, Jan 6 1878, 87
3429 LOMTZ, Franklin R, HAMMOND, Annie C, July 10 78, 87
3430 LARCH, Charles, MOORE, Lizzie, April 2d 1879, 87
3431 LANDERKIN, Thomas L, 2d wife, DEGRANGE, Augusta, Oct 21 1879, 87
3432 LORNTZ, Albert C, FIGGINS, Annie M, Nov 27th 1879, 87
3433 LEGG, Edward K, (@Edgar K), WEBSTER, Ellen T, of Geo/(not listed as Miss), June 18th 1880, 87
3434 LAMOTT, Daniel M (Rev), Pastor of Woodsboro Church, FAIR, Laura, (not listed as Miss), Jan 1st 1881, 87
3435 LEWIS, Maurice H, of Henry, CASTLE, Elizabeth C, (not listed as Miss), Sep 1881, 87
3436 LANE, John M, FALCONER, Maria O, of Wm H, June 6th 1882, 87

3437 LEIBHERTZ, William H, (@LEBHERZ), BENNETT, Maggie S, of Lewis, Nov 25 1882, 87
3438 LEASE, N Calvin, HAINES, Fannie C, March 15th 1883, 87
3439 LINTHICUM, John L (Hon), MAIN, M H, March 17th 1883, 87
3440 LEILICH, M C, BURCK, Genevive, of Lewis, June 11th 1883, 87
3441 LAYMAN, Lenoard J, BAUMGARDNER, Nora D, of H'y, July 1st 1883, 87
3442 LENOX, Arthur E, BARTGIS, Nannie, of James, Dec 27th 1883, 87
3443 LAYMAN, Clarence L, BAUMGARDNER, Lillie K, March 25 1885, 87
3444 LOY, Isaiah N, PERRY, Mary, September 1 1885, 87
3445 LERCH, George W, COOK, Sallie A, February 25 1886, 87
3446 LLOYD, Henry (Gov), SAPPLEFORT, Mary E, October 18 1886, 87
3447 LAKINS, Daniel T, ROPP, Lizzie R, November 10 1886, 87
3448 LEASE, Wm M, MORNINGSTAR, Annie, December 8 1886, 87
3449 LEASE, Edward C, CRONISE, Fannie, December 29 1886, 87
3450 LEILICH, George R, of Michael, KINTZ, Lillian, February 3d 1887, 87
3451 LONG, James W, PERRY, Katie J, (niece of Ja's P), February 16 1887, 87
3452 LOPEZ, Harry (Capt), Salvation Army, FISHER, Florence, of Wm, June 22 1887, 87
3453 LEA, Edward, (@LEE, Edgar), NEIGHBORS, Lotta H, (@Lola), November 15 1887, 87
3454 LEIN, Lincoln R, KEMP, Dora E, February 14 1888, 87
3455 LEATHERMAN, D I (Dr), (@Daniel J), WASTLER, Katie, (@WISSLER), March 13 1888, 87
3456 LARE, Wm H, KABRICK, Cordelia E, May 23 1888, 87
3457 LAYMAN, Robert L, BRENGLE, Annie V, February 19 1889, 87
3458 LEASE, Cha's W, REAGAN, Alice V, (@RAGAN), May 23 1889, 87
3459 LAMBRIGHT, James L, HOUSE, Georgeana, (@HEISER), Sept 10 1889, 87
3460 LEASE, Milliard F, DARNER, Fannie G, (@DANNER), Oct 10 1889, 87
3461 LAYMAN, George H, 2d wife, BRIGHTWELL, Sarah E, Oct 20 1889, 87
3462 LAYMAN, George W, SMITH, Annie E, December 31 1889, 87
3463 LAMBERT, George D, WHITMORE, Mollie, January 16 1890, 87
3464 LADOW, Robert V, (@LA DOW), BALTZELL, Francis M, of Wm H, April 10 1890, 87
3465 LAKIN, John S, COCKRAN, Ella B, (@COCHRAN), April 15 1890, 87
3466 LAMBERT, Murray, of D M, MUSSETTER, Mollie, (@Mary E), May 4 1890, 87
3467 LINK, A D Garl, BOWES, Grace E, Sept 25 1890, 87
3468 LAMBRIGHT, Harry, WHISNER, Lilla, Oct 28 1890, 87
3469 LEDERERER, Henry A, RICHARDSON, Fannie L, of Geo W, Nov 19 1890, 88
3470 METZGER, Jacob, GARDNER, Elizabeth (Mrs), (RIEHL), Feby 11 1821, 90
3471 MARKEY, Frederick, of David, DILL, Eliza, of John, April 30 1821, 90
3472 MCDADE, Samuel, ASPER, Elizabeth, July 22 1821, 90
3473 MCKIERNAN, Peter, STONEBRAKER, Mary, Augt 12 1821, 90
3474 MIERS, Wm H, BIRELY, Sophia, of Fred'k, July 30 1822, 90
3475 MANTZ, Peter (Jun'r), MOBLEY, Elizabeth, Jany 7th 1823, 90
3476 MARGUERT, John, of Mich'l, KOONS, Julianna, Harpersferry, March 24 1823, 90
3477 MALAMBRE, John, GETZENDANNER, Catharine, "BAER", May 13 1823, 90
3478 MILLER, Benjamin M, WYLLIE, Sarah (Mrs), May 13 1823, 90
3479 MARSHALL, Richard H, POTTS, Harriott M, of Judge Rich'd, June 12 1823, 90
3480 MICHAEL, David, FOUT, Elizabeth, of Wm, Augt 19 1823, 90
3481 MCPHERSON, John Junior, JOHNSON, Frances, Decr 9 1823, 90
3482 MCPHERSON, Horatio, of Col John, BUCHANAN, Mary, of Judge Tho's, Decr 11 1823, 90
3483 MCCREERY, James M, DARKIS, Mary Ann, Decr 21 1823, 90

3484 **MYERS**, Jacob, **NEWENS**, Christianna, of Tho's, Jany 22 1824, 90
3485 **MANTZ**, Peregrine, of Isaac, **MILLER**, Nancy, Va, Decr 1823, 90
3486 **MOBLEY**, Eli, **MAYBERRY**, Sophia, of Justenian, April 15 1824, 90
3487 **MCNAIR**, James, **WAYS**, Sarah, of Basil, May 18 1824, 90
3488 **MILLER**, John, of Daniel/3d wife, **NORRIS**, Sarah, Decr 14 1824, 90
3489 **MCDERMOTT**, John, **MCGEE**, Mary, Feby 3 1825, 90
3490 **MARTIN**, John, (Jailor)/2d wife, **TRAVERS**, Miss, (* Elizabeth), May 5 1825, 90
3491 **MARTIN**, David, of Jon, **WIEST**, Elizabeth, of Jacob, June 30 1825, 90
3492 **MCCREA**, Thompson (Dr), **DUKEHART**, Sophia, Octr 27 1825, 90
3493 **MARTIN**, Jacob, of John, **BRENEISEN**, Mary, Feby 14 1826, 90
3494 **MARKELL**, Jacob, 2d wife, **MILLER**, Rebecca, of Gottlob, Feby 23 1826, 90
3495 **MOBLEY**, Levi, **LAMBRECHT**, Rebecca, of Philip, April 27 1826, 90
3496 **MOTTER**, John S, **SMITH**, Mary Ann, of Geo, May 16 1826, 90
3497 **MURAT**, Achille, of Pr Joachiam, **GRAY**, Cath D (Mrs), Tallahassee, July 12 1826, 90
3498 **MCPHERSON**, Edward B, of Col John, **TALBOTT**, Anna, of Jos, Decr 5 1826, 90
3499 **MCLANE**, Rezin, **KEMP**, Charlotte, January 1827, 90
3500 **MANSON**, William, **SIFFORD**, Sarah Ann, of Christian, April 12 1827, 90
3501 **MATTHIAS**, John (Capt'n), **CLEMSON**, Sarah (Mrs), Septr 25 1827, 90
3502 **MOORE**, Alfred L, **SHIPLEY**, Ann G, Octr 2d 1827, 90
3503 **MORRIS**, John G (Rev), **HAY**, Eliza, of York, Pa, Nov 1 1827, 90
3504 **MATTHEWS**, Jeremiah, **ONLEY**, Eleanor, Colored Friends, Decr 20 1827, 90
3505 **MYERS**, Valentine, of Geo, **SOUDER**, Sarah A, Feby 12 1828, 90
3506 **MARTIN**, William C, **YOUNG**, Elizabeth, of And'w Jun'r, July 24 1828, 90
3507 **MIDDLETON**, Robert White, **SCHREINER**, A Elizabeth, July 27 1828, 90
3508 **MUIR**, Robert D, **HYNSON**, Clarissa C, Augt 27 1828, 90
3509 **MAHONEY**, Wm, of Barney, **SPRINGER**, Eliza, of Wm, Octr 9 1828, 90
3510 **MEALEY**, Isaiah, 1st wife, **STUB**, Elizabeth (Mrs), "WIDRICK", Jany 8 1829, 90
3511 **MORELAND**, John, **WILCOXON**, Elizabeth, of Wm, Jany 25 1829, 90
3512 **MANTZ**, Henry, of David, **BRANSON**, Sophia, Balto, Feby 12 1829, 91
3513 **METZGER**, George, of Jacob, **ACKERMAN**, Sarah, Lancaster, Pa, April 19 1829, 91
3514 **MCCULLOUGH**, John W (Rev), **DUNCAN**, Mary Louisa, May 26 1829, 91
3515 **MORGAN**, Wm Virgo, 2d wife & sisters, **BROADRUP**, Sarah, Octr 14 1829, 91
3516 **MCLANE**, George, **COOKERLY**, Amelia, Nov 1829, 91
3517 **METZGER**, William, of Jacob, **TRAIL**, Harriett, Montgomery Co, Decr 20 1829, 91
3518 **MCNEILL**, Francis A (Rev), **CRONISE**, Mary, of Simon, Feby 1 1830, 91
3519 **MCDONALD**, David, **SMITH**, Henrietta, of Henry/"ZIMMERMAN", Feby 28 1830, 91
3520 **MILLER**, Edward (Dr), of John Sam'l, **WATSON**, Harriott C, Octr 14 1830, 91
3521 **MEDTART**, Jacob (Rev), **LEGGITT**, Ann D, Nov 23 1830, 91
3522 **MANN**, Charles (Rev), **JACKSON**, Mary C, April 12 1831, 91
3523 **MCMULLIN**, Cha's P, **HAUER**, Elizabeth, of Geo, March 20 1832, 91
3524 **MARKEY**, David Jacob, of David, **BENTZ**, Susan, of Jacob, July 24 1832, 91
3525 **MILLER**, Daniel, **RIEHL**, Catharine (Mrs), widow of Fred'k, Octr 16 1832, 91
3526 **MICHAEL**, William, of Wm, **ZIELER**, Ann, of Adam, Nov 27 1832, 91
3527 **MCLANE**, Cyrus, **FLEMING**, Sarah, of Jos, Septr 25 1833, 91
3528 **MCCAHAN**, George, **LAMBRECHT**, Mary A, Decr 31 1833, 91
3529 **MANTZ**, Charles, of John/(1st wife), **GROVE**, Mary, of John D, April 11 1834, 91
3530 **MANTZ**, John Andrew, of John, **SCHAUMAN**, Eliza, April 24 1834, 91

3531 MCKINSTRY, Cha's W, LOVEDER, Ann, April 27 1834, 91
3532 MICHAEL, Jacob R, of Wm, HALLEY, Catharine, March 31 1835, "MAYBERRY", 91
3533 MCPHERSON, Wm S (Dr), 2d wife, NETH, Harriott (Mrs), July 21 1835, Annapolis, 91
3534 MCLANE, Wm W, SCHLEIGH, Margret C, Augt 20 1835, 91
3535 MCMACKIN, Edward, KILLIAN, Susan, of Philip, Septr 10 1835, 91
3536 MILLER, John F, of Mich'l, HEIM, Ann B, of David, Octr 27 1835, 91
3537 MAULSBY, Wm Pinkney, of Israel D, NELSON, Emily C T, of Roger, Nov 30 1835, 91
3538 MANN, Stephen T, HERZOG, Ann M, (HARTSOCK), March 8 1836, 91
3539 MEYERLE', Frederick, ROTH, Catharine, May 5 1836, 91
3540 MILLER, Joshua, CRUM, Susan, of Isaac, May 24 1836, 91
3541 MAULSBY, David J, of Israel D, NELSON, Sarah, of Roger, Septr 1 1836, 91
3542 MAGRUDER, Arthur John, GELWICKS, Eleanora, of Geo C, Octr 18 1836, 91
3543 MANNSTAEDT, Charles, HEMMEL, Cecelia M, of Jacob, Octr 20 1836, 91
3544 MAHONEY, Martin M, of Barney, SCHATZ, Margaret, April 13 1837, 91
3545 MARTIN, Cha's (Rev Dr), CARLTON, Eliza Jannett, of Tho's, May 11 1837, 91
3546 MARKELL, Wm W, SALMON, Mary A E, of Geo, Feby 20 1838, 91
3547 MACOMB, John Navarre (Lieut), MACOMB, Czarina, March 7 1838, 91
3548 MANTZ, Caspar, of Isaac, ELDER, Elizabeth, May 29 1838, 91
3549 MARANDER, Jacob, KONIG, Catharine, of Lewis "KING", June 28 1838, 91
3550 MEDTART, Jacob (Rev), 2d wife, BENNER, Miss, June 21 1838, 91
3551 METZGER, Gerhart, of Jacob, JONES, Elizabeth Ann, Septr 20 1838, 91
3552 STEVENS, Mason T (Gov), of Detroit, PHELPS, Julia E, of N York, Nov 1 1838, 91
3553 MCLEAN, Samuel, VORE, Harriott, March 26 1839, 91
3554 MOTTER, William, SPRIGG, Columbia, May 2 1839, 92
3555 MAYOR, Jesse, SMITH, Lydia, May 2 1839, 92
3556 MILLER, William, PRICE, Sarah, Septr 22 1829, 92
3557 MILLER, David H, of John, HALLAR, Christianna, of Joshua, Septr 26 1839, 92
3558 MICHAEL, Daniel, GEISBERT, Hester Ann, Nov 19 1839, 92
3559 MILLER, Harrison, HALLER, Elizabeth, of Peter, Jany 23 1840, 92
3560 MITCHELL, John T, LEARNED, Elizabeth, Jefferson, April 7 1840, 92
3561 MARKELL, George, of John, MARKELL, Sophia, of Jacob, April 23 1840, 92
3562 MITCHELL, Joseph J, HORSEY, Caroline, of Outerbridge, April 23 1840, 92
3563 MAYER, Bartel, his 2d wife, YOUNG, Philipina, Augt 20 1840, 92
3564 MCLANAHAN, Wm M B, SMITH, Ann R, of Geo, Septr 8 1840, 92
3565 MCFERRAN, John, MARSHALL, Ann, Octr 1840, 92
3566 MILLER, Geo Ezra, HOLTZAPPEL, Rebecca, Octr 15 1840, 92
3567 MYERS, Joel, HOOVER, Sarah A, Nov 12 1840, 92
3568 MCPHERSON, Rob't G, of Robert G, WASHINGTON, Milicent F, Va, Decr 10 1840, 92
3569 MILLER, Samuel M, HAYS, Ann J, Sharpsburg, Md, Feby 9 1841, 92
3570 MAIN, Mahlon, BISER, Catharine, March 28 1841, 92
3571 MOTTER, Jacob, TROXELL, Jemima, Emmittsburg, April 15 1841, 92
3572 MCALEER, Hugh, of John, GAITHER, Louisa, of Stuart, May 4 1841, 92
3573 MCSHERRY, James, SPURRIER, Eliza, Septr 30 1841, 92
3574 MCPHERSON, John, of Wm S/1st wife, HAMMOND, Ann J, Feby 24 1842, 92
3575 MCCLEERY, John, of Cumberland, MCCULLEY, Mary, of John J, June 9 1842, 92
3576 MILLER, David F K, of John W, WISE, Rosanna, of Fred'k, Septr 27 1842, 92
3577 MARKELL, Louis, of John, BRUNNER, Mary Ann, of John of J, Octr 27 1842, 92

3578 MASON, John Thompson (Hon), of Md, COWAN, Margaret Augusta, Pa, Decr 14 1842, 92
3579 MARTIN, John (Jun'r), WALLING, Miss, of David/(*Rebecca), Decr 27 1842, 92
3580 MCPHERSON, Edward B, 2d wife, YOUNG, Mary Jane (Mrs), Missouri, Decr 6 1842, 92
3581 MORGAN, Levi, CRIST, Eveline, Decr 29 1842, 92
3582 MASON, Elisha, HOFFMAN, Juliann, of Geo, Jany 29 1843, 92
3583 MANTZ, Alexander K, of Cyrus, BIER, Sophia B, of Jacob/Balto, Mar 9 1843, 92
3584 MICHAEL, Andrew, 2d wife, PIERCE, Martha, Manor, May 16 1843, 92
3585 MYERS, Wm, of Christopher, LITTLEJOHN, Jane, Geo Town, July 5 1843, 92
3586 MANKIN, James A, INGMAN, Mary (Mrs), (TURNER), July 3 1843, 92
3587 MITTNACHT, Geo H, 2d wife, ARMITAGE, Abigail L, Balto, July 12 1843, 92
3588 MAYNARD, Benjamin, CLAGGETT, M K, Septr 21 1843, 92
3589 MCLEAN, Tho's L (Rev), CROMWELL, Charlotte A, of Philemon, Septr 28 1843, 92
3590 MARSH, Mason R, of Joel, GETZENDANNER, Cath E, of Jefferson, Nov 9 1843, 92
3591 MILLER, Wm Baker, of Va, MANTZ, Ellen, of Cyrus, Decr 19 1843, 92
3592 MORSELL, Joshua (Rev), MCCHESLEY, Jane G, Jany 25 1844, 92
3593 MALAMBRE, George, 2d wife & sisters, MAYES, Emiline, April 30 1844, 92
3594 MOORE, John T, of Geo, WISONG, Mary E, of Isaac, June 4 1844, 92
3595 MERRICK, Wm M, WICKLIFFE, Mary B, Kentucky, Octr 15 1844, 92
3596 MILLER, John (Rev), 1st wife, BENEDICT, Margaret, Octr 1844, 93
3597 MARKELL, John S, of Uniontown, Pa, WALLING, Emma, of James, Nov 19 1844, 93
3598 MAHONEY, David L, WASKEY, Sarah A R, May 15 1845, 93
3599 MORGAN, Romulus G, of Rev Gerard, BALDERSON, Mary Annie, of John, Feby 19 1846, 93
3600 MANTZ, Milton, of Cyrus, MARKEY, Ann C, of Fred'k, March 15 1846, 93
3601 MILLER, Geo D, of Chestertown, Md, LITTLE, Christianna, of Jacob, May 4 1846, 93
3602 MYERS, Cha's H, of Balto, JACKSON, Mary M, "MANTZ""ROBERTSON, May 27 1846, 93
3603 MATTHEWS, Samuel G, CROMWELL, Catharine, of Philemon/(not listed as Miss), Septr 1 1846, 93
3604 MILLER, Harrison, (GETZENDANNER), SHAFER, Sarah Ann, of Jacob, Octr 29 1846, 93
3605 MADDOX, Thomas (Dr), CLAGGETT, Mary P, Nov 10 1846, 93
3606 MANTZ, Francis, of Peter, MILLER, Barbara Ann, of Jno W, Feby 8 1847, 93
3607 MUMFORD, Geo A, LIGHTNER, Mary Ann, March 7 1847, 93
3608 MANTZ, William, of Peter, HENDERSON, Lucy Jane, of Rob't, March 16 1847, 93
3609 MOFFET, John Newland (Rev), 2d wife, SMITH, Frances, Brooklyn, NY, Mar 22 1847, 93
3610 MANTZ, George, of Gideon, WHITE, Sarah A, Washington, DC, May 9 1847, 93
3611 MOBLEY, William, BALDWIN, A M, (*Ann), Septr 16 1847, 93
3612 MANTZ, Emauel, of Peter/1st wife, POOLE, Elizabeth, of Wm, Octr 31 1847, 93
3613 MILLER, Geo A, REIGART, Mary Emeline, of Philip/Lancaster, Pa, Nov 23 1847, 93
3614 MAUGHT, Andrew C H, "MACHT", LONG, Mary A K, of Christopher, May 9 1848, 93
3615 MAGRUDER, H C, (*Hezekiah), DALRYMPLE, Guilimina, May 30 1848, 93
3616 MILLER, Mich'l Henry, of Michael, COOKERLY, Matilda, of Jacob, Augt 31 1848, 93
3617 MURRAY, Edward (Lieut), USA, HARDING, Louisa, of John L, Octr 12 1848, 93
3618 MCLEAN, Geo W, SHRIVER, Eliza Jane, of James, Nov 7 1848, 93
3619 MONTGOMERY, James (Jun'r), ANDERSON, Ann H, Nov 8 1848, 93
3620 MOFFIT, Wm R, of Balto, WALLING, Martha A, of James, Decr 12 1848, 93
3621 MCCARTNEY, Michael, HUGHES, Florida, Feby 14 1849, 93
3622 MARTZ, Geo D, OTT, Mary Ann Louisa, March 8 1849, 93

3623 MECHLI, Eli, SCHOLL, Elizabeth C, of John, April 26 1849, 93
3624 MINES, John L, WILLSON, Martha R, of Dr Wm M B, June 5 1849, 93
3625 MCDADE, David Martin, of Sam'l, WARTHEN, Isabella, June 24 1849, 93
3626 MARTIN, Charles (Rev Dr), 2d wife, CUTTER, Harriett A, of N York, Septr 10 1849, 93
3627 MCLAIN, John S, O'NEAL, Elizabeth, Nov 11 1849, 93
3628 MURRAY, Robert, SMALL, Elizabeth Ann (Mrs), widow of Capt'n Wm/her 3d husband, Jany 6 1850, 93
3629 MERGARDT, Conrad, ROKLE, Elizabeth, of Henry, Jany 1 1850, 93
3630 MEHRLING, George, of J Geo, ENGELBRECHT, Barbara, of Adam, July 14 1850, 93
3631 MACGILL, Robert H, SHRIVER, Isabella J, of John S/Balto, July 25 1850, 93
3632 MCCOLLAM, John A, BALDERSON, Drusilla, of John, Jany 7 1851, 93
3633 MCHENRY, Luke Tiernan, KUHRE, Margaret E, Feby 20 1851, 93
3634 MCELVY, James C, HIPPENSTEEL, Mary C, March 4 1851, 93
3635 MORNINGSTAR, George, ("MORGANSTERN"), MADARY, Harriott, March 27 1851, 93
3636 MILLER, Wm S, of Geo, BUCKEY, Mary R, of Dan'l/"DIETRICK", May 13 1851, 93
3637 MORNINGSTAR, Henry, NUSZBAUM, Lydia Ann, "MORGANSTERN", June 17 1851, 93
3638 MONTGOMERY, Harvey F (Dr), BALTZELL, Eliza A, of Dr John, June 24 1851, 94
3639 MCCLEERY, Andrew, of Robert, RIA, Martha E, July 31 1851, at Emmittsburg, 94
3640 MONTGOMERY, Samuel, of Balto, KEEFER, Loretta, of Jacob, Augt 17 1851, in Balto, 94
3641 MICHAEL, Ezra, RAMSBURG, Eliza, Septr 7 1851, Glade, 94
3642 MCCLEERY, Wm H, of Wm, ROBESON, Celina, Octr 7 1851, Brookville, Indianna, 94
3643 MCCLINTOCK, John (Rev), EMORY, Catharine W (Mrs), Octr 9 1851, Carlisle, Pa, 94
3644 MOSER, Peter, FOX, Harriott, Octr 20 1851, 94
3645 MCCORMICK, George, MUMFORD, Margaret, Octr 28 1851, 94
3646 MANTZ, Emanuel, of Peter/2d wife, GROVE, Manzella M, of Jacob, Nov 11 1851, 94
3647 MIDDLETON, Samuel, of Phila, ZACHARIAS, Annie C, of Dr Dan'l, Nov 26 1851, 94
3648 MARKELL, Frederick, of Jacob, THOMAS, Cath Susan, of Geo, Nov 27 1851, 94
3649 MCKENNY, Sam'l W (Capt), MCMAHON, Agnes Biddy, "LOWELL", Decr 20 1851, 94
3650 MYERS, George, BIRELY, Maria, Feby 27 1852, 94
3651 MUMFORD, John H, FRAZIER, Ann Catherine, of Jeremiah, March 25 1852, 94
3652 MIDDLEKAUFF, E, KEMP, Margaret V, of Henry, April 13 1852, 94
3653 MERMAN, Washington P, 1st wife, LOWE, Ann Elizabeth, of Geo, Septr 28 1852, 94
3654 MULHORN, John, BARNES, Anna Eliza, (not listed as Miss), Octr 28 1852, 94
3655 MEALEY, Lewis H, of Isaiah, MILLER, Frances A, of Jacob T C, Decr 7 1852, 94
3656 MCCLERY, Perry Beall, of Robert, DOUB, Jane E, of Joshua, Jany 26 1853, 94
3657 MARKELL, Charles, of John, TRAIL, Charlotte A, of Edward, March 1 1853, 94
3658 MOTTER, John C, LEITER, Miss, of Peter/(*Ann Elizabeth LIGHTER), March 1 1853, 94
3659 MCPHERSON, John H T, of Rob't G, HENRY, Mary G, in Balto, March 31 1853, 94
3660 MCTAVISH, Charles Carroll, SCOTT, Marcella, of Gen'l Winfield, June 29 1853, 94
3661 MOBLEY, Lewis H, of Levi, SCHREINER, Catharine Virginia, of John, Augt 17 1853, 94
3662 MOBLEY, Levi M, of Levi, MCMULLIN, Margaret, of Cha's P, Septr 4 1853, 94
3663 MYERS, David L, SPECHT, Susan E, Septr 15 1853, 94
3664 MILLER, Reinhardt, 2d wife, NO BRIDES NAME GIVEN, Miss, in Balto, Octr 1853, 94
3665 MURRAY, Joshua Thomas, HALLER, Ann Maria, Octr 12 1853, 94
3666 MEDCALFE, Leonard T, HAMILTON, Catharine, of Woodward, Octr 30 1853, 94
3667 MCCARTNEY, John T, of Michael, PAYNE, Harriott E, of Jos, Nov 1 1853, 94
3668 MITCHELL, John T, 2d wife, NEWTON, Maria L, Balto, Nov 22 1853, 94

3669 MEHRLING, Caspar, of John Geo, NICKEL, Margaret Elizabeth, of Jacob, Feby 15 1854, 94
3670 MARTIN, John, HEMMELL, Kate M, of John D/Balto, May 4 1854, 94
3671 MURPHY, John R, MUMFORD, Mary Ann, Octr 5 1854, 94
3672 MCKUSTER, James, GUIE, Ellen, Kaighn Point, Phila, Sept 19 1854, 94
3673 MARTIN, Daniel, DARNELL, Elizabeth, Delaware, Ohio/ "ROHR", Octr 18 1854, 94
3674 MORNINGSTAR, Wm, KLEIN, Margaret, of Stephen, Decr 21 1854, 94
3675 MILLER, David E, REESE, Annie G, March 29 1855, 94
3676 MCDERMOTT, James, PORTER, Rose M, of John W/St Louis, Mo, June 7 1855, 94
3677 MCERMOTT, James W, of John, HOUCK, Annie, of John/"BURGESS", Septr 20 1855, 94
3678 MORGAN, Geo C, (St Marys Co), BALTZELL, Alice, of Dr John, Octr 18 1855, 94
3679 MENSENDICK, Charles, STARCKE, Agnes (Mrs), Jany 12 1856, 94
3680 MYERS, Wm H, NULL, Melissa, March 13 1856, 95
3681 MARTZ, Wm H, FAVORITE, Deborah, Creagerstown, March 20 1856, 95
3682 MOTTER, John S, RUDISILL, Martha M (Mrs), April 6 1856, 95
3683 MAIN, Lewis H, THOMAS, Elenora Sophia, of Peter, May 8 1856, 95
3684 MILLER, Geo W, GREENTREE, Anna, of Ezra/"QUINN", May 8 1856, 95
3685 MANTZ, Edward, of John, SHRIVER, Elizabeth, Meckanickstown, May 20 1856, 95
3686 MCGRIFFITH, John, NORRIS, Rachel Ann, Woodsboro, June 6 1856, 95
3687 MCDONNELL, Jacob, GRINDER, Mary Ann Sevilla, Augt 1856, 95
3688 MAYNARD, Howard G, CHISWELL, S Newton, Septr 14 1856, 95
3689 MARTIN, John T, (Carpenter), BELL, Mary E, Octr 2 1856, 95
3690 MURPHY, James Dennis, CARLIN, Ann, of Wm/"LEASE", Octr 29 1856, 95
3691 MILLER, John (Rev), 2d wife, MCDOWELL, Sally C P, (Mrs Frank THOMAS), Nov 3 1856, 95
3692 MACGILL, Lloyd T (Dr), 1st wife, RIGGS, Mary O, Nov 12 1856, 95
3693 MARKELL, Francis, of John, DELAPLANE, Caroline M, Decr 11 1856, 95
3694 MERCER, Robert S (Rev), NELSON, Annie M, of Nathan, Decr 18 1856, 95
3695 MOTTER, Edward S (Dr), of John S, BRENGLE, Mary Amelia, of Alfred F, March 19 1857, 95
3696 MORGAN, Peter, KUSTER, W, (*Wilhelmina), April 5 1857, 95
3697 MCCREA, John, BEALL, Henrietta, April 20 1857, 95
3698 MILLER, Cha's M, of Dr John Sam'l, NIXDORFF, Julia M, of Henry, June 2 1857, 95
3699 MANTZ, Peter, of Peter, BUZZARD, Elizabeth (Mrs), Balto, Augt 13 1857, 95
3700 MILLER, John, WINSINTER, Rose, Nov 9 1857, 95
3701 MEALEY, Charles E, of Isaiah/1st wife, STALEY, Sarah Jane, of Geo, Decr 3 1857, 95
3702 MCPHERSON, Maynard, of Dr Wm S, FITZHUGH, Mary P, of Peregrine, Decr 8 1857, 95
3703 MARTZ, Geo Jacob (Rev), NUNNEMAKER, Carrie, Norristown, Pa, Decr 3 1857, 95
3704 MILLER, Jacob M, of John W, LEASE, Jane, of Wm, Decr 29 1857, 95
3705 MCPHERSON, John, of Wm/2d wife, DUKE, Elizabeth (Mrs), widow of Green H, Feby 25 1858, 95
3706 MEASELL, David L, CREAGER, Susan E, March 25 1858, 95
3707 MASON, Richard R (Rev), JOHNS, Nannie Van Dyke, of Rev John/Va, April 14 1858, Va, 95
3708 MEYERS, George W, THOMAS, Ann Margaret, Manor, April 13 1858, 95
3709 MATTHEWS, Jonas, 2d wife, RICE, Mary Rebecca (Mrs), "BIRELY", May 6 1858, 95
3710 MCMULLIN, Fayette (Gov), Gov of Washington Territory, WOODS, Mary, July 12 1858, 95
3711 MOREY, Albert, of Dayton, Ohio, BAKER, Carrie, "BAKER""COE""MICHAEL", Septr 7 1858, 95

3712 MAYNARD, Dennis, HOBBS, Clara, of Wm, Octr 1858, 95
3713 MARKER, Enos, BRANDENBURG, Lucinda C, Midd valley, Nov 2 1858, 95
3714 MCKIM, Robert V, ALBERT, Mary S, of Jacob/Balto, Decr 28 1858, 95
3715 MALLEN, Tho's S, DEVILBISS, Maggie H, in Balto, Jany 4 1859, 95
3716 MERRYMAN, Sam'l H B, CLUNET, Martha Adele, of Victor, Jany 25 1859, 95
3717 MYERS, A A, of Lancaster, Pa, LOWELL, Kate, of Wm, March 1 1859, 95
3718 MOSSBURG, Edward T, SCHARFF, Mary T, March 31 1859, 95
3719 MICHAEL, Wm H, SUMMERS, Linah, Midd Valley, May 19 1859, 95
3720 MIDDLEKAUFF, G G, CUNNINGHAM, Mary V, Hagerstown, June 1859, 95
3721 MANTZ, David Allen, of Henry, MILLER, Julia A, "QUINN", June 16 1859, 95
3722 MORGAN, Tho's W, of Tho's W, HOSKINS, M Lizzie, of Geo, June 21 1859, 96
3723 MORNINGSTAR, Philip S, PENN, Sarah Ann, July 31 1859, 96
3724 MACKLEY, John A, KENNEDY, Harriett Ann, of David, Augt 31 1859, 96
3725 MARTIN, Wm Pinkney, of Wm C, MERRITT, Mary Georgianna, Balto, Octr 6 1859, 96
3726 MOXLEY, Reuben M, HOWARD, Amanda C, Octr 20 1859, 96
3727 MALONE, William, FITZPATRICK, Catharine, Nov 7 1859, 96
3728 MYERS, Cha's H, GOLDEN, Mahala Jane, Ironton, Ohio, Feby 1 1860, 96
3729 MUMMA, Jesse N, "MUMMY", SHEALEY, Susan E, March 6 1860, 96
3730 METCALFE, Henry Z, FULTON, Mary S, March 1 1860, 96
3731 MCDEVITT, Cha's W, ENGEL, Christianna L, of John, March 13 1860, 96
3732 MAESCHE, J F, (*# John F WAESCHE), BELT, Maggie E, March 21 1860, 96
3733 MAIN, Daniel A, BISER, Catharine, March 25 1860, 96
3734 MYERS, J Oliver, of John, YARBOROUGH, Mary Reed, N Carolina, April 3 1860, 96
3735 MEHRLING, Daniel, 2d wife, WEBSTER, Mary E, in Washington City, April 12 1860, 96
3736 MCCLELLAND, Geo Brinton (Capt'n), MARCY, Mary E, of Maj Randolph B, May 22 1860, 96
3737 MILLER, Washington M, KEADEL, Martha E, Sabillesville, Augt 9 1860, 96
3738 MCDANIEL, J Milton, ELKINS, Fannie, of Jos, Septr 27 1860, 96
3739 MILLER, Lewis H, of John W, STORM, Lydia R, of P Leon'd, Octr 24 1860, 96
3740 MICHAEL, John H, BRANDENBURG, Sarah Ann, Midd Valley, Nov 8 1860, 96
3741 MOORE, Geo M, of Geo, FRENCH, Mary, Washington City, Decr 20 1860, 96
3742 MARKER, Wesley, MICHAEL, Charlotte, Jany 22 1861, 96
3743 MURPHY, Geo W, SCHRINER, Julia A, of Basil E, Feby 21 1861, 96
3744 MILLER, Daniel C, COBLENTZ, Fannie C, of Henry, Feby 12 1861, 96
3745 MITCHELL, John Tho's, SLICER, Llewellen, of Rev Henry/Balto, Feby 27 1861, 96
3746 MCGINNIS, Wm C, SUMAN, Annie M H, of John, March 3d 1861, 96
3747 MAIN, George J, COBLENTZ, Sarah V, March 28 1861, 96
3748 MARKEY, Frederick A, of David J, CREAGER, Manelia S, of Eph'm, April 27 1861, 96
3749 MCCAHAN, Geo L, of Geo, CRANGLE, Mary L, Balto, April 30 1861, 96
3750 MEHRLING, John, of Geo, HANE, Susan, July 30 1861, 96
3751 MARTIN, Oliver H, of Wm C, JAMISON, Lucy, Balto, July 30 1861, 96
3752 MERCER, Edward, GIBBONS, Sabrina C, Nov 20 1861, 96
3753 MANTZ, Charles, of John/2d wife, MILLER, Annie U, of Geo/"DIETRICH", Decr 11 1861, 96
3754 MARKER, Joshua, LEMBACH, Susan C, Midd val, Decr 12 1861, 96
3755 MARTZ, Lewis J, STALEY, Margaret C, Feby 6 1862, 96
3756 MEDDERS, Albert, BOYD, Caroline Virginia, of David, March 5 1862, 96

3757 MICHAEL, Wm H, SPECHT, Jane E, of Jacob, April 15 1862, 96
3758 MUSSEETER, Charles F, KOHLENBERG, Maggie L, of Adam, Septr 16 1862, 96
3759 MILFORD, John W, BURTON, Sarah, Cumberland, Md, Octr 28 1862, 96
3760 MUMMA, Nathaniel, SCHLOSSER, Elizabeth, Nov 4 1862, 96
3761 MAGRUDER, Jonas E, MILLER, Columbia Ann, of Jacob T C, Nov 2 1862, 96
3762 MCPHERSON, Edward (Hon), of John B, CRAWFORD, Annie D, Gettysburg, Pa, Nov 12 1862, 96
3763 MAINHART, Wm H, KETROW, Caroline B, Jany 8 1863, 96
3764 MCBRIDE, Abraham, GOODMAN, Matilda, Jany 8 1863, 97
3765 MARTZ, Wilson N, WHITMORE, Phoebe A C, Feby 17 1863, 97
3766 MORRIS, James, of 3d Delaware Regt, JONES, Ann, Mrs, widow of Tho's/her 3d husband, April 5 1863, 97
3767 MARTIN, David C (Dr), BRASHEARS, Bettie, of Tho's, May 5 1863, "ROHR", 97
3768 MEALEY, Cha's E, 2d wife, PHLEEGER, Rebecca, of John, May 21 1863, 97
3769 MICHAEL, Jacob, of David, HANN, Susan, May 11 1863, Balto, 97
3770 MCGINNIS, Sam'l D, GRIMES, Sarah Jane, May 26 1863, 97
3771 MARTIN, Dan'l Tho's, WILES, Ann Elizabeth, July 9 1863, 97
3772 MAYNARD, Warren, PYFER, Rachel E, of Wm B, Octr 8 1863, 97
3773 MILLER, Calvin R, of John F, ERVIN, Mary Virginia, Nov 14 1863, 97
3774 MILLER, Cha's W, of Dan'l of A/1st wife, STARR, Augusta A, of Maurice T, Decr 8 1863, 97
3775 MCCAHAN, John E, PEARCE, Lydia E, N Market, Decr 22 1863, 97
3776 MAYER, Max, GOLDENBERG, Henrietta, Jany 10 1864, 97
3777 MERRILL, Squire G, FISHER, Ann Mary, of Hugh, Jany 19 1864, 97
3778 MERRICK, Richard T (Capt), MCQUIRE, Miss, Washington, Feby 1864, 97
3779 MCCAHAN, E Luther, of Geo, TALBOTT, Elizabeth A, Balto, Feby 11 1864, 97
3780 MYER, James (Jun'r), MANTZ, Laura V, of Cha's, May 10 1864, 97
3781 MUSSEETER, Plummer J, BAKER, Elizabeth, June 16 1864, 97
3782 MERCER, Wm E, WEBSTER, Ada S, Fairview, July 12 1864, 97
3783 MERSHON, Stacy B, RAMSBURG, Martha M, of Wm H/ N York, July 22 1864, 97
3784 MACGILL, Lloyd T (Dr), 2d wife, EDWARDS, Miss, Decr 7 1864, 97
3785 MILLER, Joseph G, COCKLIN, Sarah C, Dauphin Co, Pa, Jany 19 1865, 97
3786 MORGAN, N J B (Rev), BALDWIN, Martha E, Balto, April 26 1865, 97
3787 MERCER, Cornelius, REICH, Annie R, of Philip, May 17 1865, 97
3788 MUMFORD, M Esau, GUNDLACK, Charlotte, June 20 1865, 97
3789 MCAVOY, Edward, of N York, PETERS, Mary Ellen, of Wm, June 27 1865, 97
3790 MCBRIDE, S Foster, YOUNG, Susan H, of Henry, July 24 1865, 97
3791 MCLANE, Rufus A, DERR, Margaret Jane, of Dan'l, Septr 23 1865, 97
3792 MARTIN, Cha's (Rev Dr), 3d wife, ROBINSON, Lucinda C, Nov 8 1865, 97
3793 MATTOON, Charles B, WEST, Alice, "DEETER", Nov 21 1865, 97
3794 MAYNARD, Tho's, STEVENSON, Susan, Decr 19 1865, 97
3795 MAYER, Albert Marshall (Prof), GOLDSBOROUGH, Kitty Duckett, of Dr Cha's, Decr 27 1865, 97
3796 MEALEY, Milton, 2d wife, SHEETS, Susan (Mrs), Jany 2 1866, 97
3797 MILLER, Henry, of Conrad, BUSING, Elizabeth, of Fred'k, June 27 1866, 97
3798 MARRIOTT, Charles W, FRIDAY, Susan A E, Augt 16 1866, 97
3799 MULL, James M, WHIP, Cornelia C, Septr 4 1866, 97

3800 *MCLANE*, Cha's A, *GARROTT*, Emma O, Septr 6 1866, 97
3801 *MIDDLEKAUFF*, J A, *MORELAND*, Elizabeth, Mrs, "WILCOXON", Octr 11 1866, 97
3802 *MEYER*, Charles G, *FOX*, S W, of Ernest A C, Nov 27 1866, 97
3803 *MCCLELLAN*, Curwin B (Maj), *CARMACK*, Nellie, of Eph'm, Decr 25 1866, Curwin, 97
3804 *MILLER*, Milton, of John W, *KLEIN*, Susan, of Stephen, Decr 26 1866, 97
3805 *MSHERRY*, James (Junior), *MCALEER*, Clara L, of Hugh, Jany 1867, 97
3806 *MEHRLING*, August, of Lewis, *DREHER*, Mary Caroline, Feby 13 1867, 98
3807 *MEREDITH*, John A, *HARDING*, Lucinda C, near N Market, May 23 1867, 98
3808 *MAIN*, Cornelius M, *LIPPS*, Sophia B, of John, June 11 1867, 98
3809 *MORGAN*, James, *ROWE*, Minnie, Septr 19 1867, 98
3810 *MEASELL*, Charles, *BRUNNER*, Kate, of Lewis, Octr 17 1867, 98
3811 *MANN*, Cha's B, of Stephen S, *EADER*, Annie C, of Tho's, Octr 16 1867, 98
3812 *MAGRUDER*, C C, *TURNER*, Ellen C, of Tho's, Jany 2 1868, 98
3813 *MULL*, George H, *GETZENDANNER*, Martha A, of Jefferson, March 10 1868, 98
3814 *MEHRLING*, George, *KIMMEL*, Mary C, April 30 1868, 98
3815 *MURRAY*, Edward B, *ENGEL*, Mary Ann, "MCAULY", Augt 11 1868, 98
3816 *MASER*, Frederick, *KLIPP*, Elizabeth, "of Schneider Maister KLIPP", Nov 8 1868, 98
3817 *MOBLEY*, Wm L, of Levi, *ALBAUGH*, Mary E, of Lewis/"Liberty", Jany 15 1859, 98
3818 *MILLER*, No first name given, *BARNES*, Miss, Jany 21 1869, 98
3819 *MCCLINTOCK*, H H, *CALLIFLOWER*, Cornelia E, of Rev Wm F, Jany 28 1869, 98
3820 *MOSER*, Abraham, *SCHIEDTKNECHT*, Mary Elizabeth, Jany 14 1869, 98
3821 *MOBERLY*, David H, of Levi, *DERTZEBAUGH*, Mary Jane, of John W, Feby 25 1869, 98
3822 *MELIUS*, Louis, of Conrad, *VAUGHAN*, Lottie Amelia, Parkersburg, Va, June 1 1869, 98
3823 *MORGAN*, George, of Tho's W, *SCHLEY*, Mary M, of Edward, June 22 1869, 98
3824 *MILLER*, Thomas G, *KAUFFMAN*, Cleantha M, of Warner, June 23 1869, 98
3825 *MATTHEWS*, Fred'k W, of Miss, *PETTITT*, Isabella, "BEALL", June 16 1869, 98
3826 *MITCHELL*, Tho's E (Dr), 2d wife, *RAMSBURGH*, Charlotte L, of Lewis, Octr 5 1869, 98
3827 *MAYNARD*, S S (Dr), *FULTON*, Maggie, of John, Octr 5 1869, 98
3828 *MARTIN*, Joseph R, *STONE*, Susan R, Decr 21 1869, 98
3829 *MOBLEY*, Hiram, of Levi, *BUCHFELTER*, Maggie, Decr 28 1869, 98
3830 *MCDONALD*, Frank P, *FLEMING*, Hallie M, of J Randolph, Feby 22 1870, 98
3831 *MCCAFFNEY*, Wm H, of Mich'l, *KOOGLE*, Jeanette, of Adam, May 3 1870, 98
3832 *MERMAN*, Washington P, 2d wife, *BAYER*, Elizabeth C (Mrs), "SCHMIDT", May 22 1870, 98
3833 *MAIN*, Joshua, *STALEY*, Susan E, Septr 27 1870, 98
3834 *MARK*, Geo W, *STEVENS*, Ann J, of Balto, Nov 1 1870, 98
3835 *MORNINGSTAR*, Philip H, *WHITE*, Mary Ellen, Nov 15 1870, 98
3836 *MEHRLING*, Henry, of Lewis, *ADAM*, Mary E, of Wm, March 21 1871, 98
3837 *MYERS*, John J, of Balto, *THOMAS*, Maggie E, of David O, April 27 1871, 98
3838 *MCGILL*, Samuel (Dr), of Dr John Tho's, *FAUNTLEROY*, Lizzie R, April 27 1871, Va, 98
3839 *MAYNARD*, Sollers S, *THOMAS*, Clayonia F, of Lewis M, Jan 2 1872, 98
3840 *MARKEY*, Henry S, of D J, *SHAFFER*, Isabel L, Jan 25 1872, 98
3841 *MAULSBY*, Wm Pinkney (Hon Sen'r), 2d wife, *FISHER*, Annie E M (Mrs), March 20 1872, 98
3842 *MCCARDELL*, Adrian C, *STONEBRAKER*, Alforetta, April 11 1872, 98
3843 *MCLELLAN*, Curwin B (Maj), of USA/2d wife, *GILBERT*, Alice Victoria, Ap 30 1872, 98
3844 *MCCAFFREY*, Aloysius B, of Mich'l, *HARDING*, A Virgine, of Ph H, May 21 1872, 98

3845 MCKENZIE, James E, *FIRESTONE*, Teresa E, of Henry, Septr 13 1872, 98
3846 MARSH, George W P, *STONE*, Julia A W, March 28 1872, 98
3847 MANTZ, Cyrus, of Milton, *COOPER*, Emma, Balto, Octr 31 1872, 98
3848 MULHORN, John E, of John, *FAUBEL*, Barbara A, Nov 14 1872, 99
3849 MORRISON, James F, *SIFFORD*, Irene C, of John, Nov 26 1872, 99
3850 MASON, Wm Pinkney, *MCGILL*, Elizab Ruthven, of Dr Th J, Decr 26 1872, 99
3851 MAGRUDER, Wm F, *EBBERTS*, Sarah E, Decr 31 1872, 99
3852 MARTZ, David H, *HOUCK*, Laura F, Feb 13 1873, 99
3853 MILLER, Cha's W, of Dan'l/(Post Master)/2d wife, *CASTLE*, Emma F, of Dan'l, Feb 20 1873, 99
3854 MEALEY, Charles E, of Isaiah/3d wife, *MARRIOTT*, Mary Rose, of A W, March 11 1873, 99
3855 MORGAN, Napoleon B, *BRUCHEY*, Mary E, (not listed as Miss), March 10 1873, 99
3856 MULLIN, S Calvin (Prof), *WILHIDE*, Maggie M (Mrs), "HUNT", March 12 1873, 99
3857 MCSHERRY, Edward C (Dr), of James, *CANN*, Bertie, of Rev Tho's M, March 25 1873, 99
3858 MOSER, Amideas C, *BALTZELL*, Virginia C, March 27 1873, 99
3859 MCSHERRY, Edward C (Dr), of James, *CANN*, Bertie, of Rev Thos M, March 25 1873, repeated from above, 99
3860 MILLER, D S, of Upper Sandusk, O, *WHITTER*, Fany, of Tho's, April 10 1873, Balto, 99
3861 MOSER, Emideas C, *BALTZELL*, Virginia J, March 27 1873, repeated from above, 99
3862 MILLER, Alburtus A, *LAMBERT*, Georgetta J G, of Geo, July 3 1873, 99
3863 MAIN, Carson H, *JACOBS*, Charlotte, Augt 7 1873, 99
3864 MANTZ, Wm Eugene G Mantz, of Emanuel, *DELP*, Annie M C, Octr 23 1873, 99
3865 MILLER, Simon S (Rev), *BISER*, Mary G, of Geo C, Nov 25 1873, 99
3866 MANTZ, F Miller, of Frank, *BECKETT*, Annie B, Feb 17 1874, 99
3867 MCCUTCHEON, Tho's, of Pittsburgh, *CRONISE*, Nellie, of Sam'l, Ap 28 1874, 99
3868 MULLENDORE, Oliver S, *HORNER*, Eliza F, Septr 9 1874, 99
3869 MEIER, George E, *DONNELLY*, Mary E, Augt 31 1874, 99
3870 MOLESWORTH, Joshua, *CONDON*, Susan J, Nov 12 1874, 99
3871 MARKEY, J Hanshew, of David J, *WILLIARD*, Ida M, of Ezra, Nov 24 1874, 99
3872 MCGILL, Wardlaw (Dr), of Dr J Th, *PEARRE*, Georgia, of Geo A, Decr 17 1874, 99
3873 MCPHERSON, Wm W, of Rob't G, *BUTLER*, Gettie, Decr 23 1874, Minn, 99
3874 MOBERLY, Edmund F, *STALEY*, Addie A, Jan 12 1875, 99
3875 MCPHERSON, Wm W, of Rob't G/(repeated from above), *BUTLER*, Gettle, Minna, Decr 23 1874, 99
3876 MORRIS, Wm L, *DILL*, Georgianna, of John F, March 16 1875, 99
3877 MAIN, James M C, *WILHIDE*, Mollie E, March 11 1875, 99
3878 MEASELL, J F, *SPONSELLER*, Catharine A, March 23 1875, 99
3879 MUSSER, Francis T, *MCDEVITT*, Susan R, March 25 1875, 99
3880 MAYN, David Y, *BOPST*, Fannie May, April 20 1875, 99
3881 MOTTER, John C, *MARKEN*, Ellie B, of Josiah R, May 20 1875, 99
3882 MOORE, Wm H, of John T, *KAHLE*, Jennie L, Sep 16 1875, 99
3883 MILLER, Wm H, of Utica/2 wife, *SCHLEY*, Jennie, of Dr Fairfax, Sep 29 1875, 99
3884 MEHRLING, Jacob, of Caspar, *JORDAN*, Lydia, Nov 16 1875, 99
3885 MYERS, A (Rev), *BITTLE*, S L (Mrs), of Rev D H, Nov 24 1875, 99
3886 MACGILL, Rob't H, 2d wife, *RIGGS*, Amelia J, Decr 15 1875, 99
3887 MILLER, Frank P, *CRAMER*, Cora M, Jan 20 1876, 99
3888 MOBERLY, Lewis C, of L H, *WINTERS*, Mollie A, Balto, Feb 22 1876, 99

3889 MOORE, John T (Junr), SCOTT, Mary Ella, April 4 1876, 99
3890 MONTGOMERY, Wm T, 2d wife, SHAFFNER, Ellen J R, July 27 1876, 100
3891 MILLER, John, WISNER, Mary M, of M'l, July 1876, 100
3892 MAULSBY, Wm P (Jun'r), PIGMAN, Henrietta H, of Hanson B, Nov 16 1876, 100
3893 MULL, Geo F (Prof), HIGBEE, Annie F, Mercersb, Octr 11 1877, 100
3894 MACGILL, John S, SCHAEFFER, Ella V, of L M, Octr 24 1877, 100
3895 MERCHANT, John W, RIDENOUR, Ella, Octr 30 1877, 100
3896 MINDELL, C B, of Phila, ENGLISH, Mary J, March 15th 1878, 100
3897 MCCOY, Edward, of Balto, TAYLOR, Harriet Ann, (not listed as Miss), Mar 28 1878, 100
3898 MEYER, Herman L, of this city, SHAWBRAKER, Margaret E, Jan 14 1879, 100
3899 MULHOM, John E, of this city, FUGITT, Mary E, of Winchester, Mar 27 1878, 100
3900 MAINHART, Charles C, HORINE, E F, Feb 18th 1879, 100
3901 MCGILL, Robert, MCGILL, Era R, Sept 3d 1879, 100
3902 MARRIOTT, Alphes W, ROBINSON, Barbara, Sept 18th 1879, 100
3903 MILLER, Edgar L, of George, KNAUFF, Mary E, of Cha's/ (not listed as Miss), Aug 22 1880, 100
3904 MASON, Temple, RAGER, Maud D, (not listed as Miss), Oct 3d 1880, 100
3905 MARKELL, Louis, of Geo, SMITH, Mary K, of Geo Wm/(not listed as Miss), Nov 4th 1880, 100
3906 MOBERLY, Geo R, of Lewis, BARNES, Mary C, (not listed as Miss), Jan 13th 1881, 100
3907 MOBERLY, J Wm, of Lewis, STONE, Florence J, (not listed as Miss), March 20th 1881, 100
3908 MULNIX, Lorenzo E, HENDRICKSON, Mollie J, (not listed as Miss), May 19th 1881, 100
3909 MILLER, James H, of Geo, GITTINGER, Sallie R, of Edward/ (not listed as Miss), June 1st 1881, 100
3910 MURRAY, James A, DERR, Fannie J, of Wm/ (not listed as Miss), Oct 26th 1881, 100
3911 MCCONNES, Omer, (@ MCCANNER, Owen), KLINE, Ella, of Josiah, December 29 1881, 100
3912 MCDANNIEL, A S, HUBERT, Mary E, (of Albert), February 15 1882, 100
3913 MOORE, Elmer E, PHOEBUS, Catharine H E, of Bnj, May 11th 1882, 100
3914 MULLHORN, George W, MANSFIELD, Mary, (not listed as Miss), Oct 17th 1882, 100
3915 MENDENHALL, H G (Rev), BREATON, Lucretia M, Niece of Calvin PAGE, Oct 19th 1882, (not listed as Miss), 100
3916 MILLER, Charles B, TAYLOR, Ida C, ditto marks of prior record, Oct 22d 1882, {niece of Calvin PAGE compile}, 100
3917 MILLER, S E, WACHTER, Olive A, Oct 25th 1882, 100
3918 MOBERLY, Charles E, (@MOBBERLY), SCHLEIGH, Nellie V, of Fred/(@SLEIGH), Nov 29th 1882, 100
3919 MILLER, Jacob, HANSHEW, Caroline V, of Hary, Decr 28th 1882, 100
3920 MINES, Wm M, GAMBRILL, Annie M, 2nd husband/(not listed as Miss), April 19th 1883, 100
3921 MCLEAN, Donald, RITCHIE, Emily M, of John, April 24th 1883, 100
3922 MARKELL, Frank H, of Frank, KELLER, Mary H, of Dewitt (not listed as Miss), Septmber 19th 1883, 100
3923 MCGILL, Ernest (Rev), MCPHERSON, Mary B, October 2d 1883, 100
3924 MORGAN, Napoleon B, ORR, Sabina, (not listed as Miss), Oct 18th 1883, 100
3925 MYERS, Joseph H, of Harpers Ferry, ROSENOUR, Amelia, of B, May 25 1884, 100
3926 MCBRIDE, A C, ROUTZAHN, Annie E, June 3 1884, 100

3927 **MILLER**, Wm V, **MCCARDELL**, Nettie R, Oct 15 1884, 100
3928 **MORT**, Allen B, (@MANTZ), **MCGILL**, Belle W, of Dr Tho's/(@Arabella), Nov 12 1884, 100
3929 **MYERS**, Joseph, **RUBENSTEIN**, Pauline, March 15 1885, 100
3930 **MAYTON**, James C (Dr), **MCDERITT**, Nannie M, March 25 1885, 100
3931 **MOORE**, Joseph F, **PILES**, Clara J, (@PYLES), May 21 1885, 100
3932 **MYER**, Edward F, **GITTINGS**, Lillie G, May 21 1885, 100a
3933 **MCPHERSON**, Robert G (Jr), **HACKLETON**, Ethel, June 29 1885, 100a
3934 **MILLER**, Charles H, **RAMSBURG**, Emma, Oct 7 1885, 100a
3935 **MCCLOUW**, Charles E, **GITTINGER**, Mary C, Oct 14 1885, 100a
3936 **MOFFETT**, Jacob, **REICH**, Lillian C, October 27 1885, 100a
3937 **MULLINIX**, Thomas P, 2d wife, **BYRNES**, Mollie C, (@BYRNE), November 5 1885, 100a
3938 **MCKENZIE**, J S (Dr), **STAPLETON**, Jullia E, December 8 1885, 100a
3939 **MCMANTO**, Dennis, (@MCMAN), **WALLING**, Lilly, of Henry, July 14 1886, 100a
3940 **MARTIN**, Charles R, **MOBERLY**, Nannie G, of Lewis, October 20 1886, 100a
3941 **MARTZ**, Wm C, (@MANTZ, Willie C), **SHAFFER**, M C, (@SCHAEFFER, Mollie E), October 28t 1886, 100a
3942 **MAYNARD**, Grafton, **CASTER**, Emma, (@CARTER), October 27 1886, 100a
3943 **METZ**, Frank M (Dr), **WINEBRENNER**, Mollie L, February 25 1887, 100a
3944 **MONEY**, Wm W, **MURPHY**, Ella M, of Dennis, June 14 1887, 100a
3945 **MCDANIEL**, James E, **LAMAR**, Carrie K, July 13 1887, 100a
3946 **MILLER**, J Marshal, **HARDING**, Fannie V, November 10 1887, 100a
3947 **MARSHALL**, John W, **PRETTYJOHN**, Annie M W, "STAUFFER"/(@PETTYJOHN), November 15 1887, 100a
3948 **MCKINNEY**, A F, 2 wife/(@Andrew), **DELASHMUTT**, Annie, November 19 1887, 100a
3949 **MYERS**, Geo M, **DASHIEL**, Lizzie K, of Rev J H, January 25 1888, 100a
3950 **MESBEY**, Tho's G, (@MOSSBURG), **HILLIARD**, Clara B, February 21 1888, 100a
3951 **MILLER**, Daniel B, **BROWN**, Hattie, (@Harriet), February 23 1888, 100a
3952 **MICHAEL**, Edward L, **SMITH**, Susan E, of Hy, Feb 28 1888, 100a
3953 **MOBERLY**, Marion S, of Lewis, **KLINE**, Irene T, May 31 1888, 100a
3954 **MOBERLY**, Robert E, of Lewis, **BRENGLE**, Rosa M, August 2 1888, 100a
3955 **MOORE**, J H (Rev), 3d wife/(@John H), **CUNNINGHAM**, Bessie, of B Amos/(@Elizabeth G), Oct 24 1888, 100a
3956 **MICHAEL**, Harry C, of Jacob(@Henry), **LOCKNER**, Nannie R, of Nich, Oct 30 1888, 100a
3957 **MAINHARDT**, Lewis D, (@MAINHART), **HORINE**, Gothe' M, (@Lottie M), October 30 1888, 100a
3958 **MILLER**, Cha's M, **STULL**, Fannie E, November 14 1888, 100a
3959 **MARTZ**, George S, **WARNER**, Clara, (#), November 28 1888, 100a
3960 **MILLER**, George M C, **DERR**, Daisy, January 15 1889, 100a
3961 **MILLER**, Wm, **O'HARA**, Clara, January 31 1889, 100a
3962 **MILLER**, Frederick, **FULTON**, Alice, April 3 1889, 100a
3963 **MYERS**, Thomas H, **BURCK**, Florence C, (@BURCH), April 30 1889, 100a
3964 **MILLER**, Wm L, **WEIKERT**, Mamie, May 22 1889, 100a
3965 **MYERS**, G Edward, (@George E), **STEWART**, Mary E, September 12 1889, 100a
3966 **MANTZ**, Peter, **KOLB**, Ella, Sept 23 1889, 100a
3967 **MELCHER**, Wm H, (@MELCHIOR), **STEINER**, Grace, Sept 26 1889, 100a
3968 **MCCORMICK**, John M, 2d wife, **TUCKER**, Bessie C, Oct 9 1889, 100a
3969 **MERCHANT**, George, **BOWSE**, Almira J, {last name illegible-compiler}, October 22 1889, 100b

3970 MURPHY, Richard N, *RIDDLEMOSER*, Cora M, Oct 31 1889, 100b
3971 MCKINSTRY, Robert, *GAULT*, Maggie, November 28 1889, 100b
3972 MCGINNIS, George B, *JACOBS*, Katie C, November 28 1889, 100b
3973 MCCLOW, Oliver E, 2d wife, *SMITH*, Margie E, January 14 1890, 100b
3974 MARTIN, Wm N, *MILLER*, Isabella V, of Wm S, February 12 1890, 100b
3975 MERCER, Ralph, *EDMONDS*, Ella, April 8 1890, 100b
3976 MARTELLE, Lewis P, *BURCK*, Carrie R, April 13 1890, 100b
3977 MORNINGSTAR, George C, *BOHN*, Annie E, April 24 1890, 100b
3978 MILLER, Franklin L, *ROUTZAHN*, Mollie A, May 20 1890, 100b
3979 MCBURDETT, George B, *SMITH*, Annie E, May 21 1890, 100b
3980 MANTZ, Frank, of Wm, *NEER*, R L, June 25 1890, 100b
3981 MUNSHOWER, Cha's E, *YINGER*, Emma L, Sep 9 1890, 100b
3982 MEHRLING, Wm H, of August, *LYONS*, Carrie O, (@LOYNS), Sept 30 1890, 100b
3983 MICHAEL, Jesse H, *SHAWEN*, Lizzie, Oct 28 1891, 100b
3984 MCSHERRY, J Roger, of Judge Ja's, *ROSS*, Cornelia R, of C W, Oct 30 1891, {overwritten 29 1890-compiler}, 100b
3985 MYERS, Edward, of Oliver, *PYRELKE*, Mary, (last name illegible-compiler}, Nov 11 1891, 100b
3986 MOLER, Robert L, *STRONG*, Mollie, Dec 23 1890, 100b
3987 MARKER, John H, *PHILOWER*, Bertha M, Dec 26 1890, 100b
3988 MILLER, Harvey C, *VALENTINE*, Annie F, Dec 31st 1890, 100b
3989 QUYNN, William, 1st wife, *BRANSON*, Margaret, Balto, Feby 6 1821, 102
3990 NEWPORT, Adam, *KEHLER*, Margaret, "KELLY" of Jacob, May 12 1822, 102
3991 NORRIS, Basil, 2d wife, *CHARLTON*, Jane, of Usher, Nov 12 1822, 102
3992 NEILL, John W, Tailor, *PEPPER*, Miss, Phila, March 1823, 102
3993 NELSON, Madison, of Gen'l Roger, *MARCILLY*, Josephine, April 22 1823, 102
3994 QUYNN, William, 2d wife, *WHITTINGTON*, Louisa (Mrs), LOKEY/Geo town, DC, April 27 1823, 102
3995 OTT, Thomas, *LINN*, Mary, of Philip, Septr 2d 1823, 102
3996 NESZBAUM, David, *GEDULTIG*, Rebecca, Octr 13 1825, 102
3997 NAGLE, Charles, *ROLLINGTON*, Sophia, of John, April 6 1826, 102
3998 NEAL, Joseph, *FISCHER*, Minerva, of Adam, Augt 27 1826, 102
3999 NORRIS, Wm, of Barnabas, *NAYLOR*, Mahala, Decr 7 1826, 102
4000 NORRIS, Samuel, of Barnabas, *HOUCK*, Harriott, of Peter, May 3 1827, 102
4001 NICHOLS, James, *MCGUIRE*, R A, May 24 1827, 102
4002 ORDNER, George, *MARTIN*, Sarah, June 17 1827, 102
4003 NOAH, Mordicai Manassah, *JACKSON*, Rebecca, N York, Nov 28 1827, 102
4004 OTT, John, of Michael, *OTT*, Mary (Mrs), his brother Tho's widow, Feby 3 1828, 102
4005 NUSZ, Cyrus, *GROVE*, Susan, April 10 1828, 102
4006 NICHOLS, Seth H, 1st wife, *HEICHLER*, Catherine, of Henry, May 5 1829, 102
4007 NICHOLS, George (Junior), *BEAVANS*, Mary Ann, Octr 24 1830, 102
4008 OTIS, William, *LATE*, Mary A C, of Mich'l, March 12 1832, 102
4009 NICKEL, Jacob, of Adam, *RAGAN*, Elizabeth, May 29 1832, 102
4010 NIXDORFF, Tobias, 2d wife, *BIXLER*, Angelina A, Balto, Feby 7 1833, 102
4011 NEYHOFF, Christian, *KIEFFER*, Susan, April 10 1833, 102
4012 NEY, Adam, *BURGESS*, Elizabeth, April 23 1833, 102
4013 OGLE, James, *HOUCK*, Harriott, of John, April 26 1833, 102

4014 OURAND, David, WALKER, Ann L, of John/Glade/(omitted before), Decr 1830, 102
4015 NUSZ, Frederick, 2d wife, ZIELER, Barbara (Mrs), widow of Geo, July 29 1834, 102
4016 ORDNER, Daniel, of Peter, HANSHEW, Susan B, of Fred'k, April 28 1835, 102
4017 NORRIS, Matthias, of Barnabas, FORD, Susan, July 30 1835, 102
4018 ORNDORFF, Henry, WICKHAM, Harriott, Feby 18 1836, 102
4019 NEWELL, Daniel (Rev), RITCHIE, Annalinah, of Col John, June 16 1836, 102
4020 O'NEILL, Tho's H, of Horatio/1st wife, WEBB, Tacy, of Jos B, Decr 6 1836, 102
4021 NEY, John (Sen'r), 2d wife, GILBERT, Julietta, April 18 1837, 102
4022 NEILL, Alexander (Jun'r), NELSON, Mary S, of John, April 20 1837, 102
4023 NICHOLS, John, LAMBRECHT, Sophia, Augt 15 1837, 102
4024 NELSON, John, of Gen'l Roger/2d wife, TENANT, Matilda, Balto, March 13 1838, 102
4025 O'NEAL, Israel C, DOLL, Catharine, of Jacob, March 29 1838, 102
4026 NORRIS, Lot, GAITHER, Elizabeth Ann, of Wm, June 28 1838, 102
4027 ORDNER, Peter, of Peter, HAUPT, Ann Rebecca, Middletown, Jany 6 1839, 102
4028 NUSZBAUM, Daniel, BORING, Sarah, March 23 1839, 102
4029 NICHOLS, John Randolph, of Peter, MYERS, Catharine, of Israel, May 2 1839, 102
4030 NAUMANN, John C V, GEITZ, Mary, Augt 1839, 102
4031 NEALL, Joseph H, STONER, Eliza Ann, of Ezra "STEINER", Nov 19 1839, 103
4032 OSBOURN, James W, SCHERER, Sophia H, of Lewis, June 18 1840, 103
4033 OGLE, Joachim, KESSLER, Matilda, of Jacob/Tiffin, O, June 18 1840, 103
4034 NUSSBAUM, Jacob, 2d wife & sisters, EBERHARDT, Matilda (Mrs), June 28 1840, 103
4035 NUSZ, William, of Henry, LEONARD, Louisa, Feby 11 1841, 103
4036 ORDNER, John, of Peter, WAYS, Isabella, of Basil, April 15 1841, 103
4037 NELSON, Wm Burrows, of John, WORTHINGTON, Comfort M, Feby 15 1842, 103
4038 NICHOLS, Seth H, 2d wife, MIMM, Mary Ann, April 8 1842, 103
4039 OWENS, Hugh, BAUGHER, Elizabeth (Mrs), widow of John B, May 2 1843, 103
4040 NUSZ, George M, of Jacob, HALLER, Susan, of Henry, Feby 29 1844, 103
4041 NICHOLS, Edward, of Peter, KANTNER, Elizabeth, of Geo, Septr 5 1844, 103
4042 NORRIS, James Lawson, of Barnabas, BAKER, Ann Rebecca, Septr 4 1845, 103
4043 O'NEALL, Thomas H, of Horatio G/2d wife, HALBERT, Emeline, June 16 1846, 103
4044 O'NEIL, James, YANITZ, Mary, June 30 1846, 103
4045 QUYNN, John T, of John, HANSHEW, Mary Margaret, of Henry, Nov 24 1846, 103
4046 NUSZBAUM, John, RIGGS, Susan J, April 22 1847, 103
4047 QUYNN, Allen G, of John, HAUER, Harriott, of Dan'l Jun'r, July 13 1847, 103
4048 OLLAND, Henry, "ALLAND", LENTZ, Ann, Septr 25 1847, 103
4049 NOLAND, Michael, MAGUIRE, Jane, April 23 1848, 103
4050 NEED, John, TRAINER, Mary, April 27 1848, 103
4051 OGLE, John, ECKIS, Juliann, June 11 1848, 103
4052 NORRIS, Geo Wash Lafayette, CONRAD, Elizabeth, of Jos, Augt 1 1848, 103
4053 NICKEL, Daniel, of Adam, CHESNUT, Caroline, in Balto, Augt 16 1848, 103
4054 OGLE, Vincent, FREANER, Margaret, of Hagerstown, Decr 26 1848, 103
4055 O'LEARY, Thomas, HOFFMAN, Elizab Steiner, of Wm C, Jany 16 1849, 103
4056 NICODEMUS, Nathan, of John/1st wife, SCHOLL, Mary E, of Elias, Jany 16 1849, 103
4057 NEIDIG, Benjamin, SMITH, Mary M, May 1 1849, 103
4058 NELSON, Joseph R, 1st wife, CARSON, Eliza A, of York, Pa, July 3 1849, 103
4059 NUSZ, Hiram M, of Ezra, MOBLEY, Mary Ann, of Levi, Octr 4 1849, 103
4060 O'DONNOHUE, James, SIMPSON, Mary S, of John/Geo Town, DC, Nov 1849, 103

4061 O'NEILL, John H, of Patrick, BECKWITH, Catharine, Ohio, Nov 27 1849, 103
4062 NICHOLAS, Robert Carter, 2d wife, MCGOWAN, Eliza, Jany 24 1850, 103
4063 OSTERLY, Frederick, of Geo, ROSS, Maria, "ROSZ", March 10 1850, 103
4064 OSTERLY, George (Junior), 1st wife, BORCHER, Elizabeth, "BAYER", Octr 27 1851, 103
4065 NICODEMUS, John Lewis, of John, CASSELL, Nancy, Decr 17 1850, 103
4066 NOTTNGAEL, Lenhardt, STEPHAN, Maria, Decr 15 1850, 103
4067 NOTTNAGEL, John Jacob, SAHM, Philipina, of Peter, Feby 4 1851, 103
4068 NUSZ, Oliver T, of Ezra, INGMAN, Cecelia, of Joshua, Feby 11 1851, 103
4069 NELSON, Stephen B, FOUTZ, Agnes Ann, of Joseph, April 8 1851, 103
4070 OHLER, Solomon, CLEMM, Mary A, Glade, June 22 1851, 103
4071 O'NEALL, Singleton H, of Horatio G, HAYS, Sarah E, July 10 1851, 103
4072 NOEL, J K, (* John K NOLIN), DONNE, Eliza A, of John Aug's, Septr 24 1851, 103
4073 OHLER, Levi S, HOUCK, Catharine, Glade, May 2 1852, 104
4074 OTT, Jacob D, HOUCK, Margaret Ann, June 20 1852, 104
4075 NORWOOD, William, RYAN, Barbara Ellen, June 27 1852, 104
4076 OLDFIELD, Granville S (Junior), STEVENS, Virginia, of Commodore, Septr 15 1852, Balto, 104
4077 OVERTON, John Brooke, PIMM, Mary Elizabeth, Decr 23 1852, 104
4078 NICODEMUS, Nathan, 2d wife, FORREST, Mary C, Feby 8 1853, 104
4079 NUSZ, Sylvester J, of Ezra, SUMAN, Ann Cecelia, April 20 1853, 104
4080 OTTO, William, GRAHE', Augusta (Mrs), "BEHRENS", June 10 1853, 104
4081 NICODEMUS, John (Sen'r), 2d wife, WRIGHT, Mary, Octr 11 1853, 104
4082 QUEEN, J T, (*John Theodore), HALLER, Louisa M, of Joshua, Nov 30 1853, 104
4083 NICODEMUS, J Luther, of Boonsboro, SMITH, Eveline, of George, Nov 29 1853, 104
4084 OGLE, John Oliver, of John/1st wife, BELLEAU, Margaret W (Mrs), Glasgow, Mo, Decr 29 1853, 104
4085 NICHOLS, William, 2d wife, THOMAS, Ellen H, Decr 28 1853, 104
4086 QUANTRILL, Archibald R, 2d wife, SANDS, Mary, of Geo W/"CRONISE", Feby 8 1854, 104
4087 NELSON, Nathan, 3d wife, WAGERS, Elizabeth M, Feby 26 1854, 104
4088 NUSZ, Peter Elias, of Cyrus, MCDEVITT, Mary M, March 14 1954, 104
4089 NULL, George, SWEADNER, Mary Louisa, Liberty, June 8 1854, 104
4090 NICODEMUS, Martin L, CARTER, Lucinda, Augt 15 1854, 104
4091 NEIDIG, Isaac, of Abraham, BOWERS, Mary Jane, of Dan'l, Octr 31 1854, 104
4092 NELSON, Arthur, BYNGE, Ellen, "BING", Feby 14 1855, 104
4093 OBENDORFFER, Cha's Leonard, 2d wife, WEINICH, Margaret, March 14 1855, 104
4094 NEAL, George Henry Clay, of Joseph, TONGUE, Ann Amelia, "FISCHER"/Fauquier Co, Va, March 20 1855, 104
4095 OTT, Samuel J, STENGEN, Catherine, of Fred'k/Funkstown, Jany 31 1856, 104
4096 O'NEILL, Howard D, MACMANUS, Alice, Zanesville, Ohio, May 15 1856, 104
4097 NIXDORFF, Samuel, of Tobias, PURDY, Susan R, Nov 13 1856, 104
4098 O'BRIAN, George W, FOGEL, Minerva A, Jany 2 1857, 104
4099 OGLE, George W, HINEA, Elizabeth, Jany 29 1857, 104
4100 NUSZ, James W Fred'k, RICKERD, Rachel M, Shookstown, March 17 1857, 104
4101 O'DONNOHUE, Florence (Dr), STALLINGS, Ellen M, of Jos, June 16 1857, 104
4102 NEIDIG, Maurice O, RYERSON, Lizza A, Muscatine, Iowa, June 2 1858, 104
4103 ORME, Walter A, GRIFFITH, Emeline, of Phelemon, July 27 1858, 104
4104 NALLS, G W, (*George W), FUNK, Catharine E, (*FINK), Augt 16 1858, 104

4105 *OGLE*, John Oliver, of John/2d wife, *LEEBRICK*, Matilda A, Wayne Co, Ind, Septr 22 1858, 104

4106 *OBERLEIN*, Christian, *HEYSER*, Augusta, Octr 3 1858, 104

4107 *ORRISON*, Andrew, *ADKINS*, Malinda, Octr 12 1858, 104

4108 *NOLTE'*, Albert, his brothers widow, *NOLTE'*, Margaret Beck (Mrs), Nov 18 1858, 104

4109 *NAZERENUS*, John, 2d wife, *FISCHBACH*, Matilda (Mrs), March 9 1859, 104

4110 *NICHOLS*, John, *HUNTER*, Mary C, Point of Rocks, Augt 16 1859, 104

4111 *NELSON*, John H, of Henry, *ADAMS*, Jennette, of Valentine/4th daughter, Octr 4 1859, 104

4112 *OVIEDO*, De Don Esteban Santa Cruz, *BARTLETT*, Frances Amelia, Octr 13 1859, N York, 104

4113 *O'BOYLE*, John H, *DELASHMUTT*, Sarah E, of Elias L, Octr 20 1859, 104

4114 *OTT*, John, (Painter), *DUVALL*, Augusta, of John, Decr 28 1859, 104

4115 *NEYHOFF*, Joseph A, *ROGERS*, Susan V, Balto, Decr 22 1859, 105

4116 *NORRIS*, John D, *SMITH*, Susan Caroline, Decr 27 1859, 105

4117 *OGLE*, Thomas A, *MEALY*, Anna Lucretia, Jany 24 1860, 105

4118 *NELSON*, Robert, aged 80 years/2d wife, *KOON*, Catharine, aged 65 years, Feby 16 1860, 105

4119 *O'NEAL*, Israel C, 2d wife, *CANDLER*, Annie E (Mrs), Balto, Feby 18 1860, 105

4120 *O'NEAL*, John L, son of Israel C, *HAMMONTREE*, Dorcus M, Balto, March 27 1860, 105

4121 *NICKEL*, Adam Luther, of Jacob, *SCHRAYER*, Cornelia C, of Solomon W, April 10 1860, 105

4122 *NUSSBAUM*, Philip Henry, of Jacob, *JAMES*, Lydia A R, of Washington, April 17 1860, 105

4123 *NORRIS*, Lloyd, *BISHOP*, Sophia E, May 6 1860, 105

4124 *NOONAN*, Joseph H, *KEMP*, M Ellen, of David/"Rocky Springs", June 5 1860, 105

4125 *OTTO*, James H B, *FLOWERS*, Ann E W, of Rev Benj'n C/"Lewistown", Augt 9 1860, 105

4126 *NAGLE*, Charles W, of Cha's, *WILCOX*, Annie, Baltimore, Octr 25 1860, 105

4127 *NAILL*, Franklin A, *SLUSS*, Susan C, "SCHLOSS", Octr 25 1860, 105

4128 *OVELMAN*, William J, *SIX*, Jane E, Octr 30 1860, 105

4129 *NAILL*, William W, *BAILE*, Ann, of Abner, Jany 15 1861, 105

4130 *NULL*, George W, *MAIN*, Ann Maria, Creagerstown, Jany 31 1861, 105

4131 *NOONAN*, Edward W, of John, *BYRNE*, M C, Galena, Ill, Feby 11 1861, 105

4132 *NELSON*, Joseph R, 2d wife, *BROOKS*, Eliza, March 26 1861, 105

4133 *O'DONNOHUE*, No first name given, (*Dennis), *HARDING*, Miss, of Norman B/(*M Louisa), April 2 1861, 105

4134 *OWENS*, John, of California, *KOONTZ*, Sophia M, of George, Octr 8 1862, 105

4135 *NORTON*, W H, 5th Connecticut Regt, *FUNK*, Fannie A, Nov 27 1862, 105

4136 *OTTER*, Joseph D, *MAYBURRY*, Mary, of Justinian/Balto, April 13 1863, 105

4137 *NOTABIT*, Quesoda, *LITTLEWITT*, Elmira Elizabeth, (not listed as Miss)/N York, March 6 1863, 105

4138 *NEWBANKS*, Charles Edward, *HOTZ*, Sarah C, of Martin, May 15 1863, 105

4139 *ORRICK*, George W, *BRINING*, Amelia G, Boonsborough, Augt 4 1863, 105

4140 *NICODEMUS*, Wm H, *BROWNING*, Jennie A, Nov 18 1863, 105

4141 *NORRIS*, William Lee, *WELSH*, Rachel B, Nov 12 1863, 105

4142 *NUSSBAUM*, Adam F, *LONG*, Mary E, (not listed as Miss)/Glade, April 6 1864, 105

4143 *NIXDORFF*, T S, *EVERHART*, Sue, Balto, Nov 15 1864, 105

4144 *NICKEL*, Christian, *BERKLEY*, Nancy (Mrs), July 9 1865, 105

4145 **NYMAN**, Lewis B, **WIEST**, Catharine T, Washington Co, Feby 13 1866, 105
4146 *O'CONNELL*, Michael, **LIDAY**, Margaret, March 16 1866, 105
4147 *NAX*, Francis (Prof), 2d wife, **BARTELLE**, Mary, May 22 1866, 105
4148 **NEAL**, Lewis (Dr), **HALLER**, Alice L, of Mich'l H, Nov 8 1866, 105
4149 **NICODEMUS**, Eli, **SCHERER**, Mary, of John, Octr 8 1867, 105
4150 **NEIDHARDT**, Rudolph A, **BRENGEL**, Caroline, of Nicholus, Nov 5 1867, 105
4151 **NUSSBAUM**, McHenry P, **SNYDER**, Sarah J, Nov 28 1867, 105
4152 **NICHOLS**, Charles S, of Edward, **HEMSTONE**, Louisa, Jany 2 1868, 105
4153 **NICODEMUS**, H Baxter, **FULTON**, Alice C, July 16 1868, 105
4154 **OWEN**, Edward W, of Montgomery Co, **BRENNER**, Henrietta, of Wm, Nov 17 1868, 105
4155 **NELSON**, Robert, 3d wife, **DORSEY**, Ann, May 27 1869, 105
4156 **NIXDORFF**, Lewis M, of Henry, **MILLER**, Eliza P, Octr 20 1869, 105
4157 **NOONAN**, Francis H (Dr), of John, **THOMAS**, Fanny, of Lewis M, Nov 9 1869, 106
4158 **OSBORNE**, F M W, **MORGAN**, R Adelaide, of Romulus G/BALDERSON, Decr 7 1869, 106
4159 **OATES**, Cha's T, of John, **SMITH**, Catherine, of Balto, May 18 1870, 106
4160 **NOONAN**, Joseph J, of John/2d wife, **ROGERS**, M E Anna, Octr 27 1870, 106
4161 **NELSON**, Edward (Dr), of Madison, **WILLSON**, Hallie M, of John J, Decr 15 1870, 106
4162 **OSBOURN**, Alexander L, of Va, **SMITH**, Fannie V, of John, May 30 1871, 106
4163 **NUSZ**, J F, **LEACHEY**, Agnes V, Augt 1 1871, 106
4164 **NICHOLS**, Clayton, of Seth H, **STIER**, Miss, of Hamilton, Augt 1871, "Hoax" listed begin & end, 106
4165 **OULD**, E A (Dr), of NY, **MCLANAHAN**, Alice, of Wm M B, Nov 23 1871, 106
4166 **O'HARRA**, John, **BAER**, Mollie L, Bartonsville, March 28 1872, 106
4167 **NELSON**, Frederick J, of Madison, **SCHISSLER**, Kate S, of Hiram, Nov 12 1872, 106
4168 **NEWELL**, Wm H (Dr), **NEWTON**, Jennie W, New Jersey, April 22 1873, 106
4169 **OLAND**, Carlton E, **CRAVER**, Margaret C, Octr 15 1873, 106
4170 **OFFUTT**, John L, of Tenn, **CANDLER**, Adelaide, Jan 7 1874, 106
4171 **OTT**, Geo W (Jun'r), of John, **HITESHEW**, Jennie, Jan 13 1874, 106
4172 **NICODEMUS**, Isaac C (Jun'r), **RECK**, Martha C, Octr 29 1874, 106
4173 **OWEN**, Robert Dale, **KELLOGG**, Lottie Walton, June 23 1876, 106
4174 **O'HARRA**, Charles E, **ESWORTHY**, Fannie, Nov 28 1876, 106
4175 **OCKMAY**, James H (Rev), age 66, *death*, Colored Methodist, May 13 1877, 106
4176 **OBENDERFFER**, Fred'k W, **GETZENDANNER**, Jennie, of Jacob R, Jan 22 1878, 106
4177 **NEIDIG**, Wm C, **WINEBRENNER**, Emma B, (not listed as Miss), April 14th 1880, 106
4178 **NEIGHBORS**, Rodger M, **BRENNEMAN**, Anna M, F 16th 1881, 106
4179 **NUSZ**, Edward L, **BOBST**, Clementine A, (not listed as Miss), Feb 24th 1881, 106
4180 **NEIBOLD**, John W, **EISLER**, Mary E, of Geo, June 9th 1881, 106
4181 **ODEN**, Edward W, **WELTY**, Ada E, April 11th 1882, 106
4182 **NUSZ**, William L, **EICHNER**, Mollie, August 1 1882, 106
4183 **NUSSBAUM**, Philip J, of Henry, **DUTROW**, Fannie E, Feb 6th 1883, 106
4184 **QUINN**, Timothy W, **DIXON**, Ella, Nov 7th 1883, 106
4185 **QUINN**, Thomas N, **BAER**, Sallie, August 10 1884, 106
4186 **ODEN**, Melville H, **KNODE**, Mary E, (@KANODE), Sept 30 1884, 106
4187 **NUSZ**, Charles L, **COWAN**, Emma, December 31 1884, 106
4188 **OWENS**, John, **TRUNDLE**, Maggie A, January 28 1885, 106
4189 **NELSON**, Abraham T A Nelson, **HOPKINS**, Alice, November 11th 1885, 106
4190 **NICHOLS**, Lewis B, **JUNIA**, Minnie, January 9 1886, 106

4191 OTT, John Warren, ELEGAN, Della, October 27t 1886, 106
4192 NELSON, Holy H, COOK, Miss, November 23 1886, 106
4193 QUYNN, Cha's W, of John T, WILLIAMS, Hattie E, April 21 1887, 106
4194 QUINN, Jacob P, MULL, Ann M, February 23 1888, 106
4195 NUSZ, Fleton E, (@Fleeton), STONE, Sophie E, June 7 1888, 106
4196 NEIGHBORS, Eutah D (Dr), DERR, Ella M, July 24, 106
4197 NAU, George H, STOUFFER, E Katie, Taneytown, Dec 18 1888, 106
4198 OGLE, Calvin, MARTIN, Ella, March 5 1889, 106
4199 PFLEIDERER, Jacob, WAGNER, Elizabeth, "Deutsch", Septr 19 1822, 110
4200 POOL, Cornelius, THORN, Ann, Decr 16 1823, 110
4201 PAMPELL, Frederick W, HUGHES, Kassandra, May 16 1824, 110
4202 PUMPHREY, Vachel, FLEMING, Mary, June 3 1824, 110
4203 POOL, Valentine, HOUX, Rebecca, of Jacob, Septr 9 1824, 110
4204 PRINCE, Thomas C, 1st wife, GEYER, Rebecca, Septr 26 1824, 110
4205 PARKER, James, BALTZELL, Ann Polly, of John Jacob/in Balto, Feby 1825, 110
4206 PATTENGALL, Samuel, BOWMAN, Henrietta, of Jacob, Septr 27 1825, 110
4207 PORTER, John W, "Printer", ROLLINGTON, Elizabeth, of John, Octr 12 1826, 110
4208 POTTS, Geo Murdoch, of Richard, RINGGOLD, Cornelia, of Sam'l, Nov 16 1826, 110
4209 PETTIT, John Phillips, KESLEY, Jane Philips, Decr 9 1827, 110
4210 PHILLIPS, Warren W, CREAGER, Catharine P, of Geo, April 1 1828, 110
4211 PAMPELL, Godfrey, EICHELBERGER, Mahala, of Peter, Jany 1829, 110
4212 PRYOR, George E (Dr), GRAFF, Caroline, of Sebas, Feby 10 1829, 110
4213 PERKINS, Joseph L, HOWARD, Ann, "MEIXELL""REICH", March 17 1829, 110
4214 POE, Neilson, CLEMM, Josephine E, Nov 30 1831, 110
4215 PROBY, James, STOLTZ, Rachel, July 22 1832, 110
4216 PETTIT, Henry M, BEALL, Jane M A, of Wm M, Septr 11 1832, 110
4217 POOL, Eli, 2d wife, BIGGS, Susan, of Wm, Septr 23 1832, 110
4218 PLOWMAN, Nathan, LYON, Adrianna, of Dr Isaac, May 30 1833, 110
4219 PRICE, Benjamin, KENNEDY, Sarah A, May 20 1834, 110
4220 POOL, Eli, 2d wife & sisters, BIGGS, Elizabeth, of Wm, Decr 14 1834, 110
4221 PHELPS, Philo F (Rev), SINGER, Catharine, April 9 1835, 110
4222 PHILLIPS, Richard H (Rev), THOM, Eleanor, Va, Nov 1835, 110
4223 PHILLER, Eli, "FILLER", DAYHOFF, Maria, May 1 1836, 110
4224 PRINCE, Thomas C, 2d wife, KRUMBEIN, Catharine, of Jac, Augt 1 1837, 110
4225 PHILLIPS, Greenbury, PEACOCK, Elizabeth, Balto, Feby 1 1838, 110
4226 PIGMAN, Hanson Briscoe, of Beene S, SHRIVER, Mary E, Balto, May 23 1839, 110
4227 PLAINE, Stephen, SPONSELLER, Ann, of Jacob, Nov 8 1838, 110
4228 PHLEEGER, John, 2d wife, KEMP, Miss, (*Susan), Augt 1838, 110
4229 PICKLE, John, GEISINGER, Sarah Elizabeth, of Capt David "USN", Augt 1 1839, 110
4230 PYFER, Wm B, of Philip, PYFER, Hannah Melville, of Henry, Octr 24 1839, 110
4231 PALMER, Wm Thompson, of Jos Mortimer, KIEFFER, Mary E, of Ch'n, Nov 28 1839, 110
4232 POFFENBERGER, B T, GELWICKS, Louisa S, July 16 1840, 110
4233 POFFENBERGER, Jacob, WALLECK, Eliza Ann, Decr 3 1840, 110
4234 PORTER, Richard, PORTER, Eliza Silvester, of John A, Feby 7 1841, 110
4235 PADGET, George M, THOMAS, Elizabeth, April 6 1841, 110
4236 PITTS, William, of Rev John, ZANE, Elizabeth, Wheeling, Va, April 27 1841, 110
4237 PRESTON, Sam'l B, of Cha's/1st wife, GARROTT, Sarah, Septr 28 1841, 110

4238 *PERCEIVAL*, Charles F, *SCHULTZ*, Julia Ann, of Henry, Octr 23 1841, 110
4239 *POPE*, John H, *DOLL*, Caroline, of Jacob, Decr 21 1841, 110
4240 *PHEBUS*, James H, of Peter, *WILLS*, Elizabeth Catharine, of Mich'l, Jany 8 1842, 110
4241 *BRUCKER*, John Simon, *LANGE*, Sophia (Mrs), "ROLKE", March 27 1842, 111
4242 *PHILLIPS*, William (Rev), *HOOK*, Martha M W, of Tho's, April 19 1842, 111
4243 *PHEBUS*, George, of Peter, *GROVE*, Margaret, of Reuben, March 2 1843, 111
4244 *PEARRE*, George A, of Wm, *WORTHINGTON*, Mary S, Cumberland, Octr 31 1843, 111
4245 *PITTS*, Charles H, of Rev John, *REYNOLDS*, Elizabeth, Indianna, June 25 1844, 111
4246 *PETERS*, William, of Cha's, *DAYHOFF*, Uralh Ann, of James/(*Urith), April 15 1845, 111
4247 *PIPPINGER*, Andrew, *HOUX*, Ann E, April 3 1845, 111
4248 *PASSAVANT*, Wm A (Rev), *WALTER*, Eliza, in Balto, May 1 1845, 111
4249 *PACELEY*, William, *EMLEY*, Ann Sophia, of David M, Nov 6 1845, 111
4250 *POWDER*, John D, *HINDES*, Elizabeth H, Balto, Nov 18 1845, 111
4251 *POOLE*, Tho's E D, *GAITHER*, Margaret R, Liberty, April 14 1846, 111
4252 *PRESTON*, Wm P, *SMITH*, Margaret W, Harford Co, Md, Augt 12 1846, 111
4253 *PEARCE*, James A (Hon), US Senator, *RINGGOLD*, Matilda C, March 22 1847, 111
4254 *PHILLIPS*, Noah (Col), 2d wife, *GASSAWAY*, Elizabeth (Mrs), Feby 15 1848, 111
4255 *PACELEY*, Howard, *MCDADE*, Avis Rebecca, of Sam'l, Feby 1 1848, 111
4256 *PEYTON*, Thomas Jefferson, *JOHNS*, Catharine Ross, of Rev John, Feby 24 1848, Va, 111
4257 *POOL*, John, of Henry, *WILLS*, Ann Mary, March 26 1848, 111
4258 *PERRIE*, John (Dr), *WILCOXON*, Sarah A (Mrs), widow of Horatio, Octr 12 1848, 111
4259 *PAGE*, Jackson, *ANDERS*, Charlotte, Octr 12 1848, 111
4260 *PECK*, O T X, (*Orlando), *TYLER*, Susan E, 3d daugh of Dr Wm, April 3 1849, 111
4261 *PLAINE*, Hiram, *STAUFFER*, Ann E, of John, April 24 1849, 111
4262 *PLUMMER*, Reuben N, *HAMILTON*, Penelope L, June 10 1849, 111
4263 *PAYNE*, John W, of Joseph, *DOLL*, Ann Rebecca, of Jacob, Septr 12 1849, 111
4264 *POSEY*, B N, *DALRYMPLE*, Adelaide, Octr 4 1849, 111
4265 *PAINE*, Robert Treat, *PORTER*, Catharine S, Balto, Decr 4 1849, 111
4266 *PHEBUS*, John, of Peter, *BOLEY'*, Elizabeth, of Jacob, April 18 1850, 111
4267 *PHILLIPS*, John L, *DEMME'*, Rosa C, of Rev Cha's R/Phila, Nov 5 1850, 111
4268 *POOL*, David, "Tobacconist", *LAWRENCE*, Rebecca, New York, Feby 13 1851, 111
4269 *PHILLIPS*, Theodore B, "Jew", *TIPPETT*, Anna H, of Rev Cha's B, Feby 18 1851, 111
4270 *PRINCE*, Thomas C, 3d wife, *COX*, Sevilla, of George, March 31 1851, 111
4271 *PORTER*, John Alfred, *BAER*, Catharine (Mrs), widow of John/"ROWE", Septr 5 1851, 111
4272 *POOLE*, Peter, *SCHUETENHELM*, Eliza A, April 5 1852, 111
4273 *POTTS*, Richard (Dr), of Geo M, *MCPHERSON*, Rebecca, June 1 1852, 111
4274 *POWERS*, Wm H, *GRAILEY*, Elizabeth, of Michael/ "GRELE'", Nov 16 1852, 111
4275 *PEARRE*, Tho's Otho, *POOLE*, Clementine V, Jany 11 1853, 111
4276 *PAGE*, Calvin, *BRUA*, Lucretia, "BREWER", May 11 1853, 111
4277 *POWELL*, Cha's Edward, *BARTH*, Julia Ann, Balto, April 30 1854, 111
4278 *PHEBUS*, Peter, of Peter/2d wife, *BOWMAN*, Emeline, Septr 24 1854, 111
4279 *PICKING*, John T, *WACHTER*, Susan B, of George, Decr 25 1855, 111
4280 *PARTON*, James, *ELDRIDGE*, Sarah Payson (Mrs), "Fanny Fern"/NY, Jany 5 1856, 111
4281 *POLE*, George W, *SIMMONS*, Ann Sophia, of Maj James, March 27 1856, 111
4282 *PHLEEGER*, Edward, of John, *LYNN*, Jane H, Clark Co, Ohio, May 3 1856, 111
4283 *PITCHER*, Thomas, *KOONTZ*, Georgianna V, of John, May 23 1856, 112
4284 *POTTERFIELD*, John D, *JENKINS*, Sally Ann, Jany 7 1857, 112

4285 PHEBUS, Benjamin F, of Peter, HERGESHEIMER, Annie E, of Peter, Decr 30 1856, 112
4286 POOLE, George, FORD, Mary, April 2 1857, 112
4287 PHLEUGER, John H, HAFFER, Julia, April 7 1857, 112
4288 PEARRE, Wm H, LINDSEY, Julia A, Liberty, Nov 5 1857, 112
4289 PERRY, Wm W, RIDDELMOSER, Ellie, of Sam'l D, Nov 23 1857, 112
4290 PROBST, Geo C (Rev), MCDANIEL, Camilla E, Decr 15 1857, 112
4291 PAMPILL, David Ezra, (PAMPELL), ELY, Harriett A, of Ezra, Jany 24 1858, 112
4292 PAYNE, Joseph F, of Jos, ECKMAN, Mary, Feby 14 1858, 112
4293 PRINCE, Lemuel Tho's, of Tho's C, SMITH, Mollie F E, Balto, April 21 1858, 112
4294 PAGE, Walker Y, TYLER, Nannie C, of Dr Wm, June 1 1858, 112
4295 PADGETT, Robert J, HAMILL, Ann J, July 27 1858, 112
4296 POTTERFIELD, Jacob A, HEIM, Maria Louisa, "Knoxville", Septr 16 1858, 112
4297 PFEIFFER, Abraham, RUPPRECHT, Elizabeth, Decr 18 1858, 112
4298 POFFENBERGER, Josiah, HUMERICK, Virginia S, Myersville, Jany 11 1859, 112
4299 POWER, Hamilton H, WILLIARD, Jennie M, Decr 8 1859, 112
4300 PHEBUS, Charles E, LEAKINS, Martha J, Decr 27 1859, 112
4301 PICKING, Wm H, of Tho's, CRAMER, Margaret E, of Philip, March 8 1860, 112
4302 PELTON, James B, STEVENS, Margaret A, March 13 1860, 112
4303 PUZENAT, Lawrence A, BAKER, Emily Cassin, April 4 1860, 112
4304 PEARRE, James, of Wm, DELASHMUTT, Ann Rebecca, of E L, May 16 1860, 112
4305 PRENTICE, Clarence J, of Geo D/Ky, De FALKENSTEIN, Amelia, July 14 1860, in Paris, 112
4306 PREY, John W, ALEXANDER, Lucinda, Septr 6 1860, 112
4307 PORTER, Robert, ALBAUGH, Sallie, of Solomon, Octr 11 1860, 112
4308 PITTINGER, John, WARNER, Sarah, Woodsborough, Octr 11 1860, 112
4309 PEARRE, James W, LINDSEY, S Marion, Feby 14 1861, 112
4310 PHLEEGER, Frederick K, of John, MEALEY, Georgianna, of Isaiah, May 14 1861, 112
4311 PICKING, Thomas, 2d wife, CRAMER, Barbara, of Philip H, June 5 1861, 112
4312 POOLE, Daniel, DIEHL, Hannah, "Double Pipe Creek", Nov 26 1861, 112
4313 PERRY, Thomas (Hon), of Cumberland, LONEY, E Catharine, of John (not listed as Miss), Decr 4 1861, 112
4314 PALMER, Jacob E, MILLER, Catharine Matilda, Decr 31 1861, 112
4315 PENNINGTON, Edgar, LONG, Annie M, January 29 1862, 112
4316 PINCKNEY, Howard (Dr), "of N York", SCHLEY, Clara, of Maj Henry, April 21 1863, 112
4317 PARSONS, Simon, HOGG, Harriott A, of Sam'l R, Nov 5 1863, 112
4318 POOLE, Hanson, of Wm, NORRIS, Elizabeth, Nov 12 1863, 112
4319 PURCELL, Thomas, of Orleans Co, NY, KEEN, Emma J, Decr 3 1863, 112
4320 PEARRE, Wm H, 2d wife, BUCKINGHAM, Ruth N, Feby 18 1864, 112
4321 POOLE, Joseph H, MEALEY, Kate, Jany 9 1866, 112
4322 POPE, Thomas E, of Wm, RICE, Martha M, of Rev Lewis, Jany 23 1866, 112
4323 PRESTON, Samuel B, of Cha's/2d wife, THRASHER, C E (Mrs), Jany 10 1866, 112
4324 PEGLEY, John S, YOUNG, Almira V, of Allen M, Jany 16 1866, 112
4325 POFFENBERBER, Wm Luther, ROUZAHN, Manzella S, of Adam, Jany 22 1866, 113
4326 PRICE, Wesley, MILLER, Sally A, of this city, May 1 1866, 113
4327 PATTERSON, Samuel S, HALLER, Carrie M, of Nicholas T, Jany 29 1867, 113
4328 PERRY, E Augustus, FOX, Victoria V, Mount Pleasant, March 21 1867, 113
4329 PURNELL, Samuel, of Elkton, DUNOTT, Emma, of Dr Justus, March 10 1868, 113
4330 POTTS, Arthur, of Geo M, MOBBERLY, Helen, of Dr Eldred W, Jany 21 1869, 113

4331 *PARRAMORE*, Thomas, of E Shore, Va, *ARMSTRONG*, Henrietta J, of Rev Wm, Jany 27 1869, 113
4332 *PHEBUS*, James H, of Ja's H, *LAMB*, Mary Jane, June 10 1869, 113
4333 *PENDLETON*, Robert N, *GIBSON*, Fannie H, of Dr J Gregg GIBSON, June 16 1869, 113
4334 *PHILBY*, Thaddeus S, *PELTZ*, Mary T, July 9 1869, 113
4335 *PARSONS*, W Irving, of Mason/2d wife, *ALBAUGH*, L Jane, of Val A, April 14 1870, 113
4336 *PERRYMAN*, Edward G (Rev), 2d wife, *JOHNSON*, Julia Johns, of Wm, Decr 1 1870, 113
4337 *PERKINS*, Cha's Allen, *DE BOURBON*, Dona Maria Isabel, Princess, Nov 12 1870, Lisbon, 113
4338 *PAMPELL*, Jerome E, of Fred'k W, *MORGAN*, Ary Ann, Jan 31 1871, 113
4339 *PHLEEGER*, Louis, *WINTER*, Alvira E, of Tho's, June 29 1871, 113
4340 *POPE*, Wm H, of John H, *LINTON*, Mary A, Octr 19 1871, Balto, 113
4341 *POOLE*, Geo W, *WEDDEL*, Mary, Octr 19 1871, 113
4342 *PHOEBUS*, Charles O, (Hoax), *YOUNG*, Mary E, July 29 1872, (Hoax), 113
4343 *PFEFFER*, Baron, of Lucerne, Switzerland, *SLIDELL*, Miss, of Hon John, Septr 7 1872, 113
4344 *PRICE*, John E, *ORDEMAN*, Mollie C, Septr 24 1872, 113
4345 *PARKER*, William, *WILSON*, Kate, Feb 6 1873, 113
4346 *PHOEBUS*, George T, of John, *SEIBERT*, Harriet Ann, of Geo, April 13 1873, 113
4347 *PORTER*, Charles, *WALTER*, Kate, of John, April 3 1873, 113
4348 *POOLE*, Charles A, *NUSZ*, Vic T, May 5 1873, 113
4349 *PESCHAU*, Ferdinand (Rev), *MYERS*, Clara Jane, Gettysburg, Pa, June 3 1873, 113
4350 *PECK*, Charles M, *MCSHERRY*, Gertie, of James, Nov 27 1873, 113
4351 *PHEBUS*, Cha's O, of James H, *BURRIER*, Sarah E, May 14 1874, 113
4352 *PETERS*, Oscar A, *DELCHER*, Maggie A, Balto, June 9 1874, 113
4353 *PARSON*, Wm E (Rev), *NAILLE*, Annie R, Japan, Augt 18 1874, 113
4354 *PHELPS*, Joshua O, *CARPENTER*, Louisa, Septr 27 1874, 113
4355 *PEARRE*, James W, 2d wife, *HOWARD*, Victoria C, of Edw, Nov 24 1874, 113
4356 *PENDLETON*, Wm C, Printer, *BITTLE*, Julia F, of Rev D'd F, June 17 1875, 113
4357 *PARTON*, James, 2d wife, *ELDRIDGE*, Miss, "Fanny Fern"/NY, Feb 10 1876, 113
4358 *POPP*, John M, *LAMBRIGHT*, Laura Cath, in Balto, Octr 30 1876, 113
4359 *PLUMLEY*, Edgar, *TRASK*, Mary S (Mrs), Rev CANN, Decr 26 1876, 113
4360 *PRIMROSE*, Pers (Capt'n), *SCHINDEL*, Kate M, Hagerstown, June 1877, 113
4361 *PRICE*, John T, *SUMAN*, Clara V, Septr 18th 1879, 113
4362 *PAMPELL*, P Frank, of Henry, *HITSELBERGER*, Fannie E, (not listed as Miss), Feb 5 1880, (@HITZELBERGER), 113
4363 *PHOEBUS*, George W, of Benj, *MATHIAS*, Fannie, (not listed as Miss), Sept 7th 1880, 113
4364 *PHOEBUS*, George W, of Benj, *FISHER*, Elizabeth J, (not listed as Miss), May 24th 1881, 113
4365 *PEARRE*, Aubrey, of Balto/(@Aubray), *SIFFORD*, Nannie J, of John, July 13th 1881, 113
4366 *PAYGNE*, Joseph, 2d wife/(@PAYNE), *STAUB*, Emma, February 20th 1882, 113
4367 *PHEBUS*, Eugene McM, of James, *MILLER*, Florence O, Decr 14th 1882, 114
4368 *PAGE*, Dudley, of Calvin, *BLAKE*, Nellie P, Jan 16th 1883, Gunamay match {illegible}, 114
4369 *POOLE*, Ernest F, *RILEY*, Annie R, June 5th 1883, 114
4370 *POOLE*, George E, *MCCLOW*, Sadie, Octr 3d 1883, 114
4371 *PAISLEY*, George A, (@PAISELEY), *LAMBERT*, Willetta M, of Geo, Nov 27 1884, 114
4372 *PICKING*, Harry B, *BRENNEMAN*, Ella M, March 10 1885, 114
4373 *PHILLIPPS*, Lewis A, "Dun", *SCHOLL*, Lilly A, October 19 1886, 114

4374 **PURNELL**, Oscar O, of Wm H/(@PURCELL), *STEVENS*, Mary A, (@STEPHENS), Feb 5 1887, 114
4375 *PHLEEGER*, Clarence M, **GONSO**, Fannie, (@GONSON), February 16 1888, 114
4376 *PEARSON*, Cha's S, **CONNOR**, Alice C, February 23 1888, 114
4377 *PYLES*, Isaac J, **HEFFNER**, Lucretia R, April 19 1888, 114
4378 *PETERS*, Edward C, **VINSON**, Mammie G, of Judge John T, June 27 1888, 114
4379 *POWELL*, Milton L, **HOLDCRAFT**, Annie C, August 23 1888, 114
4380 *PERRY*, H Clay, **MEHRLING**, Margaret C, of George, Nov 15 1888, 114
4381 *PICKING*, Cha's T, **BRAGONIER**, Carrie M, of Alf, March 5 1889, 114
4382 *PAYNE*, Edward R, **MARTIN**, Laura E, June 12 1889, 114
4383 *PRINCE*, W Edgar, **HILLIARY**, Nannie, November 14 1889, 114
4384 *PURNELL*, Wm H (Jr), **RITCHIE**, Catharine L, of John, May 5 1890, 114
4385 *RAMSBURGH*, Lewis, 1st wife, **STEINER**, Charlotte, of Col Stephen, May 1 1821, 116
4386 *RIEHL*, Jacob, **BOSELL**, Catharine, Decr 9 1821, 116
4387 *REESE*, Jacob, **DERR**, Catharine, of John, June 6 1822, 116
4388 *ROWE*, Nicholas, of Jacob, **TROUT**, Mary, June 15 1823, 116
4389 *RUSSELL*, William C, **SEQUIN**, Emma F, Nov 6 1823, 116
4390 *RUMMEL*, George, **DEVILBISS**, Elizabeth, July 27 1824, 116
4391 *REYNALD*, John, of Hugh, **WINN**, Susan B, in Balto, Decr 23 1824, 116
4392 *REDMAN*, John, **JARBOE**, Catharine, Feby 10 1825, 116
4393 *RAYMOND*, James, **THOMPSON**, Miss, of Judge Wm/NY, Octr 1825, NY, 116
4394 *RICKERD*, Henry J, **ORDNER**, Caroline, of Peter, May 18 1826, 116
4395 *REINHART*, William, of Geo, **BARRICK**, Rebecca, Glade, Feby 8 1827, 116
4396 *RICHMAND*, Francis, 2d wife, **POWELL**, Catharine, Middtown, March 1827, 116
4397 *RICE*, George, of Geo, **TRAGO**, Harriet, "TRAGER", March 15 1827, 116
4398 *ROLLINGTON*, Wm M, **DAVIS**, Eleanor, Augt 20 1827, 116
4399 *RENN*, Isaac, **WILLIARD**, Martha (Mrs), Septr 20 1827, 116
4400 *ROOT*, Daniel, of D, **BRENGLE**, Mary, of Nicholas, Nov 26 1827, 116
4401 *RICKERD*, Jonathan, **LAMBRECHT**, Cristianna, of Geo, June 12 1828, 116
4402 *RUTTER*, John, **MAYBERRY**, Henrietta, of Justinian, July 1 1828, 116
4403 *RHODES*, John, **RICE**, Ann Minerva, of Geo, Nov 6 1828, 116
4404 *ROOF*, Joseph A, **KRIEGELOH**, Christianna, April 5 1829, 116
4405 *REICH*, Philip, **AYRES**, Rebecca D H, April 12 1829, 116
4406 *RENNEBERGER*, Otho, **BENSON**, Catharine, June 23 1829, 116
4407 *RICHTER*, John, **COOKERLY**, Catharine, June 18 1829, 116
4408 *ROACH*, Robert, 2d wife, **BAUSMAN**, Eliza, "BIRELY", Jany 7 1830, 116
4409 *RICE*, William, of Geo, **BIRELY**, Rebecca, of Wm, April 22 1830, 116
4410 *RANCK*, Solomon, **MERMAN**, Sarah, of Tho's, July 12 1830, 116
4411 *RANDALL*, Nicholas A, **WORTHINGTON**, Mary E, Augt 5 1830, 116
4412 *RITCHIE*, Albert (Dr), of Col John/1st wife, **DAVIS**, Catharine, of Ign, Nov 23 1830, 116
4413 *RICHMOND*, Jacob, **COBLENTZ**, Rebecca, March 8 1831, 116
4414 *RAUZAHN*, Joseph, **LEITER**, Elizabeth, of Henry, April 14 1831, 116
4415 *ROSS*, William J, 1st wife, **DAVIS**, Ann Maria, in Allegany Co, May 5 1831, 116
4416 *REICH*, John (Jun'r), **HOFFMAN**, Juliann, of John/"MUHLHEIM", July 17 1831, 116
4417 *RICE*, George, of James, **MICHAEL**, Margaret, of Wm, Octr 2d 1831, 116
4418 *RAMSBURG*, John, of John, **MCCOUBERY**, Margaret Jane, May 8 1832, 116
4419 *RAMSBURG*, Elias, of John, **HOUCK**, Catharine, of John, Octr 11 1832, 116

4420 ROWE, Charles G, of Michael, *CLOSE*, Elizabeth, July 21 1833, 116
4421 RAMSBURGH, Lewis, 2d wife, *BRISCOE*, Susan B D, of James/"Kentucky", Septr 17 1833, 116
4422 RAUCH, Frederick A (Rev), *MOORE*, Phebe B, Pa, July 9 1833, 116
4423 ROBERTS, William, *RIGNEY*, Sophia E, "HEISELY", Feby 4 1834, 116
4424 REINHART, David, of Geo, *CRONISE*, Jane Rebecca, of Jacob, March 27 1834, 116
4425 REID, William, *FISH*, Henrietta, Point of Rocks, May 3 1834, 116
4426 RAMSBURG, Jacob, of John, *EBERT*, Ann Rebecca, of John, Nov 11 1834, 116
4427 REIGHLEY, Charles (Rev), *CRONISE*, Caroline E, of Simon, Jany 5 1835, 117
4428 ROHR, Jacob, "Post Master"/2d wife, *RAMSBURG*, Elizabeth (Mrs), widow of Stephen, Nov 12 1835, 117
4429 RIGNEY, Wm H, of John, *HENDERSON*, Mary, of Robert/(this ought to be, Feby 24 1835, the line above), 117
4430 RICE, Grafton J, of Geo, *BIRELY*, Margaret, of William, March 27 1836, 117
4431 ROLKE, Geo Augustus, of John, *TURNER*, Mary A, of Isaac, May 17 1836, 117
4432 REED, Benjamin F, *PANCOAST*, Catharine, of Sam'l, June 17 1836, 117
4433 RIDDELMOSER, Samuel D, *MAGRUDER*, Elizabeth C, Middval, Nov 5 1836, 117
4434 ROHR, Philip C, of Dav, *MCMULLEN*, Malinda, Decr 29 1836, 117
4435 RITSCHY, Adam, *ULRICH*, Nancy (Mrs), "GROVE", Jany 12 1837, 117
4436 RAUCH, Charles, *BOCK*, Anna, "Deutsch", March 27 1837, 117
4437 RAMSAY, Thomas, *WATKINS*, Matilda (Mrs), Colored friends, May 15 1837, 117
4438 ROCKWELL, Elihu H, *WIESTLING*, Rachel (Mrs), "WAGNER"/"Liberty", July 12 1837, 117
4439 RYPMA, Karl J, *THOMAS*, Catharine A, of Wm/"HAUSER", Septr 25 1837, 117
4440 ROMAN, James Dixon, *KENNEDY*, Louisa, "Hagerstown", Septr 26 1837, 117
4441 RIEHL, Otho, of Mich'l, *HANE*, Catharine M, of John, Octr 15 1837, 117
4442 RIES, Benjamin, *SIMPSON*, Elizabeth, of John/Geo Town, DCa, Decr 14 1837, 117
4443 RUDISIL, Thomas, *SNYDER*, Ann Mary, Jany 4 1838, 117
4444 REMSBERG, Josiah, of Christian, *LEITER*, Mary Ann, of H'y, March 22 1838, 117
4445 RHODES, No first name given, *CUNNINGHAM*, Eliza, GeoTown, DCa, March 6 1838, 117
4446 RICHARDS, Luther (Jun'r), *REITZELL*, Elizabeth, of John/Lancaster, Pa, June 12 1838, 117
4447 RENN, John H, *HOUSE*, Sarah A R, Octr 25 1838, 117
4448 RAHAUSER, Frederick (Rev), 2d wife, *KIEFFER*, Hannah (Mrs), Pa, Octr 17 1838, 117
4449 RANNEBERGER, Philip, *BEALL*, Sarah Eleanor P, Feby 5 1839, 117
4450 REINHART, George, *FOUT*, Many M, of Wm, April 11 1839, 117
4451 REDDICK, Leonard, *WALTZ*, Jemima, June 13 1839, 117
4452 RAMSBURG, John F, *BARRICK*, Ann M E, Augt 29 1839, 117
4453 RHODES, Henry, 2d wife, *ENGLES*, Ann Elizabeth, of Silas, Septr 12 1839, 117
4454 RAMSDALE, Alonzo M, *WALKER*, Margaret, of John, Septr 13 1840, 117
4455 REED, William, *LOY*, Elizabeth Elvira, March 18 1841, 117
4456 ROSS, Wm J, of Wm/2d wife, *STOKES*, Eliza H, in Balto, April 22 1841, 117
4457 ROHLING, F, (*Frederick Wm), *KOHLER*, Ann Catharine, (*KOEHLE), June 30 1841, 117
4458 REINHART, Andrew, *HILTON*, Rebecca E, July 1 1841, 117
4459 REYNALDS, James W, 2d wife, *WOOLTZ*, Ann Barbara, of Geo, July 20 1841, 117
4460 ROACH, James J, of Rob't, *HAMBLET*, Sarah N, Balto, Octr 3 1841, 117
4461 RHODES, Henry, 3d wife, *DIFFENDERFFER*, Matilda E (Mrs), Balto, Nov 16 1841, 117
4462 RAMSBURG, Wm Henry, of John, *LEITER*, Cath A Rebecca, of Henry, May 26 1842, 117
4463 REED, John, of Jacob, *HALLER*, Rebecca, of Jacob, May 26 1842, 117

4464 RODNER, No first name given, BERGER, Maria, Deutsch, May 1842, 117
4465 ROBERTSON, James H, of Alexander, MYERS, Emily A, Balto, June 14 1842, 117
4466 RENNEBERGER, Philip, 2d wife, STOVER, Margaret, March 2 1843, 117
4467 RAMSBURG, Dennis, BRENGLE, Lydia A E, May 11 1843, 117
4468 RHINE, John (Jun'r), MONTGOMERY, Caroline L, of Col John, Decr 28 1843, 117
4469 ROWE, Ezra M, of Mich'l (Sen'r), LANDERKIN, Mary C, April 8 1844, 118
4470 RAMSAY, Thomas, NO BRIDES NAME GIVEN, Colored friends, April 21 1844, 118
4471 RIGNEY, John T, of John, QUYNN, Mary C, of Wm/Balto, Augt 22 1844, 118
4472 ROSS, John, Cherokee Chief, STAPLER, Mary B, Phila, Septr 2 1844, 118
4473 ROLKE, John, of Christian/1st wife, MEDCALFE, Juliann, Decr 12 1844, 118
4474 ROLKE, Charles, of Christian, BRASHEAR, Rebecca, Jany 9 1845, 118
4475 RAMSBURG, Edward, PACELEY, Catharine, May 12 1845, 118
4476 RICKERT, John, "Germany", BRANDT, Sophia, Septr 4 1845, 118
4477 ROBINSON, John, of Rev Henry, KUNKEL, Elizabeth, of John, Jany 28 1846, 118
4478 RITTER, J Alfred, MARTIN, Catharine E, (not listed as Miss)/"ROHR", Feby 17 1846, 118
4479 RAMSAY, James M, TYLER, Mary Eleanor Addison, of Dr Wm, April 14 1846, 118
4480 ROSENBACH, Henry, BINSWANGER, Fanny, Balto & Cumberland, May 16 1846, 118
4481 RAMSBURG, Wm M, FEGLER, Miranda, "VOGLER", May 21 1846, 118
4482 RAMSBURG, David J, GEESEY, Catharine, (not listed as Miss), Septr 10 1846, 118
4483 RICHARDS, Abraham, STOCKMAN, Barbara A R, Octr 22 1846, 118
4484 RITCHIE, Albert (Dr), 2d wife, PACKARD, Louisa, at Albany, NY, July 8 1847, 118
4485 REED, Isaac, of Jacob, DOYLE, Mary Jane, of Lawrence, Septr 19 1847, 118
4486 ROSENMERCKEL, Henry, ENGELBRECHT, Margaretta, of Adam, Jany 9 1848, 118
4487 RUSE, William N, KEPHART, Louisa, of Peter, Augt 10 1848, 118
4488 RINGER, Robert W, HAGAN, Catharine, of Peter, Augt 8 1848, 118
4489 ROLKE, John, of Christian/2d wife, ALBRIGHT, Susan R, Octr 10 1848, 118
4490 RAUZAHN, Cyrus, HARP, Lydia, Midd valley, Nov 2 1848, 118
4491 RHODES, George T, WILES, Mary Jane, Nov 2 1848, 118
4492 RUTTER, Albert J, WALSH, Biddy, Balto, Jany 1 1849, 118
4493 REMSBERG, Geo P, KEMP, Mary, of David, Febu 13 1849, 118
4494 RIEHL, Nicholas, of Michael, PAMPSELL, Sarah Ann, of Fred'k, Octr 1849, 118
4495 RITCHIE, Wm Henry, FAIRBANKS, Elizabeth Ann, Octr 24 1849, 118
4496 ROGERS, William B, BARTGIS, Mary E, of Matt E, Decr 24 1849, 118
4497 ROSS, Worthington, MCPHERSON, Ann G, of Col John, Jany 22 1850, 118
4498 ROLKE, Peter, of John, ANDERSON, Mary A, Feby 28 1850, 118
4499 ROBINSON, Robert S, LAMBRECHT, Margaret (Mrs), widow of Perry "BOWERS", June 2 1850, 118
4500 RAUZAHN, John A, HARBAUGH, Catharine N, June 17 1850, 118
4501 RICE, David S, MANTZ, Mary Elizabeth, of Peter, May 13 1851, 118
4502 RAMSBURG, Frederick, BOBST, Elizabeth, May 22 1851, 118
4503 RICE, Albert T, MANTZ, Sabina, of Gideon, June 26 1851, 118
4504 RITTER, Obediah D, UPPERMAN, Dilia, Georgetown, DCa, July 24 1851, 118
4505 ROSS, James F, PRINCE, Henrietta F, Niece of Thos C/Balto, Septr 1 1851, 118
4506 RIDGELY, T Graham, BAER, Debbie Ridgely, of Dr M S/Balto, Octr 7 1851, 118
4507 RODEROCK, Wm, LEASE, Elenora, "Linganore", March 18 1852, 118
4508 RODEROCK, John P, SPONSELLER, Catharine Ann, (not listed as Miss)/"Linganore", March 25 1852, 118

4509 RIDGE, Ephraim, DOMER, Eva Maria, Augt 26 1852, 118
4510 RINGEL, George, ROSZ, Christina, Septr 1852, 118
4511 RIDENAUER, Daniel, KING, Ann Maria, Septr 30 1852, 119
4512 RHODERICK, George W, HAINES, Isabella, Nov 16 1852, 119
4513 RICE, Perry A, FINDLEY, Eliabeth, "Mercersburg, Pa", Decr 21 1852, 119
4514 REICH, William, of John, BROWN, Lucie B J, Carroll Co, April 20 1853, 119
4515 RAINFORD, Philip (Col), JEFFERSON, Fannie A, of Hamilton, Missouri, May 4 1853, Missouri, 119
4516 RAINFERT, John, RICKERS, Anna Catharine, June 12 1853, 119
4517 ROLKE, Henry, of Christian, MUMFORD, Kate, Nov 29 1853, 119
4518 REA, Charles H, ANGELL, Julia H, Decr 15 1853, 119
4519 ROLKE, F Augustus, WITTLER, Emily, May 2d 1854, 119
4520 RIEHL, John H, of Jacob, STONE, Catharine Margretta, Octr 16 1854, 119
4521 RHODRICK, John S L, COLLEBERRY, Mary Elizabeth, "Liberty", Nov 5 1854, 119
4522 RISSLER, George, DUTROW, Francina, of John, Nov 30 1854, 119
4523 RIDER, John H, KENNEDY, C Elizabeth, March 28 1855, 119
4524 RINGEL, Christopherr, BECKER, Mary, April 8 1855, 119
4525 ROSS, Adam, "ROSZ", MILLER, Christianna, Septr 2 1855, 119
4526 RIDGE, George W, HANKEY, Mary E, Creagerstown, Septr 13 1855, 119
4527 ROSS, George, BUCK, Mary, of Wm, Jany 1 1856, 119
4528 RICHARDSON, Samuel S (Dr), GAMBRILL, Ann Margaret, of Cha's A, April 30 1856, 119
4529 RIGGS, Plummer J, WOOD, Mary, May 5 1856, 119
4530 RAMSBURG, Uriah D, STALEY, Anna S, of Peter S, May 29 1856, 119
4531 RHODES, Francis Tho's, of John, MANTZ, E Jane, of Gideon, July 23 1856, 119
4532 RUNKELS, John B, VANZANT, Ellen V, Augt 28 1856, 119
4533 RILEY, C McGinnis, RHINE, Susan E, Octr 23 1856, 119
4534 RIZER, Geo Hoffman, (Hoffman overwritten)/2d wife, PATTENGALL, Mary, Nov 10 1856, 119
4535 ROTHSCHILD, Alphonse, of James, ROTHSCHILD, Leonora, of Lionel, March 4 1857, 119
4536 RABOLD, Matthias, FIEGE, Rebecca, "FEAGA"/Cumberland, April 9 1857, 119
4537 RUSSELL, Wm H, SHORT, Mary Virginia, "Point of Rocks", Octr 10 1857, 119
4538 RUSSELL, David, O'LEARY, Mary Jane, of Augustine D, Octr 13 1857, 119
4539 ROLKE, Geo A, of Henry/1st wife, MIX, Charlotte C, Octr 20 1857, 119
4540 RUSSELL, Tho's W, WENTZELL, Elizabeth E, of Wm H/Harpersferry, Nov 4 1857, 119
4541 RUSSELL, William, WOOD, Susanna S, N Market/"Quakers", Decr 1857, 119
4542 RAUZAHN, Noah, SMITH, Elizabeth, Decr 17 1857, 119
4543 ROGERS, J O, MANTZ, Louisa, of Gideon, Jany 12 1858, 119
4544 ROLLE', Justin Albert, LUEBER, Helen M, of Francis/Geotown, DCa, Jany 6 1858, 119
4545 RAMSBURGH, John T, ZIMMERMAN, Elizabeth, Tiffin, Ohio, Jany 14 1858, 119
4546 RITCHIE, John, of Dr Albert, MAULSBY, Bettie H, of Wm P, May 5 1858, 119
4547 REED, John, MARMADUKE, Mary, Va/in Presbyterian Church, May 13 1858, 119
4548 RHODERICK, Geo C, KOOGLE, Mary Ellen, of Adam, Octr 7 1858, 119
4549 RIGGS, Joel H, REIGEL, Catharine M, Octr 7 1858, 119
4550 RUPRECHT, Wm Henry (Jun'r), DUFT, Eva Catharine, March 6 1859, 119
4551 REINEKE', E William (Rev), KNODE, Mary E, of Wm H/Wash Co, March 10 1859, 119
4552 RUNNER, Daniel P, OTT, Harriott, of Peter, March 27 1859, 119
4553 ROHR, Henry, HOFFMAN, Elizabeth, March 29 1859, 120

4554 RICE, John, MANTZ, Sophie, of Henry/Balto, April 28 1859, 120
4555 RAMSBURG, John Stephen, of Elias, BEESON, Drue H, Uniontown, Pa, May 18 1859, 120
4556 RAMSBURGH, Nelson D, HARMAN, Eliza Ann, Septr 15 1859, 120
4557 RICHARDSON, James (Dr), BURTON, Mary Jane, of Henry, Octr 20 1859, 120
4558 RITCHIE, Wm Henry, 2d wife, RAY, Elizabeth A, Balto, Octr 13 1859, 120
4559 ROHRBACH, Martin N, BRUNNER, Ellen C, of John of J, Nov 3 1859, 120
4560 REESE, Lewis H, STALEY, Louisa, of Ezra, Jany 12 1860, 120
4561 RHODERICK, Washington W, YASTE, Amanda, Midd'n, Feby 16 1860, 120
4562 REMSBERG, Geo P, SNOOTS, Ann E, of Va, Feby 28 1860, 120
4563 RAMSBURG, Alexander, CRONISE, Hannah Sophia, of Fred'k, Feby 20 1860, 120
4564 RAMSBURG, Stephen G, WELLER, Barbara Ann A, Feby 1 1860, 120
4565 ROLKE', Edward, of Christian, HEMBRY, Alice V, of John, March 20 1860, 120
4566 REINHART, Ephraim F, COLES, Miss, Springfield, O, March 22 1860, 120
4567 RUNKELS, Wm, HARDING, Barbara Ann, March 25 1860, 120
4568 RICE, M Tyler, DUVALL, Alta Zerah, April 6 1860, 120
4569 RIPPERN, Hanson T, COOKERLY, Anna M, March 22 1860, 120
4570 RAUZAHN, Edward L, of Joseph, WEINBRENNER, Harriet A, of Ch'n, May 29 1860, 120
4571 ROBERTSON, Thomas W, BENDER, Emily Clagett, of John, July 1 1860, 120
4572 RHINE, John W, LEASE, Catharine, Linganore, Septr 6 1860, 120
4573 REINHART, Jacob (Dr), GRAYBILL, Maggie, of Peter, Septr 11 1860, 120
4574 RUDY, Tho's Carlton, LEITER, Mary Ellen, of Peter, Decr 13 1860, 120
4575 RAMSBURG, Joshua, COBLENTZ, Louisa, of David, Feby 14 1861, 120
4576 ROTHSCHILD, Simon, PUMPERNICKEL, Betsey, Poughkepsie, NY, April 1 1861, 120
4577 REED, James W, JOHNSON, Ann West, July 31 1861, 120
4578 RICHARDSON, James A, COLLINS, Margaret E, Septr 17 1861, 120
4579 RICHARDSON, Ignatius Davis, RAMSBURGH, Jane Briscoe, of Lewis, Octr 24 1861, 120
4580 ROSS, Charles W, of Wm J, POTTS, Cornelia R, of Geo M, Decr 12 1861, 120
4581 RAUZAHN, Daniel H, FULTON, Margaret C, Decr 26 1861, 120
4582 RICE, Job, of Geo/Ex-shff, KAUFFMAN, Frances M L, of Wm, Decr 31 1861, 120
4583 RODERICK, Maurice H, THOMAS, Ann Rebecca, Jefferson, Jany 23 1862, 120
4584 RENNER, Elias, EISENNAGEL, Eliza, Feby 13 1862, 120
4585 REAM, Isaac L, COOK, Mary A, Jefferson, March 6 1862, 120
4586 RAMSBURGH, Tho's C, BISHOP, Phebe A, Feby 20 1862, 120
4587 ROUZER, John, 2d wife, PARRISH, Emma Kate, of Nich's M, March 20 1862, 120
4588 ROBINSON, Cornelius, DERRY, Jennie, March 23 1862, 120
4589 REIFSNIDER, John, LEINARD, Ellen, Emmittsburg, March 24 1862, 120
4590 ROBERTS, George S, CARMACK, Laura A, of Hanson, April 17 1862, 120
4591 ROGERS, John B, SNYDER, Lucinda, (at D W BROOKS), Augt 20 1862, 120
4592 RUDY, George E, COCHREN, Elmira C, Nov 4 1862, 120
4593 RAMSBURG, Valerius Elias, of Jacob/1st wife, PAYNE, Amanda H, Geo Town, DCa, Nov 11 1862, 120
4594 ROOP, Josiah L, GOODMAN, Ellen, Nov 19 1862, 120
4595 RHODES, Henry G, PEARCE, E Jane, Nov 19 1862, 121
4596 ROWAN, Michael, CUNNINGHAM, Ellen, Nov 19 1862, 121
4597 REMSBURG, George J, SMITH, Susan E, Middletown, Jany 29 1863, 121
4598 RICKETTS, Richard, 2d wife, HEAD, Ann Catharine, of Cecelius, Feby 12 1863, 121
4599 RIORDAN, Michael, COURTNAY, Mary, Balto, Feby 8 1863, 121

4600 *ROLKE*, Daniel E, of Henry, *YOUNG*, Mary Catharine, of Joshua, March 10 1863, 121
4601 *ROBERTS*, James E (Serg't), 3d Wisconsin Reg't, *MELIUS*, Mary (Mrs), of Conrad, March 11 1863, 121
4602 *ROLLINS*, George W, of Wisconsin, *LEILICH*, Louisa, of Jacob, April 9 1863, 121
4603 *RAHTER*, Adolphus C, *YANTIS*, Elizabeth, Woodsboro, Septr 3 1863, 121
4604 *RIDDELMOSER*, Lewis, *STUB*, Alice A E, Fairview, Octr 14 1863, 121
4605 *RODERICK*, D Webster, *CHILCOTE*, Mary P, of Rich'd, Nov 3 1863, 121
4606 *RUNCKELS*, Joseph, *COOKERLY*, Eliza W, Decr 22 1863, 121
4607 *RIFFLE*, Thomas, *MILLER*, Ava M V, of Dr Edward/Balto, Feby 22 1864, 121
4608 *ROLKE*, George A, of Henry/2d wife, *JORDON*, Mary J, April 11 1864, 121
4609 *ROOP*, John W, *STIMMEL*, Sarah Ann, April 5 1864, 121
4610 *RICE*, Wm P, of George, *FOUT*, Susan C, of Peter S, Decr 14 1864, 121
4611 *REICH*, Raymond C, of Philip, *DELASHMUTT*, Phebe, of Elias L, Jany 3 1865, 121
4612 *RIGNEY*, John C, *CONNOR*, Elizabeth C, Phila & Balto, Decr 25 1864, 121
4613 *REHLINGER*, Christian, *MEHRLING*, Margaret, April 4 1865, 121
4614 *REIGART*, John M, *MIDDLETON*, Frances Augusta, of Rob't W, "5th daugh", May 2 1865, 121
4615 *REICH*, Henry C, of John, *DELASHMUTT*, Rachel, of Elias L, May 11 1865, 121
4616 *RENNER*, Edward L, *ESWORTHY*, Mary P, May 27 1865, 121
4617 *RIPPON*, Jerome, *HARRIS*, Mary Ann, June 6 1865, 121
4618 *RICE*, Wm H, *CAREY*, Barbara J, of James, July 5 1865, 121
4619 *RENNER*, Peter, *LOWE*, Jane Ann, of Theodore, July 11 1865, 121
4620 *RAMEN*, William, of Phila, *HOBIE*, Elizabeth, of Fred'k City, Augt 12 1865, 121
4621 *RICKERD*, Nicholas F, *LEWIS*, Mary Jane, Septr 7 1865, 121
4622 *RAUZAHN*, Carlton P, *YOUNG*, Charlotte P, of Sam'l, Nov 21 1865, 121
4623 *RAUZAHN*, Joseph L, *COBLENTZ*, Ella A E, Nov 30 1865, 121
4624 *RANNEBERGER*, Robert, *EADER*, Virginia, of Lewis/"Cornety {County-compiler}, Feby 22 1866, 121
4625 *RAUZAHN*, Alfred H, *HAGAN*, Ann Rebecca, July 19 1866, 121
4626 *RIGDEN*, James, *SALTER*, Ann Marie, of Wm E, Septr 27 1866, 121
4627 *ROHRBACH*, Wm H H, *PETTINGALL*, Linda R, Midd valley, Nov 8 1866, 121
4628 *RAUZAHN*, Wm H, *MAIN*, Kate S, Jany 10 1867, 121
4629 *RICHARDSON*, Geo F, *TITLOW*, Margaret Lucretia, of Dan'l, Augt 8 1867, 121
4630 *RAMSBURG*, Newton A, of John, *KEECH*, Sallie M, of St Marys Co, Octr 22 1867, 121
4631 *REHLINGER*, Geo H, *HITESHEW*, Laura A, "REILING", Nov 10 1867, 121
4632 *RAMSBURG*, Valerius Elias, of Jacob/2d wife, *ROSS*, Anna, Geo Town, DC, Nov 11 1867, 121
4633 *REMSBERG*, Washington J, *HARGETT*, Mary C, of John H, May 1867, 121
4634 *RIZER*, Geo Hoffman, 3d wife, *KEEFER*, Caroline, of Christian, Jany 6 1868, 121
4635 *REESE*, Wm D, 2d wife, *HOOPER*, Sallie M, Balto, Jany 16 1868, 121
4636 *ROSENMERCKEL*, Henry (Jun'r), *ARMBRUSTER*, Annie E, (not listed as Miss)/Cumberland, Jany 30 1868, 121
4637 *RUTHERFORD*, J Edward, Dauphin Co, Pa, *MCPHERSON*, Anna H, J of Wm, Feby 18 1868, 122
4638 *REMSBERG*, Calvin F, of (erased), *HARGETT*, Emma J, of John H, March 12 1868, 122
4639 *ROLKE*, G F William, *GETZENDANNER*, Mary C, of Eli of Adam, Nov 5 1868, 122
4640 *REINHART*, Winfield G, *DEVILBISS*, Minnie M, of Reuben, Mar 23 1869, 122
4641 *RUTHERFORD*, S Harvey, of Pa, *SCHOLL*, Fannie E, of Dennis, Feby 9 1871, 122

4642 RHODERICK, Mahlon Theodore, of Mahlon, DERR, Laura Jane, of David, March 9 1871, 122
4643 ROUZER, John R (Col), WILLMAN, Julia A E (Mrs), March 4 1871, 122
4644 RENN, J Calvin, ZIMMERMAN, Mary E, of Rev Wm H, March 30 1871, 122
4645 RICE, J Edward, of Grafton J, DYER, Mary M, June 1 1871, 122
4646 RAMSBURG, Cornelius Stille', NOURSE, Sarah, of Rev J E/GeoTown, Septr 13 1871, 122
4647 RAMSBURGH, Lewis J, of Lewis, DORSEY, Emma J, Feby 8 1872, 122
4648 RAELINGER, Lewis D, TRUNNELL, Ida L R, Feby 24 1872, 122
4649 RITTER, Charles, of J Alfred, KINZER, Laura Eugenia, Augt 6 1872, 122
4650 ROOT, Daniel, of D, SWEADNER, Rebecca (Mrs), (Liberty), Septr 3 1872, 122
4651 RHODES, Calvin A, of John, STEINER, Susan Sophia, of John A, Octr 15 1872, 122
4652 RAMSBURG, John H, of Josiah, NICHOLS, Alice M, of Edw, Octr 30 1872, 122
4653 REMSBERG, Charles T, CLAGETT, Maggie B, of Tho's, Nov 27 1872, 122
4654 ROBERTSON, Cha's H, of James H, BRENGLE, Laura V, of Sam T, March 20 1873, 122
4655 RAMSBURG, Robert M, CAMDEN, Dora E, May 29 1873, 122
4656 RUPLEY, Theodore N, RAMSBURG, Fannie, of Wm H, June 12 1873, 122
4657 RUSE, Addison R, KUSSMAUL, Alice, Augt 13 1873, 122
4658 ROELKEY, Charles, of John, BRENGLE, Laura, of Ezra, Sept 16 1873, 122
4659 ROUZER, Charles B, of Gettysburg, Pa, SCHELL, Laura, of Cha's D, Nov 13 1873, 122
4660 REMSBERG, Albert J (Dr), BEALL, Mary Alice, March 12 1874, 122
4661 RILEY, Wm McKendree (Rev), BAKER, Fannie J, of H'y, Apl 16 1874, 122
4662 ROWE, Enoch Louis, of Ezra, RENNER, Mary, May 19 1874, 122
4663 RICE, Benj'n F, CUNNINGHAM, Alice L, of B A, June 16 1874, 122
4664 REIDENOUR, Joseph A, ZIMMERMAN, Ellen V, of Wm H, Nov 19 1874, 122
4665 REIGEL, Reuben E, DERR, Emma J, of Geo W, no date given, Polo, Illinois, 122
4666 REILLY, James, of Baton Rouge, TOPPER, Annie R, of A J, Jan 19 1875, 122
4667 RUDOLPH, Max, 2d wife, GRUND, Mary, Feb 18 1875, 122
4668 REIFSNIDER, Charles D, SHRIVER, Lizzie, of Edw, March 11 1875, 122
4669 RICKERD, Wm H, BEALL, Nannie, May 16 1875, 122
4670 REED, Albert W, of Indiana, REIFSNIDER, Louisa E, of John, May 27 1875, 122
4671 RITCHIE, Albert, of Dr Albert, CABELL, Lizzie Caskie, Octr 27 1875, 122
4672 REAL, George A, HAMMOND, Mary A, RIORDON, May 10 1876, 122
4673 ROGERS, Albert Holland, ZELLER, Emma R, of J Fred'k, Nov 14 1876, 122
4674 RAMSBURG, Dennis C, ROELKEY, Fannie D, of John, Decr 19 1876, 122
4675 ROBERTS, Woodward A, BAKER, Sarah A, June 14 1877, 122
4676 RAGER, Adolphus S, BAKER, Caroline E, June 20 1877, 122
4677 RENNER, John P, CHILCOTE, Mollie, of Tho's M, Oct 31 1877, 122
4678 REHLINGER, Henry, 2d wife, HARRINGTON, Sarah C (Mrs), Nov 25 1877, 122
4679 RAMSBURG, Marshall O, OGLE, Mary E, (not listed as Miss), Decr 18 1877, 123
4680 ROCHE, James R (Maj), of San Francisco, MITCHELL, Eliza L, Dec 4th 1879, 123
4681 RAGER, Rufus A, BOYER, Susan L, June 9th 1881, 123
4682 REICH, John H, BELT, Ellen C, December 7th 1881, 123
4683 ROWE, Charles H, LAMBERT, Catharine E, (of Nich), March 20th 1882, 123
4684 RIDENOUER, Joseph A, 2 wife, WISE, Ida V, April 6th 1882, 123
4685 REICH, Isaac S, ZIMMERMAN, Annie, May 24th 1882, 123
4686 RHODES, G Mantz, KOLB, Ida M, July 25 1882, (SALTER), 123
4687 REPP, John S, (second wife), JONES, Esther, August 29 1882, 123

4688 RULAND, Conrad, STEWART, Katie L, Feb 14 1883, 123
4689 RIGDON, James, 2 wife, HOOPER, Vima H, (@Lavinia), Feb 20th 1883, 123
4690 ROWE, Eugene W, EICHELBERGER, Annie M, April 25 1883, 123
4691 RAMSBURG, Clinton E, (@REMSBURG), BRENNEMAN, Allie G, of Joh/(@Alice G BENEMAN), Dec 11th 1883, 123
4692 RHODES, Wm H, CARMACK, Maggie E, (@Margaret E), January 31 1884, 123
4693 RICE, Thomas P, STEINER, Lillian C, of H F, Dec 3d 1884, 123
4694 RODOCK, George S, QUYNN, Mollie T, February 4 1885, 123
4695 RANNELS, William E, (@RANELS), GROFF, Jennie, of Ja's, April 21 1885, 123
4696 RHODERICK, George C (Jr), GROSS, Clemma B, May 7 1885, 123
4697 ROBERTS, William, SMITH, Emma, June 22 1885, 123
4698 RAMSBURG, Wm H, KUNKEL, Hallie P, July 29 1885, 123
4699 RICE, David S, FOUT, Ora, (@Orie), September 17 1885, 123
4700 RICHARDSON, J Lynn, DENNIS, Alice, October 6 1885, 123
4701 REULING, Henry C, {illegible}, LAMPE, Annie C, December 22 1885, 123
4702 ROUTZAHN, Martin B, WILLARD, Rosa M, of Tho's/(@Rosanna), January 19 1886, 123
4703 RAMSEY, Alexander, RENNE, Desie, February 3d 1886, 123
4704 ROHRBACK, Martin N, 2d wife, MARKEY, Susie, February 9 1886, 123
4705 RODGERS, Henry W, DENNIS, Fannie J, of Geo R, Feb 16th 1886, 123
4706 RICE, George W, BADGER, Georgia C, September 13 1886, 123
4707 ROSENSTOCK, Aaron, HUDLEBERGER, Isabella, September 16 1886, 123
4708 ROGERS, Charles W, BO__IE, Emily P, of the D & D/{surname illegible}, January 12 1887, {Deaf and Dumb compiler}, 123
4709 RICHARDSON, Davis, MARION, Annie M, inte west {in the west-compiler}, September 13 1887, inte west, 123
4710 RIDER, Wm E, WOODWARD, Nettie G, of Jacob, September 21 1887, 123
4711 RUMPF, Wm H, ESTERLY, Bettie, of Geo, September 21 1887, 123
4712 ROHRBACK, Cha's, of M N, JARBOE, Maggie, of Tho's, October 22 1887, 123
4713 RIDENOUR, John H, SNYDER, Laura, November 23 1887, 123
4714 RICKERDS, Wm H, LERCH, Emma V, of Henry, January 31 1888, 123
4715 RHODERICK, Wm, (@RODERICK), MERCER, Clara V, February 15 1888, 123
4716 RUDY, Walter R, ROUTZAHN, Laura, Sept 12 1888, 123
4717 RUDY, Wm L, COST, Mary E, Oct 10 1888, 123
4718 ROBINSON, David, (@ROBERSON), THOMAS, Rachel, Nov 5 1888, Colored, 123
4719 RIDGELEY, Wm D, NUSZ, Rose G, Oct 3 1889, 123
4720 REED, George A, (@READ), FORNEY, Allie R, (@Rebecca A), January 9 1890, 123
4721 ROWE, Paulus, BENNETT, Mary Ellen, (News office), Dec 31 1890, 123
4722 RYAN, Tobias Monroe, YOUNG, Emma A, of David, July 9 1889, 123
4723 SALMON, George, of Edw, SMITH, Catharine, of Dan'l, April 1819, 126
4724 SCHLEY, Frederick Augustus, 2d wife, LYNN, Francina C, of David, Jany 11 1821, 126
4725 SPRINGER, Daniel, of Wm, ROSE, Elizabeth, Octr 5 1820, 126
4726 STEINER, Stephen (Col), 2d wife, BAUSMAN, Elizabeth (Mrs), "BIRELY", May 15 1821, 126
4727 STINCHCOMB, Beal C, 2d wife, HAMILTON, Miss, (*Mary HAMBLETON), June 26 1821, 126
4728 SPRINGER, Thomas (Dr), of Wm, KELLER, Mary, of Mich'l/MiddTown, July 8 1821, 126
4729 STUP, Daniel, of Jacob, WIDRICK, Elizabeth, March 31 1822, 126
4730 SCHULTZ, Martin, CREEGER, Sabina, March 26 1822, 126

4731 SCHNAUFFER, George, 2d wife, RENNEBERGER, Eliza, April 11 1822, 126
4732 SHIPMAN, John, FISCHER, Miranda, of Adam, April 25 1822, 126
4733 SCHWEIGERT, Michael, BERRY, Nancy, May 1822, 126
4734 SMITH, John D, GOMBER, Christianna, of John, June 30 1822, 126
4735 STUTCHBURY, Wm R, SHAFER, Dorethea (Mrs), widow of Conrad, her 3d husband, Nov 26 1822, 126
4736 SIMMONS, Sam'l F, of John H, WHIFFING, Sarah P, of James, April 1 1823, 126
4737 SCHNEIDER, John, of Poland, WHIP, Mary, April 8 1823, 126
4738 SMALLWOOD, Wm Cooper, ROLLINGTON, Rosanna, of John, May 6 1823, 126
4739 SCHATZ, Jacob, SULTZER, Rebecca, June 17 1823, 126
4740 SPRENGLE, David, RUTH, Caroline M, "MEDDERT", Octr 2d 1823, 126
4741 SHAFFNER, Peter R, HART, Ann Maria, of Adam, Octr 19 1823, 126
4742 SCHELL, Enos, of Charles, BEATTY, Charlotte (Mrs), widow of John Mich'l, Octr 30 1823, 126
4743 STEINER, Christian, of Henry, WELTZHEIMER, Rebecca, of Dr Lewis, Decr 7 1823, 126
4744 SIM, Thomas (Dr), 1st wife, GIBSON, Harriott, "Woodsboro", June 22 1824, 126
4745 SCHLEY, William, of John, RINGGOLD, Ann, of Gen'l Sam'l, Septr 28 1824, 126
4746 SIMMS, Henry, BRENGLE, Margaret, of Nich's/Mount Pleasant, Nov 2 1824, 126
4747 SCHELLMAN, Jacob (Jun'r), WHIP, Charlotte, Decr 16 1824, 126
4748 SIMPSON, Thomas, KLEINERT, Wilhelmina, of Francis, Jany 9 1825, 126
4749 STAUFFER, John, of Joseph, STONER, Eleanor, (of Ab'm), March 15 1825, 126
4750 SCHWEITZER, Henry, EICKEL, Anna, April 4 1825, 126
4751 STICKEL, George, LEXTON, Sarah, May 30 1825, 126
4752 SHAFER, Noah A, BRENGLE, Matilda, of Peter, Augt 4 1825, 126
4753 SHOOK, Samuel B, RICE, Susan, of Tho's, Feby 5 1826, 126
4754 SMITH, Alexander, of Henry, COOKERLY, Margaret, March 28 1826, 126
4755 SMALL, William (Capt'n), 1st wife, TURBUTT, Maria, of Nicholas, Septr 12 1826, 126
4756 SINN, William, of Henry, LOCKE, Catharine J R, Nov 18 1826, 126
4757 SPECHT, Jacob, WISSINGER, Catharine, Feby 4 1827, 126
4758 SCHERER, Jacob (Rev), SPOON, Elizabeth (Mrs), N Carolina/by D J HAUER, Jany 9 1827, 126
4759 SMALL, William, "Shoemaker", NORRIS, Harriott, of Barnabas, March 22 1827, 126
4760 SMITH, Daniel Grove, of Henry/1st wife, BUCKEY, Eleanor, of Peter, May 8 1827, 126
4761 SHIELDS, Jefferson (Dr), GRABILL, Henrietta, July 26 1827, 126
4762 STAUFFER, Jacob, of Henry, LINN, Susan, (of Philip), Septr 23 1827, 126
4763 SHAFER, Peter, 2d wife, BRUNNER, Elizabeth, Septr 23 1827, 126
4764 SIMMONS, John H (Col), 2d wife, BEALL, Henrietta, of Elisha, Septr 15 1827, 126
4765 STALEY, Cornelius, 1st wife, CRONISE, Catharine, of John, Nov 15 1827, 127
4766 SCHLEY, Edward, of John, BRENGLE, E Margaret, of John, Decr 4 1827, 127
4767 STUP, Samuel, SMITH, Elizabeth, March 13 1828, 127
4768 SCHREINER, Henry J, EBBERTS, Susan, of Mich'l, July 25 1828, 127
4769 SHRINER, Cornelius, 1st wife, SCHOLL, Rebecca, of Christian, March 17 1829, 127
4770 STOVER, James, FLEMING, Alice, March 19 1829, 127
4771 SOWERS, Peter, 2d wife, HERZOG, Pamilia (Mrs), "HARTSOCK", May 3 1829, 127
4772 SCHREINER, John, NICHOLS, Louisa, of Peter, July 14 1829, 127
4773 SHOPE, George B, 2d wife, KELLER, Louisa, of Henry T, Augt 16 1829, 127
4774 STURGIS, Henry, SINN, Ann Eliza, of Henry, Octr 19 1829, 127

4775 STONER, Jacob, of Benedict "STEINER", HOUCK, Mary, of John/"County", Octr 25 1829, 127
4776 SHADWELL, Henry, KINKERLY, Susan, Nov 1 1829, 127
4777 STALEY, Cornelius, 2d wife, SCHNEBLY, Rowanna, Washington County, Nov 24 1829, 127
4778 SMITH, George (Jun'r), 1st wife, BAUGHER, Lydia, of Sam'l "BAGER", Nov 26 1829, 127
4779 SHAW, John, RICHARDS, Harriott, "Jac ROWE", May 27 1830, 127
4780 SIMMONS, Zachariah T, of John H, HELFENSTEIN, Louisa C, of Rev Jona'n, May 27 1830, 127
4781 SHOLL, John, (Grocer), COXEN, Sarah Ann, July 20 1830, 127
4782 SCHOLL, Elias, of Christian/1st wife, SCHERER, Susan, of Lewis, Jany 27 1831, 127
4783 STONER, Christian, of John/1st wife, SMITH, Ann M, of Henry/"Hatter", May 19 1831, 127
4784 SKINNER, Henry S, RILEY, Ann W D, (not listed as Miss), May 19 1831, 127
4785 SCHLEY, David, of John/2d wife, CLEMM, Georgiana M, May 25 1831, 127
4786 STRAEFFER, Michael, DRESSEL, Elizabeth, Cincinati, Ohio, May 19 1831, 127
4787 SCHLEICH, Daniel H, BECK, Mary Ann (Mrs), "MAYBERRY", July 12 1831, 127
4788 SHAFER, Jonathan, 2d wife, KREPS, Eliza (Mrs), Boonsboro, Septr 15 1831, 127
4789 STORM, Peter Leonard, 1st wife, RIEHL, Harriott, of Fred'k, Octr 12 1831, 127
4790 STICKEL, William, of Solomon, REIDENAUER, Sarah, Wm'sport, Nov 1 1831, 127
4791 SCHLEY, John Tho's, of John/1st wife, MCCLURE, Georgianna V, of Balto, Nov 29 1831, 127
4792 SMITH, Ezra, of George, MYERS, Mary, of Israel, April 5 1832, 127
4793 STUP, Joseph, of Jacob, HOUCK, Elizabeth, of John, April 10 1832, 127
4794 STUBBINS, John A, KLEIN, Sophia, of Stephen, April 19 1832, 127
4795 STALEY, Isaac, SHAFER, Miss, (*Susanna SHAEFFER), May 4 1832, 127
4796 SCHOLL, Daniel, of Christian, THOMAS, Susan, of Mich'l, May 10 1832, 127
4797 STUP, David, of Jacob, BAST, Susan, of Henry, Septr 20 1832, 127
4798 STEINER, Daniel, of Col Stephen, LARKIN, Julian (Mrs), "BURGESS", Septr 27 1832, 127
4799 STEDDING, Christean L, FISCHER, Catharine, of Jacob/"STREHLMACHER", Octr 21 1832, 127
4800 SMITH, Daniel Grove, of Henry/2d wife, BUCKEY, Eliza, of Peter, Jany 22 1833, 127
4801 STOKES, Robert Y, TYLER, Harriott D, of Dr Bradley, Jany 24 1833, 127
4802 SCHAEFFER, Frederick, from Germany, ORDNER, Elizabeth, of Peter, Jany 28 1833, 127
4803 SCHATZ, Henry, MYERS, Maria S, of Geo, March 21 1833, 127
4804 SMITH, Emanuel, 1st wife, HOUCK, Margaret, of John/County, May 28 1833, 127
4805 SCHERMAN, Peter, SCHELLE', Catharine (Mrs), of Fred'k, June 18 1833, 127
4806 SHARP, George W, SNYDER, Caroline Rebecca, of Nicholas, Decr 10 1833, 127
4807 SCHNAUFFER, Geo, of Geo, WIRTS, Mary Ann, Decr 12 1833, 128
4808 STALEY, Ezra, 1st wife, BRUNNER, Sophia, Decr 24 1833, 128
4809 SAUNDERS, John (Capt'n), SCHLEICH, Mary (Mrs), of Hagerstown, Jany 9 1834, 128
4810 SMITH, Augustus G, of Henry, JOHNSTON, Ann M, Leesburg, Va, March 25 1834, 128
4811 SCHUMACHER, Francis, 2d wife, SCHERER, Catharine (Mrs), 'NICKEL", Jany 28 1834, 128
4812 SCHINDLER, David, of Dan'l, BRUNNER, Catharine, of Elias, April 10 1834, 128
4813 STALLINGS, Joseph (Lieut), US Navy, HARDING, Elizabeth, of John L, July 10 1834, 128
4814 SCHELL, Joseph, of Cha's, GRABILL, Catharine Ann, Septr 16 1834, 128
4815 SIMMONS, John Adams, of Zachariah, FESSLER, Rosanna, of John, Decr 2 1834, 128
4816 SNYDER, John, of Dan'l Fairman, SPRINGER, Ann Rebecca, of Wm, Decr 4 1834, 128

4817 SCHELLMAN, Tho's C P (Rev), STEINER, Henrietta, of Capt Henry, Decr 29 1834, 128
4818 SANDERS, John Locher (Rev), SPAYTH, Lydia E, Tiffin, Ohio, Jany 20 1835, 128
4819 STAYMAN, Geo Fred'k, GUYTON, Ruth A, March 15 1835, 128
4820 STEIN, Louis, "Germany", FAUL, Elizabeth, March 17 1835, 128
4821 SHAW, John, HARTZ, Matilda (Mrs), widow of Joseph/"FRANZ", April 12 1835, 128
4822 STOFFEL, Peter, 1st wife, COX, Susan Livingston, of George, May 10 1835, 128
4823 SMITH, George, of Geo/2d wife, NIXDORFF, Mary C, of Henry, June 11 1835, 128
4824 STUP, John, KEMP, Lydia A, of Frederick, June 11 1835, 128
4825 SCHOEN, John, WAYS, Margaret, of Basil, June 11 1835, 128
4826 STANLEY, George, TURNEY, Ellen, "FRITCHIE", July 9 1835, 128
4827 STAIT, William, SCHLOSSER, Naomi G, of Geo, July 16 1835, 128
4828 SIMMS, William, LOWERY, Matilda, Baltimore, Septr 15 1835, 128
4829 SCHNEIDER, William H, WERNER, Mary, Octr 22 1835, 128
4830 SIMMS, Henry, 2d wife, LUGENBEEL, Martha E (Mrs), Nov 17 1835, 128
4831 SHEPHERD, Abijah, KELLER, Charlotte (Mrs), Decr 6 1835, 128
4832 STALEY, Henry S, CONNOR, Ann Rebecca, Decr 17 1835, 128
4833 SINN, John George, of Henry, STUTLER, Catharine E, Feby 7 1836, 128
4834 SALTER, William Ent, KILLIAN, Mary Ann, of Philip, March 6 1836, 128
4835 SINN, Jacob, of Philip, COLE, Amelia, April 19 1836, 128
4836 SCHOLL, Elias, of Christian/2d wife, DUTROW, Mary, June 15 1836, 128
4837 SIM, Thomas (Dr), 2d wife, WAGNER, Mary C, June 21 1836, 128
4838 STRAEFFER, Jacob M, CALEY, Rebecca, Cincinnati, O, Nov 17 1836, 128
4839 SPARROW, Allen, SKAGGS, Eliza, Decr 1 1836, 128
4840 STONER, Jonathan, BARNHART, Sarah, March 20 1837, 128
4841 SHRIVER, Charles, of Ab'm, THOMAS, Ann Eliza, April 4 1837, 128
4842 STEINER, John Alexander, 1st wife, MYERS, Sophia, of Israel, April 3d 1837, 128
4843 SINN, Daniel, of Philip, LAMBRECHT, Susan, of Geo, April 18 1837, 128
4844 SHRIVER, Edward, of Ab'm, STEPHENSON, Elizabeth L (Mrs), "REIGART", Augt 30 1837, 128
4845 STORCH, Theophilus (Rev), LYNCH, Mary Jane, of Wm, Nov 16 1837, 128
4846 STEINER, John J, of Capt Henry, BOYER, Frances Hanna, Tiffin, O, Decr 21 1837, 128
4847 STONER, Dennis, of John, SMITH, Charlotte, of Henry, Jany 16 1838, 128
4848 SCHLEY, James McCannon, of F A, STULL, Ellen N, of Otho H W, Feby 10 1838, 128
4849 STEINER, David C, WIEST, Elizabeth, of Jacob, March 18 1838, 129
4850 SINN, John Thomas, LOVEDER, Catharine, May 31 1838, 129
4851 STOCKMAN, David, WASKEY, Elizabeth, June 7 1838, 129
4852 SMITH, Wm H, WEINBRENNER, Elizabeth E, of Jacob, July 12 1838, Ohio, 129
4853 SCHERER, Valentine, BOLLENBACHER, Julia, Augt 28 1838, 129
4854 SMALL, William (Capt), "Brewer"/2d wife, HEWETT, Elizabeth, "DONEY", Septr 12 1838, 129
4855 SMITH, Eli, SMITH, Theresa, "Church Street", Septr 16 1838, 129
4856 STOFFEL, Peter, 2d wife, WARE, Elizabeth, Septr 30 1838, 129
4857 SCHUETENHELM, Reuben, LEASE, Elizabeth, Nov 1 1838, 129
4858 SCHELL, Charles D, of Enos, BEATTY, Cornelia Ann, March 28 1839, 129
4859 SPARROW, Wilson, STOCKMAN, Elizabeth, March 28 1839, 129
4860 SINN, Philip Henry, of Philip, BIRELY, Mary E, of Wm, April 11 1839, 129
4861 STOCKMAN, Wm Perry, UTCHISON, Matilda A, April 16 1839, 129

4862 SHAW, Zachariah, RITER, Elizabeth (Mrs), April 25 1839, 129
4863 SNYDER, William, PLAIN, Sarah A, N Market, April 25 1839, 129
4864 SHAWEN, Grafton, BENTZ, Christianna, of Wm, May 15 1839, 129
4865 SCHELLE', Jacob Frederick, LEHAY, Ellen, Balto, June 16 1839, 129
4866 SCHLEY, George, of Fred A, HALL, Mary, of Tho's B HALL/Hagerstown, June 26 1839, 129
4867 SANDERSON, Thomas, of Wm Raymond, PEARSON, Hannah A, of Jos, June 25 1839, 129
4868 SCHRODER, Henry H, RETTGERING, Johanna, July 11 1839, 129
4869 SCHEIB, Henry (Rev), EISENBRANT, Lisette D, Balto, Septr 8 1839, 129
4870 SMITH, Robert, EICHELBERGER, Rebecca, Octr 24 1839, 129
4871 SHIPLEY, Samuel, MICHAEL, Ann, Octr 29 1839, 129
4872 SUMAN, William R, CROMWELL, Rachel C, Nov 21 1839, 129
4873 SMITH, David F, of Henry, FORD, Susan E, in Balto, Decr 15 1839, 129
4874 STOKES, William H (Dr), TYLER, Mary, of Dr Bradly, Decr 19 1839, 129
4875 STUP, George, of Jacob/1st wife, HOUCK, Barbara, of John C/O, March 29 1850, 129
4876 SMITH, Christian, of George, BURKITT, Mary, April 9 1840, 129
4877 SHANK, Geo Washington, 1st wife, BAKER, Serepta A, March 26 1840, 129
4878 STRIDER, James W, of Va/1st wife, WEBSTER, Georgetta, of Geo, April 28 1840, 129
4879 SCHROEDER, Frederick, 1st wife, HORNUNG, Catharine, May 14 1840, 129
4880 SCHIEWETZ, Christian, RAELING, Elizabeth, May 26 1840, 129
4881 SMITH, Benjamin, GOWING, Ellen, "Colored friends", June 11 1840, 129
4882 SCHLUND, Joshua, SCHIETZ, Margaret, July 21 1840, 129
4883 SNOOK, Josiah, ECKMAN, Jane Sophia, Glade, Septr 10 1840, 129
4884 STULL, Joshua, SNOOK, Elizabeth, Septr 17 1840, 129
4885 SMITH, Jonathan, CUTSAIL, Nancy, Septr 17 1840, 129
4886 SHOEMAKER, Dennis, FOGEL, Lydia A, Nov 12 1840, 129
4887 SAYLER, Henry, DONSEIF, Catharine E, Nov 17 1840, 129
4888 STAUB, John W, BISHOP, Eve, Lewistown, Decr 24 1840, 129
4889 SHRINER, Cornelius, 2d wife, BARRICK, Mary, of Geo, March 9 1841, 129
4890 SHAFER, John H, SHAWEN, Sarah A, March 9 1841, 129
4891 SMITH, Daniel, HOFFMAN, Harriett, March 18 1841, 130
4892 SHELLMAN, James M (Col), JONES, Catharine G, in Balto, May 11 1841, 130
4893 SPEDDEN, Edward M, O'NEAL, Caroline, of Hor G, May 6 1841, 130
4894 SHEID, Walter H, THOMAS, Susanna, (not listed as Miss), May 6 1841, 130
4895 STRAEFFER, Daniel, of Mich'l, MENCHE', Lydia, May 27 1841, 130
4896 SCHOLL, Lewis V, MAYNARD, Jemima, of Tho's, Augt 3 1841, 130
4897 SNOOK, Dennis, BUCKEY, Matilda, of John/"Hatter", Augt 26 1841, 130
4898 STRAEFFER, John, of Mich'l, CULLER, Julia A, Octr 21 1841, 130
4899 SCHLEY, John Edward, of Henry/1st wife, TOWNER, Ann F, Va, Octr 14 1841, 130
4900 SHIPLEY, Wm G, CRONISE, Maria, of Jacob, Nov 4 1841, 130
4901 SENTZELL, Matthias, WILSON, Jane Ann, "at Berlin", Nov 18 1841, 130
4902 STEVENSON, Wm, TANEY, Elizabeth Maynadier, of Roger B/Balto, Nov 18 1841, 130
4903 SAPPINGTON, Thomas (Dr), of Tho's, DALEY, Teresa Ann, of John, Nov 25 1841, 130
4904 STEPHEN, Cha's H (Dr), BALCH, Virginia, of Lewis P W/Leestown, Va, Decr 21 1841, 130
4905 SINN, Edward, of Henry, ELKINS, Eveline, of Wm, Feby 3 1842, 130
4906 SCHULTZ, Jefferson, of Conrad/Balto/2d wife, DEBRULER, Louisa, of our City, April 12 1842, 130

4907 SHEARER, Lewis V, of Lewis/1st wife, *BUSH*, Margaret Ann, Winchester, Va, April 14 1842, 130
4908 SEEMANN, Christian, *ATTIG*, Catharine, March 1842, 130
4909 SCHMIDT, Jacob, 1st wife, *WALTER*, Catharine, "sister of John", May 16 1842, 130
4910 SCHOLL, Dennis, *BARTGIS*, Margaret, of Matthias E, Augt 17 1842, 130
4911 ST JOHN, Wm, *CREAGER*, Mary E, of Geo/Middletown, Septr 8 1842, 130
4912 SIMMONS, James, *SIMMONS*, Eleanor Howard, of Zachariah, Septr 13 1842, 130
4913 SHAWEN, George J, *JACOBS*, Rachel, Nov 10 1842, 130
4914 SAMS, Carleton C (Dr), *WEVER*, Charlotte D, of Caspar W, Nov 8 1842, 130
4915 SAUERMANN, William, *KERSHAW*, Sarah, "GERSHONG", Nov 10 1842, 130
4916 SIMMONS, Isaac, *TORRANCE*, Elizabeth R, of Jame, Nov 17 1842, 130
4917 STEINER, Jacob F, of Henry/"HALLER", *CRAMER*, Sophia, of Jacob, March 2 1843, 130
4918 STAUFFER, Simon, of Joseph, *CRAMER*, Ann R, of David, May 1843, 130
4919 SMITH, John F, *MILLER*, Mary Ann, Fairview, May 30 1843, 130
4920 SCHLEY, Frederick Augustus, 3d wife, *HALL*, Barbara, of Tho's B, June 15 1843, 130
4921 SUMAN, Israel W, *WISE*, Caroline E, of Fred'k, Septr 5 1843, 130
4922 SAHM, Christian, *SAUERMANN*, Louisa, Septr 26 1843, 130
4923 STAUFFER, Henry, of Joseph, *MAGRUDER*, Matilda, Jany 9 1844, 130
4924 SUMAN, John J (Rev), *SPENCE*, Agnes, of "Canada", Jany 11 1844, 130
4925 SCHULTZ, Wm D, of Henry, *WALKER*, Mary, of John/Glade, Feby 14 1844, Glade, 130
4926 SLACK, Cornelius, *LEASE*, Louisa Elizabeth, of Carlisle, Pa, Feby 15 1844, 130
4927 STALEY, John A, 1st wife, *HINCKEL*, Charlotte, Feby 22 1844, 130
4928 SHIPLEY, Nicholas Hall, *CONTEE*, Margaret, Feby 22 1844, 130
4929 STALEY, Daniel L, *MCDEVITT*, Sarah A, March 28 1844, 130
4930 STOUT, James M, *WEINBRENNER*, Sevilla, April 25 1844, 130
4931 SAPPINGTON, Greenbury (Dr), of Col Tho's, *PEARRE*, Sarah E, Augt 15 1844, 130
4932 STEINER, John Alexander, 2d wife, *BRUNNER*, Mary, of Jacob, Septr 19 1844, 130
4933 SCHLOSSER, Peter G, 1st wife, *MCCOLLUM*, Catharine, Octr 14 1844, 131
4934 SCHISSLER, Hiram (Dr), *GIBSON*, Margretta R M, at York, Pa, Octr 15 1844, 131
4935 SCHLEY, John Edward, of Henry/2d wife & sisters, *TOWNER*, Mary Virginia, Octr 24 1844, 131
4936 STONER, Augustus, *HAMMOND*, Susanna Ann, Decr 12 1844, 131
4937 SCHABACKER, George, of Adam, *KIEFFER*, Matilda, "STOFFEL", Decr 24 1844, 131
4938 SMITH, Franklin J (Dr), *GOERING*, Henrietta E, Feby 14 1845, 131
4939 SAPPINGTON, Thomas (Col), "Reg of Wills"/2d wife, *KLEIN*, Louisa, March 27 1845, 131
4940 SCHUETENHELM, Thomas, *HARRIS*, Elizabeth, April 6 1845, 131
4941 SCHAEFFER, David Krebs (Dr), of Rev D F, *LATE*, Margaret C, April 8 1845, 131
4942 SCHELL, Charles D, of Ezra, *LAMBRECHT*, Harriett, of Michael, June 3 1845, 131
4943 SNYDER, John, *LAMBRECHT*, Rachel, of George, June 2 1845, 131
4944 SMITH, Henry, DILL's "Henry", *NO BRIDES NAME GIVEN*, Miss, Colored friends, Septr 11 1845, 131
4945 SIMPSON, Charles B, *GETZENDANNER*, Margy G, of Geo/"SALMON", Nov 6 1845, "SALMON", 131
4946 SCHAFF, Philip (Rev DD), *SCHLEY*, Mary E, of David, Decr 10 1845, 131
4947 STIMMEL, Edward B, of John, *BARRICK*, Mary Jane, Decr 11 1845, 131
4948 STARTZMAN, Christian (Rev), *ANKNEY*, Eliza, Washington Co, Jany 12 1846, 131
4949 SNOUFFER, Benjamin J, *MOFFET*, Ellen E, Feby 19 1846, 131

4950 SENEKER, Emanuel, CHILCOAT, Ellen, April 21 1846, 131
4951 STONE, Francis S, SHORB, Maria Francina, April 30 1846, 131
4952 SHAW, Wm H, FROSCHAUER, Isabella, May 3 1846, 131
4953 STEHLE', Henry J, DOLL, Louisa B, of Ezra, May 12 1846, 131
4954 SHAW, John A, RUTHERFORD, Virginia, of Benj'n, May 145 1846, 131
4955 STANTON, William, JOHNSTON, Sophia S, of Arthur/Hagerstown, July 1846, 131
4956 SHANK, John P, ADAMS, Sarah A R, of Valentine, Augt 26 1846, 131
4957 STUP, George, of Jacob/2d wife, STALEY, Louisa M, of Geo, Nov 19 1846, 131
4958 STRIDER, James W, "STREITER"/2d wife, QUIGLEY, Lucy, Jefferson Co, Va, Decr 3 1846, 131
4959 SHAWEN, Cornelius, ALBERT, Isabella V, of John L, Feby 17 1847, 131
4960 STUNKEL, Frederick, HUGO, Maria, Feby 21 1847, 131
4961 STALEY, Joshua, BRUBAKER, Ann E, of John, March 4 1847, 131
4962 SCHLEY, Fairfax (Dr), of Henry, STEINER, Rebecca L, of Christ'n, March 18 1847, 131
4963 SMITH, Emanuel, 2d wife, CRAMER, Margaret E, Glade, May 20 1847, 131
4964 SCHROEDER, Frederick, 2d wife & sisters, HORNUNG, Sophia W, Augt 1 1847, 131
4965 STULL, David, MILLER, Charlotte, Augt 31 1847, 131
4966 SHRIVER, Wm Eltinge, of Ab'm, PULLEN, Cornelia, in Balto, Octr 16 1847, 131
4967 SALKE', Fredrich Wilhelm, ROLKE', Lena, of Christ'n, Nov 25 1847, 131
4968 SCHABACKER, Jno Jacob, BOLASKI, Catharine, Jany 13 1848, 131
4969 STEINER, Henry C, of Henry, ROHR, Ann Elizabeth, of Jacob, Feby 3 1848, 131
4970 SIM, Thomas (Dr), 3d wife, DAVIS, Lucy Ann, April 13 1848, 131
4971 STORM, Peter Leonard, 2d wife, BURROWS, Isabella, April 16 1848, 131
4972 STUNKEL, Cha's H, HUGO, Clara M, April 23 1848, 131
4973 SPECHT, David, 2d wife, SCHAEFFER, Elizabeth (Mrs), widow of John A, May 11 1848, 131
4974 STEWART, Geo Lee, MORGAN, Elizabeth Augusta, of Tho's W, May 16 1848, 131
4975 STEINER, Frederick, "Miller by trade", WUSSEL, Margaret, May 18 1848, 132
4976 STORCH, Theophilus (Rev), 2d wife, BAKER, Emma, of Cha's H/Phila, Augt 31 1848, 132
4977 SCHELL, George W, of Ezra/1st wife, BATSON, Jane, Septr 5 1848, 132
4978 STONE, Henry A, CRUM, Ann M, near Jefferson, Octr 12 1848, 132
4979 SPONSELLER, John J, LEASE, Martha, Nov 9 1848, 132
4980 SANDERS, Benedict J, NOONAN, Mary Ann, Nov 14 1848, 132
4981 SHANK, Geo P, KREIS, Margaret A, Nov 30 1848, 132
4982 SPONSILLER, William, PRINCE, Mary, of Tho's C, Nov 30 1848, 132
4983 SCHLEY, Charles, of Henry, JOHNSON, Harriett, of Dr Cha's W, Decr 5 1848, 132
4984 SCHELLMAN, Daniel J, ZIMMERMAN, Caroline S, of Geo, Decr 19 1848, 132
4985 SWEADNER, Daniel (Jun'r), CARR, Clementine, of Tho's, Decr 26 1848, 132
4986 STEELE, John Nevitt, DAVIS, Rosa Nelson (Mrs), January 22 1849, 132
4987 SCHNAUFFER, Johusa J, WHITE, Ann Jemima, April 10 1849, 132
4988 SCHMUCKER, Sam'l S (Rev), 3d wife, WAGNER, Esther M, April 24 1849, 132
4989 SCHEEL, Philip Augustus, ANNACKER, Catharine, April 27 1849, 132
4990 STALEY, Jonathan A, 1st wife, STALEY, Mary E, March 24 1849, 132
4991 SHUE, Jacob J, HAND, Emily J, Balto, May 22 1849, 132
4992 SPANGLER, Wm H, SMITH, Abbie, of New England, May 15 1849, 132
4993 STEVENSON, Andrew (Hon), of Va, SCHAFF, Mary, of Dr John, June 28 1849, 132
4994 SHRIVER, Abraham Ferree, GLOVER, Mary Jane, of Cha's, July 31 1849, 132

The Joseph Engelbrecht Marriage Ledger of Frederick Co., MD 1820-1890 *Marriage List*

4995 SHOPE, Wm B, of Geo B, KREBS, Julea Beaford, Balto, Octr 23 1849, 132
4996 STEINER, Frederick Birely (Capt'n), of Stephen, MUNDER, Catharine, Balto, Feby 21 1850, 132
4997 SHRIVER, Thomas, 2d wife, CONKLIN, Mary, Cumberland, Feby 7 1850, 132
4998 STALEY, Joshua, STALEY, Susanna, July 25 1850, 132
4999 STAUFFER, Daniel E, GEESEY, Sarah J, Octr 24 1850, 132
5000 SHEETS, Levi D (Dr), BAUGHER, Virginia, of Isaac, Octr 31 1850, 132
5001 SNYDER, Henry M, MILES, Harriott Ann, Octr 15 1850, 132
5002 STALEY, Wm Albert, SHOOK, Susanna, Nov 7 1850, 132
5003 SHRIVER, John A, Balto, BRENGLE, Olevia, of Law J, Nov 6 1850, 132
5004 SUMAN, Issac P, GANZAU, Mary E, of Jac, Decr 3 1850, 132
5005 SCHLOSSER, George, 2d wife, DERR, Catharine (Mrs), Jany 4 1851, 132
5006 SCHLEY, John Tho's, of John/2d wife, HALLER, Sophia H, of Joseph/"QUYNN", Jany 22 1851, 132
5007 SMOOT, John H, DUVALL, Julia, of Daniel, Jany 30 1851, 132
5008 STIMMEL, John, of John B, PARSONS, Hanna E, Woodsboro, Feby 10 1851, 132
5009 SANDERSON, Nelson Brown, BANTZ, Sophia Meadishin, Col'd friends, June 5 1851, 132
5010 SMELTZER, J P (Rev), EICHELBERGER, Ann, of Martin/Woodsboro, June 17 1851, 132
5011 SHIPLEY, Nimrod Owings (Dr), WRIGHT, Eliva, of Jesse, Nov 4 1851, 132
5012 SENSENEY, Geo E, GALLAHER, Mary Ellen, of John S/Va, Nov 4 1851, 132
5013 SEIDENSTRICKER, John B, CRAGG, Mary H, Balto, Nov 11 1851, 132
5014 SHAFFNER, Peter R, of P R, SALMON, Ann C, Washington, DCa, Decr 21 1851, 132
5015 STALEY, John A, 2d wife, SHOOK, Henrietta, Decr 25 1851, 132
5016 SCHEFFER, Henry, HALLER, Cecelia, of Jacob/(not listed as Miss), Jany 4 1852, 132
5017 SHRIVER, James, MEYER, Jeannie, of Tho's/Balto, Jany 21 1852, 133
5018 SHEETS, Wm Henry, PHELPS, Susan Ann, N Market, April 1 1852, 133
5019 SMALL, William, ADAMS, Emily, of John/Balto, May 20 1852, 133
5020 SINN, William E, of Wm, BONN, Ann Eliza, Balto, May 20 1852, 133
5021 SMITH, Frisby (Dr), GERHART, Elizabeth B, of Rev Isaac, May 26 1852, 133
5022 SAWYER, Henry Hudson, SHANK, Henrietta E, of Ezra, Septr 14 1852, 133
5023 SHIPLEY, Benjamin W, MUNSEED, Mary J, Septr 23 1852, 133
5024 SCHLUCKBIER, Peter, ELECK, Anna M, Octr 13 1852, 133
5025 SPONSELLER, Arthur T, RODEROCK, Jane R, Octr 21 1852, 133
5026 SCHULTZ, Edward T, of Henry, MARTIN, Susan R, of David/Balto, Nov 18 1852, 133
5027 SEABROOK, John H, EICHELBERGER, Mary M, of Jos, Nov 25 1852, 133
5028 SCHAEFFER, Luther Melancthon, of Rev D F, LATE, Ann Rebecca, of Mich'l, Feby 16 1853, 133
5029 SUESZ, Friedrich, GRAHE', Louisa, March 21 1853, 133
5030 SCHAAFF, Luther, WISE, Mary E, Jefferson, May 4 1853, 133
5031 SULTZER, Henry P, FEASTER, Mary Catharine, May 4 1853, 133
5032 SAUNDERS, John, RICKERT, Caroline, June 14 1853, 133
5033 SAUERWEIN, Christopher, SCHERER, Louisa K, July 7 1853, 133
5034 SHAWEN, Wm Henry, CRAVER, Hester Ann, July 21 1853, 133
5035 SHOOK, John Wm, MORNINGSTAR, Mary Ann, Augt 10 1853, 133
5036 SMALLWOOD, Wm Cooper (Jun'r), ZIEGLER, Julia E, Augt 1 1853, 133
5037 SHAFER, Wm A, GALLION, Emily A, of John P, Septr 13 1853, 133
5038 SCHLEY, Alfred, of David, ENGLAND, Harriett A, Liberty, Octr 12 1853, 133

5039 SCHLEY, Wm Louis, of David, KOCH, Kate M, at York, Pa, Octr 18 1853, 133
5040 STEI, Philip, DUPEL, Elizabeth, Nov 20 1853, 133
5041 SMITH, George Wm, of Geo, HOWARD, S Virginia, of Edward, Nov 22 1853, 133
5042 SPECHT, Jacob, his 3d wife & her 2d husband, HERGESHEIMER, Sophia (Mrs), Nov 24 1853, 133
5043 SCHELL, George W, of Ezra/2d wife, WELSH, Mary E, Decr 22 1853, 133
5044 SAPPINGTON, Sidney A (Dr), of Tho's, WAGNER, Margaret, Decr 27 1853, 133
5045 SHRIVER, Thomas, 3d wife, SHERWOOD, E C, Cumberland/(not listed as Miss), Feby 5 1854, 133
5046 STIMMELL, Cornelius, BARTHOLOW, Miss, (*Ann), Feby 21 1854, 133
5047 SCHWARTZ, John, WILLS, Arietta, "ORNDORFF", March 16 1854, 133
5048 SIMMONS, Simon Cyrus, of Zachariah, MYERS, Mary M (Mrs), "JACKSON", April 27 1854, 133
5049 SHAFER, Peter, 3d wife, HARGETT, Elizabeth Matthews (Mrs), "widow of Peter", June 4 1854, 133
5050 SMALTZ, John Henry (Dr), of Rev J H, NAGLEE, Caroline L, Phila, June 8 1854, 133
5051 SPRINGER, Thomas, of Daniel, NORRIS, Frances Rebecca, Septr 8 1854, 133
5052 SHIPLEY, Wm H, SILENCE, Elizabeth M (Mrs), Septr 19 1854, 133
5053 STOCKMAN, Lewis A, FULMER, Susan, Octr 5 1854, 133
5054 SAPPINGTON, Richard (Dr), SMITH, Aralanta R, Balto, Octr 18 1854, 133
5055 SCHMIDT, Christian, BAUMANN, Margaret S, (not listed as Miss), Nov 26 1854, 133
5056 SHAFER, George F, MANTZ, Margaret, of Peter, Decr 7 1854, 133
5057 SNYDER, Henry, KAUFFMAN, Mary Ann, Decr 12 1854, 133
5058 STEVENS, Wm F, of Balto, ROLKE', Christina, of Christ'n, Decr 14 1854, 133
5059 SLIFER, William, RAMSURG, Charlotte E, Middle'nvalley, Jany 16 1855, 134
5060 SMITH, Washington, OGLE, Julia A, Jany 25 1855, 134
5061 SMITH, William, RHODES, Mary E, "Point of Rocks", Feby 1 1855, 134
5062 STUP, William D, BRUNNER, Eleanor, Feby 15 1855, 134
5063 SCHULTZ, Theodore, of Geo, DILL, Mary M, of Joshua, March 20 1855, 134
5064 STEWARD, Thomas, FEIT, Mary, of Jacob/Cincinnati, March 1855, 134
5065 SELBY, Hamilton, MULLICAN, Jane, May 3 1855, 134
5066 SMITH, John Gomber, MICHAEL, Laura, of Jacob, May 8 1855, 134
5067 SMITH, Thomas A, HENDRY, Ann A, of Charles, May 8 1855, 134
5068 SCHUCKMANN, Friedrick, HOFFMAN, Louisa, "Pub in church", May 20 1855, 134
5069 SAUNDERS, Walter, MARBLE, Caroline E, at Mount Vernon, Ohio, May 31 1855, 134
5070 SEABROOK, Wm L W, THOMAS, Philipina, of Levin, Septr 4 1855, 134
5071 STULL, Frederick A, HOLTZ, Annie N, Decr 25 1855, 134
5072 SOUDER, John P, CRIST, Annie M, Jany 16 1856, 134
5073 SHAFER, Jonathan A, WHITMER, Ann R, of Nicholas, Feby 12 1856, 134
5074 SOHN, E C (Dr), of Ohio/(*Edward), BARRICK, Catharine E, Feby 27 1856, 134
5075 SCHULTZ, Alexander, of Henry, MYERS, Lizzie E, of John J/Balto, May 29 1856, 134
5076 STEINER, Herman Frank, of Henry, FOUT, Othetta L, of Otho, July 9 1856, 134
5077 SIMPSON, Tho's W (Dr), 1st wife, SIM, Sarah G, of Dr Tho's/Liberty, July 22 1856, 134
5078 STIMMEL, Amos, OTT, Julia Ann S, Septr 11 1856, 134
5079 SHREEVE, Jesse (Rev), 1st wife, HUPMAN, Margaret A, Balto, Otr 16 1856, 134
5080 STURGES, Flavius Josephus, 1st wife, STEPHENS, Ann Maria, Schley written above Josephus, Octr 21 1856, 134
5081 SIMMONS, J Samuel, SHRIVER, Ann Eliza (Mrs), widow of Cha's, Nov 13 1856, 134

5082 STOKES, William, of R Y, FITZHUGH, Sophia A, of Benj G, Decr 9 1856, 134
5083 SCHRODER, Henry Cha's August, SANDMEYER, Gertrude, Decr 23 1856, 134
5084 SUESSEROTT, Benj'n C (Rev), SCHMUCKER, Josephine, of Rev Sam'l S SCHMUCKER, Decr 24 1856, 134
5085 SIMPSON, Richard W, ROOT, Ann M, of Daniel, Decr 31 1856, 134
5086 SHRYOCK, Henry V, GRIMES, Julia A, Jany 29 1857, 134
5087 STUP, John A, ANGELBERGER, Ann S, March 19 1857, 134
5088 STONER, William, FRALEY, Ellen, March 31 1857, 134
5089 SCHREINER, Randolph, of John, RIEHL, Mary M, of Otho, May 5 1857, 134
5090 SAYLER, George, ALCOTT, Mary A (Mrs), Glade, June 7 1857, 134
5091 SNYDER, Samuel (Junior), RICE, Jane, of George, June 14 1857, 134
5092 SNYDER, Wm E (Rev), 2d wife, ORNER, Mary J, at Reading, Pa, Septr 3 1847, 134
5093 SEISS, F S Oscar, SCOTT, Margaret M, Octr 1 1857, 134
5094 SCOTT, Wm Amos, GANZAU, Catharine M, of Jacob, Octr 6 1857, 134
5095 SNOOK, John W, ADKINS, Matilda Ann, Glade, Nov 10 1857, 134
5096 STALEY, Cornelius A, 1st wife, MAIN, Eveline, Nov 29 1857, 134
5097 SPARKS, Robert, HAMMOND, Catharine, of Walter C, Decr 17 1857, 134
5098 SCHLEICH, Frederick W, MILLER, Mary C, of Conrad, Jany 6 1858, 134
5099 SEMMES, Benedict I, REYNOLDS, Sallie F, of Kentucky, Decr 8 1857, 134
5100 SHUNK, James F, of Gov Francis R, BLACK, Rebeka, of Jerry S/Pa, March 10 1858, 134
5101 SELLMAN, Wm T, PLUMMER, Ann Jennie, of Wm, March 9 1858, 135
5102 SAHM, Peter (Jun'r), MAUGHT, Mary A B, of Sam'l/"MACHT", March 25 1858, 135
5103 SCHRAYER, Solomon W, his 3d wife, EADER, Mary Ann (Mrs), widow of Geo her 2d husband, March 25 1858, 135
5104 STUP, John H, SHOOK, Mary Ann, April 7 1858, 135
5105 SCHAERER, Daniel, ROLKE', Amelia (Mrs), widow of F Augustus, April 13 1858, 135
5106 SHAY, W C, Editor "York Repub", UPP, Annie, York, Pa, April 15 1858, 135
5107 STEWARD, Wm H, WOODWARD, Alice E, of Baldwin, April 20 1858, 135
5108 SHRINER, Edward A, of Cornelius, DERR, Margaret A, of John, April 27 1858, 135
5109 STAUFFER, David R, of John, BURRIER, Mary C C, of Daniel, May 20 1858, 135
5110 SCHAEFFER, Wm G, of Rev D F/1st wife, MILLER, Ada, Balto, June 10 1858, 135
5111 SUNDAY, Daniel, FREY, Catharine, June 17 1858, 135
5112 SHOPE, Charles E, of Geo B, SALTER, Catharine Sophia, of Wm E, June 29 1858, 135
5113 SENTMAN, S (Rev), 2d wife, LEHMAN, Sallie A, Phila, July 1858, 135
5114 SOWERS, Samuel (Rev), MATTHEWS, Margaret, Augt 12 1858, 135
5115 SHOOK, Lewis A, HARGETT, Ann R, of Peter, Septr 28 1858, 135
5116 SNYDER, Samuel, DERR, Orpha E, Octr 12 1858, 135
5117 SCHWARTZ, Benjamin F, BOYER, Mary, Urbana, Nov 10 1858, 135
5118 SHUCK, Samuel, DURBIN, Annie, of Col Wm/Cumberland, Decr 9 1858, 135
5119 SAFFELL, T R, (*James T B), SANDERS, Annstener, Midd valley, Decr 21 1858, 135
5120 SHAW, George W, HOLBURNNER, Sarah J, Woodsboro, Decr 23 1858, 135
5121 SHAFER, Benjamin F, MCCAULEY, Hanna Virginia, of Sam'l/Wash Co, Decr 30 1858, 135
5122 SCHULTZ, Martin, of N York, BISHOP, Anna (Madam), "the Singer"/London, Decr 20 1858, 135
5123 SHIPLEY, Wm H, RIGGS, Hettie R, Jany 4 1859, 135
5124 SMITH, Wm T, WILKINSON, Ann Rebecca, Balto, Jany 11 1859, 135
5125 SHARPLESS, Townsend, of Phila, JOLLIFFE, Elizabeth, Va/Quakers/(not listed as Miss),

Jany 12 1859, 135

5126 *SCHLEY*, Frederick, of John, *WASHINGTON*, Florence, of Rich'd C, Feby 3 1859, 135

5127 *STOCKMAN*, George W, *FRAZIER*, Amelia Ann, of Jeremiah, Feby 22 1859, 135

5128 *SCHULTZ*, Louis H, of Geo, *THATER*, Nellie, Balto, March 7 1859, 135

5129 *SHANK*, William, *BRINKMAN*, Margaret (Mrs), March 10 1859, 135

5130 *SLICK*, Abednigo, *PARRISH*, Elizabeth H, Mechanicstown, March 22 1859, 135

5131 *STAIR*, Henry W, of York, Pa, *MILLER*, Marion, of Joshua M, March 22 1859, 135

5132 *SNADER*, Jesse W, *REINHART*, Sarah M, of Rev David, March 22 1859, 135

5133 *STODDARD*, Marshall W, *SNYDER*, Kate B, of Sam'l/Bellvue, Nebra, April 2 1859, 135

5134 *SCHRODEL*, John, *NEUBRANDT*, Caroline, of John, April 5 1859, 135

5135 *SALTZGIVER*, George, *WACHTER*, Maria M, of Rev Michael, April 12 1859, 135

5136 *SCHINDLER*, Jonathan, of David, *SMITH*, Cordelia E, "Rockey Springs", May 8 1859, 135

5137 *SHEELEIGH*, Matthias (Rev), *DILLER*, Sabina M, "Lebanon, Pa", May 3 1859, 135

5138 *SIMPSON*, Basil J H, *NUSSBAUM*, Laura J, "Liberty", May 3 1859, 135

5139 *STANLEY*, Edward (Hon), 2d wife, *BALDWIN*, Cornelia, California, May 10 1854, 135

5140 *SCOTT*, Samuel J, *HARMAN*, Mary Jane, "Graceham", May 18 1859, 135

5141 *SUMMERS*, S, (*Sylvester), *MARLOW*, L H, of Hanson/(*Louisa Hanson), May 23 1859, 135

5142 *STUMP*, Emanuel D, *WEBSTER*, Harriett, June 2 1859, 135

5143 *SCHUBER*, Lewis, *DUSING*, Mary A C, Wolfsville, June 23 1859, 136

5144 *SNOUFFER*, John B, *SHREVE*, Annie, Octr 20 1859, 136

5145 *STEIN*, Jacob, *SCHAFF*, Sarah, Octr 27 1859, 136

5146 *STULL*, John A, *RAMSBURG*, Ann S, Nov 3 1859, 136

5147 *SHAW*, Wm A, *SLIFER*, Ann V, Nov 10 1859, 136

5148 *SCHAAFF*, Francis, *RHODES*, Elmira E, Jefferson, Nov 24 1859, 136

5149 *SNYDER*, Martin H, *SCHILDKNECHT*, Elouisa M, Nov 27 1859, 136

5150 *STIER*, Frederick A, *DORSEY*, Ann E, Jany 5 1860, 136

5151 *SCHAAFF*, William, *TUCKER*, Margaret, Jany 12 1860, 136

5152 *SMITH*, George W, *BURRIER*, Jane, Jany 19 1860, 136

5153 *STRICKLAND*, Silas A (Hon), *SNYDER*, Mary Tucker, of Sam'l/Nebraska, Feby 2 1860, 136

5154 *SAYLER*, John H, *LEDGEWOOD*, Martha Jane, Feby 9 1860, 136

5155 *SCHADE*, Heinrich, *HERWIG*, Wilhelmina, Feby 12 1860, 136

5156 *SHANK*, Michael, 2d wife, *GILBERT*, Susan M, Woodsboro, Feby 12 1860, 136

5157 *SEGER*, Peter, "Blacksmith", *WAERNER*, Ann Maria, "WERNER", Feby 16 1860, 136

5158 *SMITH*, Samuel Lewis, *LEITER*, Ann Catharine, March 6 1860, 136

5159 *STUP*, George L, *WRIGHT*, Emily J, March 22 1860, 136

5160 *STEVENS*, Richard M, *STEDDING*, Mary A, of Ch'n/Balto, May 3 1860, 136

5161 *SPECHT*, Jacob (Junior), *RENN*, Mary Jane, of Isaac, May 15 1860, 136

5162 *SNOUFFER*, Archibald F, *ALNUTT*, Rebecca D, of J H, May 15 1860, 136

5163 *SCOTT*, Douglas (Capt'n), *DEBODISCO*, Harriett "WILLIAMS" (Mrs), Georgetown, DC, May 29 1860, 136

5164 *SCHILDKNECHT*, Wm, *MOSER*, Susanna (Mrs), Middletown, June 12 1860, 136

5165 *SELBY*, John S, 2d wife, *CONRADT*, Margaret R, of Geo M/Balto, June 21 1860, 136

5166 *STOCKSCHLEGER*, Amos, *MARTIN*, Catharine E, Septr 11 1860, 136

5167 *SHANK*, George W, 2d wife, *YANTIS*, Balinda E (Mrs), widow of D F, Octr 2 1860, 136

5168 *SHIELDS*, Maxwell P, *MUSSELMAN*, Sue M, of John, Nov 8 1860, 136

5169 *SPURRIER*, Grafton D, *GOUVERNEUR*, Elizabeth K Bibb, of Sam'l L, Nov 21 1860, 136

5170 *STAUFFER*, Ezra S, *SLINGLUFF*, Fannie H, of Carroll Co, Nov 21 1860, 136
5171 *SAPPINGTON*, Augustus A (Dr), *MANTZ*, Irene, of Caspar, Nov 29 1860, 136
5172 *SIFFORD*, John E, of John, *HUNT*, Susan, of Asbury H, Decr 5 1860, 136
5173 *SCHLEGEL*, George W, "SLAGLE", *CULLER*, Mary A C, Midd valley, Decr 12 1860, 136
5174 *SAMPLE*, Jerome, *BIGGS*, Julia Ann, Decr 13 1860, 136
5175 *SIMPSON*, Tho's W (Dr), 2d wife, *MAYNARD*, Virginia, of Tho's G, Jany 3 1861, 136
5176 *SAYLER*, D R, (*Daniel), *PFOUTZ*, Sarah Ellen, Jany 17 1861, 136
5177 *SMITH*, James T, *PALMER*, Eleanor Augusta, of Wm T, Feby 5 1861, 136
5178 *STULL*, George L, *YOUNG*, Hanna A M, (not listed as Miss), Feby 7 1861, 136
5179 *STEIN*, Lewis, of Louis, *CROMWELL*, Leonora Lydia, of Geo W, Feby 20 1861, 136
5180 *SENSENEY*, John Q, *HOWARD*, Marion, of Isaac, Feby 20 1861, 136
5181 *SIMPSON*, John A, 1st wife, *BAYER*, Rebecca, of Tho's, March 5 1861, 136
5182 *STEVENS*, Reuben G, *STUP*, Loretto, March 12 1861, 136
5183 *STONE*, Henry C, *GLAZE*, Elizabeth, March 13 1861, 136
5184 *STAUFFER*, Daniel, *JONES*, Nettie, of Edward, March 19 1861, 136
5185 *SLINGLIFF*, Louis Philip, *CROMWELL*, M Alverda, of Tho's, March 19 1861, 137
5186 *STEINER*, George F, "Alex'a, Va/of Jonathan, *SINN*, Amanda M, of Jno Geo, April 2 1861, 137
5187 *STEWART*, Wm, *RAMSBURG*, Isabella, April 1 1861, 136
5188 *STRAILMAN*, Francis T, *LIPPENCOTT*, Annie, Petersburg, Va, May 14 1861, 137
5189 *SHOWER*, Theodore A (Dr), Balto Co, *GOMBER*, Sallie A, of Ezra M, June 4 1861, 137
5190 *STANSBURY*, Geo W, *SHANK*, Sarah N, of Ezra, July 27 1861, 137
5191 *SENTZILL*, Charles H, *RICHARDSON*, Leah Fannie, Augt 8 1861, 137
5192 *SINN*, Edward T, of Philip of Henry, *EDSALL*, Emma L, Fort Lee, N Jersey, Augt 7 1861, 137
5193 *SPRING*, Gardner (Rev), aged 80, *WILLIAMS*, Grosvenor Abigail, aged 65/N York, Augt 14 1861, 137
5194 *STOCKMAN*, Philip W, *KELLER*, Lydia E, Septr 27 1861, 137
5195 *SMALL*, Wm D, *WARDECKER*, Mary Louisa, Octr 6 1861, 137
5196 *STUP*, Edward Lewis, *WICKHAM*, Victoria, Octr 16 1861, 137
5197 *STALEY*, Cornelius A, 2d wife, *MEASELL*, Mary Ann C, Octr 27 1861, 137
5198 *SIECRIST*, Charles H, *KLEIN*, Harriett M, Octr 10 1861, 137
5199 *SPECHT*, Lewis, *MICHAEL*, Mary E, of Henry, Nov 5 1861, 137
5200 *SPONSELLER*, Jacob C, *BAER*, Mary, Nov 7 1861, 137
5201 *SEFTON*, John W, *PFOUTZ*, Deborah L, Nov 13 1861, 137
5202 *SHOOK*, Greenberry G, *GROVE*, Barbara A, Nov 28 1861, 137
5203 *SHORB*, William T, *STAMBAUGH*, Elizabeth, Decr 5 1861, 137
5204 *SAVAGE*, C H (Rev), (*Coleman SAVIDGE), *CREAGER*, Ada, of Ephraim/(*Alice), Decr 24 1861, 137
5205 *SCHILDT*, William, *BOSTIAN*, Sophia, Jany 12 1862, 137
5206 *SHREEVE*, Jesse (Rev), 2d wife, *TAYLOR*, Emily C, Balto, Jany 16 1862, 137
5207 *SMITH*, George L, *SHANK*, Mary A, Jany 16 1862, 137
5208 *SCHLEY*, Eugene L, of John T, *HARDIE*, Georgianna, Phila, Decr 1861, 137
5209 *STONE*, John T, *SHAFER*, Mary Manilla, Jany 28 1862, 137
5210 *SHANKS*, Andrew T, of Oshkosh, Wisc Volunteers, *HOFFMAN*, Annie E, of Ezra, Feby 11 1862, 137
5211 *SHENKEL*, David, *STULL*, Harriett, Feby 16 1862, 137
5212 *SHAFER*, David L, *THOMAS*, Eliza A, March 18 1862, 137

5213 SCHLEGEL, Martin, "SLAGLE", KEMP, Juliann, April 8 1862, 137
5214 SCHOLL, Randolph C, of Elias, WOODS, Louisa, April 17 1862, 137
5215 SEVRINGHAUS, J D (Rev), KNODE, Maria E, May 11 1862, 137
5216 STAUFFER, Wm J, KLEIN, Cordelia E, of Jonathan, June 8 1862, 137
5217 STONE, George H, CANNON, Lucinda R, June 12 1862, 137
5218 SANDHOUSE, John, STEPHENS, Elizabeth, June 12 1862, 137
5219 STAULI, John L, METHENY, Catharine, Augt 6 1862, 137
5220 SELL, Edwin M, REMSBERG, Mahala C, Lewistown, Augt 21 1862, 137
5221 SMITH, George C, FRALEY, Margaret, "FROLICH", Nov 15 1862, 137
5222 SIMON, Lewis, SHOOK, Margaret, of Henry, Nov 27 1862, 137
5223 SMITH, John Tho's, of Ezra, TRAYER, Susan Emma, Decr 18 1862, 137
5224 SWIGERT, D Amos, of Va, FISHER, E Jane, of Barney/in Balt, Decr 25 1862, 137
5225 SNYDER, John A, SHANK, Jane R D, Decr 25 1862, 137
5226 SLIFER, George C, MITCHELL, Jane C, of Wm H, Jany 8 1863, 137
5227 SIM, J Tho's (Dr), son of Dr Tho's, VARDEN, Mary, of Rev Josiah, Jany 15 1863, 138
5228 STRATTON, Cha's S, WARREN, Levinia, Bridgeport, Conn/Both Dwarfs, Feby 10 1863, 138
5229 SCHOLL, Wm H, of Elias, WOOD, Elizabeth, Glade, March 5 1863, 138
5230 SPECHT, Michael, COPELAND, Elizabeth Ann, March 19 1863, 138
5231 SCHROEDER, Francis T, COPELAND, Mary Jane, March 19 1863, 138
5232 STARR, Maurice T, 3d wife, HINES, Elizabeth, Liberty, April 2d 1863, 138
5233 STUBE, Andrew, SCHRODEL, Rosanna, April 7 1863, 138
5234 SCHNEIDER, Henry, BECKER, Louisa Jane, Balto, April 7 1863, 138
5235 STOCKMAN, John N, BISER, Amanda C, Jefferson, April 9 1863, 138
5236 SCHOLL, David M, of Elias, STEINER, Florence G, of Rev Jesse, April 14 1863, 138
5237 SPECHT, Francis T, KERTZENDORFFER, Alice V, of Jos, May 21 1863, 138
5238 SINN, John Henry, of J Tho's, FACKLER, Mary, "FOGLER"/"Ab KEMP", June 23 1863, 138
5239 SCHLEY, Winfield Scott (Lieut), US Navy/of John T, FRANKLIN, Ann R, Septr 10 1863, 138
5240 STONE, George E, GETZENDANNER, Lydia A, Septr 24 1863, 138
5241 SNOOK, Dennis R, HARPER, Lottie C, of Richard/"KELLER", Octr 8 1863, 138
5242 STEVENS, Flavius J, BARRICK, Sue C, "Mount Pleasant", Octr 27 1863, 138
5243 SMITH, John E, RINGER, Catharine E (Mrs), "Boonsboro", Octr 28 1863, 138
5244 STARR, J Washington, ANDERSON, Rebecca S, of Aden, Nov 10 1863, 138
5245 SPRAGUE, Wm (Ex Gov), of R J, CHASE, Kate, of Salmon P, Nov 12 1863, 138
5246 SMITH, Wm H, FESSLER, Laura, of Henry B, Nov 17 1863, 138
5247 STUP, Francis T, GROVE, Anna M R, Decr 24 1863, 138
5248 SEHN, Jacob, WEBSTER, Cornelia A, Jany 5 1864, 138
5249 SWEET, Edward P, RICHARDSON, Sophia E, Feby 18 1864, 138
5250 SMALLWOOD, Charles, "of Wm Cooper", REINHART, Lizzie L, March 6 1864, 138
5251 STEWART, Wm, of COLE's Cavalry, HARKER, Ann R (Mrs), "Carlin KENEGE", March 9 1864, 138
5252 STOFFEL, John, 3d Wiscon Reg't, ADAMS, Anna, of Andreas, March 13 1864, 138
5253 SHAFER, Thomas M, HOUCK, Susan C, of Daniel, March 15 1864, 138
5254 SAHM, Jacob (Jun'r), ENGELBRECHT, Rebecca R, of Mich'l, May 8 1864, 138
5255 SNYDER, George, "Milk-man"/2d wife, WEIDMAN, L Adaline, Augt 16 1864, 138
5256 STALEY, Ezra, 2d wife, ZIEGLER, Mary, Octr 4 1864, 138
5257 SMITH, John A, SHORB, Mrs, in Rom Cath Church/(*Cornelia V), Octr 11 1864, 138

5258 SCHULTZ, Conrad, 2d wife, HOFFMAN, Caroline (Mrs), Nov 8 1864, 138
5259 STONE, Wm Bradley, SHAFER, Susie Virginia, Nov 10 1864, 138
5260 SPATES, Charles, Tailor, TUTWEILER, Mary E, Decr 15 1864, 138
5261 SNOOK, Jacob H, 2d wife, DUTROW, Lydia, Decr 20 1864, 138
5262 SPANGLER, Jacob, DOFLER, Ruth (Mrs), widow of Jacob, Jany 19 1865, 138
5263 STARR, Lycurgus N, STONER, Alice, Feby 2 1865, 138
5264 SOWERS, Jacob, GILTZ, Mary (Mrs), "KEYSER", Feby 7 1865, 138
5265 SCHREINER, Alfred, LINDSEY, Emma Jane, "LUGENBEEL", March 2 1865, 138
5266 STUP, Joseph C, KAUFFMAN, Alice V, March 14 1865, 138
5267 STALEY, John W, MISS, Sarah E, "Shookstown", March 21 1865, 138
5268 SEESE, Wm L, BOSTICK, Georgianna, April 3 1865, 138
5269 SHAFER, Edward, BRAIN, Ann Rebecca, April 27 1865, 139
5270 STONE, Cornelius W, STALEY, Lydia Ann, May 18 1865, 139
5271 STIMMELL, John S, RITCHIE, Esther Ann, June 22 1865, 139
5272 STALEY, Gideon (Lieut), of Ezra, NEYHOFF, Maggie, of Ch'n, July 13 1865, 139
5273 SMITH, Frank M (Capt), of D F, NICHOLSON, Mary E, Balto, Octr 4 1865, 139
5274 SMITH, David M, Ed Exam, PIPER, Mary Ellen, Octr 25 1865, 139
5275 SHIMER, J C (Dr), REIFSNIDER, Georgia B, of John, Nov 6 1865, 139
5276 STULL, Dennis, his 2d wife, RHODES, Sarah S, Nov 12 1865, 139
5277 STANLEY, George W, PALMER, M Josephine, of Wm T, Nov 21 1865, 139
5278 SPARROW, Wm Tho's, LONG, Sarah A C, of Christ'n, Nov 21 1865, 139
5279 SHAFER, John A, WASKEY, Mary F, Nov 30 1835, 139
5280 STRIDER, Isaac H, of Va, REICH, Sallie, of Philip, Jany 23 1866, 139
5281 STORM, John P L, KIRWAN, Louisa C (Mrs), Jany 23 1866, 139
5282 STOCKMAN, Luther F, GATTON, Harriott, Jany 18 1866, 139
5283 SCHAEFFER, Christian M, 2d wife, WINTER, Tillie, of Tho's, Feby 21 1866, 139
5284 SCHOLL, Lewis P, of Elias, LINK, Sarah, Glade, March 1 1866, 139
5285 SMITH, Francis (Dr), PALMER, Molly, of Balto, April 26 1866, 139
5286 SCHREINER, Edward Stanley, of Henry J, OGLE, Harriott, of James, May 22 1866, 139
5287 SHIPLEY, Wm H, KETLER, Mary E, Septr 27 1866, 139
5288 SUMNER, Charles (Hon), HOOPER, Alice (Mrs), Boston/"Mason", Octr 17 1866, 139
5289 SHUTT, Augustus, O'LEARY, Mattie A, of Augustine D, Octr 25 1866, 139
5290 STEINER, Lewis H (Dr), SMYTH, Sarah S, of Guilford, Conn, Octr 30 1866, 139
5291 STIPES, Daniel E, WATERS, Martha E, Nov 13 1866, 139
5292 SHIPLEY, Edwin M, BENNETT, Elizabeth S, "HIGGINS", Decr 20 1866, 139
5293 SCHAEFFER, Tho's H (Dr), YOUNG, Bettie, of Montg'y Co, Feby 19 1867, 139
5294 SHIPLEY, John J, GAVER, Louisa C, March 14 1867, 139
5295 STEWART, Clement, DRINKHOUSE, Harriott H, Easton, Pa, June 27 1867, 139
5296 SIMPSON, John A, 2d wife, PAMPEL, Mary C, of Henry, July 18 1867, 139
5297 SCHLEY, John, of David, SMITH, E Bella, Indiana, Augt 22 1867, 139
5298 SAUERWEIN, Cha's D, of Balto, ORVIER, Marie Gabriella, of Paris, France, Augt 23 1867, 139
5299 SPARROW, Allen T, BISER, Ann R, Jany 16 1868, 139
5300 SMITH, Eugene R (Rev), KRAFT, Sophia S, of Jacob, Feby 4 1868, 139
5301 SINN, John George, of Henry/2d wife, HOWARD, Susan, April 1868, 139
5302 STALEY, Cornelius, SERVER, Laura V, April 28 1868, 139
5303 SCHUTENHELM, Arthur, STAMBAUGH, Ann V, May 5 1868, 139

5304 STAYMAN, V D, of Geo F, *LAMB*, Sarah, Delaware, Ohio, June 2d 1868, 139
5305 SPONSELLER, Stockton, *BREITNER*, Julia, "Harpersferry", July 15 1868, 139
5306 SCHLEY, Arthur, *MACKEY*, Zulika D, Balto, July 23 1868, 139
5307 STALEY, Joseph E, *ANGELBERGER*, Clara A E, Septr 5 1868, 139
5308 SHIPLEY, Samuel N, *SCHLEICH*, Nellie, Septr 23 1868, 139
5309 SHEARER, John D, *BRUNNER*, Sallie A, Septr 30 1868, 139
5310 SCHWARIN, John B, *WARNER*, Mary C, Octr 1 1868, 139
5311 STAUFFER, J Dorsey, of Simon, *MILLER*, Annie, of Harrison/Glade, Octr 13 1868, 140
5312 SPECHT, David, hid 3d wife, *THOMAS*, Ann E (Mrs), Octr 27 1868, 140
5313 SPONSELLER, George, *THOMAS*, Sarah R (Mrs), Nov 25 1868, 140
5314 STAMBAUGH, J E (Dr), *SMITH*, Lou, "Woodsboro", Nov 25 1868, 140
5315 SLIFER, George C, *KARN*, Emma J, Nov 26 1868, 140
5316 SIMMONS, Charles E (Capt'n), of Shanghai, India, *HOUCK*, Martha Matilda, of Ezra, Decr 3 1868, 140
5317 SMITH, Charles C, of Geo, *HINKS*, Mariann N, of Sam'l, Decr 29 1868, 140
5318 STUP, Elijah C, *BROWN*, Mary A R, Jany 19 1869, 140
5319 STEINER, James O, of Jacob, *RHODERICK*, Marietta, of Mahlon, Jany 27 1869, 140
5320 STIMMELL, Philip, *HARRISON*, Georgianna, Jany 28 1869, 140
5321 STALEY, Lewis H, *WHIP*, Mary F, March 9 1869, 140
5322 SPECHT, David, his 3d wife, *THOMAS*, Ann (Mrs), her 2d husband, March 1869, 140
5323 SINN, Geo Philip, of Daniel, *MEEKS*, Minnie C, April 13 1869, Mt Vernon, Ny, 140
5324 SCHMIDT, Jacob, 2d wife, *HAGAN*, Lizzie C (Mrs), "PUTTS", July 6 1869, 140
5325 SINN, Jacob C, of Jacob, *UMBERGER*, Sarah W, Septr 16 1869, 140
5326 STERN, Philip, of Aaron, *GOLDENBERG*, Julia, Octr 6 1869, "Jews", 140
5327 STAUFFER, S Theodore, of Henry/1st wife, *CLAGETT*, Louisa, of Tho's, Octr 12 1869, 140
5328 SHAFER, Clavin L, *THOMAS*, Bettie B, of Ab'm, Nov 18 1869, 140
5329 SCHMIDT, Jacob (Junior), *STALEY*, Ann, of John A, Nov 23 1869, 140
5330 SCHAEFFER, Wm C, *STONE*, Mary Jane, Nov 25 1869, 140
5331 SEYMOUR, Aaron W, *FOUT*, Fannie E, of Greenbury, Nov 17 1869, 140
5332 SHOPE, Lyndhurst T, *STEELE*, Alice L, of Dan'l, Nov 25 1869, 140
5333 SMITH, James J (Dr), *WRIGHTSON*, Josephine B, of E Shore, Decr 30 1869, 140
5334 SCHLEY, Buchanan, of Fred'k A, *ROMAN*, Rebecca, of B F, Jany 4 1870, 140
5335 SCHAEFFER, Wm G, of Rev David F/2d wife, *LYON*, Molly J (Mrs), "FICKEY"/Balto, Jany 18 1870, 140
5336 STAUFFER, David V, *WALKER*, Alice, Feby 15 1870, 140
5337 SALTER, Geo E, of Wm Ent SALTER, *STULL*, Nettie, Feby 17 1870, 140
5338 SELBY, John W, *BENDER*, Lizzie, of Henry, April 19 1870, 140
5339 STALEY, Lewis M, *ZIMMERMAN*, Lethe S, May 18 1870, 140
5340 SMITH, Geo C, of Christian, *RHODERICK*, Olive E (Mrs), of Ohio, May 25 1870, 140
5341 SINCLAIR, James F, of Clark Co, Va, *CANDLER*, Sidonia V, of L W, June 9 1870, 140
5342 SCHELL, George, of Cha's D, *MEHRLING*, Lizzie, of Geo, Augt 30 1870, 140
5343 SMITH, Hauer P, of Christian, *CARLIN*, Clara V, of Jos, Septr 28 1870, 140
5344 SMITH, Christopher P, *ELY*, Helen R, Octr 20 1870, 140
5345 SHRINER, Geo W B, of Cornelius, *EADER*, Alice, of Wm, Nov 2 1870, 140
5346 SINN, Charles W, of J George, *SCHMIDT*, Carrie, of Jacob, Nov 16 1870, 140
5347 SHIPLEY, Isaac, *STEVENS*, Ella, Jan 18 1871, "ELDRIDGE", 140
5348 STEINER, John W, *MILLER*, Mary S, January 19 1871, 140

5349 SCHUTENHELM, Geo, BRENGLE, Debbie, of Ezra M, March 16 1871, 140
5350 STALEY, Daniel A, CARPENTER, Martha, March 21 1871, 140
5351 SPENCER, Albertus, JOHNSON, Fannie C, of Col Tho's, April 27 1871, 140
5352 SHOOK, Daniel H, KINTZ, Harriett A, of Fred'k, June 1871, 140
5353 SCHLEIGH, Daniel F, ELKINS, Laura V, of Jos D, July 26 1871, 141
5354 STONE, Wm D, KREPS, Ellen, Augt 31 1871, 141
5355 STALEY, Jonathan, 2d wife, LAMBERT, Jane E (Mrs), "SHOOK", Octr 5 1871, 141
5356 SIMPSON, Richard W, 2d wife, MCCONKEY, Marian L, Septr 26 1871, 141
5357 STURGIS, Flavius Josephus, SCHLEY written above Josephus, FULMER, Delia, Octr 25 1871, 2d wife, 141
5358 SCHEFFLER, John W, of Cha's, ENGELBRECHT, Kate, of J Adam, Octr 26 1871, 141
5359 STALEY, Edward M, BREITHEIMER, Mary Augusta, Octr 26 1871, 141
5360 SICKLES, Daniel E (Gen'l), US Min Spain/2d wife, CREIGH, Miss, Nov 1871, Madrid, 141
5361 SCHROEDER, George A, of Fred'k, WOLFE, Mollie A, Jan 10 1872, 141
5362 SWEADNER, Richard, BEALL, Octavia E, Jan 16 1872, Liberty, 141
5363 STAUB, Wm H, MAIN, Susan S, Jan 18 1872, 141
5364 SCHILDTKNECHT, Josiah, HESSONG, Rebecca D, Jany 30 1872, 141
5365 STONE, Luther M, of John, GRIFFIN, Evaline L, March 5 1872, 141
5366 SMITH, David H, of David F, WILLIARD, Julia C, Augt 14 1872, 141
5367 SNYDER, Jacob F, of Montgomery Co, WALTER, Alice V, of John, Septr 3 1872, 141
5368 SCHLEY, Jacob S, SHELDON, Lizzie A, Octr 24 1872, Balto, 141
5369 STEINER, Charles H, of Gen'l John A, MUMMA, Laura W, Septr 26 1872, 141
5370 STRAILMAN, Wm C, of Henry, KEINS, Maggie E, Octr 1872, 141
5371 STOKES, Bradley T, of Rob't Y, ROBERTSON, Grace P, of James H, Decr 7 1872, 141
5372 SADTLER, Sam'l P (Prof), BRIDGES, M Julia, Decr 17 1872, Balto, 141
5373 STEINER, Wm R, of Jacob/"STONER", YARBOROUGH, Amanda J, Feb 12 1873, 141
5374 STAUFFER, S Theodore, of H'y/2d wife, OFFUTT, C Courtnay, (#), May 13 1873, 141
5375 SCHMIDT, Francis Wm, of Jacob, HOOPER, Mary, of Jackey, July 3 1873, 141
5376 SOCKALEXIS, Gov, GLOSSIAM, Moddim, July 1873, Penopscot Indians, 141
5377 SCHILL, George W, BELT, Mary E, July 17 1873, 141
5378 STEINMETZ, Andrew, HOUCK, Johanna E, Augt 7 1873, 141
5379 STIMMEL, Joseph, GOODMAN, Rebecca, Septr 11 1873, 141
5380 STULL, Daniel L, MARTZ, Julia C, Octr 9 1873, 141
5381 SCHLEY, Towner, of Jno Edw, HARRISON, Ida Virg, Octr 22 1873, 141
5382 SCHLEY, Geo J, of David, STURGEON, Mary V, Balt, Nov 20 1873, 141
5383 STEINER, Wm H, of Henry C, COLTON, Ida, Nov 19 1873, 141
5384 SHAWBAKER, Jacob M, of Geo, ROELKE, Anna M, of Peter, Nov 27 1873, 141
5385 SIMMONS, Simon Cyrus, of Zachariah/2d wife, HOUCK, Georgia A, of Ezra, Decr 3 1873, 141
5386 SHIPLEY, George E, HENDRY, Emma C, of Cha's, Decr 3 1873, 141
5387 STAUFFER, H Clay, CRAMER, Jennie, Decr 23 1873, 141
5388 STULL, Horace E, HOUCK, Laura, Feby 3 1874, 141
5389 STULL, Edward J, OLAND, Lucretia S, Feb 5 1874, 141
5390 (STORK, Theophilus (Rev DD), aged 60/Phila, died March 24 1874), 141
5391 SARTORIS, Algernon C F, GRANT, Nellie W, of President U S, May 21 1874, 141
5392 STONE, Joseph D, MCDEVITT, Harriet E, Septr 23 1874, 141
5393 SCHONFELD, Alexander, HARTMAN, Rosa, of Simon, Sep 24 1874, 141

5394 STALEY, D H, DYER, Kate E, Octr 15 1874, 141
5395 SPARROW, Henry C, KOOGLE, Amanda, Octr 14 1874, 142
5396 SHEPHERD, P Dodge, CUNNINGHAM, Sallie A, of B A, Octr 19 1874, 142
5397 STAUFFER, Geo Wesley, NEIDIG, Clara A, of Isaac, Nov 10 1874, 142
5398 SHAFF, Geo P, RIDENAUER, Sallie A, Jan 23 1875, 142
5399 SWEADNER, John (Capt'n), ENGEL, Martha S, Feb 11 1875, 142
5400 STALEY, Howard, ROUTZAHN, Lottie E, March 4 1875, 142
5401 SHAFFNER, Geo W, EXNER, Mary (Mrs), April 12 1875, "FEY", 142
5402 SMITH, Nicholas (Col), of Ky, GREELEY, Ida, of Horace, May 1 1875, N York, 142
5403 SHERIDAN, Philip H (Maj Gen'l), RUCKER, Irene, of D H, June 3 1875, Chicago, 142
5404 SMITH, James A (Lieut), USN, HAGAN, Lou M, of Igns, June 21 1875, 142
5405 SIEDLING, George F C, FRALEY, Clara N, of H'y, Aug 8 1875, 142
5406 SCHUTZE, Cha's W, PHLEEGER, Fannie, Aug 17 1875, 142
5407 SOELKEY, Wm H, SCHWEITZER, Emma V, July 8 1875, Balto, 142
5408 SCHEEL, John Geo, ESTERLY, Rosa A, Octr 21 1875, "OSTERLE'", 142
5409 SCHWARZ, Geo W, of Chicago, FULTON, Emma W, of C C, Nov 3 1875, 142
5410 SNOOK, William Galileo, SCHAEFFER, Katie V, of David, Nov 23 1875, 142
5411 SAYLER, C Edward, ANDERS, L R, of Aaron, Decr 7 1875, 142
5412 SWAYNE, H'y Stuart, DAVIS, Sallie Worthington, of Judge, Decr 22 1875, Ill's, 142
5413 SCHAFFER, S B (Rev), RUPLEY, Sallie C, Jan 4 1876, 142
5414 SMITH, John J, of Em'l, GROSHON, Mary E, of Geo S, May 2 1876, 142
5415 SHILLING, Wm B, 2d wife, CASTLE, Ellie, of Henry, June 8 1876, 142
5416 STOCKMAN, Daniel M, HARGETT, Anna M, Sep 28 1876, 142
5417 SWAIN, Milton, of Balto, MOBERLY, Mollie L, of Lewis H, Nov 2 1876, 142
5418 STARR, Lycurgus N, HOOD, Matilda, Nov 2 1876, 142
5419 SAYLER, D P (Rev), ROHRER, Sarah K, Nov 16 1876, 142
5420 SPAHR, Milton O, REMSBURG, Alice L C, of Edw'd, Nov 21 1876, 142
5421 (SMITH, John, age 73, Jos G MILLER "Brother in law", died Decr 9 1876), 142
5422 SIMMONS, Wm A, of John A, ELY, M Ella, of Isaac H, Jan 3 1877, 142
5423 STOKES, Geo H, of James, STOKES, Nellie, of Wm, July 17 1877, 142
5424 SIMMONS, Louis, of John A, BRENGLE, Mary E, of Sam'l T {barely legible compler}, July 11 1877, 142
5425 STRICKER, Thomas, REYNOLDS, Annie E, Octr 3 1877, 142
5426 STALEY, Horace E, FEAGA, Cordelia C, Octr 11 1877, 142
5427 SCHILDTKNECHT, J M, LUDY, Manzella M, Nov 29 1877, 142
5428 SCHULTZ, Conrad, BLANK, Ellen, Dec 27 1877, 142
5429 SYMMS, Wm, WELCH, Lallah M, of Rev Joel J, Decr 26 1877, Ohio, 142
5430 SCHLOSSER, Peter G, 2d wife, BUCK, Mary J, of Cumberland/(not listed as Miss), Feb 3d 1878, 142
5431 SAPPINGTON, Geo K, FRAZIER, Bettie, March 12th 1878, 142
5432 SCHAFFER, Howard J, EAKLE, Laura V, July 17th 1878, 142
5433 SMITH, R Emmit, HOPWOOD, Maggie J, 10/17 1878, {no month listed compiler}, 142
5434 SPONSELLER, Eugene, HAHN, Mary, Aug 3rd 1879, 142
5435 SHEPHERD, Job K, KIRKLAND, Mary E, Sept 11th 1879, 142
5436 SMITH, John F, DERTZBAUGH, Clara J, Nov 27th 1879, 142
5437 STONEBRAKER, Daniel, ENGLISH, Sophie L, of James J/(not listed as Miss), Jan 21 1880, 143

5438 *SMITH*, John, "Butcher", *STOTTLEMYER*, Alice V, (not listed as Miss), Jan 29th 1880, 143
5439 *STONER*, C Edward, *YOUNG*, Maggie E, of David/(not listed as Miss), March 11th 1880, 143
5440 *STALEY*, Milton, of Kansas/formly this city, *HIGGINGS*, Hattie M, of St L/(not listed as Miss), Feb 3d 1880, 143
5441 *SCHMIDT*, J Henry, of Jacob, *KEHLER*, Jennie, Dec 7 1880, 143
5442 *SCHLEY*, B H (Maj), *GAITHER*, Sophia, June 9th 1881, 143
5443 *SHRYOCK*, Harry C, of Balto, *MYERS*, Bettie B, January 3d 1882, 143
5444 *STOCKMAN*, Emory W, *WHISTNER*, Annie, (of Michael), March 9th 1882, 143
5445 *SMITH*, Clayton, *CRIST*, Mellie, August 24 1882, 143
5446 *STARR*, Jesse W, 2d wife, *FAUBLE*, Mary E, September 12t 1882, 143
5447 *SMITH*, D Sidney T, *BRUNNER*, Mary E, Sept 20 1882, 143
5448 *STULL*, Bradley T, *SNYDER*, Lillia A, Oct 19th 1882, 143
5449 *SENSENSEY*, Silas D, *REPP*, A Mary, of John S, Oct 24t 1882, 143
5450 *STONE*, Cornelius, 2d wife, *WOLFE*, Orfie, Oct 26 1882, 143
5451 *STULL*, Daniel Z, *LENHART*, Ida, Nov 23d 1882, 143
5452 *SMITH*, Lewis C, *DERR*, Joanna M, of Daniel, Nov 29 1882, 143
5453 *SMITH*, Thomas A, of Urbana, *ALBAUGH*, Frances M (Mrs), Jan 17 1883, 143
5454 *SELDIN*, Cha's P, *REIFSNIDER*, Rosa V, of Jno, Jan 17th 1883, 143
5455 *SAPPINGTON*, Frank B, *ANGEL*, Mary R, June 6t 1883, 143
5456 *SHARETTS*, Wm P, *GRIFFIN*, Frances M, (not listed as Miss), June 22d 1883, 143
5457 *SKINNER*, Henry, *GETZ*, Margaret, (not listed as Miss), June 27th 1883, both of the D & D Inst, 143
5458 *SCHMIDT*, Jacob F, 2d wife, *FOUT*, Laura R, Oct 16t 1883, 143
5459 *STEINER*, Frank M, *OTT*, Florence E, of John, October 31st 1883, 143
5460 *SHEFFLER*, George T M, *GETZENDANNER*, Minnie R, Nov 7th 1883, 143
5461 *SYLCURK*, Samuel K, *MORGAN*, Margaret M, (not listed as Miss), Jan 17th 1882, 143
5462 *SNYDER*, M Scott, *CLOUGH*, Nellie, Dec 24 1883, 143
5463 *SNYDER*, Elmer E, *MEDCALF*, Emily S, January 13th 1884, 143
5464 *SPONSELLER*, John R, *SAUNDERS*, Laura Bella, of Cap Walter (#), April 10 1884, 143
5465 *STORM*, Richard P, of Peter L, *MARTIN*, Martha E, of Oliver, April 16th 1884, 143
5466 *SCHLEY*, Gilmer, *WILSON*, E Lullie, of N J, April 15 1884, 143
5467 *SMITH*, H Gates, *REICH*, Lucie B, April 30 1884, 143
5468 *STALEY*, Charles B, *WILSON*, Rebecca N, of N J, May 6 1884, 143
5469 *SHOCK*, Wallace, *BESANT*, Fannie R, of Jas H, Nov 10 1884, 143
5470 *SHAFER*, Carlton, *ANDREW*, Louise, November 19 1884, 143
5471 *SCHLEY*, Steiner, *KUNKEL*, Lillian F, of J Baker, January 28 1885, 143
5472 *SCHROEDER*, Frank J, *SCHOLL*, Lillie M, May 6 1885, 143
5473 *SLOAN*, John Q, *PEARRIE*, Claudie, of Jas, June 11 1885, 143
5474 *SMITH*, Dorsey H, *ECKSTEIN*, Ella V, September 1 1885, 143
5475 *SCHELL*, John Edward, *FLEMING*, Ida M, Oct 21 1885, 143
5476 *SCHLEY*, Thomas H, {X over H}, *CLAGGETT*, Mary M, December 29th 1885, 143
5477 *SMITH*, T Oden, *MITCHELL*, Eleanor, of Henry, February 23 1886, 143
5478 *STALEY*, Fleet E, *HEDGES*, Mary J, March 31 1886, 143
5479 *SCHLUGH*, David B, *PLUMMER*, Eleanor, July 14 1886, 143
5480 *SCHLEY*, Frank (Prof), *EADER*, Helen, October 14th 1886, 143
5481 *STULL*, Eugene, *SUMMERS*, Della, October 18 1886, 143

5482 *STEINER*, Ira F, *RUSE*, Irene, November 3 1886, 143
5483 *SNAPP*, George O, *BAUMGARDNER*, Ella, December 2d 1886, 144
5484 *SCHUFFLER*, Martin L, *POOLE*, Irene, December 16th 1886, 144
5485 *SNYDER*, Charles H, *FORNEY*, M Ella, February 23 1887, 144
5486 *SHOOK*, H McC, *KUHN*, Sallie E, April 19 1887, 144
5487 *STALEY*, Henry (Prof), of Gideon, *HOFFMAN*, Fanny, May 18 1887, 144
5488 *STOKES*, R Harry, *BAKER*, Catharine, June 15 1887, 144
5489 *SUTHERDARD*, B Ward T, *ELY*, Nellie M, June 23 1887, 144
5490 *STRAILMAN*, Cha's J D, *BAER*, Lydia E, August 23 1887, 144
5491 *SCHELL*, J H Nicholas, of Cha's, *BIGGS*, Ida Mary, of Joshua, September 1 1887, 144
5492 *SCHAEFFER*, Wm G, *FAUBLE*, Annie E, October 5 1887, 144
5493 *SCHLEY*, Alfred (Capt), *WALTZ*, Nannie, October 10 1887, (Runaway), 144
5494 *STOUCH*, M Harry (Rev), *HAUER*, Maggie H, November 17 1887, 144
5495 *SIMPSON*, Willie E, *NULL*, Sarah E, December 23 1887, 144
5496 *SHIELDS*, John T, *MICHELL*, Annie E V, February 9 1888, 144
5497 *SAPPINGTON*, Sidney, *STITELY*, Rosa A, February 14 1888, entire entry crossed through, 144
5498 *SMITH*, Cha's E, *SMITH*, Florence B, February 9 1888, 144
5499 *SAPPINGTON*, Sidney, *STITELY*, Rose A, February 14 1888, 144
5500 *STOUT*, Cha's M, *WALTZ*, Rene M, March 8 1888, 144
5501 *SMITH*, Wm C W, *MCCROSKEY*, Ada, April 25 1888, 144
5502 *SIMPSON*, Tho's A, *SMITH*, Maggie, May 1888, 144
5503 *STITELEY*, U S Grant, *REILEY*, Miss, Sept 7 1888, 144
5504 *SUMMERS*, Andrew J, *MERCER*, Alice, Oct 16 1888, 144
5505 *STAUFFER*, J Dorsey, *CRAMER*, Alice, Octr 17 1888, 144
5506 *SHEARER*, Daniel T, *HAMMOND*, Effie C, January 8 1889, 144
5507 *STUP*, Thomas, *THOMAS*, Hester, Jan 21 1889, 144
5508 *SYKES*, Wm J, *SNOUFFER*, Gussie, of A J, February 7 1889, 144
5509 *SHOOK*, John H, *LEASE*, Etta, February 20 1889, 144
5510 *STULL*, Carlton L, *KOLB*, Mary M, of David H, March 20 1889, 144
5511 *SHAFER*, Cha's, *KLINE*, Emma, April 17 1889, 144
5512 *SCHULTZ*, Lewis P, *TAYLOR*, Mamie B, (DILL), May 22 1889, 144
5513 *STORM*, Wm B, of Peter L, *BARTGIS*, Fanny E, of Hiram, June 12 1889, 144
5514 *SHADE*, Christian, *RUNKLES*, Cementine, August 27 1889, 144
5515 *SNYDER*, Luther, *NULL*, Idahalia, August 27 1889, 144
5516 *SHOPE*, E Isler, *PALMER*, Madaline, October 21 1889, 144
5517 *SCHILDT*, Harry F, *EYLER*, Jennie H, October 30 1889, 144
5518 *SAHM*, Harry J, *DERR*, Etta G, November 2 1889, 144
5519 *SNYDER*, Wm F, *WALTER*, Florence M, November 5 1889, 144
5520 *SIMPSON*, Cha's E, *HANE*, Mary C, November 6 1889, 144
5521 *SCHROEDER*, Clarence F, *YOUNG*, Harriet G, November 13 1889, 144
5522 *SHANK*, Cha's, *STIMMELL*, Katie F, November 28 1889, 144
5523 *SWEARING*, Cha's A, *HERGESHEIMER*, Annie S, December 3 1889, 144
5524 *SMITH*, George, *SPENCER*, Annie M, December 24 1889, 144
5525 *SCHAEFFER*, James C, *HEMLER*, Nannie D, December 31 1889, 144
5526 *STULL*, Cha's S, *CRUM*, Ella, January 1 1890, 145
5527 *SMITH*, Arthur C, *GROVE*, Laura V, February 4 1890, 145

5528 STEWARD, Wm J, NICHOLS, Clara K, (NICOLS-illegible}, February 11 1890, 145
5529 SHEPHERD, Joseph K, HALLER, Emma R (Mrs), 2d husband, April 22 1890, 145
5530 SCHAEFFER, Warren, GRASER, Mary C, April 24 1890, 145
5531 SMITH, Zachariah G, KEENEY, Catharine A, May 19 1890, 145
5532 SHENCK, John J (Prof), AHALT, J Pearl, June 18 1890, 145
5533 SHRINER, E Derr, GETZENDANNER, Nannie, December 17 1890, 145
5534 STALEY, Harry J, DEAN, Amelia V, Dec 5 1890, 145
5535 SMITH, James, KLINE, Mollie, Dec 24 1890, 145
5536 STOCKMAN, Wm M, FISHER, Sarah Ada, Dec 23 1890, 145
5537 STRINE, A Pierce, CRUM, Sarah L, Dec 24 1890, 145
5538 STEPHEY, Samuel D, WINTERS, Daisy, Dec 25 1890, 145
5539 SHANK, Cha's McClelland, KELLER, Annie D, of H'y, Dec 24 1890, 145
5540 TULLY, Aquilla, GLEASON, Margaret (Mrs), "LOWE", Decr 30 1821, 146
5541 TRAIL, Edward, RAMSBURGH, Lydia, of Jacob, Jany 17 1822, 146
5542 TEHAN, John, 1st wife, CARLIN, Catharine, of James, Decr 28 1823, 146
5543 TRAIL, Baker, LEAPLEY, Miss, (*Mary Barbara), April 1824, 146
5544 THOMAS, Leonard (Junior), TABLER, Catharine, June 3 1824, 146
5545 TORMEY, Patrick, JAMISON, Jane, May 24 1825, 146
5546 TRAVERSE, Boyle, HOFFMAN, Catharine, Octr 16 1825, 146
5547 THOMPSON, Cornelius, WILLIAMS, Catharine, (not listed as Miss), Septr 7 1826, OGLE "Colored", 146
5548 TYLER, Wm Bradley (Dr), 2d wife, MCPHERSON, Maria (Mrs), widow of Rob't G, May 17 1827, 146
5549 TRISLER, George, 3d wife, KURTZ, Susan, Balto, Octr 11 1827, 146
5550 TABLER, Abraham, SMITH, Juliann, "Zion Church", Nov 15 1827, 146
5551 THOMAS, Peter, CROMWELL, Harriott (Mrs), Jany 1828, 146
5552 TRAGO, William, GETZENDANNER, Eveline, May 25 1828, 146
5553 TAYLOR, John Wesley, SAUNDERS, Elizabeth, June 5 1828, 146
5554 TICE, Henry Nicholas, of Geo, KUNKEL, Barbara A, of John, Augt 4 1829, 146
5555 THOMSON, Wm J, of John P, DAVIS, Margretta, of Ignatius/(not listed as Miss), April 15 1830, 146
5556 THOMAS, George, of Henry/2d wife, THOMAS, Ann Maria, June 1 1830, 146
5557 TORRENCE, James, COST, Mary Ann (Mrs), Jany 19 1832, 146
5558 TALBOTT, Mahlon, of Joseph, CHARLTON, Louisa, March 29 1832, 146
5559 THOMAS, Samuel, "Manor"/2d wife, JOHNSON, Julian C, Septr 8 1832, 146
5560 TYLER, Samuel, "Lawyer", BAYLY, Catharine, of John, April 16 1833, 146
5561 TURNER, John C, LITTLEJOHN, Elizabeth T, May 9 1833, 146
5562 TIDBALL, Robert M, RINGGOLD, Maria A (Mrs), June 22 1833, 146
5563 THOMAS, Levin, "Manor"/2d wife, MARKEY, Eliza, of Fred'k "DILL", Octr 15 1833, 146
5564 THOMAS, Eli, SHOOK, Christianna, "SCHUCK", June 1 1834, 146
5565 THOMSON, John P, 3d wife, HAMNER, Mary, Decr 19 1834, 146
5566 TEHAN, John, 2d wife, YOUNG, Elizabeth A, Septr 3 1835, 146
5567 TINGSTROM, Peter, SIMMONS, Mary A, Feby 4 1836, 146
5568 TYLER, Geo Murdoch, of Wm Bradley, LATE, Ann Maria, March 29 1836, 146
5569 TITLOW, James, of Adam, MILLER, Catharine, of John W, April 10 1836, 146
5570 THOMAS, George, of Henry/3d wife, HARGETT, Juliann, of John, April 21 1836, 146
5571 TITLOW, John, of John, MOXLEY, Ann, July 12 1836, 146

5572 TYLER, Wm C, of A Arundel Co, *JOHNSON*, Eleanor M (Mrs), of Dr Cha's W, Septr 1 1836, 146

5573 TURBUTT, Edward, of Nicholas, *SPANGLER*, Elizabeth S, of York, Pa, March 28 1837, 146

5574 THOMAS, David O, of Michael, *STAUFFER*, Elizabeth, of Jos, April 5 1838, 146

5575 THOMAS, Christian, *KEMP*, Mary Elizabeth, of Walter B, May 3 1838, 146

5576 TRUNDLE, Hezekiah L, *NICHOLLS*, Mary, Montgomery Co, April 23 1839, 146

5577 THOMAS, Christian Keefer, *BUCKEY*, Eveline Virginia, June 6 1839, 146

5578 TRAPNELL, Joseph (Junior, Rev), *WATKINS*, Emily, at Annapolis, June 18 1839, 146

5579 TRAIL, Oscar, *KEMP*, Sarah A E, of Lewis/in Balto, Jany 28 1840, 146

5580 THOMAS, John N, *CROSS*, Elizabeth, Feby 1840, 146

5581 TRUESCOTT, George, *MERMAN*, Hannah, March 27 1840, 146

5582 TURNER, Isaac, *KNEPP*, Parmelia (Mrs), N Lisbon, June 16 1840, 147

5583 TUCKER, William J, *KEPHART*, Catharine, of Peter, June 25 1840, 147

5584 TITLOW, Isaac, *ELY*, Elizabeth, of Wm, May 3 1840, 147

5585 THOMAS, John B, of Levin, *THOMAS*, Charlotte, Octr 22 1840, 147

5586 TYSON, Jonathan, 2d wife, *BAER*, Elizabeth W D, of Dr Jacob, April 6 1841, 147

5587 THOMAS, Francis (Hon), *MCDOWELL*, Sarah C P, of Hon James/Va, June 8 1841, 147

5588 TYLER, Samuel (Dr), of Dr Wm, *BALTZELL*, Lucretia Josephine, of Tho's/Balto, Nov 29 1842, 147

5589 THOMAS, Lewis M, of Mich'l, *SCHREBLY*, Susan, of Washington Co, May 18 1843, 147

5590 TOLLINGER, George, *KANTNER*, Mary C, of Geo, July 20 1843, 147

5591 TYLER, John, Pres US/2d wife, *GARDINER*, Julia, of River Head, L I, N York, June 26 1844, 147

5592 TALL, Erasmus, "Jacob" Xed out Stephen alias, *LIFE*, Mary, "of Bobby", Augt 18 1844, 1st wife, 147

5593 TYLER, Wm (Junior, Dr), *ROBINSON*, Jane, of Rev Henry, Octr 8 1844, 147

5594 THOMAS, John (Junior, Capt'n), *ANDERSON*, Ann (Mrs), Decr 4 1844, 147

5595 THOMAS, Ezra M, *STOCKMAN*, Amanda, Decr 12 1844, 147

5596 THOMAS, Abraham W, *RHODES*, Catharine M, July 5 1845, 147

5597 THOMAS, Richard, *DUTROW*, Amanda, Septr 2 1845, 147

5598 THOMAS, Charles E, *HALLER*, Catherine E, "Jefferson", March 31 1846, 147

5599 TROUT, Joseph H, *BREMMERMAN*, Amelia E, May 28 1846, 147

5600 TRUNDLE, John G, *STONE*, Louisa M, May 27 1847, 147

5601 THOMAS, Charles Edward, *DUTROW*, Eliza Jane, June 17 1847, 147

5602 TANEYHILL, Aaron, *WEEMS*, Elizabeth, of Rev James/Colored, Nov 30 1848, 147

5603 THOMPSON, Cha's West (Rev), *PRESCOTT*, Caroline, Newberryport, Mass, April 19 1849, 147

5604 TRACY, Elias, *MORGAN*, Eveline, Nov 8 1849, 147

5605 THRASHER, Tho's R L, *LONG*, Amanda A F, April 16 1850, 147

5606 TRAIL, Charles E, of Edward, *MCELFRESH*, Arianna, of Jno H, Feby 26 1851, 147

5607 TRAFFORD, John, of N Jersey, *DORSEY*, Rachel, of Dr Lloyd, March 11 1851, 147

5608 THOMAS, Lewis E, *DIXON*, Sophia E, May 29 1851, 147

5609 TOCHMAN, Gaspard (Maj), *JAGELLO*, Apollonia, "JALACHICH", Augt 1851, 147

5610 TWIGGS, David E (Maj Gen'l), USA/2d wife, *HUNT*, Tabitha (Mrs), Octr 8 1851, 147

5611 TAYLOR, Francis (Col), *TANEY*, Sophia Brooke, of Roger B, June 15 1852, 147

5612 TASISTRO, Louis F, *QUINN*, Catharine, of Norfolk, Va, April 16 1853, 147

5613 TRAVERSE, John Henry, of Boyle, *BAYER*, Maria, of Tho's, May 1853, 147

5614 TREGO, John Thos, of Balto, *NORRIS*, Nellie J, of Basil, Octr 18 1853, 147

5615 TODD, William H, of Wm, STAUFFER, Susan Catharine, of John, May 9 1854, 147
5616 THOMPSON, Samuel C, DARBY, Jane, of Walter, Augt 9 1854, 147
5617 TOWERS, John T, Mayor of Washington City, PALMER, Eliza, Octr 31 1854, 147
5618 THOMAS, George P, KEMP, Maria, Balto, no date given, 147
5619 TITLOW, John, of John, FILLER, Benjamina, Cha'stown, Va, Feby 20 1855, 147
5620 TRAIL, Lewis Ramsburgh, of Edward, TICE, Ellen, of Henry N, June 28 1855, 147
5621 TUBMAN, Benjamin G, THOMSON, Margret Jane, of Wm J, Octr 23 1855, 147
5622 TRAYER, J Varden, BENNETT, Ann Virginia, Decr 31 1855, 147
5623 THOMAS, George D, of Levin, LAMAR, Martha L J, Ohio, Jany 3 1856, 147
5624 TORRYSON, John R, YOUNG, Margaret E, March 27 1856, 148
5625 TULLEY, Alfred H, BACHELOR, Martha J, Balto, July 15 1856, 148
5626 THOMAS, Abraham, RHODES, Susan M, Decr 16 1856, 148
5627 TRUNDLE, John A, PLUMMER, Martha E, Augt 18 1857, 148
5628 THOMAS, George E, BOYER, Cordelia Jane, of Peter, Octr 22 1857, 148
5629 TAYLOR, Bayard, 2d wife, HANSEN, Marie, Gotha, Germany, Octr 27 1857, 148
5630 TOPPER, James G, ASHBAUGH, Margaret G, of John, Jany 12 1858, 148
5631 TAYLOR, John, BASFORD, Susan, March 31 1858, 148
5632 TAYLOR, John J, BARRICK, Mary Jane, May 11 1858, 148
5633 TASKER, Wm (Rev), 2d wife, DAVIS, Eliza (Mrs), "Colored friends", Jany 6 1859, 148
5634 TRESIDE, Thomas, HEMBRY, Ann E, of John, March 13 1859, 148
5635 THOMAS, J D (Rev), (*James), BUCKEY, Marion E, of Dan'l/(*Harriet), Octr 13 1859, 148
5636 THOMAS, Wm H, HANNA, Susan K, (not listed as Miss), Nov 2 1859, 148
5637 TASKER, Frank, of Wm, SNIVELY, Rebecca, Col'd friends, Nov 10 1859, 148
5638 THOMSON, James Hamner, of John P, BAKER, Virginia, of Geo W, Nov 15 1859, 148
5639 TURNER, Eli, BRYON, Lucy, Mount Pleasant, May 31 1860, 148
5640 TORMEY, Leonard J, JENKINS, Ellen M, of Alfred/(not listed as Miss), Nov 21 1860, Balto, 148
5641 TOMS, Lawson J, COCHRAN, Susan R, Burkitsville, Jany 3 1861, 148
5642 TALL, Erasmus, "Jacob"/2d wife, MILLER, Rebecca, "Dan KLEIN", Jany 16 1861, 148
5643 TENNISON, James T S, MCCARTHY, Maggie L, Niece of John NOONAN, Nov 26 1861, 148
5644 TRAYER, Thomas, SMITH, Henrietta, of Ezra of Geo, April 29 1862, 148
5645 THOMAS, Bruce (Dr), CUNNINGHAM, E Virginia, of B Amos, Octr 29 1862, 148
5646 THOMPSON, George W, FREY, Lucy, Nov 24 1862, 148
5647 THOMPSON, Cha's W, 8th Reg't Md Vol, EADER, Annie M, "County", Jany 26 1863, 148
5648 TRUNDLE, Thomas, REICH, Sophia E, of John, April 9 1863, 148
5649 TYSON, Robert, GAMBRILL, Janie, of Cha's A/Balto, June 4 1863, 148
5650 TRAPNELL, Joseph (Junior, Rev), 2d wife, MARSHALL, Ellen C (Mrs), Octr 13 1863, 148
5651 TORRENCE, Josiah S, BISER, Mary E, at Dayton, Ohio, Octr 21 1863, 148
5652 TRAIL, Charles H, HARPER, Alberta, Nov 25 1863, 148
5653 THOMAS, George C, SMITH, E Jennie, Decr 1 1863, 148
5654 TODD, Wm N, of Balto, NEIDIG, Mary Jane (Mrs), "of Dan'l BOWERS"/Glade, July 16 1864, de, 148
5655 TRAVIS, Le Grand H, of N York, CARMACK, Kate E, of Sam'l, Augt 2 1864, 148
5656 TALBOTT, Joseph Howell, of Balto Co, EADER, Annie M, Septr 22 1864, 148
5657 TUCKER, Wm C, of St Louis, Mo, SMALLWOOD, Harriott, of Wm C, Octr 3 1864, 148
5658 THOMAS, H Fenton, DOFLER, Mary L, of Jacob, Jany 26 1865, 148

5659 *TREICH*, Ferdinand F, *MEYER*, Annie C, of Geo, May 1 1865, 148
5660 *TABLER*, Charles W, of Wm B, *SINN*, Kate, of John Tho's, July 18 1865, 148
5661 *THOMPSON*, Archibald, of Ohio, *BECK*, Mary V, of John J, Octr 1 1865, 148
5662 *TIDINGS*, Richard T, *MAIN*, Mary E, Octr 5 1865, 148
5663 *THOMAS*, John F, *ZIMMERMAN*, Mary E, Octr 24 1865, 148
5664 *TYLER*, Robert Bradley (Dr), of Wm Bradley/1st wife, *BRENGLE*, E Jane, of Law J, Nov 15 1865, 148
5665 *TITLOW*, Samuel S, *GUYTON*, Sarah J, Decr 12 1865, 148
5666 *THOMSON*, Ignatius Davis (Dr), of Wm J, *MAYNARD*, Julia S, Decr 19 1865, 149
5667 *TORBUTT*, A T S (Maj Gen'l), US Army, *CURRY*, Mary E, Jany 18 1866, 149
5668 *TYLER*, John A, *LOGUE*, Kate, of Lewis/Baltimore, Feby 15 1866, 149
5669 *THOMAS*, Otho T, *BREADY*, Mary Jane, of Geo/"BRIE"/Manor, Feby 20 1866, 149
5670 *THORN*, Ellis C (Dr), of Pittsburg, *CRONISE*, Tavie C V, of Sam'l, April 25 1866, 149
5671 *TORMEY*, John M, of Patrick, *CURLEY*, Barbara, of Pa/in Balto, April 26 1866, 149
5672 *TRIMMER*, Samuel, *HOUCK*, Mary E E, of David, June 5 1866, 149
5673 *THOMAS*, Samuel, *HARGETT*, Annie M, of John H, Augt 22 1866, 149
5674 *TOMS*, William E, *BUHRMAN*, Hanna E, Augt 28 1866, 149
5675 *TOMPKINS*, John A (Col), of R Island, *SHRIVER*, Anne S, of Gen'l Edward, Feby 26 1867, 149
5676 *TAYLOR*, Charles J, of Griffin, *NELSON*, Fannie, of Wm B, March 12 1868, 149
5677 *THOMSON*, Merideth Davis, of Wm J, *BROCKENBROUGH*, Letice, Va, June 3 1868, 149
5678 *TWENTY*, George L, "ZWANZIEGER", *MAIN*, Marietta C, June 18 1868, 149
5679 *TYLER*, Robert Bradley (Dr), of Dr Wm B/2d wife, *SHRIVER*, Emma, of Edw, March 11 1869, 149
5680 *THOMAS*, Edward F, *KURTZ*, Alice, in Balto, May 20 1869, 149
5681 *TRASK*, Brainard P, of Fitchburg, Mass, *CANN*, Mary S, of Rev Tho's M, July 13 1869, 149
5682 *TRAIL*, Allen, of Edward, *WILSON*, Mary Grace, St Louis, July 15 1869, 149
5683 *THOMAS*, Granville, *DAVIS*, Nannie, of James L, Nov 23 1869, 149
5684 *THOMAS*, Robert, *NOLLTE'*, Marietta, of J C L, Feby 10 1870, 149
5685 *TRAIL*, Lewis W, of Oscar, *GOLDSBOROUGH*, Zoe, of Dr Cha's, Jan 17 1871, 149
5686 *TYSON*, Jacob Baer, of Jonathan, *MANN*, Amelia, of Stephen S, May 17 1871, 149
5687 *TOMPSON*, Sam'l J, *RITTER*, Annie S, of J Alfred, June 7 1871, 149
5688 *TOLLINGER*, George D, *BARTON*, Anna M, May 21 1871, Reading, Pa, 149
5689 *TYLER*, George, of Wm C, *ROBERTSON*, Alice, of James H, Septr 13 1871, 149
5690 *TROUT*, David C C, *MELDRUM*, Anna M, April 14 1873, 149
5691 *TITZEL*, John M (Rev), *ALLISON*, Mary C, Augt 12 1873, Ger Ref, 149
5692 *THOMAS*, David O, of Cha's, *QUYNN*, Maria V, of Allen G, Octr 30 1873, 149
5693 *THOMAS*, Charles F, *BAKER*, Sarah C, of D'l, Nov 11 1873, 149
5694 *TYLER*, Geo T (Rev), *SINN*, Mary (Mrs), "FACKLER", April 27 1874, 149
5695 *THOMAS*, Silas E, *CONRAD*, Katie E, April 30 1874, 149
5696 (*THOMAS*, Ann (Mrs), age 78, "ANDERSON"/wife of Col John, died July 1 1874), 149
5697 *TYERYAR*, Rudolph, "THEIERJAHR", *PHILLIPS*, Alice V, Jan 26 1875, 149
5698 *THOMAS*, James (Rev), *WACHTER*, Rebecca, Feb 1875, 149
5699 *THOMAS*, Calvin A, *BUXTON*, Alice B, Decr 1 1875, 149
5700 *TRAPNELL*, E W (Dr), *MARLOW*, Edmonia, Jan 6 1876, 149
5701 *THOMAS*, Francis Philip (Hon), (P F), *MAY*, Clintonia G, Balto, Jan 29 1876, 149
5702 *TYSON*, Cha's B, of Jona, *HALLER*, Hettie P, of Ch's W, Octr 25 1876, 149

5703 TYSON, Henry B, of Jona/1st wife, JOHNSON, M Eugenia, of Benj, May 8 1877, 149
5704 THOMAS, John G, MANTZ, Sallie E, of Wm, Decr 18 1877, 149
5705 TYSON, C Dorsey, MORGAN, Mary A, Oct 16th 1878, 149
5706 TAYLOR, William, SULTZ, Lavinia, Octr 15th 1878, 149
5707 TREGALLAS, Samuel, SCHRYOCK, Lena, Oct 29th 1878, 149
5708 THOMAS, William, HOUCK, Margaret E, March 5th 1879, 150
5709 TREGALLAS, John N, GETZENDANNER, Fannie, (not listed as Miss), April 20th 1880, "BUCKEY", 150
5710 THOMAS, John B, 2d wife, MCCLEERY, Harriet S, (not listed as Miss), June 2d 1880, 150
5711 TYLER, W Ottis, GOLDSBOROUGH, Minnie, June 7th 1881, 150
5712 TAYLER, George W, WALTZ, Hellen M, March 29t 1882, 150
5713 TYSON, C Dorsey, 2d wife, POTTER, Lillian, September 9 1885, 150
5714 TITLOW, Cha's R ##NIS, 2d wife, ADAMS, Margaret (Mrs), September 1 1886, 150
5715 TYSON, Nathaniel S, SCHAEFFER, Margaret (Mrs), November 30 1886, 150
5716 TYSON, Henry B, 2 wife, CASTLE, Mary E V, September 6 1887, 150
5717 TUCKER, Wm, FALK, Mary, November 9 1887, 150
5718 THOMAS, Cha's, MCKINNEY, Maggie, Sept 12 1888, 150
5719 TEAGUE, J L (Rev), CROMWELL, Mary, October 3 1888, M E South, 150
5720 TALBOTT, Harry (Dr), HEDGES, Lillie, of L E, Dec 15 1888, 150
5721 TRAIL, Cha's B, WINEBRENER, Grace E, July 30 1889, 150
5722 TAYLOR, Harry S, BROWN, Mildred L, October 24 1889, of Benj F, 150
5723 THOMPSON, John M, CONDON, Amelia, Dec 18 1890, 150
5724 UPTON, Levi T, MICHAEL, Adelia E, Dec 9 1832, 154
5725 VARDEN, Josiah (Rev), CLEMSON, Elizabeth S, Septr 23 1835, 154
5726 VEIT, J Jacob, 2d wife, HENRY, Barbara, "HEINRICH", April 3 1837, 154
5727 VAN BUREN, John H W, "Baker", PHILIPS, Mary (Mrs), July 20 1837, 154
5728 VORE, William, CHAMBERS, Sarah, June 12 1838, 154
5729 UMBERGER, Michael, MOBLEY, Margaret, Jany 23 1840, 154
5730 NO SURNAME GIVEN, Victoria, Queen of England, SAXE COBURG, Albert, Prince, Feby 10 1840, 154
5731 ULRICH, Geo William, HALLER, Margaret A E, of Jacob, March 30 1841, 154
5732 VAN BUREN, John, of Martin, VANDERPOOL, Elizabeth, June 22 1841, 154
5733 UNKEFER, Francis S, "UNGEFEHR", JONES, Elizabeth, of Joshua, Octr 26 1841, 154
5734 VEIT, J Jacob, 3d wife/(*VIRT), FRAAS, Mrs, (*Margaret FROS), April 18 1850, 154
5735 UNGLESBEE, G W, HEIM, Ann Catharine, of Lewis, May 27 1852, 154
5736 VANFOSSEN, Wm H, STEELE, Catharine, Septr 13 1852, 154
5737 VANFOSSEN, Arnold, 2d wife, HERRINGTON, Julia A, Octr 17 1852, 154
5738 VANCOURT, J B, MITTNACHT, Amelia, of Geo H/Balto, Jany 17 1853, 154
5739 UPPERMAN, Joseph, METZGER, Margaret, March 28 1854, 154
5740 VALENTINE, James C, WILES, Lyida A, May 13 1858, 154
5741 VALK, John M, AUBEL, Catharine, Augt 30 1857, 154
5742 VAN LINBURG, M, CASS, Isabella, of Lew CASS, Augt 23 1858, 154
5743 ULRICH, Sam'l, SKINNER, Ann R, Hagerstown, June 2 1859, 154
5744 VANFOSSEN, Geo W, of Levi, TRUSCOTT, Sarah C, of Geo, Feby 13 1861, 154
5745 UTERMEHLE, Charles H, of Washington, KOLB, Naomi, of Dan'l, Nov 5 1861, 154
5746 VANECKER, J William, of Pittsburg, GETZENDANNER, Ada Augusta, of Cha's, Augt 13 1863, 154

5747 VIRTZ, James M W (Capt), REED, Lydia C, of Va, Octr 8 1863, 154
5748 VANDERGRIFF, Edward, CRUM, Mary E, of Wm, April 18 1864, 154
5749 VON BLUCHER, G (Capt'n), of 31st N York Battery, STIPES, Madora, June 11 1864, 154
5750 VEITCH, John Wesley, HOWARD, Annie E, of Edward, May 9 1865, 154
5751 VANSANT, J Wehrley, MYERS, Amelia, Balto, May 14 1865, 154
5752 VALENTINE, Geo S, WELTY, Kate N, Octr 30 1865, 154
5753 URNER, Milton G, HAMMOND, Laura A, of Dr Rich'd C, Jany 10 1866, 154
5754 VANFOSSEN, Eldred M, of Levi, TOLLINGER, Lizzie, June 13 1869, 154
5755 UHLER, John H, DEEDS, Virginia, Augt 3 1869, 154
5756 VION, Leon, BANTZ, Fannie, of Nimrod/Mo, Septr 20 1871, 154
5757 VANSANT, Oliver, FRIZZELL, Mary Ellen, Octr 8 1872, 154
5758 VERNON, Geo W F (Col), TODD, Sallie A, Augt 18 1873, 154
5759 VANFOSSEN, W Scott, of Levi, DUTROW, Hattie L, Nov 27 1873, 154
5760 ULRICH, John, of Wm, DEAN, Mary A, Octr 14 1874, 154
5761 VANFOSSEN, Wm J, STAUFFER, C V, Decr 19 1876, 154
5762 VEIT, John Jacob, SHOOK, Kate M, Decr 12 1877, 154
5763 UTERMEHLE, Charles H, 1st wife, STOKES, Sophie, Feb 6t 1884, 154
5764 VANFOSSEN, Gilmer, of Arnold, STITELY, Katie C, February 1 1887, 154
5765 VEITCH, Benj E, MCCARN, Minnie M, in Chicago, July 10 1888, 154
5766 UNGER, Edward C, PORTER, Aggie, Oct 14 1890, 154
5767 WORTHINGTON, Reuben, SMITH, Rebecca, of Dr Jos S, Decr 26 1820, 156
5768 WACHTER, Michael (Rev), WIEST, Margaret, of Jacob, Decr 12 1820, 156
5769 WINNULL, John, GEWEYER, Catharine, of Leonard, April 10 1821, 156
5770 WEVER, James S, TRISLER, Henrietta, of Geo, July 3 1821, 156
5771 WILLSON, Wm M B (Dr), WOOTTON, Martha, Nov 29 1821, 156
5772 WARNER, Michael (Jun'r), KREBS, Caroline, of Geo/Phil'a, May 9 1822, 156
5773 WALLING, James, of John, RITTER, Caroline, June 13 1822, 156
5774 WOLPERT, Frederick, FAUTH, Christianna, Septr 22 1822, 156
5775 WEBB, Joseph B, 2d wife, FOGEL, Mary, May 6 1823, 156
5776 WRIGHT, John, "Tailor", YOUNG, Mrs, (*Sophia), June 24 1823, 156
5777 WALLING, David, of Joseph, KAUFFMAN, Eliza, of Henry, July 14 1823, 156
5778 WILLIARD, Jacob G, GETZENDANNER, Christianna, of Lawyer Jacob, Septr 18 1823, 156
5779 WINTER, John (Rev), 1st wife, EMMITT, Henrietta, of Wm, Jany 6 1824, 156
5780 WOLFE, George, KINKERLY, Mary Ann, March 5 1825, 156
5781 WITHY, Calvin, ZIELER, Louisa, of Adam, April 28 1825, 156
5782 WAGNER, Conrad, SPECHT, Catharine, May 19 1825, 156
5783 WELLESLEY, Marquis of, PATTERSON, Mary Ann (Mrs), Octr 29 1825, Dublin, 156
5784 WATERS, William (Dr), HITE, Frances Conway, of Yost, Decr 22 1825, 156
5785 WHEELER, Bennett J, SHOPE, Mary, Augt 17 1826, 156
5786 WILSON, Robert, "Plasterer", WINCKS, Eleanor, Nov 2 1826, 156
5787 WARTHAN, Ignatius, MOORE, Nancy, Nov 5 1826, 156
5788 WINTER, Thomas, of Benj'n, FORTNEY, Elizabeth, May 10 1827, 156
5789 WOLFE, Adam, WELTZHEIMER, Caroline, of Dr Lewis, Decr 12 1826, 156
5790 WILLIS, William, 2d wife, GAYLORD, Elizabeth (Mrs), March 23 1828, 156
5791 WORTHINGTON, Cha's, BRASHEAR, Ann, June 23 1829, 156
5792 WINNULL, William, NO BRIDES NAME GIVEN, Miss, Balto, July 5 1829, 156
5793 WALKER, John (Junior), KEMP, Elizabeth, of David, Septr 15 1829, 156

The Joseph Engelbrecht Marriage Ledger of Frederick Co., MD 1820-1890 *Marriage List*

5794 WHIP, John, BREEDY, Polly, March 25 1830, 156
5795 WALLING, David, of Jos/2d wife, HOOVER, Miss, of York, Pa/(*Sarah Ann), Nov 7 1830, 156
5796 WOODWARD, Baldwin, WOODWARD, Lydia A, of John, Nov 1831, 156
5797 WEBSTER, John B, FRAZIER, Mahala, Sept 9 1832, 156
5798 WALKER, Perry, THOMAS, Harriott, "Colored friends", Octr 27 1833, 156
5799 WAYS, Samuel, of Basil, WALLING, Susan, of Jos, April 1 1834, 156
5800 WILSON, Charles, SHRIVER, Mary, of Ab'm, April 24 1834, 156
5801 WORMAN, Andrew D, of Moses, CRONISE, Sophia M, of John, April 28 1835, 156
5802 WEBER, William, of John B, PHILLIPS, Mary, May 12 1835, 156
5803 WALKER, Samuel, "of Ireland", CROUGH, Rosanna (Mrs), "CONNOR", January 1836, 156
5804 WILCOXON, John, of Wm, IJAMS, Rebecca, of Jacob, Septr 29 1836, 156
5805 WITMORE, Noah, BREITENBACH, Mary, Octr 17 1836, 156
5806 WILLIAMS, John H, SHRIVER, Ellen, of Ab'm, Nov 17 1836, 156
5807 WALKER, William, of John/Glade, SCHERER, Sarah, of Lewis, Feby 23 1837, 156
5808 WOOLTZ, Tobias, of Geo, GRAY, Eliza Ann, Geotown, DCa, April 29 1837, 156
5809 WEBSTER, Joseph, of Geo/1st wife, MCCABE, Eliza G, Balto, Augt 30 1837, 157
5810 WATKINS, John, HAUER, Margaret Ann, of Adam (Adam underline), Feby 22 1838, (Henry written over Adam), 157
5811 WAGNER, Samuel, of Rev Dan'l, REITZELL, Miss, York, Pa, March 1838, 157
5812 WORNER, Christopher, NICHEL, Louisa, of Adam, May 31 1838, 157
5813 WACHTER, John George, SCHAUB, Frances, Ohio, July 8 1838, 157
5814 WILLSON, John J, of Tho's P, TYLER, Ann, of Dr Wm Bradley TYLER, Augt 14 1838, 157
5815 WACHTER, Daniel, KEYSER, Catharine Ann, May 16 1839, 157
5816 WATERS, Baker, MAGRUDER, Rachel (Mrs), Montgomery Co, Md, June 1838, 157
5817 WACHTELL, Frederick, CROCKEN, Martha Ann, Octr 31 1839, 157
5818 WALKER, Joseph W, of John, LEE, Sarah Frances, Washington City, Feby 16 1840, 157
5819 WHITTAKER, James, LYON, Olivia, of Dr Isaac/Cincinnati, Ohio, Feby 19 1840, 157
5820 WILKINSON, William, TITLOW, Ellen, of Adam, April 12 1840, 157
5821 WALKER, Jacob, of John, RAMSBURG, Ann Mary, of John, May 17 1840, 157
5822 WATSON, Isaac Cooper, BITZENBERGER, Mary Ann, May 24 1840, 157
5823 WILSON, Adam, SHRYOCK, Mary A, Octr 29 1840, 157
5824 WISE, Henry A (Hon), 2d wife, SERGEANT, Sarah, of Hon John, Nov 26 1840, 157
5825 WATTS, Albert, NORRIS, Francina, Boonsboro, Feby 11 1841, 157
5826 WILLIARD, John, WASMUS, Louisa Ann, Gettysburg, March 9 1841, 157
5827 WILLIARD, Geo W (Rev), LITTLE, Louisa C, Mercersburg, Pa, April 28 1841, 157
5828 WISONG, William A, of Isaac, MUNDER, Caroline W, May 20 1841, 157
5829 WEBB, Tho's H, HAMILTON, Pamelia, of John/"EVITT", June 17 1841, 157
5830 WINECOFF, Jesse (Rev), 1st wife, HAUSER, Sophia, of Wm/Allegany Co, Octr 1841, 157
5831 WENTZELL, Wm H, of Alex'r, BUCKEY, Mary C, of John, Octr 28 1841, 157
5832 WOODWARD, Horace, NEYHOFF, Ann Rebecca, "Gabriel", Decr 1841, 157
5833 WOODWARD, George, of John, ECKES, Susan, Decr 1841, 157
5834 WEBSTER, Joseph, of Geo/2d wife, HANON, Margretta F, Balto, Jany 18 1842, 157
5835 WALLER, William, TYLER, Elizabeth, of President John TYLER, Jany 31 1842, 157
5836 WOODWARD, John J, of John, OTT, Ann Eliza, of Peter, March 24 1842, 157
5837 WARFIELD, Surrat D (Junior), GORE, Clarissa Jane, April 12 1842, 157
5838 WORMAN, John R, ENGLISH, Ruth Ann, of Richard, April 14 1842, 157

5839 WILL, John W, *BURALL*, Sydney J, Augt 1842, 157
5840 WEBSTER, William T, *FIELDS*, Malinda, Septr 1 1842, 157
5841 WOODWARD, Alexander, of John, *BURALL*, Ellen, Septr 4 1842, 157
5842 WATERS, Franklin (Dr), *HILLEARY*, Sarah T W, Octr 4 1842, 157
5843 WHITTER, Thomas, 2d wife, *HANE*, Susan, of John, Octr 9 1842, 157
5844 WOOD, Basil, *HAMMOND*, Charlotte C, Octr 18 1842, 157
5845 WEBSTER, Stephen J, *STOCKMAN*, Elizabeth, April 13 1843, 157
5846 WATTS, Reuben, *KOONTZ*, Sophia N, of John, Augt 22 1843, 157
5847 WINDSOR, George Washington, *MURRAY*, Elizabeth E, Octr 10 1843, 157
5848 WALLING, Henry J, of Jos, *FLEMING*, Catharine, May 23 1844, 157
5849 WAGENER, John, "Tailor", *BURGEE*, Emily, at Urbana, Decr 19 1844, 157
5850 WEBSTER, John D, *DOGGET*, Mary E, March 18 1845, 157
5851 WISSINGER, George (Capt'n), 2d wife, *WINCKLER*, Harriott, Geotown, Septr 1 1845, 158
5852 WALSH, Wm H, *CONRADT*, Ann Regina, of Ch'n Gottloeb/Balto, Septr 11 1845, 158
5853 WALKER, Cha's W, of John, *SWEADNER*, Jane Rebecca, of Dan'l, Feby 24 1846, 158
5854 WACHTER, Henry, *KEYSER*, Sarah, April 7 1846, 158
5855 WICKLIFFE, Robert (Junior), *VAN HOUTIN*, Josephine, at Turin, April 7 1846, 158
5856 WILLIARD, Henry, *ADLUM*, Sarah Ann, Jefferson, July 28 1846, 158
5857 WAYS, John T, *MYERS*, Sarah, Septr 17 1846, 158
5858 WAGNER, Dennis D, *HARRITT*, Sophia E, Octr 11 1846, 158
5859 WERTENBAKER, George W S, *DAVIS*, Elizabeth, of Luke, Nov 24 1846, 158
5860 WYSONG, Tho's T (Rev), *PRESTON*, Sarah F, Balto, Decr 10 1846, 158
5861 WARTHEN, James H, *HALLER*, Ann E, of Tobias, Sen'r, Decr 24 1846, 158
5862 WEBSTER, George T, *HOLMES*, Elizabeth, "CASSEL", Jany 5 1847, 158
5863 WITHERSPOON, Alex'r S (Dr), *KUHN*, Louisa Adelaide, of Capt Jos Lew, May 20 1847, 158
5864 WALKER, Samuel D, of John, *TODD*, Rebecca R, of Wm, May 25 1847, 158
5865 WALTER, John, *PAMPELL*, Elizabeth, of Fred'k W, June 27 1847, 158
5866 WHEELER, John Francis Ragis, *MORELAND*, Margaret, of John, July 15 1847, 158
5867 WOODSIDE, John Thomas, *EICHELBERGER*, Margaret, of Geo M, July 27 1847, 158
5868 WOODWARD, Eli, *DUVALL*, Henrietta D, Decr 29 1847, 158
5869 WORMAN, Wm D, of Moses, *GITTINGER*, Mary E, of Geo, Feby 15 1848, 158
5870 WAYS, Joseph, of Basil, *MILLER*, Miss, of Conrad/(*Elizabeth), July 2 1848, 158
5871 WISONG, George Rutherford, of Isaac, *DILL*, Henrietta, of Joshua, July 19 1848, 158
5872 WACHTER, John J, *WILES*, Barbara, Octr 15 1848, 158
5873 WACHTER, David F, *MURRAY*, Sarah A, Nov 15 1848, 158
5874 WATERS, Leander, *LEATHER*, Mary A C, June 12 1849, 158
5875 WINTHROP, Robert C (Hon), *WILLS*, Mrs, Boston, Nov 6 1849, 158
5876 WAGNER, John A, *THOMSON*, Elizabeth, March 31 1850, 158
5877 WORTHINGTON, Tho's C, *DAVIS*, Louisa, of Dr Tho's, June 20 1850, 158
5878 WACHTER, Leander (Dr), of Rev Mich'l, *LANDERS*, Elizabeth, July 24 1850, 158
5879 WEST, Joseph, *KOONTZ*, Ann Maria, of John, Septr 15 1850, 158
5880 WATERS, Cyrus (Rev), of Horatio, *GAMBRILL*, Emily S, Septr 24 1850, 158
5881 WADE, Thomas, of N Y State, *KOONTZ*, Lizzie, of Geo, Octr 24 1850, 158
5882 WINTER, John (Rev), 3d wife, *GOLDSBOROUGH*, Sarah E, Nov 11 1850, 158
5883 WAESCHE, Henry, *SCHERER*, Elizabeth, Feby 4 1851, 158
5884 WEINBRENNER, George, *STAMBAUGH*, Susan, Feby 6 1851, 158

5885 *WEDDEL*, John P, *FOSTER*, Martha Angeline, (not listed as Miss), March 6 1951, 158

5886 *WACHTER*, George M, of Rev Mich'l, *FOX*, Juliann, May 14 1851, 158

5887 *WILCOXON*, Andrew Jackson, of Wm, *GETZENDANNER*, Anna Mary, of Dan'l, April 15 1851, 158

5888 *WILLIAMS*, James, *ETCHISON*, Ruth, May 29 1851, 158

5889 *WEINBRENNER*, Geo A, of Ch'n/1st wife, *CRONISE*, Mary Ann, of Sam'l, Octr 16 1851, 158

5890 *WATKINSON*, Stephen, *HILTON*, Willie Elizabeth, Octr 16 1851, 158

5891 *WELLER*, Charles, *MILLER*, Sarah Jane, "sister of Joseph G MILLER", Nov 18 1851, 158

5892 *WISONG*, Jacob, of Isaac, *DUERING*, Mary Jane, Balto, Jany 15 1852, 158

5893 *WAHRENFELTSZ*, Josiah L, *EASTERDAY*, Susan E, "OSTERTAG", January 27 1852, 159

5894 *WHITMORE*, William, of Nicholas, *BRUBAKER*, Sarah, of John, Feby 25 1852, 159

5895 *WEDDEL*, James M, *DORSEY*, Alverda E, March 23 1852, 159

5896 *WAYS*, Wm Henry, *KUHN*, Mary Elizabeth, May 20 1852, 159

5897 *WILLIARD*, Ezra, *BISER*, Laura, Septr 1 1852, 159

5898 *WACHTER*, Lewis H, *PACELEY*, Amanda A, Septr 2 1852, 159

5899 *WALKER*, Wilson C, *NO BRIDES NAME GIVEN*, Miss, Phila, Septr 1852, 159

5900 *WENTZELL*, Alexander S, of Alex'r, *LEWIS*, Harriott A, Va, Nov 9 1852, 159

5901 *WEAGLEY*, James R, *ADAMS*, Valletta, of Valentine, Nov 24 1852, 159

5902 *WELFLEY*, John (Rev), 1st wife, *EADER*, Amelia Margaret, of Tho's, March 24 1853, 159

5903 *WATTS*, W W, *WIEST*, Susan, of Jacob/Balto, May 24 1853, 159

5904 *WOOD*, Elias, *SWAMLEY*, Amanda M, N Market, May 25 1853, 159

5905 *WHEALEY*, Geo W, *HAGAN*, Isabella F, "WHALEY"/(not listed as Miss), June 8 1853, 159

5906 *WEST*, Allen W, *LOY*, Catharine Margaret, Octr 18 1853, 159

5907 *WACHTER*, Jacob M, of Rev Mich'l, *ANDERS*, Sarah Ann, Decr 13 1853, 159

5908 *WEBSTER*, Geo Frederick, of Geo, *TRAIL*, Susan Ellen, of Edward, Feby 8 1854, 159

5909 *WILSON*, Frederick R, *SCHLEY*, S Cornelia, of David, March 15 1854, 159

5910 *WALLACE*, Tho's B, *GAINES*, Lucy B (Mrs), "BRISCOE"/"Lexington, Missouri", March 28 1854, 159

5911 *WASKEY*, Eli C, *THOMAS*, Susan R, "Manor", April 20 1854, 159

5912 *WIEST*, Frederick A, *DAVIS*, Harriott S, Balto, May 16 1854, 159

5913 *WELLER*, John B (Hon), 2d wife, *STANTON*, Lizzie W (Mrs), "BUCKELBANK"/California, June 20 1854, 159

5914 *WATERS*, Tilghman, *BRISCOE*, Ellen M, "Montgomery Co", Augt 1 1854, 159

5915 *WELSH*, Joel J, *APPLETON*, Mariania L, "Liberty, Indianna", Octr 17 1854, 159

5916 *WOODWARD*, Cha's B, of Baldwin, *HOLTZ*, Valletta J R, Nov 29 1854, 159

5917 *WOLFE*, Cha's Edward, of Adam, *HARKINS*, Louisa A, Balto, Decr 21 1854, 159

5918 *WASHBURN*, Sanford (Rev), *CROMWELL*, Caroline, of N Y State/Illinois, Decr 28 1854, 159

5919 *WOODVILLE*, Wm (Junior), *SCHLEY*, Ann Cadwalader, of Wm/Balto, January 9 1855, 159

5920 *WATERS*, Harry W D, 2d wife, *GRIFFITH*, Emily H, April 17 1855, 159

5921 *WILEY*, James, *BRUBAKER*, Mary Jane, of Jon, May 15 1855, 159

5922 *WEINBRENNER*, Edward J, *EBERT*, Caroline M R, of Benj'n, May 22 1855, 159

5923 *WORDON*, A Graham, "of Michigan", *NILES*, Geannie Ogden, of W OGDEN, June 12 1855, 159

5924 *WHITE*, Wm B, "of Bermuda", *RIORDEN*, Margaret E, Septr 4 1855, 159

5925 *WILLS*, Wm H, *LAMBRIGHT*, Mary Jane, of John, Octr 23 1855, 159

5926 *WELLER*, John, *GETZENDANNER*, Anna Kate, of Ab'm, Decr 19 1855, 159

5927 *WEBER*, Herrmann, 2d wife, *EISENHAUER*, Catharine (Mrs), Jany 1 1856, 159

5928 *WILES*, Frederick, *JACKSON*, Sarah, "Woodsboro", Jany 24 1856, 159
5929 *WEIRMAN*, Thaddeus S, *RHEAM*, Hanna R, Feby 6 1856, 159
5930 *WRIGHT*, No first name given, *LOVELY*, Mary Ann Margaret (Mrs), "CONNOR" "DADISMAN", Feby 1856, 159
5931 *WESTWOOD*, Henry Clay (Rev), *CHILD*, Emily J, Balto, March 27 1856, 159
5932 *WAYS*, Daniel F S, of Tho's/1st wife, *BURGESS*, Minerva, April 20 1856, 159
5933 *WORTHINGTON*, John T, *SIMMONS*, Mary R D, "Urbana", May 27 1856, 159
5934 *WILSON*, John (Rev), *HALBERT*, Hanna, at Staunton, Va, Augt 5 1856, 159
5935 *WARFIELD*, James H B (Dr), *WYNKOOP*, Ann M, Septr 11 1856, 160
5936 *WATERS*, Richard L, *HOBBS*, Annie Virginia, of Rezin, Octr 7 1856, 160
5937 *WILHIDE*, Robert L, *GRIMES*, Augusta A, Octr 9 1856, 160
5938 *WELTY*, Philip H, *MOBLEY*, Ann R, of Levi, Nov 6 1856, 160
5939 *WILMAN*, John L, *WILLHIDE*, Julia, Feby 4 1857, 160
5940 *WILLIS*, Wm B R, *BLAGROVE*, Harriett (Mrs), "LEASE"/"Washington City", April 2 1857, 160
5941 *WOODWARD*, Jacob C, *BUCHFELTER*, Hanna, June 2 1857, 160
5942 *WILLIAMS*, John H (Dr), *EICHELBERGER*, Elizabeth Jane, of Job D, June 18 1857, 160
5943 *WALTER*, Albert, *BECKER*, Christianna, June 28 1857, 160
5944 *WHEELER*, Joseph A, 1st wife, *PILES*, Mary A, Septr 6 1857, 160
5945 *WORTHINGTON*, Charles E, *LOGAN*, Maria L, Septr 1857, 160
5946 *WATERS*, Horatio (Jun'r), *HOGG*, Rachel Olevia, of Sam'l R, Septr 15 1857, 160
5947 *WILLIAMS*, Edward, Georgetown, DC, *TYLER*, Lizzie, of Samuel TYLER, Esq'r, Nov 10 1857, 160
5948 *WEEDON*, James H, *GIDDINGS*, Fannie E, of James, Decr 8 1857, 160
5949 *WELFLEY*, John (Rev), 2d wife, *ZIEGLER*, Catharine M (Mrs), Pa, Decr 23 1857, 160
5950 *WALKER*, Joseph W, "Printer"/2d wife, *BIGHAM*, Mary E, Pa, Jany 7 1858, 160
5951 *WEINBRENNER*, Geo A, 2d wife, *CRONISE*, Lizzie A, of Sam'l, Jany 27 1858, 160
5952 *WHITMORE*, Nicholas (Junior), *ZIMMERMAN*, Elizabeth Ann V, Feby 18 1858, 160
5953 *WELLER*, Martin D, *GEDULTIG*, Mary Jane, Glade, March 23 1858, 160
5954 *WILLIARD*, Lewis A, *SPARROW*, Cornelia A, of John W, March 31 1858, 160
5955 *WINTER*, Francis B, of Tho's, *STONE*, Lucy, of Georgetown, DCa, May 3 1858, 160
5956 *WOLFE*, George H, of Adam, *HEAGY*, Molly A, Balto, June 15 1858, 160
5957 *WOLFE*, William S, of Adam, *JONES*, Kate A, of Morris/Balto, July 22 1858, 160
5958 *WASKEY*, Leonard T, *BLESSING*, Lucinda C, Septr 28 1858, 160
5959 *WOOD*, J N (Dr), (*Isaac Newton), *NORRIS*, Lydia A, Octr 5 1858, 160
5960 *WEIKERT*, George, *BAKER*, Serepta, Woodsboro, Octr 18 1858, 160
5961 *WORNER*, Christian, *BECKER*, Mary, Octr 19 1858, 160
5962 *WITMER*, Charles (Rev), *SMITH*, Mary Helen, Emmittsburg, Nov 1858, 160
5963 *WILSON*, S C (Col), *WALLING*, Corrie E, Balto, Decr 4 1858, 160
5964 *WALTZ*, Samuel E D, *BROWN*, Hester Ann, Decr 28 1858, 160
5965 *WEST*, Patrick McGill, *MCGILL*, Ellenora Arabella, June 1 1859, 160
5966 *WILLSON*, Leonidas (Rev), 2d wife, *HARRIS*, Maria E, Clarksburg, April 4 1859, 160
5967 *WEBER*, Wm Eldridge, *SHEPHERD*, Virginia L, Cumberland, June 7 1859, 160
5968 *WAMPLER*, Wm A, *PEARRE*, Mattie A, of Wm, June 16 1859, 160
5969 *WILLIAMS*, Levi, *JONES*, Charity, Le's RAMSBURG/Colored friends, Septr 15 1859, 160
5970 *WOOD*, Wm J W, *SAMPLE*, Anna L, Octr 5 1859, 160
5971 *WELLER*, Ephraim E, *BENNETT*, Margaret A, of Wash A, Octr 6 1859, 160

5972 WHITE, Benjamin Nicholson, *DAMER*, Lititia Hannah, in Ireland, Nov 10 1859, 160
5973 WHALEY, Wm H, *KOSTER*, Sophia, of Henry, Nov 13 1859, 160
5974 WILSON, Nathaniel J, *ALBAUGH*, Ann Sophia, of Ab's, Nov 16 1859, 160
5975 WALSH, Wm, of Sligo, Ireland, *WEBB*, Mary Jane, Nov 24 1859, 160
5976 WILLHIDE, John L, *BLESSING*, Susan, "Carroll & Fred Co", Decr 22 1859, 160
5977 WETNIGHT, Abraham, *BRANDENBURG*, Mary C, Feby 16 1860, 161
5978 WOLFE, William, *DRONENBERGER*, Susan, March 15 or Apl 12 1860, 161
5979 WATERS, William (Dr), 2d wife, *TIMBERLAKE*, Mildred C (Mrs), April 3 1860, 161
5980 WALKER, Patrick Henry, *MITTNACHT*, Rosa B, May 31 1860, Balto, 161
5981 WEBSTER, Sidney, *FISH*, Miss, of Hon Hamilton FISH, June 7 1860, N York, 161
5982 WEST, Erasmus, *HAYS*, M Louisa, of Mrs KETTURAH, Septr 4 1860, 161
5983 WINDSOR, Wm B, *DUTROW*, Harriott E, of Jos, Septr 11 1860, 161
5984 WEIRMAN, John E, *LITTLE*, Maria Louisa C, Septr 18 1860, Mechanickstown, 161
5985 WILCOX, Henry Martyn, of Chicago, *MARTIN*, Emma V, of Rev Dr Cha's, Octr 18 1860, 161
5986 WALDRON, Francis, *HILLEARY*, Ellen W, Nov 28 1860, 161
5987 WILLHIDE, E M, of Joseph, *HUNT*, Margaret M, of Rev Wm, Decr 25 1860, 161
5988 WOOD, Fernando (Hon), Mayor of N York/3d wife, *MILLS*, Miss, Decr 27 1860, 161
5989 WATERS, Richard C, "HARGETT", *SMITH*, Ann Eliza, Feby 7 1861, 161
5990 WHITMORE, John M, of Nicholas, *HOPWOOD*, Ellen Adelia, of James, Feby 13 1861, 161
5991 WILE, John A, of Daniel, *TRAIL*, Ellen B, widow of Lewis R/"TICE", Feby 13 1861, 161
5992 WOLFE, Elilhu R, of Samuel, *MCDEVITT*, Margaret A E, Feby 21 1861, 161
5993 WINDPIGLER, David, *JACOBS*, Mary Jane, July 28 1861, 161
5994 WILLIAMS, James, *INGMAN*, Harriott, of Joshua, Septr 26 1861, 161
5995 WILLIARD, Adam, *MERO*, Anna, Waynesboro, Pa, Octr 17 1861, 161
5996 WEDDLE, Tho's P, US Army, *FINNEY*, Mary Fannie, of James, Decr 30 1861, 161
5997 WATERS, James K, *HILL*, Ann M, March 13 1862, 161
5998 WORTHINGTON, Nicholas (Capt'n), *DORSEY*, Nettie, of Harry W, May 15 1862, 161
5999 WINANS, Ross (Jun'r), of Balto/2d wife, *MUNSON*, Miss, of Peterson, NJ, June 1862, 161
6000 WHITMORE, Nicholas (Sen'r), 2d wife, *MILLER*, Rebecca (Mrs), "Holtzappel", Nov 16 1862, 161
6001 WELLER, Amos T, *WHITTER*, Mary M, Nov 18 1862, 161
6002 WOLFE, Levi J, of Samuel, *LUTZ*, Annie C, Decr 4 1862, 161
6003 WALTMAN, Wm A, *WELLER*, Mary Ellen, Jany 6 1863, 161
6004 WACHTER, Ezra C, *STULL*, Julia B, Glade, March 20 1863, 161
6005 WINER, Wm, *KAUFFMAN*, Annie V, of Warner/Balto, March 25 1863, 161
6006 WOODS, John, US Army, *DYER*, Mary, April 14 1863, 161
6007 WOODERS, Thomas, US Army, *EBRECHT*, Margaret Ann, of John, May 27 1863, 161
6008 WHITLOCK, William, *CROCKEN*, Ann Eliza, of James J/Balto, Octr 5 1863, 161
6009 WEIR, Robert F (Dr), US Army/1st wife, *MCPHERSON*, Maria, of Robert G, Octr 8 1863, 161
6010 WEINBERG, Samuel, *LOWENSTEIN*, Amelia, "Jews", Octr 11 1863, 161
6011 WIGLEY, Wm A, *GEWEYER*, Malinda, widow of Wm GEWEYER, March 10 1864, 161
6012 WEINBRENNER, David C, *MARKEY*, Rebecca B, of David J, Octr 12 1864, 161
6013 WESLEY, John, *RICE*, Alice O, of Geo, Octr 5 1864, 161
6014 WAHRENFELSZ, Ezra, 2d wife, *BISER*, Elizabeth, Decr 1 1864, 161
6015 WHEELER, T M, (*Thomas), *LEWIS*, Martha L, of Jacob, Decr 8 1864, 161

6016 WEITZELL, Godfrey (Maj Gen'l), BOGAN, Louise, Cincinnati, Jany 12 1865, 161
6017 WILLIAMSON, Warren R, 3d wife, SMITH, Ann Rebecca, March 9 1865, 161
6018 WAHRENFELTSZ, Samuel, TOOMS, Frances V, March 16 1865, 161
6019 WOODWARD, Geo L, BROWN, Sarah J, June 2 1865, 162
6020 WALTERS, John W, PAMPELL, Amelia, of Fred'k W, July 18 1865, 162
6021 WOODWARD, Milton A, of John J, NICKEL, Fannie, of Jacob, Septr 19 1865, 162
6022 WARE, Charles R, BRAIN, Mary C, of John, Octr 11 1865, 162
6023 WILLIAMS, James E, SMITH, Augusta Palmer (Mrs), Decr 31 1865, 162
6024 WILLIAMS, Robert (Maj), DOUGLAS, Adele Cutts (Mrs), "of Stephen A", Jany 23 1866, 162
6025 WHIP, George C, HARRISON, Sarah F, Jany 16 1866, 162
6026 WORTHINGTON, Tho's G, BEELER, Mary E, of Joseph, Jany 17 1866, 162
6027 WILLIAMS, Ludwig Alexander, ANGELBERGER, Harriette Antoinette, Feby 15 1866, 162
6028 WACHTER, Wesley A, SMITH, Susanna S, Glade, March 29 1866, 162
6029 WAYS, Sam'l D (Jun'r), LUTER, Sallie E, Augt 30 1866, 162
6030 WILCOXON, John, of Wm/2d wife, MEALEY, Martha E, of Isaiah, Octr 30 1866, 162
6031 WACHTER, Urias, MARTZ, Marietta E, Decr 4 1866, 162
6032 WOODWARD, Charles, of Horace, TRIECH, Jennie D, of John B, Decr 11 1866, 162
6033 WERNSING, Herman, SAHM, Catharine, of Jacob, Feby 2d 1867, 162
6034 WINTER, Frederick, 2d wife, NO BRIDES NAME GIVEN, Mrs, in Hagerstown, March 5 1867, 162
6035 WACHTER, Lewis F, of Geo, BRENGEL, Catharine E, of Nich's, April 9 1867, 162
6036 WOLFE, James Polk, of Samuel, HALLER, Amelia, of Tho's, Augt 1867, 162
6037 WATERS, Washington (Dr), 2d wife, WATERS, Ellen M (Mrs), "of Tilghman", Augt 22 1867, 162
6038 WORTHINGTON, Nicholas J, SIMMONS, Alice, of J Sam'l, Octr 17 1867, 162
6039 WILLIARD, Joseph, KARN, Etta, Burkittsville, Octr 15 1867, 162
6040 WICKHAM, Augustus, YOUNG, Winnie, of Henry, Octr 29 1867, 162
6041 WILLIAMSON, James J, LORENTZ, Emma S, Middletown, Nov 28 1867, 162
6042 WESTON, Nathaniel, BARNEY, Annie, of Ai BARNEY/San Rafel, Cal'a, Nov 28 1867, 162
6043 WHITMORE, Randolph, MARTZ, Annie V, Decr 17 1867, 162
6044 WINSLOW, Benj'n F, of Vermot, MIDDLETON, Mary P, of Rob't W, Decr 31 1867, 162
6045 WALTER, James N, MCLEAN, Mary E, of Rev Tho's L, July 21 1868, 162
6046 WHITTAKER, Andrew J, KOLB, Louisa C, of Dan'l, Septr 9 1868, 162
6047 WATKINS, Frank D, LYON, Augusta P D, of Rev John C, Octr 16 1868, 162
6048 WAGNER, Wm H (Dr), BARRICK, Laura R, of Ezra/Glade, Decr 16 1868, 162
6049 WOODWARD, Leonidas S, of Phila, TREICH, Adelaide L, of J B, Feby 22 1869, 162
6050 WACHTER, Gideon R, KEYSER, Alice G, March 18 1869, 162
6051 WINCHESTER, Mordaunt C, of Benj F, INGMAN, Alice Maude, of Amb, Augt 19 1869, 162
6052 WILCOXON, Rufus H, of John, MCLANE, Ann V, of Wm W, Augt 19 1869, 162
6053 WINTER, John T, of Tho's, HIRST, Allie R, of Rev Wm, Octr 20 1869, GeoTown, DC, 162
6054 WELSH, Edward H, of Ohio, WISONG, Ellen Sophia, of Isaac, Nov 8 1869, 162
6055 WAGNER, Grafton J, DUTROW, Lizzie, Nov 18 1869, Glade, 162
6056 WARFIELD, Cecelius E, of Howard Co, THOMAS, Laura W, of D O, Jany 18 1870, 162
6057 WILMER, Wm, KAUFFMAN, Helen S, of Warner/Balto, May 5 1870, 162
6058 WHALEN, John W, HOLBRUNNER, Sue J, of Tho's M, May 18 1870, 162
6059 WESSELS, Litleton B, ARMSTRONG, Belle H, of Balto, June 1870, 162

6060 WEBSTER, Tho's C S, STONE, Margaret M, Nov 3 1870, 162
6061 WOLFE, Samuel, 2d wife, SHORB, Sarah M, Nov 22 1870, 163
6062 WALLIS, Albert E (Rev), DUVALL, Columbia (Mrs), "DUTROW", March 9 1871, 163
6063 WHIP, I Newton, SHELLMAN, Ann Maria, of Dan'l, March 16 1871, 163
6064 WILLIARD, Cha's F M, BOWLUS, Mary F, of Sephen R, March 23 1871, 163
6065 WILLIAMS, Henry, of John H, STOKES, Nettie, of Robert Y, May 30 1871, 163
6066 WHITE, John H, of Huntsville, Alabama, JOHNSON, S Bird, of Dr James, Septr 6 1871, 163
6067 WILLIAMSON, Joseph A, MCGILL, Eleanor West, of Dr Tho's J, Nov 8 1871, 163
6068 WAHRENFELTSZ, Daniel, STOTTELMEYER, Clara V, Octr 5 1871, Midd valley, 163
6069 WEDDELL, Luther L, KNODLE, Mary M, Jan 15 1872, Myersville, 163
6070 WEINBRENNER, Reverdy J, HILL, Anna Lavina, Septr 12 1872, 163
6071 WILLIAMS, Robert, of Wm'sburg, Va, JOHNSON, Sarah E, of Fred'k, Md, Octr 3 1872, 163
6072 WALTER, William, of John, SNYDER, Jennie, of Jacob F, Mar 18 1873, 163
6073 WHITE, Samuel, MYERS, Mary E, July 10 1873, Col'd friends, 163
6074 WOLFE, Thomas M, of Adam, AGNEW, Sydney (Mrs), Nov 5 1873, 163
6075 WOODWARD, Alexander, 2d wife, GOFF, Martha G (Mrs), Nov 3 1873, 163
6076 WASHINGTON, George, JOHNSON, Winnie, Jan 10 1874, Colored, 163
6077 WESTENBERG, Bernhard O F H De, BIRCKHEAD, Jane Allen, (not listed as Miss), Feb 26 1874, Balto, 163
6078 WAYS, David F S, of Tho's/2d wife, MCCLELLAND, Alice A, (not listed as Miss), May 27 1874, 163
6079 WACHTER, Edward S, STONE, Alice H, June 10 1874, 163
6080 WEINBRENNER, Tho's J, YOUNG, Sarah L, July 9 1874, 163
6081 WILSON, John K, KUNKEL, Mary B, of J B K, Octr 7 1874, 163
6082 WALKER, James E, MARKELL, Annie, of Geo, Nov 3 1874, 163
6083 WARD, Frank X, EVANS, Toppie, of Topham EVANS, Nov 11 1874, 163
6084 WHEELER, Joseph A, 2d wife, STEELE, Mary J, of Dan'l, Jan 12 1875, 163
6085 WAESCHE, J Theodore, COVER, Cassandra, of E N COVER, Jan 26 1875, 163
6086 WRIGHT, Geo W, of Va, FOUT, Isadore, Apl 27 1875, "GETZENDANNER", 163
6087 WILLIAMS, Robert H (Rev), SANDERSON, Mary Pearson, of Tho's, June 15 1875, 163
6088 WACHTER, Wm H, CRAVER, Laura C, Jan 4 1876, 163
6089 WINCKELMANN, Geo, BALOF, Wilhelmina, March 29 1876, 163
6090 WAYS, William H (Jun'r), WILCOXON, Maggie H, of John, Apl 27 1876, 163
6091 WALTER, Cha's G, of John, APPEL, Carrie C, Augt 1 1876, 163
6092 WELLER, W F, SUMAN, Annie R, of Wm Rand, Octr 25 1876, 163
6093 WORMAN, Andrew D (Dr), 2d wife, DUTROW, Sarah A S (Mrs), 3d husband, Feb 22 1877, 163
6094 WATTS, Wm E, HART, Mamie A, of Ja A, July 25 1877, Iowa, 163
6095 WHITMAN, Fred'k W, RIGNEY, Lillia J, of John T, Octr 3 1877, Balto, 163
6096 WALLING, Joseph H J, STALEY, Laura V, Octr 18 1877, 163
6097 WISNER, John H, of Mich'l, BRUCHY, Mary C, Nov 21 1877, 163
6098 WEDDELL, Frederick, KILLIAN, Susan, Decr 20 1877, 163
6099 WATERS, Frank, KOLB, Laura, Oct 31st 1878, 163
6100 WINEBRENNER, G C, NO BRIDES NAME GIVEN, Laura V, youngest daughter of H'y LORENTZ, Nov 1st 1878, 163
6101 WALTZ, Williard F (Lieut), HILTON, Cora, Nov 10th 1878, 163
6102 WILLARD, John, WISONG, Jennie, July 1st 1879, 163

6103 WRIGHT, Edward W E, CARTER, E H, "TROXELLS"(not listed as Miss), April 27th 1880, 164
6104 WALLING, Samuel, HEFFRON, Mary J, (not listed as Miss), May 21st 1880, 164
6105 WARFIELD, James R, WELTZ, Mollie K, "MOBERLY"(not listed as Miss), May 25th 1880, 164
6106 WEBSTER, William, of Fairview, HAUR, Belle S, of Jno, Nov 18th 1880, 164
6107 WRIGHT, James P, of Baltimore, HUNT, Mamie E, of Asbury/(not listed as Miss), Feb 10 1881, 164
6108 WORMAN, George M, REPP, Amanda A, of John S/(name not listed as Miss), Feb 24th 1881, 164
6109 WEAST, John C, NOTNAGLE, Annie F, of J J/(not listed as Miss), March 17th 1881, 164
6110 WATERS, Harry, GEISSINGER, Mary J, March 29th 1883, 164
6111 WILCOXON, Wm M, KELLER, Lizzie C, of Dewitt, May 22d 1883, 164
6112 WORMAN, Wm J, BROWN, Mary E, of H C, May 14 1884, 164
6113 WARD, Cha's F, RENNMICKEL, Annie L, Aug 5 1884, (ENGELBRECHT), 164
6114 WILCOXON, Charles J, HORN, Mary E, April 29 1885, 164
6115 WOODWARD, John L, of Jacob, PATTTERSON, Allie, August 20 1885, 164
6116 WALLACE, Albert E, 2 wife, DUTROW, Rebbecca E, November 10t 1885, 164
6117 WACHTER, Charles S, RODERICK, Emma J, December 24 1885, 164
6118 WRIGHT, Lewis M, WILLIARD, Mollie E, of Tho's, January 19t 1886, 164
6119 WHALLEY, George W, PERRY, Delia, February 26t 1886, 164
6120 WHISTNER, John, SCHELL, Amelia, April 7 1886, 164
6121 WOLFE, Charles C, MCDANIEL, Florence C, August 24 1886, (SINN), 164
6122 WEAGLEY, C W C (Dr), FOUT, Emma, November 1/6 1886, ADAMS, 164
6123 WEBSTER, George, CARSON, Bertha, December 4 1886, 164
6124 WOODWOARD, Wm A, of Alex, FAGAN, Emma, of Tho's, February 8 1887, 164
6125 WINEBERG, George H, CARLIN, Martha, April 14 1887, 164
6126 WILLIARD, Thomas E, RHODERICK, Hammine, June 9 1887, in Jefferson, 164
6127 WILLIARD, Thomas H, 2d wife, BLESSING, Matilda G, August 9 1887, 164
6128 WHITING, Edward, MYERS, Lilly, August 10 1887, 164
6129 WOOD, Melvine P, (# Melvin), WOOD, Ann M, August 17 1887, 164
6130 WILCOX, Arthur V, COZZENS, Marian, October 5 1887, Prospect Hall, 164
6131 WHITE, M Wales, DUVALL, Nellie E, December 27 1887, 164
6132 WOLFE, Frances E S, REAMY, Mary J, January 17t 1888, 164
6133 WHITE, J Carroll, GROVE, Carrie E, of Manassa, January 26 1888, 164
6134 WOLFE, Geo D, PLUNKETT, Lucy, February 8 1888, 164
6135 WAGNER, Arthur C, MARKS, Mary C, of Lemuel, February 9 1888, 164
6136 WITLOW, Harry G, MILLER, Jennie, of Jas/Jos G, February 14 1888, 164
6137 WACHTER, Steiner R, MICHAEL, Phoebe A, February 16 1888, 164
6138 WATSON, Wm H, EBERT, Grace A, of Valerius, Fbruary 14/17 1888, 164
6139 WILSON, Tyler, BUCHEY, Hattie, March 24 1888, 164
6140 WAITE, Frank H, FRAZIER, Fanny M, June 13 1888, 164
6141 WHISTNER, Cha's D, of Michael, HAFNER, Minnie T, June 13 1888, 164
6142 WILSON, George J, 2d wife, VANFOSSEN, C Katie, November 7 1888, 164
6143 WALTERS, Edward, GRIFFITH, Mary, of P H, January 15 1889, 164
6144 WINEBRENER, Samuel E, WOENER, Mollie L, March 13 1889, 164
6145 WINTER, Howard S, SNYDER, Lizzie, March 26 1889, 164

6146 WILLIS, Wm, MARTIN, Lutue K, April 17 1889, of Dr D C, 164
6147 WILKNER, J M, JACKSON, Carrie E, May 14 1889, 164
6148 WARD, John, JAMES, Katie, May 18 1889, 164
6149 WEINER, R J, DAVIS, Margaret J, May 20 1889, 165
6150 WILLIAR, George W, HOUSER, Lullie, May 22 1889, 165
6151 WOOD, Howard S, WARDER, Jennie S, Sept 2 1889, 165
6152 WILLIAR, Allen Q, KEMP, Nettie J, Sept 10 1889, 165
6153 WICKHAM, Robert, MCKENSIE, Annie, October 16 1889, 165
6154 WOODWARD, Elmer E, BOWES, Ida M, December 9 1889, 165
6155 WALLACE, George L, GITTINGER, Josephine, of Lewis, January 11 1890, 165
6156 WEBB, Lucian, QUINN, Ella C, April 10 1890, 165
6157 WEBSTER, Joseph, OGLE, Katie E, April 16 1890, 165
6158 WORTHINGTON, Glenn H, ALVEY, Julia, April 30 1890, 165
6159 WILSON, Christian T, of N J, SMITH, Georgetta, June 30 1890, 165
6160 WALKER, J C, BARTGIS, Clara V, of James, September 30 1890, 165
6161 WERTHEIMER, Myer, HANSHEW, Edith M, Oct 14 1890, 165
6162 WACHTER, Martin L, BELL, Florence, Oct 21 1890, 165
6163 WETZEL, Wm Grant, POOLE, Sarah Ellen, Dec 23 1890, 165
6164 WILLIAR, Alonza M, WILLHIDE, Jennie M, Dec 25 1890, 165
6165 WALKER, W A, DAY, Laura A, Dec 24 1890, 165
6166 YOUNG, David, JONES, Margaret, Septr 6 1821, 166
6167 YOUNG, Jacob, of Middletown, LEAB, Sophia, of Jacob, May 22 1827, 166
6168 ZIELER, Henry, of George, RINEY, Miss, June 3 1828, 166
6169 ZIMMERMAN, John, STRAEFFER, Catharine, Decr 23 1828, 166
6170 YOUNG, Henry, of And'w (Jun'r), HILTON, Susan G, of Clement, July 23 1830, 166
6171 YOUNG, Lewis, EMLEY, Rebecca (Mrs), "KLEIN', Septr 8 1831, 166
6172 ZECHER, Caspar, 2d wife, FINK, Margaret, Octr 28 1832, 166
6173 YOUNG, John, of Conrad C, KRUMBEIN, Margaret, of Jacob, May 30 1833, 166
6174 YEAKLE, Jacob, GALEZIO, Sarah, of Cha's, April 12 1835, 166
6175 YOUNG, Perry A, of And'w (Jun'r), HERGESHEIMER, Mary A, of Jos, June 18 1835, 166
6176 ZIEGLER, Henry L, DERTZBAUGH, Margaret, of Geo, March 27 1836, 166
6177 ZIMMERMAN, Samuel, GREENWALD, Susan, of Ch'n, Decr 27 1836, 166
6178 YOUNG, Jacob, of Middletown/2d wife, PERRY, Ann L (Mrs), of Wm/"Blind", Decr 7 1837, 166
6179 ZIMMERMAN, Michael, of Geo, WOOD, Hannah, Decr 19 1837, "sheriff", 166
6180 ZIMMERMAN, Joshua J, BEARD, Susan M, June 25 1838, 166
6181 ZEPP, Thomas, KOONTZ, Jane E, of John, March 12 1839, 166
6182 YANTIS, David F, BAKER, Balinda E, of Brooke, May 30 1839, 166
6183 ZIMMERMAN, Geo F, MCNAIR, Ann, June 3 1839, 166
6184 ZIMMERMAN, Geo J, of Christian, MEGAHLY, Mary Elizabeth Eichelberger, April 7 1840, 166
6185 ZIMMERMAN, Wm H (Rev), of Henry, CRONISE, Mary E, of John, April 9 1840, 166
6186 YOUNG, Alexander H, COST, Serena S, of Christian, Septr 1 1840, 166
6187 ZIMMERMAN, John, of J/2d wife, SCHATZ, Miss, Octr 1840, 166
6188 YOUNG, William, DERTZBAUGH, Mary, Decr 10 1840, 166
6189 ZIMMERMAN, Elias, GREENWALD, Maria, of Ch'n, Nov 30 1841, 166
6190 YOUNG, Allen M, DUVALL, Ann Rebecca, of Marsh M, Decr 1841, 166

6191 YOUNG, Tilghman H, DELAUTER, Mary, May 29 1842, 166
6192 ZANTZINGER, Wm C, FISCHER, Harriott Ann, of Wm, Jany 16 1844, 166
6193 YOUNG, Abraham, SAHM, Louisa (Mrs), widow of Christian, Augt 27 1844, 166
6194 YEAKLE, William, KLEIN, Mary L, of Caspar, Octr 19 1845, 166
6195 YULEE, David Levy (Hon), of Florida, WICKLIFFE, Annie C, of Cha's A, April 7 1846, 166
6196 ZUMPFSTEIN, Frederick, BRENGEL, Catharine, of Dan'l, Augt 3 1847, 166
6197 YOUNG, Wm B (Dr), COOKERLY, Rebecca, of Jacob, Decr 7 1847, 166
6198 YECK, Charles, SCHWEIGOEFFER, Louisa, Feby 9 1848, 166
6199 ZOLLICHOFFER, Wm (Dr), BURGESS, Jemima A (Mrs), May 9 1848, 166
6200 YOUNG, John, JACOBS, Mary E, Augt 18 1848, 166
6201 ZIEGLER, Jacob Henry, HARRISON, Rosanna, of Zeph, Nov 2 1848, 166
6202 ZIMMERMAN, John J, of J/3d wife, BAYER, Rebecca, of Jacob, Decr 25 1849, 166
6203 ZIMMERMAN, Samuel J, SCHELLMAN, Catharine E, of Jacob, April 2 1850, 166
6204 YOUNG, Henry, of And'w/2d wife, MARSH, Catharine, of Joel, Augt 18 1850, 166
6205 ZIMMERMAN, Horace J, ALBAUGH, Mary C, of Val A, Octr 24 1850, 166
6206 ZIMMERMAN, Josiah B, HOLTZ, Ellen B, April 22 1851, 166
6207 ZIMMERMAN, Geo F S, of John P, HERRING, Mary J C, of Hy/"HOUCK, Decr 17 1851, 166
6208 ZIMMERMAN, John A Jackson, FIRESTONE, Mary M, of Joshua, April 4 1852, 167
6209 YOUNG, Isaac, HARN, Catharine A R, Octr 26 1852, 167
6210 ZIMMERMAN, Jonathan T, SMITH, Mary C, Nov 18 1852, 167
6211 YOUNG, Daniel, SMELTZER, Sarah C, Decr 21 1852, 167
6212 ZIMMERMAN, Wm, REMSBURG, Henrietta, May 25 1853, 167
6213 ZIMMERMAN, David V, MILLER, Ann R, Octr 13 1853, 167
6214 ZIMMERMAN, Ephraim J, THOMAS, Maria E, May 18 1854, 167
6215 YOUNG, Reuben W, HERGESHEIMER, Caroline V, of Dan'l, Decr 13 1854, 167
6216 ZIMMERMAN, E Jacob, RAMSBURG, Rebecca, Jany 29 1856, 167
6217 ZIMMERMAN, J N, (*J Nicholas, Jun'r), MEASELL, Julia A S, (*MEASLE), March 6 1856, 167
6218 YOUNG, Henry, of And'w, Jun'r/3d wife, BUCKSTON, Columbia, "KOONTZ", June 26 1856, 167
6219 YOUNG, Oliver F, of Henry of Andr'w, Jun'r, GROVE, Harriett, of Reuben, Septr 17 1856, 167
6220 YANTIS, George B, GILBERT, Ann M, July 26 1857, 167
6221 ZIMMERMAN, G M, Dr, (*George M), EICHELBERGER, Susan M, Creagerstown, Nov 30 1857, 167
6222 YOUNG, Alexander H, DORSEY, Virginia Torrence, of Dr Lloyd, Octr 12 1858, 167
6223 ZEDRICKS, Henry, 2d wife, NEAL, Rebecca, of Sam'l/Colored friends, Decr 5 1860, 167
6224 ZIMMERMAN, Hiram, SEECRIST, Harriett Ann, Decr 13 1860, 167
6225 YINGER, George Caspar, "JUNGER"/1st wife, GRELE', Susan A, of Mich'l, July 24 1861, 167
6226 YEAKLE, Wm Henry, of Jacob, SHOOK, Louisa, Augt 29 1861, 167
6227 ZIMMERMAN, Simon A, DENMAN, Susan E, Jany 30 1862, 167
6228 YOUNG, McClintock (Jun'r), MOBBERLY, Louisa, of Dr Eldred W, June 19 1862, 167
6229 ZIEGLER, Wm H, of Henry L, HALLER, Mary Ellen, of David H, March 31 1863, 167
6230 YASTE, Cha's Milton, CRUM, Laura V, of Wm/"PHILLIPS", March 17 1864, 167
6231 ZIMMERMAN, Hiram Z, HOUCK, Anna M, March 17 1864, 167
6232 ZIMMERMAN, Lewis M, WACHTER, Mollie, April 4 1864, 167

6233 **YEAKLE**, James B, of Jacob, **BENNETT**, Annie M, of Lewis H, Octr 6 1864, 167
6234 **YOUNG**, Edward, of John, **KNAUFF**, Susan, of Jacob, Nov 23 1864, 167
6235 **ZIEGLER**, John George, **MCELFRESH**, Mary T, June 1 1865, 167
6236 **ZIMMERMAN**, John M, **CASTLE**, Annie M, "Jefferson", June 8 1865, 167
6237 **YOUNG**, John R, **BUCHFELTER**, Kate, of John, June 27 1865, 167
6238 **ZACHARIAS**, John F, **MILLER**, Ann R, of John W, Nov 5 1865, 167
6239 **ZIMMERMAN**, Wm W, of Michael, **CASTLE**, Kate C, of Dan'l of T, Octr 25 1866, 167
6240 **ZIMMERMAN**, John M, **KOHLENBERG**, Lydia E, of Adam, Nov 15 1866, 167
6241 **ZIMMERMAN**, Charles A, **VAN CAMP**, Orsena S R, of Dr Aaron, June 5 1867, 167
6242 **YINGER**, George Caspar, "JUNGER"/2d wife, **GERLICH**, Elizabeth, Octr 10 1867, 167
6243 **YINGER**, Lawrence, "JUNGER", **SWOPE**, Laura, of Warner, May 5 1868, 167
6244 **YELLOTT**, John J, of Balto Co, **TRAIL**, Mary V, of Edward, June 2 1868, 167
6245 **YOUNG**, John W, **SCHILDT**, Mary E, April 12 1870, 167
6246 **YOUNG**, Geo W, **ALBAUGH**, Mary E, of Allen, April 17 1870, 167
6247 **ZIMMERMAN**, Columbus A, **BISHOP**, Josephine E, Augt 25 1870, 167
6248 **ZIELER**, David M, of John D, **LEITER**, Emma M, of John, Feby 21 1872, 167
6249 **ZIMMERMAN**, Zachary E, of Edw, **BAER**, Ann C, of Peter, July 17 1872, 167
6250 **ZIMMERMAN**, Geo H, **FRAZIER**, Florence V, of D'd, Octr 23 1873, 168
6251 **YOUNG**, Warren D, of H'y, **REYNOLDS**, Cordelia C, Apl 12 1874, 168
6252 **YOUNG**, Daniel J, **ZIMMERMAN**, Sallie P, Septr 22 1874, 168
6253 **ZIMMERMAN**, Wm N, **WILLIARD**, Mary E, Septr 24 1874, 168
6254 **ZIMMERMAN**, Gideon M, **WILSON**, Matilda, Octr 15 1874, 168
6255 **ZIMMERMAN**, Elton G, **ZIMMERMAN**, Laura M, of Horace J, Feb 4 1875, 168
6256 **YAGER**, Jacob, **FUNK**, Mary E V, March 2 1875, 168
6257 **YINGER**, Charles, of Nich's, **MOBERLY**, Laura E, of L H, Aug 12 1875, 168
6258 **ZELLERS**, C Edward, **BAER**, Mary E, of Peter, Nov 11 1875, 168
6259 **YINGER**, Fred'k, **KILLIAN**, Julia A C, of Ph, Octr 26 1876, 168
6260 **ZIELER**, Charles E, of David, **LAMBERT**, Emma J, of Fred'k, June 14 1877, 168
6261 **ZOLLICKOFF**, David Keener, **THOMPSON**, Malinda, Octr 17 1877, 168
6262 **YOUNG**, Cha's Allen, of Allen M, **BARNES**, Alice V, Nov 29 1877, 168
6263 **ZELLER**, G Herman, **SCHECKELS**, Ella, Nov 27 1877, 168
6264 **YOUNG**, Charles, **HANSHEW**, Annie K, of Fritchie/(not listed as Miss), Jan 8th 1880, 168
6265 **ZEIGLER**, Charles C, **SHEARER**, Carrie C, (not listed as Miss), Feb 26th 1880, 168
6266 **YOAST**, George, of Balto, **KOCH**, Mary E, of Peter, June 7th 1881, 168
6267 **ZIMMERMAN**, Keller C, **FLEMMING**, Laura K, of J Alfred/(not listed as Miss), Nov 2d 1881, 168
6268 **YINGER**, John F, **ALBAUGH**, Sarah E, March 21st 1882, 168
6269 **YEAKLE**, Aquilla R, **HANE**, Fannie B, of Jacob D, Octr 31st 1882, 168
6270 **ZIMMERMAN**, Albert F, **CRONISE**, Nettie, of Joseph, Jan 10 1883, 168
6271 **ZIELER**, David M, 2d wife, **HAMBRIGHT**, Annie, April 5 1883, 168
6272 **ZIMMERMAN**, Wm H, **BURCH**, Jessie E, Dec 1st 1883, 168
6273 **YINGER**, Lewis H, **PHOEBUS**, Florence M, of Benj, Septr 17 1884, 168
6274 **ZORLCK**, Jac, of D, **HAUER**, Minnie F, of Luther, Nov 26 1884, 168
6275 **YOUNG**, Howard W, **HAMMOND**, Maggie, January 28 1886, 168
6276 **ZIMMERMAN**, Cephus H, **DERR**, Ella C, of Dav, November 10 1886, 168
6277 **ZITTLE**, Joseph A, **LEONARD**, Jennie V, February 15 1887, 168
6278 **YASTE**, Edward, **DIXON**, Minnie, December 8 1887, 168

6279 *ZACHARIAS*, Edward, of Rev Daniel, ***ELLIOTT***, Ethel, December 30 1887, 168
6280 *YOUNG*, O Harry, ***STORM***, Florence, April 24 1888, 168
6281 *ZUMBRUM*, G K, ***PERRY***, Ella, May 24 1888, 168
6282 *ZIMMERMAN*, Clayton, ***HIBEARY***, Bettie, August 30 1888, 168
6283 *ZIMMERMAN*, Wm M, ***WHALEY***, Georgie F, March 13 1889, 168
6284 *ZIMMERMAN*, B F, ***ROELKEY***, Minnie, April 30 1889, 168
6285 *ZOLLICKOFFER*, A Howard, ***MEHRING***, Ida H, February 4 1890, (Taneytown, 168
6286 *ZIMMERMAN*, David E, ***MOBERLY***, Nanie R, of C E, Oct 1 1890, 168
6287 *ZACHARIAS*, Horace C, ***WILCOXON***, Tempie E, Oct 22 1890, 168
6288 *YINGER*, Christian, ***SMITH***, Rosa E, Decr 25 1890, 168
6289 *ZIMMERMAN*, Harvey S, ***MARTIN***, Mazeppa, Dec 25 1890, 168

Addendums to Marriage Ledger

1) Loose sheet on family of Mrs. Christianna HUMMELL

Mrs Christianna HUMMELL had one son and two daughters-her son John Died Octr 9 1826 aged 50. -her daughter Mary married Jacob FIRESTONE and she died Decr 17 1832 aged 52. Mrs Catharine MARKEY (afterwards married Hy GARNHART) married David MARKEY (David J MARKEY is her son) Mrs HUMMELL after her husband's death married Philip FEAGA, the father of George FEAGA, Frederick FEAGA & Mrs Christianna SCHOLL.

2) List of Births on last page of ledger (page 236)

Born		Married
ER	Decr 23 1783	spring of 1802, January 9
Eliza	June 4 1803	May 29 1825
Elias	Septr 22 1804	Octr 11 1832
Peter	March 15 1808	
John	Nov 14 1809	May 8 1832
Jacob	Nov 18 1811	Nov 11 1834
Ann Rebecca	Decr 26 1813	March 21 1833
William Henry	Octr 2 1815	May 26 1842
Ann Mary	July 1 1817	May 17 1840
Catharine	Septr 25 1819	Decr 24 1840

    Copied July 23 1869

3) List of Deaths on last page of ledger (page 236)

        When they died

Mrs Rebecca RAMSBURG Died Feb 2 1863 aged 79-1-10
" Elias RAMSBURG Died July 14 1869 aged 64-9-22
" Eliza ENGELBRECHT Died December 30 1872 69-6-26
" John RAMSBURG Died December 22 1875 66-1-8
" Peter RAMSBURG Died January 6 1877 68-9-22
" Jacob RAMSBURG Died Decr 15 1877 66 years & 27 days
" William RAMSBURG June 3 1880 65 years & " Mary WALKER Died January 13 1882 62 years
   Jacob WALKER Died Dec 19 1892 6/79-6-29
" Ann Rebecca BRUNNER died May 14 1887 aged 73-4-18
   John Stephen RAMSBURG
" Drue H RAMSBURG

de MONTIJO
  Eugenia: 379
AAB
  John: 93
ABB
  Margaret: 355
ABBOTT
  Elenora V: 61
  Francis P (Dr): 67
  George A: 91 2132
  John: 11
  John H: 119
  Nettie: 2132
ABEL
  Jacob: 60
ABELE
  F W: 1067
ABELL
  A S: 696
  Helen M: 696
  Margart: 2136
ABRECHT
  Luther N: 53
ABSHESKY
  Theodore F: 106
ACHEY
  Charles F: 55
ACKERMAN
  Lizzie: 1773
  Sarah: 3513
  Serena Elizabeth: 1999
ACRES
  Jinette V: 1852
  Nettie V: 1852
ADAM
  Andreas: 125 132 3378
  Andrew J: 86
  Annie R: 3378
  Catharine C: 1738
  Henry: 45 125
  Mary E: 3836
  Val: 572
  William: 132
  Wm: 1738 3836
ADAMS
  Ab'm Tho's: 48
  Ada C: 2731
  Andreas: 5252
  Anna: 5252
  Anne E: 1110
  Elizabeth: 535
  Ellenora M: 885
  Emily: 5019
  Jennette: 4111
  John: 5019
  John Q: 123
  Margaret (Mrs): 5714
  Martha Jane: 46
  Mary (Mrs): 225
  No First Name Given: 1401 6122
  Phebe H: 1081
  R J: 2731
  Sarah A R: 4956
  Valentine: 1 37 48 885 4111 4956 5901
  Valletta: 5901
  Washington: 43
ADDISON
  John D: 70
ADELSBERGER
  Daniel G: 84
ADKINS
  Malinda: 4107
  Mary: 1568
  Matilda Ann: 5095
ADLESBERGER
  George A E: 2124
  Georgianna: 2124
ADLUM
  No First Name Given: 1152
  Sarah Ann: 5856
AGASSIZ
  Louis (Prof): 35
AGNEW
  Sophia: 2435
  Sydney (Mrs): 6074
AHALT
  Amanda C: 2479
  Carlton P: 92
  J Pearl: 5532
  Joshua: 89
  Matthias S: 95
  Sam'l: 2479
AHL
  Romma: 115
AKERS
  Jinette V: 1852
  Nettie V: 1852
ALAND
  Carlton E: 126
ALBACH
  Allen: 21
  Andrew H: 83
  Grafton: 22
  John W: 4
  Solomon: 22
  Valentine A: 8
ALBAUGH
  Ab's: 5974
  Abraham A: 42
  Adeline A: 2345
  Allen: 6246
  Ann Sophia: 5974
  Annie A: 2056
  Blanche: 2718
  Charles E: 90
  Christian T: 61 120
  Daniel (Elder): 102
  Daniel I: 74 74
  Edward: 96
  Edward S: 131
  Emma Jane: 2826
  Ephraim: 2046
  Frances M (Mrs): 5453
  Geo F: 118
  Henry Clay: 69
  James S: 136
  Jeremiah W: 40
  Joshua: 51
  L Jane: 4335
  Laura V: 2046
  Lewis: 3817
  Lewis A: 96
  Mary C: 6205
  Mary E: 3817 6246
  Maurice: 36
  Miss: 2345
  Sallie: 4307
  Sarah E: 6268
  Sarah Susan: 1689 2817
  Solo: 131
  Solomon: 2345 2826 4307
  Susie: 1131
  Val A: 51 69 2056 4335 6205
  William H: 3
  Wm H: 101
ALBERT
  Augustus: 44
  Charlotte E: 1680
  Isabella V: 4959
  Jacob: 3714
  John L: 5 1680 4959
  Margaret: 327
  Mary S: 3714
ALBRIGHT

Susan R: 4489
ALCOTT
  Mary A (Mrs): 5090
ALDRIDGE
  Singleton A: 133
ALEXANDER
  G W: 65
  Lucinda: 4306
  Matilda: 2188
ALLAND
  Frederick: 27
  Henry: 4048
  Mrs: 28
ALLARD
  Euphremia: 1022
ALLEMAN
  Munroe J (Rev): 30
ALLEN
  Balinda E (Mrs): 2323
  Charlotte: 2579
  Charlotte (Mrs): 3356
  Isaac Hollingsworth: 17
  Mervin (Rev): 13
  Sallie J: 3036
ALLEND
  Henry: 31
ALLISON
  John: 6
  Mary C: 5691
  Richard T: 39
ALNUTT
  J H: 5162
  Rebecca D: 5162
ALSTON
  David M: 140
ALTMAN
  Jacob G: 71
  John M: 111
  John Michael: 41
ALTPETER
  George: 129
ALVEY
  Julia: 6158
AMBROSE
  Henry W: 113
AMELUNG
  Emma: 2969
AMES
  Hon: 122
ANDERS
  Aaron: 34 5411

Caleb A: 63
Cha's A: 105
Charles C: 135
Charlotte: 4259
George J: 57
James W: 82
John M: 76
Joshua: 75
L R: 5411
Margaret: 76
Sarah Ann: 5907
Susan: 422
Thomas: 56
Upton: 50 68
Wm: 47
Wm H: 85 110
ANDERSON
  Aden: 2788 5244
  Ann: 5696
  Ann (Mrs): 5594
  Ann H: 3619
  Archer: 78
  Cecelia R: 2414
  Edward: 139
  Eugenia H (Mrs): 3277
  Geo W (Rev): 52
  J W: 19
  Jesse: 138
  Johanna: 3087
  Julius H: 117
  Kitty Ann: 1878
  Lavinia: 2788
  Mary A: 4498
  Minnie J: 1849
  No First Name Given: 23
  Oliver P: 103
  Rebecca S: 5244
  Tho's W: 66
  Wm Pickney: 32
  Wm R: 104
  Wm S: 25
ANDREW
  Louise: 5470
ANDREWS
  Solomon (Jun'r Dr): 54
ANGEL
  Mary R: 5455
  Wm H: 38
ANGELBERGER
  Ann S: 5087
  Clara A E: 5307
  David S: 29
  Geo: 1653

Geo D: 49
Harriette Antoinette: 6027
Jacob M: 33
John P: 64
Joseph: 14
Luther Henry: 59
Mary S: 2533
Philip S: 124
Rebecca: 1653
ANGELL
  David: 80
  Julia H: 4518
  Sophronia: 1920
ANGEVINE
  Wm H: 108
ANKNEY
  Eliza: 4948
ANNACKER
  Catharine: 4989
ANNAN
  Andrew A: 137
  Jane: 1921
  Robert L (Dr): 121
ANSPACH
  Fred'k R: 24
  Fred'k R (Rev): 81
APP
  Conrad: 28
APPEL
  Carrie C: 6091
APPLER
  Arthur M: 79
APPLETON
  Mariania L: 5915
ARAGO
  Cha's Gabriel: 94
ARBUCKLE
  Mary: 776
ARCHBALD
  Elizabeth (Mrs): 1148
ARMBRUSTER
  Annie E: 4636
ARMITAGE
  Abigail L: 3587
ARMOUR
  Charles Lee: 88
  Ja's U: 3244
  James E U: 20
  James U: 2 10
  Jane M: 3244
  Jas U: 1938

Julia A: 1938
ARMPRISLER
Louisa: 2316
ARMSTRONG
Archibald: 77
Belle H: 6059
Henrietta J: 4331
Wm (Dr): 4331
Wm (Rev): 7
ARNOLD
Annie E: 1027
Catharine (Mrs): 1508
Ja's Madison: 1027
James M: 100
James Madison: 12
Sophia: 1894
ARTHUR
Catharine E: 1620
S A McNair: 72
ARTZ
Christian Burr: 26
Edwin: 99
ASCHBACH
Aquilla: 109
ASCHEMEIER
William: 62
ASHBAUGH
John: 608 5630
Margaret G: 5630
Mary J: 608
Sam'l D: 116
Wm H: 73
ASHBURY
Prudence: 205
ASHENHUST
John J: 128
ASHERMAN
David: 97
Mary M: 479
Tilghman: 87
ASHLEY
Elizabeth (Mrs): 908
ASPER
Elizabeth: 3472
ATHERTON
Benjamin: 107
ATKINS
Polly: 1164
ATKINSON
Harriott L: 2023
J Edward (Dr): 114

ATLEE
Abe J: 112
ATTICK
Albert S: 134
ATTIG
Catharine: 4908
John: 46
Philip: 15
ATWATER
Dorrence: 130
AUBEL
Catharine: 1643 5741
AUBERT
Albert H: 58
Ann Rebecca: 2293
Jacob: 9 1024 2293
Louisa: 1024
AUL
Jacob: 16
AULD
Amy Y: 2082
AYRES
Rebecca D H: 4405
B___ING
Mary C: 1842
BA??ER
Julia C: 751
BABCOCK
Hiram: 619
BABEL
Ch'n: 3406
Christian: 1720
George Andrew: 638
J Christian: 608
Maggie E: 1783
Margaret Caroline: 1720
Mary E: 3406
BACHARACH
N E: 675
BACHELOR
Martha J: 5625
BACHMAN
Charlotte: 1558
George: 152
Henry C (Rev): 499
John W: 285
BACON
Amelia A: 1896
Ann: 165
BADEN
Eliza Ann: 257

BADGER
Georgia C: 4706
BAER
Ann C: 6249
Ann E: 828
Caroline: 3320
Catharine (Mrs): 4271
Cha's J (Dr): 299
Charlotte (Mrs): 1511
Debbie Ridgely: 4506
Elizabeth Schellman: 492
Elizabeth W D: 5586
Emma: 1140
Ezra: 163
Fannie: 1006
George: 291
George W: 566
Henry: 392 514
Jacob (Dr): 5586
James J: 585
John: 154 163 1006 3320 4271
John R: 578
Juliann: 1534
Kate: 2624
Lydia E: 5490
M S (Dr): 4506
Margaret: 2199
Mary: 5200
Mary E: 2535 6258
Mich'l: 492 828
Mich'l T (Dr): 585
Michael: 1511
Mollie L: 4166
No First Name Given: 3477
Peter: 6249 6258
Rachel Ann: 1767
Sallie: 4185
Sarah A (Mrs): 183
William H: 659
Wm: 2199
BAETZHOTZ
John: 155
BAGER
Sam'l: 4778
Samuel B: 147
BAILE
Abner: 4129
Ann: 4129
David C: 434
Jesse: 640
Kitty Ann: 1289
M Ellen: 640

BAILEY
- Otho: 268
- Sarah: 1212

BAKER
- A H: 593
- Aaron: 1040
- Amanda S: 2444
- Ann Rebecca: 4042
- Balinda E: 6182
- Benjamin E: 697
- Brooke: 6182
- Camillus S: 336
- Camillus W: 501
- Caroline E: 4676
- Carrie: 3711
- Catharine: 920 2886 5488
- Cha's H: 4976
- Cha's J: 733
- Clementine A: 2523
- D'l: 5693
- Edw: 2523
- Edward: 259 660
- Elizabeth: 3781
- Emily Cassin: 4303
- Emma: 4976
- Emma J (Mrs): 579
- Ephraim: 387
- Ezra: 160 431
- Fannie J: 4661
- Francis M (Rev): 331
- Fred'k: 660
- Geo W: 5638
- H'y: 4661
- Harrison: 512
- Henry: 231
- Henry W: 705
- Jacob: 438
- James T: 639
- John: 210 686
- John P: 515
- Joseph D: 685 763
- Joseph G: 433
- Julia E: 438
- Katie: 2130
- Lizzie A (Mrs): 592
- Lucretia: 1838
- Maggie E: 1040
- Mary A (Mrs): 1404
- Mary S: 2819
- Nathan: 535
- Nathan L: 524
- No First Name Given: 3711
- R B: 485
- Sarah A: 4675
- Sarah C: 5693
- Sarah Jane: 2486
- Serepta: 5960
- Serepta A: 4877
- Susan C: 2600
- Virginia: 5638
- Washington: 697
- Wm B: 270
- Wm Harrison (Dr): 245

BALCH
- Catharine: 864
- L P W (Sen'r): 864
- Lewis P W: 4904
- Lewis P W (Rev): 228 349
- Thomas: 373
- Virginia: 4904

BALDERSON
- Drusilla: 3632
- John: 308 3599 3632
- Mary Annie: 3599
- No First Name Given: 4158

BALDWIN
- A M: 3611
- Ann: 3611
- Cornelia: 5139
- Martha E: 3786

BALEY
- Eliza: 2233
- Susan: 1254

BALL
- Caroline E: 1591
- Cha's N: 563
- John: 755
- Owen D: 262
- William: 473

BALLINGER
- Herrman: 400

BALOF
- Wilhelmina: 6089

BALTZELL
- Alice: 3678
- Ann Polly: 4205
- Catharine: 2877
- Clara L: 306
- Eliza A: 3638
- Ellen: 1560
- Fannie: 3107
- Francis M: 3464
- Hezekiah: 426
- James M: 361
- John: 153
- John (Dr): 146 1560 3107 3638 3678
- John Jacob: 4205
- Josephine: 3164
- Juliann: 475
- Lucretia Josephine: 5588
- Robert C: 581
- Rosa: 2856
- Sarah A: 2384
- Tho's: 306 5588
- Virginia C: 3858
- Virginia J: 3861
- Wesley: 488
- Wm: 2856
- Wm H: 3464
- Wm H (Dr): 404 3164

BALTZLEY
- Christana: 2557

BANDELL
- Geo W: 562

BANNISTER
- R Harry: 622

BANTZ
- A Sydney: 369
- Catharine A S: 1260
- Clarence: 650
- Daniel Z: 761
- Edward (Dr): 330
- Elizabeth Maria: 1507
- Eugene H: 590
- Fannie: 5756
- Fannie M: 2542
- Gideon: 590 629 1260 1287
- Gideon (Junior): 203
- Harry H: 621
- Julia Ada: 1287
- Mollie: 1091
- Nimrod: 177 5756
- No First Name Given: 718 1786
- Peter Sowers: 519 558
- Sophia Meadishin: 5009
- Theodora: 3407
- Theodore Marion: 629
- Theodore S: 274
- William S: 250
- Wm: 761
- Wm S: 386 641 3407
- Wm T: 621

BARBER
- Cha's: 493
- Llyod H: 724

BARCLAY

R G (Dr): 489
BARGEE
  Caroline C: 725
  Miles: 283
BARIER
  Saddie E: 1807
BARKER
  Samuel: 193
BARNES
  Alice: 678
  Alice V: 6262
  Anna Eliza: 3654
  John: 662
  John R: 606
  Mary C: 3906
  Miss: 3818
  Rachel: 3315
  Samuel T: 602
  Tho's: 602 678
BARNETT
  Annie E: 621
BARNEY
  Ai: 6042
  Annie: 6042
  Jerome A: 598
BARNHART
  Sarah: 4840
  Sarah Jane (Mrs): 68
BARNITZ
  Sarah R: 2291
BARNUM
  Phineas Taylor: 658
BARON
  Isabella: 188
BARRAUD
  Courtney C: 2427
BARRETT
  E (Mrs): 3212
  Ellen: 2308
BARRETTE
  Exile: 2740
BARRICK
  Ann M E: 4452
  Catharine: 1188
  Catharine E: 5074
  Cha's J: 673
  Christian: 460
  Clarissa: 2277
  Ella A: 2580
  Ezra: 6048
  Ezra E: 239

  Fred'k: 860
  Geo: 4889
  Geo P: 298
  George D: 762
  John C: 665
  John W: 238 318
  Joseph: 393
  Josiah: 453
  Juliann: 860
  Laura R: 6048
  Lavinia E: 2606
  Mary: 4889
  Mary J: 3349
  Mary Jane: 4947 5632
  Matilda S: 1048
  Presley Jones: 557
  Rand J: 2606
  Rebecca: 4395
  Samuel: 145
  Sue C: 5242
  Susan M: 1692
  Theodore: 475
  Wm T: 484
BARTELLE
  Mary: 4147
BARTGIS
  Anna R: 1433
  Clara V: 6160
  Dewitt Clinton: 374
  Doc: 699
  Eliza: 791
  Fanny E: 5513
  Geo W L: 606
  Geo Washington Lafay: 300
  Hiram: 338 5513
  Ja's: 1411
  James: 351 3442
  James W: 706
  John A: 710
  John M: 303
  Maggie E: 606
  Margaret: 4910
  Martin L: 401
  Mary E: 4496
  Mathias E: 699
  Matt E: 4496
  Matthias E: 4910
  Nannie: 3442
  Nellie J: 1411
BARTGOS
  James: 6160
BARTH
  Julia Ann: 4277

BARTHELOW
  Wm D: 751
BARTHMANN
  Valentine: 312
BARTHOLOW
  Ann: 5046
  J Presley: 413
  John: 375
  Marshall A: 690
  Mary A: 971
  Miss: 5046
  Wm H: 671
BARTIS
  Frederick Trenck: 292
BARTLETT
  Frances Amelia: 4112
BARTON
  Anna M: 5688
  John: 635
BASCH
  Elizabeth: 2154
BASCOM
  Henry B (Rev DD): 226
BASFORD
  Elizabeth: 470
  George: 554
  J Henry: 411
  Jacob: 548
  Susan: 5631
BAST
  Elias: 217
  Henry: 4797
  Isaac: 246 624
  Israel: 234 520
  John H: 570
  Samuel L: 624
  Susan: 4797
BATERY
  Annie: 3183
BATSON
  Daniel: 759
  Ella C: 1832
  Jane: 4977
  John B: 384
BAUER
  John G: 506
BAUERLEIN
  John Geo: 267
BAUFELTER
  George: 634
  Sallie R: 688

BAUGHER
- Amanda: 1563
- Ann E: 501
- Charles H: 693
- Daniel B: 276
- Elizabeth (Mrs): 4039
- Isaac: 324 415 501 835 1563 5000
- John B: 4039
- John David: 487
- John F: 415
- Lizzie: 592
- Louisa: 835
- Lydia: 4778
- Oscar: 324
- Sevilla: 1329
- Susanna (Mrs): 1609
- Virginia: 5000

BAUGHMAN
- Corrinne F: 1425
- John W: 1425
- L Victor (Col): 696

BAUMAN
- Frederick: 447
- George: 289
- George W: 743

BAUMANN
- Anna B: 2994
- Margaret S: 5055

BAUMGARDNER
- Carrie V: 3215
- Cha's: 3215
- Ella: 5483
- Geo T: 736
- H'y: 3441
- Ida A M: 1797
- Jno: 736
- Lillie K: 3443
- Nora D: 3441

BAUMGARTNER
- Elizabeth: 1764
- Henry: 409

BAUMGERTNER
- Barbara A: 3347
- Charles: 594
- John: 534
- Tho's: 3347

BAUSMAN
- Eliza: 4408
- Elizabeth (Mrs): 4726

BAY
- Fannie: 2613

BAYER
- Annie: 1649
- Elizabeth C (Mrs): 3832
- Francis: 457
- Henry: 222
- Jacob: 6202
- Jacob M: 423
- John H F: 707
- Lewis: 689
- Maria: 5613
- No First Name Given: 4064
- Rebecca: 5181 6202
- Tho's: 423 5181 5613
- Thomas: 178

BAYLEY
- George W: 282

BAYLY
- Catharine: 5560
- F W: 694
- John: 5560

BEACH
- Philip S: 559

BEACHT
- Joseph F: 728

BEAHEY
- John: 201

BEAKLEY
- Susan A: 1328

BEALE
- Wm T: 749

BEALL
- Amelia A: 2100
- Elisha: 184 4764
- Eliza: 1933
- Enoch: 227
- Evan F: 486
- Frances: 2901
- Geo W: 184
- Harriott M: 1974
- Henrietta: 3697 4764
- James B: 202
- Jane M A: 4216
- John H: 322
- Lucinda: 838
- Martha M: 2267
- Mary Alice: 4660
- Mary E: 394
- Nannie: 4669
- No First Name Given: 2562 3825
- Octavia E: 5362
- Sarah Eleanor P: 4449
- Wm M: 2267 2901 4216
- Wm T: 254

BEAMER
- Nelson: 655

BEAN
- Samuel: 607

BEAR
- Cha's J (Dr): 720
- Emma L: 1140

BEARD
- John W: 451
- Mary Ann: 1552
- Sarah: 1862
- Sarah V: 636
- Solomon: 230
- Susan M: 6180

BEATTY
- Afrebee Philip: 218
- Alex'r P: 683
- Charlotte (Mrs): 4742
- Cornelia Ann: 4858
- Elie: 272
- John Mich'l: 4742
- Joseph E (Dr): 555
- Nettie: 2135
- Wm H: 538

BEAUFORT
- Fannie: 3149

BEAVANS
- Mary Ann: 4007

BEAVERS
- Julia A: 2993

BECHENBAUGH
- Geo: 601
- John M (Dr): 601

BECHT
- Wm H: 360

BECHTEL
- Hannah: 851
- J: 290
- John: 290
- Miss: 851
- Samuel: 370

BECHTOLL
- Harvey: 491

BECK
- Adam: 410
- Agnes: 410
- Cath Ann (Mrs): 1691
- Edward: 260
- Emma: 2131
- Harriett E: 484

Ida E: 1430
James M: 568
John: 328
John J: 345 1691 5661
Laura V: 3121
Mary Ann (Mrs): 4787
Mary V: 5661
Nicholas: 450
Osborn: 339
BECKENBACH
Maria: 2891
Mary A: 2958
Rebecca: 3045
Sophia: 149
BECKENBAUGH
Geo: 3322
George (Sen'r): 546
George W: 497
Isabella C: 3322
Wm W: 313
BECKER
Christiana: 1758
Christianna: 5943
George: 389
Henry: 657
John: 565
Lewis: 1758
Louis P: 657
Louisa Jane: 5234
Mary: 4524 5961
BECKETT
Annie B: 3866
BECKLEY
Constantine F: 609
Gabriel: 609
BECKLIE
Gabriel: 293
BECKWITH
Catharine: 4061
Elizabeth: 3096
Mary: 1467
BECROFT
John L: 525
BEDDINGER
John A: 422
BEDFORD
Mary E: 873
BEDHEIMER
George: 715
BEDINGER
Susan Peyton: 1487
BEEBE

Charles: 586
BEELER
Henry S: 721
Joseph: 6026
Mary E: 6026
BEESON
Drue H: 4555
BEGGETT
Elizabeth: 1613
BEHRENS
Augusta: 4080
BEIDEL
Andrew: 394
Christopher: 354
BELKNAP
Wm W (Hon): 651
BELL
Ann: 2917
Caroline (Mrs): 2382
Catharine: 3249
Emanuel: 470
Florence: 6162
H: 435
Herbert: 616
John: 164
Laura: 2704
Laura V: 2543
Mary E: 3689
Sarah Catharine: 437
Tho's: 307
Thomas: 252
BELLEAU
Margaret W (Mrs): 4084
BELMONT
August: 346
BELT
Alfred M (Dr): 709
Ellen C: 4682
J Lawrence: 764
Loretto: 1723
Maggie E: 3732
Mary E: 5377
T H (Jun'r): 617
T Hanson: 344
BENDER
Edward: 377
Elizabeth J: 107
Emily Clagett: 4571
Francis T: 661
Henry: 5338
Jacob: 382
John: 107 144 325 377 382

398 4571
John H: 341
Lizzie: 5338
Mary Catharine: 325
BENEDICT
Margaret: 3596
BENEMAN
Alice G: 4691
BENNER
Francis: 618
Miss: 3550
BENNETT
Ann Elizabeth: 844
Ann Virginia: 5622
Anne M: 2715
Annie M: 6233
C M: 3129
Daniel: 737
David: 2337
David T: 405
Eleanora: 2593
Elizabeth S: 5292
Emma J: 1400
Frank: 737
Hannah: 2405
John: 2715
John H: 541
Joseph S: 335
Lewis: 3437
Lewis H: 249 541 682 1400 6233
Lewis T: 682
Lydia A M: 2337
Maggie S: 3437
Margaret A: 5971
Mary Ellen: 4721
Mary M: 1362
Nettie J: 716
No First Name Given: 2125
Robert: 402
Tilghman: 1362 2405
Tilghman B: 221
Wash A: 5971
BENSON
Ann: 180
Catharine: 4406
BENTLINGER
Adam T: 644
Catharine R: 1756
Fred'k: 1756
Frederick: 223
BENTZ
Anna M: 3034

Catharine: 2168
Christianna: 4864
Dan'l: 305 3034
Daniel: 196 445 754
Elizabeth: 2148 2786
Ezra: 205
Geo: 205 1922 2148
Geo Wm Wallace: 708
George W: 437
Harriott: 1922
Henry: 367
Horatio Wm: 315
Jacob: 2168 2208 3524
Jacob M: 321
John: 159 2786
Lawrence: 348
Lewis: 576
Louisa: 2208
Mary Elizabeth (Mrs): 305
Susan: 3524
Wm: 321 367 437 445 4864

BERGAN
Joshua: 713

BERGEN
Louis: 719

BERGER
Francis A: 325
Henry: 233
John W: 448
Maria: 4464
Philip: 233 279

BERKLEY
Nancy (Mrs): 4144

BERNARD
Mary: 892
Rob't: 892

BERNHARDT
Margaretta: 1540

BERNHART
Catharine: 210

BERRY
John: 150
Nancy: 4733

BERTERMAN
John: 425

BESANT
Fannie R: 5469
Jas H: 5469

BEST
Cha's E T: 739
George W: 504
Henry L: 403

John F: 197
John T: 553
Lydia E: 2693
Nathaniel L: 552
Wm H: 529

BETES
Miss: 2202

BETSON
Samuel P: 556

BETTS
Ida: 2571
Samuel C: 580

BETTY
Nettie: 2135

BETZEN
Margaret C: 1701

BEVAN
Joseph: 216

BIBBY
James Monroe: 427

BICKHARD
Susie M: 3204

BIECHLEY
Conrad: 2034
Mary: 2034

BIELFELD
Salome: 656

BIER
Jacob: 3583
Sophia B: 3583

BIGGS
Billy: 263
Catharine: 3231
Elisha H: 536 649
Elizabeth: 4220
Elizabeth M: 2846
Frederick: 832
Ida Mary: 5491
James: 677
James M: 263
Joshua: 5491
Julia Ann: 5174
Rebecca: 2890
Susan: 832 4217
William: 148
Wm: 2890 3231 4217 4220

BIGHAM
Mary E: 5950

BILLINGSLEA
James L (Dr): 577

BILLY

John C: 542

BING
Ellen: 4092

BINGER
Catharine: 505
Catherine (overwritt: 2950

BINGHAM
Daniel H: 165

BINNIX
Tho's H: 243

BINSWANGER
Fanny: 4480

BIRCH
Joseph H: 615

BIRCKHEAD
Jane Allen: 6077

BIRDWELL
Catharine P: 1610

BIRELY
Caroline: 1500
Charles S: 723
Charlotte C: 2205
Elizabeth: 4726
Ettie R: 1123
Fannie: 1431
Fred'k: 3474
Geo K: 1431
George Krebs: 474
J Wm: 640 646
John Wm: 280
Lizzie: 3196
Margaret: 4430
Maria: 3650
Mary E: 4860
Mary Rebecca: 515 3709
No First Name Given: 4408
Philip Henry Clay: 640
Rebecca: 4409
Sophia: 3474
Valentine: 311
William: 4430
Wm: 1500 2205 4860
Wm C: 646
Wm F: 760

BIRNIE
Clotworthy (Jun'r): 170

BISCH
Marie: 1410
Victor (Col): 1410

BISER
Amanda C: 5235
Ann R: 5299

Catharine: 3570 3733
Clarence S: 741
Daniel G: 472
David: 513
Elizabeth: 6014
G S: 758
Geo C: 3865
James P: 589
John G: 247
John W: 530
Laura: 5897
Mary E: 5651
Mary G: 3865
Thaddeus: 758
Tilghman (Dr): 173
Wm Henry: 583

BISHOP
Anna (Madam): 5122
Edwin: 352
Eve: 4888
Joseph: 712
Josephine E: 6247
Mark: 410
Phebe A: 4586
Sophia E: 4123

BITTEL
Elizabeth: 1955
Tho's F: 477

BITTLE
D H (Rev): 3885
D'd F (Rev): 4356
Elmer: 732
Julia F: 4356
S L (Mrs): 3885
Wm Metzger: 522

BITZENBERGER
Ann Elzab: 2446
Juliann: 3296
Mary Ann: 5822

BIXLER
Angelina A: 4010
Wm Tell: 306

BIZER
Martha V: 3203

BLACK
Cha's G: 757
Geo W Z (Col): 648
Jerry S: 5100
Mary J: 1224
Rebeka: 5100

BLACKBURN
Richard S: 198

BLACKISTON
Jennie: 650

BLACKSTONE
B H: 738
Benjamin C: 189
Benjamin H: 419
Wm C: 738

BLADEN
James H: 747

BLAGROVE
Harriett (Mrs): 5940

BLAIR
Edmonia: 1435
John: 187

BLAKE
Nellie P: 4368
William: 334

BLAND
I H: 604

BLANDY
Charles G: 722

BLANEY
Cha's E: 496

BLANK
Ellen: 5428
John H: 429

BLAUDEN
James H: 747

BLENDEN
Louisea: 3195

BLESSING
Ab'm: 1576
Abraham (Jun'r): 172
Elizabeth E: 2524
Francis T: 412
George W: 572
Loretto A: 517
Lucinda C: 5958
Matilda G: 6127
Parker George: 399
Penelope A M: 1576
S V: 584
Susan: 5976
Wm H: 550

BLISS
Betty "TAYLOR" (Mrs): 1297
Wm W S (Col): 333

BLOCHER
John: 220

BLUEJACKET
Cha's: 1990
Sallie: 1990

BLUEMENAUER
Catharine: 2400

BLUME
Michael: 257

BLUMENAUER
Caroline: 2491
Cath (Mrs): 2794
Catharine: 3246
Geo: 3246
Geo W: 688
George: 258 310 327
Henry: 355 464 2794
John: 731
John N: 680
Michael: 288 310
Michael (Sen'r): 505
Nicholas: 269
Nicholas J: 727

BLUMENAUR
Daniel: 742

BLUMENBERG
Katie: 3428

BLUNT
Wm W: 507

BO__IE
Emily P: 4708

BOARDWELL
Daniel B: 540

BOBST
Alice M: 3390
Clementine A: 4179
Elizabeth: 4502
Henrietta: 1968
Joshua D: 390
Mahala Ann: 3293
Rowanna: 93
Sarah A: 347
William: 326
William M: 714

BOCK
Anna: 4436

BODISCE
Alexander de: 242

BOETLER
Edward M: 730

BOGAN
J Nich Andrew (Dr): 1465
Louise: 6016

BOGEN
Caroline: 1465

BOGGERT
　Harvey: 455
BOGGS
　Sarah Ann: 2298
BOGUE
　John J: 378
BOHN
　Annie E: 3977
　Daniel: 533
BOLASKI
　Catharine: 4968
BOLASKY
　Susan (Mrs): 1520
BOLEY
　Annie: 1649
BOLEY'
　Elizabeth: 4266
　Jacob: 4266
BOLINGER
　Werner: 320
BOLLEBACHER
　Peter: 211
BOLLENBACHER
　Julia: 4853
BOLLER
　Henry A: 362
BOLUND
　Daniel: 266
BONAPART
　Cha's Joseph: 669
　Jerome Napoleon (Col): 632
BONAPARTE
　Louis Napoleon 3d: 379
BOND
　Isaac: 452
　John R: 407
BONINE
　Tho's W: 439
BONN
　Ann Eliza: 5020
　Frederick (Rev): 571
BOOGER
　Susan: 2456
BOOGHER
　Elizabeth A: 224
BOON
　Ann: 3001
　Martha R: 2328
BOONE
　Alexius: 774
　Benedict: 344
　Caroline: 774
　Clara: 344
　Edward: 301
　H Jerningham (Dr): 314
　Tho's J: 224
BOOTH
　Nathaniel: 287
BOPST
　Bine: 753
　Byron: 753
　Fannie May: 3880
　John: 701
　John H: 543
　Milton B: 591
BORCHER
　Elizabeth: 1598 4064
　Miss Elizabeth: 1598
BORDER
　Sallie: 3413
BORGER
　William: 388
BORING
　Sarah: 4028
BOSELL
　Catharine: 4386
BOSLEY
　Emma: 2060
BOSSLER
　David (Rev): 212
BOSTEAN
　Solomon: 253
BOSTIAN
　Sophia: 5205
BOSTICK
　Georgianna: 5268
BOSTON
　Jacob: 200
BOSWELL
　Priscilla: 2897
BOTELER
　Alice V (Mrs): 568
　Henry: 181 297
　Jefferson O: 442 568
　M W: 2026
BOTHEIMER
　Ferdinand: 240
BOTTLEMAY
　Vernon: 458
BOUIC
　Rufus A: 654
BOULDIN
　William J (Jr): 704
BOULIGNY
　J E (Hon): 490
BOUST
　Lewis C: 717
BOWEN
　James E: 561
BOWER
　Wm D: 726
BOWERS
　Alfred B: 441
　Allen T: 424
　Cora E: 2663
　Dan'l: 3274 4091 5654
　Daniel: 408
　H A (Mrs): 651
　John: 444
　Margaret: 3274 4499
　Mary Jane: 4091
　Reuben G: 516
　Wm D: 414
　Wm H: 478
　Wm W (Rev): 449
BOWERSOX
　Mattie: 1387
BOWES
　Grace E: 3467
　Harry W: 726
　Ida M: 6154
　J'm: 2663
BOWIE
　Catharine: 1201
　Washington: 599
BOWLING
　Anna: 959
BOWLUS
　Catharine: 3241
　David: 149 645
　Edw (Dr): 645
　George: 180
　Josiah: 537
　Mary F: 6064
　Samuel: 208
　Sephen R: 6064
BOWMAN
　Emeline: 4278
　Henrietta: 4206
　Jacob: 4206
　Tho's (Rev): 256
BOWSE
　Almira J: 3969

BOYD
  A McKendree: 603
  Andrew: 271 1028
  Asbury McKendree: 438
  Caroline Virginia: 3756
  Charles (Doctr): 363
  David: 262 363 438 603 664 664 2760 3756
  Elizabeth: 262
  John J: 316
  Mary: 2760
  Mary E: 1028
  No First Name Given: 532 2852
  Wilson Rowan: 483
BOYER
  Alice E: 3116
  Cordelia Jane: 5628
  Elizabeth: 1598
  Emma V: 1453
  Frances Hanna: 4846
  Jesse J: 511
  Margaret: 1983
  Mary: 5117
  Oliver: 463
  Peter: 5628
  Samuel L: 672
  Sarah: 1636
  Susan L: 4681
  Sydney Jane: 1316
  Tho's S: 765
BOYLE
  James: 286
BRACE
  Wm D: 750
BRADBURN
  Kate E: 1068
BRADENBERG
  Matthias: 517
BRADLEY
  Wm H: 744
BRADSHAW
  Wm H: 539
BRADY
  Charles G: 722
  David F S: 509
  George C: 443
BRAGONIER
  Alf: 4381
  Carrie M: 4381
  Charles H: 703
BRAIN
  Ann Rebecca: 5269
  John: 6022
  Mary C: 6022
BRANDENBURG
  Charlotte: 3335
  James A: 462
  Joel: 436
  John N: 304
  Lucinda C: 3713
  Lydia: 2512
  Mary C: 5977
  Mary E: 2707
  Sarah Ann: 3740
BRANDT
  Henry: 264
  Sophia: 4476
BRANE
  George: 232
  Henry: 229
BRANSON
  Margaret: 3989
  Sophia: 3512
BRANT
  Elizabeth (Mrs): 1771
BRASHEAR
  Ann: 5791
  Belt (Dr): 1149
  Bettie: 1264
  Caroline R: 918
  Mary C: 2803
  Rebecca: 4474
  S L: 2800
  S Louisa: 2800
  Sarah: 1149
  Tho's (Col): 1264
  Tho's C: 2803
  Thomas: 179
BRASHEARS
  Bettie: 3767
  Tho's: 3767
BRAUN
  Henry: 2156
  Mary: 2156
BRAWNER
  Joseph: 366
BREADY
  C Edward: 605
  Elizabeth A: 944
  Geo: 944 5669
  Mary Jane: 5669
BREATON
  Lucretia M: 3915
BRECKINRIDGE
  Robert J (Rev): 317
  Wm C P: 465
BREEDY
  George: 191
  Polly: 5794
BREIDTHAUPT
  Frederick: 277
BREITENBACH
  Mary: 5805
BREITHEIMER
  Mary Augusta: 5359
BREITNER
  Julia: 5305
BREMMERMAN
  Amelia E: 5599
BRENDEL
  Ann Amelia: 1980
  Cha's H: 596
  Franklin A: 630
  H'y G: 630
  Henry G: 1980
BRENEISEN
  Mary: 3493
BRENGEL
  Caroline: 2893 4150
  Catharine: 6196
  Catharine E: 6035
  Dan'l: 6196
  Daniel (Sen'r): 219
  Elizabeth: 248
  J Nicholas: 275
  Jacob: 2893
  Nich's: 6035
  Nicholus: 4150
BRENGLE
  Alfred F: 186 3011 3695
  Ann Maria: 1513
  Ann R: 1913
  Annie V: 3457
  Barbara (Mrs): 383
  Catharine: 1476
  Ch'n: 2428 2889
  Cha's: 183
  Cha's B: 687
  Christ'n: 183
  Christian: 545
  Christian (Jun'r): 329
  Christian (Sen'r): 213
  Daniel: 199
  Debbie: 5349
  E Jane: 5664

E Margaret: 4766
Edward A: 633
Eliza (Mrs): 2889
Elizabeth C: 3023
Ezra: 4658
Ezra M: 1753 5349
Fannie M: 1817
Francis: 215
Geo L: 244
George M: 610
Henrietta E: 3011
Jacob: 143 186 343 545 2889
James S: 567
John: 4766
John (Capt): 171 209
John (Capt'n): 199 1513
John W: 461
Laura: 4658
Laura V: 4654
Law J: 567 5003 5664
Lawrence J: 171 209 3023
Lewis A: 204
Lewis A (Junior): 508
Louisa: 186
Lydia A E: 4467
M Lizzie: 1753
Margaret: 4746
Mary: 4400
Mary Amelia: 3695
Mary C: 2226
Mary E: 5424
Mary Susan: 2428
Matilda: 4752
Nich: 186
Nich's: 4746
Nicholas: 521 1476 2791 4400
Olevia: 5003
Peter: 204 215 1913 2226 4752
Rachel E: 2791
Rosa M: 3954
Sam: 1817
Sam T: 4654
Sam'l T: 5424
Sam'l Tho's: 385
Wm: 143 343
Wm H: 329
Wm H (Jun'r): 668

BRENNEMAN
Allie G: 4691
Anna M: 4178
Ella M: 4372

Joh: 4691

BRENNER
Applonia: 676
Henrietta: 4154
Mary J: 132
William: 175
Wm: 151 4154

BRENT
R W H (Rev): 236

BRETTELL
J Cha's (Rev): 295

BREWER
Eliza Jane: 432
Ellen: 2844
Jacob Newton: 432
John H C: 494
Lucretia: 4276

BRIDGES
M Julia: 5372
Wm James: 532

BRIE
Geo: 5669
Mary Jane: 5669
No First Name Given: 944

BRIEN
Isabel Ann: 3300
John McPerson: 169
John McPherson: 188
Luke Tierman: 323
Rob't C: 323
Robert Coleman: 162
Wm C: 194

BRIGHTLY
Marcy: 141

BRIGHTWELL
Martha: 1741
Sarah E: 3461

BRINING
Amelia G: 4139
Kate M: 2498

BRINKMAN
Margaret (Mrs): 5129

BRISCOE
Andrew Jackson: 294
Ellen M: 5914
James: 4421
Lucy B: 5910
Susan B D: 4421

BRISH
David: 329
Harriott A R: 2381
Henry C: 156

John H: 503
John M: 158 2381
Mary: 329
Wm H: 503

BROADBENT
G S (Rev): 623
Wm (Jun'r, Dr): 582

BROADRUF
Cornelius A: 420

BROADRUP
Cornelius A: 531 587
George E: 551
Sarah: 3515

BROBST
John Frederick (Rev): 357

BROCKE
Theodore: 498

BROCKENBROUGH
Letice: 5677

BRODERICK
Gertrude E: 2142

BROGUMIER
Anna Mary: 2992
Jacob: 2992

BROMWELL
Gussie: 620

BROOKE
John Thompson (Rev): 168

BROOKER
Joseph H: 564

BROOKS
Cha's S: 454
D W: 4591
David W: 643 1964
Eliza: 4132
Elizab: 1964
Mora B (Mrs): 1716

BROSIUS
John W: 612 729

BROSS
Barbara C A: 2620

BROWER
Isaac (Maj): 278

BROWN
B F: 2635
Benj F: 5722
Benjamin F: 372
D Anderton: 161
Daniel: 637
Daniel E: 684
E Lincoln (Dr): 237

Fannie V: 1802
Florence: 2635
Florence G: 1421
Geo H: 476
H C: 6112
Harriet: 3951
Hattie: 3951
Helena: 2546
Henry: 600
Hester Ann: 5964
James: 745
John: 510
John R: 273
John Wilson: 492
Lucie B J: 4514
Margaret E: 1077
Martin L: 523 573
Mary: 2156
Mary A R: 5318
Mary C: 1957
Mary E: 2393 6112
Mary Elizabeth: 3340
Mary L: 263
Mary M E: 3108
Mildred L: 5722
Nelson: 356
No First Name Given: 613
R M G (Lieut): 718
S Elmer: 711
Sarah J: 6019
William: 364
Wm A: 380
Wm H: 466
Wm S: 174 319 2393
Wm T: 476
Zachariah: 332

BROWNING
Basil D: 502
Elias: 625
Jennie A: 4140
Richard M: 767

BRUA
Jacob Newton: 432
Lucretia: 4276

BRUBACHER
Ann: 1155
John: 166

BRUBAKER
Ann E: 4961
Isabella: 1618
John: 1618 4961 5894
John Wm: 666
Jon: 5921

Mary Jane: 5921
Sarah: 5894

BRUCHEY
Mary E: 3855
Sallie A: 1141
Sidney A: 1760

BRUCHY
Mary C: 6097

BRUCKER
John Simon: 4241

BRUGONIER
Alfred: 500
Wm W: 406

BRUMETT
Michael: 207

BRUNNER
Ann Rebecca: a3
Annie M: 714
Caroline: 386
Catharine: 4812
Charles A: 528
Edward Jacob: 376
Edward Livingston: 628
Eleanor: 5062
Elias: 185 4812
Elizabeth: 4763
Ellen C: 4559
Frances E: 2415 3194
Franklin: 642
Henrietta: 58
Henry: 255
Isaac: 241
J: 176 386 3577 4559
Jacob: 58 4932
John: 176 386 3577 4559
John H: 305 611
Jonathan: 185 195 309
Kate: 3810
Lewis: 123 190 528 628 642 3810
Lewis A (Rev): 350 2067
Mary: 4932
Mary Ann: 3577
Mary E: 5447
Mary L: 2067
Mattie S: 2133
Rebecca: 8 858
Rhoda: 836
Sallie A: 5309
Sophia: 4808
Susan: 123
Valentine Stickel: 381
Wm L: 481

BRUST
Caspar: 653 656 663 1019
Caspar (Jun'r): 526
Cha's C: 766
Charles: 663
Conrad: 469
George: 656
Henry: 653
John Nicholas: 746
Margaret: 1019
O Nicholas: 746

BRUTCHEY
Henry: 342
Jacob: 142
Jacob (Sen'r): 358
Mary E: 753

BRUTSCHE
Barbara Ann (Mrs): 3324

BRUTSCHY
Basil: 397
John H: 495
Joseph: 446
Mary C: 595 1015

BRYON
Lucy: 5639

BUCHANAN
James: 3047
Mary: 3482
No First Name Given: 2832
Tho's (Judge): 3482

BUCHER
Jemima: 1471
Sarah Elizabeth: 343
Susan: 2456

BUCHEY
Hattie: 6139

BUCHFELTER
Hanna: 5941
John: 6237
Kate: 6237
Maggie: 3829

BUCHHEIMER
Conrad: 248
George: 396
Mary (Mrs): 2406

BUCK
Jerome B: 569
John M: 428
Mary: 4527
Mary J: 5430
Wm: 4527

BUCKELBANK

Lizzie W: 5913
BUCKEY
Ann: 2167
Basil V: 674
Catharine Louisa: 2761
Charles: 430
Dan'l: 284 3636 5635
Daniel: 214
Edward E: 518
Eleanor: 4760
Eliza: 4800
Elizabeth: 2203 3060
Elizabeth M: 1906
Eveline Virginia: 5577
Francis T: 626
G Jacob: 3163
Geo: 214 2203
Geo J: 681
Geo Jacob: 347
Geo P: 418
Geo Wm: 588
George Wm: 302
Harriet: 5635
Harriott C: 284
Jacob: 192 677
Jacob E: 725
Jacob M: 284
John: 2761 4897 5831
Laura V: 3163
Marion E: 5635
Mary C: 5831
Mary E: 1893
Mary L: 677
Mary R: 3636
Matilda: 4897
Mich'l: 430
Michael: 225
No First Name Given: 5709
Peter: 1893 2167 4760 4800
Richard Root: 359
Washington: 182 3060
BUCKIGNANI
Antonio: 467
BUCKINGHAM
Ruth N: 4320
BUCKLES
Alice A: 2096
BUCKSTON
Columbia: 6218
BUDDINTON
Wm Ives (Rev): 251
BUDDY
Philip: 365

BUESING
Etta C: 2666
Wm H: 2666
BUFFINGTON
Kate A: 2966
BUHRMAN
Alfred (Rev): 353
Cha's A: 670
David H: 560
Ephraim H: 527
Florence: 1763
Hanna E: 5674
Harvey (Dr): 652
Jacob: 549
Mary E: 523
Mollie: 732
Seraphine: 1666
Upton: 670 732 1763
BUL
Ole: 627
BULER
Henry S: 721
BULFIELD
H (Rev): 2691
Lydia H: 2691
BUNKLEY
Josephine M: 54
BURALL
Cameron: 756
Ellen: 5841
George W: 698
Oliver: 417 471
Sydney J: 5839
William: 395
BURCH
Florence C: 3963
Jessie E: 6272
Sarah A: 1535
BURCK
Amelia P: 3157
Anna Mary: 2088
Carrie R: 3976
Cha's W: 752
Christiana V: 1845
Florence C: 3963
Francis Tho's (Dr): 679
Genevive: 3440
John: 440
Joseph: 676
Lewis: 3440
Mary F: 2478
Philip: 421

Philip H: 691
Wm: 421
BURG
Caroline: 2955
Philip: 2955
BURGEE
Emily: 5849
Harriott: 1596
BURGER
Charles E: 716
Henry C: 678
BURGESS
Eleanor: 2157
Elizabeth: 4012
Jemima A (Mrs): 6199
John E F: 740
Julian: 4798
Mary Catharine: 303
Minerva: 5932
No First Name Given: 3677
Sarah D: 1877
BURGHEIM
Philip Fahnenberg de: 459
BURK
Lewis A: 702
BURKE
Lucinda: 1202
Wm B: 1202
BURKHART
Charles H: 167
Elizabeth: 2373
Ezra G W: 371
Wm F: 261
BURKITT
Henrietta: 1673
Henrietta C: 2313
Mary: 4876
Newton: 157 2313
BURNES
Cha's W: 235
BURRAS
Daniel E: 692
BURRIER
Calvin S: 647
Cha's D: 547
Daniel: 5109
Eli: 1334
Jane: 5152
John W: 595
Lewis H: 636
Mary C C: 5109
Sarah E: 4351

Simon E: 575
Susan: 1334
Wm H: 391

BURROWS
Isabella: 4971

BURTON
Columbia T: 604
Henry: 4557
James H: 468
James Henry: 574
John C: 340
Mary Jane: 4557
Mary Parks: 234
R Henry: 604
Sarah: 3759

BURUCKER
Clementine: 91
Ida: 2688
J Louis: 597
John S: 2043 2688
John Simon: 265
Mary E: 2043
Oscar M: 734

BUSBY
Marg't M J: 84

BUSER
Ann: 2187
Elizabeth: 2169

BUSEY
Ezra F (Rev): 416
Wm G: 482

BUSH
Margaret Ann: 4907

BUSHEY
Ann M: 2036
Frances V: 622
J M: 622
Jacob: 631 2036
Jacob M: 620
T Frank: 631

BUSING
Elizabeth: 3797
Fred'k: 3797
Wm F: 480

BUSSARD
Daniel R: 735
Lucinda: 1792

BUTCHER
Margaret: 3278

BUTLER
Ann E: 191
B F: 122

Blanche: 122
Cha's J: 667
Charles E: 667
Edward M: 730
Frank G: 700
Gettie: 3873
Gettle: 3875
Harman: 3326
John Geo (Rev DD): 592
Kennedy H (Lieut): 544
Mary Elizabeth: 3326
Ormon Fischer: 383
Ormond F: 191
Ormond F (Junior): 296
Pierce: 206
Richard F: 281
Samuel J: 456

BUTTERWORTH
Marian: 772

BUTTLER
Geo C: 695

BUTTS
Isabella E: 3175
Joseph: 479

BUXTON
Alice B: 5699
Brook (Jun'r): 579
No First Name Given: 579
Susan B: 3137

BUZZARD
David: 368
Elizabeth (Mrs): 3699
Lydia: 1914

BYERLY
Ettie: 1123
J Davis: 614
Jacob: 337 614

BYERS
Ann R: 1331

BYNGE
Ellen: 4092

BYRN
Samuel L: 748

BYRNE
M C: 4131
Mary: 1252
Michael: 1252
Mollie C: 3937

BYRNES
Mollie C: 3937

BYRNS
S L: 748

CABELL
Lizzie Caskie: 4671

CAHEN
Felix: 1089

CAHOON
Joel B: 800

CAIN
John: 891

CALEY
Rebecca: 4838

CALHOUN
Mary: 2924

CALLAHAN
Rose: 3000

CALLIFLOWER
Cornelia E: 3819
Wm F (Rev): 3819

CALVIN
Jos: 1040

CAMBRELING
Churchill C (Hon): 813

CAMDEN
Dora E: 4655

CAMPBELL
Abner: 790 3150
Cha's A: 1143
Edward: 785
Jennie: 2834
John B H: 870
Lizzie: 3150
Mortimer S: 1003
Randolph: 772
Robert H: 1108

CANDLER
Adelaide: 4170
Annie E (Mrs): 4119
Augusta B: 1398
Daniel H: 828
Eveline: 820
L W: 5341
Sidonia V: 5341

CANN
(Rev): 4359
Bertie: 3857 3859
Geo W: 1071
Mary S: 5681
Tho's M: 5681
Tho's M (Rev): 1071 3857 3859

CANNON
Ann Levina: 1189

Anna S: 531
Lucinda R: 5217
CANOUGH
No First Name Given: 227
CANTWELL
James: 831
CAPEL
Joseph: 915
CAREY
Annie M: 377
Barbara J: 4618
Cyrus: 776
Eleanor: 156
Elizabeth C: 35
George G: 974
James: 1138 4618
James (Jun'r): 1021
John: 377
John T H: 945
CARLIN
Agnes: 1255
Alverta: 3027
Ann: 3690
Anne R: 2477
Catharine: 5542
Ceclia: 1009
Clara V: 5343
David: 823 2477
Eliza A: 398
Frank B: 951
George T: 969
Henry: 797
James: 338 771 807 951 1255 3027 5542
John T: 1093
Jos: 5343
Joseph: 863 2065
Margaret P: 1600
Martha: 6125
Mary E: 2065
Matilda E: 338
Tho's: 789 797 823 863 1009
Tho's (Junior): 794
Wm: 789 1600 3690
CARLISLE
David: 896
CARLLEY
Mary H: 1543
CARLTON
Ann Rebecca: 204
Eliza Jannett: 3545
Tho's: 204 3545

William: 841
CARMACK
Ann Sophia: 2324
Christian S: 815
Eph'm: 3803
Ephraim: 804
Hanson: 829 4590
Jacob: 786
Kate E: 5655
Laura A: 4590
Maggie E: 4692
Margaret E: 4692
Mary E: 466
Nellie: 3803
Sam'l: 2324 5655
Sam'l Philip: 954
CARNES
Sarah Ann: 392
William: 803
CARNS
Wm H: 1060
CARPENTER
John M: 852
Louisa: 4354
Marcie: 3026
Mark C: 1030
Martha: 5350
CARR
Clementine: 4985
Tho's: 4985
CARROLL
Anna: 2431
D H (Rev): 1028
Harriott: 3240
John Lee (Gov): 1088
R G Harper: 1070
CARSANOVIA
J N: 991
CARSON
Alonzo: 1059
Ambrose: 1059
Bertha: 6123
Eliza A: 4058
Lyle: 2629
CARTER
Cha's C: 1110
E H: 6103
Emma: 3942
Grafton: 1036
Henry: 922
Lucinda: 4090
Walter S: 1043

CARTY
Alton B: 1111
Cha's P: 1041
Clarance C: 1042
Clarence C: 1115
Daisy: 1117
Dassie E: 1117
Jos W L: 1041 1042 1117
Joseph W L: 862 1007 1144
CARUTHERS
Elizabeth W: 1283
CASHOUR
Charles W F: 1102
CASS
Isabella: 5742
Lew: 5742
CASSADY
Francis Stansbury (R: 909
CASSEL
Dan'l: 2340
No First Name Given: 5862
CASSELL
Nancy: 4065
CASSIN
John: 968
Sophia A: 965
Stephen (Com): 965 968
CASTER
Emma: 3942
CASTLE
Abraham H: 868
Abraham P: 1087
Annie: 3170
Annie M: 6236
Birdie B: 2726
Charles A: 1103
Dan'l: 3853 6239
Daniel: 1108
Elizabeth: 2339
Elizabeth C: 3435
Ellie: 5415
Emma F: 3853
George T: 847
George T (Capt'n): 1017
Henry: 5415
James (Jun'r): 809
James W: 964
Jennie: 1108
Kate C: 6239
Mary E V: 5716
Rezin Josephus: 940
T: 6239

Tho's F: 993
Thomas M: 1034
CAUGHY
No First Name Given: 906
CAUSTIN
Miss: 3140
CECILL
George M: 1038
Samuel T: 946
CELAPHANE
Joshua: 2773
Matilda: 2773
CESNOLA
Cavaliere Luigi Palm: 994
CHALMERS
Sadie: 3216
CHAMBERLAIN
Benjamin W: 1139
CHAMBERS
Ezekiel F: 1223
James: 890
Laura: 1223
Sarah: 5728
Tho's J: 1001
William: 867
CHAMBLIN
Laura R: 3306
CHANEY
Elias: 775
Richard G (Rev): 895
CHANY
Geneva: 1833
CHAPLINE
J Thomas: 1037
CHAPMAN
John Lee: 1065
CHARD
Henrietta: 1279
CHARLES
Mary Ann Traill: 2434
CHARLESWORTH
Solomon: 801
CHARLTON
Jane: 3991
John W: 780
John W (Jun'r Rev): 1025
Louisa: 5558
Usher: 3991
CHASE
Kate: 5245
Nettie: 2586

S P (Judge): 2586
Salmon P: 5245
CHESNUT
Caroline: 4053
CHESTER
Wm G: 1099
CHEW
A Richard: 1129
Jos H: 1098
Thomas: 1104
CHILCOAT
Ellen: 4950
CHILCOATE
Tho's M: 4677
CHILCOTE
Mary P: 4605
Mollie: 4677
Rich'd: 4605
Thomas M: 913
CHILD
Emily J: 5931
CHILDS
Geo F: 1128
CHILTON
Wm F: 1122
CHINIGUY
Charles (Rev): 1022
CHISWELL
Geo W: 881
John N (Capt'n): 1055
Joseph: 1418
Joseph N: 1124
Rachie: 1418
S Newton: 3688
Virginia: 755
CHLEY
David: 4785
CHRISTIANCY
J P (Hon): 1085
CISIL
Ada: 3201
CISSELL
Jonas: 1012
Mary E: 2997
Richard S T: 892
Wm Martin: 961
CLABAUGH
Charles B: 1140
G M Dall: 1114
Geo M: 1123
Mary E: 2359

N: 2359
Norman B: 886
Susie E: 2672
Usher: 1082
CLAGETT
Grafton A (Dr): 3029
Kate A C: 3029
Louisa: 5327
Maggie B: 4653
Mollie: 645
Tho's: 645 4653 5327
CLAGGETT
Ellen Moale: 1160
Horace W: 1135
Laura E: 2000
M K: 3588
Mary: 2912
Mary M: 5476
Mary P: 3605
Sarah: 1213
Sophie E: 1136
Tho's John: 924
CLAPHAM
Josiah Henry: 970
CLAPP
C Clinton: 983
CLAPSADDLE
Catharine E: 1554
Miss: 1554
CLARK
Asa: 1145
Carrie (Mrs): 655
Eliza A L: 1495
Elizab Jane: 2802
John F: 1006
Joseph P: 1014
Mary C W: 1910
Mary M: 3124
Samuel (Rev): 777
CLARKE
Catharine (Mrs): 1201
Ja's C: 2848
James Charles: 907
Jennie O: 2848
Rolurt B: 950
CLARKSON
Freeman (Rev): 864
CLARY
Cordelia Ann: 1194
Frederick S: 914
Nathaniel H: 971
Upton: 816

CLAY
  Adam H: 873
  Cinderella: 2460
  Miss: 465
  Sarah A: 1211
  Tho's Hart: 465
  William: 931
  Zebulon: 2460
CLAYBAUGH
  Harriott: 829
CLEAVLAND
  Sylvester: 877
CLEM
  A: 840
  Barbara: 2375
  George: 920
  George A: 840
  George H: 980
  Harriett: 904
  John: 904
  Miranda Priscilla: 83
  Peter C: 836
  Philip H: 871
  Sarah Ann E: 973
CLEMENT
  Wm H: 846
CLEMM
  Georgiana M: 4785
  Josephine E: 4214
  Mary A: 4070
CLEMSON
  Elizabeth S: 5725
  Harrison T: 844
  Juliett: 278
  Sarah (Mrs): 3501
CLERAMER
  Minnie: 1142
CLEVELAND
  Deborah A: 281
CLINE
  Caspar: 932 1056
  George Tho's: 1005
  George W: 975
  Maggie C: 1130
  Margaret: 1130
  Nicholas: 1130
  Nicholas O: 1056
CLINGAN
  Amanda S H: 1813
  Annie E: 1750
  Hester E: 949
  John F: 1750
  Lewis S: 992
  Thomas: 949
  Winchester: 781 949
CLINGHAN
  Wm (Rev): 783
CLINGMAN
  Enoch G: 837
CLOSE
  Elijah: 832
  Elizabeth: 4420
  Virginia C: 1039
CLOUD
  Jesse: 1606
  Maria H: 1606
CLOUGH
  Nellie: 5462
CLUNET
  Martha Adele: 3716
  Victor: 3716
CLUNETT
  Victor: 810
CLURER
  Charles W: 1118
COATES
  Isaac: 934
COBB
  Edward L: 1002
  Lucie D: 2089
COBLENTZ
  David: 4575
  Edward T: 985
  Ella A E: 4623
  Fannie C: 3744
  Geo G: 1126
  Henry: 3744
  John C: 1058
  Leonora: 2929
  Louisa: 4575
  Malinda A: 330
  Mary Ellen: 3389
  Mollie C: 1111
  Rebecca: 4413
  Sarah V: 3747
  Stephen B: 1046
COBURN
  Jacob D: 1009
  James R: 799
COCHRAN
  Ella B: 3465
  Mary: 2061
  Susan R: 5641
COCHREN
  Elmira C: 4592
  Lewis R: 1072
COCKEY
  Bella S: 1106
  Caroline C: 184
  Nannie: 729
  S G: 1106
  Sebastian G: 811
COCKLIN
  Sarah C: 3785
COCKRAN
  Ella B: 3465
COE
  Catherine (Mrs): 210
  Emma: 428
  No First Name Given: 3711
COHEN
  Arnoldine (Mrs): 2987
COLBATH
  Martin P: 1027
COLBERT
  Wm B: 1052
COLBY
  Wm J: 1015
COLE
  Amelia: 4835
  Cha's: 1050 1078
  Charles: 875
  Charles Edwin: 1050
  Clara V: 2849
  David: 899
  Fannie R: 1359
  Geo A: 899
  George A: 792
  Lamartine: 1078
  Lewis M: 856 1359
  Mary Emily: 451
  No First Name Given: 5251
  Wm G: 849 1068
  Wm H: 1068
COLEGATE
  Catharine V: 2362
  Edward: 845
  George: 814
COLEMAN
  Chester: 788
  George: 784
  M Ann: 2342
COLES
  Miss: 4566

COLFAX
　Schuyler: 1049
COLLEBERRY
　Annie R: 1314
　Mary Elizabeth: 4521
COLLIER
　Sarah: 661
COLLIFLOWER
　Henry: 1013
　Laura C: 2055
　Willie A: 1035
　Wm F: 2055
　Wm F (Rev): 839 1035
COLLINS
　Cha's E: 1029
　Elisha: 857
　Lydia A (Mrs): 588
　Margaret E: 4578
　Wm O: 861
COLLIS
　Cha's H T, Capt'n: 999
COLTON
　Ida: 5383
COLVOCORESSES
　Geo M: 876
COLYER
　Nancy: 3327
COMFORT
　H C (Rev): 1035
COMPHER
　Candace V: 1855
CONDON
　Amelia: 5723
　Frank C: 1066
　Joseph: 918
　Richard W: 956
　Susan J: 3870
CONKLIN
　Mary: 4997
　Wm J: 1117
CONLEY
　Harrison: 591 822 941
　Rose A: 591
CONN
　Ella T: 1450
　John T: 958
CONNER
　Hebert: 1119
　James: 615
　James A O: 853
　Mollie E: 615

CONNOR
　Alice C: 4376
　Ann Rebecca: 4832
　Elizabeth C: 4612
　Geo J: 901
　Henry: 818
　Ida M: 667
　James: 855
　Mary Ann Margaret: 5930
　Mary Ann Margt: 3265
　Rosanna: 787 5803
　Tho's: 787 818 901 3265
CONOWAY
　Solomon Freeborn: 824
CONRAD
　A Cordelia: 2504
　Caroline W: 1747
　Elizabeth: 4052
　Ettie: 1775
　Fannie M: 106
　Henry: 929
　James P: 1077
　John: 830 2495
　John D: 960
　Jos: 830 834 929 4052
　Katie E: 5695
　Margaret: 2495
　Wm: 834
　Wm J: 1051
CONRADI
　F A (Rev): 1067
CONRADT
　Ann Regina: 5852
　Ch'n Gottloeb: 5852
　Christian G: 773
　Geo M: 5165
　Margaret R: 5165
　Theophilus M: 880
CONTEE
　Alice Lee: 2882
　Margaret: 4928
　Richard: 959
CONVERSE
　Freeman: 817
COOK
　Alexander A: 826
　Benjamin F: 948
　Frank W (Dr): 1044
　Henrietta R: 3073
　John: 793 854 912
　Joseph D: 977
　Luther M E: 912

　Mary A: 4585
　Miss: 4192
　Sallie A: 3445
　Wm F Nelson: 1125
COOKE
　Mary Ann E: 2807
COOKERLY
　Amelia: 3516
　Anna M: 4569
　Catharine: 4407
　Eliza W: 4606
　George W: 1116
　Jacob: 3616 6197
　Margaret: 4754
　Matilda: 3616
　Rebecca: 6197
COOKSEY
　Wm T: 1076
COOKSON
　John C: 939
COOLEY
　Ruth Ann: 1529
COOMBS
　Martha Ann: 2746
　Wm H O: 1064
COOMES
　Joseph W: 859
COOPER
　Adderly: 1020
　David: 885 1401
　David (Hon): 927
　E Minnie: 1401
　Emma: 3847
　James (Gen'l): 990
　John: 990
COPELAND
　Elizabeth Ann: 5230
　James W: 943
　Lottie R: 2549
　Mary Jane: 5231
COPPERSMITH
　Lewis F: 835
CORBIN
　Samuel M: 883
CORCORAN
　Louisa M: 1659
　W W: 1659
CORNELL
　Georgie A: 2585
　Mary: 3146
CORNER

James: 416
S Jane: 416
CORNING
Albion J: 1069
Jasper: 1106
CORRICK
Annie S: 2643
CORRISON
Geo Wm: 1000
COSSMAN
Louisa M A: 449
COST
Catharine: 2743
Christian: 6186
Elias: 2743
Henry: 967 1372
Mary A S (Mrs): 1372
Mary Ann (Mrs): 5557
Mary E: 4717
Serena S: 6186
COURTNAY
James F: 1063
Mary: 4599
COUSINS
Lewis W: 1105
COUTCHLEY
Lillie M: 1819
COVELL
Lydia (Mrs): 662
COVER
Cassandra: 6085
Cyrus: 905
E N: 6085
John: 2569
John M: 942
Lizzie: 577
Mary L: 2569
COWAN
Emma: 4187
Margaret Augusta: 3578
COX
Caroline: 376
George: 4270 4822
Sevilla: 4270
Susan Livingston: 4822
COXEN
Sarah Ann: 4781
COYLE
Margaret: 1942
COZENS
Wm J (Maj): 1130

COZZENS
Marian: 6130
CRABB
Margaret (Mrs): 2199
CRABSTER
Elmira J: 1916
CRAFT
Sophia: 546
CRAGG
Mary H: 5013
CRAIG
Geo W: 1016
CRAIGHEAD
Matilda H: 1614
CRAMER
Ada M: 1101
Agnes: 2268
Albert J: 987
Alice: 2574 5505
Amos: 1981
Ann R: 4918
Barbara: 4311
Catharine: 197 1925
Catharine B: 504
Catharine S: 3065
Cha's C: 962
Columbus A: 928 982
Cora M: 3887
David: 4918
David K: 1100
E Joh: 699
E_than: 1141
Edward A: 1127
Ephraim: 1127
Ethan Allen: 910
Ezra: 2268
Ezra L: 1101
Ezra Lewis: 923
Geo L: 1095
Geo W: 1073
George: 869
George W: 989
Harriet: 239
Harry B: 1137
Henry: 1141
Henry E: 1141
Ida V: 699
Jacob: 819 889 2988 4917
Jacob W: 1026
Jennie: 5387
Jeremiah C: 1039
Jeremiah H: 884

John A: 1097
John David: 887 986
John P: 1033
Katie J: 738
Maggie E: 2492
Mamie L: 1454
Margaret: 1981
Margaret E: 4301 4963
Margret: 1573
Martha: 1340
Mary Ann: 984
Mary E: 679
Mary L: 1454
Mary M: 1612
Mary R: 280
Ph: 989
Philip: 3065 4301
Philip H: 280 4311
Sophia: 4917
Susan D: 2988
William: 902
Willie: 1131
Wm C: 1131
CRAMPTON
Garrott: 1136
Henry G: 1075
J D Garrott: 1136
John W: 879
CRANGLE
Mary L: 3749
CRAVER
George W: 1010
Grafton H: 973
Hester Ann: 5034
Laura C: 6088
Margaret C: 4169
Simon P: 882
CRAW
Edwin A: 1008
CRAWFORD
Ann Elizabeth: 979
Annie D: 3762
Cha's T: 1146
Emily: 2799
Emma F: 2669
Malinda (Mrs): 2040
Margaret: 2411
Tho's L: 1090
CREAGER
Ada: 5204
Alice: 5204
Andrew J: 1031
Carrie E: 623

Catharine P: 4210
Clarissa E: 110
Eliza A: 420
Eph'm: 623 3748
Ephraim: 1080 5204
Esau D: 900
F A W (Lieut): 1053
Geo: 4210 4911
John Wesley: 1024
Lewis (Dr): 157
Manelia S: 3748
Mannassah: 957
Margaret (Mrs): 2898
Martha S: 2565
Mary A: 3294
Mary E: 4911
Noble H: 1080
Rebecca: 157
Simon: 936 988
Sophia: 3287
Susan E: 3706

CREEGER
Henrietta S: 573
Sabina: 4730

CREIGH
Miss: 5360

CREIGHTON
Johnston Blakely (Li: 919

CREMINS
John: 952

CRIMMINS
John: 952

CRISE
Geo H: 1092
Mollie O: 1415

CRISSAMER
Anna: 1626

CRIST
Annie M: 5072
Annie O: 2024
Eveline: 3581
Grafton B: 953
Jacob: 850 1587
Joseph: 796 913 2024
Josephine: 1587
Margret E: 913
Mellie: 5445
William: 1109

CRITTENDEN
John J: 908

CROCETCHER
Jane: 1129

CROCKEN
Ann Eliza: 6008
James J: 791 6008
Martha Ann: 5817

CROFT
S F: 1084

CROMWELL
Ann Rebecca: 461
Annie B: 3387
Caroline: 5918
Catharine: 3603
Cha's C: 1081
Charlotte A: 3589
Elizabeth R: 295
Ellen: 2785
Ellen B: 958
Geo W: 1081 5179
George W: 806 926
Harriott (Mrs): 5551
Henrietta G: 1599
J Charles: 1096
John: 779 958 1599
Joseph W: 894
Leonora Lydia: 5179
Lucy Ann: 1499
M Alverda: 5185
Margaret (Mrs): 2982
Margaret Ellen: 2508
Mary: 5719
Mary A: 1204
Mary E: 2420
Netta: 112
Philemon: 827 1062 2785 3589 3603
Rachel C: 4872
Richard: 774
Susan: 514
Tho's: 5185
Tho's T: 827 1062
Wm Eldridge: 979
Wm H H: 917

CRONE
Charlotte A V: 513
Conrad: 2942
John E: 981

CRONISE
B Franklin: 878
Caroline E: 4427
Catharine: 4765
Eliza: 1159
Ella: 3131
Fannie: 3449
Fred'k: 963 1958 4563
Frederick: 2407
Geo W: 963
Gideon: 1023
Hannah Sophia: 4563
Henry: 2879
Isaac: 812 860
J Calvin: 1040
J Stoll (Dr): 872
Jacob: 872 1159 4424 4900
Jane Rebecca: 4424
John: 778 812 858 860 4765 5801 6185
Jonathan K: 947
Joseph: 858 3131 6270
Lizzie A: 5951
Louisa J: 2357
Lydia A: 1958
Maria: 4900
Mary: 3518
Mary Ann: 5889
Mary E: 6185
Nellie: 3867
Nettie: 6270
No First Name Given: 4086
Rebecca: 2407
Sam'l: 898 947 978 1023 1268 2357 3867 5670 5889 5951
Samuel: 778
Simon: 898 978 3518 4427
Sophia M: 5801
Susan: 2879
Susan H: 1268
Tavie C V: 5670
Wm H V: 1047

CROOK
Geo Wash Musgrave: 976

CROPSEY
Frances J: 805

CROSS
Elizabeth: 5580
Lewis (Junior): 768
Robert: 833

CROUCH
James O: 1011

CROUGH
Michael: 787
Rosanna (Mrs): 5803

CROUSE
George V: 921
Harriott S: 1967
John L (Dr): 966
Nannie H: 541

William A: 1019
Wm A: 1133
Wm F: 1054
CROW
John: 874
CROWN
Elizabeth V: 536
S Curtis: 944
CRUM
Alice C: 2514
Ann M: 4978
Ann Maria: 1646
Ann Rebecca: 2251
Caspar: 1018
Catharine: 1506
Charles J: 1121
Ella: 5526
Frances Matilda: 36
Geo M: 1061
Geo W (Dr): 893
Hanson: 1048
Isaac: 795 798 802 1506 1646 2166 2820 3093 3540
Isaac B: 997
Issac L: 1032
Jennie: 2032
John: 802 984 1086
Laura V: 6230
Lewis: 998 1074
Louisa M: 3093
Mary E: 5748
Nancy, Mrs: 2166
Sarah L: 5537
Simon: 996
Stephen Basford: 825
Susan: 3540
Susan E: 2820
William: 798
William E: 938
Wm: 997 2032 2514 5748 6230
CRUMBAUGH
F B: 647
Flora C: 126 647
Geo F B: 916
Gideon: 1681
Harriet E: 40
Margret A: 1681
Simon C (Rev): 935
Simon Calvin: 911
CRUTCHLEY
Elias: 838 2344
Lucinda (Mrs): 2344

CUBITZ
A Elizabeth: 2440
George: 1057
CULLER
America E: 2608
Andrew Jacob: 1147
C C (Rev): 930
Charles K: 1142
Cordelia S: 1075
Dan'l L: 2540
Daniel: 821
David: 955
Ella R: 2540
Henry: 821 865
Henry (Col): 1079
Henry (Jun'r): 866
J Harman: 972
Jacob A: 1147
Joanna Virginia: 1718
John J: 903
John J S: 1120
Julia A: 4898
Mary A C: 5173
Peter: 851 1075 1718
Philip: 865
CUMINGS
Mora B: 1716
CUMMING
Aug's J: 454 494
Aug't J: 1004
Fannie: 494
Mora B: 454
Wm A: 1004
CUMMINGHAM
Emma N: 685
CUNNINGHAM
Alice L: 4663
B A: 4663 5396
B Amos: 1122 2398 3955 5645
Benj'n Amos: 820
Bessie: 3955
Celia: 1122
Daniel T: 782
E Virginia: 5645
Eliza: 4445
Elizabeth G: 3955
Ellen: 4596
John R H: 937
Mary R: 2398
Mary V: 3720
Philip: 888
Sallie A: 5396

Wm Armstrong: 995
Wm F: 1045
CURFMAN
Sarah: 3318
William: 770
Wm: 843 3318
Wm H: 1083
CURLEY
Barbara: 5671
CURRAN
Robert N: 1113
CURRANS
Elijah: 808 1635
Emma C: 1635
CURRY
Mary E: 5667
CURTIS
George C: 965
J B Gregg: 1094
John: 848
CUSHMAN
Philip: 769
CUSHWA
Geo W: 1091
CUSTARD
Adam: 2053 2451
Annie Virginia: 2053
Martha A S: 2451
CUSTUS
Wm H: 842
CUTSAIL
Ann J: 624
Charles: 1112
Clayton E: 1107
J J: 1107
J Milton: 1132
Joseph M: 1132
Nancy: 4885
Wm H: 925 933
CUTSHALL
Katie M: 762
Wm B: 1134
CUTTER
Harriett A: 3626
Wm J (Rev): 897
CUTTS
Ada: 1284
Adele: 6024
De FALKENSTEIN
Amelia: 4305
DADE

Maruice: 1418
Mary A: 2243
DADISMAN
Almira E: 1582
Ezra: 1184 1344 1693 1969
Jacob: 1170 1184 1344 1582
Mary Ann Margaret: 5930
Mary Jane: 1969
No First Name Given: 901 3265
Sarah: 1693
Sophia: 6
DAHLGREN
John Vinton: 1455
DAIGEN
Owen: 1235
DAIGER
No First Name Given: 1343
DALE
M Frances: 3360
DALEY
John: 4903
Teresa Ann: 4903
DALL
John R: 2804
Lydia A: 2804
Meloria: 693
DALRYMPLE
Adelaide: 4264
Eleanora (Mrs): 2752
Guilimina: 3615
DAMER
Lititia Hannah: 5972
DAMON
Cha's L: 1341
DANDRIDGE
Edmund P: 1396
Philip P: 1297
DANIELS
M E: 1460
DANNER
Cha's H: 1442
Charlotte: 1479
Hannah M: 1374
Mary Ann: 1586
Robert T: 1434
Wm H: 1456
DANNIER
Fannie: 3460
DARBY
Darius: 1265

Jane: 5616
Martha A P: 2429
Walter: 5616
Walter C: 2429
Zachary Taylor: 1398
DARCUS
William: 1275
DARKIS
Mary Ann: 3483
DARKUS
David F: 1340
DARNALL
Rachel: 488
Rob't: 488
DARNELL
Elizabeth: 3673
Lizzie: 2520
DARNER
Fannie G: 3460
DASHIEL
J H (Rev): 3949
Lizzie K: 3949
DATESMAN
Ann Maria: 930
DATZBAUGH
Fannie S: 1811
DAUGHADAY
Joseph: 1279
DAVIDISON
Bradly H: 1436
DAVIDSON
Patrick (Rev): 1173
Samuel P: 1173
DAVIS
Ann Maria: 4415
Annie: 686
Catharine: 4412
Eleanor: 4398
Eliza (Mrs): 5633
Elizabeth: 2829 5859
Geo L L: 1223
Hallie: 1786
Harriott S: 5912
Henry G: 1260
Henry G (Hon): 1786
Henry Winter (Hon): 1285
Ign: 4412
Ignatius: 1149 1179 1190 1217 1223 5555
Isaac Y: 1280
Ja's L: 995 1283
James: 1183

James L: 937 1179 2829 5683
John J: 1217
John K: 1446
Judge: 5412
Katie B: 718
Laura J: 3377
Laura V: 586
Levi: 1166 1193
Louisa: 5877
Lucy Ann: 4970
Luke: 5859
Margaret J: 6149
Margretta: 5555
Mary E: 2459
Mattie C: 937
Miss: 2829
Molly: 995
Nannie: 5683
Richard W (Dr): 1149
Robert E: 1356
Rosa Nelson (Mrs): 4986
S Hamner (Rev): 1283
Sallie Worthington: 5412
Sam'l R: 1406
Tho's (Dr): 5877
Tho's I: 1190
Tyler: 586
William: 1309
William C: 1368
Wm: 1449
Wm M: 1294
Zachariah H: 1194
DAVISON
Morris: 1347
DAWSON
Philip: 1177 1196
Wm C (Hon): 1269
DAY
Daniel: 1301
Ellen Channing: 669
Enoch G: 1176
Laura A: 6165
DAYHOFF
Elizabeth: 928
F M: 1448
James: 4246
John J: 1339
Joshua T: 1306
Maria: 1526 4223
Nancy G: 3242
Uralh Ann: 4246
Urith: 4246

Urith A: 2572
DE BOURBON
Dona Maria Isabel: 4337
DE CANNAY
The Marquis: 1300
DE GARMADNDIER
Carlos: 1425
DE VIERS
B F: 1452
DE VRIES
Benjamin: 1452
DE YOE
Luther (Rev): 1457
DEAN
Amelia V: 5534
Annie M C: 2071
Geo Albert: 1349
George W: 1385
Henry A: 1337
Henry C: 1405
James H: 1369
John: 1385
John A: 1399
Margaret: 3066
Margaret Ann: 2236
Mary A: 5760
Robert: 1240
Sam'l M: 1342
William: 1188
Wm E: 1259
Wm Houston R: 1336 1348
DEAVER
G Clinton (Prof): 1393
DEBODISCO
Harriett "WILLIAMS": 5163
DEBRING
Gertrude: 1840
Ida Gertrude: 1840
Lucy M (Mrs): 3142
DEBRULER
Louisa: 4906
DECK
Joseph: 1258
DECKER
Deborah: 1205
DEEDS
Virginia: 5755
DEETER
Alexander R: 1231
Jacob (Jun'r): 1271
No First Name Given: 3793

DEGRANGE
Augusta: 3431
Catharine M: 367
Cha's A: 1421
D W F: 1388
David J: 1320 1354
Garnett S: 1407
George W: 1272
Henry Clay: 1362
Jane R C: 1087
John: 367 1148 1272 1320 1354 1386 1388
Margaret: 1512
Peter: 1362 1512
Peter (Jun'r): 1169
Wm F: 1386
Wm M: 1329
DELAPLAINE
Theo: 1431
Wm T: 1431
DELAPLANE
Caroline M: 3693
Joshua: 1244
Theodore: 1232
William: 1276
DELASHMUT
Basel: 695
Elias E: 1420
Margaret M: 695
DELASHMUTH
Lizzie V: 1116
DELASHMUTT
Andrew J: 1248 2119
Ann Rebecca: 4304
Annie: 3948
Arthur: 1282
Basil: 1247
Basil J: 1239
Catharine Ann: 1574
E L: 4304
E T H: 1412
E Van (Dr): 1310
Elias L: 1383 4113 4611 4615
John A: 1441
Lynn: 1463
Phebe: 4611
Philip R: 1410
Rachel: 4615
Sarah E: 4113
Virginia R: 2119
Wm G: 1370
DELAUTER
Ann S: 25

John H: 1333
Mary: 6191
Sarah: 1787
DELCHER
Maggie A: 4352
DELP
Annie M C: 3864
DEMME
C K (Rev): 3297
DEMME'
Cha's R (Rev): 4267
Marianna S: 3297
Rosa C: 4267
DEMUTH
Geo A: 1361
Josiah: 1319
DENEGRE
Wm P (@): 1419
DENMAN
Susan E: 6227
DENNIS
Alice: 4700
Fannie J: 4705
Geo: 4705
Geo R, Col: 1346
George R: 1253
Louis E: 1408
DEPFER
Frederick: 1206
DEPKIN
J Harry: 1415
DERBY
Ella V: 1071
DERING
Sarach C: 2552
DERN
George M: 1381
DERR
Abraham: 1221
Catharine: 1485 4387
Catharine (Mrs): 5005
Catharine E: 298
Charles E: 1376
Daisy: 3960
Dan'l: 1351 1390 1628 3791
Daniel: 1182 5452
Dav: 6276
David: 4642
Eliza: 2254
Elizabeth: 1857
Elizabeth C: 1628

Ella C: 6276
Ella M: 4196
Emma J: 4665
Etta G: 5518
Eugene L: 1402
Fannie J: 3910
Geo F: 1355
Geo W: 4665
George C: 1351
George Washington: 1215
Hiram: 1416
Jacob: 1167 1485
Joanna M: 5452
John: 1198 1312 1322 1379 1402 1857 1863 4387 5108
John (Jun'r): 1172
John P: 1312
John W: 2254
Laura Jane: 4642
Luther C: 1367
Luthur: 1835
Margaret A: 5108
Margaret Jane: 3791
Mary: 1863
Mary Irene: 1835
Millard Taylor: 1390
Orpha E: 5116
William R: 1379
Wm: 3910
Wm H: 1225

DERRY
Jennie: 4588

DERTZABAUGH
Georgetta: 701

DERTZBACH
George Wm: 1236

DERTZBAUGH
Catharine: 1182
Christianna: 1238
Clara J: 5436
Geo: 1182 1238 6176
Henry: 1400
John W: 1219
Katie: 2126
Margaret: 6176
Mary: 6188
No First Name Given: 103 1377

DERTZEBAUGH
John W: 3821
Mary Jane: 3821

DETER
Wm H: 1440

DETRICK
Peter: 1445

DETZBAUGH
Fannie: 1811

DEVILBISS
Abner C: 1321
Ada: 1452
Cath Sophia: 238
Catharine: 3225
Catharine M: 2332
Cha's W: 1257
David: 819 1207 2332
Eliza: 840
Elizabeth: 4390
Elizabeth Jane: 1207
Ezra M: 1317
Geo: 238
George W: 1277 1289
Hannah: 433
Isaiah: 1243
James E (Dr): 1387
John Hanson: 1286
Joseph: 1281
Lee/Levi (@ #): 1437
Lucretia A: 819
Maggie H: 3715
Mary Catharine: 3091
Minnie M: 4640
Reuben: 4640
Solomon D: 1268

DEVITT
David B: 1150 1171
David M: 1263

DIDIER
Josephine: 352

DIEFENTHAL
Cha's A: 1332

DIEFFENDERFER
Wm: 1433

DIEHL
Adam: 1382
Albert (Jun'r): 1392
Albrecht: 1295
Hannah: 4312
Nathan: 1389
Nelson: 1382
T S (Dr): 1450

DIELMAN
Addie J: 2843
Henry (Prof): 2843

DIETER
Wm H: 1440

DIETRICH
Christian: 1181
Edington: 1360
Henry: 1159 1380
J H: 1274
J Stoll: 1380
No First Name Given: 3753
Philip: 1187

DIETRICK
Lewis F: 1298 1443
No First Name Given: 3031 3636

DIFFENDAL
T Bernard: 1447

DIFFENDERFFER
Matilda E (Mrs): 4461

DIFFINDAL
Charles L: 1426

DILL
Charles L: 1224
Edward W: 1216
Eliza: 3471
Ellen Virginia: 282
Emma J: 618
Ezra: 282 1203 1205 1212 1216 1224
George T: 1234
Georgianna: 3876
Henrietta: 5871
John: 3471
John F: 618 1211 3876
John Tho's: 1212
Joshua: 1211 1234 5063 5871
Joshua J: 1411
Leonard Augustus: 1189
Lewis H: 1227 1429
Lewis M: 1411
Mary M: 5063
No First Name Given: 4944 5512 5563
Tho's P: 1203
Wm H: 1205

DILLER
Jacob: 1228
Sabina M: 5137

DIMMICH
Clementine: 1731
Joseph E: 1315
Mich'l: 1731

DINDEMAN
Conrad: 1156

DINTERMAN
  Jacob E: 1391
DIX
  Morgan (Rev DD & LLD: 1395
DIXON
  Alice L: 3126
  Ann R: 865
  Ann Reb: 824
  B F: 1273
  Benjamin: 1273
  Benjamin S: 1358
  Caroline: 393
  Cha's T: 1327
  Charles F: 1365
  Eliza: 1517
  Elizabeth: 1308
  Ella: 4184
  Frank: 1144
  Haines: 393 824 1242 1517
  Hellen: 99
  Ida N: 2097
  John: 1338
  John W: 1245
  Joshua: 1186
  Lilly C: 2687
  Mary E A: 1749
  Mary Jane: 502
  Minnie: 1144 6278
  Richard P: 1432
  Sophia E: 589 5608
  Thomas: 1311
  Thomas H: 1414
  William: 1180
  Wm: 1308 1327
  Wm H: 589 1261
  Wm T: 1464
DODGE
  Daniel (Rev): 1175
DOFLER
  Christianna: 2916
  Geo: 1214 2904 2916
  George (Jun'r): 1174
  Jacob: 1214 1342 5262 5658
  Jonathan: 1157
  Mary L: 5658
  Rebecca: 2904
  Ruth (Mrs): 5262
  Ruth "MURRAY" (Mrs): 1342
DOGGET
  Mary E: 5850
DOLL
  Ann Rebecca: 4263
  Barbara: 2910
  Caroline: 4239
  Catharine: 4025
  Cha's J: 1454
  Charles D: 1461
  Charlotte: 2915
  Clifford H: 1417
  Daniel: 1210
  David: 1154 2975
  Ezra: 1153 1256 4953
  Geo Jos: 1256
  Geo W: 1302
  J Edward: 1409
  Ja's: 2910
  Jacob: 1210 2915 4025 4239 4263
  John: 1461
  John L: 1255 1409
  Jos: 176
  Leander Z: 1345
  Lewis H: 1323
  Louisa B: 4953
  Mary R: 2273
  Melville E: 1374
  No First Name Given: 764
  Samuel V: 1373
  Sophia: 176
  Susanna E: 2975
  Tho's: 2273
  Thomas: 1152
  Wm D: 1241
DOMER
  David: 1249
  Eva Maria: 4509
  Maria (Mrs): 1249
  Susan Elizabeth: 47
DOMY
  Lilly: 1443
DONELSON
  Andrew J (Maj): 1209
DONEY
  No First Name Given: 4854
DONNALLY
  Elizabeth R: 378
  Patrick: 378
DONNE
  Eliza A: 4072
  John Aug's: 4072
  John Augustus: 1165
DONNEBERGER
  Geo: 1318
DONNELLY
  Mary E: 3869
DONOLDSON
  Donald: 1352
DONSEIF
  Catharine E: 4887
DORCUS
  Edward T: 1438
DORFF
  Geo: 11 2956
  Juliann: 11
  No First Name Given: 61
  Sophia: 2956
DORFFLER
  Ch'n: 1307
  Christian: 1229
  Louis: 1307
DORSEY
  Alverda E: 5895
  Ann: 4155
  Ann E: 5150
  Augustus P: 1195
  Clagett W: 3054
  Claggett W: 975
  Edwin (Rev): 3385
  Emma J: 4647
  Harriet Ann: 975 3054
  Harry W: 507 1218 5998
  Harry W (Jun'r Dr): 1313
  Ignatius W: 1384
  James: 1308
  Joanna M: 553
  Joseph J: 1330
  Lizzie M: 507
  Lloyd (Dr): 5607 6222
  Maria: 2739
  Mary Elleanor: 3385
  Mary T: 3310
  Nettie: 5998
  Nicholas J (Dr): 1293
  Nimrod: 1304
  Rachel: 5607
  Richard H: 1378
  Robert E (Dr): 1163
  Roderick W: 1264
  Susan H: 1911
  Virginia Torrence: 6222
  W L: 1326
  Wm H B: 1375
  Wm L: 1326
DOTY
  E W: 1458
DOUB
  Effie R: 2138

Ezra (Capt'n): 1296
Jane E: 3656
Joshua: 1155 1246
Josiah: 1328
Lewis P: 1335
Valentine Wm Otterbe: 1250
Wm H: 1246

DOUBB
Charles V: 1435

DOUD
Francis A: 1262

DOUGHERTY
Jennie I: 1850
John S: 1252

DOUGLAS
Adele Cutts (Mrs): 6024
Rob't (Rev): 601
Stephen A: 6024
Stephen Arnold (Hon): 1284

DOUGLASS
Annie: 601
John T: 1230
Robert: 1353
William: 1192

DOULE
Joshua: 3656

DOWDLE
Old Wm: 1164

DOWNEY
Jesse Wright: 1403
John: 1233
Maggie M: 2573
Maria: 215
William: 1226
Wm: 215 2573

DOWNING
Maggie W: 611

DOWNS
John T: 1202

DOYLE
George: 1158
Lawrence: 997 1151 4485
Margaret: 997
Mary Jane: 4485

DRAPER
Margaret: 391
Minerva: 1491

DREHER
Mary Caroline: 3806

DRESSEL
Elizabeth: 4786

DRILL
Andrew: 1162
Henry C: 1291
Ollie B: 1459

DRINKHOUSE
Ellie R: 1971
Harriott H: 5295

DRIXELL
Elizabeth: 1455

DRONEBERGER
John Tho's: 1334

DRONENBERGER
Susan: 5978

DRURY
Rosanna: 1475

DRYDEN
J Merideth: 1359

DRYSDALE
James M: 1350
Lieut: 1350

DU VAL
Singleton: 1160

DUBOSE
D M: 1299

DUCKETT
Thomas: 1168 1201

DUDDERAR
David W: 1371

DUDDERER
John: 3056
Joseph H: 1204
Molly Jane: 3056

DUDERAR
Dennis: 1314

DUDERER
Ellie V: 3081

DUDERRAR
Charlotte E: 1605

DUDLEY
Ruth A: 1368

DUDREAR
Richard R: 1424

DUER
Mary Ann: 1868

DUERING
Mary Jane: 5892

DUFFIE
Margaret: 1607

DUFFINDORFER
Wm E: 1433

DUFT
Eva Catharine: 4550

DUGAN
Wm H: 1278

DUKE
Annie M E: 2037
Elizabeth (Mrs): 3705
Green H: 1197 2037 3705

DUKEHART
John M: 1366
John P: 1287
Sophia: 3492

DULANY
James H (Rev): 1324

DULL
Annie M: 2700
H'y: 2700

DUNAWIN
Phebe A: 486
Tho's: 486

DUNCAN
Mary Louisa: 3514
Sarah: 1885

DUNGAN
Jane: 1288
Levi: 1161
Martha (Mrs): 1547
William H: 1270
Wm L W: 1439

DUNKHORST
Dorus: 2453
H'y: 2453

DUNLAP
Worthington: 1254

DUNLOP
Henry (Col): 482
Lizzie: 482
Mary Ann: 291

DUNN
Barbara: 2876
Miss: 2185

DUNOTT
Emma: 4329
Justus (Dr): 4329
Thomas J (Dr): 1364

DUPEL
Elizabeth: 5040

DURBIN
Annie: 5118
Elizabeth: 220
James: 1178

Wm: 220
Wm (Col): 5118
DURGEN
Stephen: 1292
DURMIN
Edward F: 1451
DURNEY
Mary T: 2093
DUSCHE
George J: 1423
DUSING
Mary A C: 5143
DUST
Lewis: 1357
DUTROW
Amanda: 5597
Catharine: 2998
Catharine A: 2527
Columbia: 6062
Columbia F: 1303
Cromwell: 1305
E Frank: 2558
Eliza: 2925
Eliza Jane: 5601
Fannie E: 4183
Francina: 4522
Harriott E: 5983
Hattie L: 5759
Jacob W: 1363
John: 4522
Jos: 5983
Joseph S: 1394
Lizzie: 6055
Lydia: 5261
Mary: 4836
Philip H: 1207
R Claude: 1430
Randolph: 1200 1404 2558
Rebbecca E: 6116
Rebecca: 2229
Richard J: 1401
Robert H: 1199
Sam'l: 1303
Samuel: 1372
Sarah A S (Mrs): 6093
DUVAL
M (Maj'r): 1208
Malachi: 1208
DUVALL
A: 3046
Alex'r Tho's Hawkins: 1237 1267

Alta Zerah: 4568
Ann Rebecca: 6190
Annette P: 1818
Annie D: 635
Augusta: 4114
Benjamin F: 1316
Benjamin W: 1251
Columbia (Mrs): 6062
Daniel: 5007
Ellen Jane: 1236
Grafton: 1303
Grafton (Dr): 1163 1213
Henrietta D: 5868
Henry: 1213
J Ijams: 1397
James E: 1377
James L H: 1220
John: 1191 1222 4114
John W: 1238
Julia: 5007
Julia A: 116
Luther: 1422
Marsh M: 6190
Marsh Mareen: 1185 1222
Marsh Maureen: 1191
Nellie E: 6131
No First Name Given: 1449
Rebecca: 231
Ruth: 1282 3208
Sarah Ann: 1163
Tho's: 1236 1238 1282 1397
Wilber H: 1444
Wilbur H: 1413
Wm H E: 1422
Wm Luther: 1325
Wm T: 116 1185 1331
Wm W: 1266
Zerua Ann: 2220
DYE
Elizabeth: 1579
DYER
Edward: 1288
Elizabeth Ellen: 3395
Harry W: 1427
John H: 1428
John W: 1290
Kate E: 5394
Marion: 1453
Martha J: 73
Mary: 6006
Mary E (Mrs): 1757
Mary M: 4645
Sallie C: 2057

Walter R: 1462
EADER
Ab'm: 1471 1473 1485
Alice: 5345
Amelia Margaret: 5902
Ann Maria (Mrs): 2953
Annie C: 3811
Annie E: 629
Annie M: 5647 5656
August: 1804
Augustus L: 1661
Cha's E: 1642
Cha's W: 1582
Charles E: 1806
Charles M: 1804
Chas: 1806
Darias: 1473
David: 1476
David Nicholas: 1607
Edward: 1498 1541
Edward J M: 1805
Eliza C: 3361
Elizabeth (Mrs): 3247
Geo: 5103
George: 1485 1491 1501
Helen: 5480
Isabella Ann: 1578
Jane: 2944
John: 1491 1498 1501 1583
Jonathan: 1610
L B: 1607
Lewis: 4624
Lewis A: 1658
Lewis B: 1476 1610 1642 1687 1760 3361
Mannassah: 1583
Mary Ann (Mrs): 5103
Peter Mantz: 1760
Susan: 2940
Tho's: 1578 1661 3811 5902
Thomas: 2940
Thomas S: 1821
Virginia: 4624
W H: 1687
William: 1523
Wm: 629 1471 2944 5345
EAER
Wm: 1582
EAGLE
E Frances: 1247
George W: 1636
Lycurges: 1713
Sally E: 1621

William: 1494 1529 1711
William H: 1605
Wm: 1247 1621
EAKLE
Laura V: 5432
Susan A: 2539
EARDMAN
Frederick F: 1735
EARLY
John: 2270
Margaret: 2270
EARNSHAW
Georg: 1822
Olive R: 2423
EARY
Theresa: 1128
EASTBURN
Robinson: 775
Sarah: 775
EASTER
Hamilton: 1697
EASTERDAY
Daniel: 1551
Geo E: 1751
Joseph: 1765
Martin VanBuren: 1728
Susan E: 5893
EATON
Elizabeth A J: 980
Henry: 1535
John H (Hon): 1496
Mary L (Mrs): 467
EATY
Henry B: 1499
EAVES
Katie: 2134
Mary Jane: 2501
EBAUGH
Emma: 766
EBBERTS
Annie M (Mrs): 3427
Catharine E: 1935
Geo Fred'k Erdman: 1762
Jos: 1935
Jos M: 3411
Joseph: 1573
Joseph Matthias: 1550
Louisa C: 1169
Mary E: 3411
Mich'l: 1895 4768
Michael: 1169
Sarah E: 3851

Susan: 4768
Thomas H O: 1803
Wilhelmina: 1895
Wm: 1573 1762 1803
EBEL
Jacob: 1639
EBERHARDT
Matilda (Mrs): 4034
EBERT
Adam: 1601
Adam S: 1596
Ann Rebecca: 4426
Augustus F: 1507
Augustus H: 1764
B: 1794
Benj: 1406
Benj'n: 1611 1764 5922
Benjamin: 1500
Caroline M R: 5922
Charles S: 1792
Charlotte: 1601
Edward C: 1794
Emanuel: 1474
Fannie V: 1375
Geo Adam: 1596
Grace A: 6138
John: 1478 1500 1558 1579
1611 1794 1815 1821 4426
John M: 1549 1774
John Wm: 1774
Katie R: 1821
Laura V: 1768
Rebecca M: 1406
Valerius: 1375 1558 6138
Valerius (Jun'r): 1739
Vals: 1792
William H: 1815
Wm: 1579 1768
EBNECHT
Ann Rebecca: 401
John: 401
EBRECHT
Amanthe E: 3343
Cornelia: 3380
George F: 1772
Georgianna: 1271
James: 1787
John: 1271 3380 6007
John (Jonathan): 1509
Jonathan: 1772
Luther N: 1631
Margaret Ann: 6007
No First Name Given: 540

William: 1566
EBUR
E M (Lieut): 1712
Edwin: 1712
ECKER
Albert W: 1850
ECKERD
Titus: 1665
ECKES
Harriett E: 2319
Susan: 5833
ECKIS
Juliann: 4051
ECKLES
Grace M: 2661
ECKMAN
Jane Sophia: 4883
John W: 1620
Mary: 4292
ECKSTEIN
Annie M: 2589
Ch'n: 610
Chr'n: 2589
Christian: 3138
Christian H: 1784
Ella V: 5474
Lizzie: 610
Louisea E: 2647
Mary C: 3138
No First Name Given: 1833
EDGAR
Caro'e Leroy (Mrs): 632
EDMONDS
Ella: 3975
EDMONSON
Ellen: 1919
EDMONSTON
Richard A: 1600
EDSALL
Emma L: 5192
EDWARDS
Miss: 3784
Samuel: 1601
EGE
Andrew Gailbraith: 1614
EGLESTOWN
Lucy: 1448
EICHEL
H L: 1662
EICHELBERGER
Abraham J: 1854

Ann: 5010
Ann M: 1251
Ann Maria: 1912
Annie M: 4690
Catherine: 320
Elizabeth Jane: 5942
Emma J: 673
Frances M: 2603
Francis M: 1819
Geo M: 5867
Geo M (Col): 1902
Grayson: 1563 2603
J Dix: 1606
Job D: 5942
Jos: 5027
Lewis (Rev): 1502 1538
Mahala: 4211
Margaret: 5867
Martin: 1486 5010
Martin J: 1704
Mary: 400
Mary Jane: 314
Mary M: 5027
Nancy: 1902
Peter: 4211
Rebecca: 4870
Samuel: 1682
Sarah Jane: 1566
Singleton: 1719
Susan M: 6221
Wm H: 1767

EICHENBROD
Daniel: 1542

EICHHOLTZ
Jesse: 1633
Lydia: 1645

EICHLER
Mary Ann Elizabeth (: 964

EICHNER
John: 1675
Mollie: 4182

EICKEL
Anna: 4750

EIDEMILLER
Mary Ann: 3283

EILER
Jeremiah: 1701
Juliann: 524

EINSTEIN
No First Name Given: 2441
Samuel: 1616

EISENBRANDT
Henry W R: 1672

EISENBRANT
Lisette D: 4869

EISENHART
J Schmucker: 1655

EISENHAUER
Balthaser: 1619
Catharine (Mrs): 5927
John: 1734
Joseph F: 1766

EISENNAGEL
Eliza: 4584

EISLER
Geo: 4180
Mary E: 4180

EISSLER
Daniel G: 1832

ELDER
Elizabeth: 3548

ELDRIDGE
Clarke: 1795
Miss: 4357
No First Name Given: 5347
Olen Emory (Rev): 1788
Sarah Payson (Mrs): 4280
Wm C: 1795

ELECK
Anna M: 5024

ELEGAN
Della: 4191

ELGEN
John: 1685

ELIOTT
Agnes: 1796
Jas: 1796
Robert (Rev DD): 1472

ELKINS
Edward J: 1829
Eveline: 4905
Fannie: 3738
Henry M (Dr): 1681
Jos: 3738
Jos D: 5353
Joseph D: 1565
Laura V: 5353
Margaret: 2928
Missouri M: 3184
Stephen B (Hon): 1786
Wm: 2928 4905

ELLIOTT
Curtis E: 1667

Ethel: 6279
Grafton W: 1691
James: 1564
James H: 1855
Tho's: 1479

ELLIS
Crosby W: 1561
Dan'l: 1641
Daniel: 1555
John D: 1747
Joseph: 1570
Mollie V: 712
Susan R: 1641
William: 1552

ELLSWORTH
Frederick: 1487

ELVINS
William R: 1465

ELY
Catharine: 2222
Dan'l: 1161
David W: 1589
Elizabeth: 5584
Ezra: 1488 1741 4291
Harriett A: 4291
Helen R: 5344
Isaac: 727
Isaac H: 1603 5422
James: 1741
M Ella: 5422
Maggie: 727
Martha (Mrs): 1161
Nellie M: 5489
William J: 1650
Wm: 1589 2222 5584

EMBRECHT
John: 3343

EMERICK
Margaret: 897

EMERY
John H: 1785
Olive P: 2607

EMLEY
Ann Sophia: 4249
David M: 1482 4249
Rebecca (Mrs): 6171

EMMART
Joseph: 1776

EMMITT
Emily: 212
Henrietta: 5779
Wm: 5779

EMMRUN
  Joseph -- (Dr): 1839
EMORY
  Catharine W (Mrs): 3643
EMRY
  Wm H: 1808
ENBELBRECHT
  Margaret (Mrs): 2321
ENGEL
  Christianna L: 3731
  Ezra: 1678
  John: 3731
  Lydia A: 576
  Martha S: 5399
  Mary Ann: 3815
  Rebecca (Mrs): 2903
ENGELBRECHT
  A Lincoln: 1852
  Adam: 3630 4486
  Agnes: 1017
  Barbara: 3630
  Catharine: 2150
  Eliza: a3
  Florence K: 3178
  Geo: 1017 1840 3178
  George: 1513 1628 1836
  J Adam: 5358
  Jacob: 1481
  John: 1591 1840
  John Adam: 1586 1628
  John Conrad: 1591
  Kate: 5358
  Lewis W: 1846
  Luther M: 1727
  Margaretta: 4486
  Mary Ann: 3057
  Mich'l: 1481 3057 5254
  Michael: 1533
  No First Name Given: 6113
  Philipp Melancthon: 1630
  Rebecca R: 5254
  William: 1505
  Wm: 1727
ENGLAND
  Caroline: 2170
  Catherine: 175
  Harriet L: 1722
  Harriett A: 5038
  Henrietta: 2438
  James W: 1722
  John W: 1721
  Juliann: 1176
  Sarah: 151

ENGLAR
  Samuel L: 1826
ENGLE
  John R: 1623
ENGLEBRIGHT
  John: 1483
  Mich'l: 1483
ENGLES
  Ann Elizabeth: 4453
  Catharine: 2941
  Cristianna: 200
  Silas: 200 4453
ENGLISH
  George N: 1837
  Isabella: 2744
  James J: 1575 5437
  Jonathan W: 1363
  Mary J: 3896
  Rich'd: 2744
  Richard: 1575 5838
  Ruth Ann: 1363 5838
  Sophie L: 5437
ENNIS
  Mary C: 3132
ENOLE
  Annie R: 2014
ENRIGHT
  P J: 1714
  Patrick: 1714
ENSHAW
  Georg: 1822
ENT
  Charles W: 1578
  Geo W (Capt): 172 1578
  Mary: 172
  No First Name Given: 1576
  Otho George: 1527
ERDMAN
  Barbara: 1929
ERITT
  No First Name Given: 2755
ERNSPWILLER
  Henry: 2756
ERNSTBERGER
  Catherine: 155
EROIN
  Wm T: 1673
ERVIN
  Hariett (Mrs): 2015
  Mary Virginia: 3773
ESKSTEIN

  Ch'n: 1779
  Wm F: 1779
ESTERLY
  Bettie: 4711
  Bettie E: 1772
  Clara: 1810
  Frederick: 1593
  Geo: 1598 4711
  George: 1825
  George (Jun'r): 1653
  John P: 1770
  Mollie: 1848
  Philip: 1693
  Rosa A: 5408
  William: 1709
ESWORTHY
  Fannie: 4174
  Harriet: 1831
  James: 1585
  Joseph W: 1671
  Mary P: 4616
ETCHISON
  Annie M: 1002
  Frank B: 1847
  Grace: 2137
  Helen M: 79
  Henry N: 1841
  Lenora: 1458
  Marshal C L: 1801
  Perry G: 2454
  Ruth: 5888
  Sarah Roberta: 2454
  Tho's: 1002
  Tho's H: 79
ETSCHBERGER
  Berthia C: 1203
EULER
  Andrew Jackson: 1689
  Margaret: 230
EULISS
  Mary: 2750
EUSTIS
  George (Hon): 1659
EVANS
  Corilla: 932
  F James: 1649
  French S (Rev): 1699
  M Topham: 1580
  Richard K: 1802
  Tho's B (Dr): 1698
  Topham: 6083
  Toppie: 6083

EVERHART
  Cornelia: 138
  Geo F: 1732
  O T: 1660
  Serauda E C: 38
  Sue: 4143

EVERS
  Wm (Rev): 1763

EVES
  Katie: 2134
  Peter: 1608

EVITT
  Joseph: 1468
  No First Name Given: 5829
  Woodward: 1467 1468

EXNER
  J Sebastian: 1730
  Mary (Mrs): 1730 5401

EYLER
  Emeline: 1033
  Ephraim: 1740 1851
  Jennie H: 5517
  Joseph H: 1679
  Laura: 2839
  Tho's W: 1848

EYSTER
  D A S: 1576
  David: 1576

FACKLER
  Mary: 5238 5694

FAGAN
  Allen C: 1810
  Charles: 1715
  Elizabeth: 1524
  Emma: 6124
  Geo: 1524 2330
  George (Jun'r): 1556
  Mary Jane: 2330
  Tho's: 6124
  Thomas: 1587 1695 1810

FAHRENSTOCK
  Matilda: 2895

FAIR
  Laura: 3434

FAIRBANKS
  Elizabeth Ann: 4495

FALCONER
  Maria O: 3436
  Wm H: 3436

FALK
  Eva M: 3002

  John M: 1643
  Mary: 5717

FALLON
  John F: 1725

FARROW
  Mollie C: 1025
  Wm H: 1750

FAUBEL
  Barbara A: 3848
  Catharine A: 315
  David: 1512 1518
  Jacob: 315 1571
  John: 1759
  John Jacob: 1571
  Joseph D: 1536
  Lydia A: 1510
  Solomon: 1554

FAUBLE
  Alice: 3176
  Annie E: 5492
  Barbara: 692
  John: 1843
  Mary E: 5446

FAUL
  Elizabeth: 4820
  Maria: 2911

FAUNTLEROY
  Lizzie R: 3838

FAUST
  Wm: 1817
  Wm A J: 1817

FAUTH
  Christianna: 5774

FAVORITE
  Deborah: 3681
  Henry: 1702
  Wm L: 1645

FAVOURTIE
  C: 1704

FAY
  Caroline C: 67
  Theodore S: 1651
  Thodore S: 67

FEAGA
  Christianna: a1
  Cordelia C: 5426
  Elmer B: 1828
  Frederick: a1
  George: a1
  George (Sen'r): 1562
  Philip: a1
  Rebecca: 4536

FEARHAKE
  Adolphus (Jun'r): 1796

FEASTER
  Benjamin: 1632
  John H: 1718
  Mary Catharine: 5031

FEESTER
  Kate A: 1789

FEETE
  Daniel (Rev): 1771
  Harrison: 1531
  Henry: 1789
  Wm C: 1789

FEGLER
  Miranda: 4481

FEIGHLER
  Joseph: 1581

FEIGLEY
  Daniel F: 1816

FEINAUER
  Mary K (Mrs): 1784

FEINAUR
  Mary K: 1784

FEIT
  J Jacob: 1595
  Jacob: 1528 5064
  Mary: 5064

FEITZ
  Geo V: 1703

FELDHEIMER
  Theresa: 2140

FELTY
  Rachel C: 1199

FERREE
  Daniel: 1517

FERRELL
  Martha Ann: 2796

FERTICH
  John: 1514

FESSLER
  Caroline R: 2309
  Henry B: 5246
  Henry Baer: 1519
  John: 2309 4815
  Laura: 5246
  Rosanna: 4815
  Susan: 585

FETTE'
  Dorothea: 2234
  Eliza M: 3289
  Johanna: 890

Melle': 2234, 3289
FETTERLING
Geo R: 1618
FEW
Howell: 1495
William: 1469
FEY
No First Name Given: 5401
FICKEY
Molly J: 5335
FIDE
Susan: 1669
FIEGE
Catharine M: 2285
Charles E: 1710
Fred'k: 1559
George: 1562
Philip: 1559
Rebecca: 4536
FIELD
Maggie: 759
FIELDS
James: 1737
Malinda: 5840
FIGGINS
Annie M: 3432
James: 1644
FILBY
C Lizzie: 2716
Mary: 2070
Samuel L: 1807
FILLER
Benjamina: 5619
Eli: 1526 4223
FILLMORE
Millard (Hon): 1647
FINCH
Ann Catharine: 345
Cath Ann: 1691
John: 345 1557 1589
Julia: 1589
No First Name Given: 2517
Wm: 1557
FINDLEY
Eliabeth: 4513
FINE
John: 1664
FINGER
John Adam: 1480
FINK
Catharine E: 4104

Lizzie: 2825
Margaret: 6172
Mary: 3264
FINLAYSON
L A: 1752
FINNEY
Ch'n Keefer: 1634
James: 1511 5996
Mary Fannie: 5996
FINNY
Clark: 1652
FIRESTONE
Frederick: 1569
Henry: 3845
Henry M: 1548
Jacob: 1548 a1
Joshua: 1503 1708 6208
Martin Luther: 1708
Mary M: 6208
Oscar F: 1824
Teresa E: 3845
FIROR
Calvin L: 1676
Ephraim: 1613
FIROUR
B U: 1833
FISCHBACH
Margaret: 125
Matilda (Mrs): 4109
FISCHER
Adam: 216 3998 4732
Ann E: 839
Anna M: 1762
Catharine: 4799
Catharine B: 506
Elizabeth: 1675
Frederick: 1842
George Jacob: 1522
Harriott Ann: 6192
Jacob: 4799
Julia: 3040
Margaret: 1892
Mary: 388
Minerva: 3998
Miranda: 4732
No First Name Given: 2774 4094
Sarah: 216
William (Dr): 1466
Wm: 6192
FISH
Hamilton (Hon): 5981

Henrietta: 2947 4425
Miss: 5981
Nancy: 658
Preserved: 1545
FISHER
Adam: 1892
Ann Mary: 3777
Annie E M (Mrs): 3841
Barney: 1617 1646 1696 1726 5224
Cha's: 1835
Charles: 1745
Clara Ida): 2714
E Jane: 5224
Elizabeth J: 4364
Florence: 3452
George J: 1799
Grace J: 2714
Hugh: 1625 3777
Ida L: 2090
John: 1637
Joseph R: 1543
Lewis: 1577 1646 1726
Lucinda J: 3101
Moses: 1812
Parks: 1729
Sarah Ada: 5536
Warner: 1696
William: 1657
Wm: 3452
Wm H: 1617 1749
FITCH
Mortimer C: 1692
Tho's W: 1780
FITZGERALD
Aaron (Capt): 1544
Maria: 1477
FITZHUGH
Benj G: 5082
Mary P: 3702
Peregrine: 3702
Sophia A: 5082
FITZPATRICK
Biddy: 2171
Catharine: 3727
Daniel: 1484
FITZSIMMONS
Sophia: 2821
FLAREY
Elizabeth (Mrs): 2996
FLEET
John A: 1588

FLEIGHNER
 Charles: 1809
FLEISCHMAN
 Carl: 1758
 Elizabeth (Mrs): 3112
 John H: 1758
FLEMING
 Alice: 4770
 Alice E: 1712
 Amelia: 2162
 Anna V H: 1960
 Arthur: 2162
 Catharine: 5848
 Charles F: 1641
 Charlotte: 10
 Eleanor: 2189
 Elizabeth: 2336
 Fannie: 1715
 Hallie M: 3830
 Ida M: 5475
 J Alfred: 1627
 J Randolph: 3830
 John: 1516
 John C: 1622
 John E: 1706 1800
 Jos: 2189 3527
 Jos P: 390 1622 1627 1960
 Joseph P: 1490 1609
 Julia A E: 390
 Katie H: 1102
 Mary: 4202
 Richard: 1773
 Robert: 1754 1798
 Robert C: 1621
 Sarah: 2196 2255 3527
 Tho's A (Dr): 1515 1641 1706 1712 1715 1754 1798
 Wm: 1838
 Wm Randolph: 1572
FLEMMING
 J Alfred: 6267
 Laura K: 6267
 Marianna: 872
 W Norman: 1733
FLING
 Thomas: 1612
FLOOK
 Eveline E: 2765
 Jacob: 2765
 Jonas: 1746
 Jonas E: 1684
 Sarah A (Mrs): 1275
FLORENCE
 No First Name Given: 1677
FLOWERS
 Ann E W: 4125
 Benj'n C (Rev): 4125
 Benjamin C (Rev): 1530
 Michael: 1508
 No First Name Given: 1894
FLOYD
 J Walker: 1755
FOGEL
 Emeline: 1001
 Lydia A: 4886
 Margaret R: 1682
 Mary: 5775
 Michael: 1686
 Minerva A: 4098
 Rebecca: 455
FOGLE
 Flora E: 136
 Margaret: 253
FOGLER
 Henry: 1547
 Henry (Jun'r): 1477
 Mary: 5238
 No First Name Given: 834
FOLLAND
 John: 1731
FOOTE
 Henry S: 1663
FORD
 A W (Dr): 1791
 Cha's W: 1849
 Eveline R: 3043
 John B: 1567
 John T: 1599
 Lulie B: 1143
 Mary: 4286
 No First Name Given: 1567
 Robert: 1560
 Susan: 4017
 Susan E: 4873
 Wm Henry: 1723
FOREMAN
 Cha's V: 1656
 Mary W: 3156
FORMAN
 O T/S: 1813
FORNEY
 Allie R: 4720
 M Ella: 5485
 Rebecca A: 4720
 Samuel J: 1853
 Susan S: 581
FORREST
 Elizabeth: 2521
 Mary C: 4078
 Summerfield: 1635
FORTNEY
 Elizabeth: 5788
 Lucretia R: 2536
FORWARD
 Annie E: 927
FOSSETT
 Francis C: 1707
FOSTEN
 Euphrosina: 2468
FOSTER
 Martha Angeline: 5885
 Rachel: 3386
FOUKE
 Isaac: 1604
FOUT
 Baltzer: 1470 1590 1880
 Barbara Ann: 3308
 Bradley T: 1757
 Catharine: 1550
 Catharine (Mrs): 2926
 Charles B: 1748
 Charlotte: 1244
 Clayton O: 1834
 Cyrus A: 1790
 Dan'l: 1506
 Daniel: 1489 1497 1504
 David: 1076
 David J: 1590
 Elizabeth: 1171 3480
 Emma: 6122
 Fannie E: 5331
 Geo: 3397
 Geo H: 1394
 Geo Wm: 1738
 George: 1532
 George H: 1831
 George Henry: 1615
 Grafton: 1539 2044
 Greenberry: 1537
 Greenbury: 5331
 Greenbury G: 1683
 Isadore: 6086
 Isadore V: 2044
 Jacob: 141
 John H: 1521
 Julia M: 2052
 Laura R: 5458

Lewis: 960 1489 1497 1504 1769
Lewis F: 1775
Lillie F: 1076
Many M: 4450
Margaret: 1494
Margaret E: 886
Marshal: 1820
Mary A: 1404
Mary C: 3397
Michael W: 1592
Olivia: 960
Ora: 4699
Orie: 4699
Othetta L: 5076
Otho: 1506 2926 3308 5076
Otho F: 1777
P T: 1790
Peter: 1171 1550
Peter S: 886 1492 1748 1757 2052
Peter T: 1615
Rebecca: 1880
Sophia: 141
Sue A: 1394
Susan C: 4610
Wm: 1494 1521 1592 3480 4450

FOUTZ
Agnes Ann: 4069
Geo W: 1724
Joseph: 4069

FOWLER
David Q: 1688
Oliver Perry: 1668
Samuel L: 1670

FOX
Adolph: 1408
Adolphus: 1042 1742
Ann Elizabeth: 1276
Ann J: 726
Baltzer: 1276
Cha's B: 726 1742
Cha's H O: 1638
Charles J: 1525
Christine Wilhelmina: 2986
Corona: 756
E A C: 1797
Eliza A: 2107
Emma Francisco: 1408
Ernest A C: 671 3802
Ernst A C: 1720 1761
Ernst Augs: 1761

Geo H: 652
George F V: 1814
Harriott: 3644
Henry C: 1744
Ida V: 671
Jacob: 1073
James H: 1674
Johanna: 1042
John F A: 1811
Joseph C: 1666
Juliann: 5886
Lewis M: 1797
Margaret: 245
Maria: 292
Maria J: 2078
Mollie E: 1073
Orlando B: 1716
Rebecca (Mrs): 2314
S W: 3802
Singleton E: 1753
Sophia: 652
Sophronia: 756
Thomas E: 1756
Victoria V: 4328
William A: 1568

FRAAS
George: 1540
Mrs: 1595 5734

FRAIM
Ann M: 2295

FRALEY
Alice R: 1376
August: 1440
Clara N: 5405
Cora H: 1440
Ella: 2860
Ellen: 2860 5088
Eutoka G: 1414
H'y: 634
Henry: 1367 1524
Jennetta: 634
John F: 1690
Lewis: 1845
Lizzie: 3059
Mahlon Augustus: 1700
Margaret: 5221
Victoria: 1367

FRANCE
Louisa M: 590

FRANKLIN
Ann R: 5239
Benjamin (Dr): 1793

FRANTZ
No First Name Given: 142

FRANZ
Matilda: 4821

FRAYLEY
H'y: 5405

FRAZIER
Amelia Ann: 5127
Ann Catherine: 3651
Ann Elizabeth: 917
Ann Mary: 1629
Bettie: 5431
D'd: 2127 6250
David: 135 1594 1818
Ernst D: 1818
Fanny M: 6140
Fielder: 1475
Florence V: 6250
Ida: 1413
Jennie R: 2667
Jeremiah: 246 1546 1594 3651 5127
Jeremiah H: 1629
Lillie R: 135
Luther: 1584 2667
Mahala: 5797
Margaret: 246
Nannie: 2127
Sylvester A: 1626
Virginia R: 2667
Wm: 1546
Wm H: 1669

FREANER
Margaret: 4054

FREDERICK
Wm Nicholas Charles: 1648

FREED
J D (Rev): 1823

FREEZE
Wm O: 1830

FRENCH
Ford Jones: 1624
Mary: 3741

FRENSCHBACH
Frederick: 1520

FREY
Catharine: 5111
George: 1640
Henry: 1730
Joseph: 1493
Lucy: 5646
Mary P: 166
Robert: 1827

FRIDAY
    Henry: 1597
    Henry (Jun'r): 1574
    John M (Rev): 1778
    Susan A E: 3798
FRIEND
    Edward H: 1680
    Rachel Ann: 941
FRIEZE
    Mary A: 1319
FRISBY
    Edgar: 1768
FRISLER
    Geo: 5770
FRITCHIE
    No First Name Given: 4826
FRITZ
    Laura V: 689
FRIZZELL
    Mary Ellen: 5757
FROLICH
    Alice: 1376
    Henry: 1367 1524
    John F: 1690
    Lizzie: 3059
    Mahlon Augustus: 1700
    Margaret: 5221
    Victoria: 1367
FROMKE
    August: 2577
    Henry W: 1783
    Matilda D: 2577
FROS
    Margaret: 5734
FROSCHAUER
    Adam: 1510 1694 2902
    Ann M: 988
    Geo C: 1705
    Geo W: 1534
    Isabella: 4952
    John M: 1694
    No First Name Given: 1900
    Sevilla: 3222
    Sophia: 2902
FROSS
    Mary M: 3055
FROST
    Eli: 1736
FUGITT
    Mary E: 3899
FULL
    Madera: 385
FULLER
    Adelia: 703
FULMER
    Ann R: 3042
    Delia: 5357
    John Lewis: 1654
    Mary Catharine: 2551
    Susan: 5053
FULTON
    Alice: 3962
    Alice C: 4153
    C C: 5409
    C Henry: 1743
    Emma W: 5409
    John: 3827
    Joseph: 1602
    Lee Calvin L: 1717
    Maggie: 3827
    Margaret C: 4581
    Mary S: 3730
FULTZ
    Mary Cath: 2404
FUNDENBURG
    Ann Maria: 237
    Juliann: 2762
FUNK
    Catharine E: 4104
    Fannie A: 4135
    Mary E V: 6256
    Minnie L: 1428
    Wm H: 1844
FURUHR
    Ephraim: 1613
FUSS
    Jeremiah: 1553
GAINES
    Edmund P (Gen'l): 1910
    Lucy B (Mrs): 5910
GAITHER
    Annie E: 336
    Elizabeth Ann: 4026
    George: 1976
    Lott: 1942
    Louisa: 3572
    Margaret R: 4251
    S Jane: 950
    Sophia: 5442
    Stuart: 336 950 1856 3572
    Wm: 4026
GALBRAITH
    Sam'l H: 2055
GALE
    Susan M (Mrs): 81
GALEZIO
    Cha's: 2206 6174
    Margaret: 2206
    Sarah: 6174
GALLAGHER
    Harry P (Dr): 2142
    Tho's: 1873
GALLAHER
    John S: 5012
    Mary Ellen: 5012
GALLE
    Catharine V: 1708
GALLE'
    Henry: 1936
GALLIAN
    John P: 2015
GALLION
    Ann Louisa: 1336
    Emily A: 5037
    Geo F: 2036
    John P: 989 1336 2036 5037
    Molly E: 989
GALLOWAY
    Nelson: 1998
GAMBRILL
    Ann Margaret: 4528
    Annie M: 3920
    Cha's A: 1882 1902 4528 5649
    Emily S: 5880
    Horace D: 2020
    James H: 2004
    Janie: 5649
    Nettie: 3185
GAMEZ
    Harold H: 2141
GANNON
    Catharine C: 528
    James M: 1957
    Wm E: 2064 2096
GANSAU
    Fannie S: 1794
GANTT
    Edward Anderson: 1878
GANTZAN
    Mary (Mrs): 1555
GANZAN
    George: 1934
    Henry: 1996

GANZAU
  Catharine M: 5094
  Jac: 5004
  Jacob: 5094
  Margaret: 2775
  Mary E: 5004
GARDINER
  Julia: 5591
GARDNER
  Elizabeth (Mrs): 3470
  Frederick: 1872
  Geo: 1858
  Henry: 1858
  Jacob: 1891
  James F: 2032
  John A P: 2117
  Mich'l: 1906
  Oliver P: 1906
GARLETZSKI
  Louis: 2011
GARNAND
  Geo R: 2144
GARNER
  Caroline: 1686
  Daniel (Rev): 1982
GARNHART
  Hy: a1
GARRETSON
  Nimrod: 1922
GARROTT
  Edward: 2101
  Emma O: 3800
  Joseph B: 2063
  Lee: 2139
  Sarah: 4237
  W M: 2026
GARROTT
  Willard N: 2121
GARTER
  Clementine V: 1998
GARVER
  Wm H: 1781 2083
GASEY
  Theodore: 1956
GASSAWAY
  Elizabeth (Mrs): 4254
GASTON
  Jane: 2999
GATCHELL
  Hugh McElderry: 2049
GATRELL
  James L: 1876
GATTON
  Harriott: 5282
GAUGH
  Daniel: 1958
  Eve: 2485
GAULT
  Adam: 1935
  Maggie: 3971
GAVER
  Elizabeth: 896
  Emma Susan: 2563
  Louisa C: 5294
  Mahala: 208
GAW
  U Annie: 567
GAYBRECHT
  Wm: 2018
GAYLORD
  Elizabeth (Mrs): 5790
GEAR
  Josiah: 1979
GEARY
  John W (Hon): 1986
GEBHARDT
  Geo: 2174
  Mary Ann: 2174
GEBHART
  John (Sen'r): 1883
GEBRECHT
  Wm: 2018
GEDULTIG
  Cha's H: 2039
  Mary Jane: 5953
  Rebecca: 3996
GEESEY
  Catharine: 4482
  John T: 1931
  Sarah J: 4999
  Susan R: 1031
GEETIG
  John: 1871
GEHRNETT
  Barb Ann (Mrs): 131
GEIGER
  John W: 2067
GEISBERT
  Christian: 2002
  Hester Ann: 3558
  Samuel C: 2127
  Stephen: 2127
  Wm H: 2118
GEISELMAN
  Michael: 1978
  Wm H: 2054
GEISENHAINER
  Augustus T (Rev): 2022
GEISINGER
  Annie A: 2564
  Barbara (Mrs): 2197
  David (Capt): 4229
  George D: 2128
  John J: 2003
  John W: 2078
  Sam'l L: 1638 2003 2564
  Sarah Catharine: 1638
  Sarah Elizabeth: 4229
  Tho's E: 2091
GEISSINGER
  Mary J: 6110
GEITZ
  Charles: 289
  Marg't: 289
  Mary: 4030
  Miss: 289
GELTZ
  John E: 1972
GELWICKS
  Ann Maria: 2192
  Cha's A (Rev): 1984
  Eleanora: 3542
  Geo C: 2192 2396 3542
  Louisa S: 4232
  Virginia F: 2396
GENNETZ
  John: 1983
GENSLEY
  Elizabeth: 2735
GENSLY
  Susan: 1866
GENTZEN
  Susan: 1866
GENZEN
  Elizabeth: 2735
GENZENBACH
  Cha's H: 2095
GEORGE
  Stewart: 2130
GEPHART
  Henrietta: 2210
  John: 1933 2210
  John (Jun'r): 1937

Simon Cronise: 1933
Solomon A: 1944

GERDEMANN
J W (Rev): 2085

GERE
John A (Rev): 1887

GERHART
E V (DD): 2089
Elizabeth B: 5021
Isaac (Rev): 5021

GERLACH
Henry: 2048
Jacob: 2088

GERLACK
Annie M (Mrs): 2664

GERLICH
Elizabeth: 6242

GERNAND
Jacob: 499
Joseph: 1967
Sarah E: 499

GERSER
George M: 2102

GERSHONG
Sarah: 4915

GETTINGER
Ed: 1854
Harriott R: 1963
John: 1963
Minnie: 1854

GETZ
Charles B: 2001
Margaret: 5457
Mary A: 802

GETZEBDANNER
Jacob (Col): 150

GETZEMDAMMER
Daniel: 2068

GETZENDANNER
Ab'm: 5926
Abraham: 1893
Ada Augusta: 5746
Adam: 863 1525 4639
Alexander: 1888
Ann Rebecca: 2325
Anna Kate: 5926
Anna Mary: 5887
Cath E: 3271 3590
Catharine: 3477
Catharine E: 1525
Catherine (Mrs): 2894
Ch'n: 1859 1865 1866 1897
Cha's: 1897 1940 5746
Charles: 1866
Christian: 1917 1940 2060 2060
Christianna: 5778
Dan'l: 1939 2047 5887
Daniel: 1863
Daniel (Jun'r): 1966
Edw T: 1382
Edward T: 1939 2068
Eli: 4639
Eveline: 5552
F Marion: 2072
Fannie: 5709
Geo: 1865 4945
Geo W: 2029
Hannah: 1858
Henry: 1861
Henry (Jun'r): 1867
Jacob: 1888 5778
Jacob (Col): 1186 2005
Jacob A J: 1952
Jacob R: 1960 4176
Jefferson: 3813
Jennie: 4176
John: 1857 1863 1893
John D: 1926 2044 2069
John J: 2005
John W: 2044
John W (Dr): 2076
Jonathan: 1857 1926 1960 1995 2065 2325 3271
Josiah: 1889
Katie: 2128
Laura V: 1382
Lawyer Jacob: 5778
Lydia A: 5240
M Eugene: 2047
Margaret (Mrs): 619
Margy G: 4945
Martha A: 3813
Martha V: 2076
Mary: 150
Mary A: 290
Mary C: 4639
Mich'l Jefferson: 1862
Minnie R: 5460
Nannie: 5533
Nettie: 745
No First Name Given: 3604 6086
Rebecca: 23 159
Samuel P: 2069
Sarah L: 863
Sol: 2128
Solomon: 1859
Solomon J: 2027
Sophia: 1186
Tho's E: 1995 2065

GETZMACHER
Wm Tho's J: 1989

GEWEYER
Catharine: 5769
Geo: 1928
George: 1864
Leonard: 1864 5769
Malinda: 6011
William: 1928
Wm: 6011

GEYER
John Wesley (Dr): 1971
Rebecca: 4204
W F: 2053

GEYSER
Sam'l: 1971

GIBBONS
Annie E: 3074
David: 2038
Jacob: 1870
John: 1870
Sabrina C: 3752
Susan: 2529

GIBBS
George W: 1914

GIBSON
Alexander E (Rev): 1970
Caroline G: 2805
Fannie H: 4333
Harriott: 4744
Horatio Gates: 2023
J Gregg (Dr): 1932 4333
Joshua Gregg (Dr): 2042
Margretta R M: 4934

GIDDINGS
Fannie E: 5948
James: 5948

GIESEY
S H (Rev): 1997

GIGUS
Henry: 1975

GILBERT
Alice Victoria: 3843
Ann M: 6220
Charles M: 2104
Daniel: 1901

David: 1884 2092
F Marshal: 2079
Geo A (Jr): 2129
George: 1964
George A: 2092
H Clay: 2094
James: 2086
James L: 2087
John A: 1991
John W: 1909
Julietta: 4021
Solomon: 1923
Susan M: 5156
Wm H: 2056
Wm L: 2134

GILDEA
John H: 2125

GILDZ
Mary Ann C: 1934
Rebecca: 339

GILLISS
M A B: 2995
Marianne A B: 2263

GILPIN
Charles: 1938

GILSON
Ella B: 747

GILTZ
Mary (Mrs): 5264

GINN
Mary: 476

GISE
Daniel W: 2143

GIST
G N: 2057
Newton H: 1896

GITTINGER
Edward: 3909
Edward Allen: 1999
Ella C: 2722
Frances B: 1379
Geo: 2028 2071 5869
Geo M: 2106
George: 1875 1953
Henry M: 2116
J Howard: 1947
J William: 1913
John: 1947
John E: 2071
Josephine: 6155
Lewis: 6155
Lewis C: 2028

Margaret J: 723
Mary C: 3935
Mary E: 5869
Myrile: 2111
Sallie R: 3909
Samuel J: 2133
Tho's C: 2046
Wm: 1379 2046
Z Ja's: 2106
Zachariah James: 1945

GITTINGS
Ella C: 2722
Lillie G: 3932

GIVINS
Charles: 1961

GLABSTER
Martin: 2132

GLADHILL
J Levi: 2100
John T (Rev): 2074

GLASNER
Annie R: 2104

GLAZE
Elizabeth: 5183
Joseph: 1981
Mary Ann: 1627
Zachariah: 2014

GLEASON
Margaret (Mrs): 5540

GLEIS
George Leonard: 2040
Mary M: 396

GLENN
Lewis W: 1868

GLESSNER
Amanda M: 2439
Geo M: 2439
Geo W: 1959
Geo W (Rev): 3048
Mary C: 3048
Wm: 1959
Wm (Capt'n): 1969
Wm T: 1969

GLISAN
Samuel: 1950

GLONINGER
Frederick: 1962

GLOSSIAM
Moddim: 5376

GLOVER
Cha's: 4994

Cora E: 3028
Mary Jane: 4994
Phebe: 813

GOBRICHER
Sussman (Rev): 1987

GOEBRICKER
Meyer: 2110

GOERING
Henrietta E: 4938

GOFF
Martha G (Mrs): 6075

GOLDBOROUGH
Leander W (Dr): 1885

GOLDEN
Mahala Jane: 3728
Margaret J: 2008

GOLDENBERG
Daniel: 2013
Henrietta: 3776
Henry: 1994
Julia: 5326
No First Name Given: 2140

GOLDSBOROUGH
Catharine E W: 1168
Cha's (Dr): 3795 5685
Cha's E: 2010
Cha's W (Dr): 1907
Cha's W (Jun'r Dr): 2035
Edw Y: 2082
Edward Y (Dr): 1874
John (Dr): 2025
Kitty Duckett: 3795
Minnie: 5711
Sarah E: 5882
Wm: 1168
Zoe: 5685

GOLDSCHMIDT
Otto: 1948

GOLDSMITH
Myer B: 2140

GOMBER
Christianna: 4734
Eza M: 2051
Ezra: 992
Ezra M: 1892 5189
John: 2051 4734
Minerva E: 992
No First Name Given: 1688 2284
Sallie A: 5189

GONDER
Thomas E: 2050

GONSO
 Fannie: 4375
 Laura: 1385
 Margaret: 2775
 Wm H: 1385
GONSON
 Fannie: 4375
GONTER
 John: 1898
GOODFELLOW
 Charles: 2030
GOODMAN
 Ellen: 4594
 Matilda: 3764
 Rebecca: 5379
GOODMANSON
 Peter: 1895
GOODMASON
 Peter: 1915
GOODSELL
 Wm Henry: 2073
GORDON
 Elizabeth: 1869
 Sarah: 1151
 Wm: 1869
GORE
 Clarissa Jane: 5837
 Jonathan: 1990
GORMLEY
 Matthew: 2093
 Thomas: 1993
GORRELL
 Molly A H: 2377
GORSUCH
 A P: 1894
 Abraham: 1894
 Robert: 1920
GORTON
 Emma V: 1349
GOSNELL
 Kate C: 2615
 L Ward: 2097
 Stewart F: 2105
GOSNER
 John: 1954
GOSSNEL
 Stewart F: 2105
GOSSNELL
 Ann Firoda: 1685
GOSZ
 Lorentz: 1905

GOUVENEUR
 Ruth M: 2853
 Sam: 2853
GOUVENIR
 Rose Di C: 2713
GOUVERNEUR
 Elizabeth K Bibb: 5169
 Sam'l L: 5169
 Samuel L: 1949
GOWING
 Ellen: 4881
GRABILL
 Catharine Ann: 4814
 Charlotte: 2260
 Henrietta: 4761
 J M, (Rev): 1988
GRACE
 Mary: 1258
GRACY
 John: 2041
GRAEF
 Gustav: 1929
GRAFF
 Caroline: 4212
 Geo: 1561
 Mary C: 1561
 Sebas: 4212
GRAHAM
 Arthur S: 2135
 Augustus: 788
 Eliza: 788
GRAHAME
 Ann R: 2768
 James: 1879 2037
 John (Maj): 1860
 Tho's J: 1860 2768
 Tho's J (Dr): 1974 2037
GRAHE
 Fred'k H: 2090
 John H C: 2075
 Julius: 2075 2090
 Julius A: 2109
 Sophia: 1145
 Theodore: 1927
GRAHE'
 Augusta (Mrs): 4080
 Louisa: 5029
GRAILEY
 Elizabeth: 4274
 Michael: 4274
GRANT

 Fred'k D (Col): 1782 2084
 Nellie W: 5391
 U S: 1782 5391
 Ulysses S: 2084
GRASER
 Ella M: 3214
 Mary C: 5530
GRAY
 Ann E: 471
 Cath D (Mrs): 3497
 Eliza Ann: 5808
 John F: 2000
 Peter: 1980
GRAYBILL
 Maggie: 4573
 Peter: 4573
GRAYSIN
 Lafayette: 2115
GRAZER
 Ella M: 3214
GREAGER
 George: 2112
GREBRICKKER
 Meyer: 2110
GREELEY
 Horace: 5402
 Ida: 5402
GREEN
 Benedict: 2526
 George W: 1977
 Hanson T C: 2024
 John Henry Francis: 2120
 John T: 1941 2019
 Mary C: 2841
 Sallie E: 2526
 Tho's W (Rev): 1877
 Wm: 2126
 Wm E: 2006
GREENBAUM
 Rachel: 719
GREENHOLTZ
 Jacob: 1900
GREENTREE
 Anna: 3684
 Eliza W: 1634
 Ezra: 1634 1652 1963 3684
 Howard: 1839 1963
 Isabella: 1652
 Mary Elizabeth: 2984
 Nettie H: 1839
 No First Name Given: 3180
GREENWALD

Ch'n: 1273 6177 6189
Christian: 1886
Emanuel (Rev): 1899
Maria: 6189
Mary C: 1273
Susan: 6177

GREENWOOD
Geo E: 2031

GREER
J Allen: 2059

GRELE
Elizabeth: 4274
Michael: 4274

GRELE'
Elizabeth: 2555
Mich'l: 6225
Susan A: 6225

GREUZARD
Louis: 1890

GRIER
Maggie A: 2541
Rob't S (Rev): 2541
Robert (Rev): 1921
Robert S (Rev): 1985

GRIFFIN
Evaline L: 5365
Frances M: 5456
Mahala C: 2633
William H: 2103

GRIFFING
George H: 2033

GRIFFITH
Clarence: 2137
Emanuel R: 1918
Emeline: 4103
Emily H: 5920
Florence C: 1847
John J: 2136
Leah: 881
Lebbeus: 1908
Mary: 6143
P H: 6143
Phelemon: 4103
Wm T: 1881

GRIM
Edward O: 1903
Sarah: 2868
Tho's C: 1925

GRIMES
Albert: 1919
Ann A W: 969
Augusta A: 5937
Frances M: 1943
Gassaway S (Dr): 1911
Julia A: 5086
Levi F: 1992
Millie: 3016
Napoleon B: 2062
Sarah Jane: 3770

GRIMM
Ann Sophia: 431

GRINDER
Jacob: 1904
Mary Ann Sevilla: 3687

GROFF
Cha's L R: 2138
David: 2113
Eli G: 2016
Fannie: 1424
Ja's: 4695
Jennie: 4695
Joseph: 1424

GROH
Joseph A: 2108

GROSBACH
Olivia: 2530

GROSHON
Abraham E: 1912
Geo S: 2045 2070 5414
George M: 2045 2070
Mary E: 5414

GROSS
Catharine: 1872
Clemma B: 4696
John: 2122
Wm H: 2081

GROSSNICKEL
D'l: 2578
Emanuel: 2034
Penelope A: 2578
Peter: 1955

GROVE
Alice B: 2042
Amelia: 3221
Anna M R: 5247
Annie J: 3127
Barbara A: 5202
Carrie E: 6133
Catharine: 2408
Christie S: 3382
Daniel R: 2007
David: 1968
Edward P: 2114
Elias: 2009
Emanuel M: 2058
Geo W: 2098
Greenberry F: 2066
Hannah: 9
Harriett: 6219
Hiram J: 2012
Jacob: 2042 2424 3221 3309 3646
Jeremiah C: 2017
Joan: 2424
John D: 3529
John R: 2119
Laura V: 5527
Lauretto: 1539
Leon'd S: 2066 3127
Leonard S: 1880 2077
Louisa: 626
Lydia Ann: 335
Manassa: 6133
Mannassah: 1951
Manzella M: 3646
Margaret: 143 2386 4243
Mary: 3529
Mary Ann R: 3309
Nancy: 4435
R Bella: 710
Reuben: 335 938 1968 2009 2408 4243 6219
Reuben E: 2021
Susan: 938 4005
Susan L: 3190
William P: 2052

GROVER
George M: 1916
Leonard B: 1973
Theresa: 2736

GROVERMAN
Fannie: 1402

GRUBB
Lydia Ellen: 970

GRUMBEIN
Alice M: 597
Calvin J: 2043
Dan'l: 2043

GRUMBINE
David George: 2124
Grayson?: 2124
Ida M: 3181
Issac M: 2107
John A: 2099
Rosa C: 2670
Wm: 2131

GRUND

Mary: 4667
Michael: 1946
GRUNDEL
   Eve Mary: 450
GRUSSER
   No First Name Given: 2468
GUE
   William H: 2008
GUELPH
   Victoria: 18
GUERAND
   Leonide M: 1063
GUIE
   Ellen: 3672
   Margaret: 402
   Rebecca: 915
GUIRY
   Wm G: 1965
GULL
   Ignatius: 2123
GULPH
   Victoria Adelaide M: 1648
GUMMEL
   Louisa: 571
GUNDLACK
   Charlotte: 3788
GUNDLOCK
   August: 2061
   Conrad: 2080
GUNN
   Walter (Rev): 1924
GUNTON
   Elizabeth Livingston: 251
   Harriott: 1466
GUYTON
   Ab'm: 1869
   Albert G: 2409
   Albert Gallatin: 1869
   Harriott J: 2409
   Mary: 423
   Ruth A: 4819
   Sarah (Mrs): 783
   Sarah J: 5665
GWYNN
   Robert: 1930
HABERCORN
   Sarah: 526
HABERKERN
   John L: 2646
HACK
   Mary Ann: 2757

HACKLETON
   Ethel: 3933
HADDAWAY
   S W (Rev): 2618
HADERMAN
   Carl Julien: 2177
HAFER
   Cha's H D: 2677
   Cha's M: 2676
   Samuel: 2408
HAFFER
   Julia: 4287
HAFFNER
   Elmer: 2733
   William A: 2664
HAFNER
   Eugene: 2696
   Minnie T: 6141
HAGAN
   Ann Rebecca: 4625
   Catharine: 4488
   Cha's M C: 2658
   Eugene M: 2670
   Francis T: 2539
   Henry: 2315
   Henry J D: 2693
   Ignatius: 2354
   Igns: 5404
   Igntius: 1405
   Isabella F: 5905
   John: 2212 2464 2498 2547 2670
   John C: 2498
   Lizzie C (Mrs): 5324
   Lou M: 5404
   Maggie E: 1405
   Mary A: 2960
   Michael: 2658
   Michael P: 2380
   Norman B H: 2684
   Peter: 2212 2257 2315 4488
   Peter A: 2547
   Stephen: 2257
   Wm E: 2464
HAGER
   Christian: 2197
   John: 2324
   Lena: 2030
   Lewis: 2478
   Martin: 2345
HAHN
   Charles N: 2676

Henry A: 2616
J W: 2605
Lewis E: 2654
Malinda Ann: 1633
Mary: 5434
Matilda: 362
Sarah A: 3097
Sophia L: 1032
William: 2403
Wm H: 2675
HAHNENKAMPF
   Mary Elizabeth: 2927
HAHRMAN
   Wm H: 2568
HAINES
   Annie: 2697
   Dorothy (Mrs): 1242
   Fannie C: 3438
   Francis R: 2587
   Granville S: 2366
   Hannah A: 1705
   Isabella: 4512
   Nicholas: 2499
   Thomas J: 2460
HALBERT
   Emeline: 4043
   Hanna: 5934
HALE
   Ann Virginia: 527
HALEY
   William: 2171
HALL
   B Franklin: 2534
   Barbara: 4920
   John: 2196
   Mary: 4866
   Mary Ann: 2237
   Ralph G: 2683
   Robert C: 2398
   Sarah, Mrs: 2255
   Tho's B: 4866 4920
HALLAR
   Cha's W: 2235
   Christianna: 3557
   Elisha: 2202
   Joseph: 1915
   Joshua: 2235 3557
   Mary: 1915
   Philip: 2155 2195
HALLEBAUGH
   Joel V: 2317
HALLER

Abner Davis: 2417
Alice L: 4148
Alice Virginia: 63
Alice Z: 1332
Amelia: 6036
Ann E: 5861
Ann Maria: 3665
Arthur N: 2706
Carrie M: 4327
Catharine: 1198 2403 2753 2880
Catharine A: 3284
Catherine E: 5598
Cecelia: 5016
Ch W: 63
Ch's W: 5702
Charles E: 2589
Christopher: 2146
Dan'l: 2585 2636
Daniel: 2192 2399 3012
Daniel G: 2585
David E: 2404 2674
David H: 2247 2628 6229
Eleanora L: 2399
Elizab: 293
Elizabeth: 3559
Elizabeth C: 529
Emma R (Mrs): 5529
Ezra: 1332 2203
Florence: 1827
Frank B: 2661
Geo W: 2153 2274
Grant L: 2690
Henry: 293 1546 2231 3284 4040
Henry W: 2520
Hettie P: 5702
Isaac H: 2535
Jacob: 2305 2305 2360 2589 2753 4463 5016 5731
Jacob (S & F): 2403
Jacob B: 2154
Jacob Junior: 2347
Jacob L: 2568
James S: 2636
John: 2156
John Alexander: 2146
John P (Rev): 2628
Joseph: 2185 5006
Joseph C: 2662
Joshua: 2880 4082
Julia Virginia: 71
Lottie: 3158
Louisa M: 4082
Lucie V: 3155
M H: 694
Margaret: 1546
Margaret A C: 3012
Margaret A E: 5731
Maria L: 439
Mary: 1498
Mary (Mrs): 1541
Mary E: 2568
Mary Ellen: 6229
Mary M: 694
Mich'l H: 529 687 2404 2520 4148
Michael: 2674
Michael H: 2205
Nich: 2661
Nicholas: 2645 2690
Nicholas T: 2273 4327
No First Name Given: 4917
Oscar L: 2652
Peter: 1198 1498 2153 2156 2185 2192 2203 2207 2247 3559
Phil: 2417
Philip: 439
Rebecca: 4463
S Loretto: 687
Samuel: 2207
Silas L: 2637
Sophia H: 5006
Susan: 4040
Tho's: 3155 6036
Tho's Grason: 2484
Thomas: 2252 2309
Thomas H: 2663
Tobias: 2205 2252 2645 2662
Tobias (Sen'r): 5861
Tobias W: 2231 2535
William: 2274 2360
Wm T: 2647

HALLEY
Catharine: 3532
Leonard: 2339
Mary A: 187
No First Name Given: 1688

HALLOWAY
A C (Rev): 2507

HALSEY
Eliza F: 876

HAMBLET
Sarah N: 4460

HAMBLETON
Mary: 4727

HAMBRIGHT
Annie: 6271

HAMIL
Henry P (Rev): 2695

HAMILL
Ann J: 4295

HAMILTON
Ann: 2755
Annie E: 2594
Benjamin: 2236
Catharine: 3666
Catharine (Mrs): 2389
Clara: 2141
Geo W: 2609
Isabella: 848
James D: 2630
John: 2245 2245 2482 2594 5829
John W: 2496
Mary: 4727
Miss: 4727
Pamelia: 5829
Penelope L: 4262
Randolph: 2601
Wm T: 2141
Wm T (Hon): 2457
Woodward: 2389 2496 3666
Woodward Evitt: 2222

HAMMACK
Emma L (Mrs): 1726

HAMMITT
Julia B: 2685
Susan B: 2685
Thomas P: 2511

HAMMOND
Ann J: 3574
Anna M: 2352
Annie C: 3429
Augustus (Rev): 2397
Burgess: 3167
Carrie B: 2041
Catharine: 2747 5097
Cha's: 2263
Charles S: 2263
Charlotte C: 5844
Clara: 2851
Dawson V: 2296 2352
Denton: 1403 2292 2314
Effie C: 5506
Elizabeth R: 2292
Emma: 2079
Grafton: 740 2164 2455

Hattie: 3167
John D: 2721
Laura A: 5753
Louisa (Mrs): 1301
M A B (Mrs): 2995
Maggie: 6275
Maria L: 2783
Mary A: 4672
Mary M: 1378
Mary Virginia: 2397
Miss: 1403
Nettie L: 740
Oliver B: 2463
Rich'd C (Dr): 5753
Richard F (Dr): 2268
Richard T (Dr): 1378
Susanna Ann: 4936
T (Dr): 2079
Upton J: 2328
Walter C: 2268 5097
Wm Edgar: 2454
Wm P: 2289

HAMMONTREE
Dorcus M: 4120

HAMNER
Elizabeth G: 1179
James G (Rev): 2194
Mary: 5565
Tho's L (Rev): 2282

HAMPFSTEIN
Christian: 2243

HAMPTON
Louisa: 489

HAMTRAMCK
John F: 2265

HAND
Emily J: 4991

HANDSCHUH
Kate: 1057

HANE
Catharine: 2244
Catharine M: 4441
Christianna C: 2918
Daniel: 2302
David: 2244
Fannie B: 6269
Frank T: 2600
Jacob D: 2302 6269
John: 2918 4441 5843
Mary C: 5520
Susan: 3750 5843

HANES
Emeline H: 1978

HANKEY
Mary E: 4526

HANN
R F: 2671
Susan: 3769

HANNA
Susan K: 5636

HANON
Margretta F: 5834

HANSEN
Marie: 5629

HANSHEW
Annie K: 6264
Caroline V: 3919
Daniel Stover: 2593
Edith M: 6161
Fred'k: 4016
Fritchie: 2451 6264
H'y: 2593
Hary: 3919
Henry: 119 2159 2451 4045
Henry E: 2297 2597
John: 2152 2297
Julia M: 119
Mary Margaret: 4045
Susan B: 4016

HANSON
Geo A: 2427
Sarah R: 2921

HARBACH
Charles M: 2553

HARBAUGH
Catharine N: 4500
Geo S: 2313
Harriott Josephine: 491
Henrietta C (Mrs): 1673
James P: 2450
John S: 2433
Levi C: 2370
Morgan: 2218
Simon W: 2500
Susan: 560

HARD
Edward D: 2248

HARDEN
Ellen: 957
William (Rev): 2371
Wm (Rev): 2425

HARDIE
Georgianna: 5208

HARDING
A Virgine: 3844
Alice R: 2050
Ardene: 2626
Barbara Ann: 4567
Basil: 2372
Bruce: 2720
Eleanora: 991
Elizabeth: 4813
Ellen: 957
Fannie V: 3946
James M: 2617
James Marshall: 2255
John B (Rev): 2673
John L: 991 2232 2255 2390 3617 4813
Lewis D: 2580
Lewis R: 2443
Louisa: 3617
Lucinda C: 3807
M Louisa: 4133
Margaret Ann: 1950
Marshall F: 2617
Mary: 177
Miss: 4133
Norman B: 2050 2232 4133
Norman Bruce: 2720
O P: 2626
Ph H: 3844
Sarah Ann: 2217

HARDINGER
Basil: 2372

HARDMAN
Elmore: 2504

HARDT
Charlotte: 2579 3356
Geo: 3356
Geo H: 2579
George: 2169 2233 2355
John: 1096 2150
John Conrad: 2326
Maggie C: 1096
Margaret C: 862
Peter: 2169 2233
Wm Mc: 2648

HARDY
Benjamin: 2173
Hamilton S: 2632

HARE
John J: 2577

HARGER
M: 2338

HARGETT
Ann Eliza: 2823

Ann M: 821
Ann R: 5115
Anna M: 5416
Annie M: 5673
Catharine B: 847
Charles E: 2641
Curtis F: 2522
David: 2229 2349
David Z: 2524
Douglas G: 2640
Edward S: 2702
Elizabeth Matthews (: 5049
Emma J: 4638
Francis A: 2615
Geo B: 2536
Harriott V: 429
John: 847 2227 2253 2356 5570
John B: 2440
John E: 2513
John H: 2191 2522 4633 4638 5673
John William: 2253
Juliann: 5570
Luther F: 2551 2638
Mary C: 2559 4633
No First Name Given: 5989
Peter: 2191 2228 5049 5115
Sam: 2640
Sam'l: 2559 2631
Samuel: 2227
Schaeffer T: 2631
Simeon W: 2633

HARGROVE
Maggie R: 1993

HARKER
Ann R (Mrs): 5251
Joseph: 2477

HARKEY
James M (Rev): 2310
James S: 2570
S W (Rev): 2570
Simeon W (Rev DD): 2544
Sydney L (Rev): 2322

HARKINS
Louisa A: 5917

HARKNESS
John C: 2401

HARLAN
James (Hon): 3393
Mary: 3393
Sarah: 2871

HARLEY
Elizabeth: 1664
G W Truman: 2392

HARMAN
Ann Maria: 2953
Eliza Ann: 4556
George: 2379
Jacob: 2885
Margaret: 2885
Mary Jane: 5140

HARN
Catharine A R: 6209
Elizabeth C: 3304
Levi O: 2220
Wesley J: 2447

HARP
Daniel V: 2480
Elizabeth: 1542
Lydia: 4490
M D: 2731
Mary A: 1335

HARPER
Alberta: 5652
Emma: 3077
James Emory: 2560
Lottie C: 5241
Richard: 2213 5241
Robert G: 2394

HARRINGTON
Adolphus H: 2624
Sarah C (Mrs): 4678

HARRIS
Amanda: 3405
Ann Virginia: 3319
Chancey (Capt): 2523
Edward: 2176 2481
Elizabeth: 4940
Geo W: 2538
George W: 2493
Henry R: 2277 3405
John: 2509
Josephine: 552
Maria E: 5966
Martin E: 2704
Mary Ann: 4617
My Elizabeth: 22
N J: 2523
Wm C: 2343

HARRISON
Edward: 2396
Geo W: 2556
Georgetta: 1059
Georgianna: 5320
Ida Virg: 5381

James W: 2529
Joseph: 2446
Joshia: 2286
Josiah: 1059 2051
Luther F: 2682
Lydia Ann: 855
Mary E: 2051 2547
Nimrod F: 2409
Orra: 2421
P Leonard (Rev): 2542
Rosanna: 6201
Sarah Ann (Mrs): 2038
Sarah F: 6025
Wm: 2502
Wm (Dr): 2502
Wm G: 2204
Wm H: 2619
Wm Henry (Rev): 2311
Zeph: 615 2286 2311 2396 2542 6201
Zephaniah: 855

HARRITT
Sophia E: 5858

HARRY
Wm H H: 2559

HARSHBERGER
Henry S: 2294

HARSHMAN
Israel: 2602
W W (Prof): 2732

HART
Adam: 2193 4741
Alice F: 3037
Ann Margaret: 867
Ann Maria: 4741
Caspar J: 2607
Catherine (Mrs): 189
Elias: 2303
Ja A: 6094
Jacob: 2193 2399 2607 3037
Jacob A: 2399
John: 867 2165
Mamie A: 6094
Susan V: 3147

HARTBAUER
Charlotte: 447
William: 2249
Wm: 447

HARTMAN
Annie M: 2601
Annie O H: 1829
Cecelia: 274
Frances O: 2343

Juliann: 203
Matilda: 256
Rosa: 5393
Simon: 2503 5393
Valentine: 2594

HARTSOCK
Ann M: 3538
Annie: 2081
Cha's T: 2703
Clarence L: 2717
Noah: 2321
Pamilia: 4771
S M (Rev): 2566
Wm: 2699

HARTT
Frederick P: 2400

HARTZ
Catherine: 142
Franz: 2188
Joseph: 2188 4821
Matilda (Mrs): 4821

HARWETEL
Ella: 760

HARWOOD
Emma: 1120

HASSELBACH
George: 2217
John: 2217

HATCH
Madaline C: 44
William S: 2161
Wm S: 44

HATTON
Nancy: 148

HAUER
Adam: 2239 5810
Annie M: 539
Catharine E: 337
Cha's N: 2716
Charlotte C: 1624
D J: 4758
Dan'l (Jun'r): 337 1572 2276 4047
Dan'l J (Rev): 1624 1873
Daniel Jacob (Rev): 2179
Elizabeth: 3523
Fritchie H: 2672
Geo: 3523
Geo N: 2376
Geo Wm: 2681
George: 2672
Harriott: 4047
Henry: 2376 5810
J Fisher: 2651 2667
Jane C: 3388
John: 539 2239 3388
Luther: 6274
Maggie H: 5494
Margaret Ann: 5810
Matilda: 1572
Minnie F: 6274
Nicholas D: 2276

HAUGH
Addison G: 2578
Clemmie A: 134
John W: 2462
Laura C V: 2105
Solomon: 2362
Susannah: 51
Wm: 2462
Wm H: 2369

HAUPT
Ann Rebecca: 4027
Jacob N D: 2439

HAUR
Belle S: 6106
Jno: 6106

HAUSER
Dennis D: 2474
Frank T: 2489
No First Name Given: 2112 4439
Paul: 2709
Sophia: 5830
Wm: 5830

HAVER
Dan'l J (Rev): 1732
Mary E: 1732

HAVILAND
Anna: 1697
James C: 1697

HAWKEN
Mary: 2299

HAWMAN
Philip Jefferson: 2183
Rebecca: 1185

HAY
Ann: 1904
Ch A (Rev): 2611
Charles A (Rev): 2291
Edwin B: 2635
Eliza: 3503
Mary Jane: 2611
Penelope Lynn: 1538

HAYDEN
James E: 2583
William: 2680

HAYDON
John A: 2595

HAYS
Ann J: 3569
Elizabeth (Mrs): 2751
Harriet A: 660
John B: 2456
M Louisa: 5982
Marietta: 312
No First Name Given: 2301
Sarah E: 4071

HEAD
Ann Catharine: 4598
Cecelius: 4598

HEAGY
G W (Dr): 2359
Jacob: 2407
Molly A: 5956

HEALD
William: 2323

HEARD
Fannie M: 1805
J Wilson: 2346
Wm K: 2659

HEATH
Grove: 2514

HECK
H Ridgely: 2612
John: 2612

HECKATHORN
Ch'n: 1008
Susan E: 1008

HECKENTHORN
Christian: 2242
Sophia: 19

HECKMAN
A Sophia: 3083
Sophia: 1864

HEDGE
Christian E: 2723
Clinton E: 2723

HEDGES
Andrew: 2147
Baily: 2266
Daniel A: 2332
Eneas: 2147
Enos: 1225 2332 2444
Henry S: 2492

John: 2221
Julia A: 3213
Julia Ann R: 1225
L E: 5720
Lewis A: 2494
Lillie: 5720
Lycurgus E: 2444
Mary J: 5478
Samuel H: 2700

HEEFNER
Philip: 2694

HEETER
John: 2495

HEFFNER
Catharine A: 2002
John H: 2375
John J: 2510
John P: 2655
Lewis C: 2415 2533
Lucretia R: 4377
Mary L: 516
Samuel P: 2344
Susan: 3302
William A: 2664
Wm W: 2285

HEFFRON
Mary J: 6104

HEFNER
Eugene: 2696
Fannie: 2649
Julius: 2696
Philip: 2694

HEFRON
Nathaniel: 2621

HEGESHEIMER
David J: 2278
Joseph: 2278

HEICHLER
Catherine: 4006
Henry: 4006

HEIDECKER
Henry: 2262

HEIGERD
Henry (Rev): 2472

HEIM
Andrew: 2312
Ann B: 3536
Ann Catharine: 5735
Charles G: 2582
Daniel L: 2625
David: 3536
David C: 2448
Edward P: 2367
Elias: 2163
Euphrosina (Mrs): 600
Jacob B: 2284 2582
James: 2363
Lewis: 5735
Lewis A: 600
Lewis Augustus: 2468
Maria Louisa: 4296
Mary Ann: 3258
Mary Mansilla: 1000
Sarah Rebecca: 1654
Susan C: 368
Tho's A: 2312
William D: 2208
Wm G: 2613
Wm H: 2561

HEIMER
Andrew: 2284

HEIMS
Maurice H: 2692

HEINER
Elias (Rev): 2216
John (Dr): 2260

HEINLEIN
Frederick: 2453

HEINRICH
Barbara: 1528 5726

HEINTZ
Adam: 2283 2521
Jacob Junior: 2501

HEISE
Henry L D: 2506

HEISELY
No First Name Given: 4423

HEISER
Georgeana: 3459
Levi F: 2519

HEISKELL
Elizabeth K: 427
Mary E: 1779

HEISTERMANN
Adolph: 2406

HEIT
Jacob: 2382

HEITSCHUH
Philip: 2259

HELDEBRAND
Amanda Melvina: 1608
Ann M: 551
John: 1608

Joseph D: 2531
Lewis H: 2422
Lewis M: 2471

HELFENSTEIN
Albert G: 2295
Catharine: 790
Cha's J: 2413
Ernest (Rev): 2725
Jona'n (Rev): 4780
Jonathan (Rev): 790 2295
Louisa C: 4780

HELFFENSTEIN
Cyrus G: 2437

HEMBRY
Alice V: 4565
Ann E: 5634
Arrabella: 3113
Elizabeth: 2923
Isaacher: 2419
Issacher: 2336
John: 2230 3064 3113 4565 5634
Mary Elizabeth: 3064
Matthew: 2923

HEMLER
Nannie D: 5525

HEMMEL
Cecelia M: 3543
Jacob: 3219 3543
John D: 2200
Margaret: 3219

HEMMELL
Jacob: 108
John D: 2334 3670
Kate M: 3670
Rosie: 108

HEMP
Clayton R: 2668

HEMSTON
Christian: 2243

HEMSTONE
Armstead T: 2320
Louisa: 4152

HEMSWORTH
Eliza A: 807

HENDERSON
Andrew: 3379
Deborah: 2965
Lucy Jane: 3608
Maggie J: 3379
Maria Cath: 2269
Mary: 4429

Mary (Mrs): 1986
Rob't: 2269 2965 3608
Robert: 4429
HENDRICKSON
Ephraim: 2414
John D: 2665
Mollie J: 3908
HENDRY
Ann A: 5067
Cha's: 70 1721 5386
Charles: 5067
Charles Junior: 2438
Emma C: 5386
Martha C: 70
Mary E: 1721
HENKE'
William D: 2467
HENNEY
Edward: 2705
HENNINGTON
Frances: 525
HENRY
Barbara: 1528 5726
Cornelia: 3376
Mary G: 3659
T Walton: 2342
HEPBURN
John Marshall: 2579
HERBACH
Mary An: 1174
HERBERT
John: 2378
Sarah C: 3267
HERBESHEIMER
Dan'l: 6215
HERD
Catharine: 182
Elizabeth: 1873
HERGESHEIMER
Ann Rebecca: 2317
Annie E: 4285
Annie S: 5523
Caroline V: 6215
Catherine: 334
Cha's A: 2571
Dan'l: 334
Daniel: 2170
Emma: 674
Florence R: 1814
Geo P: 2436
Ja's: 674
Jacob: 2449 2526

James: 2269
Jane Rebecca: 1575
Jos: 1575 3285 6175
Louisa: 3285
Mary A: 6175
Peter: 2180 2449 2526 4285
Sam'l: 2317 2571
Samuel: 2175 2271
Sophia (Mrs): 5042
HERGSPERGER
John: 2689
HERNDON
Jackson L: 2491
HERONIMUS
R S Dean: 2429
HERR
Rebecca: 3353
HERRING
Adam: 2193
Ann Sophia: 2307
Catharine: 189 2165
Daniel: 2306
Edward: 2705
Edward L: 2512
Geo Edward: 2461
H'y: 6207
Henry: 2158
John H A: 2316
Lloyd H: 2432
Mary: 2193
Mary J C: 6207
HERRINGTON
Elizabeth: 2948
Geo: 2386
Julia A: 5737
HERRMAN
Mich'l: 2517
HERRMANN
Lena: 1357
Maggie: 2517
Michael: 2555
HERSCHBERGER
Aaron B: 2479
HERSCHMAN
Anna M: 628
David W: 2488
HERSHBERGER
John: 2689
Tilghman T: 2656
HERTZ
Elizabeth: 2283
HERWIG

August: 2395
Wilhelmina: 5155
HERZOG
Ann M: 3538
Pamilia (Mrs): 4771
HESCH
Ann M M: 3115
HESS
L Araminta: 3420
HESSEN
Matilda E: 2383
HESSER
George Jacob: 2470
HESSONG
Rebecca D: 5364
HETTERLY
Elizabeth C: 426
HEUSER
Christian: 2288
HEWELL
James L: 2337
HEWES
Cha's K: 2707
HEWETT
Elizabeth: 4854
Mary Jane: 961
HEWITT
Melissa: 436
HEYSER
Augusta: 4106
Lewis F: 2622
William: 2148
HIBEARY
Bettie: 6282
HICKMAN
Mary E (Mrs): 1671
HICKSON
Susanna: 3
HIGBEE
Annie F: 3893
HIGGINGS
Hattie M: 5440
HIGGINS
No First Name Given: 5292
HIGH
Joseph A: 2416
HIGHTMAN
Frank: 2724
Jennie: 2730
Jos: 2730

Mary E: 2727
HILDEBRAND
　Annie E: 3210
　Cha's R: 2728
　Frank T: 2715
　Frederick: 2550
　Geo H: 2565
　Samuel T: 2576
　Wm H: 2333
HILDEBRIDEL
　Sarah: 998
HILDT
　Geo (Rev): 2610
　Geo C: 2610
HILL
　Ann M: 5997
　Anna Lavina: 6070
　C H: 2650
　Christopher: 2381 2423
　Cornelius H: 2603
　George S: 2599
　Margretta E: 443
　Maria: 1888
　Noah: 2657
HILLEARY
　Ann Perry: 924
　Bertha: 2101
　Edward J: 2358
　Elizabeth M: 324
　Ellen W: 5986
　Emma W: 705
　Laura Clagett: 2101
　Sarah T W: 5842
　Thomas: 2329
　Wm: 705
　Wm H: 2101
HILLIARD
　Clara B: 3950
HILLIARY
　Nannie: 4383
HILTNER
　Wm: 2660
HILTON
　Alice: 1347
　Ann F: 792
　Clement: 792 2240 6170
　Cora: 6101
　H'y K: 1347 2612
　Henry K: 1325
　Henry Konig: 2238
　Lovetto C: 2612
　Lucretia: 57

Margaret Ann: 2248
Mary S: 1325
No First Name Given: 1436
Rebecca E: 4458
Rosanna: 222
Susan G: 6170
William H: 2240
Willie Elizabeth: 5890
Wm H: 2698
HIMES
　John A (Prof): 2611
　William H: 2452
HIMMELL
　Francis B: 1093
HINCKEL
　Charlotte: 4927
HINDES
　Elizabeth H: 4250
HINEA
　Elizabeth: 4099
　Jacob H: 2485
HINES
　Elizabeth: 5232
　James C: 2364
HINKEL
　Moses M (Rev): 2162
　Nathaniel H: 2223
HINKS
　Cha's D: 2391 3134
　Mariann N: 5317
　Mary V: 3134
　Sam'l: 5317
　Samuel: 2272
HIPPENSTEEL
　Mary C: 3634
HIPSLEY
　Levi F (Dr): 2387
HIRST
　Allie R: 6053
　Wm (Rev): 6053
HISSEY
　Mary Ann: 2355
HITE
　Caroline M: 214
　Frances Conway: 5784
　Yost: 5784
HITESHEW
　Jennie: 4171
　Laura A: 4631
　Philip: 2259 2483
　Philip L (Capt'n): 2528

Sophia E: 2483
HITSELBERGER
　Fannie E: 4362
HITZELBERGER
　Fannie E: 4362
HOATS
　Morris: 2729
HOBBS
　Albert: 2487
　Amelia: 480
　Annie Virginia: 5936
　Charles S: 2483
　Clara: 3712
　Jackson: 2335
　Laura: 1384
　Mary A: 2675
　Mollie: 1447
　Rezin: 2206 2483 5936
　Samuel A: 2475
　Wm: 3712
HOBIE
　Elizabeth: 4620
　Phil: 4620
HOBLITZELL
　William: 2210
HOCH
　Catharine: 547
　David: 2598
　George: 2620
　Rebecca: 2837
　Sam'l: 547 2598 2620 2837
HOCK
　John: 158
HOCKENHEIMER
　Sadie A: 2684
HOCKENSMITH
　Jennie: 2092
HODDINOTT
　Charles: 2258 2518
HODGEKISS
　Lydia: 2296
HOEFER
　Sarah: 2976
HOES
　Russell R: 2713
HOESTER
　Jeanneta Ludovike Ch: 2989
HOFF
　John F (Rev): 2241
　John J: 2686

Peter: 2190
HOFFMAN
Ann Mary: 3217
Annie E: 5210
Caroline (Mrs): 5258
Catharine: 5546
Daniel: 2411
Elizab Steiner: 4055
Elizabeth: 4553
Ellen E: 2798
Ezra: 2178 2275 2405 2537 5210
Fanny: 5487
Francis: 2251
Geo: 2280 3582
George: 2537
Harriett: 4891
Henry: 2515
Jacob: 2178 2211 2211 2275 2368 2405
John: 2172 2508 3217 4416
John Nicholas (Rev): 2184
Jos Cromwell: 2418
Joseph K: 2678
Josephine V: 1354
Juliann: 3582 4416
Louisa: 5068
Malinda: 2280
Mary: 1834
Mary A: 809
Sarah: 232
Wm C: 2234 2508 2546 4055
Wm Christian: 2172 2552
Wm Fette': 2546
Wm O: 2626
HOFFMEIER
John W (Rev): 2215
HOFFORD
Harriet: 2553
HOGG
Harriott A: 4317
John Kunkel: 2575
Lizzie Robinson: 1296
Rachel Olevia: 5946
Sam'l B: 2237
Sam'l R: 1296 2575 4317 5946
Samuel R: 2281
William: 2237
HOKE
Catharine: 547
David: 2598
George: 2620

George B: 2722
Rebecca: 2837
Sam'l: 547
HOLBRUNNER
Charles W: 2643
John H: 2383
John M: 2516
Lydia A: 3348
Margaret: 996
Maria L: 105
Sarah E: 3374
Sue J: 6058
Tho's M: 2331 6058
HOLBURNNER
Sarah J: 5120
HOLDCRAFT
Annie C: 4379
John: 2712
No First Name Given: 2124
Patrick J: 2527
HOLLAND
Miss: 1023
Sally: 1023
HOLLIDAY
Daniel: 2353
Susan (Mrs): 101
HOLLINGSWORTH
J T: 2365
HOLLODAY
Margaret: 3254
HOLLOW
Maggie V: 654
HOLMES
Alice E: 3174
Charles E H: 2554
Elizabeth: 5862
John L: 2319
M Scott: 2340
Mary A: 2758
Sam'l A: 2590
Wm F: 2642
HOLMS
Emma: 1138
HOLT
Alexander Stephens: 2525
Sophia: 2110
HOLTER
Elizabeth: 2363
HOLTZ
Albert B: 2420
Annie N: 5071
Benedict M: 2351

Ellen B: 6206
John Oliver: 2357
Valletta J R: 5916
HOLTZAPPEL
Rebecca: 3566 6000
HOLTZINGER
Teresa: 1619
HOLTZMAN
Bernard H: 2280
Eliza A: 1228
HONORE
Ida M: 1782 2084
HOOD
Benjamin: 2264
George: 2410
James M: 2298 2604
James T: 2564
Marion E: 2669
Matilda: 5418
Rachel: 1909
Sallie E: 1090
Wm E: 2708
HOOK
Martha M W: 4242
Tho's: 4242
HOOKER
Joseph (Maj Gen'l): 2530
HOOPER
Ab'm: 1918 2584 2627
Abraham: 2219
Alice (Mrs): 5288
Almo: 2718
Ann Eliza: 2936
Cha's: 2602
Elizabeth: 2867
Elmer: 2718
Emma V: 2064
Ettie: 743
Ida L: 1104
Jackey: 5375
Jacky: 2389
James: 2459
John: 2219 2230 2300 2341 2389 2459 2936
John (Sen'r): 2419
John H: 2614
Juliann: 2230
Laura E: 2692
Lavinia: 4689
Marietta: 743
Mary: 2419 5375
Mary (Mrs): 1918

Mary Cath: 2602
Mary K: 2689
Mary S (Mrs): 2518
Miss: 2936
Oscar: 2581
Sallie M: 4635
Tho's: 2064 2300 2614
Vima H: 4689
William: 2341
Wm: 2581
Wm H: 2428 2584 2627

HOOPWOOD
Emma J: 1823
Jas: 1823

HOOVER
Allen D: 2714
Christian: 2412
John: 2572
Julia C: 666
Lucy: 1559
Miss: 5795
Sarah A: 3567
Sarah Ann: 5795

HOPKINS
Alice: 4189
Evans: 2145
Harriet O: 1393
Howard H (Dr): 2573
James H: 2591

HOPWOOD
Charles L: 2549
Ellen Adelia: 5990
Francis Tho's: 2588
Ja's: 2465 2557
James: 2214 2588 5990
James W: 2557
Joshua: 1501 2214
Maggie J: 5433
Mahlon Augustus: 2465
Mary: 1501
Matilda J: 2356
Wm: 2187

HORINE
Adam F: 2442
Carlton R: 2608
E F: 3900
Ezra S: 2402
Gothe' M: 3957
John F: 2430
Lottie M: 3957
Martin L: 2727
Mary M: 3094
Peter M: 2563

Sarah S: 1751
Tobias: 1751 3094

HORN
Lewis: 2653
Mary E: 6114

HORNER
Eli: 2435
Eliza F: 3868
Elizabeth: 318
O A (Maj'r): 2541

HORNUNG
Catharine: 4879
George: 2373
Sophia W: 4964

HORSEY
Caroline: 3562
Outerbridge: 2431 3562

HORTON
James: 2244

HORWETEL
Lewis: 2469

HOSKINS
Geo: 3722
George: 2174
M Lizzie: 3722

HOSKINSON
Elizabeth: 2426
Hilleary: 2426
Mary P: 879

HOTTEL
F B: 2623

HOTZ
Ann Elizabeth: 1339
Charles E: 2649
Martin: 1339 4138
Sarah C: 4138

HOUCK
Anna M: 6231
Annie: 3677
Asbury Hemphill: 2307
Barbara: 4875
Caroline: 2158
Catharine: 4073 4419
Catharine S: 2792
Charles: 2445
Charles E: 2666
Charlotte: 1490
D Edward: 2644
Daniel: 5253
Daniel J: 2293
David: 2490 2543 5672
David E: 2543

Edward: 2279
Edwin S: 2685
Eliza: 158
Elizabeth: 3084 4793
Ellen: 1227
Ezra: 2168 2545 2545 2558 2574 2792 5316 5385
Fannie M: 3191
Geo: 2158 2168
Geo John: 2256
George: 2558
George John: 3084
Georgia A: 5385
Harriott: 4000 4013
Henry: 2226 2548
Henry G: 2318
Henry J: 2548
Henry T: 2250
Isaac J: 2505
Jacob: 2256 2261
Jacob (Dr): 2250
Jacob R: 2567
James: 2574
Johanna E: 5378
John: 1227 1490 2226 2445 3400 3677 4013 4419 4775 4793, 4806
John (Junior): 2270
John (Sen'r): 2157
John C/O: 4875
John W: 2490
Laura: 5388
Laura F: 3852
Margaret: 4804
Margaret Ann: 4074
Margaret E: 5708
Martha Matilda: 5316
Mary: 3400 4775
Mary E E: 5672
Mary J: 2567
No First Name Given: 1323 6207
Peter: 2374 4000
Susan C: 5253
Susanna: 3426
Thomas: 2711
Thomas Theodore: 2711

HOUCX
Jacob: 4203

HOUFF
Charles J: 2592
John J: 2686

HOUGHTON

Cha's S: 2726

HOUPT
George W: 2458
Josiah: 2466

HOUSE
Eli C P: 2327
Eliza Ann: 2402
George C: 2710
Georgeana: 3459
Martin W E: 2304
Sarah A R: 4447
Wm W: 2308

HOUSEHOLDER
Wm H: 2476

HOUSER
Lullie: 6150

HOUSTON
Ja's F: 2434
James F: 1564 1930
John: 2182
Lizzie: 1930
Mary A Trail (Mrs): 1752
Sam T: 1752
Samuel: 2182
Samuel T: 2434
Sarah A: 1564

HOUX
Ann E: 4247
David F: 2209
Geo Jacob: 1192 2287
Harriet: 2553
Jacob: 2209
Matthias: 2287
Rebecca: 4203
Sophia: 1192

HOVES
William: 2473

HOWARD
Amanda C: 3726
Ann: 4213
Ann M: 3053
Annie E: 5750
Annie M: 2810
Caroline M: 2619
Cha's: 2167 2189
Cha's T: 2569
Charles: 2166
Charles E: 2424
Dorcus: 2155
Edw: 4355
Edward: 939 2167 2424 2540 2980 5041 5750

Emily: 939
George W (Prof): 2441
Hulda M: 2795
Isaac: 5180
James: 2201
James M: 2679
James W: 2639
John C: 2198
John S: 2160
John T: 2517
Marion: 5180
Mary Elizabeth: 2980
S Virginia: 5041
Sarah Ann (Mrs): 625
Susan: 5301
Tho's: 2166 2569
Thomas: 2189
Victoria C: 4355
William: 2330
Wm H: 2540

HOWE
No First Name Given: 2181
Wm E: 2687

HOY
Clementine V: 424

HOYT
Henry, Dr: 2199
Wm Sprague: 2586

HUBBARD
Alexander J: 2393 2629

HUBERT
Albert: 3912
Mary E: 3912

HUDDLESTONE
Sarah Jane: 3286

HUDLEBERGER
Isabella: 4707

HUDSON
Fannie L: 1064
Herschel: 2361
John A: 1064 2246

HUFFER
Cha's S: 2730
Jos L: 2007
Julia: 2007

HUGHES
Barbara Ann: 3324
Catharine: 194 1156
Daniel (Maj): 2151
Edward: 2225
Emily: 773
Emma: 3007

Eugene: 2634
Florida: 3621
James: 2385
Kassandra: 4201
Nancy J: 2433
No First Name Given: 2225
Renie: 1449
Ross: 2186
Victoria A: 2772
Wm H: 2325

HUGO
Clara M: 4972
Dorothea: 3095
Maria: 4960
Wilhelmina (Mrs): 2262

HULL
C Elmer: 2697
G W: 2486
H Clay: 2606
Harriott: 1889
Henrietta: 933
Joel: 2384
Julius: 933
Louisa: 3235
Lydia A: 406
Sarah Ann: 902
Sarah J: 69
Tideman (Dr): 2254
Wm H: 2688

HULSEMANN
B H: 2642
Elizab M: 2642

HUMERICK
Virginia S: 4298

HUMMELL
Catharine: a1
Christianna (Mrs): a1
John: a1
Mary: a1

HUMRICHOUSE
Cha's W: 2299
Charles: 2149

HUNEBERG
W B: 2691

HUNT
Asbury: 6107
Asbury H: 5172
Asbury Hemphill: 2224 2307
Caroline: 2977
David Boyd: 2377
Jesse Johns: 2348
Job: 2267 2348

Louisa Alice: 2665
Maggie M: 3856
Mamie E: 6107
Margaret M: 5987
Robert J (Dr): 2350
Samuel: 2267
Susan: 5172
Tabitha (Mrs): 5610
Wm (Rev): 2977 5987

HUNTER
Henry Lee: 2562
Mary C: 4110
Rebecca: 168

HUNTON
Tho's: 2701

HUNTRESS
Hiram: 2532

HUPMAN
Margaret A: 5079

HURDLE
Malinda: 296

HURLEY
George E: 2290
Lucinda Jane: 1383

HURST
Mary Ann: 2223

HUTH
Firdenand W: 2497

HUXFORD
David C: 2388

HYACINTHE
Pere (Rev): 2596

HYATT
Asa: 332
George W: 2719
Lucy M: 332

HYNSON
Clarissa C: 3508

IDE
E Louis (Prof): 2813
Ernst Henry Cha's: 2813
Ernst Henry Chas: 2814

IJAMS
J P: 1397
Jacob: 5804
Jacob W: 2810
Josham M: 319
Mary V: 1397
Plummer: 319 852
Rebecca: 852 5804
Richard: 2780

ILER
Andrew Jackson: 2817

INGALLS
Mary J: 3333

INGMAN
Alice: 713
Alice Maude: 6051
Amb: 6051
Ambrose: 2761
Cecelia: 4068
Harriott: 5994
Joshua: 4068 5994
Mahlon: 2764
Mary (Mrs): 3586

INISHWILLER
H: 2756

IRELY
Wm: 4409

IRVIN
Washington B: 2825

JACKLARD
Augustus P: 2811

JACKSON
Andrew (Junior): 2754
Carrie E: 6147
David: 2742
Mary C: 3522
Mary M: 3602 5048
Rebecca: 4003
Sarah: 5928

JACLARD
Augustus P: 2805
Clara (Mrs): 1292

JACOBS
Adam L: 2815
Benjamin L: 2792
Charlotte: 3863
Corbin: 2792
George W: 2755
Katie C: 3972
Mary E: 6200
Mary Jane: 5993
Michael J: 2773
Philip: 2755
Philip A: 2824
Rachel: 4913
Rosa: 2696

JAGELLO
Apollonia: 5609

JALACHIAH
Apollonia: 5609

JAMES
Charity A: 405
Dan'l: 2869
Edward: 2857
Emmanuel C: 2827
Harry: 2860
Joshua H: 2819
Julia A C: 2630
Katie: 6148
Lydia A R: 4122
Mary M: 561
Sydney Ann: 2869
Washington: 405 561 2753 2826 4122
Wm H: 2826

JAMISON
Henry M: 2740 2758
J Vincent: 2850
Jane: 5545
Joseph: 2746
Joseph L: 2856
Lucinda B: 728
Lucy: 3751
Mary Jane: 285
Sylvester Baker: 2786

JANNEY
Annie V: 1459

JANSEN
Cha's W: 2840
Elizabeth: 2256
Erasmus: 2256 2769
Eugene: 2840

JARBOE
Alexander H: 2736
Catharine: 4392
Eleanor Ann: 247
Fannie: 1683
Harriett E: 1947
Henry J: 2765
John: 2751
John S W: 2787
Maggie: 4712
Martha: 1951
Tho's: 4712

JAY
Anna: 228
Wm: 228

JEFF
Ann Liberia: 3047

JEFFERSON
Fannie A: 4515
Hamilton: 2745

JEFFERY

E T: 2848

JENKINS
Alfred: 5640
Edward Austin: 2836
Ellen M: 5640
Geo W: 2793
Ida: 1078
Martin Luther: 2796
Mary Jane: 2322
Sally Ann: 4284
Thomas: 2821
Wm (Rev): 2750 2796

JENKS
W R C: 2818

JENNESS
Clara: 2457

JOHNS
Arthur Shaaff: 2835
Catharine Ross: 4256
John (Rev DD): 2759 2806
John (Rev): 2734 2835 3707 4256
Nannie Van Dyke: 3707

JOHNSON
Ann J: 785
Ann West: 4577
Baker: 831
Baker (Col): 1860 2734 2737 2739 2749
Baker A: 2772
Benj: 5703
Bradley Tyler: 2782
Caroline: 1860
Cha's D W: 2738
Cha's H (Dr): 4983
Cha's W: 2769
Cha's W (Dr): 2749 2782 5572
Dall: 2858
David: 2785
DeWitt Clinton: 2804
Eleanor M (Mrs): 5572
Eliza: 7
Elizabeth: 2899
Elizabeth D: 1233
Ellen Cuyler: 43
Emma: 3398
Eugene A: 2840
Fannie C: 5351
Frances: 3481
Geo: 2853
Geo (Dr): 2859
Geo H: 2762 2812
Geo P: 2859
George (Dr): 2799
Harriett: 4983
J Graham: 2854
James (Dr): 6066
James T (Dr): 2777
Jane E: 86
John: 2744 2841
John D (Dr): 2816
John S: 2808
Julia Johns: 4336
Julian C: 5559
Julianna: 2734
M Eugenia: 5703
Margaret R: 1879
Mary A: 697
No First Name Given: 2201 2204
Otis: 2838
Rebecca H: 1267
Rich'd Potts (Dr): 2779
Richard P: 2855
Ross: 2783
S Bird: 6066
Samuel: 2797
Sarah E: 6071
Sophia: 831
Susan W: 2914
T W (Dr): 1233
Tho's (Col): 43 86 5351
Tho's Roger: 2829
Tho's W: 2804 2839
Tho's W (Dr): 2752 2914
Thomas (Major): 2743
Thomas R: 2803
William C: 2853
Winnie: 6076
Wm: 2739 4336
Wm F: 697
Wm Francis: 2767
Wm S: 2748
Wm T: 2795
Wood P: 2861
Worth: 2768 2779 2783
Worth'g: 2799
Worthington: 2737 2854
Worthington R: 2768
Zachariah: 2784

JOHNSTON
Ann M: 4810
Arthur: 4955
Gershom D: 2828
Henry E: 2832
Isabella: 1522
Leonidas: 2791
Louis: 2851
Robert: 2770
Sophia S: 4955
Worthington R: 2839

JOLLIFFE
Elizabeth: 5125

JONES
A Sherridan (Prof): 2831
Alexander: 2842
Allen A: 2830
Ann (Mrs): 2771
Ann M: 1897
Ann, Mrs: 3766
Aubury: 532 1043 2760 2834
Benjamin: 2820
Catharine G: 4892
Cha's A (Rev): 2852
Cha's Joseph: 2802
Charity: 5969
Charlotte: 768
David T: 2809
Edward: 2833 5184
Elizabeth: 5733
Elizabeth Ann: 3551
Emma F: 706
Esther: 4687
George Francis: 2845
Harvey E: 2834
Henry: 2747 2763
J R: 2800
John: 2741
John R: 2788 2800
Jos H (Rev): 2774 2778 2802 2844
Jos H Claggett: 2778
Joseph: 2847
Joseph Chas: 2774
Joshua: 5733
Joshua (Dr): 2771
Kate A: 5957
Maggie S: 3104
Margaret: 6166
Mary A: 3117
Mary A B: 1043
Mary Ann: 1530
Maurice: 2837
Morris: 5957
Morris J: 2757
Nettie: 5184
Philip R: 2801
Sallie: 2695
Seth C: 2849

Spencer Cone: 2844
Susan H G: 532
Tho's: 3766
Thomas: 2766
Virginia: 1352
William H: 2781 2789
William T: 2790
Wm H: 2822 2846

JORDAN
Lewis: 2735
Lydia: 3884

JORDON
Mary J: 4608

JOURDAN
Charles H (Prof): 2843

JOY
Geo R: 2823
George R: 2798
Hezekiah: 2807
Mary Ann: 3255

JUDY
Francis L: 2775
Wm A: 2776

JUNGER
George Caspar: 6225 6242
Lawrence: 6243

JUNIA
Minnie: 4190

JUNKER
John: 2794

KABLE
John J: 3081

KABRICK
Cordelia E: 3456

KAHENDAH
No First Name Given: 3047

KAHLE
Jennie L: 3882

KAILOR
David: 3033
David (Capt'n): 3058
James H: 3079
Mary Jane: 3033

KALKLOSCHER
Sarah E V: 3099
Zachary Taylor: 3099

KAMAHAMAHA 4th
No First Name Given: 3017

KANAUFF
C E: 739

KANDEL
Elizabeth: 2190
Jacob: 2190

KANN
Jacob: 2974 3069
Jacob (Sen'r): 2987

KANODE
Jacob: 3214
Mary E: 4186

KANTER
Geo: 2347
J: 2975

KANTNER
Elizabeth: 4041
Geo: 1309 4041 5590
George: 2905
Henrietta F: 1309
John J: 2975
Mary C: 5590
Sarah: 1484 2347

KARH
Josephus: 3094

KARN
Eliza Ann: 2942
Emma J: 5315
Etta: 6039
Ezra L: 3152 3154
Lewis H: 3132
Miss: 2942
Nettie L: 3154

KARNS
M Jane: 2436

KAUFFMAN
Alice V: 5266
Ann Cath: 2499
Annie V: 2561 6005
Cleantha M: 3824
Clifford T: 3156
Conrad: 2899 2998
Edward S: 3133
Eliza: 5777
Emma J: 2087
Frances M L: 4582
Geo L: 3191
Helen S: 6057
Henry: 1290 2146 2499 2935 3061 3220 5777
Henry (Jun'r): 2915
Ida A: 3144
Jacob H: 3061
John: 2884 2998
John Henry: 2899
Joseph: 3039
Louisa: 3220
Martin L: 3085
Mary: 2146
Mary Ann: 5057
Mary E: 1290
Peter S: 1757
Warner: 2561 2935 3824 6005 6057
Wesley H: 3114
Wm: 2087 4582

KAUFMAN
Geo L: 3191
John: 3191

KAY
J W: 3041

KEADEL
Martha E: 3737

KEAFAUVER
Daniel Carlton: 3056
Geo H: 3086
Horatio: 3048
Jacob: 972 2929
Lucinda C: 972

KEALHOFER
George: 2927

KEATINGE
John M: 3063

KEECH
Henry H (Dr): 3051
Sallie M: 4630

KEEDY
Clayton O: 3165
Walter H: 3090

KEEFER
Adelia Margaret: 868
Alice V: 442
Amanda C: 3370
Caroline: 4634
Catharine: 301
Ch'n: 2934
Charles E: 3189
Charlotte: 1511
Christian: 4634
Edward P: 3101
Ellen S: 2787
Geo W: 3064
Harriet Virginia: 1291
Hiram: 1808 2880 3021 3101
J Henry: 442
Jacob: 868 2787 2890 3640
Jennie C: 2045
John: 1409 3003

John H: 3190
John Henry: 3027
Katie: 1808
L Elmer: 3198
Lewis Elmer: 3198
Lewis H: 3027
Loretta: 3640
M Ella: 1409
Margaret: 946
Mich'l: 2045 3134
Michael: 2934
Michael C: 3134
Nannie C: 1115
No First Name Given: 1943
Peter: 3064
Peter H: 3370
Rebecca: 3224
Sam'l: 3003
Theodore P: 2972
Wm E: 3021

KEELIKOLAUI
H E L: 1280

KEEN
Emma J: 4319
Laura Virginia: 1389

KEENAN
Annie Amelia Gibson: 983
James: 983

KEENEY
Catharine A: 5531

KEFFER
Harry W: 3195
Lewis H: 3195

KEHLER
Elizabeth: 144
Ella V: 602
Fred'k: 3128
Frederick: 602 2928 2928
Frederick W: 3128
Henry: 144 797
Henry Junior: 2889
Jacob: 2476
Jennie: 5441
Margaret: 3990
Mary: 2476
Sallie H: 1800
Sarah: 797

KEIFER
George: 3190
John H/(@KEEFER): 3190

KEINS
Laura V: 3139

Maggie E: 5370

KEISER
Charles: 3206
Samuel: 3019

KEITH
Christianna: 1208
James: 1208

KELLER
Adam: 2891 2944 3046
Adeline: 21
Alice Grace: 1147
Andrew M: 3073
Ann Amelia: 1706
Ann Elizabeth: 2310
Annie D: 5539
Benjamin H: 2966
C: 3277
Caroline M: 2297
Cha's F: 2940 2977
Charles E: 3066 3179
Charles J: 2963
Charlotte (Mrs): 4831
Conrad: 2963
Daniel: 2991
Dewitt: 3922 6111
Dewitt Clinton: 3026
Edward L: 3182
Eugenia H: 3277
Ezra (Rev): 2920
Fred'k: 3026 3277
Frederick: 2963
Frederick H: 2970
Grace: 1147
H'y: 5539
Henry T: 3245 4773
Jacob: 2213 2297 2310 2867
 2944 2966 2970 2977
Jennie C V: 2120
Joel: 3086 3096
John H: 2973
John J: 3072
Jonathan: 2913
Kate A: 2005
Laura V: 1083
Lizzie C: 6111
Louisa: 4773
Lydia E: 5194
Margaret: 2609
Mary: 4728
Mary H: 3922
Mary Ida: 2648
Mary R: 3086
Mich'l: 4728

Michael: 2898
No First Name Given: 5241
Rebecca: 3245
Rudolph: 2867
Sophia: 178 2213
Theophilus: 2005 2910
Willard C: 3185
Wm H: 3187

KELLOGG
Lottie Walton: 4173

KELLY
Catharine: 1184
Eliza: 1687
Henry: 2928
Jacob: 3990
James: 2916
John: 3082 3153
Margaret: 3990
Margaret A: 201
Mary A: 1315
Miss: 782

KELTY
Wm H R: 3065

KEMBLE
Fanny: 206

KEMP
A Bella: 2681
A M: 3161
Ab: 5238
Abraham: 3111
C Edward: 3199
C Thomas: 3209
Calvin F: 3110
Caroline A: 3282
Catharine: 1861
Ch'n: 2863
Cha's L: 3023
Cha's Wesley: 3018
Charles E: 3199
Charlotte: 3499
D Clinton: 3194
D L: 3192
Dan'l S: 2644
Daniel: 2863 2895
Daniel M: 2887 3001
David: 48 923 2881 3123
 3282 4124 4493 5793
David Columbus: 3123
Dora E: 3454
E Cornelia: 3375
Elizabeth: 5793
Ellen C: 3338
Emily B D: 2010

Fred'k: 1861
Frederick: 3013 4824
George: 2876
Harriott: 2863
Henrietta: 923 2390
Henry: 1580 2863 2895 3652
Henry Junior: 2883
J Wm: 3155
Jennie: 2644
John: 2938
John Milton: 3077
John Quincy Adams: 3127
Jonathan: 2864
Joshua V: 2988
Juliann: 5213
L Brengle: 3177
Lavinia Ellen: 1580
Lewis: 5579
Lewis (Col): 2390 3023 3031
Lewis G: 3031
Lydia A: 4824
M Ellen: 4124
Margaret: 916
Margaret V: 3652
Maria: 5618
Mary: 4493
Mary Ann: 887
Mary Elizabeth: 5575
Miss: 4228
Nettie J: 6152
Peter: 887 2874 2925 3011 3018 3375
Peter (Rev): 2864 2874 2925
Rebecca S: 1220
Sarah A: 48
Sarah A E: 5579
Stephen: 3013
Susan: 780 4228
Virginia R: 114
W H Clay: 3155
Walter B: 5575
William: 2962
Wm: 3197
Wm H: 3011
Wm H C: 2968
Wm H H: 3139
Wm L E: 3141
Wm M (Dr): 2914 2969

KENDARD
Francis C: 3188
KENEASTER
Lucy C: 1041
KENEGE
Ann R: 5251
Carlin: 5251
David: 823 2904
Elizabeth: 1871
Joseph: 1871
Mary: 823

KENNEDY
C Elizabeth: 4523
Daniel F: 3062
David: 3724
George T: 3014
Harriett Ann: 3724
John: 3168
John C: 2995
John W: 2932
Joseph: 3029
Louisa: 4440
Sarah A: 4219
Thomas F: 3157

KENNY
Moses S: 2982

KENT
Joseph (Gov): 2882

KEOHLER
Reginald: 3200

KEPHART
Caroline: 1707
Catharine: 5583
Charlotte: 1470
Geo: 1470
Geo R: 2981
Louisa: 4487
M Ellen: 3313
Peter: 1707 2784 2981 3313 4487 5583
Susan R: 2784

KEPLER
Henry S (Rev): 2921

KEPLINGER
Annie: 2122

KERETZER
Cora: 3160

KERN
Annie A (Mrs): 1056 3125
Bettie: 509
Emeleugene Davoust: 2989
James: 509
Sarah Ann: 392
William: 803

KERR
John Bosman (Hon): 2978

KERSCHNER
Elizabeth: 2288
Jonathan: 2919

KERSHAW
Sarah: 4915

KERTZENDORFFER
Alice V: 5237
Henrietta: 412
Jos: 412 2304 5237
Rebecca E: 2304

KESLEY
Jane Philips: 4209

KESSELRING
George: 2958

KESSLER
Ann Catharine: 1516
Catharine: 795
David: 795
Henry: 2897
Ida V: 2845
Jacob: 1516 4033
Lloyd A: 2845 2980
Maria: 15
Matilda: 4033
No First Name Given: 36 3093
Rebecca: 3288
Thomas: 3211
Wm H H: 3068

KETLER
Geo: 3120
George: 2950
George F: 3120
Mary E: 5287

KETRO
George: 2894

KETROW
Caroline B: 3763
Henry: 2946
Sarah E: 3368

KETTLER
Catherine (Mrs): 505

KETTLEWELL
Glover: 3158

KETTURAH
Mrs: 5982

KETZILBERGER
Geo L: 3091

KEY
Joseph H: 3107
William T: 3164

KEYS
Charles: 2990

KEYSER
  Alice G: 6050
  Ann E: 1972
  Annie: 1439
  Benjamin: 2959
  Catharine Ann: 5815
  Cha's David: 3088
  Elizabeth: 796
  Jacob: 2930 3060
  John C: 3097
  Louis: 3136
  Mary: 5264
  Philip: 3060
  Sarah: 5854

KEYSER & SHULL
  No First Name Given: 3136

KIDD
  John C: 3053
  Wm: 3201

KIDWELL
  Henry: 2947

KIEFFE
  Geo: 2358

KIEFFER
  Adam: 2892
  Caroline: 2985
  Ch'n: 4231
  Charles H: 3034
  Christian: 2888
  Dennis P: 2956
  Frederick: 2923
  Geo: 2985
  Hannah (Mrs): 4448
  Hiram: 3012 3034
  Hiram M: 3012
  J Spangler (Rev): 3124
  Jacob: 2907
  John Henry: 2906
  Lizzie G C: 3312
  Mary A: 2358
  Mary E: 4231
  Matilda: 4937
  Michael: 2911
  Nicholas: 2902
  Peter: 2888 2956
  Sam'l: 2923
  Susan: 4011

KIEHNE
  Augustus: 3083
  Caroline A: 3024
  Frederick C: 3037
  Lewis F: 3118

KIETH
  James: 1208

KIGNEY
  Magy M: 3188

KILGOUR
  J Mortimer: 3149
  John A (Rev): 3149

KILLIAM
  Wm H: 3163

KILLIAN
  James: 3162
  John Edward: 3142
  Julia A C: 6259
  Mary Ann: 4834
  Ph: 6259
  Philip: 2936 3535 4834
  Susan: 3535 6098

KILLINGSORTH
  J C: 3105

KILLITTZ
  Herrman: 2965

KILPATRICK
  Susan C: 2472

KIMBALL
  Julius H: 3130

KIMMEL
  Anthony: 2869
  Anthony Zaarr: 3050
  Mary C: 3814

KIMMELL
  Emma M: 2698

KINDLEY
  G Wesley: 3180

KING
  Ann Maria: 4511
  Augustus: 3083
  Caroline A: 3024
  Catharine: 1891 3549
  Chas F R: 3022
  Christian: 3055
  Christianna: 2961
  Conrad: 2948
  Frederick C: 3037
  Henrietta: 594
  Henry: 1121 2657 2955 3112
  J Bell: 3208
  Jane: 2657
  Jesse W: 3042
  John: 2997
  Katie L: 1121
  Lewis: 2997 3022 3055 3549
  Lewis F: 3118
  Louis: 3350
  Mary: 3350
  Mary A: 684
  Rebecca: 2009
  Rufus: 2933
  Wm: 3170

KINGHORN
  Mary E: 2979

KINKERLY
  Mary Ann: 5780
  Susan: 4776

KINLEY
  William: 2984

KINNA
  Emma: 1107
  Mary (Mrs): 3058
  Thomas: 3045
  William: 3008

KINNEY
  Emma: 1107

KINTZ
  Cha's F: 3161
  David C: 3151
  Fred'k: 5352
  Harriett A: 5352
  Jacob: 3184
  Lewis: 3204
  Lillian: 3450
  Sarah J: 3110
  Wm F: 3144

KINZER
  Laura Eugenia: 4649

KIRACOFE
  J W (Rev): 3137

KIRBY
  Charles A: 2937
  Elizabeth: 2482
  Wm: 2482

KIRCHHOFF
  J W: 3137

KIRK
  Philip Howard: 3145

KIRKLAND
  Mary E: 5435

KIRKLEY
  Joseph W: 3093

KIRKPATRICK
  John C (Dr): 3131

KIRWAN
  Louisa C (Mrs): 5281

KISTER

Sally: 1660
KITTO
John T: 3078
KLAARMUNN
John: 3075
KLAUBER
Susan: 2209
KLAY
William: 2985
KLEIN
Andrew: 497
Caspar: 825 932 3125 6194
Cordelia E: 5216
Dan: 5642
Daniel: 2943
Edward D: 3074
Ephraim H: 3098
Geo W: 3054
H Thomas: 3113
Harriett M: 5198
Harriott: 825
Henry: 2871
John H: 3108
Jonathan: 3024 5216
Joseph T: 3024
Louisa: 4939
Margaret: 3674
Mary L: 6194
Mollie A: 497
Nicholas O: 3125
No First Name Given: 440
Peter: 2939 3009
Rebecca: 1482 6171
Sarah: 1304
Sophia: 4794
Stephen: 1482 2871 2908 2908 2943 3113 3674 3804 4794
Susan: 3804
Wm E: 3057
KLEINERT
Francis: 4748
Frederick: 1518
Susan: 1518
Wilhelmina: 4748
KLEISZ
Solomon: 2868
KLESSNER
Wm: 2903
KLINE
Charles T: 3173
Ella: 3911
Emma: 5511
H Lewis: 3178
H Tho's: 731
Irene T: 3953
John F: 3203
Josiah: 3911
Julia A: 731
Mollie: 5535
Wm: 3173
KLING
Tho's E: 3193
KLINK
John D: 3016
KLIPP
Elizabeth: 3816
John: 3147
Paul: 3146
Schneider Maister: 3816
KLOTZ
James: 2951
Robert: 3186
KNAUFF
Ann: 3013
Cha's: 3903
Charles E: 2992
Elizabeth: 152
F Gertrude: 739
Howard A: 3126
Jacob: 926 2238 2872 2979 3013 3126 6234
Margaret: 2238
Maria: 227
Mary A E: 926
Mary E: 3903
Susan: 6234
William: 2979
KNEPP
Parmelia (Mrs): 5582
KNIGHT
Abel: 3084
Ealt: 3160
John: 2901
No First Name Given: 613
Samuel: 3122
KNIGHTON
Francis: 3100
KNILL
William: 3020
KNIPPLE
Mary A: 510
KNOCK
Cha's F: 3210
James H: 3174
KNODE
Alice V: 1132
Cornelius: 2912
John: 2879
Maria E: 5215
Mary E: 4186 4551
No First Name Given: 2879
Sam'l C: 3076
Wm H: 4551
KNODLE
John: 2922
Josiah: 3032
Mary M: 6069
KNOTT
Columbus: 3150
John O (Rev): 3202
Rosella: 163
KNOX
Samuel (Rev): 2866
KOCH
Jacob: 3092
Kate M: 5039
Mary E: 6266
Peter: 6266
Philip: 2873
KOCHLER
Wm: 3025
KOEHLE
Ann Catharine: 4457
KOEHLER
Herrmann C: 3067
KOESTER
Lewis: 3176
KOHLENBERG
Adam: 104 2949 3087 3121 3758 6240
Emma R: 2637
Geo Ragan: 3087
George T: 3121
Harriet A: 104
Leonora: 1245
Lydia E: 6240
Maggie L: 3758
KOHLER
Ann Catharine: 4457
KOHLHAAS
Frederick: 2931
KOLB
Alfred B: 3169
Alice Virginia: 2086
Ann E: 1281

Ann R: 357
Caroline: 1152
Catharine: 1154
Charlotte A: 1996
Dan'l: 3007 5745 6046
Daniel: 2893
David: 3143
David H: 3030 5510
Ella: 3966
Fred'k: 3129
Frederick: 2909 2964 2996
Ida M: 4686
J Mich'l: 638
Jacob M: 3007
John Mich'l: 3080
John Michael: 2918
Laura: 6099
Lewis A: 3106
Louisa C: 6046
Marceline: 638
Mary Alice: 749
Mary M: 5510
Mich'l: 781 2893 2909 2917
Michael: 2964
Michael Grosch: 2917
Naomi: 5745
Nimrod Owing: 3080
Raemor: 357
Sophia: 781
Sophie M A: 2683
Valentine Brunner: 3129
William: 2926
William H: 3071
Wilson W (Dr): 2885 3030
Wm: 2086 2918 2926 3104 3117 3143
Wm Augustus: 3104 3117

KONIG
Catharine: 3549
Cha's F R: 3022
Christian: 3055
Conrad: 2948
Henrietta: 594
Henry: 594 2955 3112
John: 2997
Lewis: 2997 3022 3055 3549
Louis: 3350
Mary: 3350

KONIGSBACKER
Samson: 3109
Solomon: 3070

KOOGLE
Adam: 3384 3831 4548

Amanda: 5395
Annie: 1127
Carleton E: 3166
Cha's W: 3103
Clinton M: 3181
Emiline: 537
Geo Washington: 3102
George: 3033
Hallie A: 3384
Jeanette: 3831
Jennie: 1127
John: 3049
Mary Ellen: 4548

KOON
Catharine: 4118

KOONS
Julianna: 3476
Robert L: 3196

KOONTZ
A Lilly: 702
Adele: 1816
Ann Maria: 5879
Ann Sophia: 2745
Annie R: 1736
Cha's F: 3000
Cornelia E: 609
Ed: 1816
Edward: 609 2870 3043 3138 3138 3175
Elleanor Matilda: 874
Geo: 1736 2973 2999 5881
Geo S: 2999
George: 2878 4134
Georgianna V: 4283
Godfrey: 895 2875 2953
Henrietta C: 2258
Henry: 563 2745 2862 2870 2971 3015 3043
Jane E: 6181
John: 563 874 2258 2862 2971 3015 4283 5846 5879 6181
John J: 3095
Lizzie: 5881
Margaret: 1884
Margaret C (Mrs): 563
Minerva: 2973
No First Name Given: 6218
Robert L: 3196
Sallie E: 895
Samuel C: 3154
Sophia M: 4134
Sophia N: 5846

W A: 3167

KOPP
William (Rev): 3035
Wolfgang: 2994

KOREL
John: 3010

KOST
J K (Rev): 3036

KOSTER
Henry: 2484 2900 5973
Martha E: 2484
Sophia: 5973

KOSZTA
Martin: 3005

KRAFT
Jacob: 5300
Sophia S: 5300

KRAGER
Olevia: 2340

KRAGLER
Siegmund: 3006

KRAMER
Ann Rebecca: 2968
Daniel: 2865
John Adam: 3044

KRANTZ
Frederick: 3171
John D: 2960
Wm H: 2993 3116

KRAPP
Jabez: 3089

KRAPT
Dorathea: 2983

KRAUTH
Charles Porterfield: 2954
Frederick K: 2957
Louisa A: 564

KREBS
Caroline: 5772
Delia: 2550
Geo: 2896 5772
Geo W: 2896
Julea Beaford: 4995
Mary Ann: 909

KREH
Ann M M (Mrs): 1086
Cha's: 3205
Charles F: 3172
Frank L A: 3212
Henry: 3216
John: 1086 2961 3115 3183

John E: 3183
Lewis: 3002 3216
Lizzie: 691
Mary C: 2678
Mollie: 2678
Theo: 1086
Theodore: 3115
Theodore F: 3159

KREIDLER
James H: 2941

KREIG
Jesse: 3207

KREIS
Lydia A S: 50
Margaret A: 4981

KREMER
Michael: 2983

KREPS
Eliza (Mrs): 4788
Ellen: 5354

KRIEG
Jesse: 3207

KRIEGELOH
Christianna: 4404

KROH
Henry Ferdinand Theo: 2986

KROHL
Julius H: 3038

KROHN
Conrad: 2942
No First Name Given: 981

KRUG
Elizabeth: 1478
John Andrew (Rev): 1478

KRUMBEIN
Catharine: 4224
Daniel M: 2945
Jac: 4224
Jacob: 6173
Margaret: 6173

KUDRY
Clayton O: 3165

KUHL
John: 2976

KUHN
Cyrus C: 3028
Henry: 804
Henry (Dr): 2877
Jos Lew (Capt): 5863
Leander H: 3052
Louisa Adelaide: 5863
M: 1462
Mary Elizabeth: 5896
Mary M: 804
Matilda: 3299
Mollie M: 1462
Sallie E: 5486
Wm E: 3059

KUHNE
Christianna: 2961
Rebecca: 2009

KUHRE
Margaret E: 3633

KULLING
John (Rev): 3040

KULLMAN
Caroline (Mrs): 219

KUNKEL
Barbara: 2281
Barbara A: 5554
Elizabeth: 4477
Hallie P: 4698
J: 2281
J B K: 6081
J Baker: 3140 5471
Jacob M: 2967 3135
John: 3004 3140 4477 5554
John Baker: 2952
John J: 3135
Lillian F: 5471
Mary B: 6081
Philip H: 3004

KURTZ
Alice: 5680
Benjamin (Rev): 2886 2924
Susan: 5549
T Newton: 3148
Wm Newton: 3148

KUSHWA
John D: 911
Kate: 911

KUSSMAUL
Alice: 4657
John: 3119
Lewis F: 3215
P Frank: 3213

KUSTER
W: 3696
Wilhelmina: 3696

LA DOW
Robert V: 3464

LADOW
Robert V: 3464

LADSON
Wm Henry: 3300

LAKE
Orange E (Rev): 3421

LAKIN
John H: 3273
John S: 3465
William H: 3338

LAKINS
Daniel T: 3447
Martha A M: 2938

LALEY
William H: 3346
Wm H: 3285

LAMAR
Annie M: 605
Baker J: 3375 3398
Benoni S: 3260
Carrie K: 3945
Martha L J: 5623
Mary Ann: 173
Miss: 173
Rich'd J: 3375 3387 3396
Richard D: 3413
Richard J: 3257 3282
Robert G: 3396
Wm K: 3387

LAMB
Mary Jane: 4332
Sarah: 5304

LAMBERT
Catharine E: 4683
Charles: 3345
D M: 3466
Daniel T: 3316
David Michael: 3321
Emma J: 6260
Fred'k: 3090 3321 3345 3418 6260
Frederick: 3243
Geo: 3862 4371
George D: 3463
Georgetta J G: 3862
Hallie A: 3090
Jane E (Mrs): 5355
John: 374 3233 3309 3316
John George: 3309
Joseph: 3258
Malinda A C: 3141
Mary: 217 374
Murray: 3466
Nich: 4683

Tho's F: 3418
Willetta M: 4371
LAMBRECHT
Ann C: 1642
Ann Sophia: 348
Cath E: 3243
Catharine: 366 1890
Cristianna: 4401
David: 3302
Frederick: 3248
Geo: 1890 3248 3274 4401 4843
George: 4943
Harriett: 4942
Henry: 3225
Jacob: 403 3227 3242
James W: 3327
John: 1642 3231 3299 3302 3319 3327 3378
John W: 3319 3378
Joseph: 3339
Lydia: 1527
Margaret (Mrs): 4499
Mary A: 3528
Mary Jane: 403
Mich'l: 348 1527 3243
Michael: 4942
Perry: 3274 4499
Philip: 3299 3495
Philip D: 3268
Rachel: 4943
Rebecca: 3495
Sophia: 4023
Susan: 4843
Susan T E: 889
LAMBRIGHT
Harry: 3468
James L: 3459
John: 5925
Laura Cath: 4358
Mary Jane: 5925
Philip H: 3422
LAMOTT
Daniel M (Rev): 3434
Elizabeth: 1472
LAMPE
Annie C: 4701
Christian L C: 3406
Henrietta: 425
J Henry: 3373
Julius Junior: 3350
Louisa: 62
LANCASTER
John Henry: 3351
LANDAUER
Abraham: 3428
LANDERKIN
Mary C: 4469
Tho's C: 3290
Thomas L: 3431
LANDERS
Elizabeth: 5878
Wm H: 3382
LANDIS
Emma: 1044
Jesse: 1044
LANE
Harriett: 2832
John M: 3436
M Kate: 3076
LANGE
Catharine: 2950
Catharine (Mrs): 505
Constantin: 3250
Sophia (Mrs): 265 4241
LANGLEY
Grace: 734
John W (Rev): 3314
LANSDALE
John: 3281
LARCH
Charles: 3430
LARE
David W: 3325
Edw: 3386
Edward: 3245 3376
George H: 3333
Henry C: 3252
Lewis G: 3386
Maria (Mrs): 2401
William: 3235
Wm: 3315
Wm H: 3456
Wm L: 3315 3348
LARKIN
Julian (Mrs): 4798
Olevia M C: 1670
LARKING
Jacob (Rev): 1670
LATE
Ann Maria: 5568
Ann Rebecca: 5028
George: 3311
George W: 3294
Jacob: 1504
Margaret C: 4941
Mary A: 1504
Mary A C: 4008
Mich'l: 4008 5028
LATRILLE
Robert Horatio: 3363
LATROBE
Ferdinand C: 3357
LAUERMAN
Charlotte: 1206
LAUMAN
Margaret: 229
LAUPHEIMER
Belle: 675
LAURENT
Frederick C: 3297
LAVENTUNE
Samuel: 3370
LAWRENCE
Caspar: 1005
Frances: 1005
No First Name Given: 2350
Otho: 3412
Rebecca: 4268
Richard H: 3412
LAWYER
Henry: 3292
LAYMAN
Clarence L: 3443
Geo H: 3364
George H: 3461
George W: 3462
Lenoard J: 3441
Robert L: 3457
Susan H M: 1427
LEA
Edward: 3453
LEAB
Sophia: 6167
LEACHEY
Agnes V: 4163
Annie E: 633
LEAH
Charlotte: 2207
Jacob: 2207 6167
LEAKIN
Julia E: 1571
Ruth: 2881
LEAKINS
Martha J: 4300
Mary E: 533

Senia E: 85

LEAPLEY
Mary Barbara: 5543
Miss: 5543

LEARNED
Elizabeth: 3560

LEASE
A Calvin: 3395
Amos: 3400
Andrew Jackson: 3335
Ann Cath (Mrs): 1694
Barbara Ann: 341
Cath (Mrs): 2200
Catharine: 1483 4572
Cha's E: 3326
Cha's W: 3458
David H: 3355
Edward C: 3449
Elenora: 4507
Elizabeth: 878 4857
Emma C: 1423
Etta: 5509
Ezra: 3289
Franklin M: 3402
Geo: 326 341 789 1483 3224 3293 3326
Geo Henry: 3284
Geo W: 3293
George: 3223
George (Junior): 3221
Harriett: 5940
Harry: 2245
Henry: 3247
Jane: 3704
Jemima: 2815
Josiah: 3368
Louisa Elizabeth: 4926
Maggie V: 2706
Margaret: 2706
Margart E: 557
Martha: 4979
Mary: 1583 2245
Matilda: 322
Milliard F: 3460
N Calvin: 3438
Nicholas: 2200 3284 3289
No First Name Given: 1600 3690
Oliver D: 3372
Otho: 3232
Robert: 3362
Sarah: 789
Sarah E: 326

Tho's U: 3342
Upton: 3301
William: 3224
Wm: 878 3355 3704
Wm (Jun'r): 1694
Wm H: 3369
Wm M: 3448

LEATHER
Ann R: 2443
David: 3354
Henrietta L: 2369
James: 3303
John: 2369 3303
John (Major): 2443
Luther J: 3337
Mary A C: 5874

LEATHERMAN
D I (Dr): 3455
Daniel J: 3455
Josiah: 3305
Marshall (Dr): 3417

LEBHERZ
William H: 3437

LECHLEITER
Agnes: 261
Alexander A: 3353
Harriet T: 1941
John H: 3287
Mary A: 3339

LEDERERER
Henry A: 3469

LEDGEWOOD
Martha Jane: 5154

LEE
Edgar: 3453
Ellen: 3263
George: 3219
Harriett S: 2811
Henrietta Edmonia: 2035
John: 3240
Margaret (Mrs): 308
Mary D: 1070
Mary Digges: 1949
Sarah Frances: 5818
Tho's: 1070
Tho's Lim: 3262
Wm: 1949 3263

LEEBRICK
Matilda A: 4105

LEFEVER
John Beforegod: 3254

LEFEVRE

Jacob A (Rev): 3331

LEGG
Edgar K: 3433
Edward K: 3433

LEGGE
J Frank: 3407

LEGGITT
Ann D: 3521

LEGROFT
George: 3388

LEHAY
Ellen: 4865

LEHMAN
Jacob: 3222
Sallie A: 5113

LEIBHERTZ
William H: 3437

LEILICH
Anna Magdelena: 1905
Annie: 1306
Francis T: 3411
George R: 3450
Jacob: 569 1306 3246 4602
Louisa: 4602
M C: 3440
Maria L: 569
Michael: 3283 3399 3411 3450

LEIN
Lincoln R: 3454

LEINARD
Ellen: 4589

LEISHER
Susan: 2240

LEISTER
Albert: 3365

LEITER
Ann Catharine: 5158
Cath A Rebecca: 4462
Daniel J: 3415
Elizabeth: 4414
Elizabeth (Mrs): 641
Emma M: 6248
Ezra K: 3410
H'y: 4444
Henry: 3241 3288 4414 4462
Henry Junior: 3271
John: 3288 6248
Lawson: 3241
Mary Ann: 4444
Mary Ellen: 4574
Miss: 3658

Peter: 3658 4574
Samuel L H: 3389
Solomon: 3266
LEMBACH
Susan C: 3754
LEMMEIER
Fred'k G: 3249
LEMMON
Miss: 2315
LENHART
Henry W: 3328
Ida: 5451
Juliann L: 3365
Mary A R: 3337
LENOX
Arthur E: 3442
LENTZ
Ann: 31 4048
LEONARD
Jennie V: 6277
Louisa: 4035
Mary R: 3014
Tho's: 3380
LEOPOLD
Geo A (Rev): 3244
Matthias: 3264
LERCH
Emma V: 4714
George W: 3445
Henry: 4714
Lizzie: 3205
Mary M: 3205
LESTER
Joseph R: 3392
LEUTWEIN
Anna: 1651
LEVERING
Righter: 3277
LEVI
Miss: 999
LEVY
Ann R C: 181
Cha's V S: 3404
David: 181 2149
John Leonard: 3237
Maria C: 2149
No First Name Given: 2820
LEWIS
Cha's J: 1139
Charles (Capt): 3217
Charles J: 3384
Emily: 2335
Emogine: 748
Francis J: 3394
George T: 3383
Hannah M: 976
Harriott A: 5900
Henry: 3435
Imogene: 748
Jacob: 976 2566 3359 3379 6015
John: 3291
John S: 3379
Katie: 1139
Martha L: 6015
Mary E: 2566
Mary Jane: 4621
Maurice H: 3435
S Candace: 1777
Sam'l: 3272
Samuel B: 3275
Susan C: 3021
William H: 3361
Wm D: 3021 3251
LEWYT
Caroline: 3069
S H: 3069
LEXTON
Sarah: 4751
LIDAY
Charlotte (Mrs): 2579
Henrietta: 905
Henry: 3356
Joseph: 3296
Julia A: 1302
Margaret: 4146
LIDIE
Clara: 1098
LIEDEMAN
John L: 3424
LIFE
Bobby: 5592
Mary: 5592
Miss: 2275
Sarah: 2211
LIGGET
Charles A: 3360
John J (Dr): 3405
LIGHTER
Ann Elizabeth: 3658
Peter: 3658
LIGHTNER
Ann M: 2473
Jonathan Coleman: 3340
Mary Ann: 3607
Presley T: 3349
Wesley J: 3426
LIGON
Tho's Watkins (Gov): 3310
LILLY
Mattie: 1798
Rebecca: 2870
LINCOLN
Ab'm: 3393
Robert T: 3393
LIND
Jenny: 1948
LINDSAY
Samuel J: 3238
Sarah A (Mrs): 2016
LINDSEY
Benjamin F: 3358
Emma Jane: 5265
George: 3377
Julia A: 4288
R Robinson: 3312
S Marion: 4309
LINK
A D Garl: 3467
Catharine: 982
Daniel (Lieut): 3371
Lewis: 3330
Mary F: 74
Sarah: 5284
LINN
Edw: 646
Henry: 779
Mary: 3995
Maud E: 761
Philip: 3995 4762
Susan: 4762
LINTHICUM
Ellen M: 283
John L (Hon): 3439
LINTON
Ann Mary: 1231
Benj'n: 1231
Henry: 3220 3228
Mary A: 4340
Samuel: 3324
LIPPENCOTT
Annie: 5188
LIPPS
John: 3253 3403 3425 3808
John C: 3391

Lewis: 3425
Sophia B: 3808
Thomas: 3403
LIPSCOMB
George B: 3308
Mary Ellen: 287
LISCHER
Louisa R (Mrs): 2544
LITTLE
Benjamin Rush (Dr): 3317
Christianna: 3601
Daniel: 3278
Harriett Ann: 2935
Harry: 3427
Isabella: 90
Jacob: 2935 3601
John L: 3145 3313
Louisa C: 5827
Maria Louisa C: 5984
Nannie E: 3145
William: 3229
LITTLEJOHN
Elizabeth T: 5561
Francis Geisinger: 3286
Geo: 3226
Jane: 3585
John: 3226
LITTLEWITT
Elmira Elizabeth: 4137
LLOYD
Henry (Gov): 3446
Maggie: 2621
William: 3259
Wm Ambrose: 3218
LOANE
Martha F: 496
LOATS
John: 3295
LOCHNER
Geo: 3323 3347
Nicholas: 3347
Wm M: 3323
LOCHR
Henry C: 2401
Maria: 2401
LOCKE
Catharine J R: 4756
LOCKNER
Annie E: 1016
Geo: 1016
Nannie R: 3956
Nich: 3956

LOCKWOOD
Ellisence: 3325
LOEHR
Edward: 3245
Geo: 3235 3245
William: 3235
LOEWENSTEIN
David: 3401
LOGAN
James: 1099 3320
Maria L: 5945
Mora: 1099
LOGUE
Isaac: 3298
Kate: 5668
Lewis: 5668
LOH
John M: 3256
LOHMANN
Edward: 3408
LOHMEYER
H H: 3341
LOHR
David W: 3325
Edw: 3325 3333 3386
Edward: 3376
George H: 3333
Henry C: 3252
Lewis G: 3386
Wm: 3315 3348
Wm I: 3348
Wm L: 3315
LOKEY
Catharine: 2290
Louisa: 3994
Virginia R: 877
LOMTZ
Franklin R: 3429
LONEY
E Catharine: 4313
John: 4313
LONG
Amanda A F: 5605
Annie M: 4315
Charles H: 3332
Christ'n: 5278
Christopher: 3614
Elizabeth: 3266
James W: 3451
Josephus: 3374
Mary A K: 3614
Mary E: 4142

P Allison (Rev): 3420
Sarah A C: 5278
LONGWELL
John K: 3261
LOPEZ
Harry (Capt): 3452
LORENTZ
Charles H: 3414
Edwin C: 3423
Emma S: 6041
George: 3267
H'y: 6100
Henry: 3279 3414 3423
Jacob: 921
Laura V: 6100
Malinda A: 921
Wm: 3270
LORNTZ
Albert C: 3432
LOUD
Granville: 3367
LOUGH
Myrtie E: 1134
Myrtle: 1134
LOUIS
Adelaide Victoine: 2836
Enoch: 2836
LOUTHAN
Henrianna: 2063
LOVEDER
Ann: 3531
Catharine: 4850
LOVEJOY
Perry B: 3307
LOVELEY
John Emanuel: 3343
LOVELL
Joseph: 3334
Wm S, Lieut: 3329
LOVELY
Amantha E: 540
Emanuel: 3265
Mary Ann Margaret (M: 5930
LOWE
Adelaide Victoire: 2836
Ann Elizabeth: 3653
Bradley: 3280
Eliza: 3272
Enoch Louis: 3280
Geo: 3653
George: 3230

Jacob: 3272
Jane Ann: 4619
John: 3272
John M: 3256
Margaret: 5540
Margaret E: 2372
Mrs: 3272
Sarah Jane Amelia: 708
Theodore: 4619

LOWELL
Ellen Maria: 3080
James P: 3352
Kate: 3717
Miss: 3080
No First Name Given: 2354 3649
Rose: 1020
Wm: 1020 3080 3352 3717

LOWENSTEIN
Amelia: 6010
Clara M: 1809
Isaac: 3416
Jennie: 3109

LOWER
Sarah E: 1769

LOWERY
Matilda: 4828

LOWRY
Miss: 1867

LOY
Catharine Margaret: 5906
Elizabeth Elvira: 4455
Isaiah N: 3444

LOYNS
Carrie O: 3982
James W: 3318

LUCHER
Francis: 3038
Sophia: 3038

LUCKETT
Harriott B: 2320
Lloyd: 2320
Mountjoy Bailey: 3269
Nelson (Col): 3236
Wm F (Dr): 3409

LUDWIG
Ann Rebecca: 2286

LUDY
Manzella M: 5427

LUEBER
Helen M: 4544

LUEHER
Francis: 4544

LUELIER
Francis: 3234

LUGENBEEL
Ann Rebecca: 2506
Basil: 3239
Elizabeth: 1172
Henry G: 3344
Jamima A (Mrs): 1062
John H: 3304
Lillie: 1085
Maria S: 1270
Martha E (Mrs): 4830
Mary Margaret: 1007
Moses: 1007 1270
No First Name Given: 5265
Pickney (Lieut): 3276
Sarah A: 2016
Tho's E S: 3336

LUTER
Sallie E: 6029

LUTZ
Annie C: 6002
Charles: 3390
John: 3419
Mich'l: 3419

LYETH
Anna: 1345
Ida: 1776
J McF: 1776
John Mc: 3397
John McF: 1345
John T: 3397

LYNCH
Eugene H: 3263
John A: 3322
Mary Jane: 4845
Thomas: 3255
Wm: 3306 3381 4845
Wm B: 3306 3381

LYNN
A Luther: 3385
David: 4724
Francina C: 4724
Jane H: 4282

LYON
Adrianna: 4218
Augusta P D: 6047
Isaac (Dr): 837 4218 5819
John C (Rev): 6047
Molly J (Mrs): 5335
Olivia: 5819
Sarah: 837

LYONS
Carrie O: 3982
Mary: 934

MABURRY
Fannie L: 3100
Justin: 3100

MACGILL
John S: 3894
Lloyd T (Dr): 3692 3784
Mary E: 3135
Rob't H: 3135 3886
Robert H: 3631

MACHT
Andrew C H: 3614
Mary A B: 5102
Sam'l: 5102
Sarah E: 89

MACKEY
Zulika D: 5306

MACKLEY
John A: 3724
Mary A: 3152

MACMANUS
Alice: 4096

MACOMB
Czarina: 3547
John Navarre (Lieut): 3547

MADARY
Harriott: 3635

MADDOX
Thomas (Dr): 3605

MAESCHE
J F: 3732

MAGRUDER
Arthur John: 3542
C C: 3812
Elizabeth C: 4433
H C: 3615
Hezekiah: 3615
Jonas E: 3761
Matilda: 4923
Rachel (Mrs): 5816
Wm F: 3851

MAGUIRE
Jane: 4049

MAHONEY
Ann: 803
Barney: 3509 3544
David L: 3598
Effie A: 2709

Margaret: 2066
Martin: 1548
Martin M: 3544
Mary Ann: 1548
Wm: 3509
MAHONY
Mary J (Mrs): 1765
MAIN
Amanda C: 3103
Ann Maria: 4130
Carson H: 3863
Catharine E: 985
Charlotte Cath: 2814
Cornelius M: 3808
Daniel A: 3733
Eveline: 5096
George J: 3747
James M C: 3877
Joshua: 3833
Kate S: 4628
Laura Bell: 2704
Lewis H: 3683
M H: 3439
Mahlon: 3570
Marietta C: 5678
Mary E: 5662
Nettie: 2622
Rowanna R: 3111
Susan S: 5363
MAINHARDT
Lewis D: 3957
MAINHART
Charles C: 3900
Lewis D: 3957
Mary A: 1399
Wm H: 3763
MALAMBRE
George: 3593
John: 3477
MALLEN
Tho's S: 3715
MALONE
William: 3727
MANAHAN
Eurith: 2447
MANKIN
James A: 3586
Latitia: 1175
MANN
Allie: 1084
Amelia: 5686
Annie M: 1661

Cha's B: 3811
Charles (Rev): 3522
Josephine: 3067
M Virginia: 639
Stephen: 1084
Stephen S: 3067 3811 5686
Stephen T: 639 1661 3538
MANNSTADT
Mary R: 1662
MANNSTAEDT
Catharine T: 2793
Cha's: 2793
Charles: 3543
MANSELL
Jeabel H: 2859
MANSFIELD
Mary: 3914
MANSON
William: 3500
MANTZ
Alexander K: 3583
Allen B: 3928
Ann: 1150
Anna C (Mrs): 2801
Caroline: 271
Caspar: 3548 5171
Catharine: 1265
Cha's: 607 2623 2816 3780
Charles: 3529 3753
Christianna E: 793
Cyrus: 270 271 3583 3591 3600 3847
David: 2742 3512
David Allen: 3721
E Jane: 4531
Edward: 549 3685
Elizabeth: 270
Elizabeth (Mrs): 549
Ellen: 3591
Emanuel: 3646 3864
Emauel: 3612
Emma: 2623
F Miller: 3866
Francis: 3606
Frank: 3866 3980
George: 3610
Gideon: 1265 1945 3610 4503 4531 4543
Henry: 1366 3512 3721 4554
Ida: 1804
Irene: 5171
Isaac: 793 826 1150 3485
Isabella: 2816

John: 3529 3530 3685 3753
John Andrew: 3530
Laura V: 3780
Louisa: 4543
Margaret: 5056
Mary: 826 1945 2742
Mary E: 607
Mary Elizabeth: 4501
Milton: 2801 3600 3847
Minnie: 721
No First Name Given: 3188 3602
Peregrine: 3485
Peter: 3606 3608 3612 3646 3699 3699 3966 4501 5056
Peter (Jun'r): 3475
Quincey: 3198
Rebecca: 1366
Sabina: 4503
Sallie E: 5704
Sophie: 4554
William: 3608
Willie C: 3941
Wm: 3980 5704
Wm Eugene G Mantz: 3864
MARANDER
Jacob: 3549
MARBLE
Caroline E: 5069
MARCILLY
Josephine: 3993
MARCKLEY
Barbara (Mrs): 1480
MARCY
Mary E: 3736
Randolph B (Maj): 3736
MARGUERT
John: 3476
Mich'l: 3476
MARION
Annie M: 4709
MARK
Geo W: 3834
MARKELL
Annie: 6082
Charles: 3657
Francis: 3693
Frank: 3922
Frank H: 3922
Frederick: 3648
Geo: 614 1380 3905 6082
George: 3561

Hallie: 1380
Jacob: 3494 3561 3648
John: 2770 3561 3577 3657 3693
John S: 3597
Louis: 3577 3905
Mary: 614 2770
Mary M: 763
Sophia: 3561
Wm W: 3546

MARKEN
Ellie B: 3881
Hellen: 1761
Josiah R: 1761 3881

MARKER
Enos: 3713
John H: 3987
Joshua: 3754
Rebecca: 3049
Wesley: 3742

MARKEY
Ann C: 3600
Anna C: 2801
Catharine (Mrs): a1
D J: 3840
David: 3471 3524 a1
David J: 1970 3748 3871 6012 a1
David Jacob: 3392 3524
Eliza: 5563
Fred'k: 1594 3600 5563
Frederick: 3471
Frederick A: 3748
Henry S: 3840
J Hanshew: 3871
Lucy E: 3392
Mary Ellen: 1970
Matilda E: 1594
Rebecca B: 6012
Susie: 4704

MARKS
Lemuel: 6135
Mary C: 6135

MARLOW
Ann R: 1592
Edmonia: 5700
Hanson: 1592 5141
L H: 5141
Louisa Hanson: 5141

MARMADUKE
Mary: 4547

MARMAN
Juliann E: 2246

MARNIE
Sarah J: 3071

MARRIOTT
A W: 3854
Alphes W: 3902
Charles W: 3798
Lizzie: 2597
Mary Lizzie: 2597
Mary Rose: 3854

MARSH
Catharine: 6204
George W P: 3846
Joel: 1696 3590 6204
Mary A: 1696
Mason R: 3590

MARSHALL
Ann: 3565
Ellen C (Mrs): 5650
Hannah: 2741
John W: 3947
Richard H: 3479

MARTELL
Jacob: 1341 1719
Kate: 1719
Mary: 1341

MARTELLE
Lewis P: 3976

MARTIN
Catharine E: 4478 5166
Cha's (Rev Dr): 3545 3792 5985
Charles (Rev Dr): 3626
Charles R: 3940
D C (Dr): 6146
Dan'l Tho's: 3771
Daniel: 3673
David: 3491 5026
David C (Dr): 3767
Ella: 4198
Emma V: 5985
Jacob: 3493
Jane: 2931
John: 3490 3493 3670
John (Jun'r): 3579
John T: 3689
Jon: 3491
Joseph R: 3828
Laura E: 4382
Lutue K: 6146
Martha E: 5465
Mary A M: 2416
Mary Ann: 1221
Mazeppa: 6289

Oliver: 5465
Oliver H: 3751
Rosanna: 842
Sarah: 4002
Sophia: 356
Susan R: 5026
William C: 3506
Wm C: 2416 3725 3751
Wm N: 3974
Wm Pinkney: 3725

MARTZ
Annie V: 6043
Caroline C: 2505
Catharine S: 1936
David H: 3852
Elizabeth: 14
Geo D: 3622
Geo Jacob (Rev): 3703
George S: 3959
Julia C: 5380
Lewis J: 3755
Marietta E: 6031
Wilson N: 3765
Wm C: 3941
Wm H: 3681

MASER
Frederick: 3816

MASON
Elisha: 3582
John Thompson (Hon): 3578
John Y: 78
Mary: 235
Mary Ann: 78
Richard R (Rev): 3707
Temple: 3904
Wm Pinkney: 3850

MATHEWS
Mary Rebecca (Mrs): 515

MATHIAS
Etta: 2717
Fannie: 4363

MATLOCK
Elizabeth: 1881

MATTERN
Catharine: 1886

MATTEWS
Elizabeth: 2271

MATTHEWS
Elizabeth: 2228
Fred'k W: 3825
Jeremiah: 3504
Jonas: 3709

Margaret: 5114
Samuel G: 3603
MATTHIAS
John (Capt'n): 3501
MATTOON
Charles B: 3793
MAUGHT
Andrew C H: 3614
Mary A B: 5102
Sam'l: 5102
MAULSBY
Bettie H: 4546
David J: 3541
Emily V: 3130
Israel D: 3537 3541
Wm P: 3130 4546
Wm P (Jun'r): 3892
Wm Pinkney: 3537
Wm Pinkney (Hon Sen': 3841
MAUZY
Eugenia H: 468
MAY
Clintonia G: 5701
Lullu E: 1844
Magdalena: 389
MAYBERRY
Henrietta: 4402
Justenian: 3486
Justiman: 1737
Justinian: 4402
Laura E V: 1737
Mary Ann: 4787
No First Name Given: 3532
Sophia: 3486
MAYBURRY
Justinian: 4136
Mary: 4136
MAYER
Albert Marshall (Pro: 3795
Bartel: 3563
Johanna: 1229
Max: 3776
MAYES
Emiline: 3593
MAYHEW
Keziah: 2946
MAYN
David Y: 3880
MAYNARD
Benjamin: 3588
Dennis: 3712
Grafton: 3942
Howard G: 3688
Jemima: 4896
Julia S: 5666
Lea Ellen: 1588
S S (Dr): 3827
Sollers S: 3839
Tho's: 3794 4896
Tho's G: 5175
Virginia: 5175
Warren: 3772
MAYOR
Jesse: 3555
MAYTON
James C (Dr): 3930
MCALEER
Clara L: 3805
Hugh: 3572 3805
John: 3572
MCALLISTER
Ann A: 3369
MCAULY
No First Name Given: 3815
MCAVOY
Edward: 3789
MCBRIDE
A C: 3926
Abraham: 3764
S Foster: 3790
MCBRIEN
Isabel Ann: 3300
John: 3300
MCBURDETT
George B: 3979
MCCABE
Eliza G: 5809
MCCAFFERTY
John: 115
Mary Ellen: 115
Susannah: 1344
MCCAFFNEY
Mich'l: 3831
Wm H: 3831
MCCAFFREY
Aloysius B: 3844
MCCAHAN
Catharine: 2919
E Luther: 3779
Geo: 3749 3779
Geo L: 3749
George: 2828 3528
John E: 3775
Mary C: 2828
MCCANN
Eleanor (Mrs): 2157
MCCANNER
Owen: 3911
MCCARDELL
Adrian C: 3842
Nettie R: 3927
MCCARN
Minnie M: 5765
MCCARTHY
Maggie L: 5643
MCCARTNEY
Jane: 3268
John T: 3667
Michael: 3621 3667
MCCAULEY
Hanna Virginia: 5121
Sam'l: 5121
MCCHESLEY
Jane G: 3592
MCCLAIN
Wm: 2094
MCCLEERY
Andrew: 3639
Ellen: 340
H'y: 2866
Harriet S: 5710
John: 3575
Lizzie Hanna "KNIGHT: 613
Robert: 3639
Wm: 340 3642
Wm H: 3642
Zeraiah: 2866
MCCLELLAN
Curwin B (Maj): 3803
MCCLELLAND
Alice A: 6078
Geo Brinton (Capt'n): 3736
Leora: 2645
MCCLERY
Perry Beall: 3656
Robert: 3656
MCCLINTOCK
H H: 3819
John (Rev): 3643
MCCLOUW
Charles E: 3935
MCCLOW
Oliver E: 3973
Sadie: 4370

MCCLURE
 Georgianna V: 4791
MCCOLLAM
 John A: 3632
MCCOLLUM
 Catharine: 4933
MCCONKEY
 Marian L: 5356
MCCONNES
 Omer: 3911
MCCORMACK
 Jane Rebecca: 453
MCCORMICK
 Catharine Ann: 871
 George: 3645
 Harriett A: 1355
 John M: 3968
MCCOUBERY
 Margaret Jane: 4418
MCCOY
 Edward: 3897
MCCREA
 John: 3697
 Thompson (Dr): 3492
MCCREERY
 James M: 3483
MCCRON
 Jennie: 582
 Jon (Rev): 582
MCCROSKEY
 Ada: 5501
MCCULLEY
 John J: 2326 3575
 Mary: 3575
 Sarah Jane: 2326
MCCULLOUGH
 John W (Rev): 3514
MCCUTCHEON
 Tho's: 3867
MCDADE
 Avis Rebecca: 4255
 David Martin: 3625
 Isabella: 1640
 Margaret: 2364
 Mary: 252
 Sam'l: 1640 2364 3625 4255
 Samuel: 3472
MCDANIEL
 Camilla E: 4290
 Florence C: 6121
 J Milton: 3738

 James E: 3945
MCDANNIEL
 A S: 3912
MCDERITT
 Nannie M: 3930
MCDERMOTT
 James: 3676
 John: 1343 3489
 Katie: 1343
 Rosa M (Mrs): 1337
MCDEVITT
 Cha's W: 3731
 Elizabeth: 397
 Harriet E: 5392
 Margaret A E: 5992
 Mary M: 4088
 Sarah A: 4929
 Susan R: 3879
MCDONALD
 David: 3519
 Frank P: 3830
MCDONNELL
 Jacob: 3687
MCDOWELL
 James (Hon): 5587
 Sally C P: 3691
 Sarah C P: 5587
MCDULL
 Jennette: 3041
MCELDERRY
 Jane: 2194
MCELFRESH
 Anna Mary: 2967
 Arianna: 5606
 Jno H: 5606
 John H: 2967
 Mary T: 6235
MCELVY
 James C: 3634
MCERMOTT
 James W: 3677
 John: 3677
MCFALL
 Lucinda M (Mrs): 3005
MCFERRAN
 John: 3565
MCGEE
 Elizabeth: 500
 Mary: 3489
MCGILL
 Arabella: 3928

 Belle W: 3928
 Eleanor West: 6067
 Elizab Ruthven: 3850
 Ellen: 3236
 Ellenora Arabella: 5965
 Era R: 3901
 Ernest (Rev): 3923
 J Th (Dr): 3872
 John Tho's (Dr): 3838
 Robert: 3901
 S K: 2650
 Samuel (Dr): 3838
 Th J (Dr): 3850
 Tho's (Dr): 3928
 Tho's J (Dr): 6067
 Wardlaw (Dr): 3872
MCGINNIS
 George B: 3972
 Sam'l D: 3770
 Wm C: 3746
MCGLENNEN
 Margaret: 818
MCGOWAN
 Eliza: 4062
MCGRIFFITH
 John: 3686
MCGUIGEN
 Sarah J: 1991
MCGUIRE
 R A: 4001
MCGURN
 Alice: 3136
MCHENRY
 Luke Tiernan: 3633
 Mollie: 752
MCINTOSH
 Caroline C: 1647
MCJILTON
 Margaret C G: 1699
MCKALEB
 Sarah H: 3261
MCKENNY
 Sam'l W (Capt): 3649
MCKENSIE
 Annie: 6153
MCKENZIE
 J S (Dr): 3938
 James E: 3845
MCKIERNAN
 Peter: 3473
MCKIM

Robert V: 3714

MCKINLEY
Ann Maria: 1157

MCKINNEY
A F: 3948
Andrew: 3948
Juliann: 1235
Maggie: 5718

MCKINSTRY
Cha's W: 3531
Robert: 3971

MCKNIGHT
Jennie: 1457

MCKONKEY
Eliza: 2738

MCKUSTER
James: 3672

MCLAIN
Adelade: 2094
John S: 3627

MCLAINE
Florence M: 1416

MCLANAHAN
Alice: 4165
Martha A: 193
Wm M B: 3564 4165
Zeruah M: 2224

MCLANE
Ann V: 6052
Cha's A: 3800
Cyrus: 3527
George: 3516
Mary Lucretia: 1373
Rezin: 3499
Rufus A: 3791
Wm W: 1373 3534 6052

MCLAUGHLIN
Mary: 3062
Sarah (Mrs): 375

MCLEAN
Cha's: 2830
Donald: 3921
Geo W: 3618
Mary E: 6045
Mary F B: 2830
Samuel: 3553
Tho's L (Rev): 3589 6045

MCLELLAN
Curwin B (Maj): 3843

MCMACKIN
Edward: 3535

MCMAHON
Agnes Biddy: 3649
Mary: 2354

MCMAN
Dennis: 3939

MCMANTO
Dennis: 3939

MCMULLEN
Malinda: 4434

MCMULLIN
Cha's P: 3523 3662
Fayette (Gov): 3710
Margaret: 3662
Rebecca R: 1533
Rose Ann: 478

MCNAIR
Ann: 6183
James: 3487

MCNAMAR
Elizabeth: 2905

MCNEILL
Francis A (Rev): 3518

MCNUNALEY
No First Name Given: 2123

MCPHERSON
Alice: 1253
Alphemia J: 587
Ann G: 4497
Anna H: 4637
Cornelia: 1230
Edw B: 1230
Edward (Hon): 3762
Edward B: 3498 3580
Fannie: 1346
Horatio: 3482
John: 3574 3705
John (Col): 1253 1346 3482 3498 4497
John B: 3762
John H T: 3659
John Junior: 3481
Maria: 6009
Maria (Mrs): 5548
Mary B: 3923
Mary E: 2932
Maynard: 3702
Rebecca: 4273
Rob't G: 3568 3659 3873 5548
Robert G: 6009
Robert G (Jr): 3933
Robert J: 3568
Wm: 3705
Wm S (Dr): 2932 3533 3702
Wm T: 3574
Wm W: 3873 3875

MCPRICE
Mary M: 1451

MCQUILKEN
Sallie M: 1407

MCQUIRE
Miss: 3778

MCSHERRY
Alice M: 2595
Edward C (Dr): 3857 3859
Gertie: 4350
J Roger: 3984
Ja's: 2595
Ja's (Judge): 3984
James: 3573 3859 4350

MCTAVISH
Charles Carroll: 3660

MCVICKER
Mary: 801

MEALEY
Cha's E: 3768
Charles E: 3701 3854
Cora A: 2102
Georgianna: 4310
Isaiah: 3510 3655 3701 3854 4310 6030
Jemima: 512
Kate: 4321
Laura V: 3171
Lewis H: 3655
Martha E: 6030
Milton: 3796

MEALY
Anna Lucretia: 4117

MEASELL
Amanda: 556
Charles: 3810
David L: 3706
J F: 3878
Julia A S: 6217
Margaret S: 1311
Mary Ann C: 5197
Mary Jane: 1051

MEASLE
Julia: 6217

MECHLI
Eli: 3623

MEDCALF
Emily S: 5463

MEDCALFE
  Juliann: 4473
  Leonard T: 3666
MEDDERS
  Albert: 3756
MEDDERT
  No First Name Given: 4740
MEDTART
  Jacob (Rev): 3521 3550
MEEKS
  Minnie C: 5323
MEGAHLY
  Mary Elizabeth Eiche: 6184
MEHRING
  Ida H: 6285
MEHRLING
  August: 3806 3982
  Caspar: 3669 3884
  Casper: 2712
  Daniel: 3735
  Ella: 2712
  Geo: 3750 5342
  George: 3630 3814
  Henry: 3836
  J Geo: 3630
  Jacob: 3884
  John: 3750
  John Geo: 3669
  Lewis: 3806 3836
  Lizzie: 5342
  Margaret: 4613
  Margaret C: 4380
  Wm H: 3982
MEIER
  George E: 3869
MEIKSELL
  Eliza: 2266
  Jacob (Sen'r): 2266
MEIXELL
  No First Name Given: 4213
MELCHER
  Wm H: 3967
MELCHING
  Margaret: 2971
MELCHIOR
  William: 3967
MELDRUM
  Anna M: 5690
  Elizabeth A: 850
MELIUS
  Conrad: 3822 4601
  Louis: 3822
  Mary (Mrs): 4601
MENCHE'
  Lydia: 4895
MENDEL
  Regina: 1987
MENDENHALL
  H G (Rev): 3915
MENSENDICK
  Charles: 3679
MERCER
  Alice: 5504
  Clara V: 4715
  Cornelius: 3787
  Edward: 3752
  Fannie: 1100
  Irene: 2118
  Ralph: 3975
  Rebecca H: 1822
  Robert S (Rev): 3694
  Sarah A E: 3085
  Wm E: 3782
MERCHANT
  George: 3969
  John W: 3895
MERCIER
  Rebecca: 1822
MEREDITH
  John A: 3807
MERGARDT
  Conrad: 3629
MERIDETH
  Rebecca: 169
MERMAN
  Hannah: 5581
  Salina M: 1584
  Sarah: 4410
  Sarah, Mrs: 3256
  Tho's: 4410
  Washington P: 3653 3832
MERO
  Anna: 5995
MERRICK
  Richard T (Capt): 3778
  Wm M: 3595
MERRILL
  Miss: 2182
  Squire G: 3777
MERRIMAN
  Emilie J (Mrs): 2596
MERRITT
  Mary Georgianna: 3725
MERRYMAN
  Sam'l H B: 3716
MERSHON
  Stacy B: 3783
MESBEY
  Tho's G: 3950
MESSER
  Ann Rebecca: 940
METCALFE
  Henry Z: 3730
METHENY
  Catharine: 5219
METZ
  Frank M (Dr): 3943
METZGER
  Ann M: 321
  Catharine E: 1219
  George: 3513
  Gerhart: 3551
  Jac: 1219
  Jacob: 3470 3513 3517 3551
  Margaret: 2487 5739
  Mattie: 1759
  William: 3517
  Wm: 1759
MEYER
  Annie C: 5659
  Charles G: 3802
  Fredericca: 269
  Geo: 2575 5659
  Herman L: 3898
  Jeannie: 5017
  Justus: 3419
  Lizzie W: 2575
  Maria Elizab: 3419
  Tho's: 5017
MEYERLE'
  Frederick: 3539
MEYERS
  Ann Kate: 2276
  George W: 3708
MICHAEL
  Adelia E: 5724
  Andrew: 3584
  Ann: 4871
  Ann M (Mrs): 2305
  Annie A: 1056 3125
  Cassandra: 2412
  Catharine: 2160
  Charlotte: 3742
  Daniel: 3558

David: 3480 3769
Edward L: 3952
Emily J: 953
Ezra: 3641
Harry C: 3956
Hattie L: 3182
Henry: 3956 5199
Jacob: 3769 3956 5066
Jacob R: 3532
Jesse H: 3983
John H: 3740
Laura: 5066
Margaret: 4417
Mary Ann: 2462
Mary E: 5199
Mary E A: 309
No First Name Given: 3711
Othelia: 2892
Phoebe A: 6137
Sarah C: 2421
Sarah J: 1338
Virginia E: 1061
William: 3526
Wm: 3526 3532 4417
Wm H: 3719 3757

MICHELL
Annie E V: 5496

MICKEY
Katie M: 2680

MIDDELKAUFF
Mary: 195
Sarah: 185

MIDDLEKAUFF
E: 3652
G G: 3720
J A: 3801

MIDDLETON
Frances Augusta: 4614
Mary P: 6044
Rob't W: 4614 6044
Robert White: 3507
Samuel: 3647

MIERS
Wm H: 3474

MIESELL
Catherine Malinda: 3009

MILES
Harriott Ann: 5001
Mary E: 3133

MILFORD
John W: 3759

MILLER

A: 3774
Ada: 5110
Alburtus A: 3862
Ann: 2943
Ann Maria: 3248
Ann R: 6213 6238
Annie: 1133 5311
Annie S: 2465
Annie U: 3753
Ava M V: 4607
Barbara Ann: 3606
Benjamin M: 3478
Calvin R: 3773
Catharine: 5569
Catharine E: 236
Catharine Matilda: 4314
Cha's M: 3698 3958
Cha's W: 3774 3853
Charles B: 3916
Charles H: 3934
Charlotte: 153 2888 4965
Christianna: 4525
Clara: 3425
Clarissa E: 3102
Columbia Ann: 3761
Conrad: 3797 5098 5870
D S: 3860
Dan'l: 3774 3853
Daniel: 3488 3525
Daniel B: 3951
Daniel C: 3744
David E: 3675
David F K: 3576
David H: 3557
Edgar L: 3903
Edward (Dr): 3520 4607
Eliza P: 4156
Elizabeth: 5870
Elizabeth A: 1531
Elleanora: 3391
Emily: 817
Emma Virg'a: 1982
Eveline M: 1791
Florence O: 4367
Frances A: 3655
Frances Ann (Mrs): 1544
Frank P: 3887
Franklin L: 3978
Fred'k D: 2465
Frederick: 3962
Geo: 1274 3031 3636 3753 3909
Geo A: 3613
Geo D: 3601

Geo Ezra: 3566
Geo W: 236 3684
George: 3903
George M C: 3960
Gottlob: 3494
Harrison: 3559 3604 5311
Harvey C: 3988
Henry: 3797
Isabella V: 3974
J Marshal: 3946
J Sam'l (Dr): 153 2748
Jacob: 3919
Jacob M: 3704
Jacob T C: 593 2822 3655 3761
James H: 3909
Jane: 2991
Jas G: 6136
Jennie: 6136
Jno W: 3606
John: 2888 3488 3557 3700 3891
John (Rev): 3596 3691
John F: 3536 3773
John Sam'l: 3520
John Sam'l (Dr): 3698
John W: 2274 3576 3704 3739 3804 5569 6238
Jos G: 5421 6136
Joseph G: 3785 5891
Joshua: 3540
Joshua M: 5131
Julia A: 3721
Julia B: 3180
Juliann H: 481
Lewis H: 3739
Louisa: 1274
Mamie: 1419
Margaret: 1604
Maria: 3025
Maria Ellen: 1625
Maria M (Mrs): 1187
Marion: 5131
Mary: 2274 2509
Mary Ann: 1502 4919
Mary C: 5098
Mary S: 5348
Matilda: 2481
Mich'l: 3536
Mich'l Henry: 3616
Michael: 3616
Milton: 1133 3804
Minerva A: 2370
Miss: 5870

Nancy: 3485
No First Name Given: 3818
Rebecca: 2748 3494 5642
Rebecca (Mrs): 6000
Reinhardt: 3664
S E: 3917
Sallie A J: 593
Sally A: 4326
Samuel M: 3569
Sarah A E: 444
Sarah Jane: 5891
Sarah M: 3031
Simon S (Rev): 3865
Susan: 680
Thomas G: 3824
Virginia A R: 2822
Washington M: 3737
William: 3556
Wm: 1419 3961
Wm Baker: 3591
Wm H: 3883
Wm L: 3964
Wm S: 3636 3974
Wm T: 1791
Wm V: 3927

MILLS
Miss: 5988

MIMM
Mary Ann: 4038

MINDELL
C B: 3896

MINES
John L: 3624
Wm M: 3920

MINNICH
Ann C: 446
Catharine Ann S: 3270

MISS
Laura: 543
Sarah E: 5267
Tillie O: 715

MITCHEL
Ella M: 760

MITCHELL
Eleanor: 5477
Eliza L: 4680
Henry: 5477
Jane C: 5226
John T: 3560 3668
John Tho's: 3745
Joseph J: 3562
Tho's E (Dr): 3826

Wm H: 5226

MITTNACHT
Amelia: 5738
Geo H: 3587 5738
Rosa B: 5980

MIX
Charlotte C: 4539
Louisa E: 3022

MOATH
Miss: 1436

MOBBERLY
Amanda Elizab: 2933
Anna: 2777
Charles E: 3918
Eldred W (Dr): 2777 4330 6228
Helen: 4330
Louisa: 268 6228

MOBERLY
C E: 6286
Cha's: 2682
Charles E: 3918
David H: 3821
Edmund F: 3874
Geo R: 3906
J Wm: 3907
Katie: 1112
L H: 3888 6257
Laura E: 6257
Levi: 3821
Lewis: 1112 3906 3907 3940 3953 3954
Lewis C: 3888
Lewis H: 5417
Marion S: 3953
Mary M: 2682
Mary O: 2694
May A: 2694
Mollie L: 1114 5417
Nanie R: 6286
Nannie G: 3940
No First Name Given: 6105
Robert E: 3954
Rowanna V: 2556

MOBLEY
Ann R: 5938
Eli: 3486
Elizabeth: 3475
Hiram: 3829
Levi: 3495 3661 3662 3817 3829 4059 5938
Levi M: 3662
Lewis H: 3661

Margaret: 5729
Mary Ann: 4059
William: 3611
Wm L: 3817

MOFFAT
Gracie: 1463

MOFFET
Ellen E: 4949
John Newland (Rev): 3609

MOFFETT
Jacob: 3936

MOFFIT
Wm R: 3620

MOHLER
Margaret: 3098

MOIECSELL
Jacob (Sen'r): 2922
Violetta B: 2922

MOLER
Robert L: 3986

MOLESWORTH
Joshua: 3870
Rachel: 1266

MOLICH
Eliza: 3341

MONEY
Wm W: 3944

MONTGOMERY
Caroline L: 4468
Emily O: 1240
Fannie R: 3193
Harvey F (Dr): 3638
James (Jun'r): 3619
Jennette R: 3314
Joanna: 1327
John (Col): 1327 3314 4468
Samuel: 3640
Wm T: 3890

MONTHOLON
Albine Ann Yolande: 94

MOODY
Mary Winbourne: 2425

MOORE
Alfred L: 3502
Ann R: 875
Elmer E: 3913
Geo: 2789 3594 3741
Geo M: 3741
George: 853 875
J H (Rev): 3955
John H: 3955

John T: 3594 3882
John T (Junr): 3889
Joseph F: 3931
Lizzie: 3430
Margaret H: 853
Marie: 2139
Nancy: 5787
Phebe B: 4422
Rachel L: 2789
Wm H: 3882

MORELAND
Elizabeth, Mrs: 3801
John: 3511 5866
Margaret: 5866

MOREY
Albert: 3711

MORGAN
Ary Ann: 4338
Eleanor W: 2441
Elizabeth Augusta: 4974
Eveline: 5604
Geo C: 3678
George: 3823
Gerard (Rev): 3599
James: 3809
Levi: 3581
Margaret M: 5461
Mary: 3050
Mary A: 5705
Mary Ann: 799
Mary C: 2963
N J B (Rev): 3786
Napoleon B: 3855 3924
Peter: 3696
R Adelaide: 4158
Romulus G: 3599 4158
Sarah: 2091
Sarah J: 859
Sophia Rollington: 32
Tho's W: 32 859 2441 3722 3823 4974
Thomas W: 407
Virginia D: 407
Wm Virgo: 3515

MORGANSTERN
George: 3635
Henry: 3637

MORGART
Mattie: 2605

MORNINGSTAR
Annie: 2639 3448
George: 3635
George C: 3977

Henry: 3637
Mary Ann: 5035
Philip H: 3835
Philip S: 3723
Wm: 3674

MORRIS
James: 3766
John B: 1285
John G (Rev): 3503
Nancy H: 1285
Wm L: 3876

MORRISON
James F: 3849
Jane: 1162

MORSELL
Joshua (Rev): 3592

MORT
Allen B: 3928

MOSER
Abraham: 3820
Amideas C: 3858
Emideas C: 3861
Peter: 3644
Susanna (Mrs): 5164

MOSSBURG
Campsy Dell: 1125
Edward T: 3718
Thomas: 3950

MOTHLAND
Annie E: 1637

MOTT
Emma: 742

MOTTER
A C: 121
Edward S (Dr): 3695
Jacob: 3571
John C: 3658 3881
John S: 3496 3682 3695
John T: 3008
M A Virginia: 3008
Mabel: 733
William: 3554

MOUDLIN
Dennis (Rev): 2990

MOULDEN
Mary Ann: 2990

MOUNT
Eliza Ellen: 3307

MOXLEY
Ann: 5571
Margaret C: 243
Nora: 1446

Reuben M: 3726

MSHERRY
James (Junior): 3805

MUHL
Sophia: 3006

MUHLHEIM
No First Name Given: 4416

MUIR
Robert D: 3508

MULHEIM
No First Name Given: 3217

MULHOM
John E: 3899

MULHORN
Barbara (Mrs): 1900
John: 3654 3848
John E: 3848

MULL
Ann M: 4194
Geo F (Prof): 3893
George H: 3813
James M: 3799

MULLAN
Sally A: 954

MULLEN
Teresa: 3153

MULLENDORE
Oliver S: 3868

MULLHORN
George W: 3914

MULLICAN
Jane: 5065

MULLIN
S Calvin (Prof): 3856

MULLINIX
Sybelle M: 1801
Thomas P: 3937

MULNIX
Lorenzo E: 3908

MUMFORD
Geo A: 3607
John H: 3651
Kate: 4517
M Esau: 3788
Margaret: 3645
Mary Ann: 3671

MUMMA
Jesse N: 3729
Laura W: 5369
Nathaniel: 3760

MUMMY

Jesse N: 3729
MUNDER
　Caroline W: 5828
　Catharine: 4996
MUNDTS
　Mary: 2112
MUNNICH
　Jemima: 2153
MUNSEED
　Mary J: 5023
MUNSHOWER
　Cha's E: 3981
MUNSON
　Miss: 5999
MUNZ
　Mary: 2112
MUNZENBERG
　Dora: 1307
MURAT
　Achille: 3497
　Joachiam (Pr): 3497
MURPHY
　Dennis: 3944
　Ella M: 3944
　Geo W: 3743
　James Dennis: 3690
　John R: 3671
　Richard N: 3970
　Sarah A: 644
　Sarah A P: 519
MURRAY
　Edward (Lieut): 3617
　Edward B: 3815
　Elizabeth E: 5847
　James A: 3910
　Joshua Thomas: 3665
　Robert: 3628
　Ruth: 1214 1342
　Sarah A: 5873
MUSSEETER
　Charles F: 3758
　Eliza A: 2780
　Plummer J: 3781
MUSSELMAN
　John: 5168
　Sue M: 5168
MUSSER
　Catharine E: 2021
　Francis T: 3879
MUSSETER
　Sarah A: 2489

MUSSETTER
　Maggie R: 1799
　Mary E: 3466
　Mollie: 3466
MYER
　Edward F: 3932
　James (Jun'r): 3780
MYERS
　A (Rev): 3885
　A A: 3717
　Amelia: 5751
　Ann Rebecca: 3273
　Bettie B: 5443
　Catharine: 4029
　Cha's: 1109
　Cha's E: 3414
　Cha's H: 3602 3728
　Christopher: 3585
　Clara H: 3414
　Clara Jane: 4349
　Cleopatra: 2033
　David L: 3663
　Edward: 3985
　Elizabeth: 2874
　Emily A: 4465
　Evelina Virginia: 2028
　G Edward: 3965
　Geo: 3505 4803
　Geo M: 3949
　George: 3650
　George E: 3965
　Israel: 3273 4029 4792 4842
　J Oliver: 3734
　Jacob: 3484
　Joel: 3567
　John: 1698 2028 3734
　John J: 3837 5075
　Joseph: 3929
　Joseph H: 3925
　Lilly: 6128
　Lizzie E: 5075
　Lucy: 1109
　Maggie J: 1698
　Maria S: 4803
　Mary: 778 4792
　Mary E: 6073
　Mary M (Mrs): 5048
　Oliver: 3985
　Rebecca E: 943
　Rudolph: 778 2874
　Sarah: 5857
　Sophia: 4842
　Tho's J: 2033

Thomas H: 3963
Valentine: 3505
Wm: 3585
Wm H: 3680
NAGLE
　Cha's: 4126
　Charles: 3997
　Charles W: 4126
NAGLEE
　Caroline L: 5050
NAILL
　David W: 434
　Franklin A: 4127
　Mary Elizabeth: 434
　William W: 4129
NAILLE
　Annie R: 4353
NALLS
　G W: 4104
　George W: 4104
NATHAN
　Benj: 1677
　Miss: 1677
NAU
　George H: 4197
NAUMANN
　John C V: 4030
NAX
　Francis (Prof): 4147
NAYLOR
　Mahala: 3999
NAZERENUS
　Elizabeth: 264
　John: 4109
NEAL
　Eliza (Mrs): 3078
　George Henry Clay: 4094
　Joseph: 3998 4094
　Lewis (Dr): 4148
　Rebecca: 6223
　Sam'l: 616 6223
　Sarah: 1887
　Sophia F: 616
NEALL
　Joseph H: 4031
NEED
　John: 4050
NEEDWOOD
　No First Name Given: 427
NEER
　R L: 3980

NEIBOLD
John W: 4180
NEIDHARDT
Mary E: 1054
Rudolph A: 4150
Wm: 1054
NEIDIG
Abraham: 4091
Benjamin: 4057
Clara A: 5397
Isaac: 4091
Mary Jane (Mrs): 5654
Maurice O: 4102
Wm C: 4177
NEIGHBORS
Elizabeth R: 167
Eutah D (Dr): 4196
Lola: 3453
Lotta H: 3453
Rodger M: 4178
NEIHOFF
Annie L E: 2031
Christian: 2031
NEILL
Alexander (Jun'r): 4022
John W: 244 841 3992
Mary P: 841
Susan: 244
NELSON
Abraham T A Nelson: 4189
Annie M: 3694
Arthur: 4092
Edward (Dr): 4161
Emily C T: 3537
Emma F: 580
Fannie: 5676
Fannie C: 1830
Frederick J: 4167
Grace F: 2725
Henry: 4111
Holy H: 4192
John: 1217 4024 4037
John H: 4111
Joseph R: 4058 4132
Josephine V: 404
Madison: 404 580 3412 3993 4161 4167
Mary S: 4022
Molly: 1350
Nathan: 3694 4087
Nelly: 3269
Nora J: 2729
Robert: 4118 4155
Roger: 3537 3541
Roger (Gen'l): 3269 3993 4024
Rosa L: 1217
Rose E: 3412
Sallie S: 1826
Sarah: 3541
Stephen B: 4069
Wm B: 1350 5676
Wm Burrows: 4037
NEROMAN
E Susan: 2470
NESZBAUM
David: 3996
NETH
Harriott (Mrs): 3533
NEUBRANDT
Anna Mary: 3399
Caroline: 5134
Christianna: 240
John: 3399 5134
NEVINS
Mollie: 2590
NEWBANKS
Charles Edward: 4138
NEWELL
Daniel (Rev): 4019
Wm H (Dr): 4168
NEWENS
Christianna: 3484
Tho's: 3484
NEWPORT
Adam: 2341 2769 3323 3990
Louisa C: 3323
Mary Jane: 2341
Sarah M: 2769
NEWTON
Jennie W: 4168
Maria L: 3668
NEY
Adam: 4012
John (Sen'r): 4021
NEYHOFF
Ann Rebecca: 5832
Ch'n: 5272
Christian: 4011
Gabriel: 5832
Joseph A: 4115
Maggie: 5272
NICHEL
Adam: 5812
Louisa: 5812
NICHODEMUS
Addie: 1119
NICHOLAS
Robert Carter: 4062
NICHOLLS
Mary: 5576
NICHOLS
Alice M: 4652
Ann: 417 3259
Charles S: 4152
Clara K: 5528
Clara V: 3402
Clayton: 4164
Edw: 4652
Edward: 1050 4041 4152
George (Junior): 4007
James: 4001
John: 4023 4110
John Randolph: 4029
Lewis B: 4190
Louisa: 4772
Margaret: 1468
Mary: 1917
Mary A: 1876
Mary Catharine: 1050
Mary Jane: 3355
Peter: 1917 4029 4041 4772
Seth H: 4006 4038 4164
William: 4085
Wm: 3355
NICHOLSON
Mary E: 5273
NICKEL
Adam: 4009 4053
Adam Luther: 4121
Catharine: 4811
Christian: 4144
Daniel: 4053
Fannie: 6021
Jacob: 1710 3669 4009 4121 6021
Margaret Elizabeth: 3669
Martha S: 1710
NICODEMUS
Bessie: 2582
Eli: 4149
H Baxter: 4153
Isaac C (Jun'r): 4172
J Luther: 4083
John: 4056 4065
John (Sen'r): 4081
John Lewis: 4065
Margaret E: 922

Martin L: 4090
Nathan: 4056 4078
Wm H: 4140

NICOLS
Clara K: 5528

NILES
Ann Sophia: 2937
Geannie Ogden: 5923
Wm Ogden: 2937

NIXDORFF
Annie M: 3199
Henry: 2272 3698 4156 4823
Julia M: 3698
Lewis M: 4156
Mary C: 4823
Sam: 3199
Samuel: 4097
Susan: 2272
T S: 4143
Tobias: 4010 4097

NO BRIDES NAME GIVEN
Alexandra: 98
Alexandrovna: 127
Alice Maude Mary: 3366
Laura V: 6100
Miranda: 3298
Miss: 88 901 2368 3664 4944 5792 5899
Mrs: 6034
No First Name Given: 2360 4470
Princess Mastia: 130

NO SURNAME GIVEN
Albert: 18
Albert Edward: 98
Ernst Alfred: 127
Louis: 3366
Victoria: 5730

NOAH
Mordicai Manassah: 4003

NOAKES
Christianna: 1191
Rich'd: 1191

NOBLE
Sarah E: 20

NOEL
J K: 4072

NOLAND
Mary: 2764
Michael: 4049

NOLIN
John K: 4072

NOLLTE'
Fredericka: 3408
J C L: 5684
Marietta: 5684

NOLTE'
Albert: 4108
Christianna: 1392
Margaret Beck (Mrs): 4108

NOONAN
Edward W: 4131
Francis H (Dr): 4157
John: 4131 4157 4160 5643
Joseph H: 4124
Joseph J: 4160
Mary Ann: 4980

NORDHAUS
Eva: 1994

NORMAN
Mary Matilda: 2177

NORRIS
Barnabas: 3999 4000 4017 4042 4759
Basil: 3991 5614
Elizabeth: 4318
Frances Rebecca: 5051
Francina: 5825
Geo Wash Lafayette: 4052
H Annie: 3358
Harriott: 4759
James Lawson: 4042
John D: 4116
Lloyd: 4123
Lot: 4026
Lydia A: 5959
Margaret: 2862
Matthias: 4017
Nellie J: 5614
No First Name Given: 1235 1785
Rachel Ann: 3686
Sam'l: 3358
Samuel: 4000
Sarah: 3488
William Lee: 4141
Wm: 3999

NORTON
W H: 4135

NORWOOD
William: 4075

NOTABIT
Quesoda: 4137

NOTNAGLE
Annie F: 6109
J J: 6109
Joh J: 2668
Louisa: 2668

NOTTNAGEL
John Jacob: 4067

NOTTNGAEL
Lenhardt: 4066

NOURSE
J E (Rev): 4646
Sarah: 4646

NULL
George: 4089
George W: 4130
Idahalia: 5515
Mary Jane: 233
Melissa: 3680
Sarah E: 5495

NUNNEMACHER
Mary: 1709

NUNNEMAKER
Carrie: 3703

NUSSBAUM
Adam F: 4142
Henrietta: 2418
Henry: 4183
Jacob: 2418 4034 4122
Laura J: 5138
Margaret C: 3301
McHenry P: 4151
Philip Henry: 4122
Philip J: 4183

NUSZ
Ann R: 925
Anna Mary: 538
Catharine: 1515 1898
Charles L: 4187
Clara: 649
Cyrus: 925 4005 4088
Edward L: 4179
Eleanora V: 559
Ezra: 4059 4068 4079
Fleeton: 4195
Fleton E: 4195
Frederick: 1515 4015
George M: 4040
Harriott: 1493
Henry: 1898 2186 4035
Hiram M: 649 4059
J F: 4163
Jacob: 4040
James W Fred'k: 4100

Julia Ann: 2073
Mary: 2186
Oliver T: 4068
Peter Elias: 4088
Rose G: 4719
Sylvester J: 4079
Vic T: 4348
William: 4035
William L: 4182
Wm: 538 559

NUSZBAUM
Daniel: 4028
John: 4046
Lydia Ann: 3637

NYMAN
Lewis B: 4145

O'BOYLE
John H: 4113

O'BRIAN
George W: 4098

O'CONNELL
Michael: 4146

O'DONNEL
Josephine: 3262

O'DONNOHUE
Dennis: 4133
Florence (Dr): 4101
James: 4060
No First Name Given: 4133

O'HARA
Clara: 3961

O'HARRA
Charles E: 4174
John: 4166

O'LEARY
Augustine D: 4538 5289
Mary Jane: 4538
Mattie A: 5289
Thomas: 4055

O'NEAL
Caroline: 4893
Elizabeth: 3627
G (Hon): 2365 3252
Hor G: 4893
Israel C: 4025 4119 4120
John L: 4120
Maria: 2401 3252
Susan A: 2365

O'NEALL
Horatio: 4043
Horatio G: 4071
Singleton H: 4071

Thomas H: 4043

O'NEIL
James: 4044

O'NEILL
Amanda A: 1903
Horatio: 4020
Howard D: 4096
John H: 4061
Patrick: 4061
Tho's H: 4020

OATES
Catharine: 3082
Cha's T: 4159
John: 3082 4159

OBENDERFFER
Fred'k W: 4176

OBENDORFFER
Cha's Leonard: 4093

OBERLEIN
Christian: 4106

OBGORN
Laura J: 962

OCKMAY
James H (Rev): 4175

ODEN
Edward W: 4181
Mariann: 3114
Melville H: 4186

OESTERLE
Mary Ann: 288

OFFUTT
C Courtnay: 5374
John L: 4170

OGBORN
Fannie: 518
John W: 518 962

OGDEN
W: 5923

OGLE
Ann Maria: 2232
Annie F: 1323
Annie S: 2488
Calvin: 4198
Elizabeth: 1197
Eveline: 978
George W: 4099
Harriott: 5286
Ja's (Sen'r): 1197
James: 978 1323 4013 5286
James (Sen'r): 2232
Joachim: 2511 4033

John: 2488 4051 4084 4105
John Oliver: 4084 4105
Julia A: 5060
Katie E: 6157
M Tillie: 2511
Mary E: 4679
No First Name Given: 5547
Thomas A: 4117
Vincent: 4054

OHLER
Levi S: 4073
Solomon: 4070

OLAND
Carlton E: 4169
Lucretia S: 5389

OLDFIELD
Granville S (Junior): 4076

OLLAND
Henry: 4048

ONLEY
Eleanor: 3504

ORDEMAN
Emma C: 2634
H D (Capt): 2634
Mollie C: 4344

ORDNER
Caroline: 4394
Catharine: 2175
Daniel: 4016
Elizabeth: 4802
George: 4002
John: 2225 4036
Peter: 2175 4016 4027 4036 4394 4802
Sophia (Mrs): 2225

ORME
Walter A: 4103

ORNDORFF
Henry: 4018
No First Name Given: 5047

ORNER
Mary J: 5092

ORR
A V B (Rev): 452
A V B Orr (Dr): 1644
Caroline E: 452
Letitia A: 1644
Sabina: 3924

ORRICK
George W: 4139

ORRISON
Andrew: 4107

ORTNER
- Elizabeth: 300
- John: 300

ORVIER
- Marie Gabriella: 5298

OSBORNE
- F M W: 4158

OSBOURN
- Alexander L: 4162
- James W: 4032

OSTERDAG
- Daniel: 1551

OSTERLE
- Frederick: 1593
- Geo: 1770
- George (Jun'r): 1653
- Rosa A: 5408
- William: 1709

OSTERLY
- Frederick: 4063
- Geo: 4063
- George (Junior): 4064

OSTERTAG
- Joseph: 1765
- Susan E: 5893

OTIS
- William: 4008

OTT
- Ada D: 2654
- Ann Eliza: 5836
- Ann Sophia: 1241
- Florence E: 5459
- Geo W (Jun'r): 4171
- Harriott: 4552
- Jacob D: 4074
- John: 4004 4114 4171 5459
- John Warren: 4191
- Julia Ann S: 5078
- Mary: 1918 2219
- Mary (Mrs): 4004
- Mary Ann Louisa: 3622
- Mary Jane: 520
- Michael: 4004
- No First Name Given: 1235
- Peter: 1241 2219 4552 5836
- Samuel J: 4095
- Tho's: 4004
- Thomas: 3995

OTTER
- Joseph D: 4136

OTTO
- James H B: 4125

- William: 4080

OULD
- E A (Dr): 4165

OURAND
- Ann L (Mrs): 260
- David: 4014

OVELMAN
- William J: 4128

OVERTON
- Ella M: 2659
- John Brooke: 4077

OVIEDO
- De Don Esteban Santa: 4112

OWEN
- Edward W: 4154
- Robert Dale: 4173

OWENS
- Hugh: 4039
- John: 4134 4188

OYSTER
- Joyce: 2176

PACELEY
- Amanda A: 5898
- Catharine: 4475
- Emily H: 1060
- Howard: 4255
- William: 4249
- Wm: 1060

PACKARD
- Louisa: 4484

PADGET
- George M: 4235

PADGETT
- Robert J: 4295
- Ruth A: 3207

PAGE
- Calvin: 3915 3916 4276 4368
- Dudley: 4368
- Jackson: 4259
- Walker Y: 4294

PAINE
- Mary E: 511
- Robert Treat: 4265

PAISELEY
- George: 4371

PAISLEY
- George A: 4371

PALL
- Sophie: 3200

PALMER
- Carrie: 655 1014

- Eleanor Augusta: 5177
- Eliza: 5617
- Elmira: 1010
- Jacob E: 4314
- Jos Mortimer: 4231
- M Josephine: 5277
- Madaline: 5516
- Molly: 5285
- Susan Ellen: 1728
- Wm T: 655 1014 5177
- Wm Thompson: 4231

PALMER
- Wm T: 5277

PAMPEL
- Henry: 5296
- Mary C: 5296

PAMPELL
- Amelia: 6020
- David Ezra: 4291
- Elizabeth: 5865
- Fred'k W: 4338 5865 6020
- Frederick W: 4201
- Godfrey: 4211
- Henry: 4362
- Jerome E: 4338
- P Frank: 4362

PAMPILL
- David Ezra: 4291

PAMPSELL
- Sarah Ann: 4494

PAMSELL
- Fred'k: 4494

PANCOAST
- Catharine: 4432
- Sam'l: 4432

PARKER
- James: 4205
- Miss: 490
- William: 4345

PARKS
- Margaret M: 2878
- Susan: 2909

PARRAMORE
- Thomas: 4331

PARRISH
- Elizabeth H: 5130
- Emma Kate: 4587
- Nich's M: 4587

PARSON
- Wm E (Rev): 4353

PARSONS
- Hanna E: 5008

Mamie D: 664
Mason: 4335
Simon: 4317
W Irving: 4335

PARTON
James: 4280 4357

PASSAVANT
Wm A (Rev): 4248

PATTEN
Hattie E: 1113

PATTENGALL
Mary: 4534
Samuel: 4206

PATTERSON
Mary Ann (Mrs): 5783
Nancy: 2145
Samuel S: 4327

PATTINGALL
Ann: 3228
Charlotte E: 1926
Sam'l: 1926

PATTTERSON
Allie: 6115

PAYGNE
Joseph: 4366

PAYNE
Amanda H: 4593
Edward R: 4382
Harriott E: 3667
Ida G: 2099
John W: 4263
Jos: 3667 4292
Joseph: 4263 4366
Joseph F: 4292
Sarah C D: 161

PEACOCK
Elizabeth: 4225

PEARCE
E Jane: 4595
Emily B: 380
James A (Hon): 4253
Lydia E: 3775

PEARRE
Aubray: 4365
Aubrey: 4365
Geo A: 3872
George A: 4244
Georgia: 3872
James: 4304
James W: 4309 4355
Maggie A: 1371
Mary Tabitha: 2301

Mattie A: 5968
Sarah E: 4931
Tho's Otho: 4275
Wm: 2301 4244 4304 5968
Wm H: 4288 4320

PEARRIE
Claudie: 5473
Jas: 5473

PEARSON
Cha's S: 4376
Hannah A: 4867
Jos: 4867

PEBUS
Ann: 1177
Jacobus: 1177

PECK
Charles M: 4350
O T X: 4260
Orlando: 4260

PEGLEY
John S: 4324

PEISER
Ernestine: 2974

PELTON
James B: 4302

PELTZ
Mary T: 4334

PENDLETON
Robert N: 4333
Wm C: 4356

PENN
Sarah Ann: 3723

PENNELL
Virginia A: 3052

PENNINGTON
Edgar: 4315

PEPPER
Miss: 3992

PERCEIVAL
Charles F: 4238

PERKINS
Cha's Allen: 4337
Joseph L: 4213
Mary Jane: 1261

PERRIE
John (Dr): 4258

PERRY
Ann L (Mrs): 6178
Delia: 6119
E Augustus: 4328
Ella: 6281

H Clay: 4380
Ja's P: 3451
James: 1432
Katie J: 3451
Mary: 3444
Mathew C (Com): 346
Minnie N: 1432
Miss: 346
Thomas (Hon): 4313
Wm: 6178
Wm W: 4289

PERRYMAN
Edward G (Rev): 4336

PESCHAU
Ferdinand (Rev): 4349

PETERHOFF
Catherine: 102

PETERS
Cha's: 1210 4246
Edward C: 4378
Elizabeth: 4
Mary C: 1210
Mary Ellen: 3789
Oscar A: 4352
Urith A (Mrs): 2572
William: 4246
Wm: 3789

PETT
No First Name Given: 3351

PETTINGALL
Linda R: 4627

PETTIT
Hattie F: 1755
Henry M: 4216
John Phillips: 4209
Lizzie M: 2562

PETTITT
Isabella: 3825

PETTYJOHN
Annie M W: 3947

PEYTON
Thomas Jefferson: 4256

PFAUB
Catharine: 328

PFEFFER
Baron: 4343

PFEIFFER
Abraham: 4297

PFLEIDERER
Jacob: 4199

PFOUTZ

Deborah L: 5201
J's (Rev): 2054
Sarah Ellen: 5176
PHEBUS
Ann E: 2490
Benjamin F: 4285
Cha's O: 4351
Charles E: 4300
Elizabeth: 12
Eugene McM: 4367
Geo: 2386 2490
George: 4243
Ja's H: 657 4332
James: 4367
James H: 4240 4332 4351
John: 4266
Laura Permelia: 3363
Margaret (Mrs): 2386
Mary E: 657
Peter: 4240 4243 4266 4278
  4278 4285
PHELPS
Joshua O: 4354
Julia E: 3552
Philo F (Rev): 4221
Susan Ann: 5018
PHILBY
Thaddeus S: 4334
PHILIPS
Isabella: 413
Mary (Mrs): 5727
PHILLER
Eli: 4223
PHILLIPPS
Lewis A: 4373
PHILLIPS
Alice V: 5697
Ann: 798
Annie M: 1103
Deborah: 2872
Greenbury: 4225
John L: 4267
Mary: 5802
Minerva: 2198
Miranda: 1473
No First Name Given: 6230
Noah: 2198
Noah (Col): 4254
Richard H (Rev): 4222
Theodore B: 4269
Warren W: 4210
William (Rev): 4242

PHILOWER
Bertha M: 3987
PHILPOT
Violetta: 297
PHLEEGER
Clarence M: 4375
Edward: 4282
Fannie: 5406
Frederick K: 4310
John: 3768 4228 4282 4310
Louis: 4339
Rebecca: 3768
PHLEUGER
John H: 4287
PHOEBUS
Benj: 4363 4364 6273
Bnj: 3913
Catharine H E: 3913
Charles O: 4342
Clara V: 1770
Florence M: 6273
George T: 4346
George W: 4363 4364
John: 1770 4346
PICKING
Annie E: 72
Cha's T: 4381
Harry B: 4372
John T: 4279
Rebecca T: 1369
Tho's: 72 1369 4301
Thomas: 4311
Wm H: 4301
PICKINS
Margaret: 1532
PICKLE
John: 4229
PIERCE
Martha: 3584
PIERPOINT
Sarah A: 2327
PIGMAN
Beene S: 4226
Hanson: 648
Hanson B: 3892
Hanson Briscoe: 4226
Hattie B: 3051
Henrietta H: 3892
Mary Briscoe: 648
PILES
Clara J: 3931
Mary A: 5944

PIMM
Mary: 384
Mary Elizabeth: 4077
PINCKNEY
Howard (Dr): 4316
PIPER
Mary Ellen: 5274
PIPPINGER
Andrew: 4247
PITCHER
Molly N: 1080
Thomas: 4283
PITTINGER
John: 4308
PITTS
Caro: 2543
Caroline: 2382
Ch's H: 1396
Charles H: 4245
Elizabeth: 1396
John (Rev): 4236 4245
No First Name Given: 307
William: 4236
PLAIN
Sarah A: 4863
PLAINE
Hiram: 4261
Stephen: 4227
PLOWMAN
Nathan: 4218
PLUME
Kate C: 1047
PLUMLEY
Edgar: 4359
PLUMMER
Ann Jennie: 5101
Eleanor: 5479
Martha E: 5627
Reuben N: 4262
Wm: 5101
PLUNKETT
Lucy: 6134
POE
Amelia: 1907
Josephine C: 974
Neilson: 974 4214
POFFENBERBER
Wm Luther: 4325
POFFENBERGER
B T: 4232
Jacob: 4233

Josiah: 4298
Martha: 3403
POLE
George W: 4281
POLK
Esther W: 3280
James: 3280
POOL
Cornelius: 4200
David: 4268
Eli: 4217 4220
Elizabeth: 814
Henry: 4257
John: 4257
Susan: 2884
Valentine: 4203
Walter: 2884
POOLE
Ann M: 3336
Annie E: 2502
Charles A: 4348
Clementine V: 4275
Daniel: 4312
Elizabeth: 3612
Ella: 139
Emma J: 575
Ernest F: 4369
Geo W: 4341
George: 4286
George E: 4370
Hanson: 4318
Irene: 5484
John: 575
Joseph H: 4321
Kate: 1976
Laura T: 3122
Lillie: 3168
Lucretia: 2376
Mary Ann: 2908
No First Name Given: 712
Peter: 4272
Sarah E: 1744
Sarah Ellen: 6163
Tho's E D: 4251
Wm: 2376 2908 3612 4318
POPE
Catharine (Mrs): 2261
Jennie E: 2059
John H: 2059 4239 4340
Thomas E: 4322
Wm: 2261 4322
Wm H: 4340
POPP

John M: 4358
PORTER
Aggie: 5766
Catharine S: 4265
Charles: 4347
Deborah B: 2952
Eliza Silvester: 4234
Isabella S: 369
John A: 4234
John Alfred: 4271
John W: 3676 4207
Richard: 4234
Robert: 4307
Rosa: 1337
Rose M: 3676
POSEY
B N: 4264
POST
Eliza (Mrs): 1537
POTTER
Lillian: 5713
POTTERFIELD
Jacob A: 4296
John D: 4284
Nettie: 1046
POTTS
Arthur: 4330
Cornelia R: 4580
Eleanor: 2835
Elizabeth: 2151
Geo M: 2835 4273 4330 4580
Geo Murdoch: 4208
Harriott M: 3479
Mary: 2737
Rich'd: 2737
Rich'd (Judge): 3479
Richard: 4208
Richard (Dr): 4273
Richard (Sen'r): 2151
POWDER
John D: 4250
POWELL
Catharine: 4396
Cha's Edward: 4277
Milton L: 4379
POWER
Hamilton H: 4299
POWERS
Elizabeth (Mrs): 2555
Wm H: 4274
PRATHER

Ann: 1988
PRENTICE
Clarence J: 4305
Geo D: 4305
PRESCOTT
Caroline: 5603
PRESTON
Ann E: 1597
Cha's: 2235 4237 4323
Sam'l B: 4237
Samuel B: 4323
Sarah B: 2235
Sarah F: 5860
Susan (Mrs): 164
Wm P: 4252
PRETTYJOHN
Annie M W: 3947
PREY
John W: 4306
PRICE
Benjamin: 4219
John E: 4344
John T: 4361
Mary Cath: 3352
Nannie: 3105
Sarah: 3556
Wesley: 4326
PRIMROSE
Pers (Capt'n): 4360
PRINCE
Catharine Amelia: 2560
Henrietta F: 4505
Lemuel Tho's: 4293
Mary: 4982
Tho's: 2560
Tho's C: 4293 4505 4982
Thomas C: 4204 4224 4270
W Edgar: 4383
PROBST
Carrie L: 3424
Geo C (Rev): 4290
J F (Rev): 3424
PROBY
James: 4215
PROTZMAN
Kate B: 2029
PRYOR
George E (Dr): 4212
PULLEN
Cornelia: 4966
PULTZ

Lorenia: 1924
PUMPERNICKEL
  Betsey: 4576
PUMPHREY
  Vachel: 4202
PURCELL
  Oscar: 4374
  Thomas: 4319
PURDY
  Susan R: 4097
PURNELL
  Elizabeth H: 722
  Elkton: 4329
  Oscar O: 4374
  Samuel: 4329
  Wm H: 722 4374
  Wm H (Jr): 4384
PUTTS
  Lizzie C: 2464 5324
  No First Name Given: 666
PUZENAT
  Lawrence A: 4303
PYFER
  Ann C: 3004
  Elizabeth: 1263
  Hannah Melville: 4230
  Henry: 1263 4230
  Margaret M: 381
  Ph: 381
  Philip: 3004 4230
  Rachel E: 3772
  Wm B: 3772 4230
PYLES
  Clara J: 3931
  Isaac J: 4377
PYRELKE
  Mary: 3985
QUANTRILL
  Archibald R: 4086
QUEEN
  J T: 4082
  John Theodore: 4082
QUIGLEY
  Lucy: 4958
QUINN
  Catharine: 5612
  Ella C: 6156
  Jacob P: 4194
  John: 1806
  Mary M: 1806
  No First Name Given: 3684

3721
Thomas N: 4185
Timothy W: 4184
QUITMAN
  Antonia: 3329
  John A (Gen'l): 3329 3334
  Louisa T: 3334
QUYNN
  Allen G: 4047 5692
  Cha's W: 4193
  John: 4045 4047
  John T: 4045 4193
  Maria V: 5692
  Mary C: 4471
  Mollie T: 4694
  No First Name Given: 1625 5006
  William: 3989 3994
  Wm: 4471
RAAC
  Sophia: 45
RABOLD
  Matthias: 4536
RAELING
  Elizabeth: 4880
RAELINGER
  Lewis D: 4648
RAFF
  Isabelle: 1089
RAGAN
  Alice V: 3458
  Elizabeth: 4009
RAGER
  Adolphus S: 4676
  Maud D: 3904
  Rufus A: 4681
RAHAUSER
  Frederick (Rev): 4448
RAHTER
  Adolphus C: 4603
RAILING
  Catharine: 3019
RAINFERT
  John: 4516
RAINFORD
  Philip (Col): 4515
RAITT
  Lydia: 1173
RAMEN
  William: 4620
RAMKEY

Sophia: 2636
RAMSAY
  James M: 4479
  Thomas: 4437 4470
RAMSBURG
  Alexander: 4563
  Amanda Ellen: 1952
  Amanda L: 97
  Ann Mary: 5821 a2
  Ann Rebecca: 190 a2
  Ann S: 5146
  Catharine: 1549 a2
  Clinton E: 4691
  Cordelia A: 1026
  Cornelius Stille': 4646
  David J: 4482
  Dennis: 4467
  Dennis C: 4674
  Drue H: a3
  Edward: 4475
  Elias: 4419 4555 a2 a3
  Eliza: 1481 3641 a2
  Elizabeth (Mrs): 4428
  Ellen R: 508
  Emma: 3934
  ER: a2
  Fannie: 1837 4656
  Florence: 3417
  Frederick: 4502
  Isabella: 5187
  Jacob: 4426 4593 4632 a2 a3
  John: 1481 1549 4418 4418 4419 4426 4462 4630 5821 a2
  John F: 4452
  John H: 4652
  John Stephen: 4555 a3
  Joshua: 4575
  Josiah: 4652
  Le's: 5969
  Lillie M: 2710
  Marshall O: 4679
  Martha M: 3783
  Mary E: 2494
  Mattie M: 1790
  Mollie E: 2117
  Newton A: 4630
  Peter: a2 a3
  Rebecca: 6216
  Rebecca (Mrs): a3
  Robert M: 4655
  Stephen: 4428
  Stephen G: 4564

Susie: 1420
Uriah D: 4530
Valerius Elias: 4593 4632
William: a3
William Henry: a2
Wm H: 508 1420 3783 4656 4698
Wm Henry: 4462
Wm M: 4481

RAMSBURGH
Charlotte L: 3826
Jacob: 5541
Jane Briscoe: 4579
John T: 4545
Lewis: 3826 4385 4421 4579 4647
Lewis J: 4647
Lydia: 5541
Nelson D: 4556
Tho's C: 4586

RAMSDALE
Alonzo M: 4454

RAMSEY
Alexander: 4703

RAMSURG
Charlotte E: 5059

RANCK
Solomon: 4410

RANDALL
Nicholas A: 4411

RANDOLPH
Elizabeth A: 1209

RANELS
William E: 4695

RANNEBERGER
Philip: 4449
Robert: 4624

RANNELS
William E: 4695

RAUCH
Charles: 4436
Frederick A (Rev): 4422

RAUPP
Dorothea: 2378

RAUZAHN
Adam: 566 1727
Alfred H: 4625
Betty: 1727
Carlton P: 4622
Caroline: 2218 2920
Catharine: 522 566
Cyrus: 4490
Daniel H: 4581
Edward L: 4570
Harriott A (Mrs): 1743
John A: 4500
Jos: 1305
Joseph: 4414 4570
Joseph L: 4623
Loretto: 1305
Lydia Ann: 1489
Miss: 2920
Noah: 4542
Philip: 903
Sarah: 903
Wm H: 4628

RAY
Elizabeth A: 4558

RAYMER
Cordelia F: 670

RAYMOND
James: 4393

REA
Charles H: 4518

READ
George A: 4720
L E C: 2838

REAGAN
Alice V: 3458
Jane A: 3003

REAL
George A: 4672

REAM
Elizabeth Ann: 395
Isaac L: 4585

REAMY
Mary J: 6132

RECK
Martha C: 4172

REDDICK
Leonard: 4451

REDMAN
John: 4392

REED
Albert W: 4670
Benjamin F: 4432
Caroline: 307
George A: 4720
Isaac: 4485
Jacob: 4463 4485
James W: 4577
John: 4463 4547
Lydia C: 5747
William: 4455

REED
Lethe Ann: 82

REEDER
Charlotte M: 363
Jane E: 530

REEL
Ann C: 421
Miss: 421
Otho: 421

REESE
Ann: 2184
Anna M: 956
Annie G: 3675
D E (Rev): 558
Elizabeth B: 1322
Jacob: 4387
Lewis H: 4560
Mattie T: 558
Wm D: 4635

REEVES
Miss: 3345

REHLINGER
Christian: 4613
Geo H: 4631
Henry: 4678

REICH
Annie R: 3787
Dorcus H: 372
Hannah: 2172
Henry C: 4615
Isaac S: 4685
John: 2172 4514 4615 5648
John (Jun'r): 4416
John H: 4682
Lillian C: 3936
Lucie B: 5467
Mary C: 2809
No First Name Given: 1822 4213
Phebe: 1248
Philip: 372 1248 1370 2809 3787 4405 4611 5280
Raymond C: 4611
Sallie: 5280
Sarah: 37
Sophia E: 5648
Virginia S: 1370
William: 4514

REID
Mary Isabella: 994
Sam'l (Captn): 994
William: 4425

REIDENAUER
 Catherine (Mrs): 75
 Sarah: 4790
REIDENOUR
 Joseph A: 4664
REIFSCHNEIDER
 Sarah Jane: 2797
REIFSNIDER
 Charles D: 4668
 Georgia B: 5275
 Jno: 5454
 John: 4589 4670 5275
 Louisa E: 4670
 Rosa V: 5454
REIGART
 Elizabeth L: 4844
 John M: 4614
 Mary Emeline: 3613
 Philip: 3613
REIGEL
 Catharine M: 4549
 Reuben E: 4665
REIGHLEY
 Cha's (Rev): 1360
 Charles (Rev): 4427
 Elise: 1360
REILEY
 Miss: 5503
REILING
 Geo H: 4631
REILLY
 James: 4666
REIN
 Emily C: 947
 Matilda A: 898
REINDOLLAR
 Amelia J: 808
REINEKE'
 E William (Rev): 4551
REINHART
 Andrew: 4458
 David: 4424
 David (Rev): 5132
 Ephraim F: 4566
 Geo: 4395 4424
 George: 4450
 Jacob (Dr): 4573
 Lilly: 24
 Lizzie L: 5250
 Sarah M: 5132
 William: 4395

 Winfield G: 4640
REITZELL
 Elizabeth: 4446
 John: 4446
 Miss: 5811
REMSBERG
 Albert J (Dr): 4660
 Calvin F: 4638
 Charles T: 4653
 Geo P: 4493 4562
 Josiah: 4444
 Mahala C: 5220
 Mary: 2152
 Susan S: 893
 Washington J: 4633
REMSBURG
 Alice L C: 5420
 Christian: 4444
 Clinton E: 4691
 Edw'd: 5420
 George J: 4597
 Henrietta: 6212
 Kate A C: 2588
RENFRO
 Kate: 1053
RENN
 Amelia: 211
 Catharine E: 1695
 Emma Frorence: 2638
 Harriett: 548
 Isaac: 4399 5161
 J Calvin: 4644
 John H: 1320 4447
 Lauretto: 554
 Lydia Ann C: 2349
 Mary Jane: 5161
 Miss: 1695
 Ruth A C: 1320
RENNE
 Desie: 4703
RENNEBERGER
 Eliza: 4731
 Otho: 4406
 Philip: 4466
RENNER
 Edward L: 4616
 Elias: 4584
 Elizabeth: 1702 2658
 John P: 4677
 Lola E (Mrs): 1444
 Mary: 4662
 Peter: 4619

 Rebecca: 33 1333
RENNMICKEL
 Annie L: 6113
REPP
 A Mary: 5449
 Amanda A: 6108
 John S: 4687 5449 6108
 Maggie E: 1429
RETTGERING
 Johanna: 4868
 Matilda: 2259
 Melle': 2259 2262
 No First Name Given: 310 3095
 Wilhelmina: 2262
REULING
 Henry C: 4701
REYNALD
 John: 4391
REYNALDS
 Catharine A: 869
 Elizabeth: 777
 James W: 4459
 Mary Ellen: 574
 Sam'l: 869
REYNOLD
 Hugh: 4391
REYNOLDS
 Annie E: 5425
 Cordelia C: 6251
 Elizabeth: 4245
 Margaret: 1536
 Sallie F: 5099
 Susan: 2954
RHEAM
 Hanna R: 5929
RHINE
 John (Jun'r): 4468
 John W: 4572
 Susan E: 4533
RHOADES
 Ada E: 1853
RHOADS
 Dan'l: 1317
 Susan: 1317
RHODERICK
 Elizabeth: 302 1745
 Geo C: 4548
 George C (Jr): 4696
 George W: 4512
 Hammine: 6126
 Mahlon: 4642 5319

Mahlon Theodore: 4642
Marietta: 5319
Olive E (Mrs): 5340
Washington W: 4561
Wm: 4715

RHODES
Ada: 1853
Calvin A: 4651
Catharine M: 5596
Columbia A: 3018
Elmira E: 5148
Francis Tho's: 4531
G Mantz: 4686
George T: 4491
Henry: 4453 4461
Henry G: 4595
John: 3018 4403 4531 4651
Mary E: 5061
No First Name Given: 4445
Sarah S: 5276
Susan M: 5626
Wm H: 4692

RHODRICK
John S L: 4521

RIA
Martha E: 3639

RICE
Albert T: 4503
Alice O: 6013
Alverta: 2808
Amy: 1901
Ann Minerva: 4403
Benj'n F: 4663
David S: 4501 4699
Drucilla: 2510
Ella J: 2121
Geo: 643 784 1944 4397 4403 4409 4430 4582 6013
Geo (Sen'r): 849
George: 4397 4417 4610 5091
George W: 4706
Grafton J: 4430 4645
Harriett A: 643
J Edward: 4645
James: 145 4417
Jane: 5091
Job: 4582
John: 4554
Juliann: 849
Levin: 2808
Lewis (Rev): 4322
Louisa: 784
Louisa Virginia: 1944
M Tyler: 4568
Martha M: 463 4322
Mary Rebecca (Mrs): 515 3709
Miss: 145
Perry A: 4513
Perry G: 2510
Sophia: 145
Susan: 4753
Tho's: 4753
Thomas P: 4693
William: 4409
Wm H: 4618
Wm P: 4610

RICHARDS
Abraham: 4483
Harriott: 4779
Luther (Jun'r): 4446

RICHARDSON
Ann U: 870
Davis: 870 4709
Fannie L: 3469
Geo F: 4629
Geo W: 3469
Helen: 3177
Ignatius Davis: 4579
J Lynn: 4700
James (Dr): 4557
James A: 4578
Leah Fannie: 5191
Samuel S (Dr): 4528
Sophia E: 5249

RICHL
Mich'l: 4441

RICHMAND
Francis: 4396

RICHMOND
Jacob: 4413

RICHTER
John: 4407

RICKARDS
Ella F: 2109

RICKERD
Catharine: 1567
Henry J: 1567 4394
Jonathan: 4401
Nicholas F: 4621
Rachel M: 4100
Wm H: 4669

RICKERDS
Ellen F: 2109
Wm H: 4714

RICKERS
Anna Catharine: 4516

RICKERT
Caroline: 5032
John: 4476

RICKETTS
Catharine: 1567
Richard: 4598

RIDDELMOSER
Ann: 493
Ellie: 4289
Lewis: 4604
Sam'l D: 4289
Samuel D: 4433

RIDDLEMOSER
Cora M: 3970

RIDENAUER
Daniel: 4511
Sallie A: 5398

RIDENOUER
Joseph A: 4684

RIDENOUR
Ella: 3895
John H: 4713
Verna: 3206

RIDER
John H: 4523
Wm E: 4710

RIDGE
Ephraim: 4509
George W: 4526

RIDGELEY
Wm D: 4719

RIDGELY
Ellen: 637
Ruth: 146
T Graham: 4506

RIDGEWAY
Emily: 1300
John: 1300

RIEHL
Catharine (Mrs): 3525
Elizabeth: 3470
Fred'k: 3525 4789
Harriott: 4789
Jacob: 4386 4520
Jane: 3354
John: 717
John H: 4520
Mary M: 5089

Michael: 4494
Nicholas: 4494
No First Name Given: 1891
Otho: 3354 4441 5089
Princella: 717
RIES
Benjamin: 4442
RIFFLE
Thomas: 4607
RIGDEN
Columbia E: 3251
James: 4626
RIGDON
James: 4689
RIGGS
Amelia J: 3886
Hettie R: 5123
Jemima B: 2098
Joel H: 4549
Mary O: 3692
Plummer J: 4529
Susan J: 4046
RIGNEY
John: 4471
John C: 4612
John T: 4471 6095
Lillia J: 6095
Sophia E: 4423
Wm H: 4429
RILEY
Ann W D: 4784
Annie R: 4369
C McGinnis: 4533
Wm McKendree (Rev): 4661
RINEY
Miss: 6168
RINGEL
Christopherr: 4524
George: 4510
RINGER
Catharine E (Mrs): 5243
Robert W: 4488
RINGGOLD
Ann: 4745
Cornelia: 4208
Maria A (Mrs): 5562
Matilda C: 4253
Sam'l: 4208
Sam'l (Gen'l): 4745
RIORDAN
Michael: 4599
RIORDEN

Margaret E: 5924
RIORDON
No First Name Given: 4672
RIPPERN
Hanson T: 4569
RIPPON
Jerome: 4617
RISE
Sarah A (Mrs): 2655
RISER
Geo H: 544
Sarah E W: 544
RISSLER
George: 4522
RITCHIE
Albert: 4671
Albert (Dr): 4412 4484 4546 4671
Annalinah: 4019
Bettie M: 704
Catharine L: 4384
Emily M: 3921
Esther Ann: 5271
John: 704 3921 4384 4546
John (Col): 4019 4412
Susan: 1469
Wm: 1469
Wm Henry: 4495 4558
RITER
Elizabeth (Mrs): 4862
RITLER
Eartheldia: 744
Erthida: 744
J Alf: 744
RITSCHY
Adam: 3253 4435
Catharine: 3253
RITTER
Annie S: 5687
Caroline: 5773
Catharine: 1094
Catharine (Mrs): 1883
Charles: 4649
Irene: 3165
J Alfred: 2847 4478 4649 5687
Obediah D: 4504
Rose: 2847
T Alfred: 3165
RIZER
Geo H: 2631
Geo Hoffman: 4534 4634

Maggie: 2631
ROACH
James J: 4460
Rob't: 4460
Robert: 4408
ROAT
D: 4400
ROBERSON
David: 4718
ROBERTS
George S: 4590
James E (Serg't): 4601
Rachel: 2279
Sallie: 735
William: 4423 4697
Woodward A: 4675
ROBERTSON
Alexander: 4465
Alice: 5689
Cha's H: 4654
Grace P: 5371
James H: 4465 4654 5371 5689
Mary (Mrs): 2742
No First Name Given: 3602
Thomas W: 4571
ROBESON
Celina: 3642
ROBINSON
Barbara: 3902
Catharine: 3279
Cornelius: 4588
David: 4718
Henry (Rev): 857 3279 4477 5593
Jane: 5593
John: 4477
Lucinda C: 3792
Martha Ann: 857
Robert S: 4499
ROCHE
James R (Maj): 4680
Lizzie H: 483
ROCK
No First Name Given: 2155
ROCKWELL
Elihu H: 4438
RODENEISZER
Catharine: 456
RODERICK
D Webster: 4605
Ella: 765

Emma J: 6117
Maurice H: 4583
Wm: 4715
RODEROCK
Jane R: 5025
John P: 4508
Wm: 4507
RODGERS
Henry W: 4705
RODNER
No First Name Given: 4464
RODOCK
George S: 4694
RODRICK
Ella E: 765
ROELKE
Anna M: 5384
Christian: 977
Christianna: 2900
Eliza: 2247
John: 2900 3250
Medora S: 977
Peter: 5384
Sophia: 265 3250
ROELKEY
Anne: 672
Charles: 4658
Fannie D: 4674
John: 4658 4674
Mary E: 1812
Minnie: 6284
Wm: 672
ROGERS
Albert Holland: 4673
Charles W: 4708
J O: 4543
John B: 4591
M E Anna: 4160
Susan V: 4115
William B: 4496
ROHLING
F: 4457
Frederick Wm: 4457
ROHR
Ann Elizabeth: 4969
Dav: 4434
David: 3238
Eleanor A: 3238
Henry: 4553
Jacob: 179 4428 4969
Louisa: 179
No First Name Given: 3673

3767 4478
Philip C: 4434
ROHRBACH
Martin N: 4559
Wm H H: 4627
ROHRBACK
Cha's: 4712
M N: 4712
Martin N: 4704
ROHRER
Sarah K: 5419
ROKLE
Elizabeth: 3629
Henry: 3629
ROLKE
Charles: 4474
Christian: 4473 4474 4489 4517
Daniel E: 4600
F Augustus: 4519
G F William: 4639
Geo A: 4539
Geo Augustus: 4431
George A: 4608
Henry: 4517 4539 4600 4608
John: 2247 4431 4473 4489 4498
Peter: 4498
Sarah J: 1038
Sophia: 4241
Wm: 1038
ROLKE'
Amelia (Mrs): 5105
Christ'n: 4967 5058
Christian: 4565
Christina: 5058
Edward: 4565
F Augustus: 5105
Lena: 4967
ROLLE'
Justin Albert: 4544
ROLLINGTON
Eleanor (Mrs): 207
Elizabeth: 4207
John: 3997 4207 4738
Rosa: 1337
Rosanna: 4738
Sophia: 3997
Wm M: 4398
ROLLINS
George W: 4602
ROMAN

B F: 5334
James Dixon: 4440
Rebecca: 5334
ROOF
Joseph A: 4404
ROOKE
Emma: 3017
ROOP
John W: 4609
Josiah L: 4594
ROOT
Ann M: 5085
D: 4650
Daniel: 4400 4650 5085
ROPP
Lizzie R: 3447
ROSE
Elizabeth: 4725
Rebecca: 3230
ROSENBACH
Henry: 4480
ROSENMERCKEL
Henry: 4486
Henry (Jun'r): 4636
ROSENOUR
Amelia: 3925
B: 3925
ROSENSTOCK
Aaron: 4707
ROSS
Adam: 4525
Ann E: 2204
Anna: 4632
C W: 3984
Cath M: 2201
Charles W: 4580
Christianna (Mrs): 521
Cornelia R: 3984
Florence E: 1105
George: 4527
James F: 4505
John: 4472
Julianna J: 2241
Maria: 1593 4063
Maria A: 681
Mary Barbara: 2831
Peter: 1105
William J: 4415
Wm: 2201 2204 2241 4456
Wm J: 4456 4580
Worthington: 4497
ROSZ

Adam: 4525
Christina: 4510
Elizabeth M: 3373
Maria: 1593 4063
Mary Barbara: 2831

ROSZEL
Mary C: 2348
S Calvert: 2348

ROSZMAN
Barbara: 1577
Jacob: 1577

ROTH
Catharine: 3539
Mary: 279

ROTHAUER
Catharine: 1514

ROTHCHILD
James: 4535
Lionel: 4535

ROTHENHOEFFER
Catherine: 2592

ROTHSCHILD
Alphonse: 4535
Leonora: 4535
No First Name Given: 346
Simon: 4576

ROUT
Peter S: 4610

ROUTZAHN
Amanda E: 1381
Annie E: 3926
Charlotte E: 414
Joseph: 414
Laura: 4716
Lottie E: 5400
Martin B: 4702
Mollie A: 3978

ROUZAHN
Adam: 4325
Manzella S: 4325

ROUZER
Charles B: 4659
John: 4587
John R (Col): 4643
Josephine: 1676
Sallie J: 683

ROWAN
Michael: 4596

ROWE
Ann Eliza: 1488
Catharine: 3227 4271
Catherine: 154

Charles G: 4420
Charles H: 4683
Clara M: 2651
Enoch Louis: 4662
Eugene W: 4690
Ezra: 4662
Ezra M: 4469
Jac: 4779
Jacob: 2173 3227 4388
Marg't: 2173
Mary L: 2144
May: 2732
Mich'l (Sen'r): 4469
Michael: 4420
Michael (Sen'r): 1488
Minnie: 3809
Miss: 2173
Nicholas: 4388
No First Name Given: 1006 3320
Paulus: 4721

ROY
Mary Mason: 603
Wm H: 603

RUBENSTEIN
Pauline: 3929

RUCKER
D H: 5403
Irene: 5403

RUDISIL
Thomas: 4443

RUDISILL
Martha M (Mrs): 3682

RUDOLPH
Max: 4667

RUDY
George E: 4592
Tho's Carlton: 4574
Walter R: 4716
Wm L: 4717

RUE
Ellen: 854

RULAND
Conrad: 4688

RUMMEL
George: 4390

RUMPF
Wm H: 4711

RUNCKELS
Joseph: 4606

RUNKELS
John B: 4532

Theodocia A: 914
Wm: 4567

RUNKLES
Cementine: 5514
Clara E: 1126

RUNNER
Daniel P: 4552

RUPLEY
Sallie C: 5413
Theodore N: 4656

RUPPRECHT
Elizabeth: 4297

RUPRECHT
Wm Henry (Jun'r): 4550

RUSE
Addison R: 4657
Irene: 5482
William N: 4487

RUSSELL
Ann E: 1353
David: 4538
Tho's W: 4540
William: 4541
William C: 4389
Wm H: 4537

RUTH
Caroline M: 4740

RUTHERFOD
Benj'n: 2353

RUTHERFORD
Benj'n: 856 4954
Caroline: 856
Fannie M: 2353
J Edward: 4637
S Harvey: 4641
Virginia: 4954
Wm: 4637

RUTTER
Albert J: 4492
John: 4402
Loretta V: 3321

RYAN
Barbara Ellen: 4075
John (Dr): 1714
Mary A: 1714
Tobias Monroe: 4722

RYERSON
Lizza A: 4102

RYPMA
Karl J: 4439

SADTLER

Sam'l P (Prof): 5372
SAFFELL
  James T B: 5119
  T R: 5119
SAHM
  Catharine: 6033
  Christian: 4922 6193
  Harry J: 5518
  Jacob: 6033
  Jacob (Jun'r): 5254
  John Peter: 2249
  Louisa: 2249
  Louisa (Mrs): 6193
  Mary: 267
  Mary Catharine: 1603
  No First Name Given: 1118
  Peter: 4067
  Peter (Jun'r): 5102
  Philipina: 4067
SALKE'
  Fredrich Wilhelm: 4967
SALMON
  Ann C: 5014
  Edw: 4723
  Elizabeth: 1865
  Geo: 3546
  George: 4723
  Margaret: 2898
  Mary A E: 3546
  No First Name Given: 4945
SALTER
  Ann Marie: 4626
  Catharine Sophia: 5112
  Geo E: 5337
  Mary E: 3030
  No First Name Given: 4686
  William Ent: 4834
  Wm E: 3030 4626 5112
  Wm Ent: 5337
SALTZGIVER
  George: 5135
SAMPLE
  Anna L: 5970
  Jerome: 5174
SAMS
  Carleton C (Dr): 4914
SANDERS
  Annstener: 5119
  Benedict J: 4980
  John Locher (Rev): 4818
SANDERSON
  Elinnor: 2854

Mary Pearson: 6087
Nelson Brown: 5009
No First Name Given: 356
Tho's: 6087
Thomas: 4867
Wm Raymond: 4867
SANDHOUSE
  John: 5218
SANDMEYER
  Gertrude: 5083
  Louisa: 469
SANDS
  Geo W: 4086
  Mary: 4086
SAPPINGTON
  Augustus A (Dr): 5171
  Frank B: 5455
  Geo K: 5431
  Greenbury (Dr): 4931
  Richard (Dr): 5054
  Sidney: 5497 5499
  Sidney A (Dr): 5044
  Tho's: 4903 5044
  Tho's (Col): 4931
  Thomas (Col): 4939
  Thomas (Dr): 4903
SAPPLEFORT
  Mary E: 3446
SARTORIS
  Algernon C F: 5391
SAUERMANN
  Louisa: 4922
  William: 4915
SAUERWEIN
  Amelia C: 2391
  Cha's D: 5298
  Christopher: 5033
  Geo: 3331
  Kate L: 3331
SAUMAN
  Wilhelmina: 277
SAUNDERS
  Catherine: 2
  Eliza: 2972
  Elizabeth: 5553
  Jeannie C: 2782
  John: 2 3237 5032
  John (Capt'n): 4809
  Laura Bella: 5464
  Romulus: 2782
  Sarah: 3237
  Walter: 2972 5069

Walter (Cap): 5464
SAVAGE
  C H (Rev): 5204
SAVIDGE
  Coleman: 5204
SAWYER
  Henry Hudson: 5022
  Ida A: 2676
SAXE COBURG
  Albert: 5730
SAYLER
  C Edward: 5411
  Catharine E: 2516
  D P (Rev): 5419
  D R: 5176
  Daniel: 5176
  George: 5090
  Henry: 4887
  John H: 5154
  Margret E: 942
SAYWER
  Carrie V: 3143
SCHAAFF
  Dr: 2759
  Francis: 5148
  Luther: 5030
  Margaret Jane: 2759
  William: 5151
SCHAAR
  Rosina: 3075
SCHABACKER
  Adam: 4937
  Barbara: 213
  Caroline: 409
  George: 4937
  Jacob: 409
  Jno Jacob: 4968
SCHADE
  Heinrich: 5155
SCHADE'
  Wilhelmina (Mrs): 2080
SCHAEFFER
  Anna Mary: 2302
  Christian M: 5283
  D F (Rev): 2302 4941 5028 5110
  David: 5410
  David (Rev): 5335
  David Krebs (Dr): 4941
  Elizabeth (Mrs): 4973
  Ella V: 3894
  Frederick: 4802

James C: 5525
John A: 4973
Katie V: 5410
L M: 3894
Luther Melancthon: 5028
Margaret (Mrs): 5715
Mary Ann: 27
Mollie E: 3941
Peter: 27
Susanna: 907
Tho's H (Dr): 5293
Warren: 5530
Wm C: 5330
Wm G: 5110 5335 5492

SCHAERER
Daniel: 5105

SCHAFF
John (Dr): 4993
Mary: 4993
Philip (Rev DD): 4946
Sarah: 5145

SCHAFFER
Howard J: 5432
Mary: 1234
Noah A: 1234
S B (Rev): 5413

SCHALBACKER
Barbara: 383

SCHARFF
Mary T: 3718

SCHARMANN
Elizabeth: 3010

SCHATZ
Henry: 4803
Jacob: 4739
Margaret: 3544
Miss: 6187

SCHAUB
Frances: 5813

SCHAUMAN
Eliza: 3530

SCHECKELS
Ella: 6263

SCHEEL
John Geo: 5408
Philip Augustus: 4989

SCHEFFER
Henry: 5016
Lugenia F: 2480

SCHEFFLER
Cha's: 5358
John W: 5358

Margaret C: 2840

SCHEIB
Henry (Rev): 4869

SCHEIDEL
Adaline M: 1943

SCHELL
of Cha's: 1856
Amelia: 6120
Bettie: 707
Cha's: 4814 5491
Cha's D: 3061 4659 5342
Charles: 4742
Charles D: 4858 4942
Enos: 4742 4858
Ezra: 822 4942 4977 5043
George: 5342
George W: 4977 5043
J H Nicholas: 5491
John Edward: 5475
Joseph: 4814
Laura: 4659
Mary M: 3061
Rosanna Elizabeth: 822

SCHELLE
Fred'k: 4805

SCHELLE'
Catharine (Mrs): 4805
Jacob Frederick: 4865

SCHELLMAN
Catharine E: 6203
Catherine E: 30
Daniel J: 4984
Jacob: 6203
Jacob (Jun'r): 4747
Tho's C P (Rev): 4817
Wm: 30

SCHENER
No First Name Given: 1746

SCHENKEL
Sarah L: 487

SCHERER
Catharine (Mrs): 4811
Elizabeth: 5883
Jacob (Rev): 4758
John: 4149
Lewis: 4032 4782 5807
Louisa K: 5033
Louisa R: 2544
Mary: 4149
Sarah: 5807
Sophia H: 4032
Susan: 4782

Valentine: 4853

SCHERMAN
Peter: 4805

SCHIEDTKNECHT
Mary Elizabeth: 3820

SCHIETENHELM
Maggie: 3106
Mary: 3362

SCHIETZ
Margaret: 4882

SCHIEWEL
Harriott: 3233

SCHIEWETZ
Christian: 4880

SCHILDESHEIM
Amelia: 2013

SCHILDKNECHT
Elouisa M: 5149
Sarah Ann: 3305
Wm: 5164

SCHILDT
Harry F: 5517
Mary E: 6245
William: 5205

SCHILDTKNECHT
J M: 5427
Josiah: 5364

SCHILL
Geo: 1725
George W: 5377
Mary E: 1725

SCHINDEL
Kate M: 4360

SCHINDLER
Dan'l: 4812
David: 4812 5136
Jonathan: 5136
Susanna: 1551

SCHISSLER
Anna Margret: 2591
Hiram: 2591 4167
Hiram (Dr): 4934
Kate S: 4167

SCHLEGEL
George W: 5173
Martin: 5213

SCHLEICH
Daniel H: 4787
Frederick W: 5098
Mary (Mrs): 4809
Nellie: 5308

SCHLEIFER
- Mary C: 1684
- Peter: 1684

SCHLEIGH
- Daniel F: 5353
- Fred: 3918
- Margret C: 3534
- Mary C: 2346
- Nellie V: 3918

SCHLEY
- Alfred: 5038
- Alfred (Capt): 5493
- Alice: 968
- Ann Cadwalader: 5919
- Ann E: 474
- Anna M: 3317
- Antoinette: 1729
- Arthur: 5306
- B H (Maj): 5442
- Buchanan: 5334
- Charles: 4983
- Clara: 4316
- David: 904 2818 3317 4946 5038 5039 5297 5382 5909
- Edward: 474 2020 3823 4766
- Edward (Col): 968 1037
- Ellie E: 2020
- Eugene L: 5208
- F A: 4848
- Fairfax (Dr): 3883 4962
- Frank (Prof): 5480
- Fred A: 4866
- Fred'k A: 5334
- Frederick: 5126
- Frederick Augustus: 4724 4920
- Geo: 599
- Geo J: 5382
- George: 4866
- Gilmer: 5466
- Henry: 4899 4935 4962 4983
- Henry (Maj): 4316
- Jacob S: 5368
- James McCannon: 4848
- Jennie: 3883
- Jno Edw: 5381
- John: 1874 4745 4766 4785 4791 5006 5126 5297
- John Edward: 4899 4935
- John T: 1729 5208 5239
- John Tho's: 4791 5006
- Laura: 1037
- Margaret: 1874
- Mary E: 4946
- Mary M: 3823
- Nettie: 599
- No First Name Given: 5080 5357
- S Cornelia: 5909
- Steiner: 5471
- Susan S: 2818
- Thomas H: 5476
- Thomas X: 5476
- Towner: 5381
- William: 4745
- Winfield Scott (Lieu: 5239
- Wm: 5919
- Wm Louis: 5039

SCHLIMMER
- Hannah: 2469

SCHLOSS
- Susan C: 4127

SCHLOSSER
- Elizabeth: 3760
- Geo: 4827
- George: 5005
- Naomi G: 4827
- Peter G: 4933 5430

SCHLUCKBIER
- Peter: 5024

SCHLUGH
- David B: 5479

SCHLUND
- Joshua: 4882

SCHLY
- Rosa: 720

SCHMALTZ
- No First Name Given: 2338

SCHMIDT
- Annie G: 668
- Carrie: 5346
- Christian: 5055
- Elizabeth: 60 457 1639
- Elizabeth C: 3832
- Francis Wm: 5375
- J Henry: 5441
- Jacob: 457 668 1724 4909 5324 5346 5375 5441
- Jacob (Junior): 5329
- Jacob F: 5458
- Mary: 1724

SCHMIDTHEIM
- Fredericka: 2515

SCHMUCKER
- Elleanora S: 2022
- Josephine: 5084
- S S: 2022
- Sam'l (Rev): 5084
- Sam'l S (Rev): 4988

SCHNAUFFER
- Geo: 4807
- George: 4731
- Johusa J: 4987

SCHNEBLY
- Rowanna: 4777

SCHNEIDER
- Henry: 5234
- John: 4737
- William H: 4829

SCHOEN
- John: 4825

SCHOLL
- Annabel: 986
- Catharine: 2147
- Ch'n: 1875 2147
- Charlotte: 1875
- Christ'n: 196
- Christian: 4769 4782 4796 4836
- Christianna (Mrs): a1
- Dan'l: 2604
- Daniel: 4796
- David M: 5236
- Dennis: 3118 4641 4910
- Elias: 986 4056 4782 4836 5214 5229 5236 5284
- Elizabeth: 1497
- Elizabeth C: 3623
- Fannie E: 4641
- Henry: 3044
- John: 1497 2865 3044
- Lewis P: 5284
- Lewis V: 4896
- Lillie M: 5472
- Lilly A: 4373
- M Jane: 3118
- Margaret E: 2604
- Maria: 2865
- Mary E: 4056
- Mary Elizabeth: 196
- Randolph C: 5214
- Rebecca: 4769
- Serena S: 3044
- Wm H: 5229

SCHONBURG
- No First Name Given: 346

SCHONFELD
- Alexander: 5393

SCHONHOLTZ
  Fred'k: 2873
  Mary: 2873
SCHOOL
  John: 3623
SCHRAYER
  Cornelia C: 4121
  Solomon W: 4121 5103
SCHREBLY
  Susan: 5589
SCHRECK
  Mary L: 2690
SCHREINER
  A Elizabeth: 3507
  Alfred: 5265
  Catharine Virginia: 3661
  Edward Stanley: 5286
  Henry J: 4768 5286
  John: 3661 4772 5089
  Mary E: 1611
  Randolph: 5089
SCHRERFFER
  Peter: 907
SCHRINER
  Basil E: 3743
  Elizabeth R: 418
  John: 1611
  Julia A: 3743
SCHRIVER
  Ab'm: 1882
  Ann M: 1882
  James: 3618
SCHRODEL
  John: 5134
  Rosanna: 5233
SCHRODER
  Henry Cha's August: 5083
  Henry H: 4868
  Johanna D: 310
SCHROEDER
  Albertine: 2497
  Clarence F: 5521
  Francis T: 5231
  Frank J: 5472
  Fred'k: 5361
  Frederick: 4879 4964
  George A: 5361
SCHROYER
  Mary: 2581
SCHRYOCK
  Lena: 5707

SCHUBEL
  Mary: 1222
SCHUBER
  Lewis: 5143
SCHUCK
  Christianna: 5564
SCHUCKMANN
  Friedrick: 5068
SCHUETENHELM
  Eliza A: 4272
  Reuben: 4857
  Thomas: 4940
SCHUFF
  Emma F: 2855
SCHUFFLER
  Martin L: 5484
SCHULTZ
  Alexander: 5075
  Amelia S: 55
  Ann Sophia: 241
  Conrad: 4906 5258 5428
  Edward T: 5026
  Elizabeth Ann: 353
  Emma: 133
  Geo: 241 255 259 5063 5128
  H'y: 55
  Henrietta: 3172
  Henry: 4238 4925 5026 5075
  Hetta: 3172
  Jefferson: 4906
  Julia Ann: 4238
  Lewis P: 5512
  Louis H: 5128
  Margaret J: 255
  Maria Louisa: 259
  Martin: 4730 5122
  Mary M: 3209
  Sophia K: 750
  Theo: 3209
  Theodore: 3172 5063
  Wm D: 4925
SCHUMACHER
  Ann: 1746
  Francis: 4811
SCHUTENHELM
  Arthur: 5303
  Geo: 5349
  Syney Ann: 2534
SCHUTZE
  Cha's W: 5406
SCHWAERIN
  Maggie: 578

SCHWALM
  Catharine: 275
SCHWARIN
  John B: 5310
SCHWARTZ
  Benjamin F: 5117
  John: 5047
SCHWARZ
  Geo W: 5409
SCHWEIGERT
  Michael: 4733
SCHWEIGOEFFER
  Louisa: 6198
SCHWEITZER
  Emma V: 5407
  Henry: 4750
SCHWERTZELL
  No First Name Given: 2435
SCHWIETZ
  No First Name Given: 67
SCHWIN
  Elizabeth: 354
SCOTT
  Douglas (Capt'n): 5163
  Marcella: 3660
  Margaret M: 5093
  Mary Ella: 3889
  Samuel J: 5140
  Winfield (Gen'l): 3660
  Wm Amos: 5094
SCULLY
  Brida: 2123
SEABROOK
  John H: 5027
  Martha C: 1650
  Wm L W: 5070
SEACHRIST
  C W (Rev): 1464
  Salome E: 1464
SECHRIST
  Salome: 1464
SEECRIST
  Harriett Ann: 6224
SEEMAN
  Christian: 448
  Elizabeth: 448
SEEMANN
  Christian: 4908
SEESE
  Wm L: 5268

SEEVERS
  Eveline H: 311
SEFTON
  John W: 5201
  Margaret F: 1656
  Mary M: 966
SEGER
  Peter: 5157
SEHN
  Jacob: 5248
SEIBERT
  Anna: 3120
  Geo: 3120 4346
  Harriet Ann: 4346
SEIDENSTRICKER
  John B: 5013
SEIFFENSIDER
  Miss: 3070
SEISS
  F S Oscar: 5093
SELBY
  Hamilton: 5065
  John S: 5165
  John W: 5338
  Sarah Elmor: 2265
SELDIN
  Cha's P: 5454
SELL
  Edwin M: 5220
SELLMAN
  Wm T: 5101
SELLMANN
  Maggie V (Mrs): 654
SELSAM
  Emma: 3409
SEMMES
  Benedict I: 5099
SENEKER
  Emanuel: 4950
SENSENEY
  Geo E: 5012
  John Q: 5180
SENSENSEY
  Silas D: 5449
SENTMAN
  S (Rev): 5113
SENTZELL
  Bettie: 1795
  Catharine: 258
  Margaret: 619 1940

Matthias: 4901
SENTZILL
  Charles H: 5191
SEQUIN
  Emma F: 4389
SERGEANT
  John (Hon): 5824
  Sarah: 5824
SERVER
  Laura V: 5302
SEVRINGHAUS
  J D (Rev): 5215
SEYMOUR
  Aaron W: 5331
SHADE
  Christian: 5514
SHADWELL
  Henry: 4776
SHAEFFER
  Susanna: 4795
SHAFER
  Albenia E: 472
  Benjamin F: 5121
  Carlton: 5470
  Catharine E: 1939
  Cha's: 5511
  Clavin L: 5328
  Conrad: 4735
  David L: 5212
  Dorethea (Mrs): 4735
  Edward: 5269
  George F: 5056
  Hallie: 2598
  Hanson: 2598
  Harriott E: 1622
  Henrietta: 2191
  Jacob: 1622 1939 2945 3604
  John A: 5279
  John H: 4890
  Jonathan: 4788
  Jonathan A: 5073
  Katie: 2113
  Margaret: 2163
  Mary Ann: 2945
  Mary C: 1445
  Mary Manilla: 5209
  Matilda: 2576
  Miss: 4795
  Noah A: 4752
  Peter: 3311 4763 5049
  Rebecca C: 3311
  Sarah Ann: 3604

Sarah C: 2113
Susanna: 4795
Susie Virginia: 5259
Thomas M: 5253
Wm A: 5037
SHAFF
  Geo P: 5398
SHAFFER
  Isabel L: 3840
  Jacob: 276
  M C: 3941
  Susanna: 276
SHAFFNER
  Ellen J R: 3890
  Geo W: 5401
  P R: 5014
  Peter R: 4741 5014
SHANK
  Carrie V: 120
  Cha's: 5522
  Cha's McClelland: 5539
  Ezra: 120 3351 5022 5190
  Geo P: 4981
  Geo Washington: 4877
  George W: 5167
  Henrietta E: 5022
  Jane R D: 5225
  John P: 4956
  Margaret A: 3351
  Mary A: 5207
  Michael: 5156
  Sarah N: 5190
  William: 5129
SHANKS
  Andrew T: 5210
SHARETTS
  Wm P: 5456
SHARP
  George W: 4806
SHARPLESS
  Townsend: 5125
SHAW
  Ellen E: 1215
  Estella: 2723
  George W: 5120
  John: 4779 4821
  John A: 4954
  Mary Elizabeth: 945
  Sarah C: 3364
  Wm A: 5147
  Wm H: 4952
  Zachariah: 4862

SHAWBAKER
Geo: 5384
Jacob M: 5384
SHAWBRAKER
Margaret E: 3898
SHAWEN
Cornelius: 4959
George J: 4913
Grafton: 4864
Lizzie: 3983
Mary E: 351
Sarah A: 4890
Wm Henry: 5034
SHAY
W C: 5106
SHEALEY
Susan E: 3729
SHEARER
Carrie C: 6265
Daniel T: 5506
John D: 5309
Lewis: 2252 4907
Lewis V: 4907
Lydia Ann: 2252
SHEARMAN
Jane E: 350
SHEDD
Miss: 2287
SHEELEIGH
Matthias (Rev): 5137
SHEETS
Anna Mary: 963
Christianna: 3330
Levi D (Dr): 5000
Susan (Mrs): 3796
Wm Henry: 5018
SHEFFER
Dan'l: 95
Martha Jane: 95
SHEFFLER
Emeline: 2646
George T M: 5460
SHEID
Walter H: 4894
SHELBY
Virginia (Mrs): 317
SHELDON
Lizzie A: 5368
SHELLMAN
Ann Maria: 6063
Dan'l: 6063

James M (Col): 4892
SHENCK
John J (Prof): 5532
SHENKEL
David: 5211
SHEPHERD
Abijah: 4831
Job K: 5435
Joseph K: 5529
Mary (Mrs): 1545
No First Name Given: 2130
P Dodge: 5396
Susan: 2366
Virginia L: 5967
SHEPPERD
Abijah: 951
Cecelia: 951
SHERIDAN
Philip H (Maj Gen'l): 5403
SHERMAN
Maria E: 1780
W J (Gen'l): 1780
SHERWOOD
E C: 5045
Emma B: 880
Mary J: 2957
SHIELDS
Jefferson (Dr): 4761
John T: 5496
Maxwell P: 5168
SHILLING
Wm B: 5415
SHIMER
J C (Dr): 5275
SHIPLEY
Ann G: 3502
Benjamin W: 5023
Catharne: 221
Edwin M: 5292
Eliza A: 53 1631
George E: 5386
Hattie: 2708
Isaac: 5347
John J: 5294
Maggie: 2701
Mary A S: 967
Mary E: 754
Milcah Ann: 1216
Mollie: 1437
Nicholas Hall: 4928
Nimrod Owings (Dr): 5011
Samuel: 4871

Samuel N: 5308
Susan J: 3068
Tho's: 3068
Wm G: 4900
Wm H: 5052 5123 5287
SHIPMAN
Elizab Jane: 2774
Harriott A: 2394
John: 4732
SHIVERS
Fannie M: 2075
SHOCK
Wallace: 5469
SHOE
Wm: 2970
SHOEMAKER
Dennis: 4886
Elizabeth: 430
Geo: 430
Mary S E: 2711
SHOLL
John: 4781
SHOOK
Belle E: 1422
Christianna: 5564
Clementine M: 583
Daniel H: 5352
Greenberry G: 5202
H McC: 5486
Henrietta: 5015
Henry: 5222
Jane E: 3316 5355
John H: 5509
John Wm: 5035
Kate M: 5762
Lewis A: 5115
Louisa: 6226
Luretia: 1615
Margaret: 5222
Mary Ann: 5104
Samuel B: 4753
Susanna: 5002
SHOPE
Charles E: 5112
E Isler: 5516
Geo B: 4995 5112
George B: 4773
Lyndhurst T: 5332
Mary: 5785
Sophia: 2225
Wm B: 4995
SHORB

Cornelia V (Mrs): 5257
Maria Francina: 4951
Mrs: 5257
Sarah M: 6061
William T: 5203

SHORT
Mary Virginia: 4537

SHOWER
Theodore A (Dr): 5189

SHREEVE
Jesse (Rev): 5079 5206

SHREVE
Annie: 5144

SHRINER
Cornelius: 4769 4889 5108 5345
E Derr: 5533
Edward A: 5108
Geo W B: 5345
Julia C: 1200

SHRIVER
Ab'm: 4841 4844 4966 5800 5806
Abraham Ferree: 4994
And'w: 171 209
Ann Eliza (Mrs): 5081
Anne S: 5675
Cath C: 171
Cha's: 5081
Charles: 4841
Edw: 4668 5679
Edward: 4844
Eliza: 209
Eliza Jane: 3618
Elizabeth: 3685
Ellen: 5806
Emma: 5679
Gen'l Edward: 5675
Isaac: 1166 1193
Isabella J: 3631
James: 5017
John A: 5003
John S: 3631
Juliann: 1193
Lizzie: 4668
Mary: 5800
Mary E: 4226
No First Name Given: 1052
Rebecca: 1166
Sallie E: 2114
Thomas: 4997 5045
Wm Eltinge: 4966

SHRYOCK
Harry C: 5443
Henry V: 5086
Louisa E: 891
Mary A: 5823

SHUCK
Mary E: 80
Samuel: 5118

SHUE
Jacob J: 4991

SHUEY
Aggie: 1793

SHUFF
Emma F: 2855

SHUNK
Francis R (Gov): 5100
James F: 5100

SHUTT
Augustus: 5289

SICKLES
Daniel E (Gen'l): 5360

SIECRIST
Charles H: 5198

SIEDLING
George F C: 5405

SIFFORD
Adelaide Frances: 316
Caroline E: 3295
Christ'n: 2212
Christian: 3500
Cleantha E: 1310
Georgia: 1717
Irene C: 3849
John: 316 1310 1717 3295 3849 4365 5172
John E: 5172
Maria: 2212
Nannie J: 4365
Sarah Ann: 3500

SILENCE
Elizabeth M (Mrs): 5052
Emma A: 682

SIM
Bobbie: 1045
J Tho's (Dr): 5227
Sarah G: 5077
Tho's (Dr): 5077 5227
Thomas (Dr): 4744 4837 4970

SIMMONS
Alice: 6038
Ann Sophia: 4281
Balinda E: 13 2323
Charles E (Capt'n): 5316
Eleanor Howard: 4912
Emily A: 2106
Emlia: 2106
Emma: 584
Fannie S: 1441
Isaac: 4916
J Sam'l: 6038
J Samuel: 5081
James: 4912
James (Maj): 2463 4281
John (Col): 13
John A: 584 5422 5424
John Adams: 4815
John H: 4736 4780
John H (Col): 4764
Louis: 5424
Ludie: 2116
Mary A: 5567
Mary R D: 5933
Mollie: 2850
Sam'l F: 4736
Serena: 2463
Simon Cyrus: 5048 5385
Susie F: 2111
Wm A: 5422
Zachariah: 4815 4912 5048 5385
Zachariah T: 4780

SIMMS
Henry: 4746 4830
William: 4828

SIMON
Lewis: 5222

SIMPSON
Basil J H: 5138
Cha's E: 5520
Charles B: 4945
Elizabeth: 4442
Helen Maria: 3234
John: 266 4060 4442
John A: 5181 5296
Julia A: 2721
Juliet L: 1239
Mary S: 4060
Richard W: 5085 5356
Sophia: 266
Tho's A: 5502
Tho's W (Dr): 5077 5175
Thomas: 4748
Willie E: 5495

SINCLAIR
James F: 5341

SINGER

Catharine: 4221

SINN
Amanda M: 5186
Ann Eliza: 4774
Charles W: 5346
Dan'l: 534
Daniel: 4843 5323
Ed: 3187 3202
Edith M: 2143
Edw: 3396
Edward: 2143 4905
Edward T: 5192
Emma: 3187
Franny E: 534
Geo Philip: 5323
Henry: 4756 4774 4833 4905 5192 5301
J Tho's: 5238
Jacob: 100 3344 4835 5325
Jacob C: 5325
Jno Geo: 5186
John George: 4833 5301
John Henry: 5238
John Tho's: 5660
John Thomas: 4850
Kate: 3396 5660
Laura: 1973
Laura V: 646
Margaret: 779 2982
Martha: 100
Mary (Mrs): 5694
Mary A E: 3344
Mary K: 2115
No First Name Given: 958 3387 6121
Philip: 4835 4843 4860 5192
Philip Henry: 4860
Rosie M: 3202
William: 4756
William E: 5020
Wm: 1973 5020

SINNLEY
J George: 5346

SIX
Adalaine: 2660
Adelia: 2660
Jane E: 4128
John: 730
Mamie K: 730

SKAGGS
Eliza: 4839

SKINNER
Ann R: 5743

Henry: 5457
Henry S: 4784

SLACK
Cornelius: 4926

SLAGLE
George W: 5173
Martin: 5213

SLEIGH
Nellie V: 3918

SLICER
Henry (Rev): 2371 3745
Lizzie S: 2371
Llewellen: 3745

SLICK
Abednigo: 5130
Laura: 757

SLIDELL
John (Hon): 4343
Miss: 4343

SLIFER
Ann V: 5147
George C: 5226 5315
Lydia A: 1989
Margaret Ann: 955
Mary C: 1684
Peter: 1684
Sarah: 1923
William: 5059
Wm: 1923

SLINGLIFF
Louis Philip: 5185

SLINGLUFF
Fannie H: 5170

SLOAN
John Q: 5473

SLUSS
Susan C: 4127

SMALL
Charlotte: 382
Elizabeth Ann (Mrs): 3628
Lizzie A: 435
Mary: 2970
William: 4759 5019
William (Capt): 4854
William (Capt'n): 4755
Wm (Capt): 435
Wm (Capt'n): 3628
Wm D: 5195

SMALLWOOD
Charles: 5250
Harriott: 5657
Wm C: 5657

Wm Cooper: 4738 5250
Wm Cooper (Jun'r): 5036

SMALTZ
J H (Rev): 5050
John Henry (Dr): 5050

SMELTZER
Daniel: 2442
Deborah F: 2442
Elizabeth: 2432
Henry R: 1581 2432
J P (Rev): 5010
Sarah C: 6211
Sarah Catharine: 1581

SMILEY
Rachel D (Mrs): 1663

SMITH
Abbie: 4992
Alexander: 4754
Alice R: 3169
Andrew: 993
Ann C: 2284
Ann Eliza: 5989
Ann L: 2720
Ann M: 4783
Ann R: 3564
Ann Rebecca: 6017
Anna M: 464
Annie E: 3462 3979
Aralanta R: 5054
Arthur C: 5527
Augusta Palmer (Mrs): 6023
Augustus G: 4810
Benjamin: 4881
Catharine: 4723
Catherine: 4159
Cha's E: 5498
Charles C: 5317
Charlotte: 4847
Christ'n: 2584
Christian: 4876 5340 5343
Christopher P: 5344
Clara C: 1092 2617
Clara V: 2047
Clayton: 5445
Cordelia E: 5136
D F: 5273
D Sidney T: 5447
Dan'l: 4723
Daniel: 4891
Daniel Grove: 4760 4800
David F: 562 1029 4873 5366
David H: 5366
David M: 5274

Dorsey H: 5474
E Bella: 5297
E Jennie: 5653
Eli: 4855
Elizabeth: 147 769 2331 4542 4767
Ellie C: 1655
Emanuel: 4804 4963
Eml: 5414
Emma: 2430 4697
Eugene R (Rev): 5300
Eveline: 4083
Ezra: 1058 4792 5644
Fannie V: 4162
Fanny Virginia): 2861
Florence B: 5498
Frances: 3609
Frances R: 2584
Francis (Dr): 5285
Frank M (Capt): 5273
Franklin J (Dr): 4938
Frisby (Dr): 5021
Geo: 2047 3496 3564 5041 5317 5644
Geo C: 5340
Geo Wm: 3905
George: 4083 4792 4823 4876 5524
George (Jun'r): 4778
George C: 5221
George L: 5207
George W: 5152
George Wm: 5041
Georgetta: 6159
Georgianna: 993
H Gates: 5467
H'y: 3952
Hattie E: 724
Hauer P: 5343
Henrietta: 3519 5644
Henrietta E: 441
Henry: 1183 3519 4754 4760 4783 4800 4810 4847 4873 4944
Hester E (Mrs): 1841
James: 5535
James A (Lieut): 5404
James J (Dr): 5333
James T: 5177
Jennie: 2861
John: 2331 2587 4162 5421 5438
John A: 5257
John D: 2284 4734
John E: 5243
John F: 4919 5436
John Gomber: 5066
John J: 5414
John Tho's: 5223 5223
Jonathan: 4885
Jos S (Dr): 5767
Joseph: 2178
Juliann: 5550
Laura V (Mrs): 1688
Lewis C: 5452
Lizzie: 2500
Lou: 5314
Lucinda E M: 1058
Lucretia: 562
Lydia: 3555
Maggie: 5502
Margaret W: 4252
Margie E: 3973
Mary: 2178
Mary A: 2448
Mary Ann: 3496
Mary B: 304
Mary C: 6210
Mary E: 1390
Mary Helen: 5962
Mary Jane: 2312
Mary K: 3905
Mary M: 4057
Mary Virginia: 2587
Midd: 2331
Mollie F E: 4293
Nancy: 460
Nicholas (Col): 5402
R Emmit: 5433
Rebecca: 5767
Robert: 4870
Rosa E: 6288
Sallie: 2778
Sallie C: 2852
Samuel Lewis: 5158
Sevilla: 3239
Sophia: 1183
Susan Caroline: 4116
Susan E: 3952 4597
Susan R: 1029
Susanna S: 6028
T Oden: 5477
Theresa: 4855
Thomas A: 5067 5453
Urbana: 5453
Washington: 5060
William: 5061
Wm C W: 5501
Wm H: 4852 5246
Wm T: 5124
Zachariah G: 5531

SMOOT
John H: 5007

SMYTH
Sarah S: 5290

SNADER
Jesse W: 5132

SNAPP
George O: 5483

SNELL
Mary E: 294

SNIVELY
Rebecca: 5637

SNOOK
Dennis: 4897
Dennis R: 5241
Elizabeth: 4884
Elizabeth A: 1250
Jacob H: 5261
John W: 5095
Josiah: 4883
William Galileo: 5410

SNOOTS
Ann E: 4562

SNOUFFER
A J: 5508
Archibald F: 5162
Benjamin J: 4949
Bessie M: 1137
Fannie: 1124
Gussie: 5508
John B: 5144

SNYDER
Ann M: 1277
Ann Mary: 4443
Caroline Rebecca: 4806
Charles H: 5485
Dan'l Fairman: 4816
Elmer E: 5463
George: 5255
Henry: 5057
Henry M: 5001
Jacob F: 5367 6072
Jennie: 6072
John: 4816 4943
John A: 5225
Kate B: 5133
Laura: 4713
Lillia A: 5448
Lizzie: 6145

Lucinda: 4591
Luther: 5515
M Scott: 5462
Martin H: 5149
Mary Tucker: 5153
Nicholas: 4806
Olevia J: 3342
Sam'l: 5133 5153
Samuel: 5116
Samuel (Junior): 5091
Sarah J: 4151
Susanna (Mrs): 3
William: 4863
Wm E (Rev): 5092
Wm F: 5519

SOCKALEXIS
Gov: 5376

SOELKEY
Wm H: 5407

SOHN
E C (Dr): 5074
Edward: 5074

SOUDER
John P: 5072
Mary: 160
Miss: 160 2864
Sarah A: 3505
Susanna: 2864

SOUTHGATE
Angeuna E (Mrs): 2806

SOUTTER
Emily Wolsey: 1395

SOWER
No First Name Given: 210

SOWERS
H L (Mrs): 1079
Jacob: 5264
No First Name Given: 1084
Peter: 4771
Samuel (Rev): 5114

SPAHR
Milton O: 5420

SPALDING
Susan: 1859

SPANGLER
Elizabeth S: 5573
Jacob: 5262
Wm H: 4992

SPARKS
Robert: 5097

SPARROW
Allen: 4839

Allen T: 5299
Cornelia A: 5954
Henry C: 5395
John W: 5954
Wilson: 4859
Wm Tho's: 5278

SPATES
Charles: 5260

SPAYTH
Lydia E: 4818

SPEAR
Otis: 1997
Sarah Lydia: 1997

SPECHT
Catharine: 5782
David: 4973 5312 5322
Francis T: 5237
Jacob: 3757 4757 5042
Jacob (Junior): 5161
Jane E: 3757
Lewis: 5199
Mary C: 1021
Michael: 5230
Susan E: 3663

SPEDDEN
Edward M: 4893

SPENCE
Agnes: 4924

SPENCER
Albertus: 5351
Annie M: 5524

SPIELMAN
Elizabeth: 2239
Sarah E: 2766

SPONSELLER
Adam: 223
Amanda A: 223
Ann: 4227
Arthur T: 5025
Catharine A: 3878
Catharine Ann: 4508
Eugene: 5434
George: 5313
Jacob: 254 4227
Jacob C: 5200
John J: 4979
John R: 5464
Mary R: 254
Stockton: 5305

SPONSILLER
William: 4982

SPOON

Elizabeth (Mrs): 4758

SPRAGUE
R J: 5245
Wm (Ex Gov): 5245

SPRENGLE
David: 4740

SPRIGG
Columbia: 3554
Elizabeth: 811

SPRING
Gardner (Rev): 5193

SPRINGER
Ann Rebecca: 4816
Daniel: 4725 5051
Eliza: 3509
Jane L: 2913
Margaret: 299
Mary: 815
No First Name Given: 2301
Thomas: 5051
Thomas (Dr): 4728
Wm: 815 2913 3509 4725 4728 4816

SPROUT
Isabella: 2951

SPURRIER
Eliza: 3573
Grafton D: 5169
Horace: 2161
Mary (Mrs): 2161

ST JOHN
Wm: 4911

STAHLE
Katie A: 764

STAIR
Henry W: 5131

STAIT
William: 4827

STALEY
Addie A: 3874
Ann: 5329
Ann E (Mrs): 1562
Anna S: 4530
Antoinette: 2004
Catharine (Mrs): 1167
Charles B: 5468
Cornelius: 1246 2004 4765 4777 5302
Cornelius A: 5096 5197
D H: 5394
Daniel A: 5350
Daniel L: 4929

Edward M: 5359
Emma E: 1774
Ezra: 4560 4808 5256 5272
Fletch E: 5478
Geo: 3701 4957
Gideon: 5487
Gideon (Lieut): 5272
Harry J: 5534
Henry (Prof): 5487
Henry S: 4832
Horace E: 5426
Howard: 5400
Isaac: 4795
Jennie E: 2857
John A: 1774 4927 5015 5329
John W: 5267
Jonathan: 5355
Jonathan A: 4990
Joseph E: 5307
Joshua: 4961 4998
Julia Ann: 3328
Juliann Cath: 59
Laura V: 2471 6096
Lewis H: 5321
Lewis M: 5339
Louisa: 4560
Louisa M: 4957
Lydia Ann: 5270
Margaret C: 3755
Marietta C: 1246
Mary Ann R: 2333
Mary E: 2538 4990
Mary S: 64
Milton: 5440
Mitton: 5440
Naomi M: 2677
Orsena: 1828
Orthena B: 1828
Peter S: 4530
Phebe Ann: 2351
Rowanna R: 1030
Sarah Jane: 3701
Susan E: 3833
Susanna: 4998
Wm Albert: 5002

STALLINGS
Ann E: 1523
Benj'n: 1180 1523
Ellen M: 4101
Jos: 4101
Joseph (Lieut): 4813
Mary Ann: 2388
Rebecca: 1180

STAMBAUGH
Ann V: 5303
Elizabeth: 5203
J E (Dr): 5314
Susan: 5884

STANLEY
Edward (Hon): 5139
George: 4826
George W: 5277

STANSBURY
Geo W: 5190

STANTON
Lizzie W (Mrs): 5913
William: 4955

STAPLER
Mary B: 4472

STAPLETON
Jullia E: 3938

STARCKE
Agnes (Mrs): 3679

STARR
Ann L: 1937
Augusta A: 3774
Eliza Ann: 1557
J Washington: 5244
Jesse W: 5446
Lycurgus N: 5263 5418
Maurice T: 3774 5232

STARRE
Louisa: 1927

STARTZMAN
Christian (Rev): 4948

STAUB
Cora L: 2705
Emma: 4366
John W: 4888
Wm H: 5363

STAUCH
Catharina: 1946

STAUFFER
Ann E: 4261
C V: 5761
Catharine: 827
Daniel: 5184
Daniel E: 4999
David R: 5109
David V: 5336
Elizabeth: 5574
Ellen Amanda: 900
Ezra S: 5170
Geo Wesley: 5397
H Clay: 5387
H'y: 5374
Henry: 4762 4923 5327
J Dorsey: 5311 5505
Ja's: 827
Jacob: 4762
John: 900 4261 4749 5109 5615
Jos: 2887 5574
Joseph: 4749 4918 4923
Mary A: 361
No First Name Given: 3947
S Theodore: 5327 5374
Simon: 4918 5311
Susan Catharine: 5615
Susan M: 2887
Wm J: 5216

STAULI
John L: 5219

STAYMAN
Geo F: 5304
Geo Fred'k: 4819
V D: 5304

STEDDING
Ch'n: 5160
Christean L: 4799
Mary A: 5160

STEEL
Sarah: 931

STEELE
Alice L: 5332
Ann V: 1781 2083
Catharine: 5736
Dan'l: 5332 6084
John Nevitt: 4986
Mary J: 6084

STEHLE'
Henry J: 4953

STEI
Philip: 5040

STEIGERWALD
Meyer: 2001
Rose: 2001

STEIN
Amie: 2724
Charlotte: 3020
Elizabeth: 2907
Elizabeth C: 1348
Jacob: 5145
John: 3020
Lewis: 5179
Louis: 1348 4820 5179
No First Name Given: 2911

Sophia H: 365
Susan R: 1632
STEINBERG
Miss: 1616
STEINBRECHER
Elizabeth: 41
STEINER
Alice Ida: 128
Benedict: 4775
Charles H: 5369
Charlotte: 4385
Christ'n: 4962
Christian: 4743
Daniel: 4798
David C: 2554 4849
Eliza Ann: 4031
Elizabeth: 846
Ezra: 834 4031
Fannie E: 1824
Florence G: 5236
Frank M: 5459
Frederick: 4975
Frederick Birely (Ca: 4996
George F: 5186
Grace: 3967
H F: 4693
Henrietta: 4817
Henry: 910 4743 4917 4969 5076
Henry (Capt): 4817 4846
Henry (Captn): 846
Henry C: 4969 5383
Herman Frank: 5076
Ira F: 5482
Jacob: 3223 5319 5373
Jacob F: 4917
James O: 5319
Jesse (Rev): 128 5236
John A: 4651
John A (Gen'l): 5369
John Alexander: 4842 4932
John J: 4846
John W: 5348
Jonathan: 5186
Lewis H (Dr): 5290
Lillian C: 4693
Margaret: 834
Mary: 1456
Mary Ann: 3223
Rebecca L: 4962
Stephen: 4996
Stephen (Col): 4385 4726 4798

Susan R: 910
Susan Sophia: 4651
Valietta: 2554
Wm H: 5383
Wm R: 5373
STEINMETZ
Andrew: 5378
STENGEN
Catherine: 4095
Fred'k: 4095
STENGER
Cha's: 3229
Wilhelmina: 3229
STEPHAN
Maria: 4066
STEPHEN
Cha's H (Dr): 4904
STEPHENS
Ann Maria: 5080
Elizabeth: 5218
Mary: 912 4374
Sam'l: 912
STEPHENSON
Elizabeth L (Mrs): 4844
STEPHEY
Samuel D: 5538
STERETT
Ellie R (Mrs): 1971
STERN
Aaron: 3401 5326
Clara: 3401
Philip: 5326
STEVENS
Ann J: 3834
Commodore: 4076
Ella: 5347
Flavius J: 5242
Lucy Hamilton: 2978
Margaret A: 4302
Mary A: 4374
Mason T (Gov): 3552
Reuben G: 5182
Richard M: 5160
Virginia: 4076
Wm F: 5058
STEVENSON
Andrew (Hon): 4993
Susan: 3794
Wm: 4902
STEWARD
Thomas: 5064
Wm H: 5107

Wm J: 5528
STEWART
Annie F: 1012
Clement: 5295
Geo Lee: 4974
Katie L: 4688
Margaret: 458
Margaret (Mrs): 1985
Margaret Ann: 313
Mary: 3162
Mary E: 3965
Wm: 5187 5251
STICKEL
A Mary Ann: 5
George: 4751
Solomon: 4790
William: 4790
STIER
Frederick A: 5150
Hamilton: 1324 4164
Mary P: 1324
Miss: 4164
STILLY
John: 1870
Lydia (Mrs): 1870
STIMMEL
Amos: 5078
Edward B: 4947
Elizabeth C: 884
Joanna: 698
John: 4947 5008
John B: 5008
Joseph: 5379
Sarah Ann: 4609
STIMMELL
Cornelius: 5046
John S: 5271
Katie F: 5522
Mary L: 2703
Philip: 5320
STINCHCOMB
Beal C: 4727
STIPES
Catharine (Mrs): 1658
Daniel E: 5291
Madora: 5749
STITCHER
Catharine (Mrs): 845
STITELEY
U S Grant: 5503
STITELY
Katie C: 5764

Laura V: 2054
Rosa A: 5497
Rose A: 5499
STOCKETT
Mary A: 2445
STOCKMAN
Amanda: 5595
Barbara A: 3072
Barbara A R: 4483
Daniel M: 5416
David: 4851
Elizabeth: 4859 5845
Emory W: 5444
George W: 5127
John N: 5235
Lewis A: 5053
Luther F: 5282
Philip W: 5194
Sarah Ann E: 948
Susan: 2962
Wm M: 5536
Wm Perry: 4861
STOCKSCHLEGER
Amos: 5166
STODDARD
Marshall W: 5133
STOFFEL
John: 5252
No First Name Given: 2358 2902 2907 2911 2985 4937
Peter: 4822 4856
STOKES
Bradley T: 5371
Eliza H: 4456
Geo H: 5423
James: 5423
Nellie: 5423
Nettie: 6065
R Harry: 5488
R Y: 5082
Rob't Y: 5371
Robert Y: 4801 6065
Sophie: 5763
William: 5082
William H (Dr): 4874
Wm: 5423
STOLTZ
Rachel: 4215
STONE
Alice H: 6079
Catharine Margretta: 4520
Cornelius: 5450

Cornelius W: 5270
Elizabeth: 1623
Eugenia M: 2548
Florence J: 3907
Francis S: 4951
George E: 5240
George H: 5217
Henry A: 4978
Henry C: 5183
John: 5365
John T: 5209
Joseph D: 5392
Julia A W: 3846
Louisa M: 5600
Lucy: 5955
Luther M: 5365
Margaret M: 6060
Mary Jane: 5330
Sarah T: 124
Sophie E: 4195
Susan R: 3828
Susannah: 2318
Wm Bradley: 5259
Wm D: 5354
Wm H: 2548
STONEBRAKER
Alforetta: 3842
Daniel: 5437
Mary: 3473
STONER
Ab'm: 4749
Alice: 5263
Alice A: 690
Ann E: 1178
Anna Mary: 542
Augustus: 4936
C Edward: 5439
Christian: 4783
Dennis: 4847
Eleanor: 4749
Eliza: 3078
Eliza Ann: 4031
Ezra: 3078 4031
Hannah E: 1097
Jacob: 4775 5373
John: 1521 4783 4847
Jonathan: 4840
Lydia Ann: 29
Martha A E: 1356
Mary Ann: 34
Sarah A (Mrs): 2384
Susan: 1521
William: 5088

Wm R: 5373
STORCH
Theophilus (Rev): 4845 4976
STORK
Theophilus (Rev DD): 5390
STORM
Clara: 1742
Florence: 6280
John P L: 5281
Lydia Ann: 1170
Lydia R: 3739
Mary A E: 806
P L: 1742
P Leon'd: 3739
Peter: 806 1170
Peter L: 5465 5513
Peter Leonard: 4789 4971
Richard P: 5465
Salina Virginia: 1630
Wm B: 5513
STOTTELMEYER
Clara V: 6068
Rebecca: 987
S Ann: 2379
Susan M: 642
STOTTLEMYER
Alice V: 5438
STOUCH
M Harry (Rev): 5494
STOUFFER
E Katie: 4197
Fannie: 1124
Helen J: 1846
Miranda E: 805
STOUT
Cha's M: 5500
James M: 4930
STOVER
Catharine: 2159
James: 4770
John: 2159
Margaret: 4466
STOWELL
Lydia Ann: 2300
Mary A: 883
STRAEFFER
Annie M: 2012
Catharine: 6169
Daniel: 4895
Henrietta: 2939
Jacob M: 4838
John: 2012 4898

Margaret: 770
Mich: 4895
Mich'l: 4898
Michael: 4786
Miss: 770
STRAFFER
Olivia: 2653
STRAILMAN
Cha's J D: 5490
Francis T: 5188
Geo: 899
Henry: 5370
Sarah A: 899
Wm C: 5370
STRATTON
Cha's S: 5228
STRAUSBERGER
Ada J: 2827
STRAUSS
Carrie: 3416
Mich'l: 3416
STREAM
Mary A V: 2367
STREHLMACHER
No First Name Given: 4799
STREITER
James W: 4958
STRICKER
Thomas: 5425
STRICKLAND
Silas A (Hon): 5153
STRICKLER
Susan: 3035
STRIDER
Isaac H: 5280
Ja's W: 2025
James W: 4878 4958
Nannie: 2025
STRINE
A Pierce: 5537
STRINGHAM
Edwinna: 919
STROBEL
Mary Grace: 3404
Wm D (Rev): 3404
STRONG
Mollie: 3986
STROTHER
J F S: 459
Miss: 459
STUB

Alice A E: 4604
Elizabeth (Mrs): 3510
Lydia Ann (Mrs): 2964
STUBBINS
Eliza: 440
Frances: 1735
John A: 4794
STUBE
Andrew: 5233
STUFF
Otho H W: 4848
STULL
Amelia M: 1931
Ann Florence: 653
Annie S: 663
Bradley T: 5448
Carlton L: 5510
Cha's S: 5526
Christianna: 1503
Daniel L: 5380
Daniel Z: 5451
David: 4965
Dennis: 5276
Edward J: 5389
Ellen N: 4848
Emma Jane S E: 2519
Eugene: 5481
Fannie E: 3958
Florence J: 1461
Frederick A: 5071
George L: 5178
Harriett: 5211
Hester Ann Louisa: 3410
Horace E: 5388
Ida M: 3159
John A: 5146
Joshua: 4884
Julia B: 6004
Levina: 2374
Nettie: 5337
Nettie V: 2108
Rowanna: 1678
Susanna R: 882
STUMP
Emanuel D: 5142
STUNKEL
Cha's H: 4972
Frederick: 4960
STUP
Daniel: 4729
David: 4797
Edward Lewis: 5196
Elijah C: 5318

Francis T: 5247
George: 4875 4957
George L: 5159
Jacob: 4729 4793 4797 4875 4957
John: 4824
John A: 5087
John H: 5104
Joseph: 4793
Joseph C: 5266
Loretto: 5182
Samuel: 4767
Thomas: 5507
William D: 5062
STURGEON
John: 1262
Margaret: 1262
Mary V: 5382
STURGES
Flavius Josephus: 5080
STURGIS
Flavius Josephus: 5357
Henry: 4774
STUTCHBURY
Wm R: 4735
STUTLER
Catharine E: 4833
SUESSEROTT
Benj'n C (Rev): 5084
SUESZ
Friedrich: 5029
SULCER
Florence: 2733
SULLIVAN
Agnes: 2461
Dan'l (Dr): 2461
Mary: 952
Miss: 952
SULTZ
Lavinia: 5706
SULTZER
Henry P: 5031
Rebecca: 4739
SUMAN
Adelia: 3128
Alice O: 1434
Ann Cecelia: 4079
Annie M H: 3746
Annie R: 6092
Clara V: 4361
Ellen: 109
Isaac: 249 1434 2231

Israel W: 4921
Issac P: 5004
J J (Rev): 2095
John: 2449 3746
John J (Rev): 4924
Juliann C: 2231
Mary A M: 249
Rachel: 2449
Terasa A R: 2095
William R: 4872
Wm Rand: 6092

SUMMERS
Andrew J: 5504
Della: 5481
Jacob: 42
Jane: 810
Linah: 3719
Mary A: 42
Miss: 810
S: 5141
Sylvester: 5141

SUMNER
Charles (Hon): 5288

SUNDAY
Daniel: 5111

SUTHERDARD
B Ward T: 5489

SWAIN
Milton: 5417
Mollie L (Mrs): 1114

SWAINE
Elizabeth (Mrs): 3218

SWAMLEY
Amanda M: 5904

SWAN
Nellie P: 140

SWANN
Louisa: 3357
Tho's: 3357

SWAYNE
H'y Stuart: 5412

SWEADNER
Dan'l: 1321 5853
Daniel (Jun'r): 4985
Jane Rebecca: 5853
John (Capt'n): 5399
Lydia: 1321
Mary Louisa: 4089
Rebecca (Mrs): 4650
Richard: 5362

SWEARING
Cha's A: 5523

SWEET
Edward P: 5249

SWIFT
Emily: 373

SWIGERT
D Amos: 5224

SWOPE
Laura: 6243
Warner: 6243

SWORMSTEDT
Eliza Catharine: 1665

SYKES
Wm J: 5508

SYLCURK
Samuel K: 5461

SYMMS
Wm: 5429

TABLER
Abraham: 5550
Catharine: 5544
Charles W: 5660
Ida Kate: 1748
Wm B: 1748 5660

TALBOTT
Anna: 3498
Elizabeth A: 3779
Harry (Dr): 5720
Jos: 3498
Joseph: 5558
Joseph Howell: 5656
Mahlon: 5558
Mattie: 1293

TALL
Erasmus: 5592 5642
Jacob: 5592 5642
Stephen: 5592

TAMMANY
No First Name Given: 3153

TANEY
Elizabeth Maynadier: 4902
Maria Key: 39
Roger B: 39 4902 5611
Sophia Brooke: 5611

TANEYHILL
Aaron: 5602

TANKAFIELD
No First Name Given: 785

TARGEE
Helena: 2413

TASISTRO
Louis F: 5612

TASKER
Frank: 5637
Wm: 5637
Wm (Rev): 5633

TAYLER
D V (Rev): 942
George W: 5712
Maggie F: 3186

TAYLOR
Bayard: 5629
Betty: 333 1297
Betty Leigh: 2779
Charles J: 5676
Emily C: 5206
Francis (Col): 5611
Griffin: 2779 5676
Harriet Ann: 3897
Harry S: 5722
Ida C: 3916
Irene: 3423
John: 5631
John J: 5632
John Wesley: 5553
Mamie B: 5512
Margaret: 545
Mollie E: 1074
William: 5706
Zachary (Gen'l): 333
Zack (Gen'l): 1297

TEAGUE
J L (Rev): 5719

TEHAN
Anna: 612
John: 612 5542 5566

TENANT
Matilda: 4024

TENNISON
James T S: 5643

THATER
Nellie: 5128

THEIERJAHR
Rudolph: 5697

THIEMEYER
Emilie: 129

THOM
Eleanor: 4222

THOMAS
Ab'm: 5328
Abraham: 5626
Abraham W: 5596
Alice: 117
Amanda A: 1975

The Joseph Engelbrecht Marriage Ledger of Frederick Co., MD 1820-1890 *Index of Names*

Ann (Mrs): 5322 5696
Ann E (Mrs): 5312
Ann Eliza: 4841
Ann Margaret: 3708
Ann Maria: 5556
Ann Rebecca: 4583
Belvae: 2656
Bettie B: 5328
Bruce (Dr): 5645
C Keefer: 117
C Keefer (Col): 700
Calvin A: 5699
Caroline: 199
Cath Susan: 3648
Catharine A: 4439
Cha's: 5692 5718
Charles E: 5598
Charles Edward: 5601
Charles F: 5693
Charlotte: 5585
Christian: 5575
Christian Keefer: 5577
Clayonia F: 3839
D O: 6056
David O: 3837 5574 5692
E Alvida: 1412
E Amanda: 1358
Edward F: 5680
Elenora Sophia: 3683
Eli: 5564
Eliza A: 5212
Elizabeth: 4235
Elizabeth (Mrs): 1013
Ellen H: 4085
Emma K: 1803
Eveline M: 2949
Ezra M: 5595
Fanny: 4157
Francis (Hon): 5587
Francis Philip (Hon): 5701
Frank (Mrs): 3691
Gabriel: 2183
Geo: 3648
George: 5556 5570
George C: 5653
George D: 5623
George E: 5628
George P: 5618
Granville: 5683
H Fenton: 5658
Harriott: 5798
Hattie: 1426
Henry: 1492 1979 5556 5570
Hester: 5507
J D (Rev): 5635
Jacob R: 2278
James: 5635
James (Rev): 5698
Jane E: 2103
Jennie: 700
Jennie I: 758
John (Col): 5696
John (Junior, Capt'n): 5594
John B: 2656 5585 5710
John F: 5663
John G: 5704
John N: 5580
Katie: 2610
Laura W: 6056
Leonard (Junior): 5544
Levin: 2253 5070 5563 5585 5623
Lewis E: 5608
Lewis M: 2610 3839 4157 5589
Maggie E: 3837
Margaret: 2183
Margaret C: 26
Maria E: 6214
Martha: 1979
Martha C: 1195
Mary A: 550
Mary C: 3260
Mary Ellen: 2253
Mich'l: 1 4796 5589
Michael: 26 5574
Miss: 2306
Otho T: 5669
P F: 5701
Peter: 1358 3683 5551
Philipina: 5070
Rachel: 4718
Richard: 5597
Robert: 5684
Samuel: 5559 5673
Sarah A E: 198
Sarah Ellis: 2278
Sarah R (Mrs): 5313
Sevilla: 1
Silas E: 5695
Susan: 1492 4796
Susan R: 5911
Susanna: 4894
William: 5708
Wm: 199 4439
Wm H: 5636
THOMPSON
Alice: 1065
Archibald: 5661
Carter: 1088
Cha's W: 5647
Cha's West (Rev): 5603
Cornelius: 5547
Eleanora V: 2632
George W: 5646
John M: 5723
Malinda: 6261
Mary: 1196
Mary J: 659
Mary W: 1843
Miss: 4393
Mollie: 2618
Samuel C: 5616
Susan E: 2525
Wm (Judge): 4393
THOMSON
Andrew: 1165
Elizabeth: 5876
Grace: 1165
Ignatius Davis (Dr): 5666
James Hamner: 5638
John P: 5555 5565 5638
Margret Jane: 5621
Merideth Davis: 5677
Wm J: 5555 5621 5666 5677
THORN
Ann: 4200
Ellis C (Dr): 5670
THORPE
Sarah: 627
THRASHER
C E (Mrs): 4323
Tho's R L: 5605
TICE
Annie E: 2392
Barbara (Mrs): 2281
Ellen: 5620
Ellen B: 5991
Geo: 5554
H'y Nichs: 2392
Hen Nich: 2281
Henry N: 5620
Henry Nicholas: 5554
Mary (Mrs): 1467
TIDBALL
Robert M: 5562
TIDINGS
Richard T: 5662
TIERNAN
Ann Elizah: 162

Luke: 162
TIGHDY
Harriett: 833
TIMBERLAKE
Margaret L (Mrs): 1496
Mary L: 467
Mildred C (Mrs): 5979
TINGSTROM
Peter: 5567
TINTERMAN
Mary Ellen: 113
TIPPETT
Anna H: 4269
Cha's B (Rev): 4269
TITLOW
Adam: 5569 5820
Caroline: 1602
Cha's: 1825
Cha's R ##NIS: 5714
Dan'l: 4629
Eleanor: 1565
Elizabeth: 2906
Ellen: 5820
Evelina: 17
Geo: 17
Henrietta: 1570
Hester: 1825
Isaac: 5584
James: 5569
John: 1565 1570 2906 5571 5619
Juliann: 192
Maggie E: 570
Margaret: 830
Margaret Lucretia: 4629
Samuel S: 5665
Susan E: 1391
TITZEL
John M (Rev): 5691
TOBBINS
Katie E: 2686
TOCHMAN
Gaspard (Maj): 5609
TODD
Benj'n: 2387
Lucy E: 2387
Rebecca R: 5864
Sallie A: 5758
William H: 5615
Wm: 5615 5864
Wm N: 5654
TOLLINGER
George: 5590
George D: 5688
Lizzie: 5754
TOMLINSON
Catharine B: 767
TOMPKINS
John A (Col): 5675
TOMPSON
Sam'l J: 5687
TOMS
Lawson J: 5641
William E: 5674
TONEY
Ann R: 3332
TONGUE
Ann Amelia: 4094
TOOGOOD
Mary: 2763
TOOMBS
Robert: 1299
Sallie: 1299
TOOMS
Frances V: 6018
TOPPER
A J: 4666
Annie R: 4666
Clara V: 3422
James G: 5630
TORBUTT
A T S (Maj Gen'l): 5667
TORMEY
John M: 5671
Leonard J: 5640
Mary Jane: 906
Patrick: 5545 5671
TORNEY
Patrick: 906
TORRANCE
Elizabeth R: 4916
Jame: 4916
TORRENCE
James: 5557
Josiah S: 5651
TORRYSON
John R: 5624
TOWERS
John T: 5617
TOWNER
Ann F: 4899
Mary Virginia: 4935
TRACY
Elias: 5604
Molly E: 1034
TRAFFORD
John: 5607
TRAGER
Harriet: 4397
TRAGO
Catharine R: 3290
Harriet: 4397
William: 5552
Wm: 3290
TRAIL
Allen: 5682
Amanda: 2883
Ann E: 2437
Annie M: 2673
Ariana T: 709
Baker: 5543
C E (Col): 709 2673
Cha's B: 5721
Charles E: 5606
Charles H: 5652
Charlotte A: 3657
Edw: 2437
Edward: 3657 5541 5606 5620 5682 5908 6244
Ellen B: 5991
Harriett: 3517
Jona (Rev): 2437
Lewis R: 5991
Lewis Ramsburgh: 5620
Lewis W: 5685
Mary V: 6244
Oscar: 5579 5685
Susan Ellen: 5908
Theresa Ann: 473
TRAINER
Mary: 4050
TRAMMEL
Ann E: 1711
TRAPNELL
E W (Dr): 5700
Emily: 555
Jos (Jun'r): 555
Joseph (Junior, Rev): 5578 5650
Sarah: 218
TRASK
Brainard P: 5681
Mary S (Mrs): 4359
TRAVERS
Elizabeth: 3490

Miss: 3490
TRAVERSE
Boyle: 5546 5613
John Henry: 5613
TRAVIS
Le Grand H: 5655
TRAYER
J Varden: 5622
Martha Frances: 2455
Susan Emma: 5223
Thomas: 5644
TREAGO
Mary: 746
TREFZER
Ann M: 1181
TREGALLAS
John N: 5709
Samuel: 5707
TREGO
J: 1785
John T: 1785
John Thos: 5614
TREICH
Adelaide L: 6049
Ferdinand F: 5659
J B: 6049
TRESIDE
Thomas: 5634
TRESSLER
Henry B: 585
TRIECH
Jennie D: 6032
John B: 6032
TRIMMER
Samuel: 5672
TRIMPER
Maria E: 990
TRISLER
Geo: 2303
George: 5549
Henrietta: 5770
Margaret: 2303
TROGLER
Ann (Mrs): 803
TROUT
Charlotte: 174
David C C: 5690
Harriett C E: 2537
Joseph H: 5599
Julian: 411
Mary: 4388

TROXELL
Columbia H: 3394
Emma H: 1036
Jemima: 3571
Joshua: 1036 3394
TROXELLS
No First Name Given: 6103
TRUESCOTT
George: 5581
TRUNDLE
Hezekiah L: 5576
John A: 5627
John G: 5600
Maggie A: 4188
Thomas: 5648
TRUNNELL
Ida L R: 4648
TRUSCOTT
Geo: 5744
Sarah C: 5744
TUBMAN
Benjamin G: 5621
TUCKER
Bessie C: 3968
Margaret: 5151
William J: 5583
Wm: 5717
Wm C: 5657
TULLEY
Alfred H: 5625
TULLY
Aquilla: 5540
TURBUTT
Edward: 5573
Maria: 4755
Nicholas: 4755 5573
TURNER
Amelia F: 1278
Ann Barbara (Mrs): 358
Eli: 5639
Ellen C: 3812
Isaac: 4431 5582
Jennie R: 66
John C: 5561
Margaret A: 495
Mary: 1668 3586
Mary A: 4431
No First Name Given: 2764
Tho's: 66 3812
TURNEY
Ellen: 4826

TUTWEILER
Mary E: 5260
TWENTY
George L: 5678
No First Name Given: 2531
TWIGGS
David E (Maj Gen'l): 5610
TYERYAR
Rudolph: 5697
TYLER
Ann: 5814
Bradley (Dr): 4801
Bradly (Dr): 4874
Eleanor M: 2749
Elizabeth: 5835
Geo Murdoch: 5568
Geo T (Rev): 5694
George: 5689
Harriott D: 4801
John: 5591
John (President): 5835
John A: 5668
Lizzie: 5947
Lucy F: 331
Maria: 617
Mary: 4874
Mary A: 2049
Mary Eleanor Addison: 4479
Nannie C: 4294
Robert Bradley (Dr): 5664 5679
Sam'l (Dr): 2049
Samuel: 5560
Samuel (Dr): 5588
Samuel (Esq'r): 5947
Susan E: 4260
W Ottis: 5711
Wm (Dr): 331 4260 4294 4479 5588
Wm (Junior, Dr): 5593
Wm B (Dr): 5679
Wm Bradley: 5568 5664
Wm Bradley (Dr): 617 5548 5814
Wm C: 5572 5689
TYSON
C Dorsey: 5705 5713
Cha's B: 5702
Henry B: 5703 5716
Jacob Baer: 5686
Jona: 5702 5703
Jonathan: 5586 5686
Nathaniel S: 5715

Robert: 5649
TYSSOWSKI
Pelagia: 2011
UHER
Nelsie: 737
UHLER
John H: 5755
ULRICH
Geo William: 5731
John: 5760
Nancy (Mrs): 4435
Sam'l: 5743
Wm: 5760
UMBERGER
Michael: 5729
Sarah W: 5325
UMSTEAD
Catharine: 1298
J H (Rev): 1298
UNGEFEHR
Abdiel: 2289
Francis S: 5733
Harriet L: 2289
Lucy R: 96
UNGER
Edward C: 5766
UNGLESBEE
G W: 5735
UNKEFER
Abdiel: 2289
Francis S: 5733
Harriet L: 2289
Lucy R: 96
UPP
Annie: 5106
UPPERMAN
Dilia: 4504
Joseph: 5739
Margaret (Mrs): 2487
Mary E: 3092
UPTON
Levi T: 5724
URNER
Milton G: 5753
UTCHISON
Matilda A: 4861
UTERMEHLE
Charles H: 5745 5763
Washington: 5745
VALENTINE
Annie F: 3988

Geo S: 5752
James C: 5740
VALK
John M: 5741
VAM CAMP
Aaron (Dr): 6241
VAN ALLEN
Margaret (Mrs): 800
VAN ANTWERP
Eliza: 226
VAN BUREN
John: 5732
John H W: 5727
Martin: 5732
VAN CAMP
Orsena S R: 6241
VAN HORN
Anna E: 2338
VAN HOUTIN
Josephine: 5855
VAN LINBURG
M: 5742
VANANDA
Mollie A: 3415
VANCOURT
J B: 5738
VANDERGRIFF
Edward: 5748
VANDERPOOL
Elizabeth: 5732
VANDERSLOOT
Salome F: 2507
VANECKER
J William: 5746
VANFOSSEN
Annie: 2129
Arnold: 2129 5737 5764
C Katie: 6142
Clara V: 2662
Edith: 3232
Eldred M: 5754
Eli: 1351
Frances F: 1351
Geo: 736
Geo W: 5744
Gilmer: 5764
Hattie L: 736
Levi: 77 888 5744 5754 5759
Mary A: 77
Mary E: 1954
Susan: 888

W Scott: 5759
Wm H: 5736
Wm J: 5761
VANHORN
Annie: 2699
VANSANT
Ellen: 936
J Wehrley: 5751
Oliver: 5757
VANZANT
Ellen V: 4532
VARDEN
Josiah (Rev): 5227 5725
Mary: 5227
VAUGHAN
Lottie Amelia: 3822
VEIT
J Jacob: 5726 5734
John Jacob: 5762
VEITCH
Benj E: 5765
John Wesley: 5750
VERNON
Geo W F (Col): 5758
VIERS
Kate: 1004
Sam'l C: 1004
VIET
Jacob: 5734
VINSON
John T (Judge): 4378
Mammie G: 4378
VION
Leon: 5756
VIRTZ
James M W (Capt): 5747
VOGLER
No First Name Given: 4481
VON BLUCHER
G (Capt'n): 5749
VON NECHEIM
No First Name Given: 1994
VORE
Harriott: 3553
William: 5728
VOUGHT
Geo Wm: 1738
Henry: 1738
WACHTELL
Frederick: 5817

WACHTER
Charles S: 6117
Dan'l: 503
Daniel: 5815
David F: 3371 5873
Edward S: 6079
Elizabeth: 49
Elizabeth B (Mrs): 1322
Ezra C: 6004
Florence E: 665
Geo: 6035
George: 4279
George M: 5886
Gideon R: 6050
Henry: 5854
Jacob M: 5907
Jane R: 1286
John George: 5813
John J: 5872
Leander (Dr): 5878
Lewis F: 6035
Lewis H: 5898
Margaret S: 503
Maria M: 5135
Martin L: 6162
Mich'l (Rev): 5878 5886 5907
Michael (Rev): 5135 5768
Mollie: 6232
Olive A: 3917
Rebecca: 5698
Sophia E: 3371
Steiner R: 6137
Susan B: 4279
Urias: 6031
Wesley A: 6028
Wm H: 6088

WADE
Ella M: 1049
Thomas: 5881

WADSWORTH
Amelia: 2264

WAERNER
Ann Maria: 5157

WAESCHE
Henry: 5883
J Theodore: 6085
John F: 3732

WAGENER
John: 5849

WAGERS
Elizabeth M: 4087

WAGLEY
Vallie S: 3179

WAGNER
Amelia J: 56
Arthur C: 6135
Conrad: 5782
Dan'l (Rev): 5811
Dennis D: 5858
Elizabeth: 4199
Esther M: 4988
Grafton J: 6055
John A: 5876
Margaret: 16 5044
Margaret C: 3015
Mary C: 4837
Rachel: 4438
Samuel: 5811
Wm H (Dr): 6048

WAHRENFELSZ
Caroline: 2458
Ezra: 6014
Mary A R: 462
Sarah A: 2039

WAHRENFELTSZ
Daniel: 6068
Josiah L: 5893
Samuel: 6018

WAITE
Elizabeth B (Mrs): 2334
Frank H: 6140
Louisa H (Mrs): 1072

WALCUTT
Serena S A: 3123

WALDRON
Francis: 5986

WALKER
Alice: 5336
Ann L: 260 4014
Cha's W: 5853 5853
J C: 6160
Jacob: 5821 a3
James E: 6082
John: 2214 4014 4454 4925 5807 5818 5821 5864
John (Junior): 5793
Joseph W: 5818 5950
Margaret: 4454
Mary: 1965 2214 4925 a3
Mary F: 2062
Nettie: 3197
Patrick Henry: 5980
Perry: 5798
Samuel: 5803
Samuel D: 5864
W A: 6165
William: 5807
Wilson C: 5899

WALLACE
Albert E: 6116
George L: 6155
Tho's B: 5910

WALLECK
Eliza Ann: 4233

WALLER
William: 5835

WALLING
Adelia H: 286
Corrie E: 5963
David: 1556 3579 5777 5795
Elizabeth: 1556
Emma: 3597
Henry: 3939
Henry J: 5848
James: 286 3597 3620 5773
John: 3275 5773
Jos: 5795 5799 5848
Joseph: 5777
Joseph H J: 6096
Lilly: 3939
Maria: 3275
Martha A: 3620
Miss: 3579
Rebecca: 3579
Samuel: 6104
Susan: 5799

WALLIS
Albert E (Rev): 6062

WALSH
Biddy: 4492
Wm: 5975
Wm H: 5852

WALTER
Albert: 5943
Alice V: 5367
Birdie E: 1460
Carrie: 2003
Catharine: 4909
Cha's G: 6091
Christianna (Mrs): 3291
Eliza: 4248
Florence M: 5519
Jacob: 3291
James N: 6045
John: 1460 4347 4909 5367 5865 6072 6091
Kate: 4347
William: 6072

WALTERS
- Edward: 6143
- Isabella: 596
- John W: 6020

WALTMAN
- Wm A: 6003

WALTZ
- Hellen M: 5712
- Jemima: 4451
- Nannie: 5493
- Rene M: 5500
- Samuel E D: 5964
- Sarah C: 1740
- Williard F (Lieut): 6101

WAMPLER
- Wm A: 5968

WARD
- Cha's F: 6113
- Elizabeth M: 371
- Frank X: 6083
- John: 6148
- Sallie: 2350

WARDECKER
- Mary Louisa: 5195

WARDER
- Jennie S: 6151

WARE
- Charles R: 6022
- Elizabeth: 4856

WARFIELD
- Annie M: 2781
- Caroline: 250
- Catharine A: 2934
- Cecelius E: 6056
- Eliza Ann: 866
- Fanny A: 1703
- James H B (Dr): 5935
- James R: 6105
- Suratt D: 2781
- Surrat D (Junior): 5837

WARNER
- Annie C N: 1312
- Clara: 3959
- Hanna M: 2058
- Henrietta: 2179
- Maria: 2896
- Mary C: 5310
- Mich'l: 1312
- Michael (Jun'r): 5772
- Sarah: 4308

WARREN
- Levinia: 5228

WARRENFELSZ
- Amanda: 2466

WARTHAN
- Ignatius: 5787

WARTHEN
- Balinda: 1928
- Isabella: 3625
- James H: 5861
- Josephine A: 419

WASHBURN
- Sanford (Rev): 5918

WASHINGTON
- Florence: 5126
- George: 6076
- Milicent F: 3568
- Rich'd C: 5126

WASKEY
- Catharine: 2625
- Eli C: 5911
- Elizabeth: 4851
- Leonard T: 5958
- Mary F: 5279
- Sallie J: 2522
- Sarah A R: 3598

WASMUS
- Louisa Ann: 5826

WASTLER
- Katie: 3455

WATERS
- Achsah D: 2790
- Alice V: 2614
- Annie Pottinger: 1313
- Baker: 5816
- Cyrus (Rev): 5880
- Ellen (Mrs): 2227
- Ellen M (Mrs): 6037
- Frank: 6099
- Franklin (Dr): 5842
- Harry: 6110
- Harry W D: 5920
- Horatio: 5880
- Horatio (Jun'r): 5946
- James K: 5997
- Leander: 5874
- Lizzie: 1766
- Martha E: 5291
- Mary Ann: 1259
- Mary Elizabeth: 477
- Mary Jane: 1961
- Miss: 1218
- Richard C: 5989
- Richard L: 5936
- Susan: 1932
- Tilghman: 5914 6037
- Washington (Dr): 6037
- William (Dr): 5784 5979
- Wm (Dr): 1313 1932

WATKINS
- Emily: 5578
- Frank D: 6047
- John: 5810
- Matilda (Mrs): 4437

WATKINSON
- Stephen: 5890

WATSON
- Harriott C: 3520
- Isaac Cooper: 5822
- Wm H: 6138

WATTS
- Albert: 5825
- Reuben: 5846
- W W: 5903
- Wm E: 6094

WAYS
- Basil: 3487 4036 4825 5799 5870
- Daniel F S: 5932
- David F S: 6078
- Harriet A: 485
- Isabella: 4036
- John T: 5857
- Joseph: 5870
- Margaret: 4825
- Sam'l D (Jun'r): 6029
- Samuel: 5799
- Sarah: 3487
- Tho's: 5932 6078
- William H (Jun'r): 6090
- Wm Henry: 5896

WEAGLEY
- C W C (Dr): 6122
- James R: 5901
- Valetta S T: 572
- Vallie S: 3179

WEANT
- Sallie E: 3192

WEAST
- John C: 6109

WEAVER
- Theodosia: 816

WEBB
- Jos B: 273 1553 4020
- Joseph B: 5775
- Lucian: 6156

Mary Jane: 5975
Mercy Elgar: 273
Naomi Lacy: 1553
Tacy: 4020
Tho's H: 5829

WEBER
Herrmann: 5927
John B: 5802
William: 5802
Wm Eldridge: 5967

WEBSTER
Ada S: 3782
Cornelia A: 5248
Eliza V: 2450
Ellen T: 3433
Geo: 3433 4878 5809 5834 5908
Geo (Mrs): 799
Geo Frederick: 5908
George: 6123
George T: 5862
Georgetta: 4878
Harriett: 5142
John B: 5797
John D: 5850
Jos: 1733
Joseph: 5809 5834 6157
Julia: 1733
Mary E: 3735
Rosa A: 2674
Sidney: 5981
Stephen J: 5845
Tho's C S: 6060
William: 6106
William T: 5840

WECKLER
Fred'k: 118
Vickie R: 118

WEDDEL
James M: 5895
John P: 5885
Mary: 4341

WEDDELL
Candace A: 2475
Frederick: 6098
Henrietta: 2019
Luther L: 6069

WEDDLE
Tho's P: 5996

WEEDON
James H: 5948

WEEMS

Elizabeth: 5602
James (Rev): 5602

WEHNER
Margaret: 1734

WEIDMAN
L Adaline: 5255

WEIKERT
George: 5960
Mamie: 3964

WEINBERG
Samuel: 6010

WEINBRENNER
Ch'n: 1966 4570 5889
David C: 6012
Edward J: 5922
Elizabeth E: 4852
Geo A: 5889 5951
George: 5884
Harriet A: 4570
Harriott: 360
Harriott A: 1743
Jacob: 4852
Julia: 387
Margaret E: 1966
Mary Ellen: 1959
Reverdy J: 6070
Sevilla: 4930
Tho's J: 6080

WEINER
R J: 6149

WEINICH
Margaret: 4093

WEIR
Robert F (Dr): 6009

WEIRMAN
Hannah Rose (Mrs): 2812
John E: 5984
Sarah D: 2361
Thaddeus S: 5929

WEISZ
Elizabeth: 2257

WEITZELL
Godfrey (Maj Gen'l): 6016

WELCH
Joel J (Rev): 5429
Lallah M: 5429

WELFLEY
John (Rev): 5902 5949

WELKER
Harriett: 981
Julian: 1992

WELLER
Amanda C: 2006
Amos T: 6001
Barbara Ann A: 4564
Catharine E: 1977
Charles: 5891
Ephraim E: 5971
John: 5926
John B (Hon): 5913
Martin D: 5953
Mary Ellen: 6003
W F: 6092

WELLESLEY
Marquis of: 5783

WELSH
Edward H: 6054
Elizabeth: 2767
Joel J: 5915
Malinda: 3257
Mary E: 5043
Rachel B: 4141

WELTY
Ada E: 4181
Hiram: 3189
Kate N: 5752
Lucy J: 3189
Marcella: 3032
Philip H: 5938

WELTZ
Mollie K: 6105

WELTZHEIMER
Caroline: 5789
Lewis (Dr): 4743 5789
Rebecca: 4743

WENRICK
Rebecca: 2018

WENSING
Maggie E: 1118

WENTZELL
Alex'r: 5831 5900
Alexander S: 5900
Elizabeth E: 4540
Wm H: 4540 5831

WERKIN
Catherine E: 2702

WERNER
Ann Maria: 5157
Annie: 498
Catherine: 2395
Mary: 4829

WERNSING
Herman: 6033

WERTENBAKER
George W S: 5859
WERTHEIMER
Myer: 6161
Sophia: 2503
WESLEY
John: 6013
WESSELS
Litleton B: 6059
WEST
Alice: 3793
Allen W: 5906
Erasmus: 5982
Joseph: 5879
Patrick McGill: 5965
WESTENBERG
Bernhard O F H De: 6077
WESTON
Nathaniel: 6042
WESTPHALE
Augustina: 1295
WESTWOOD
Henry Clay (Rev): 5931
WETNIGHT
Abraham: 5977
Elizabeth: 87
WETZEL
Wm Grant: 6163
WEVER
Caspar W: 861 4914
Catharine Willis: 861
Charlotte D: 4914
James S: 5770
WEVERTON
No First Name Given: 861
WEYL
Amanda: 3367
C G (Rev): 3367
Chas G (Rev): 1657
Elleanor: 1657
WHALEN
Elizabeth: 3211
John W: 6058
Lizzie: 3211
Lonie C: 2719
WHALEY
Geo W: 5905
Georgie F: 6283
Wm H: 5973
WHALLEY
George W: 6119

WHEALEY
Geo W: 5905
WHEELER
Bennet: 2242
Bennett J: 5785
John F B: 1667
John Francis Ragis: 5866
Joseph A: 1330 5944 6084
Margaret (Mrs): 1667
Mary (Mrs): 2242
Mary A (Mrs): 1330
Sarah Odel: 2329
T M: 6015
Thomas: 6015
WHIFFING
James: 4736
Sarah P: 4736
WHIP
Charlotte: 4747
Cornelia C: 3799
Ella S: 1778
Emma M: 2640
Geo T: 2640
George C: 6025
I Newton: 6063
Ida E: 3151
John: 5794
Mary: 4737
Mary F: 5321
WHISNER
Lilla: 3468
WHISTNER
Annie: 5444
Cha's D: 6141
John: 6120
Michael: 5444 6141
Mollie V: 741
WHITE
Ann Jemima: 4987
Benjamin Nicholson: 5972
Elizabeth: 812
J Carroll: 6133
John: 812
John H: 6066
Luella: 137
M Wales: 6131
Mannie M: 2074
Mary E: 1135
Mary Ellen: 3835
Samuel: 6073
Sarah A: 3610
Virginia: 1055
Wm B: 5924

WHITEFORD
Anna M V: 565
WHITING
Edward: 6128
WHITLOCK
William: 6008
WHITMAN
Fred'k W: 6095
WHITMER
Ann R: 5073
Nicholas: 5073
WHITMORE
John M: 5990
Mary E: 3079
Mermelta: 2728
Mollie: 3463
Nicholas: 5894 5990
Nicholas (Junior): 5952
Nicholas (Sen'r): 6000
Phoebe A C: 3765
Randolph: 6043
William: 5894
WHITNEY
Maria: 598
WHITTAKER
Andrew J: 6046
James: 5819
WHITTER
Ann E: 2776
Ella J: 2452
Fanny: 2017
Fany: 3860
Mary M: 6001
Rebecca: 1569
Tho's: 1569 2452 2776 3860
Thomas: 5843
WHITTINGTON
John: 771 1158
Louisa (Mrs): 3994
Margaret: 1158
Mary: 771
Miss: 771
WICKES
Mary P: 370
Wm (Rev): 370
WICKHAM
Augustus: 6040
Harriott: 4018
Martha J: 1956
Robert: 6153
Victoria: 5196
WICKLIFFE

Annie C: 6195
Cha's A: 6195
Mary B: 3595
Robert (Junior): 5855

WIDRICK
Elizabeth: 3510 4729

WIEST
Catharine T: 4145
Conrad: 3346
Elizabeth: 3491 4849
Frederick A: 5912
Jacob: 2385 3491 4849 5768 5903
John: 3226
Laura V: 3346
Margaret: 3226 5768
Mary C: 2385
No First Name Given: 2554
Susan: 929 5903

WIESTLING
Rachel (Mrs): 4438

WIGGIN
Emily: 349

WIGLEY
Wm A: 6011

WILCOX
Annie: 4126
Arthur V: 6130
Henry Martyn: 5985

WILCOXON
Andrew Jackson: 5887
Ann (Mrs): 1232
Anna M: 1995
Charles J: 6114
Clara M: 711
Elizabeth: 3511 3801
Fannie A: 2528
Horatio: 4258
Jesse: 1232
John: 1365 1995 2528 5804 6030 6052 6090
Laura J: 1365
Louisa: 202
Maggie H: 6090
Rufus H: 6052
Sarah A (Mrs): 4258
Tempie E: 6287
Wm: 202 3511 5804 5887 6030
Wm M: 6111

WILD
Jeannette C: 1672

WILDMAN
Jane D: 3381

WILE
Annie C: 631
Dan'l: 631
Daniel: 5991
John A: 5991

WILES
Ann Elizabeth: 3771
Ann M: 111
Arabella: 2493
Barbara: 5872
Ellen A C: 1386
Frederick: 5928
Lyida A: 5740
Mary: 3166
Mary Ann: 1243
Mary Jane: 4491
Mary P: 2380
Mattie W: 1851
Sarah A Missouri: 3088
Tho's: 1386

WILEY
James: 5921

WILHIDE
Ann Marie: 2467
Maggie M (Mrs): 3856
Mary M: 1679
Mollie E: 3877
Robert L: 5937

WILKINSON
Ann Rebecca: 5124
William: 5820

WILKNER
J M: 6147

WILL
John W: 5839

WILLARD
Cordelia: 2641
John: 6102
Manzilla M: 92
Rosa M: 4702
Rosanna: 4702
Tho's: 4702

WILLHIDE
E M: 5987
Jennie M: 6164
John L: 5976
Joseph: 5987
Julia: 5939

WILLIAMS
Catharine: 5547
E M (Mrs): 1269
Edward: 5947
Eleanor M: 2250
Grosvenor Abigail: 5193
Harriett: 242 5163
Hattie E: 4193
Henreitta E: 3276
Henry: 6065
James: 5888 5994
James E: 6023
John H: 5806 6065
John H (Dr): 5942
Levi: 5969
Livinia: 1899
Louisa: 3148
Ludwig Alexander: 6027
Robert: 6071
Robert (Maj): 6024
Robert H (Rev): 6087
Sarah: 1713
Sarah J: 1237
Susan: 2842
Thankful: 3089

WILLIAMSON
E V: 1388
James J: 6041
Joseph A: 6067
Manzella: 2532
Warren R: 2532 6017

WILLIAR
Allen Q: 6152
Alonza M: 6164
George W: 6150
Margaret Ann (Mrs): 408
Sarah A: 1361

WILLIARD
Adam: 5995
Cha's F M: 6064
Ezra: 3871 5897
Geo W (Rev): 5827
Henry: 5856
Ida M: 3871
Jacob G: 5778
Jennie M: 4299
John: 5826
Joseph: 6039
Julia C: 5366
Lewis A: 5954
Margaret Ann: 3039
Martha (Mrs): 4399
Mary E: 6253
Mollie E: 6118
Sarah Ann: 2294

Tho's: 6118
Thomas E: 6126
Thomas H: 6127
WILLIS
Sarah Ann: 794
William: 5790
Wm: 794 6146
Wm B R: 5940
WILLMAN
Julia A E (Mrs): 4643
WILLS
Ann Mary: 4257
Arietta: 5047
Elizabeth Catharine: 4240
Henrietta: 3292
Katie: 1442
Mich'l: 1509 4240
Mrs: 5875
Rebecca: 1509
Wm H: 5925
WILLSON
Ellie: 1066
Hallie M: 4161
John J: 1066 1082 4161 5814
Leonidas (Rev): 5966
Martha R: 3624
Mary A: 2417
Mary E: 1082
Mary E A R: 2164
Tho's P: 2164 5814
Wm M B (Dr): 3624 5771
WILMAN
John L: 5939
WILMER
Wm: 6057
WILSON
Adam: 5823
Cha's: 1052
Charles: 5800
Christian T: 6159
E Lullie: 5466
Emma (Mrs): 3007
Frederick R: 5909
George J: 6142
Harriott H: 2282
Jane Ann: 4901
John (Rev): 5934
John K: 6081
Kate: 4345
Mary E: 1052
Mary Grace: 5682
Mary Isabel: 1984

Mary V: 323
Matilda: 6254
N J: 5466 5468 6159
Nathaniel J: 5974
Rebecca N: 5468
Robert: 5786
S C (Col): 5963
Tyler: 6139
WINANS
Ross (Jun'r): 5999
WINCHESTER
Alice N (Mrs): 713
Benj F: 6051
Evaline Kirkham: 415
Hiram: 415
Mordaunt C: 6051
WINCKELMANN
Geo: 6089
WINCKLER
Harriott: 5851
WINCKS
Eleanor: 5786
WINDBIGLER
Amanda L: 2422
Laura J: 2824
Mary: 1585
WINDPIGLER
David: 5993
WINDSOR
Antonie M: 1294
Drusilla: 3303
George Washington: 5847
Mary: 741
Mary Jane: 1590
Wm B: 5983
Zadock: 3303
WINE
Laura V: 2628
WINEBERG
George H: 6125
WINEBRENER
Grace E: 5721
Samuel E: 6144
WINEBRENNER
Emma B: 4177
G C: 6100
Mollie L: 3943
WINECOFF
Jesse (Rev): 5830
WINER
Annie V (Mrs): 2561

Wm: 6005
WINGATE
Matilda: 1003
WINGER
Elizabeth: 3359
WINN
Isabella: 1190
Susan B: 4391
WINNULL
Ann: 786
John: 5769
William: 5792
WINSINTER
Rose: 3700
WINSLOW
Benj'n F: 6044
WINTER
Alvira E: 4339
Anna M: 52
Benj: 5788
Benj'n: 1505
Francis B: 5955
Frederick: 6034
Howard S: 6145
John (Rev): 5779 5882
John T: 6053
Susan: 1505
Temple Ann: 3063
Tho's: 3063 4339 5283 5955 6053
Thomas: 5788
Tillie: 5283
WINTERS
Daisy: 5538
Mollie A: 3888
WINTHROP
Robert C (Hon): 5875
WINWOOD
Sarah A: 2311
WIRTS
Mary Ann: 4807
WIRTZ
Anna M: 1018
WISE
Caroline E: 4921
Fred'k: 3576 4921
Henry A (Hon): 5824
Ida V: 4684
Mary E: 5030
Rosanna: 3576
WISING

Isaac: 5871

WISNER
Caroline: 1011
Clemma E: 1417
John H: 6097
M'l: 3891
Mary M: 3891
Mich'l: 6097

WISONG
Ann E B: 1256
Ellen Sophia: 6054
Geo R: 2599
George Rutherford: 5871
Isaac: 894 1256 3594 5828 5892 6054
Jacob: 5892
Jennie: 6102
Margaret S: 894
Mary D: 2599
Mary E: 3594
William A: 5828

WISSEL
Veronica: 1962

WISSINGER
Catharine: 4757
Geo: 2180
George (Capt'n): 5851
Sophia: 2180

WISSLER
Katie: 3455

WITHERSPOON
Alex'r S (Dr): 5863

WITHY
Calvin: 2195 5781
Louisa (Mrs): 2195

WITLOW
Harry G: 6136

WITMER
Charles (Rev): 5962
Mary: 2221

WITMORE
Noah: 5805

WITTLER
Emily: 4519

WITTRICK
Margret: 2085

WOENER
Mollie L: 6144

WOLF
Florence J: 1820
Geo: 1820

WOLFE
Adam: 364 5789 5917 5956 5957 6074
Cha's Edward: 5917
Charles C: 6121
Elilhu R: 5992
Ellen: 935
Frances E S: 6132
Geo D: 6134
George: 5780
George H: 5956
James Polk: 6036
John: 359
Levi J: 6002
Mary E: 2216
Mary Margaret: 364
Mollie A: 5361
Orfie: 5450
Samuel: 5992 6002 6036 6061
Sarah: 2410
Susan Elizabeth: 359
Thomas M: 6074
William: 5978
William S: 5957

WOLFF
Ella S: 1272

WOLPERT
Frederick: 5774

WOOD
Ann M: 6129
Basil: 5844
Elias: 5904
Elizabeth: 5229
Fernando (Hon): 5988
Hannah: 6179
Howard S: 6151
Isaac Newton: 5959
J N (Dr): 5959
Mary: 4529
Melvin: 6129
Melvine P: 6129
Nancy: 1257
Sarah Ann: 1908
Susanna S: 4541
Wm J W: 5970

WOODERS
Thomas: 6007

WOODS
Ann Maria (Mrs): 1474
Eleanora: 342
John: 6006
Louisa: 5214
Mary: 3710
Mrs: 1474

WOODSIDE
John T: 1069
John Thomas: 5867
M Sheppie: 1069

WOODVILLE
Wm (Junior): 5919

WOODWARD
Alex: 2671 6124
Alex'r: 1690 3383
Alexander: 5841 6075
Alice E: 5107
Baldwin: 2813 5107 5796 5916
Catharine: 1690
Cha's B: 5916
Charles: 6032
Cora V: 2652
Eli: 5868
Elmer E: 6154
Emma Malinda: 3281
Geo L: 6019
George: 5833
Horace: 5832 6032
Ida E M: 2671
Jacob: 4710 6115
Jacob C: 5941
John: 5796 5833 5836 5841
John J: 5836 6021
John L: 6115
Jon: 2981
Leonidas S: 6049
Lydia A: 5796
Maria: 2981
Mary Jane: 3383
Milton A: 6021
Nettie G: 4710
Sally A E: 2813

WOODWOARD
Wm A: 6124

WOOLTZ
Ann Barbara: 4459
Ann Eliza: 1519
Geo: 1519 2181 4459 5808
Lydia: 2181
Tobias: 5808

WOOTTON
Martha: 5771

WORDON
A Graham: 5923

WORMAN

And'w D: 2545
Andrew D: 5801
Andrew D (Dr): 6093
George M: 6108
John R: 5838
Margaret R: 2545
Mary O: 1095
Moses: 5801 5869
Wm D: 5869
Wm J: 6112
WORNER
Christian: 5961
Christopher: 5812
WORTHINGTON
A D: 1326
Cha's: 5791
Charles E: 5945
Comfort M: 4037
Eleanor: 2858
Glenn H: 6158
Harriott A: 170
John T: 5933
Mary E: 4411
Mary S: 4244
Nicholas (Capt'n): 5998
Nicholas J: 6038
Reuben: 5767
Tho's C: 5877
Tho's G: 6026
Upton: 1326
Wm: 170
WRIGHT
Anna M: 1617
Edward W E: 6103
Eliva: 5011
Emily J: 5159
Geo W: 6086
James P: 6107
Jesse: 1226 5011
John: 5776
Lewis M: 6118
Lydia F: 1318
Margaret Jane: 1226
Mary: 4081
Mary E: 1674
No First Name Given: 5930
WRIGHTSON
Josephine B: 5333
WUSSEL
Margaret: 4975
WYLLIE
Sarah (Mrs): 3478
WYNKOOP

Ann M: 5935
WYSONG
Tho's T (Rev): 5860
YAEGER
Gottleb: 2112
YAGER
Jacob: 6256
YANDLEY
Ann: 843
YANITZ
Mary: 4044
YANTIS
Balinda E (Mrs): 5167
D F: 5167
David F: 6182
Elizabeth: 4603
George B: 6220
YARBOROUGH
Amanda J: 5373
Hattie L: 1739
Mary Reed: 3734
YARNELL
Mary D: 272
YASTE
Amanda: 4561
Cha's Milton: 6230
Cornelia F: 2077
Edward: 6278
Jane: 2679
YATES
Georgetta M F: 2027
YEAKLE
Aquilla R: 6269
Jacob: 6174 6226 6233
James B: 6233
Mary: 2875
Mary Adelia: 2125
William: 6194
Wm Henry: 6226
YECK
Charles: 6198
YELLOTT
John J: 6244
YERK
Catharine (Mrs): 366
YINGER
Annie E: 2048
Charles: 6257
Christian: 6288
Emma L: 3981
Fred'k: 6259

George Caspar: 6225 6242
John F: 6268
Lawrence: 6243
Lewis H: 6273
Mary M: 2496
Nich's: 6257
Nicholas: 2048 2496
YINGLING
Laura Belle: 1146
YOAST
George: 6266
YOE
Mollie E: 1788
YONSON
Wilhelmina: 399
YORKE
Sarah: 2754
YOUNG
Abraham: 6193
Adaline A: 1700
Alexander H: 6186 6222
Allen M: 4324 6190 6262
Almira V: 4324
And'w: 6204 6218
And'w (Jun'r): 3506 6170 6175
Andr'w (Jun'r): 6219
Bettie: 1754 5293
Carrie V: 3119
Catharine: 1953
Cha's Allen: 6262
Charles: 6264
Charlotte P: 4622
Conrad C: 6173
Daniel: 6211
Daniel J: 6252
David: 3173 4722 5439 6166
Edward: 6234
Elizabeth: 3506
Elizabeth A: 5566
Emma A: 4722
Frances H: 445
Geo W: 6246
H'y: 6251
Hanna A M: 5178
Harriet G: 5521
Henrietta C: 65
Henry: 1700 3790 6040 6170 6204 6218 6219
Howard W: 6275
Isaac: 6209
Jacob: 6167 6178
John: 65 6173 6200 6234

John R: 6237
John W: 6245
Joshua: 4600
Laura V: 103
Lewis: 6171
Maggie A: 1377
Maggie E: 5439
Margaret E: 5624
Mary Catharine: 4600
Mary E: 2474 4342
Mary Jane (Mrs): 3580
Mary K: 3173
McClintock (Jun'r): 6228
Mrs: 5776
O Harry: 6280
Oliver F: 6219
P: 65
Perry A: 6175
Philipina: 3563
Reuben W: 6215
Sam'l: 4622
Sarah E: 2072
Sarah L: 6080
Sophia (Mrs): 5776
Susan H: 3790
Susie: 1836
Tilghman H: 1754 6191
Verlinda C: 2068
Warren D: 6251
William: 6188
Winnie: 6040
Wm: 1377
Wm B (Dr): 6197

YOUNT
Addie N: 2570

YULEE
David Levy (Hon): 6195

ZACHARIAS
Annie C: 3647
Dan'l: 1364
Dan'l (Dr): 3647
Daniel (Rev): 6279
Edward: 6279
Horace C: 6287
John F: 6238
Lizzie: 1364

ZANE
Elizabeth: 4236

ZANTZINGER
Wm C: 6192

ZECHER
Caspar: 6172

ZEDRICKS
Henry: 6223

ZEIGLER
Charles C: 6265

ZELLER
Emma R: 4673
G Herman: 6263
J F: 2497
J Fred'k: 4673

ZELLERS
C Edward: 6258

ZEPP
Thomas: 6181

ZIEGLER
Alice S: 630
Catharine M (Mrs): 5949
Frederika: 2959
Henry I: 630
Henry L: 6176 6229
Jacob Henry: 6201
John George: 6235
Julia E: 5036
Mary: 5256
Wm H: 6229

ZIELER
Adam: 3526 5781
Ann: 3526
Ann M: 2305
Anna L: 2583
Barbara (Mrs): 4015
Cath: 2200
Charles E: 6260
David: 6260
David M: 6248 6271
Geo: 1153 2200 4015
George: 6168
Harriott: 1153
Henry: 6168
John D: 2583 6248
Louisa: 5781

ZIMMERMAN
Albert F: 6270
Alice: 1438
Ann E: 2756
Anna M: 2616
Annie: 4685
Annie M: 2069
B F: 6284
Caroline S: 4984
Catharine: 2930
Cephus H: 6276
Ch'n: 2930
Charles A: 6241
Christian: 6184
Clayton: 6282
Columbus A: 6247
David E: 6286
David V: 6213
E Jacob: 6216
Edw: 6249
Elias: 6189
Elizabeth: 4545
Elizabeth Ann V: 5952
Ellen Lucretia: 2513
Ellen V: 4664
Elton G: 6255
Ephraim J: 6214
Fannie V: 1815
G M, Dr: 6221
Geo: 4984 6179
Geo F: 6183
Geo F S: 6207
Geo H: 6250
Geo J: 6184
George: 6221
Gideon M: 6254
Harvey S: 6289
Henry: 6185
Hiram: 6224
Hiram Z: 6231
Horace J: 6205 6255
J: 6187 6202
J N: 6217
J Nicholas (Jun'r): 6217
John: 2756 6169 6187
John A Jackson: 6208
John J: 6202
John M: 6236 6240
John P: 6207
Jonathan T: 6210
Joshua J: 6180
Josiah B: 6206
Kate E: 3418
Keller C: 6267
Laura M: 6255
Lethe S: 5339
Lewis M: 6232
Lillie H M: 3421
Lilly Ann: 2215
Maria C: 1486
Mary E: 4644 5663
Michael: 6179 6239
Minerva: 3372
No First Name Given: 3519
Sallie P: 6252
Sam'l: 2069 2513
Samuel: 6177
Samuel J: 6203

Simon A: 6227
Susan A: 1438
Susan E (Mrs): 2627
Wm: 6212
Wm H: 2616 4664 6272
Wm H (Rev): 4644 6185
Wm M: 6283
Wm N: 6253
Wm W: 6239
Zachary E: 6249

ZITTLE
Joseph A: 6277

ZOLLICHOFFER
Carrie S: 2833
D'l (Rev): 2833
Wm (Dr): 6199

ZOLLICKOFF
David Keener: 6261

ZOLLICKOFFER
A Howard: 6285

ZORCK
D: 6274

ZORLCK
Jac: 6274

ZUMBRUM
G K: 6281

ZUMPFSTEIN
Frederick: 6196

ZWANZIEGER
George L: 5678

ZWANZIGER
Annie: 2531

both this place 2649
in the west 4709
near town 3029
of our town 1649
of our City 3105 4906
of this city 3898 3899 4326
this city 5440
valley 3410
A Arundel Co 5572
Adams 1826
Adamsville 1010
Albany, NY 4484
Albarry, NY 1647
Alex'a, Va 5186
Allegany 1580
Allegany Co 1974 4415 5830
Annapolis 3533 5578
Arrow Rock, Missouri 2564
Ashtobula Co, O 1049
Austria 3005
Balt 380 675 1065 1080 2615 2629 5224 5382
Baltimore 725 2851 4126 4828 5668 6107
Balto 22 44 68 69 74 81 115 129 146 162 169 201 263 299 303 323 352 416 428 435 439 476 483 485 492 496 546 571 582 590 606 620 621 664 684 810 833 880 974 1034 1063 1069 1072 1078 1089 1118 1160 1202 1203 1205 1212 1216 1217 1224 1262 1279 1301 1312 1330 1332 1343 1344 1349 1359 1366 1369 1389 1405 1443 1479 1495 1596 1617 1657 1662 1667 1672 1697 1699 1726 1729 1733 1737 1775 1776 1887 1896 1903 1937 1962 1973 1993 1997 2001 2010 2013 2059 2060 2087 2184 2201 2204 2240 2250 2272 2276 2323 2334 2340 2342 2348 2353 2385 2391 2404 2416 2417 2425 2445 2515 2547 2561 2577 2582 2613 2757 2801 2810 2820 2828 2896 2899 2917 2937 2954 2979 2986 2987 2999 3000 3069 3100 3104 3117 3148 3262 3325 3331 3333 3341 3357 3376 3380 3385 3386 3392 3512 3583 3587 3602 3620 3631 3640 3659 3664 3668 3670 3699 3714 3715 3725 3745 3749 3751 3769 3779 3786 3834 3837 3847 3860 3888 3897 3989 4010 4024 4053 4076 4115 4119 4120 4136 4143 4159 4205 4225 4226 4248 4250 4265 4277 4293 4340 4352 4358 4365 4391 4456 4460 4461 4465 4471 4480 4492 4505 4506 4554 4558 4599 4607 4612 4635 4791 4865 4869 4873 4892 4902 4906 4966 4991 4995 4996 5003 5013 5017 5019 5020 5026 5054 5058 5075 5079 5110 5124 5128 5160 5165 5206 5234 5273 5285 5298 5306 5335 5368 5372 5407 5417 5443 5549 5579 5588 5614 5618 5625 5640 5649 5654 5671 5680 5701 5738 5751 5792 5809 5834 5852 5860 5892 5903 5912 5917 5919 5931 5956 5957 5963 5980 5999 6005 6008 6057 6059 6077 6095 6266
Balto Co 5189 5656 6244
Bartonsville 662 4166
Baton Rouge 4666
Beallsville 1074
Bedford, Pa 1982
Beirut 489
Bellvue, Nebra 5133
Berlin 478 4901
Bermuda 1020 5924
Berne 1651
Bethel church 1057
Beyroot 489
Boonsboro 118 890 1215 1989 2572 3032 3076 3391 4083 4788 5243 5825
Boonsborough 2430 4139
Boston 1117 1948 5288 5875
Boyd 532
Bridgeport, Conn 5228
Brooklyn, NY 1697 3609
Brookville, Ind 340
Brookville, Indianna 3642
Brussels 459
Burkitsville 2942 5641
Burkittsville 3132 6039
Cal'a 2636
California 598 1047 4134 5139 5913
Calloway Co, Mo 2802
Calvert 1788
Canada 4924
Canal Dover, Ohio 2199
Carlisle, Pa 370 901 2360 3223 3643 4926
Carroll Co 418 1793 1911 2587 2797 3369 4514 5170 5976
Carroll Co, Md 510
Catoctin Furnace 1983
Cecil Co, Md 2237
Cedar Rapids, Iow 2607
Cha'stown, Va 5619

Chamb'g 2661
Chambersburg 2148
Chambersburg, Pa 935 3133
Chestertown, Md 3601
Chicago 2848 3005 5403 5409 5765 5985
Church Street 4855
Cincin, O 363 837 2530
Cincinati, Ohio 2312 4786
Cincinnati 5064 6016
Cincinnati, O 4838
Cincinnati, Ohio 5819
Clark Co, Ohio 4282
Clark Co, Va 5341
Clarksburg 5966
Conn 1008 1809
Connecticut 106 4135
Coridon, Ia 619
Cornety 4624
Council Bluffs, Iowa 3028
Country 2261
County 4624 4775 4804 5647
Creagerstown 1650 2370 3681 4130 4526 6221
Cumberland 23 1559 1933 2210 2456 2838 3051 3575 4244 4313 4480 4536 4636 4997 5045 5118 5430 5967
Cumberland, Md 464 3759
Cuml'd 220
D & D Inst 5457
Dauphin Co, Pa 3785 4637
Davie Co, NC 1664
Dayton, Ohio 330 2029 3711 5651
Delaware 3766
Delaware, O 376
Delaware, Ohio 350 3673 5304
Denmark 98
Detroit 3276 3552
Deutschlandt 2892
Double Pipe Creek 4312
Dublin 5783
Duck River, Tenn 2750
DCa 2209
E Shore 5333
E Shore, Va 4331
East Va 1283
Easton, Pa 5295

Elkton 4329
Emmitsburg 2435
Emmittsburg 121 366 1173 1921 1985 2433 2518 2756 3254 3571 3639 4589 5962
Eng 18
England 127 235
F F Seminary 637
Fairview 993 2073 2502 2529 3074 3782 4604 4919 6106
Fauquier Co, Va 4094
Fitchburg, Mass 5681
Florida 831 6195
Fort Lee, N Jersey 5192
Fred Co 5976
Fred'k City 4620
Fred'k, Md 6071
Frederick 830
Funkstown 4095
Galena, Ill 4131
Gardner, Mass 1071
Geo town, DC 3994
Geo Town 892 3585
Geo Town, DC 4060 4632
Geo Town, DCa 4442 4593
Geo.town, DCa 3038
Georgetown 205 225 430
Georgetown, DC 695 1579 5163 5947
Georgetown, DCa 969 4504 5955
Georgia 1269 1299
Geotown 266 2371 4646 5851
Geotown, DCa 4544 5808
GeoTown, DC 6053
GeoTown, DCa 4445
Germany 2907 3115 4476 4802 4820
Gettysburg 1901 2394 5826
Gettysburg, Pa 1374 1629 3353 3762 4349 4659
Glade 40 110 160 298 403 406 460 504 665 840 902 988 1026 1311 1381 1645 1904 2002 2488 2493 2516 2527 3139 3225 3349 3417 3641 4014 4070 4073 4142 4395 4883 4925 4963 5090 5095 5229 5284 5311 5654 5807 5953 6004 6028 6048 6055
Glasgow, Mo 4084
Globe Inn 365
Gloucester Co, Va 604
Gontoon 897

Gotha, Germany 5629
Graceham 466 973 1633 1991 5140
Grove 2386
Guilford, Conn 5290
Hagerstown 272 599 773 826 854 1709 2220 2299 2457 2927 3720 4054 4360 4440 4809 4866 4955 5743 6034
Hamburg 3020
Hamilton, Missouri 4515
Harbach valley 2450
Harbachs valley 3039
Harford Co 2738 3105
Harford Co, Md 4252
Harmony 2808
Harmony Grove 463
Harpers Ferry 3925
Harpersferry 468 1258 1604 3476 4540 5305
Harrisburg, Pa 3124
Hauvers 573
Henderson, Ky 958 1599
Hesse 3366
Honolulu, Hawaii 1280 3017
Howard Co 6056
Huntsville, Alabama 6066
Huntsville, TX 1053
Ijamsville 2098
Ill's 5412
Illinois 1005 1022 1081 1681 5918
Indiana 4670 5297
Indianapolis 1041 1293
Indianna 2818 2963 4245
Iowa 1681 2585 3037 3130 6094
Ireland 5803 5972
Ironton, Ohio 3728
Japan 4353
Jeff Co, Va 1599
Jefferson 984 1013 1778 2077 2251 2563 2798 2807 3073 3288 3338 3560 3590 3813 4583 4585 4978 5030 5148 5235 5598 5856 6126 6236
Jefferson Co, Va 4958
Jerseyville, Illinois 2590
Johnsville 3016
Kaighn Point 3672
Kaighns Point, NJ 402
Kaighns-point, NJ 915

Kankaky 1022
Kansas 1439 1990 3136 5440
Kemptown 1777
Kentucky 317 465 908 1009 2748 2982 3595 4421 5099
King and Queen Co, Va 2778
Knoxville 3077 4296
Ky 4305 5402
Lancaster 2295
Lancaster, Pa 2241 3513 3613 3717 4446
Lebanon, Pa 5137
Leesburg, Va 817 2282 3306 3381 4810
Leetown, Va 864 4904
Lewistown 1198 3186 4125 4888 5220
Lexington, Missouri 5910
Liberia 3047
Liberty 724 848 912 1045 1452 1623 1741 2833 3817 4089 4251 4288 4438 4521 4650 5038 5077 5138 5232 5362
Liberty, Indiana 5915
Linganore 322 1583 2245 3247 4507 4508 4572
Lisbon 4337
Lockport, NY 1067
London 349 2596 5122
Loudon Co 970
Loudon Co, Va 2993
Louisiana 1052 1237
Lucerne, Switzerland 4343
Lunenburg, N Scotia 449
M E South 5719
M Valley 1955
Madison, Wisc 627
Madrid 5360
Maine 67 3377
Manor 536 2421 2947 2949 3584 3708 5559 5669 5911
Martinsburg, Va 1272 2423
Mass 35
Mathews Co, Va 603
Md 3578 5647
Mechanickstown 2812 3685 5984
Mechanicstown 5130
Memphis, Tenn 1687
Mercersb 3893
Mercersburg, Pa 911 4513 5827
Merryland Tract 297

Michigan 990 5923
Midd 2331
Midd val 2556 3754
Midd valley 981 3045 3713 4490 4627 5119 5173 6068
Midd Valley 3719 3740
Midd.town 2193
Midd'n 4561
Middle'nvalley 5059
Middlen 1789
Middlet 3086
Middletown 1322 2007 2113 2257 2306 2825 2891 2898 2929 3046 3079 3096 3264 3266 3270 4027 4597 4911 5164 6041 6167 6178
Middletown valley 462
Middletownvalley 477 513 537 1058 1333 2466 2991
Middtown 4396
Middval 4433
MiddTown 4728
Milton, Pa 930
Milwaukie, Wisc 1307
Minn 3873
Minnisota 927
Miss 122 3825
Missouri 1230 3580
Mo 5756
Monrovia 2410
Montg'y Co 5293
Montgomery 57
Montgomery Co 1713 3517 4154 5367 5576 5914
Montgomery Co, Md 5816
Mount Pleasant 1674 1744 3330 4328 4746 5242 5639
Mount Vernon, Ohio 5069
Mt St Mary 2843
Mt Vernon, Ny 5323
Muhlenberg, Africa 2472
Muscatine, Iowa 4102
Myersville 4298 6069
N Carolina 161 1739 3734 4758
N Jersey 5607
N Lisbon 5582
N Market 471 1324 1331 1362 2008 2169 2187 2397 3775 3807 4541 4863 5018 5904
N Orleans 490 1659 1910
N Y State 5881 5918
N York 94 228 1002 1360 1395 3552 3626 3783 3789 4003 4112 4137 4316 5122 5193 5402 5655 5749 5981 5988
Nashville, Tenn 1663
Natches 3334
Nazereth, Pa 499
Nebraska 607 5153
New England 4992
New Jersey 4168
New York 813 1292 4268
New York City 2202
Newberryport, Mass 5603
Norfolk, Va 2427 2546 5612
Norristown, Pa 1771 3703
NC 2782
NJ 2523 2847
NY 346 1419 1425 1677 2003 2525 2805 2811 2957 3334 4280 4357 4393
Ohio 128 431 622 1263 1730 1899 1979 1984 2082 2452 2553 2810 3007 3029 3036 3098 3123 3423 4061 4852 5074 5340 5429 5623 5661 5813 6054
Orleans Co, NY 4319
Oshkosh, Wisc 5210
Pa 542 949 1614 1660 1732 2499 3578 4422 4448 4641 5100 5671 5949 5950
Paris 78 1300 4305
Paris, France 5298
Parkersburg, Va 3822
Parksville, Missouri 3360
Pennsylvania 1423
Petersburg, Va 5188
Peterson, NJ 5999
Phil 2417
Phil'a 5772
Phila 206 373 567 999 1300 1677 1752 1868 2298 2431 2434 2799 2952 3040 3140 3240 3297 3647 3672 3896 3992 4267 4472 4612 4976 5050 5113 5125 5208 5899 6049
Pipe Creek 2469
Pittsburg 5670 5746
Pittsburgh 1356 2591 3867
Point of Rocks 4110 4425 4537 5061
Poland 4737
Polol, Illinois 4665

Porthmouth, NH 2457
Poughkepsie, NY 4576
Prin Geo Co 2181
Prince Geo Co, Md 959
Prospect Hall 6130
Prussia 1648
R Island 5675
Reading, Pa 1309 3218 5092 5688
River Head, L I, N York 5591
Rochester, Ny 1029 3107
Rockey Springs 5136
Rockville 654 2355
Rockville, Md 1671
Rocky Spring 1051 2565
Rocky Springs 4124
Rulo, Nebraska 2571
S Carolina 2562 2595
Sabillesville 3737
Sam's Creek 956
San Francisco 4680
San Rafel, Cal'a 6042
Sandusky, O 846
Saxe Coburg 18
Schweitz 1651
Shanghai, India 5316
Sharpsburg, Md 3569
Sheph town, Va 3339
Shepherdstown, Va 2315 3345
Shookstown 4100 5267
Sligo, Ireland 5975
Snowhill 1025
So Cara 3424
Somerset, Pa 3035
South Carolina 1755
Spain 379 5360
Springfield, O 2311 4566
Springfield, Ohio 2920
St Louis 519 1337 2023 3363 5682
St Louis, Mo 2413 3676 5657
St Marys 3164
St Marys Co 3678 4630
St Petersburg 127
Staunton, Va 5934
Steubenville, Ohio 1978
Stuttgart 3040
Sugarloaf Mountain 1636

Tahiti 130
Tallahassee 3497
Taneytown 829 3261 4197 6285
Tenn 4170
Tennessee 1209 2796
Tiffin, O 4033 4846
Tiffin, Ohio 233 1516 2384 4545 4818
Tifflin, Ohio 1062
Turin 5855
Uniontown, Pa 3597 4555
Unionville 1304
Upper Sandusk, O 3860
Urbana 3398 5453 5933
Urbanna 1326 5117 5849
Utica 3883
Va 20 24 107 168 618 661 700 776 960 1079 1184 1195 1487 2035 2063 2265 2542 2806 2816 2886 2951 3081 3099 3217 3485 3568 3591 3707 3838 4162 4222 4256 4547 4562 4878 4899 4993 5012 5125 5224 5280 5587 5677 5747 6086
Verango Co, Pa 2630
Vermont 3089
Vermot 6044
W Va 650 1388 3413
Wales 98
Walkersville 916
Wash Co 4551 5121
Wash'g Co 1988
Washington 251 467 490 1716 2287 2826 3060 3778 4122 5745
Washington City 123 1068 1183 1192 1315 1610 1613 1750 1881 2011 3735 3741 5617 5818 5940
Washington Co 2912 2922 4145 4948 5589
Washington County 4777
Washington Territory 3710
Washington, DC 3610
Washington, DCa 5014
Wayne Co, Ind 4105
Waynesboro, Pa 5995
Westminster 1637 3352
Wheeling, Va 2185 4236
Williamsburg, Pa 1655
Winchester 3899
Winchester, Va 438 983 1502 2834 4907
Wiscon 5252

Wisconsin 2509 2532 4601 4602
Wm'sburg, Va 6071
Wm'sport 4790
Wmsport 1680
Wolfsville 1363 5143
Woodsboro 76 230 455 484 535 1249 1275 1340 2600 2839 2996 3686 4603 4744 5008 5010 5120 5156 5314 5928 5960
Woodsboro Church 3434
Woodsborough 410 4308
Wyandot, Ohio 2067
Wyondotte, Ohio 1736
York 203 454
York, Pa 256 274 479 1649 1808 1906 2114 2216 2291 2343 3503 4058 4934 5039 5106 5131 5573 5795 5811
Zanesville, Ohio 4096
Zion Church 5550
Zouaves de Afrique 999